WHERE BLUEBELLS CHIME

Elizabeth Elgin is the bestselling author of *All the Sweet Promises*, *Whisper on the Wind*, *I'll Bring You Buttercups* and *Daisychain Summer*. She served in the WRNS during the Second World War and met her husband on board a submarine depot ship. A keen gardener, she has two daughters and five grandsons and lives in a village in the Vale of York.

ELIZABETH ELGIN

Where Bluebells Chime

HarperCollins*Publishers*

HarperCollins*Publishers*
77–85 Fulham Palace Road,
Hammersmith, London W6 8JB

A Paperback Original 1996
3 5 7 9 8 6 4

A catalogue record for this book
is available from the British Library

ISBN 0 00 649622 9

Set in Sabon by
Rowland Phototypesetting Ltd,
Bury St Edmunds, Suffolk

Printed and bound in Great Britain by
Caledonian International
Book Manufacturing Ltd, Glasgow

To
my husband George
and to
my daughters Jane and Gillian.

The Pendenys Place Suttons

Albert Elliot — Mary Anne Pendennis

The Rowangarth Suttons

Sir Gilbert Sutton — Mary Whitecliffe

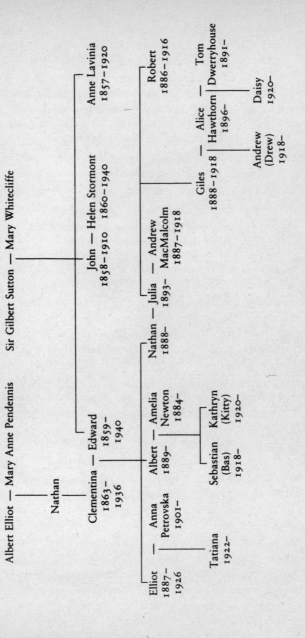

Nathan

Clementina — Edward
1863– | 1859–
1936 | 1940

Anne Lavinia
1857–1920

John — Helen Stormont
1858–1910 | 1860–1940

Elliot — Anna Petrovska
1887– | 1901–
1926

Albert — Amelia Newton
1889– | 1884–

Nathan — Julia
1888– | 1893–

Andrew MacMalcolm
1887–1918

Robert
1886–1916

Giles — Alice Hawthorn
1888–1918 | 1896–

Tom Dwerryhouse
1891–

Tatiana
1922–

Sebastian (Bas)
1918–

Kathryn (Kitty)
1920–

Andrew (Drew)
1918–

Daisy
1920–

1

June 1940

She saw Keth's letter when the alarm jangled her awake at half-past seven and reached for it, sighing contentment, turning the envelope over to read 'Open on 20 June' written across the flap. It must have arrived yesterday, or the day before and Mam had hidden it away then tiptoed into her room last night to prop it against the clock.

She gazed at the colourful American stamp and the air-mail sticker so she might stretch out the seconds before opening it, then frowned to read the postmark. Washington DC instead of Lexington as it almost always was. Why Washington? Quickly, she slit open the envelope.

My darling,

Happy birthday. Close your eyes and know I am thinking of you and wanting you and needing to touch and hold you.

I miss you so much. It should not have been like this. A week ago, I sat my last exam and I know I shall get a good degree. Now I should be packing my cases, heading for New York and a passage home, but nothing is simple any longer. The Atlantic is forbidden, now, to people like me, but I will find a way to be with you.

Since France capitulated I have thought of little else but getting home. Please, darling, take care of yourself and try to keep out of harm's way. The papers here talk about England being invaded but I can't believe it can happen – not when I am not there to take care of you and Mum.

There must be a way for us to be together and I will find it. I know you want me to stay in Kentucky, but that is not possible when I need you so desperately and love you so much.

Always remember you are mine.

Keth.

She closed her eyes tightly, trying to smile away the tears that threatened because if she were to weep on her birthday then she would weep all year, Mam said.

'The summer of 'forty I'll be back,' Keth promised, when they parted, but he could not, must not come home.

Today she was twenty and next year, when she came of age, was to have been her wedding day – well, not quite on her birthday, it being a Friday and Friday an unlucky day for weddings. That was why she had ringed round the day after; ringed it on every calendar in the house.

June 21 1941. At All Souls', Holdenby, by the Reverend Nathan Sutton. Keth Purvis to Daisy Julia Dwerryhouse.

She had read the announcement of their wedding so often in her dreamings. Daisy Purvis. Mrs Keth Purvis. She had promised never to write her married name – not before the wedding that was. As unlucky as a Friday marrying, Mam said, so she had never done it. But it hadn't stopped her saying it secretly and softly. Daisy Julia Purvis. It made a sound like a love song, like nightingales singing, like the sighing hush of silence before two lovers kiss.

The summer of 'forty. It had been her watchword; words to wear like a talisman, to say over and over when she missed him and wanted him unbearably.

Yet now the summer of 'forty had come and there should have been a letter telling her that soon he'd be sailing from New York, and would she be at Southampton – or Tilbury or Liverpool, perhaps – to meet him when he docked?

Sometimes it had been like that, but sometimes in her dreamings Keth had surprised her, had been waiting where Rowangarth Lane branched off into Brattocks Wood and the footpath that ran through the trees to Keeper's Cottage; standing there in grey flannel trousers and a white shirt, just as he had been two years ago.

The summer of 'thirty-eight, it had been – their daisychain summer – yet now that longed-for summer of 'forty had arrived and Keth was still in Kentucky. It was where, truth known, she wanted him to stay.

Don't come home, Keth. Stay in America where you'll be safe.

America wasn't at war. America was safety and young men living their lives without fear of call-up; young men knowing they could make plans, go to university, get jobs, stay alive. So she didn't really want that letter saying he was coming home because if he did, *They*, the faceless ones, would take him. There had been no heady, patriotic rush to volunteer as there was in Dada's war. This time, *They* had already put their mark on every fit young man of twenty-one and dubbed them the militia. Conscripts, really. Six weeks in barracks; forty-odd days in which to accept the discipline of life in the armed forces, to march like automatons in foot-blistering boots; learn to salute Authority and acknowledge that henceforth and for the duration of hostilities, each was no more than a surname and a number. Then away to active service, and some of them killed already.

Stay, Keth. She sent her thoughts winging high and far. *I'd rather wait four years, if four years it takes, than have you no more than a name on a gravestone in some foreign cemetery.*

She heard the creaking of the stairs and laid her lips briefly to the letter in her hand. Then she swung her feet to the floor. Mam was coming to wish her a happy birthday. Daisy forced her lips into a smile . . .

*   *   *

When Daisy said goodbye to Reuben Pickering that night, he stood at his almshouse door, waiting to wave to her as she reached the corner. She always turned for one last wave and every time she did she wondered if she would see him again. You never knew what might happen in wartime, and besides, Reuben was frail and old; very old. Over ninety, Mam said, though she would never tell how many years over ninety. You didn't remind people, especially Uncle Reuben, about their age, she admonished when Daisy once asked. So Daisy always tried, now, to treat the retired gamekeeper as if every time she saw him would be the very last and to be especially kind to him, not just for the sake of her conscience, but because she loved him very much.

Reuben was a part of her life, had always been there – a part of Mam's life, too. A sort of father, really, because Mam had never had one – or not that she remembered. That was why today in her dinner hour, Daisy had stood in a queue outside a sweet shop and when she reached the counter, had chosen humbugs because they were Reuben's favourite, though she would have to tell him she was sorry there had been no tobacco queue, but that she would try to get him some tomorrow.

Tobacco and cigarettes were even harder to come by now than humbugs. But yesterday she hadn't looked for queues during her dinner hour. Yesterday she had –

Daisy blinked her eyes as she stepped from the mellow evening sunlight and into the green-cool dimness of Brattocks Wood, breathing in the damp, mossy scent of it to calm herself, because whenever she thought of what she had done yesterday in her dinner hour, her heart started to bump – especially when she realized that before so very much longer she would have to tell her parents about it. She had almost decided it must be tonight, though it would be awful, telling them on her birthday.

Then she salved her conscience almost at once by

remembering that Sunday was to be her official birthday, with Aunt Julia calling for Reuben and bringing him to Keeper's in her car and the two of them staying for a birthday tea. It was good of Aunt Julia, come to think of it, since petrol was rationed now, and no one got half enough.

But yesterday had started badly. She had awakened and thought that this day next year should have been her wedding day and it wouldn't be, now, because of the bloody awful war. She had known with dreadful certainty it would not. Keth would not be home, now, though she knew she should be glad he was in America and out of harm's way. There was no way, now, of crossing the Atlantic unless you were a merchant seaman, sailing square-packed in convoys or unless you were in the Air Force and could fly across in a warplane.

Civilians could no longer buy a sailing ticket or a seat on a flying-boat, because all transatlantic liners were troopships, now, and flying-boats had been commandeered by the Air Force and painted in the dull colours of camouflage to be a part of Coastal Command. Besides, the Atlantic was a dangerous place to be, packed with German submarines and battleships sailing where they wanted, doing exactly as they pleased because Britain was still licking its wounds after Dunkirk and could do little to stop them.

An aircraft flew low overhead, crashing into her thoughts. She could not see it through the denseness of the branches above her but she knew it was one of the bombers from the aerodrome at Holdenby Moor. There were two squadrons there now and last night they had flown over Germany again, dropping their bombs – an act of defiance, really, when everything was in such a mess and everyone worrying about the invasion. But when it came people would make a fight of it, though in France they hadn't been given much of a chance. Hitler's armies had just marched on and on . . .

But we had the Channel – the *English* Channel – and

13

Hitler had to cross it first. And we had a navy, still, to help stop them, so perhaps it would be all right. Maybe the Germans wouldn't come.

Daisy looked down at her watch. Mam wouldn't be home from the canteen yet, nor Dada from his meeting. She squinted up at the sun dappling through the trees. Soon, when it reached the cupola of Rowangarth stable block it would start slowly to set. Blackout tonight would be at eleven o'clock and remain until daylight came about five tomorrow morning.

The blackout, Daisy frowned, was the strangest thing about the war, especially in winter when it began at teatime and lasted until long past breakfast time, next day. Last winter had been bleak and cold and very dark, and the blackout had taken a lot of getting used to. Stepping out into it, even from a dimly lit room, was like stepping into sudden blindness. So you stood there, if you had any sense, and gave yourself up the the blackness, eyes blinking until shapes could be picked out against the skyline. Shapes – outlines of buildings, that was, and trees – and especially in towns you stood still until your eyes could make out not only shapes but the white bands painted on gateposts and lampposts and telegraph poles and corners of buildings; unless you wanted a bloody nose or a black eye, of course, from walking into things you couldn't see. 'Bumped into a lamppost, did you?' people would grin, with no sympathy at all for bruises or shattered spectacles.

But there would be virtually no blackout tonight because it was June and would hardly get dark because of that extra, unnatural hour of double summertime. She must remember to think about June evenings when the drear of November was with them.

Drew, her half-brother, had joined the Royal Navy. His last letter had been from signal school where he was learning to read morse. And when he had, he'd be sent to a ship and only heaven knew where he would end up.

Once, Daisy sighed, there had been six of them: herself and Drew and Keth and Tatiana, with Bas and Kitty over from Kentucky each summer and every Christmas. Her Sutton Clan, Aunt Julia called them.

They had been golden summers and sparkling Christmases in that other life, yet now Bas and Kitty could no longer visit, and Keth was staying with them because he had gone to university in America with Bas. And with Drew gone there was only her and Tatty left to remember how it had once been; how very precious.

Tatty was eighteen now, beautiful, and fun to know. She wanted to do war work, but her Grandmother Petrovska, who never ceased to remind anyone who would listen that she was *White* Russian and a countess, had forbidden it absolutely.

Poor Tatiana. And poor Daisy, who'd better be getting home to Keeper's Cottage to tell her parents her secret. And when she told them, Mam would burst into floods of tears and Dada would shout and play merry hell so that Mam would have to tell him to watch that temper of his before it got him into trouble. And when Mam said that, Daisy would know that the worst was over and that Mam at least was on her side.

But oh, *why* had she done it – especially now?

Julia Sutton offered the letter to her mother, smiling indulgently. 'I'm to thank you, Drew says, for the soap and chocolate, but he says you mustn't bother now they're rationed – but read it for yourself . . .'

'No, dear.' Helen Sutton placed a cushion behind her head, then closed her eyes. 'My glasses are upstairs. Read it to me.'

'We-e-ll – he says to thank you for the things you sent but you're not to do it again because they can get quite a lot at the NAAFI in barracks. Soap, razor blades and cigarettes, too.'

'Oh, I do hope he hasn't started smoking.'

'I hope so, too,' Julia sighed. 'It's murder when you haven't got one.'

Cigarettes were in short supply to civilians. Shops doled them out now five at a time – if you were lucky enough to be there, that was, when a cigarette queue started.

Julia smoked; a habit begun when she was nursing in the last war. She had carried cigarettes in her apron pocket, lighting one, placing it between the lips of a wounded soldier. And then came the day when she too needed them. Cigarettes soothed, filled empty spaces in hollow stomachs, became a habit she could not break.

'And he says that when they aren't in the classroom they are cleaning the heads – I think he means the lavatories – and polishing brass and the floors, too. It's a stupid way to fight a war, Mother, if you want my opinion!'

'Maybe so.' Helen Sutton stirred restlessly. Talk of war upset her; talk of Drew being in that war was even worse. 'But I'd rather he polished floors for ever than went to sea.'

'He'll be safer at sea than he'd be if he were flying one of those bombers from Holdenby Moor. Will Stubbs said they lost three last night.' Such a terrible waste of young lives. 'Anyway, once Drew has finished his course he'll get leave, he thinks, before they find a ship to send him to. I suppose things are in a bit of a mess still, after Dunkirk.'

'I don't know why they took him if they don't know what to do with him,' Helen fretted.

'They will, in time,' Julia soothed. 'We've got to sort ourselves out, don't forget.' And who could forget Dunkirk?

But her mother was growing old. It had to be faced. Before war came – before *another* war came – Helen Sutton had looked younger than her years, but now Julia worried about her. She seemed so frail lately; hadn't eaten properly since Drew left three months ago. It was as if that Sunday last September when they knew they were at war again had turned her world upside down and she was still floundering.

'He'll be all right, won't he, Julia?'

'He'll be all right, dearest. I feel it, *know* it. Drew will come home to us.'

'Yes, he will. And I'll write to him, tomorrow – too tired tonight. Do you think you could ring for Mary, ask for my milk?'

'I'll get it myself,' Julia smiled. 'Mary is, well, *busy*, these days.'

Lately, Mary Strong was most likely to be found in the grooms' quarters above the stables. After almost twenty years of courtship, Will Stubbs had at last been pinned down. A day had been set for the wedding, the banns already called once at All Souls'.

'I tell you, Will, I'll wait no longer,' Mary had stormed. 'I'm the laughing stock of Holdenby, the way I've let you blow hot and blow cold. Well, those Nazis are coming and when they do, I want a wedding ring on my finger – is that understood?'

Will had understood. If the Germans did invade, he might as well be married as single. It would matter little. When the Nazis came – and Will had deduced they well might – they'd all be thrown into concentration camps anyway. Best do as Mary ordered and wed her.

'I never thought she'd get Will Stubbs down the aisle,' Julia smiled as she closed the door behind her.

Tilda was sleeping in the chair – in Mrs Shaw's chair – when Julia poked her head round the kitchen door and she jumped, gave a little snort, then blinked her eyes open.

'Sorry to disturb you – I've come for Mother's milk.'

'All ready.' Tilda was instantly awake.

On the kitchen table lay a small silver tray on which stood the pretty china saucer her ladyship was fond of and the glass from which she drank her nightly milk and honey. Beside it was an iron saucepan, a milk jug and honey jar and spoon. Tilda Tewk was nothing if not methodical, now she had taken over Mrs Shaw's position as Rowangarth's cook.

'I'll just pop a pan on the gas, Miss Julia. Be ready in a tick.'

'Thanks, Tilda.' Julia sat down on the chair opposite to wait. 'I called on Mrs Shaw, today. She seems to have settled in nicely, though she's sad, she said, that she had to wait for Percy Catchpole to die before she could get an almshouse to retire into.'

'There's been a lot of changes, Miss Julia, amongst the old folk. Think it was the war coming that has to answer for it. Seemed as if they just couldn't face another. But I couldn't help noticing, ma'am, that there was a letter from Sir Andrew by the late post. How is he then, and when will us see him?'

'Drew is fine, and looking forward to his first leave,' Julia smiled. 'I'll tell him you asked.'

'You do that. And tell him when he comes home as Tilda'll see he's well looked after. He'll not be eating overwell, now that he's a sailor.' Food rationing or not, young Sir Andrew would have nothing but the best when he came on leave and there'd be his favourite iced buns and cherry scones, just like Mrs Shaw used to make. Tilda Tewk had glacé cherries secreted away for just such an occasion – aye, and more sugar than anyone in this house knew about! The last war had taught her a lot about squirrelling away and this war, when it came, had not caught her napping! 'Now here's her ladyship's glass, though you'd only to ring and I'd have answered.' There was little to do now at Rowangarth, even though Mary was so taken up with her wedding and Miss Clitherow, the housekeeper, away to Scotland to the funeral of a relative. 'And when do you expect the Reverend, Miss Julia?'

'Late, I shouldn't wonder. A parishioner, you know – the Sacrament.'

18

'Ah,' Tilda nodded. Flixby Farm, it would be. The old man had been badly for months.

'Go to bed. I'll wait up,' Julia offered.

'Nay, miss, there's no hurry. Mary's still out so it'll be no bother and any road, I promised Miss Clitherow before she went that I'd check the blackout.'

'Have you heard from her, Tilda?'

'Only once, to let us know she'd got there – eventually. A terrible journey, by all accounts. Two hours late arriving, and no toilet on the train.'

'That's the war for you,' Julia sighed, wondering if anything would ever be the same again and refusing, stubbornly, even so much as to think about the threat of invasion.

Tom Dwerryhouse sat in the rocker in the darkening kitchen, reluctant to draw the thick blackout curtains, needing to suck on his pipe, sort things out in his mind.

Nothing short of a fiasco, that meeting had been, with no one knowing rightly what to do. The formation of the Local Defence Volunteers it was supposed to be; civilians who were willing to stand and fight if the Germans came. And come they would, Tom frowned, since there seemed nowhere else for them to go except Russia, and they'd signed a pact with Russia not to fight each other.

Strange, when you thought about it – Fascists and Communists, ganging up together. The two didn't mix, any fool knew that. But happen they'd only agreed the non-aggression pact because each was scared of the other. And long may it remain so. A bit of healthy mistrust was just what Hitler could do with – the need to look over his shoulder at the Russians – wonder if *they* would stab *him* in the back.

But Stalin was nowt to do with us. What was more important was getting some kind of order into the Volunteers. There had been all manner of opinions put forward and no one agreeing until in the end the Reverend had suggested he contact the Army in York and ask them to send someone over to talk to the men.

Then the Reverend had been called away to Flixby Farm and that had more or less been that. A right rabble they were – no uniforms, no rifles. Those men who owned shotguns had brought them, but the cowman from Home Farm had arrived with a hay fork over his shoulder, which was all he could muster, and hay forks – shotguns, even – weren't going to be a lot of use against tanks and trained soldiers. Hitler would pee himself laughing if he knew, and be over on the next tide!

Tom gazed into his tobacco jar, wondering if he could indulge himself with a fill. He had shared his last ounce with Reuben and only the Lord knew when he could get more.

And soon beer would be in short supply, the landlord at the Coach and Horses in Creesby had been heard to prophesy gloomily. On account of sugar being rationed, that was. No option, really, when the breweries had had their sugar cut, an' all.

But beer was the least of Tom Dwerryhouse's worries. What really bothered him was all the talk of invasion. People spoke about it in a kind of subdued panic, as if it couldn't really happen. Not to the British.

But things were bad: the French overrun and British soldiers snatched off Dunkirk beaches reeling with the shock of it. It was all on account of that Maginot Line, Tom considered gravely. Smug, the French had been. No one would ever breach *their* defences; not this war.

But they hadn't reckoned with Hitler's cunning in invading the Low Countries. Never a shot fired in anger, because his armies had just marched round the end of the invincible Maginot Line and had been in Paris before the French could say Jack Robinson. Only Hitler could have thought of pulling a fast one like that and getting away with it. A genius was he, or mad as they come?

Tom reached again for his tobacco. He needed a fill. Things were writhing inside him that only a pipe could soothe. It wasn't just the invasion and taking care of Alice and Daisy and Polly, if it happened; it was that Local Defence lot in the village. He had left Keeper's Cottage expecting to join it and be treated with the respect due to an ex-soldier, but all they'd done was witter amongst themselves, tie on their Local Defence Volunteer armbands and agree to meet another night. And there was nothing like an armband for scaring the wits out of a German Panzer Division!

'That you, love?' He half turned as the back door opened and shut.

'It's me, Dada. Mam not home, yet?'

'No, lass. She rang up from the village, summat about getting the loan of a tea urn. Be about half an hour, she said.'

'I'd better see to the blackout, then. Won't take me long, then I'll put the kettle on.'

Daisy had expected both her parents to be home; had got herself in the mood to come out with it, straight and to the point. That Mam still wasn't back had thrown her.

She pulled the curtain over the front door then walked upstairs, drawing the thick black curtains over each window. She should have asked Dada, she brooded, how long ago Mam had phoned. She was getting more and more nervous. If Mam wasn't soon home, she'd have to blurt her news out to Dada and she didn't want to do that.

Mind, she was glad they had a telephone at last. They wouldn't have got one if it hadn't been for the coming of the Land Army, and them taking over Rowangarth bothy. Aunt Julia had been glad for the land girls to have the place because since the apprentices who lived there had been called up into the militia it had stood empty, and Polly living there alone, rattling round like a pea in a tin can.

The Land Army people had had so many requests from the local farmers for land girls to help out, and Rowangarth bothy would be ideal quarters for a dozen women. A warden would be installed to run the place and a cook, too. Aunt Julia had said they could have it for the duration with pleasure if they would consider Mrs Polly Purvis as warden or cook. Mrs Purvis had given stirling service, Aunt Julia stressed, looking after the garden apprentices, and would be ideally suited to either position.

So Keth's mother was offered the cooking, and accepted gladly, especially when they'd mentioned how much wages she would be paid, as well as her bed and keep. And the GPO came to put the phone in.

That was when the engineer had asked Dada, Daisy recalled, why he didn't get a phone at Keeper's Cottage whilst they were in the area.

'There'll be a shortage of telephones before so very much longer, and that's a fact,' the GPO man said. 'Soon you'll not be able to get one for love nor money. The military'll have taken the lot!'

Daisy could have hugged Dada when he said yes and now a shiny black telephone stood importantly in the front passage at Keeper's Cottage.

For the first week, Mam had jumped a foot in the air every time it rang because Aunt Julia was tickled pink that Keeper's was on the phone at last and rang every morning for a chat. And she, Daisy, so often sat on the bottom step of the stairs, gazing at it, willing it to ring so that when she lifted it and whispered 'Holdenby 195', Keth would be on the other end, calling from Kentucky and he'd say –

But Keth couldn't call and she couldn't call Keth, not even if she didn't mind giving up a whole week's wages just to talk to him for three minutes, because civilians weren't allowed to ring America now. The under-sea cable was needed for more important things by the Government and the armed forces. Indeed, civilians were having a bad time all round, Daisy brooded. Asked not to travel on public transport unless their journey was really necessary; their food rationed, clothes so expensive in the shops that few could afford them, and no face cream nor powder nor lipstick to be had – even a shortage of razor blades, would you believe? But that was as nothing compared to what was soon to come, she thought as she pulled down the kitchen blind, drew together the blackout curtains then pulled across the bright, rose-printed curtains to cover them, because not for anything was she looking at those dreary black things night after night, Mam said.

'Shall I make a drink of tea, Dada?' Daisy switched on the light.

'Best not, sweetheart. Wait till your mam gets back.'

Since tea was rationed six months ago, the caddy on the mantelshelf was strictly under Alice's supervision.

'Dada?' Daisy sat down in the chair opposite. 'There's something –' She stopped, biting on the words.

'Aye, lass?' Her father did not shift his gaze from the empty fireplace and it gave her the chance she needed to call a halt to what she had been about to say.

'I – well, I know it's stupid to ask, but can you tell me,' she rushed on blindly, warming to her words, 'what will happen to my money if the Germans invade us? Will I get it?'

'Well, if you wait another year till you're one-and-twenty, you'll know, won't you? Not long to go now, so I wouldn't worry over much. But if you really want my opinion, that inheritance of yours is going to be the least of our worries if the Germans do get here. So let's wait and see, shall us?'

Daisy's inheritance. Money held in trust by solicitors in Winchester. Only a year to go and then it would be hers to claim, Tom brooded – if the Germans didn't come, that was; if all of them lived another year.

'Silly of me to ask.' And silly to have almost blurted

out what she had done yesterday, during her dinner hour. 'You're right, Dada. Either way now, it doesn't matter.'

And it didn't, when Drew was in the Navy and Keth was in Kentucky not able to get home, and people having to sleep in air-raid shelters and already such terrible losses by all the armed forces. When you thought about that, Daisy Dwerryhouse's fortune was immoral, almost.

It came as a relief to hear the opening of the back door and her mother calling, 'Only me . . .'

Then Mam, opening the kitchen door, hanging her coat on the peg behind it, patting her hair as she always did, popping a kiss on the top of Dada's head like always.

'Sorry I'm late, but I'd the offer of the use of a grand tea urn for the canteen. And talking of tea, set the tray, Daisy, there's a love.'

She sat down in her chair, pulling off her shoes, wiggling her toes.

Then, as she put on her slippers Daisy said, 'Mam, Dada, before we do anything – please – there's something I've got to tell you . . .'

2

'Tell us?' Tom gazed into the empty fireplace, puffing on his pipe, reluctant to look at his daughter. 'Important, is it?' Which was a daft thing to ask when the tingling behind his nose told him it was. Loving his only child as he did, he knew her like the back of his own right hand.

'Anything to do with the shop?' Alice frowned.

'Yes – and no. I don't like working there, you know.'

'But whyever not, lass?' Tom shifted his eyes to the agitated face. 'You've just had a rise without even asking for it.'

'Never mind the rise – it's still awful.' Daisy looked down at her hands.

'Oh, come now! Morris and Page is a lovely shop, and the assistants well-spoken and obliging. All the best people go there and it's beautiful inside.' Twice since her daughter went to work there, curiosity got the better of Alice and she had ventured in, treading carefully on the thick carpet, sniffing in the scent of opulence. She bought a tablet of lavender soap on the first occasion and a remnant of blue silk on the second. Paid far too much for both she'd reckoned, but the extravagance had been worth it if only to see what a nice place Daisy worked in.

'I'll grant you that, Mam. The shop is very nice, but once you are in the counting house where I work, there are no carpets – only lino on the floor. And we are crowded into one room with not enough windows in it. And as for those ladylike assistants – well, they've got Yorkshire accents like most folk. A lot of them put the posh on because it's expected of them. And obliging? Well, they get commission on what they sell and they need it, too, because their wages are worse than mine!'

'So what's been happening? Something me and your dada wouldn't like, is it?'

'Something happened, Mam, but nothing that need worry anyone but me. Yesterday morning, if you must know. There was this customer came to the outside office, complaining that we'd overcharged her. She gets things on credit, then pays at the end of the month when the accounts are sent out. Anyway, yesterday morning she said she hadn't had half the things on her bill, so I had to sort it out. She was really snotty; treated me like dirt when I showed her the sales dockets with her signature on them.'

'But accounts are nothing to do with you, love. You're a typist.'

'I know, Mam, but the girl who should have seen to it is having time off because her young man is on leave from the Army, so there was only me to do it.'

'So you told this customer where to get off, eh?' Tom knew that flash-fire temper; knew it because she had inherited it from him.

'As a matter of fact, I didn't. I just glared back at her and she said I was stupid and she'd write to the manager about me, the stuck-up bitch!'

'Now there's no need for language!' Alice snapped. 'But if you didn't answer back nor lose your temper, what's all the fuss about?'

'Oh, I *did* lose my temper, but I didn't let that one see it. When she'd slammed off, I realized it was my dinner break, so I got out as fast as I could. She got me mad when there are so many awful things happening and all she could find to worry about was her pesky account!'

'But you cooled down a bit in your dinner break?'

'Well, that's just it, you see.' Daisy swallowed hard. No getting away from it, now. 'I ate my sandwiches on a bench in the bus station, then I walked into the Labour Exchange and asked them for a form. And I filled it in. I'm changing my job. I'm not kowtowing any longer to the likes of *that* woman.'

'And would you mind telling your mam and me just what that form you filled in was all about?' The tingling behind Tom's nose was still there. That little madam standing defiant on the hearth rug had done something stupid, he knew it. 'You're not going to work on munitions, are you?'

'Oh, Daisy! Not munitions? Mary Strong went on munitions in the last war and went as yellow as saffron!'

'Nothing like that, Mam, and anyway, they'll probably not take me. You've got to have an uncle who's a peer of the realm and a godfather who's an admiral and your mam's got to have danced with the Prince of Wales when she was a deb – or so they say.'

'So what was it about?'

'About the Navy. Drew has joined and I'm joining, too, if they'll take me. The women's navy, that is. The Wrens.'

'You – are – *what*?'

'I'm joining up.'

'Oh, but you're not! We could be invaded at any time! Just what do you think me and Mam would do if you were miles and miles away? You've got to stay here, safe at home!'

'No! Drew is miles and miles away. Drew's at Devonport – so what's so special about me?' Daisy challenged.

'The fact that you're still not of age, for one thing, and I don't remember giving my permission for you to join anything,' Tom flung, suddenly triumphant.

'Oh but you did, Dada. Your signature was on the bottom of the form. I wrote it there for you!'

'Why, you – you –' His face took on an ugly red. 'Don't think you can –'

'Tom! Stop it! Just take a deep breath, won't you? Calm down, for goodness' sake. That temper of yours is going to get you into trouble one day, just see if it doesn't!'

'I won't have a bit of a lass forging my name!' His voice was low; too low.

'Well, she's done it and I'm very annoyed about it. You'll never again write your father's name, do you hear me, Daisy?'

'I won't, Mam. And I've got to have a medical first, and they say there's a waiting list to get in, so by the time they get around to me the invasion will have happened, if it's going to. And I'm truly sorry, Mam, and oh – Dada . . .'

She threw her arms round her father's neck and because he loved her unbearably he gathered her to him and stroked her hair and made little hushing sounds, just as he had always done when she was unhappy.

'I'm a fool, aren't I? I shouldn't have done it but everything's in such a mess. Drew has gone, and Bas and Kitty are in America, and Keth's with them and –' The tears came, then; great, jerking sobs from the deeps of her despair. 'I miss Keth so much. The summer of 'forty he said he'd be home – this very summer – but he won't be; he can't be! I want to see him, but I want him to stay in America, too! Can't you understand what it's like? Mam was my age when you and she said goodbye in your war, then she went to France to be near you! Try to understand how it is for me and Keth.'

'I do, lass. I do. And happen it'll be like you said. By the time you get into the Navy, we'll all know where we stand, one way or the other.' He took a handkerchief from his pocket, offering it, his expression tender with the love he felt for her. 'So dry your eyes, our Daisy. Mam and me didn't want there to be another war, and now there's nothing we can do about it except to keep our chins up and carry on as best we can. Now how about a smile?'

'I'm sorry,' Daisy sniffed. 'I really am. And I love you both very much and I don't know why I filled that form in for the Wrens – I honestly don't!'

'Oh yes you do, Daisy Dwerryhouse!' The tension had left Alice now. 'You did exactly as I did. You listened to your heart instead of to your head. There must be a daft streak somewhere in us Dwerryhouse women. Now for goodness' sake, let's have that drink of tea.' She flinched as a bomber flew over the house, the noise of its engines drowning out speech. 'My, but that one was low!'

'Aye. Loaded, they'll be. It must take a bit of doing, getting one of those things off the ground,' Tom frowned. 'Going bombing again I shouldn't wonder.'

'Again. And they're bits of lads, some of them. There was an air-gunner in the canteen a couple of nights ago; told me he was eighteen. *Eighteen!* Now I ask you, what age is that?'

'Two years younger than me, Mam,' Daisy whispered.

'So it is, love.' She raised her eyes to the ceiling. 'And there's another of them off over, an' all. Well – God go with them,' she whispered, her eyes all at once too bright, 'and bring them all safely back.'

She turned her back so Tom and Daisy should not see her tears. Drew gone and now Daisy worrying to go and oh, damn the war! Damn and blast it!

Julia Sutton was crossing the hall as her husband, Nathan, came through the front door.

'You're late.' She lifted her face for his kiss. 'How were things at Flixby?'

'The old man was sleeping when I left. He'll slip away gently. Ewart Pryce gave him an injection so he isn't in pain.'

'Ah, well – there'll be two more. Hear of one, hear of three, isn't that what they say? Want a drink?'

'Please. Have we any Scotch?'

'Enough. But can anyone tell me why things we took for granted seem just to have disappeared? The distilleries haven't suddenly been taken over, have they? The cigarette factories haven't closed down?'

Only that morning she had stood twenty minutes in a queue for five – *five*, would you believe? – cigarettes. She had been so desperate for one she'd had difficulty not lighting up in the street there and then!

'Shortage of materials, shortage of labour. Tobacco has to be brought here by sea, just like most of our food. The farmers are going to have to produce more, though they can't grow sugar nor tea . . .'

Nor petrol, Julia thought. All her June petrol coupons used, and more than a week to go before she could get any more. Only a thimbleful left in the tank.

'I'll have to start riding my bike,' she said, out of the blue. 'Do me good, I suppose . . .'

'It would. And you could tell yourself you were helping the war effort, saving petrol.'

'I wouldn't be saving anything, just eking out my ration. Thank goodness I drive a baby Austin. Your pa's Rolls would guzzle up a month's ration in two days!'

'Pa put the Rolls in mothballs ages ago, and you know it. His eyes are getting worse, though he won't admit it. He's going to have to give up driving before so very much longer.'

'But he'd be virtually marooned at Pendenys without a car,' Julia protested. 'He'll just have to get a pony and trap. Mother had one in the last war; got quite good at it.'

'And you, I seem to remember, were always to be seen biking furiously along the lanes,' he smiled fondly.

'Mm. Me and Alice both. We used to ride in the dark in winter – we had to. It was the only way to get to Denniston when we were –'

She stopped abruptly, her cheeks pinking. When she and Alice had been probationer nurses, she'd been going to say; when she'd been married to Andrew, that was, and desperate to get to France to be near him.

'A long time ago, darling.' Nathan accepted the glass she offered. 'Woman – you've drowned my whisky!'

'Sorry – only way to make it go further.' She settled herself on the floor at his feet, leaning her back against his chair. 'How old is the man who's dying?'

'Seventy-six next . . .'

'It'll be a long pull, then, when he goes.' Seventy-five slow, sombre peals on the death bell; one for each year of his life.

'No. No more passing bells. There was a letter from the Diocese office this morning. Bell ropes are to be tied up as a precaution. And we'll have to stop the church clock striking, too. No more bells nor chimes – only for the invasion, if it comes.'

'You mean not for *anything*?' Church bells and the chiming of the church clock were a part of their lives.

'Only if the invasion comes. The military will tell us when to ring them. As a warning, you see – to let people know . . .'

'Then let's hope we never hear them till it's all over and we've won!' What a chiming of bells there'd be then! *When* we won. There were some old miseries, Julia frowned, who said it would go on far longer than the last one did, especially as there seemed to be no stopping Hitler. 'Will it last four years, Nathan? Is Drew going to be away all that time?' The best years of his life, away from Rowangarth?

'Barring miracles, Julia, I think he might. There's even talk of women being directed into war work soon – compulsory, so they say. They might even send young women, if they aren't married, into the armed forces.'

'*Send* them, Nathan? But they can't! Oh, my Lord! Tom Dwerryhouse'll go berserk if they call Daisy up!'

'But, sweetheart, there's a lot of young women in the Forces already.'

'Yes – but they are volunteers, there because they want to be or because they feel they should be. But the powers that be can't take young girls from their parents and put them into uniform, dammit! And some of them are so innocent they don't know how babies get there – or get out!'

'*They* can, Julia. *They* can do anything they want if they think it's justified. It's done under the new law – the Defence of the Realm Act. They're using it, now that Italy has declared war on us, to round up people here they think might have Italian connections or sympathies. They'll intern them, just as they did to Germans living here when war broke out.'

'And serve them right, too,' Julia snorted. 'Italy declaring war on us when we were on our knees, almost, after Dunkirk! Kicking us when we were down, that's what! Mussolini is a pig! And I think I'll have a whisky, too, *and* a cigarette. I need them!'

'Yes. I think you'd better,' Nathan said; said it softly and strangely so that Julia turned sharply.

'Why?' she demanded. 'Have you some more miserable news for me?'

'Depends on how you look at it, I suppose. It's why I was so late tonight. I called in on Pa. It's been on the cards for some time; this morning it was definite. *They* want Pendenys Place . . .'

'*Taking* it, you mean? Commandeering it – lock, stock and barrel?'

'Under the Defence of the Realm Act, they told Pa. But only Pendenys. The stock and the barrels Pa has a month to shift out. They're letting him have the tower wing – what's left of it, that is – to store all the stuff in. He's getting a removal firm from Creesby to do it for him, then he's got to hand the place over. They're taking the stable block and the garages, too – even the kitchen garden.'

'But what do they want Pendenys for – a hospital?' Julia downed her drink almost at a gulp, so agitated was she. 'What on earth can they do with it?'

'I don't know anything except that *They* want it, so there's nothing anyone can do about it. Pa isn't all that much bothered – or won't be once the place has been emptied and everything locked up safely. He's going to Anna, to look after her and Tatiana at Denniston, he says.'

'But Anna's got Karl to look after her! Your pa should come here to Rowangarth.'

'Where you and Aunt Helen have me to look after you. And Denniston House isn't far away – you above all should know that.'

'Mm. About ten minutes by bike,' Julia agreed.

Nathan drained his glass, setting it on the table at his side. 'Pa seems to think Pendenys might be used for the Air Force – maybe for offices or accommodation for Holdenby Moor. It isn't far from the aerodrome, when you think about it. But I'm not so sure. All the visits were made by army people and they seemed more concerned with its seclusion and how easily it could be made secure.'

'For something hush-hush, you mean?'

'Maybe for a bolt hole for high-ups in the Government or the Civil Service if the invasion happens.'

'Or maybe for exiled foreign royals – perhaps even for our own, if they start bombing London.'

'Lord knows,' Nathan shrugged.

'And He'll not tell us,' Julia pointed out irreverently and not at all like the wife of the vicar of All Souls'. 'Hell, but I hate this war! They've taken Drew and we're waiting here for Hitler to make up his mind when he's coming! What are we to do, darling – and don't say, "Pray, then leave it in God's hands." The Germans will be praying, too, and it looks as if it's them God is listening to at the moment! No platitudes, Nathan Sutton, or I'll thump you!'

'All right – then how if we both have another Scotch? Just a small one . . .'

Julia gazed at her empty glass, then turned to smile at her husband.

'You know something, Vicar – that's a very good idea. And what the heck? We can only drink it once!'

She held out her hand for his glass, then walked to the table on which the near-empty decanter stood, frowning as she tilted it.

The Army – or whoever – was welcome to Pendenys, great ugly, ostentatious place that it was. Only Aunt Clemmy and her precious Elliot had liked it and they were both dead and buried.

Then she permitted herself a small, mischievous smile just to think of Aunt Clemmy's ghost, weeping and wailing at the front entrance, cursing the dreadful, common people who had dared to take her beloved Pendenys Place.

But what on earth did they want it for?

3

Each evening when she got home from work, Daisy expected the letter to have arrived. It would be small, she supposed, the envelope manila-coloured with 'On His Majesty's Service' printed across the top. And inside would be a tersely-worded message, telling her where and when to attend for her medical examination.

It was so long coming, though, that she began to think her application had been lost or ignored – or that the Women's Royal Naval Service had such a long list of twenty-year-old shorthand typists that they weren't all that much bothered about Daisy Dwerryhouse.

She began not to care, even to be glad, and only to scan the mantelpiece for Keth's pale blue air-mail envelopes as she opened the kitchen door.

Since war started, Keth's letters rarely came singly. Almost a week without one, then three or more would arrive, giving her news of the Kentucky Suttons and messages from Bas and Kitty, but mostly telling her he missed her and loved and wanted her. There were no more Washington postmarks and she ceased to wonder why he had been there.

She read his letters over and over, arranging them in date order. There were a great many; more than three hundred, packed tightly into shoe boxes in the bottom of her wardrobe and easily to hand because if things got worse and Holdenby was bombed, they were the first things she would grab and take down to the cellar with her.

Tonight, there had been a letter from Drew.

. . . all at once it began to make sense, fall into place. I realized, the other afternoon, that I could sort the dits and the das into letters and figures – actually read them.

Daisy frowned. Dots and dashes, did he mean?

Even so, I found it hard to believe when they told me I had passed out. I am now a telegraphist and will be going back to barracks soon for drafting.

Don't write back, Daiz, because there is a strong buzz we will be given leave. I'll try to give you a ring if it is likely to happen, though there is always a queue at the phone box and delays getting through. Don't be surprised if I just arrive without warning . . .

Drew coming on leave – but when? She felt so lonely and alone that tomorrow wouldn't be soon enough. There seemed nothing, now, to life but working, wondering, worrying – and wanting. Wanting Keth, that was; wanting him here to touch and kiss and make love to her; wanting him to stay in Kentucky so They, the faceless ones, should not take him into the Army.

She ought to be ashamed, really. Compared to some, her life hadn't changed overmuch. This far, Keth was out of harm's way, Keeper's Cottage had not been bombed, the evening air was heavy with the scent of newly cut hay and Rowangarth was still there, its sagging old roof just visible over the treetops to remind her that some things endured.

It was sad, for all that, that France had finally given in, been forced to sign a surrender in the same railway carriage in which Germany signed the Armistice at the end of the last war – Dada's war. How humiliating for the French; how Hitler must have gloated.

And now, fresh fears. German soldiers had occupied Guernsey and Jersey, and those islands almost a part of

Britain. It sent fear screaming through her just to think about it.

Only one thing was certain, Daisy admitted as sudden, silly tears filled her eyes. England – Great Britain – stood alone now, backs to the wall. This cockeyed little island was going to have to take whatever the Nazis threw at it, or give in. And since Mr Churchill had said we would never surrender, it seemed we were in for a bad time. A shiver of pure melancholy ran through her. How brave would she be when – *if* – it happened?

Keth, I need you so . . .

Mary Strong gave a final loving rub to the silver punchbowl she was polishing, then wrapped it in black tissue paper, wondering if Will was right and her ladyship really was going to hide away the silver and valuables – just in case.

If she were given a pound note for every time she had cleaned that bowl over the years, Mary sighed, she could buy the most beautiful bridal gown in York and still have a tidy pile left over.

Mind, she would still work as parlourmaid for Lady Helen when she and Will were wed. Once, it was demeaning for a married woman to work, unless she were a widow and had little choice. But war had come again and married women without encumbrances were expected to work.

Yet what concerned Rowangarth's parlourmaid more immediately was what to wear to her wedding four weeks hence. She was the first to admit she was past bridal white and anyway, a once-only dress was an extravagance she didn't subscribe to.

Now if Alice could be persuaded to make her something pretty yet sensible, she pondered, and she could find a nice matching hat, her problem would be solved.

'I'll ask Alice,' she said to Tilda, 'to make my dress – for the wedding, I mean . . .'

'I'd concentrate, if I were you,' Tilda frowned, 'on getting Miss Clitherow's sitting room seen to. She's back tomorrow and you could write your name on the top of that table of hers. I've no time, Mary, what with the bottling to see to and the raspberry jam to make!'

'Oh? And where did Tilda Tewk get sugar for jam, then?'

'Never you mind!' It wasn't only silver could be hidden away! There were twenty two-pound bags of sugar, an' all, and Hitler, if he came, could draw her teeth one by one before she'd tell them where so much as a grain was hidden. 'And don't forget, herself'll be on the night train and back here before noon!'

'Aye.' Mary wasn't likely to forget. It had been grand with the housekeeper away and just her and Tilda to see to things. 'She's been gone so long I thought we'd seen the back of her, but I'll give her room a going-over in the morning.

'Now would you favour blue for a wedding dress, Tilda, and a matching hat? And do you think Mr Catchpole would make me up a few flowers? Not a bouquet – not without a veil – maybe a little posy, though.' Miss Julia had worn blue and carried white orchids – at her first wedding, that was, to the doctor, Andrew MacMalcolm.

She lapsed again into daydreams and Tilda, who was nothing if not practical, knew better than to interrupt them. But she'd be glad when Miss Clitherow got herself back; when Mary and Will were safely wed and when – and may God forgive her for such thoughts – Hitler had made up his mind about the invasion. Maybe then, things could get back to normal – or as normal as they ever could be with a war on.

Tilda sighed, remembering the last one, then turned her thoughts to the evening meal ahead. She supposed it would be rabbit. Again.

*　　*　　*

'Do you think, dear,' Helen Sutton asked of her daughter at breakfast, 'that either Will or Catchpole could be persuaded to look after a few hens?' Eggs were rationed now, and sometimes to only one each person a week. 'Surely we could keep them on household scraps and gleanings of wheat and barley?'

'We could ask. Polly Purvis has six Rhode Island Reds at the bothy. She says they are laying well – a couple of dozen eggs a week. She gives the land girls a boiled egg apiece every Sunday for breakfast and keeps what's left for cooking. But perhaps we should ask Will? Catchpole has more than enough on his plate. He can just about manage the kitchen garden on his own, but he's not going to have the time to grow flowers.'

Growing flowers was unpatriotic, the Government pronounced. 'Dig for Victory!' the posters demanded, with people being urged to plant cabbages, leeks and peas instead of flowers.

'In the last war we ploughed up the lawns and grew potatoes,' Helen murmured. Beautiful camomile lawns were turned under the plough, but they had been hungry then. Maybe before this one was over they would be hungry again. It was a distinct possibility when so many ships carrying food were being sunk every day by U-boats.

'I'll have a think about the hens, but first I think we should seriously consider getting some help for Catchpole.'

'But how, Julia? They don't consider gardening to be a reserved occupation.' *They* had taken the garden apprentices into the militia and a waste of six years of training when you considered that two of them were in the infantry and one consigned to an army cookhouse.

'No, but growing food is important and with a bit of help our kitchen garden could supply no end of vegetables and soft fruit. Anyway, I'm going to try.'

'But where are we to find another gardener?'

'You'll see.' It was such a mad idea, Julia supposed, she

just might bring it off. 'Tell you later,' she smiled mysteriously. 'And that was the postman, if I'm not mistaken. Bet you anything you like there'll be a letter.'

From Drew, of course. No other letters mattered.

Daisy sat on the gate, waiting for Tatiana. It was where they usually met; halfway between Keeper's Cottage and Denniston House, where Tatiana lived with her mother, Anna, with Karl, the big, black-bearded Cossack, to watch over them; was where, soon, Tatiana's grandfather would be living when he handed over Pendenys Place to the Government.

Daisy hoped Rowangarth would escape. It would be awful having the military there, especially if they wanted Keeper's Cottage, too.

But They could do anything they wanted now, and no one's house – or car or boat, even – was safe if They decided they had greater need of it. For the war effort, of course. Mind, Mam thought it was a good thing about Pendenys and that Mr Edward would be better off living at Denniston. 'All on his own in that great pile of slate and stone, like living in a cathedral.'

Daisy jumped off the gate as Tatiana arrived, red-faced from pedalling.

'I am sick, sick, *sick* of old people,' she announced dramatically, leaning her cycle against the hedge. 'It was awful at Cheyne Walk!'

'Well, you're back home now,' Daisy offered mildly because she was used to her friend's fiery outbursts. Probably something to do with her being half-Russian.

'Yes, thank God! Grandmother Petrovska was her usual awful self and Uncle Igor was rushing around making sure they weren't going to be interned.'

'But they won't be. We aren't at war with the Russians.'

'Not yet, but we will be, Grandmother says. And don't call them Russians, Daisy. They are *Communists*, not real

Russians. They've made a pact with Hitler, you know.'

Daisy did know. Dada hadn't been able to understand it. Communists and Fascists should be natural enemies, he'd said.

'So what was so awful about staying with your grandma?' Daisy demanded.

'Oh, it was Grandmother, I suppose, being stubborn.' Tatiana took a deep breath, sighing it out dramatically, leaning her elbows on the gate, gazing out over the field of ripening wheat. 'Mother wants her to pack up and leave London – stay at Denniston for the duration. She thinks London will be heavily bombed soon. Stands to sense, doesn't it? Hitler's got to knock out London before he invades.'

'We-e-ll, yes . . .' It made sense, Daisy was bound to agree, running her tongue round lips gone suddenly dry.

'And all the ports, too, Uncle Igor said.'

The ports, too, and Drew was near Plymouth.

'So it was better, Mother said, for Grandmother to move out. Apart from the two aerodromes, there isn't a lot around Holdenby for the Luftwaffe to waste its bombs on.'

'So when is she coming?' Daisy had met the autocratic Countess Petrovska and felt sorry for Tatty.

'Oh, she isn't. Refused point-blank. She said if she left Cheyne Walk, They would take it because there'd be no one living in it.

' "I hef lorst my beautiful house in St Petersburg and my estate at Peterhof to the rabble. I vill not give up this one, too," ' Tatiana mimicked. 'And I suppose you can't blame her. Drew said he'd hate it if the Communists had taken Rowangarth.'

'But there aren't any Communists here.'

'No, but *They* might commandeer it, like Pendenys.'

'For goodness' sake, Tatty, don't be so miserable!'

'I can't help it. It's my Russian soul.'

'Don't be daft! You're as English as I am.'

'Half-English. I speak the mother tongue, don't forget.'

'Y-yes.' Daisy was forced to admit it. Tatiana Sutton spoke the politely correct Russian learned from her mother but she was fluent, too, in the dialect spoken by Karl, a Georgian by birth. Tatiana, when provoked, had the advantage of being able to let fly a string of Russian swear words – learned from Karl – and get away with it. 'But tell me – how was London?'

'Poor old place – it seemed a bit bewildered. Barrage balloons in all the parks and sandbags everywhere. And it's so completely dark now at nights. The shops haven't a lot to sell. Mother didn't buy a thing except a lipstick, and she had to stand in a queue for half an hour to get it. And there are uniforms everywhere. Such gorgeous men, and all of them going to war.' She sighed loudly and with regret. Such a waste when she, Tatiana Sutton, hadn't even been kissed yet – leastways, not with passion. 'It makes you want to join up, doesn't it?'

'I suppose so. As a matter of fact,' Daisy took a deep breath, 'I *have* joined up.'

'*Wha-a-t?* You mean you'll be leaving, too? But, Daisy, you *can't*! Drew's gone, and Kitty and Bas can't visit any more, and Keth's stuck in America! If you go, there'll be only me left out of the entire Clan!'

'I know, and I'm sorry I did it. But don't worry overmuch. They haven't even acknowledged my application yet, and not a word about my medical. I could be months and months waiting.'

'So what are you joining?' Tatiana was piqued.

'The Wrens, if they'll have me. It's got to be, you see, because of Drew. I hate working in that shop and I thought that if anything I could do would shorten the war by just one week, then I should do it. I want Keth home – but not till the war is over.'

'Then that does it! If you can volunteer, so can I! I think

42

I might go for the ATS. Well, the Suttons have always joined the Army, haven't they?'

'Until Drew – yes. But you can't, Tatty! Have you thought about what your grandma would say?'

'Oh, bugger Grandmother Petrovska!' Tatiana could swear in English, too. 'I'm sick of her and her everlasting black! Imagine – she's still in mourning for Czar Nicholas and him dead more than twenty years!'

'But it won't be a bed of roses. Don't expect it to be fun – in the Forces, I mean.'

'Anything would be better than having Grandmother living at Denniston, because London *will* get bombed and she *will* have to leave.'

'But your mother wouldn't let you. You're not twenty-one yet.'

'Neither are you. Did your father give his permission? My mother will say I can, anyway.'

'She won't, and you know it. Dada didn't sign for me to go. I sort of did it for him. He hit the roof!'

'Then I shall sign Mother's name. Aleksandrina Anastasia Petrovska Sutton. I know exactly how she does it.'

'Oh, don't let's talk about the war! I'm afraid, really, about the invasion.'

'So am I. They might treat us like they treated the Poles. And Grandmother wouldn't help. She'd shout at them, if they came – all sorts of insults. We'd end up against the wall, being shot!'

'Don't say things like that, *please*. Let's talk about Drew. Aunt Julia says he might be home on leave soon.'

'He might?' Tatiana brightened visibly. 'There'd be half the Clan together again.'

'Mm. And I could ask him for a few tips about the Wrens – what to say, I mean, if they ask me what I want to do.'

'So they won't put you in the cookhouse, you mean?'

'Sort of. And in the Navy they call it the galley.'

'Whatever,' Tatiana shrugged. 'But they do that, you

43

know. If you can cook, then they'd put you in an office and if you can type –'

'Which I can.'

'Exactly. They'd probably put you on a barrage balloon, or something. They do it on purpose.'

'It wouldn't be that. I think the Air Force looks after all the barrage balloons. But I stood in a queue in Woolworth's, yesterday, and guess what?' She was anxious not to talk about the war any more. 'I got a jar of cold cream.'

'Lucky dog! Tell you what – let's go back to Denniston and have a root through Mother's make-up. She's out do-gooding for the war effort. She won't be back till late.'

'Could we? What if she caught us?'

'She won't. Come on!' An aircraft flew low overhead and Tatiana squinted up into the sky. 'Ooh, just look at that! It's a Whitley.' Tatiana was good at recognizing aircraft. 'They've got some at Holdenby Moor to replace the old Hampdens. And don't you just love those aircrew boys? Aren't they marvellous? I could fall head over heels for every one of them!'

'No you couldn't, Tatty. They're very young – most of them not old enough to get married. And they get killed – all the time. But no more war talk – *please*.'

'Oh, dear. Whatever next?' Helen Sutton looked up from the evening paper she was reading as her daughter came into the room. 'Our allies, Julia, yet we've sunk the best part of the French fleet. They were anchored somewhere in North Africa and our navy just turned their guns on them. Sank them, and more than a thousand killed. Well, I hope,' she breathed, tight-lipped, 'that Drew will never be called on to do anything so awful!'

'You're right. It *is* awful. But did we have any choice, Mother? We couldn't let Hitler get his hands on those ships.'

'But the French captains wouldn't have let that happen.

A lot of their ships have already sailed into British ports – and the French fought alongside us last time, remember.'

'I know – but there's another war on now and we can't afford to use kid gloves, these days – not when we're up against it, like now. But I think I might have some good news for you. You know I said I wanted to get help for Jack Catchpole? Well, I just might be lucky. I think we're getting a land girl.'

'But I thought land girls worked on farms.'

'They work on the *land*, whether it's farmland or Rowangarth kitchen garden. They're there to help grow food and we could send no end of stuff to the Creesby shops. And a land girl could look after some hens for us. I went to the bothy – well, they call it a hostel, now – and I was lucky. Both the warden and the forewoman were in, and both of them thought Rowangarth could qualify. They were very nice and told me who to contact to get things going. We might have one before the month is out. Couldn't be in better time, either, for the soft fruit.'

'But how will Catchpole take it? He wouldn't be getting an experienced gardener, would he? I believe some land girls come from towns and can't milk a cow, even.'

'But we haven't got any cows. Anyway – can you milk a cow, Mother?'

'No. But I could learn if I had to, I suppose . . .'

'There's your answer then. She'll do just fine with Catchpole watching her. I've asked him, by the way, and he says as long as she doesn't mind getting her hands dirty and is willing to learn and doesn't give cheek, he said he would at least give it a try. So it's fingers crossed. I think they'll give us one. After all, we didn't make a fuss when they asked us to let them have the bothy, and we supplied them with a cook, don't forget.'

'If we'd said no, they'd have taken it, for all that.'

'But we didn't say no. We co-operated and did all we could to help, so they owe us a land girl.'

'I suppose so . . .' Helen Sutton was not entirely convinced, but Julia would never change, would always rush in without too much thought.

'By the way,' Helen called after her daughter's retreating back, 'Nathan wants to see you about something. He's in the library.'

And they could but try, she acknowledged as the door banged noisily shut. Yet for all that, she hoped that the young lady, if ever she arrived, didn't come complete with bright red lipstick and painted nails to match. Catchpole wouldn't like that at all.

The telephone rang shrilly and she heard Julia crossing the hall to answer it. She knew it was good news, even before the door flew open and a flushed and smiling Julia announced, 'Drew's coming on leave! Next Thursday, for ten days, he said!' She gathered her mother into her arms, hugging her fiercely. 'Isn't it wonderful? Must just tell Nathan, then I'll give Alice a ring!'

She was gone in a flurry of delight before Helen could even ask when her grandson would be arriving and if he wanted meeting at Holdenby station.

Then she smiled and picked up the framed photograph of a young sailor from the table beside her chair. His hair was cut much too short, but he smiled back at her exactly as Drew had always done.

Drew. Sir Andrew Sutton, really – Giles and Alice's son. Coming home on Thursday; home to Rowangarth.

But Thursday was all of five days away – a hundred and twenty long, slow hours away. However was she to endure them?

4

Never in her life had Agnes Clitherow been so glad to see Rowangarth. A feeling of homecoming wrapped around her and almost made her regret what she and her cousin Margaret had decided, but she shook such thoughts from her head, picked up her cases and walked, straight-backed as ever, to the kitchen door. As Rowangarth's housekeeper she had a right to enter by the front, but to do so would necessitate the ringing of the doorbell and that, at half-past six in the morning, was simply not done.

'Miss Clitherow!' Tilda gasped at the sight of the dishevelled lady who leaned against the door jamb. 'Oh, come in, do!' She guided her to a chair, all the while clucking and soothing as the occasion seemed clearly to demand, then set the kettle to boil on the gas stove. 'A good strong cup is what you need. Been travelling all night, have you?'

'Oh, Tilda!' She had indeed made the overnight journey, which from Oban to Glasgow had passed without too much discomfort. But from Glasgow to York! '*Never* take the night train!'

Packed to overflowing it had been with soldiers with respirators and kitbags, airmen with kitbags and respirators and a great many sailors with the added encumbrance of rolled and lashed hammocks and all of them sleeping and snoring not only where they ought to have been, but in corners, corridors and anywhere space was to be found.

'We were held up at Newcastle for almost an hour and if it hadn't been for an ATS girl, I don't know what I'd have done – you know what I mean . . . ?'

No need to go into intimate detail, but the resourceful

young lady had left the train, marched up to the engine driver and loudly threatened, 'Now listen 'ere, mate! If you start your bleedin' engine before me and this lady have found somewhere to have a widdle, I'll burst yer!' To which the driver replied that it looked as if they'd have time to sit there for the rest of the night and make their Wills if they were so minded, before he got the green light to move.

So embarrassing it had been and surely obvious to everyone awake that they were about to search the blacked-out railway station for the ladies' room!

'But wasn't there a lavvy on the train?' Tilda quickly sized up the cause of the upset.

'There were several, and all of them filled with luggage.' If she could have reached one, that was. They'd had the greatest difficulty getting off the train and they had struggled and pushed their way back to their compartment only to find their seats occupied by two burly sergeants who gazed at the ATS girl's single stripe and told her where she could go. Pulling rank, Miss Clitherow later discovered it was called, and bleedin' sergeants were always doing it!

'And the train was dirty and blacked out.' Except for the odd blue light bulb, that was, and if she never set foot on a train again for the entire duration of hostilities, it wouldn't bother her one iota. And that, she supposed was something of a contradiction in view of the decision she had made.

'Never you mind, Miss Clitherow, dear. Just take off your hat and wash your hands, then I'll pour you a cup.' Tilda had never seen the housekeeper so distraught, not in all her thirty-odd years at Rowangarth. 'And then I'd get a bath, if I were you, and pop straight into bed.'

'Oh, no!' A bath maybe, but she must see her ladyship as soon as maybe, thank her for the time off, then explain the position fully, a thought which brought tears to her eyes and Tilda to place a comforting arm around her shoulders – a liberty she would once never have dreamed of taking – and tell her that she was home and safe now, and must never go away again. Which immediately caused the tears to flow faster and for Miss Clitherow to murmur, amid gasps, 'Tilda! Please *don't* say that!'

The tears came again when she and her ladyship were comfortably seated in the small parlour, windows wide to the July afternoon. It was her ladyship's fault, the housekeeper reluctantly admitted, her being so genuinely pleased to see her back from her bereavement.

'We have missed you, Miss Clitherow,' Helen smiled. 'It's so good to see you again. Julia tells me your journey was very uncomfortable, but never mind – you are home now.'

'Oh dear, Lady Helen, but I'm not you see. Well, not for so very much longer.'

And she had gone on to explain how her cousin Margaret – the elder sister of Elizabeth, whose funeral Miss Clitherow had gone to attend – had begged her, almost, to leave domestic service and spend her remaining years close to kin amid the beautiful – and safe – hills and lochs of Scotland. 'It's time for you to retire, stop working for the gentry, Agnes, my dear. And it's so peaceful and quiet, here.'

Her cousin was right, of course. Apart from the blackout, there was little sign of the war in the tiny village between Oban and Connel. Just sight of the ferry from Achnacroish to Oban and the odd merchant ship making for the Sound of Mull. Certainly there were no aircraft armed with bombs and bullets, their wings heavy with fuel, struggling to take off. The bombers from RAF Holdenby Moor worried Agnes Clitherow. She flinched when they roared overhead, awoke with a start when, in the early hours of the morning, they returned from raids over Germany.

'We are safer here on the west coast. If the invasion comes it will be from the south or the east,' Margaret had urged and she was right without a doubt. Hitler's divisions occupied France, Belgium and the Netherlands, had ports and aerodromes there in plenty. 'Mark my words, Agnes, Hitler will not do the obvious. They are waiting for him to invade the south coast of England but in my opinion he'll land in Yorkshire or Northumberland. He's a sly one!'

'Not for so very much longer?' Helen's words cut into the housekeeper's troubled thoughts. 'You aren't ill, Miss Clitherow?'

'No, milady, but I am getting older, and my cousin has offered me my own room. It's so peaceful there in Scotland, and safe somehow.'

'And you don't feel safe here at Rowangarth?' Helen Sutton knew how much her housekeeper disliked having the aerodrome so near. 'You really want to go, Miss Clitherow? Are you and I to part after so long?'

'Needs must, Lady Helen. You know how old I am and I'm mindful of the fact that there would always have been shelter for me here. But I'm of a mind to end my days with Margaret in Scotland. It's why I'm giving notice now, and hoping it will be convenient for me to go in four weeks' time.'

'Miss Clitherow, you may leave as soon as you wish, but it will grieve me to see you go. I shall miss you greatly. Rowangarth will miss you.'

'Oh, milady . . .' Tears trembled on Agnes Clitherow's voice.

'Now don't upset yourself,' Helen soothed. 'Scotland isn't the other end of the world. We'll all keep in touch. But promise me one thing? You know I wish you well in your retirement, but just *if* things don't work out, I want you to know that you have only to ring me. There is room and to spare for you always here at Rowangarth. You'd never be too proud to admit that you missed us more than you thought, now would you?'

'No. I wouldn't,' she sniffed. 'This house has been like a home to me and where else would I turn, if trouble came?

And like you say, Rowangarth is only a telephone call away. But if you'll pardon me, milady – things to be done, you see . . .' And if she didn't get out of this dear little room she would break down and weep – a thing she had never done before – well, not in front of her ladyship, that was. 'Perhaps if we could talk later? It has been distressing for me, telling you.'

'And for me, too, learning I am to lose a splendid house-keeper and a dear friend. But if your mind is truly made up, then I promise not to try to persuade you to stay.'

'Thank you. Thank you for everything, milady,' the housekeeper choked as, for the first time in all her years with Lady Helen, she made a hasty, undignified exit.

Helen watched her go, heard the quiet closing of the door and the slow, sad steps along the passage outside, walking away from her.

But everything and everyone she had known and loved seemed to be leaving her now, she thought sadly. Soon there would be no one left. No one at all.

Jack Catchpole, son of the late Percy, and head – and since war started the only – gardener at Rowangarth, was not at all sure about the land girl Miss Julia had said would be coming. To help in the kitchen garden, she said, since they must grow all the food they could. Vegetables and fruits in season would help the war effort and Rowangarth, therefore, was entitled to apply for help from the Ministry of Agriculture and Fisheries – the Ag and Fish, most people called it.

What had surprised Catchpole, however, was that as in most things, Miss Julia had had her way in no time at all and now he must prepare himself for a female invasion of his domain.

He sucked on his empty pipe, contemplating the horrors of it. For one thing, she wouldn't know a weed from a seedling and for another, she wouldn't want to get her hands dirty nor break her fingernails which without a doubt would be long and painted bright red. And she would be late every morning, an' all, and make up all kinds of female excuses when she wanted time off to meet her young man or have her hair permanently waved. In short, she was not welcome.

It came as a great surprise, therefore, and something of a shock to see a young woman, smartly dressed in Land Army uniform, advancing upon him just as the kettle on the potting shed hob was coming to the boil and he had emptied his twist of tea leaves and sugar into the little brown teapot he had used for years and years. He watched her, saying not a word until she stood before him, eyes wide.

'Are you the head gardener?' she asked.

'Aye.' His eyes did not waver.

'I think you're expecting me, sir. I'm your land girl and I'm willing to learn . . .' She let go her breath in a little nervous huff.

'Aye.' Catchpole stuffed his pipe into the pocket of his shirt. 'Well, the first thing you learn in my garden is not to call me sir. My name is Jack Catchpole – *Mister* Catchpole to you. And what might your name be?'

'Grace Mary Fielding, Mr Catchpole, but people call me Gracie. Gracie Fielding – Gracie Fields, see? Well, when you come from Rochdale, what else?'

'What else indeed?' Catchpole liked Gracie Fields and her happy, brash voice. Made him laugh, Our Gracie did. 'So, young Gracie Fielding, what made you choose market gardening in general and Rowangarth in particular?'

'Oh, I didn't, Mr Catchpole – choose either, I mean. I just got sick of streets and mills and joined the Land Army so I could be in the country – and do my bit, of course. And it was the Land Army chose to send me here.'

'Mills, eh? Cotton mills?'

'Mm. All the women in our family worked in the mills,

but Mam said she wanted better for me. "Gracie isn't going in t'mill," she said and she worked extra hours to send me to the Grammar School.'

'So you got yourself a better job – kept away from the looms, then?'

'A better job – yes,' she grinned, 'but at the mill, as a wages clerk. Would make Dickie Hatburn's cat laugh, wouldn't it?'

'And who might Dickie Hatburn be?'

'Dunno, but he must have had a cat, that's for sure.' She threw back her head and laughed and her teeth were white and even. Her eyes laughed, too.

'Do you like cats, Gracie Fielding?'

'Not as much as dogs.'

'Then that's the second thing you learn in my garden. Cats is not welcome. When you see one you chase it, don't forget. Cats wait till you've made a nice soft tilth and sown your seeds careful, like, in nice straight rows, then they've the cheek to think you've done it specially for them. Soon as your back is turned, they're scratching about among your little seeds and you know what they leave behind them?'

'Oh I do, Mr Catchpole, and I'll chase them.'

'And dogs, too. Dogs're not welcome in my garden either, unless accompanied by a responsible adult and secure on the end of a lead.'

'I'm learning,' Gracie smiled.

'Then rule number three. At a quarter past ten exactly, I mash a pot of tea. Most days there's a fire in the big potting shed if we can find wood, and it's going to be one of your jobs to see that I get my tea on time.'

'Ten fifteen exactly.'

Catchpole took out his pocket watch, then glanced in the direction of the potting shed.

'Water'll just about be on the boil. Tea's in the pot. Reckon it might run to two. You'll find an extra mug on the top shelf beside the bottle marked poison.'

Gracie entered the dark shed. It smelled of earth and bone meal and smoke from the crackling wood fire in the little iron grate. On the hob a kettle was just beginning to puff steam.

She searched the top shelf to find a blue enamelled mug, rinsed it in the rainwater butt outside the door, then shook it dry. She liked Mr Catchpole and the smell of his big shed; liked his garden with its high, red-brick walls with fruit trees growing up them and she liked the straight, weed-free paths and their little clipped hedges.

'I'm glad I'm here,' she smiled, handing him the bigger mug, settling herself beside him. 'It'll be better than working on a farm, shovelling manure.'

'And what makes you think you won't be shovelling manoor here?' He jabbed the stem of his pipe in the general direction of a large, steaming heap in a distant corner of the garden. 'That manoor came here this March and there it'll stay till it's good and black and rotted down and smells as sweet as a nut. And then, I shouldn't be at all surprised, you'll shovel it into a barrow and you'll spread it down the potato rows and anywhere else I think fit for it to go. It'll be the land girl's job.'

'Rule number four,' she said gravely. 'Manure.'

'That's it. And then, when we've used up that heap – next spring, that'll be – us plants marrows there. Alus. Marrows is greedy feeders and they like growing where a manoor heap has wintered. Ground full of goodness, see. There's a great call, these days, for marrows for stuffing.'

'Stuffing,' Gracie echoed, never having eaten a stuffed marrow and making a mental note never to eat one in future.

Catchpole supped appreciatively. The lass could mash tea and she had a happy face and could take a bit of teasing.

He glanced at her outfit, taking in the khaki knee-stockings, the shirt and green tie; the short, smart jacket and the hat, tipped to the back of her bright yellow curls.

'Hope you don't intend coming to work all dressed up like that,' he remarked, eager to find just one fault.

'Bless you, luv, no! I'm wearing my walking-out togs just to make an impression. Tomorrow, I'll be wearing my dungarees and a cool shirt – and my good thick boots!'

Catchpole nodded, mollified, drained his mug then placed it on the ground at his feet.

'You got a young man, then?'

'One or two, Mr Catchpole, but none of them serious. Well, it's best not when there's a war on. Don't think I'd like having someone I cared about very much away at the war.'

'Ar.' The lass had sense. 'Still, can't sit here all morning nattering. Work to be done. Us've got to dig for victory, or so the Government tells us.'

Gaudy posters everywhere urged it. 'Dig for Victory!' they exhorted. Britain needed food, so lawns must be dug up and cabbages and potatoes planted instead. Those without gardens were offered allotments; flowerbeds in parks were planted with peas and beans and lettuces. Any grassy stretch came under the plough and this year, where children once played and dogs had been walked, wheat and oats and barley were already turning from green to gold, soon to be harvested.

Dig for victory! Every spadeful of earth turned over, every potato picked, was a second in time off the duration of the war, and Britain dug furiously.

'Then can't I stay, Mr Catchpole – start work right away?'

'You could, if you wasn't all togged up like that.'

'Then why don't I go back to the hostel and change into my dungarees? And I can pick up my sandwiches whilst I'm about it. And Mr Catchpole – why is our hostel called a bothy?'

Questions, questions! 'A bothy,' he sighed, 'is a place

where apprentice lads lived. Young gardeners, stable lads and the like. Every big house has a bothy, only once, in the old days, they were filled. Mrs Purvis looked after them all.'

'Mrs Purvis who's our cook?'

'That same lady. When the garden apprentices were taken into the militia, she had nothing to do. Lucky for her you land girls came along.'

'She's nice. She's been asking us, now the apples are ripening, to try to get her some windfalls, then she'll make us an apple pie for Sunday dinner. She's a good cook.'

'Well, you'm welcome to any windfalls you can gather here. There's a few about, over by the far wall. Now off with you, lass! I'll be over yonder when you get back, hoeing the sprouts. You know what sprouts are?'

'Course I do – but I've never seen them growing.'

'Well, from now on and for the duration, Gracie Fielding, you'm going to learn how to grow 'em – aye, and peas and beans and potatoes and more besides.'

'Suits me, Mr Catchpole.'

He watched her go. Happen he just might make something of the lass from Rochdale. She had a nice smile and a ready laugh and he'd especially looked at her fingernails, which were short cut and unpainted.

'Us'll see how you shape up, Gracie Fielding,' he murmured to her retreating back and surprised himself by noticing she had a nice, neat little bottom.

He chuckled mischievously, wondering how long it would be before the lads at the aerodrome were wolf-whistling his land girl.

Picking up the mugs, he rinsed them in the water butt and returned them to the shelf beside the bottle marked poison. Then he took the teapot and emptied the leaves on the compost heap, making a mental note to instruct Gracie about compost heaps and their value in the order of things.

He reckoned the lass would be a quick learner and was very surprised to find himself looking forward to her return.

'I see they're making the Duke of Windsor governor of the Bahamas,' Helen Sutton murmured over the top of the morning paper.

'Best place for him,' Julia grunted without looking up from her plate. 'Hope he takes *her* with him. Shouldn't wonder if Mr Churchill isn't behind the move. The man'll be out of harm's way there. Tell me something important.'

'We-e-ll, it says here that there have been air raids on Swansea and Falmouth, and convoys in the Channel have been attacked. And more raids on Clydeside and the south.'

'Looks as if we are being softened up for the invasion,' Julia shrugged.

'Don't say that, *please*.' Helen Sutton laid down her newspaper. 'Drew is in the south, don't forget.'

'Drew is just fine. I'd know inside me if he wasn't.' Julia picked up the paper, shaking it open. Newspapers were easily read these days. Sometimes containing no more than eight pages, they were quickly scanned. 'Well! Here's something you missed. That dratted Lord Haw-Haw! Last night, it says, he broadcast a final appeal to reason to the British, urging them to make peace with Germany. The cheek of the ruddy man!'

'I saw it, Julia. I didn't think it worth comment. And you know I have forbidden anyone in this house to tune in to him.'

'But people do, you know. They reckon he's a good laugh.'

'Oh, *no*! Some of the things he says are remarkably true, or so they say. He doesn't amuse *me*!'

An Englishman – no one could be quite certain of his identity – broadcast regularly from Germany. He had an arrogant, nasal voice that some likened to the braying of an ass. So Lord Haw-Haw he had become, and almost as much a part of listening in to the wireless as Tommy Handley or Henry Hall, and though no one at all admitted to having heard him, he was, nevertheless, regularly reported in the newspapers. Completely as a joke, of course!

'Well, we don't want peace with Hitler – not on his terms, anyway. Oh, wouldn't he just love rubbing our noses in it? We'll manage, Mother. He knows what he can do with his offer of peace as far as I'm concerned. And here's another bit you missed. The Government says that no more cars are to be manufactured – not for civilians, that is.'

'Civilians must make sacrifices,' Helen sniffed. She disliked cars, refusing to learn to drive. You couldn't blame her, Julia thought, when Pa had killed himself in a motor on the Brighton road, trying to reach sixty miles an hour.

'Oh, and something else,' she smiled, folding the paper. 'Alice told me last night. The LDV boys have been given uniforms at last and they're to be called the Home Guard. They're to have shoulder flashes to sew on, and tin hats, too, just as if they were soldiers. They've made Tom a corporal. I think he's quite chuffed about it. All he wants now is for them to be issued with rifles, then they'll be ready for the Jerries. If they come, of course.'

'And do you think they will, Julia? Honestly?'

'Every night I pray they won't but truly, Mother, where else is Hitler to go now? America is too far away; Russia is an unknown quantity and anyway, even Hitler wouldn't be fool enough to take on such a big country. They've already taken the Channel Islands – it's likely we'll be next. Yet Nathan says he feels that we won't be invaded. Apart from his faith in God, he says he just knows inside him we'll be all right. So let's not worry too much, uh? Every day is a bonus, so chin up, dearest. We'll manage.'

'Well, Nathan did tell me that according to the so-called experts, Hitler will hold back until some time about mid-September. Conditions would be better then, and the tides just right.'

'Well, there you are! We'll be good and ready for him come September. Let's not think about it any more for a while.'

She looked up as the door opened and a smiling Mary brought in the morning post.

'The Reverend is back from early church, Miss Julia, and there's a letter from Sir Andrew.'

Eagerly Helen reached for it, tearing it open. It occupied just half a sheet and was soon read.

She passed it to her daughter then smiling happily she said, 'He's just confirming what he told us on the phone, Mary. Drew's leave is definitely on. He says his divvy has okayed his application. What is a divvy, Julia?'

'His divisional officer, I think, but who cares as long as he's coming!'

Drew home! Her son – *Alice*'s son – coming on leave. So go to hell, Hitler! We don't want your peace, at any price!

5

Gracie gazed around her, cheese sandwich poised. Only her second day at Rowangarth, yet it seemed as though she had always worked here; as if that other life of streets and mill hooters and wage packets had never been – except for Mam and Dad, that was, and Grandad.

The air seemed to shimmer golden, dancing with butterflies. She had never before seen so many; not all at one time. To her right, rooks cawed and flapped over the distant trees. Busy getting their second broods out of the nest, Mr Catchpole told her; told her, too, how special that rookery was to Lady Sutton and how, if ever those big, black birds left to nest in some other place, sorrow and tragedy would come to the Garth Suttons, or so legend had it.

'Who are the Garth Suttons?' Idly, she flicked breadcrumbs from her overalls.

'Why, you'm working for them. There's two Sutton families hereabouts, see. Those as lives here at Rowangarth – them's the Garth Suttons – and there's the Suttons at Pendenys Place as folks call the Place Suttons. And there's Mrs Anna Sutton of Denniston House. Her's a widow and an offshoot of the Place Suttons. Now, the Garth Suttons have the breeding and the title; the Place Suttons,' he added, right eyebrow raised, 'have the brass. Mr Nathan, as is married to Miss Julia, was a Place Sutton but he's a decent gentleman, like his father . . .'

Gracie nodded, anxious not to interrupt, because people who lived in big houses – though she had come into contact with very few – intrigued her. Sometimes, on a day trip on the chara, she had passed such houses, all dignified and aloof, and wondered who lived in them and how many servants they had or if they ate off gold plates. And then her Lancashire practicality had taken over and she had tried to work out why they needed so many rooms and whoever found time to clean all the windows.

'Tell me some more, Mr Catchpole . . .'

'Not a lot to tell. I served out my apprenticeship at Pendenys. Wouldn't have done for me to do it here, not with my dad being head gardener. But I was glad to finish my time and to come to Rowangarth as under-gardener. A right martinet that Mrs Clementina Sutton at Pendenys Place was. Had her servants bobbing and curtsying all the time. Not like our Lady Helen, who don't hold with it.

'Mrs Clementina's father was a self-made millionaire and her his only child, so she copped for the lot.' His eyes took on a remembering look. 'By heck, lass, there's things I could tell you about that one. Married Mr Edward Sutton, who was born here at Rowangarth. A case of brass marrying breeding, but it didn't ever make a lady of her. An ironmaster's daughter, that's what, and she never changed. Silk purses from sows' ears, tha knows . . .'

He bit savagely into a sandwich. At midday, Jack Catchpole was in the habit of eating a good, sustaining meal with his feet under his kitchen table, but today he had been fobbed off with sandwiches, and all on account of those Spitfires. Derisively he investigated the contents of the sandwich.

'A man's expected to dig for victory on fish paste?' he snorted.

'Mrs Catchpole not very well, then?'

'Nay. Nowt like that. She's busy collecting aluminium; her and Alice Dwerryhouse and Miss Julia got it all organized.'

'The Government, you mean – wanting people's pans to melt down for planes?'

'That's it. Got a right pile already in one of the stables at Rowangarth. Folks is chucking out pans like there's no tomorrow. But I suppose we need fighters. Us lost a lot at Dunkirk, tha knows.'

Gracie knew. She had wept with pride when the soldiers were snatched off the beaches. It had been around that time, in a heady haze of patriotism, she had joined the Land Army.

'Any road,' Catchpole was eager to return to the ins and outs of the Suttons, 'young Sir Andrew comes on leave soon, we hope, from the Navy. He'll be down here for sure, having a look at the gardens. He's real fond of the orchid house – but I'll tell you later about her ladyship's special orchids, the white ones. Very sentimental about the white ones, she is.'

'So when he comes here, what do I call him?' Gracie had never met a gentleman of title before.

'Why, you gives him his rank as is due to him. "Good morning, Sir Andrew," you'll say, then like as not he'll ask you to call him Drew as folk who've known him since he was a babbie alus do. Mind, when he came of age, some started to call him Sir Andrew – but more as a politeness. The lad hasn't changed, though. He's a credit to her as had him, and her as reared him. But we haven't all day to sit here nattering.' He threw the remainder of his sand-wiches to hopefully waiting sparrows. 'There's a war on and we've got to get them potatoes and marrows ready for when the market man calls – and a score cabbages he wants, an' all.'

'But you'll tell me some more, tomorrow – about the Suttons?' Gracie begged. 'About the one who had him and the one who brought him up, I mean.' That small snippet had intrigued her. 'Did Sir Andrew have a nanny?'

'No, he didn't. But that's another story. For tomorrow,' Catchpole chuckled. He could get to like this lass. Happen, if he and Lily had had bairns of their own, one of them might have been like young Gracie. 'So on your feet, lass. Let's get digging up them potatoes – for victory!'

Though when that victory would come, he thought mournfully, only the good Lord knew – and He wasn't telling!

The first sight of Rowangarth had always been special to Drew Sutton. To walk the long slow curve of a drive lined with beeches and oaks and all at once to come upon the old house always aroused an ache of tenderness in him. But this afternoon it was particularly special and achy because he hadn't seen it for six months and only now he realized how much he had missed it.

Mullioned windows still shone a welcome; the roof still sagged and the rose-red bricks were still smothered in blowsy Bourbon roses and clematis.

God – don't let me die and lose it. The heart-thumping ache turned to panic inside him. *Let me live through this war.*

'Stupid clot!' he hissed. It wasn't down to God. It was like the old Chiefie in signal school said: you just had to accept that there was a time to be born and a time to die. And you died when – if – your number came up. So best not worry overmuch about it, Chiefie said comfortably, because worrying only wasted the time you had left.

Good old Chiefie. He'd teach them the morse code if it was the last bloody thing he did, he said at the start of their training. And taught them he had, Drew grinned. DWRX805 Telegraphist Sutton A. he was now, and seven shillings a week extra at pay parade because of it.

He pulled back his shoulders and set off at a quick pace. They always said that the longest part of any journey was the last mile home and now there was only a hundred yards to go. A hundred strides, and he was there!

He should have known someone would be waiting and watching because all at once the doors were thrown open and his mother was calling, waving, running to meet him. And Grandmother standing at the top of the steps with Nathan and Tilda and Mary.

'Drew!' Mother and son held each other tightly.

'Hullo, dearest . . .' It was all he could say because all at once there was nothing to say – nothing that mattered.

He gathered his grandmother gently in his arms, kissing her softly, whispering, 'Missed you, Gran.' And the words were hard to say so he clasped Nathan's hand tightly then kissed Mary and Tilda. And Mary blushed hotly and Tilda closed her eyes and smiled broadly. Then it all came right and all at once everything was happiness and homecoming.

'*Hecky!*' Tilda shrieked, and rushed off in a tizzy.

'She's got cherry scones in the oven,' Mary supplied, which made everyone laugh because special days at Rowangarth had always been cherry-scone days ever since anyone could remember.

'It's good to be home,' Drew laughed because suddenly it seemed as if he had never been away.

'I've just noticed,' Julia frowned. 'Where is your hat?'

'*Cap*, Mother.'

'Well, where is it – and your kit?'

'I left everything at the lodge.' Hammock, kitbag, respirator, greatcoat. In his eagerness to see Rowangarth he could carry them no further. 'I hitched a lift from Holdenby station. There was a tractor passing with a trailer behind it. People always give lifts to uniforms. He dropped me off right at the gate lodge. I'll borrow a wheelbarrow from Catchpole later, and collect my stuff.'

'But you should have phoned from York. I'd have picked you up.'

'There was a queue for the phone boxes and you know how long it takes to get through these days. Anyway, what about your petrol coupons?'

'Blow the petrol!' Drew was home. Nothing else mattered.

'Shall we all have tea?' Helen smiled. 'And will someone tell me – where did Cook find glacé cherries for the scones?'

Such things – dried fruit for cakes, too – had disappeared completely since war came, she had thought. People were even hoarding the last of their prunes now, to chop finely into pieces and hope they would pass for currants.

'I think, Mother, she has some squirrelled away in a screw-top jar – for special occasions.'

'Good old Tilda,' Drew laughed.

A cherry-scone tea in the conservatory. All at once, his war was a million miles away.

Later, when Drew had collected his kit and returned the wheelbarrow to its proper place, Julia took her son's cap and regarded it, eyebrows raised.

'HMS, Drew? HMS *what*?'

'Barracks is known as HMS *Drake*, Mother, but we can't use a ship's name now. It would tell the enemy which warships are in port, for one thing.'

'So you'll only ever have HMS on your cap?' Julia felt mildly cheated.

'Afraid so – for the duration. That's why all the signposts have been removed. We don't want to let paratroopers know exactly where they have dropped, now do we?' He was careful to make light of it, to smile as he said it, because most people thought that the invasion, if it came, would be airborne – after a softening-up of bombing, that was. 'But don't worry. The south coast, if you could see it, is thick with ack-ack guns and barrage balloons, and there are a lot of fighter stations all along the coast and around London. You'd be surprised the way we've got ourselves organized so quickly after Dunkirk,' he supplied with the authority of one who had seen almost six months' service in the armed forces.

'So do you think there'll be an invasion, Drew?' Julia was eager for any small word of comfort.

'Not until I've had my leave,' he grinned. 'I specially stipulated not until Drew Sutton had had his ten days . . .'

'They say it won't be yet. More like September-ish, when the tides are right,' Julia pressed, refusing to make light of it.

'I heard that, too. The old hands in barracks seem to think so. And by then we'll be ready for them. They've got to cross the Channel, remember.'

'They could fly men across it, Drew.'

'They could, but only in isolated pockets. They'd soon be mopped up.'

'By the Home Guard!' Julia's apprehension returned. 'But the Holdenby lot haven't been given rifles yet!'

'Mother! We've got an army, too. We got the best part of it out of France, don't forget.' It came as a shock to him to realize how worried the civilian population had become. 'Now tell me – where is that nurse who went to France? The Germans didn't frighten you and Lady then!'

'Alice and I didn't go to France to fight. We went to nurse the wounded. And you'll have to pop over to Keeper's – let her know you've arrived. Daisy won't be home from work yet, but Alice will be expecting you.' Julia reached up to place his cap jauntily on the back of his head. 'There, now you look very smart. Dinner's at seven, so don't be too long.'

Drew shifted his cap to the more orthodox position, low on his forehead, then saluted his mother smartly. Determinedly, Julia pushed her fears from her thoughts. She would *not* spoil her son's leave by worrying about what Hitler would do next. She had longed to see Drew since the day he'd left home, and the invasion could wait – until September!

Drew stood at the gate of Keeper's Cottage, gave a low, slow whistle then called, 'Hullo, there! The fleet's in!'

Alice dropped the log basket she was carrying across the yard, spinning round in amazement.

'Drew! It *is* you!' In no time she was in his arms, tears brimming. Then she pushed him away from her, dabbing her eyes with the corner of her pinafore, reaching up to cup his face in gentle hands. 'You've grown, I swear it – and you're thinner,' she accused.

'Tilda will soon feed me up,' he laughed, kissing her fondly. 'And don't cry – please don't cry.'

'I'm not crying,' she sniffed, shaping her lips into a smile, 'but it seems no time at all since you were a little thing, gazing up at me, saying, "Hullo, lady . . ."'

'And I've called you Lady ever since, haven't I?'

'That you have, love, and you've grown up into a – a *man* to be proud of.'

She never called him son. From the day he'd been born, almost, he had been Julia's; had belonged to Rowangarth, his inheritance.

'And you, Lady, are very special to me. You'll keep sending letters, you and Daisy? They're very important to sailors.'

'We'll keep them coming,' she smiled, in charge of her emotions again. 'Daisy won't be in for an hour yet, and Tom's out setting up snares. Catches as many rabbits as he can. They're like gold dust now. Everybody's after them – rabbits not being on the ration. Are you coming in?'

'Later. I've got to do the rounds first. Orders from Mother. But I'll call later on, when Daisy is home.'

'Tomorrow's her half-day off. You'll have a lot to talk about, the pair of you. The silly young madam's gone and – but she'll tell you herself.' She reached on tiptoe to kiss him again. 'You're so like Giles, you know. You get more like him every day.'

She lifted her hand, a blessing almost, as he turned at the gate to smile a goodbye.

So very like Giles Sutton, her first husband, that it made

her believe there really was a God in heaven. There had to be, or Drew would have looked like the man who fathered him – and that would have been nothing short of a tragedy.

She lifted her eyes to the late-afternoon sky. 'Thanks, at least, for that . . .' she whispered.

'No more uniform, no more war, for nine days.' Drew pulled a stem of grass, then nibbled on the soft white end. 'Duty done, Daiz. Mother insisted I visit Reuben, Mrs Shaw and Jinny Dobb – by which time the entire village would have seen me in my uniform. I think she's rather proud of me, but it's good to get into civvie clothes again.'

He gazed lazily into the dapple of leaves and sunlight above him. Hands behind her head, Daisy lay beside him in the wild garden.

'Remember, Drew, when we were kids? We used to lie here, all six of us, in the long grass, just talking – sometimes not even talking.' Just glad to be together, she supposed.

'The Clan. And now there's only you and me.'

'And Tatty, don't forget. She'll be along later. She's gone to Creesby to get her hair trimmed. She'll come, though, now she knows you're home.'

'The whole Riding knows I'm home,' Drew sighed contentedly. 'It's as if I've never been away – well, it seems like it, lying here. Wish Keth and Kitty and Bas could suddenly appear – oh, Daiz! I'm sorry!'

'Don't be. And you don't wish it half as much as I do. But I'm feeling good today. Four letters came this morning – two of them from Washington. Keth's got a job there, but not one word about what he's doing. I miss him, Drew. Half of me wants him home; the other half wants him to stay safe in America so they can't call him up. And that's an awful thing to say, isn't it, when you've been called up for six months, almost?'

'Do you think he'll manage to get back home? It's a

pretty dicey crossing from America these days, and difficult for civilians to get a permit to sail, I believe. Between you and me, Daiz, we're losing more shipping in the Atlantic than the Government tells us about. And there's no chance at all of him flying over.'

'I know. There's nothing I can do about it, I suppose. If he manages to get back – well fine. If he doesn't, at least I won't have to go through what Mam and Aunt Julia went through in their war – and, oh! I shouldn't have said that, either – not when you're already fighting, Drew. I'm sorry.'

''S all right, Daiz. And I'm not fighting – not just yet. When my leave is over, though, I think I'll get a ship pretty quickly.' He closed his eyes, breathing slowly, deeply; smiling contentment. 'But right now, I'm enjoying being here and I'm not going to think of going back till next Saturday.'

'Next Saturday is Mary's wedding. You'll miss it. She'll be ever so disappointed.'

'Yes, she said so. But we'd better not talk about weddings, had we?'

'Best not. And next year, when I'm twenty-one, don't even *think* of mentioning weddings. That's when we'd have been getting married. Expect I'll weep all day. On the other hand, though, I might not.' She sat up, arms clasped round her knees, then turning to face him she whispered, 'I might not be here, you see. I volunteered, three weeks ago, for the Wrens.'

'You did – *what*?'

'Signed up. I thought – what the heck! Drew's in the Navy so that'll do for me. I was fed up . . .'

'Fed up? We call that chocker in the Navy.'

'Okay – so I'm learning. I was chocker with that shop so I went in my dinner hour and did it. And I signed Dada's name, too. I had to because I'm still a minor. He hit the roof, Drew. In the end, Mam gave us both a telling-off and it has sort of died down now because I haven't heard another word from them.'

'Not even about your medical?'

'Nope. But I heard they were pretty choosy. Maybe I won't hear any more.'

'I think you will. There were two Wrens on my training course and they were smashing. And the Wrens who work in barracks are okay, too. You'll look great in the uniform, Daiz. One of the blokes in our mess saw your photograph and his eyes nearly popped out of his head. "Where did you find a bit of crackling like that, Sutton?" he asked me, and I told him under a gooseberry bush – that you were my sister. I'll tell him you're joining the Wrens,' he grinned. 'It'll make his day!'

'Then you'd better tell him I'm engaged, too – and, Drew, can we walk? I've got something else to tell you.'

'Which necessitates walking?'

'Yes – oh, *no*! But it's going to take a bit of explaining after so long, you see. And I hope you won't think I've been sneaky and secretive about it, but nobody knows – well, only Mam and Dada and Aunt Julia. And Keth, of course.'

'I'm curious. Where shall we go?'

'Into Brattocks the back way, then down to the elms. I want the rooks to hear it, too.'

'You believe all that nonsense about telling things to the rooks, do you?'

'Mam does! Anyway, I want to tell them!'

'Fine by me.' He held out his hand and she took it, smiling up at him, glad he was her brother – her *half*-brother.

'We-e-ll – it started when we lived in Hampshire. Do you remember Hampshire, Drew?'

'Of course I do! I loved it when Mother and I came to stay with you. I thought it was great, having you and Keth to play with. Do you remember when they told us we were related, you and me? You threw the mother of all tantrums and ran out.'

'Don't remind me! But I was jealous, you see, when they told us Mam had once been married to your father. Funny, isn't it, that Mam was once Lady Alice Sutton?'

'Don't see why, considering she married Sir Giles Sutton and they had me.'

''S'pose not. Does having a title bother you, Drew? Do the other sailors rag you about it – you being on the lower decks, I mean?'

'The blokes in the Mess don't know about it. I took good care not to tell them. I'm Telegraphist Sutton and that's the way I want it.'

'But hadn't you considered a commission? You'd be a good officer.'

'No better than a lot of others, Daiz, and anyway, I like it where I am. I've been with a decent crowd of blokes, training. I'm sorry we'll all be split up, but that's war for you – and here we are at the elms, so you'd better tell me what's bothering you because something is.'

'Not bothering me, exactly, but it's something I want you to know and like I said, I wasn't being deceitful, not telling you. I almost told you ages ago, when I told Keth, but he was so shocked by it, I decided not to . . .'

'Daisy! *Tell!*'

'All right.' She settled herself on the grass, her back to the elm tree bole, arms behind her as if she were embracing it, connecting herself and her words to it and to the rooks that nested in it. It was the way she always did it. 'Remember when Keth's father and Mr Hillier were drowned?' She took a deep, calming breath. 'And that Mr Hillier left Windrush Hall to the miners as a convalescent home – because he'd been a boy down the pit before he got so rich?'

Drew nodded, careful not to interrupt because she was finding it difficult, he knew.

'Well, he left everyone who worked for him a hundred

pounds, the rest of his money to be invested for the upkeep of the home.'

'I knew that, Daiz . . .'

'Yes, but what you don't know is that the money he left me *wasn't* a hundred pounds. Oh, I thought it was. I felt rich; thought I could spend it on bikes and toys, but Mam thought otherwise. But what I didn't know, Drew, and they didn't tell me for ages afterwards –' She turned to face him, one hand on the tree-trunk, still. 'They waited till I'd got a bit more sense, knew how not to blab about it at school. That hundred pounds I thought I'd been left was more. Much more.'

'How much more?' he asked warily.

'Mr Hillier left me ten thousand pounds!'

The words came out in a rush and it seemed like an age before Drew hissed, 'Ten thousand *pounds*?'

'Yes.' She swallowed loudly. 'I couldn't take it in, not so much money, so Dada said it would be better if I thought about it in terms of *things*; said that if I imagined a road of newly-built houses; nice houses with bathrooms, mind, – *twenty* of them – then that's what my money would buy.'

'That much money would buy Rowangarth and the stable block and the lodges and all the parkland. You're richer than me, Daiz.'

'I'm not richer than you, Drew. Rowangarth and the farms and all Holdenby village are worth more than ten thousand.'

'Not a lot more, because it's entailed. I've got to pass it on. And houses aren't what you'd call security in wartime. Hitler is bombing them or setting them on fire with incendiaries and you can't insure houses and things against enemy action – did you know that? I reckon if you've got your money in the bank then you're laughing.'

'If Hitler doesn't come before I get it. Because it won't be mine till next June. The solicitor in Winchester and Sir

Maxwell Something-or-other and Dada are Trustees and they'll only let me have bits of my money for special, necessary things like education or if I got very ill and there were doctor's bills that Dada couldn't pay. They've been very mean with it this far.'

'For your own good, I suppose.'

'I accept that, but I'd have liked to get some of it to help Keth through university when he didn't get a scholarship to Leeds, but I'd more sense than to ask.' She shrugged because she had never thought of all that money as hers, really. It had just been something there, uneasily in the background. Until now, that was. The ten years since they'd told her about it suddenly seemed to have flown by.

'Well, Keth got through university all right, as it happens. And I'm glad about the money, Daiz – or I will be when it's sunk in. Suppose Keth's had time to get used to it, now?'

'I think he has, though he never mentions it. When I told him he said that he wanted to be the breadwinner – buy things for me and not the other way round. It was a bit awkward I can tell you, so in the end we decided our children should have the bulk of it – good schools and perhaps ponies if they wanted them. The rest, Keth said, should be invested for their future. If we ever have kids, that is.'

Her voice began to tremble and her eyes filled with tears. Such very blue eyes, Drew thought, fishing for his handkerchief.

'Stop it, Daiz. Of course you'll have children.'

'Then how, will you tell me, with the flaming Atlantic between us? Have them by air mail, will we?'

'Oh you don't half go on about things. You're almost as bad as Kitty when it comes to being a drama queen.'

Thoughts of Kitty led to thoughts of Bas and again to Keth who was with them still in Kentucky – or was it Washington now? But she blinked hard on her tears and blew her nose loudly. Then she took a deep, calming breath and tilted her chin ominously.

'All right then, Drew Sutton – drama queen, am I? Well how about this, then? That money *is* in the bank, sort of. They invested it for me and on my birthday they always send Dada a statement about it. By the time I'm twenty-one, there'll be more than fifteen thousand!'

'*Fifteen!* Good grief! No wonder you wanted to tell the rooks about it!'

She stared at the grass at their feet, saying nothing, which only went to show, Drew thought, that Daisy too realized what a responsibility so much money was and hoping fervently that it wouldn't make trouble between herself and Keth.

'Tell you what,' he smiled, getting to his feet, holding out a hand to her, 'let's go over to Denniston – see if Tatty's back from Creesby yet.'

After what he'd been told, it was all he could think of to say.

6

'I suppose, Sir Andrew, you've nobbut come to see my land girl,' Catchpole chuckled.

'As a matter of fact, it was the tea I came for. Knew you'd have the kettle on just about now. But if it's served by a pretty popsy, then so much the better.' Laughing, Drew held out a hand. 'Good to see you again, Jack.'

'And you, young Drew. Welcome home. And who told you our Gracie was pretty, then?'

'Polly Purvis. Daisy and I went to see her last night.'

'Ar. And how's that lad of Polly's? Heard he'd got a job over in America. Planning on stopping there, is he?'

'Your guess is as good as mine. Polly seems to think Keth is agitating to get home, though she hopes, really, that he stays there. You can't blame her. The last war didn't do Keth's father any favours.'

'Keth'll happen be wanting to get back to Daisy, though how he'll manage it with all those U-boats about, I don't know. But there's nowt so queer as folk. If that's what Keth wants, then good luck to the lad. But here's tea, and here's our new lady gardener.'

'Good morning, Sir Andrew.' Gracie stood hesitantly, a mug in either hand. 'I saw you arrive – I've poured one for you, too.'

'Hullo, Gracie.' Drew rose to his feet. 'Let me help you.'

'Careful. These enamelled mugs are very hot.'

'Don't I know it. We use them in barracks.' His gaze took in her thick yellow curls, held captive in a bright green snood, her shirt unbuttoned to show a long, slim neck. She didn't wear make-up either and had a wide, ready smile. 'Pull up a box,' he invited.

'If you're sure that's all right?' Her eyes asked permission of the head gardener.

'Course it is, lass. Us don't stand on ceremony here. So tell us, Drew, how is the Navy treating you?'

'No complaints so far, but it's good to be home and –'

'And you'd rather forget being a sailor, eh?'

'Until I have to go back,' Drew nodded. 'It's good to get out of uniform and not to have to do everything at the double, though when I get a ship things will be a bit less hectic, they tell me.'

'So what do you plan doing with yourself, then?'

'Daisy and I might go into Creesby – see a flick tonight. But no plans at all, really. I got up late this morning. I awoke at six as usual and it was marvellous not having someone yelling, "Wakey-wakey! On yer feet! Lash up and stow!" I felt peculiar in a bed, first night home. I've got used to sleeping in a hammock. They're quite comfortable.'

'But don't you ever fall out of them?' Gracie frowned. 'And what's lash up and – and –'

'Stow. You roll up your hammock into a big sausage, then stow it in the hammock racks, all tidy. There's two ways of doing things in barracks: Chiefie's way, or the wrong way. You soon learn which,' he grinned.

'Do you like dancing, Sir Andrew?'

'Yes, I do! Is there a dance on?'

'At the aerodrome tomorrow night. There's an invitation from the sergeants' mess at Holdenby Moor pinned on the noticeboard at the hostel. They send a transport to the crossroads, the girls told me. All HM forces welcome, though it's ladies they want most – for partners, I suppose. A lot of the girls go in dresses so Daisy could come too, if she said she was a land girl.'

'And Tatty, my cousin – could she come? She's mad about the Air Force.'

'Don't see why not.'

'Then I hope you'll have a few dances with me, Gracie. I need practice.'

'That's a promise. But don't forget to wear your uniform or you'll not get in. The transport leaves at half-past seven. If you aren't there, then I'll know you can't make it.'

'We'll be there!' Well, he and Daisy, though probably Aunt Anna wouldn't let Tatty go. And that would be a pity, because Tatty was fun now. He'd forgotten how pretty she was until they'd met yesterday. 'And before I forget, Jack, Mother is coming to see you – something about keeping a few hens, she said.'

'Hens! Me? Nay, Drew. Hens in my garden wouldn't do at all!' Hens would be bothersome, like cats. Just think of the damage they could do if they got out. They'd be scratching and picking everywhere.

'She's very keen to have some. Where do you suggest they should go then?'

'Don't know, and that's for sure.' Anywhere, but in his garden!

'I like hens. Before Grandad came to live with us – he came when Gran died – he used to keep hens in his back garden,' Gracie offered. 'Well, bantams, actually. Pretty little things. Laid ever such tiny eggs. Mind, he had to keep an eye on them. Bantams are flyers – always trying to get out – but if you were to get some like Mrs Purvis has at the hostel, they wouldn't be a lot of trouble. Hers are Rhode Island Reds. They're very placid – not like bantams or Leghorns.'

'For a town lass you seem to know quite a bit about hens, Gracie Fielding.'

'Not all that much, Mr Catchpole, but I like them and if Mrs Sutton wants some hens of her own, I'd like to look after them for her. You have to give up your egg ration, though. You take your ration book to the Food Office and they cancel your egg coupons and give you chits to buy hen meal instead. It's by far the better way. You get a lot more eggs and they're lovely and fresh. You save all the scraps and potato peelings and such like, then boil them up and mix them with the meal. Hens lay well on it.'

'Then I reckon you and Mrs Sutton should have a word about it, lass. You'm welcome to her hens.'

'Would you mind, Gracie?'

'Not a bit, Sir Andrew.'

'Good. Well, that's tomorrow night settled, and the hens,' he smiled. 'And, Gracie, please call me Drew. Most people do.'

Catchpole drained his mug, observing the couple and saying not a word. Seemed it wasn't only the lads from Holdenby Moor who'd be taking a fancy to his land girl. Young Drew seemed smitten an' all. And he must remember, if Miss Julia ever did get her dratted hens, to ask Gracie to keep the droppings for him when she cleaned out their coop. Hen muck made good manure; brought tomatoes along a treat.

He sucked on his pipe. Happen a few Rhode Island Reds mightn't be such a bad idea after all. As long as they were well away from his garden, that was!

'Do let her go, Aunt Anna,' Drew urged. 'There'll be a transport laid on to get us there and I'll take good care of her. Tatiana does so want to come.'

'I'm sure you would take care of her, but a dance at the aerodrome . . . ?'

'Dada says I can go if Drew's there,' Daisy offered. 'It's all very proper. There won't be any rowdiness. The aircrew boys are very nice.'

'But it would be all blacked out and goodness knows what might happen,' Anna murmured, feeling guilty for even thinking what could take place should her daughter be enticed from the dance floor to heaven only knew where.

'But *everywhere* is blacked out, Mother! And I know

what you are thinking,' Tatiana flung. 'You think I'll get up to mischief, don't you, necking round the back of the hangars with some bloke who's after what he can get?'

'Tatiana – do *not* speak like that! I thought no such thing!' Anna's cheeks flushed pink. 'It's just that feelings run high when there's a war on and –'

'Don't worry. Tatty wouldn't be able to leave the dance. There'll be a guard on the door, most likely,' Drew hastened. 'The Air Force couldn't allow people the freedom of the aerodrome, if only for security reasons. Tatty will be fine with Daisy and me.' And girls of eighteen weren't so naïve as Aunt Anna tried to make out, he thought, though he was careful not to say so. 'I'd see her back home.'

'Mother, *please*? You know how I love dancing!'

Anna gazed down at her feet, knowing just how high feelings could run. Desperately in love with Elliot Sutton she had been at eighteen; besotted by him, desperate for his glance, his touch, his mouth on hers. But Elliot had been dead these many years and she had not shed a tear at his graveside. Nor since.

'Very well. You may go, since Drew will be with you. But you must not stay out late, remember.'

'We can't, Mrs Sutton,' Daisy was quick to point out. 'Gracie has to be back in the hostel by eleven.'

'And I won't be creeping out of the dance, don't worry. I wouldn't even have thought of such a thing if you hadn't put the idea into my head!' Tatiana flung, angry to be so humiliated before Daisy and Drew.

'Now listen to me, young lady!' Anna was becoming angry. 'If you continue to be impudent you'll not only not go to the dance, but you'll be gated for the remainder of Drew's leave. I mean it!'

'Mother, you couldn't! You *wouldn't*!' Tatiana wailed, her eyes filling with tears.

'I could, but I won't. I said you might go and you shall.

That you don't do anything foolish is surely not too much to ask?'

'It isn't!' Tatiana flung her arms around her mother. 'And I *will* be good!' She was smiling now, tears forgotten, because she could twist her mother round her little finger – had always been able to. She gave a skip of delight, then grasped Daisy's hand, pulling her towards the stairs.

'Let's go through my wardrobe,' she demanded when her bedroom door was firmly closed. 'I just love those aircrew boys and I'll die if no one asks me to dance!'

'They will. You're very pretty, Tatty. Just like Anne Rutherford. And I think,' Daisy took an emerald-green dress from the rail, 'that you should wear this one. Green really suits you. And I'd wear the gold dancing pumps with it.'

The green it would be and oh! Tatiana sighed inside her, she couldn't wait for tomorrow night. Just her luck, she thought, suddenly sober, if most of the aircrews were flying. She crossed her fingers and wished for the thickest, heaviest pea-souper there was, because only fog could ground the bombers.

And wasn't she the stupid one? Pea-soupers, in July?

The RAF transport, driven by a Waaf corporal, came to a stop at the entrance to the sergeants' mess.

'Okay, you lot! Out you get!' She let down the tail-flap with a clatter. 'And mind how you go.'

Drew jumped down first, glad to be out of the gloomy interior of the canvas-covered truck. He was the only man there and had been met with wolf-whistles from the land girls when he'd arrived with Tatiana and Daisy at the crossroads.

'Shut up, you lot!' Gracie had stepped out of the huddle of waiting women. 'This is Drew Sutton and he's on leave, so give over being so stupid. Anyone'd think you'd never seen a sailor before!'

'Not as tall and fair and handsome as this one!' someone quipped. 'Where've you been hiding him, Gracie?'

'Stop it, I told you, or you'll get me the sack! Drew's my boss – well, sort of . . .'

Drew's embarrassment and Gracie's protests had been cut short by the arrival of the transport from RAF Holdenby Moor, and they climbed aboard, laughing.

Over Brattocks Wood, a full moon was rising. It was round and white but tonight on the way home it would shine silver, help light their way, pick out shapes and ditches – even potholes in the narrow road.

'Everybody okay?' the driver asked. 'Get yourselves settled. Just one more pick-up to make. Soon be there.'

She let out the clutch, and the truck lurched forward and on to Holdenby village, where more girls waited. Later, when darkness came, she would be thankful for the moonlight. It was the very devil, driving in the blackout with headlamps painted over black except for the smallest slit in the centre. Thank heaven for white-painted kerbstones, she sighed. The times she had run off the road were too many to count.

The guardroom lay ahead and she stopped with a squealing of brakes that brought shouts and giggles from the back of the truck.

'Ladies for the sergeants' mess, plus one matelot,' she called as the red and white pole that barred the road was raised.

Tatiana shivered with delight as she jumped down into Drew's waiting arms because even though the door and all the windows of the Nissen hut that served as a mess were closed, she could hear the faint sound of music and the vibrating thunk and tap of bass and drums. She loved to dance and closed her eyes and fervently begged for her fair share of partners. It would be too awful, too degrading, if she sat out every dance when she had taken such trouble to look her best.

She need not have worried. Lady partners were thin on the ground and a cheer went up as they pushed aside the curtain that hung over the door.

Already the air was stuffy and thick with cigarette smoke. It wasn't time for the blackouts to be put into place, but the windows had been nailed up during the winter and no one had bothered trying to open them since.

They laid their coats over a table at the end of the hut and Tatiana shook her head and ran her fingers through her long dark hair. Then she turned to look into eyes almost as blue as Daisy's and smiled a breathless, 'Yes, please,' when a tall, fair sergeant asked if she would like to dance with him. He held her gently and not too closely and she matched her steps to his as they moved into a waltz.

'You haven't been here before.' It was more a statement than a question. 'I'd have seen you, if you had.'

'No. This is my first time. I was only allowed to come because my cousin is home. That's him,' she nodded. 'The sailor, dancing with the land girl. Maybe I won't be able to come again,' she sighed, wide-eyed.

'Then we'll have to make the most of tonight, won't we?' he smiled. 'I want every dance – okay? Name's Timothy Thomson – the Scottish Thomson, without the P. Tim.'

'I'm Tatiana Sutton,' she breathed, wondering why her voice wobbled and her lips were so stiff. 'Tatty – and I'm very pleased to meet you.' The words came out all in a rush.

'Tatty's a silly name. Where I come from, a tattie-bogle is a scarecrow and you're no' that. I'm very pleased to meet you, too.' His eyes challenged hers, daring her to look away, claiming her, almost. 'Tell me where you live. I want to know all about you.'

So she told him, and that her father was dead, but that very soon her grandfather would be coming to live with them when the military moved into the house they were going to take away from him.

'Is that the old castle? I've often seen it when we fly over.'

'It isn't old and it isn't a castle. It only thinks it is. It's awful, really – sort of pushy. I think Grandfather's glad to be leaving it for the duration.'

'You must be rich.'

'We aren't, actually. We might have been if Father hadn't been killed. He'd have inherited, you see. But I suppose, in the end, Bas will be stuck with it and he hates it.'

'Bas?' he frowned.

'Sebastian Sutton. He's my cousin – lives in Kentucky.'

'And why, Tatiana Sutton, do you have a Russian name?' The dance ended and he took her arm and guided her to chairs in the far corner of the floor.

'My mother is Russian. Her family left because of the Communists. She's called Aleksandrina Anastasia – Anastasia for the grand duchess. They were born on the same day, just a few hours apart.' And because all at once she felt so easy with him, she told him about her Grandmother Petrovska, who was very sniffy and always wore black, and how she was very poor because most of what they owned had been left behind in St Petersburg, which Grandmother refused to call Leningrad.

'You don't know what poor is,' he said bluntly. 'Take me, for instance. I come from a Greenock tenement. I'm bright, though. Got a free place at the local academy. Should've been at university if the war hadn't happened.'

'But you'll get there in the end,' she comforted, 'when the war is over.'

'When this war's over I'll be long dead,' he said matter-of-factly. 'The survival rate for aircrews is pretty grim, and it's grimmer for tail-gunners like me.'

'Then why did you volunteer? Did you have to?' she demanded angrily, because she had only just found him and she didn't want, ever, to lose him.

'Not really. But on the first Clydeside raid I lost family

83

and friends and I went out in a rage and signed up.'

'How old are you, Tim?'

'Twenty. And you . . . ?'

'Eighteen. Nineteen next March. But can we dance again, please?'

All at once it wasn't enough to be sitting beside him, her hand in his. She needed to be closer, his arms around her. She needed it especially because he was right; not only did aircraft go missing, but even when they got back the rear-gunner was sometimes dead. Tail-end Charlies they were called. Luftwaffe fighter pilots always shot up the gunner first.

He took her in his arms and she moved closer. 'I think I'm falling in love with you,' she whispered in her best Imperial Russian.

'What did you say?' he laughed.

'I was speaking in Russian.' She lifted her eyes to his. 'I said I think – I think you are a very good dancer.' Her cheeks flushed hotly because she had almost said it; had wanted to say it.

'Thanks. You're no' bad yourself.'

He drew her closer still and rested his cheek on her head and she relaxed against him and let go her indrawn breath in a sigh of contentment.

She wanted tonight never to end. She wanted to stay in his arms until the war was over.

'Will you ring me tomorrow?' she murmured, suddenly bold.

'If we aren't flying. No one can phone out if we're going on ops. Security, you see. But if there's no call, wish me luck when I fly over?'

'I will, Tim.' With all her heart and soul she would wish him luck; will him safely back. He *had* to get back. He couldn't get killed; not when they had only just met. Not when she loved him so much.

*   *   *

'Sssh. We'll wake them up,' Daisy breathed as their feet crunched the gravel drive that led to Denniston House.

'Can you see all right, Tatty?' Drew whispered as she fumbled her key into the lock.

'Fine, thanks.' Carefully she swung the door open, then turned to fold her arms round Drew, kissing him fondly.

'G'night, coz. 'Night, Daisy. It's been just great. Thanks for getting me in, Gracie.'

'No bother. I'll let you know next time they send us an invitation.'

At an upstairs window, Anna Sutton pulled back the curtain, peering into the moonlit night. She needn't have worried. Her daughter was safely home. She watched as Drew and Daisy and Rowangarth's land girl waved a silent good night, then slipped back into bed, listening to the sound of the closing of the front door, the slipping home of the bolts, the creaking of the second stair from the top as Tatiana crept to her room. The knob of the bedroom door turned slowly, carefully.

'I'm home,' Tatiana whispered.

The light from the landing fell on Anna's closed eyelids. Her mother was asleep. Gently she closed the door.

Anna's eyes flew open and a smile tilted the corners of her mouth. Dear, innocent Tatiana. She hoped she'd had a lovely time.

They said good night to Gracie at the bothy gate, then Daisy slipped her arm through Drew's.

'Are you coming in for a drink? Mam said she'd leave a tray for us.' She pushed open the door, still unlocked, then switched on the kitchen light, her eyes automatically turning to check the blackout curtains. 'Sit down, Drew. Won't be a minute. My, but you had a good time – danced with Gracie most of the night, didn't you?'

'Mm. I like her. She's fun. She's a good dancer, too. Taught me some new steps. She says there's a dance in Creesby on Wednesday night – shall we all go?'

'Drew Sutton, I believe you're sweet on her! You haven't fallen for her, have you?'

'Of course not!' Drew's cheeks coloured.

'You kissed her good night . . .'

'I kissed Tatty good night and I suppose I shall kiss you good night too, Daiz, but I haven't fallen for any of you!'

'Then you disappoint me. Here you are, almost twenty-three and still heart-whole. Are you going the way of all sailors with a girl in every port?'

'Sorry, Daiz, no. I'd like to have just one special girl – fall in love with her. I like Gracie. She's pretty and she's great to be with. And could you lend her a dress, do you think, for the Creesby dance; just until her mother sends her one from home, and her dancing shoes? She says it's awful going to a dance in breeches and a shirt and tie.'

'Course I will, but are you sure you aren't just a little bit in love?'

'I like Gracie a lot – I've just said so – but she isn't the one. I'll know the minute I kiss her when the right girl comes along. And when she does, you'll be the first to know, Daiz, I promise you!'

Julia lay still in bed, not wanting to move lest she awakened Nathan. Her mind buzzed with silly thoughts and tired as she was, sleep would not come.

She supposed she should try counting her blessings as her mother did. 'Better than counting sheep, dear.' And blessings Julia Sutton had aplenty. Drew was home and her husband had no fear of call-up. Nathan was fifty-two, next; her brother Giles's age, had Giles lived. Giles would've been pleased she and Nathan were married.

Why had she waited so long? Why hadn't she known Nathan loved her, had always loved her, even when he assisted at her wedding to Andrew?

Almost two years, now, since she and Nathan had been

86

married quietly in York, yet even on their first night together she felt she must surely be cheating him; that never again could she love as she had loved Andrew.

That first, long-ago loving had been deep and passionate because for an army doctor and a young VAD nurse there were no tomorrows; just here and now and living wildly their moments together. Yet in all the three years she and Andrew had been married, only ten nights were spent in his arms.

Yet being married to Nathan was equally good, but in a different way. This time it was gentler and sweeter and safer, somehow, because for her and Nathan there *was* a tomorrow.

She swung her feet to the floor then padded to the window to pull aside the curtain. Delight washed over her at the sight of trees silvered by a bright, full moon, gilding the stable block and the outline of the bothy behind the wild garden; making a mockery of the blackout.

She stood, breath indrawn. Not a sound outside. No bombers airborne tonight. Unsafe for aircraft to range the skies silhouetted darkly against the brightness, easy targets for hunting night-fighters.

Tonight the crews at Holdenby Moor were grounded and doubtless dancing without a care because tonight at least they could be sure of one tomorrow. Drew had put on his uniform and gone to that dance with Daisy and Tatty and the new land girl. Now it was almost midnight and he wasn't home yet.

'Julia . . .'

'Sorry, darling. Did I wake you?'

'I wasn't asleep. Come back to bed. Drew's a grown man now. Bet he stays out later than this at Plymouth.'

'Yes, but he's at the aerodrome and outside it's like daylight.' She pulled back the covers and lay down beside Nathan. 'On nights like this, German fighters come nuisance raiding, remember; flying in low out of the moon and shooting up our aerodromes and –'

'Julia, for goodness' sake! Drew is all right and Daisy and Tatty, too.'

'Y-yes. I suppose so. But how did you know I was thinking about Drew being out?'

'Of course you were. I know you so well that knowing what you are thinking comes easily.'

'It does?' She turned to face him, kissing him gently, her breath soft on his cheek. 'Then tell me, what am I thinking now?'

'You are thinking,' he said huskily, drawing her closer, 'that you want me to make love to you.'

'Mm.' She kissed him again. 'My darling – how well you know me . . .'

7

Yesterday, Mary Strong returned from Creesby in triumph, having found the blue silk cabbage roses with which to trim the wide-brimmed biscuit-coloured hat she was to wear to her wedding.

'I tell you, Tilda – no silk flowers to be found. I'd just about given up hope when I went down a side street and found them in a poky little shop. Dust all over everything, mind, but there they were, just what I'd been looking for and exactly the same blue as the frock!'

'Lucky,' Tilda murmured, glad that in four days Mary would be Mrs Stubbs, and wedding talk a thing of the past.

'I'll take them over to Alice to sew on the hat.' Mary eased on the biscuit-coloured wedding shoes she was breaking in for Saturday, because not for anything was she walking down the aisle at All Souls' squeaking with every step. 'Won't be more'n a couple of minutes. Table's laid for dinner – you know they want it a bit earlier, tonight?'

On account of Drew going to the dance in Creesby, that was. Daisy was going, too, and the land girl, Mary learned only that morning when she had gone to the kitchen garden with Tilda's vegetable list. Indeed, it had been the land girl's idea for Mr Catchpole to make a finger-spray of flowers instead of a posy for her to carry.

'Pale pink carnations and white gypsophila, that's what, with a little loop underneath so you can slip it over your middle finger. And a pink carnation, perhaps, for your bridegroom's buttonhole . . . ?'

Mary had taken at once to the idea though truth known she had never heard of finger-sprays before.

. . . and the bride, dressed in conflower blue and given away by Mr Thomas Dwerryhouse, carried a finger-spray of pink carnations. It would read very well in the *Creesby Advertiser.* A nice girl, that Gracie, even if she did go dancing with Sir Andrew and presumed to call him Drew after only six days' acquaintance.

She sighed, though with pleasure or relief she couldn't be sure. Relief, she supposed, to be getting wed at last.

Tatiana Sutton looked critically at her reflection in the full-length mirror and was pleased with what she saw. And she would look better still once she was able to put on her lipstick and dab a little of her precious perfume on her wrists. But the finishing touches must wait until later or her mother would become suspicious if she went to Daisy's house all dressed up. If Mama really knew where she was going she would put on her Grandmother Petrovska face and forbid the Creesby dance, even though Drew and Daisy would be there. Creesby dances were not allowed because, unlike the Holdenby hops, they were frequented by people – *men* – of unknown pedigree, who could be relied upon to take liberties with young ladies in general and Tatiana Sutton in particular.

The night following the aerodrome dance, Tim Thomson did not phone, and six Whitley bombers and six Wellingtons had thrashed and roared into the sky.

'Please Lord, *please* take care of Tim; take care of all of them,' she whispered, dry-mouthed. Then she turned to the icon above her bed and, crossing herself piously in the Russian Orthodox manner, prayed again to the Virgin and Child, just to make sure. She was relieved, on counting them home next morning, that twelve planes came in to land at Holdenby Moor.

Not long after, the phone rang and she found herself

shaking when a voice whispered, 'Hullo there, hen. Just thought I'd let you know I'm back. Can we meet?'

That was when the drawing-room door opened and she was forced to reply, 'Daisy! Hi! I think so. When?'

'The crossroads outside Holdenby,' Tim had replied, laughter in his voice. 'Tonight at seven – okay?'

'Could you make it half-past, Daisy?'

And Tim had said that half-past seven was just fine and that he looked forward to seeing her.

Tatania spent the rest of that day partly on a pale pink cloud and partly in a trough of gloom, worried lest when they met at the crossroads someone should see them, though as it turned out no one did. They had walked the narrow road that led to Holdenby Pike with never a car passing them – thanks be for petrol rationing – and Tim kissed her, which made her cheeks flame and her heart bump deliciously.

That first kiss was kind and gentle, because she hadn't quite known how to do it and blushingly told him so, though he assured her gravely that she would get much better with practice.

'Tomorrow night is a bit – well, *uncertain*,' he whispered throatily, kissing the tip of her nose, which Tatiana found thrilling, 'and I mightn't be able to phone, but Wednesday should be okay. Shall we say Wednesday – the Creesby dance? Will I call for you?'

'No, Tim! Oh, *no*!'

'But of course, you'll be going with Daisy,' he grinned. 'See you at the dance, then?'

'Yes, please,' she breathed, closing her eyes, lifting her face to his. And she parted her lips a little, just to let him know she wanted him to kiss her again.

And their second kiss had been wonderful.

Tatiana was grateful that on the morning of the Creesby dance, Grandfather Sutton made a final check of the locks of the rooms in which he had been allowed to store his furniture, then handed over two complete sets of keys to the army major waiting to take possession of Pendenys Place. That a third set of keys was still in Edward Sutton's pocket was of little consequence, he having neither the need nor the desire ever to use them. But having them meant he had not quite given up Pendenys, though why the thought should please him he had no idea.

He had readily agreed to the military commandeering the house he had lived in all his married life, his only regret being that if there really was a hereafter, then Clemmy would be reading his thoughts and sending down her wrath against him for not putting up more of a fight of it, for Pendenys had been his wife's pride and joy.

And on the Wednesday of the Creesby dance, Tatiana's mother was so occupied with making sure Grandfather Sutton was welcomed and made comfortable that she had even agreed to her daughter staying late at Daisy's house, provided she was seen safely home by eleven o'clock.

Drew and Daisy were waiting at Keeper's Cottage when, breathless from pedalling, Tatiana propped her cycle against one of the dog houses, apologizing for being late and begging them never, ever, to tell anyone about the Creesby dance.

'I won't tell Aunt Anna on you,' Drew admonished, 'but just let's hope, Tatty, that she doesn't mention it to me so I don't have to tell any lies.'

'She won't. She's going to be far too busy fussing over Grandfather ever to bother. And I'm sorry I involved you in it, Daisy,' she said contritely, as they walked to the bothy to pick up Gracie, 'but I'll die if I don't see Tim again.'

'Tatty! You haven't fallen for him?' Daisy demanded. 'For heaven's sake, you hardly know him!'

'I do, so! I've known him four days and that's time enough. Besides,' she added defiantly, 'I met him on Tuesday as well. We went to the top of Holdenby Pike and –'

'Spare us the details,' Drew grinned. 'And we won't snitch on you, Tatty, just so long as you watch it – you know what I'm getting at?'

'Of course I know and you needn't worry, Drew. I didn't come down with the last fall of snow,' she flung testily, though what she would do if Tim ever wanted to do *that*, she wasn't entirely sure. 'And I think you should mind your own business and watch yourself with the land girl. You're gone on her, aren't you?'

'No, I'm really not. I like Gracie, though, to dance with. Now for Pete's sake let's get a move on or we'll miss the bus!'

He was pleased, for all that, to see how attractive Gracie looked in the borrowed blue dress and found himself hoping that other men at the dance didn't find her equally so. They danced well together, and tonight Gracie had promised to teach him the dip and the spin; if he could get a look-in, that was, because, on seeing her legs for the first time, it had to be admitted they were wasted in breeches and dungarees!

'Are you all clued up for Saturday, then?' Julia settled herself on the hearth rug, leaning her back against Nathan's armchair.

'The wedding? Yes. I've had a chat with them both and gone over the service. Mary wants the obey bit left in,' he laughed, 'though once she's got the ring on her finger, I think we know who'll be obeying.'

'Mary has waited a long time for Will Stubbs,' Julia defended.

'Like I waited for you, wife.' There was no rancour in Nathan's voice.

'Mm. And soon we'll be having our second anniversary. Shall we have a bit of a do, if the rations will run to it? I tried to persuade Mother to have a party for her eightieth birthday, but she won't hear of it. She doesn't want reminding, she said, that she's been living on borrowed time for the last ten years. I wish she'd let us make just a little fuss. A lot of the tenants seem to be expecting it, and Tilda's saving some of the rations to make her just a little cake – with one big pink candle on it.'

'I don't think we should push her.' Nathan wound a strand of Julia's hair round his forefinger.

'You could be right, love. But we might be able to pull something off. How about a get-together for our anniversary and whilst we're about it we could toast Mother's birthday – belatedly, sort of. There are still a few bottles of decent stuff in the cellar – why leave them for Hitler's lot to get their hands on?'

'Julia! I thought we'd agreed, no more invasion talk. There isn't going to be one, I know it.'

'Oh? Got God's phone number, have you?'

'No. He's ex-directory. But it's a gut feeling I've got that we'll be all right, so let's talk about turning our anniversary into a surprise party for your mother's eightieth, because that's what you really intend, isn't it?'

'It is, actually. We'd have to be careful – make sure she didn't get wind of it.'

'You're a scheming woman, Julia Sutton.' He wasn't at all sure it was a good idea. Aunt Helen had aged visibly this last year. The coming of another war so soon after the last one had upset the elderly, many of whom would never quite push the carnage of the trenches behind them. And Drew joining the Navy hadn't helped. There were times, Nathan had to admit, when Helen's frailty worried him. 'Scheming and devious and I don't know why I love you so much.'

'I'm perfect, that's why. And stop fiddling with my hair! You're only looking for grey bits! Now – about Mother's birthday party. Pity it'll be a couple of months late, but I'm determined she'll have one. Tell you what – why don't we hold it in the parish hall? That way we'd have a better chance of keeping it a secret, though we'd have to find a way of inveigling her down there. But I'll think of something . . .'

'I'm sure you will.' His wife always got her own way; always had, ever since he could remember. But she was so open and charming in all she did that she got away with it every time. It was one of the things he loved about her. 'And I'm sorry, darling, but I promised I'd look in on Father – make sure he's settled in at Denniston. Are you coming?'

'Not tonight, if you don't mind. I'll maybe take Mother over tomorrow. And don't worry about him, Nathan. He'll be fine with Anna and Tatty. It wasn't good for him being all alone in that place. Best thing *They* ever did was commandeering Pendenys.'

'You'll have to try to find out who's taking it over, and what they intend using it for. Alice told me Tom saw a convoy of army lorries this afternoon that seemed to be heading in that direction. They aren't wasting any time, are they? Give my love to Uncle Edward, won't you?' She rose to her feet, clasping her arms around his neck, drawing him close to kiss him. 'And don't be away too long,' she murmured throatily as he left her.

Agnes Clitherow rose stiffly to her feet, the last of her possessions packed carefully into tea chests and clearly labelled for when the carrier collected them. She had delayed her departure for Scotland until after the wedding, which would give her the opportunity to say goodbye to her friends; less sad, too, since everyone would be in a happy frame of mind.

Yet leaving would not be easy. Saying goodbye to her ladyship and Miss Julia would be near-heartbreaking and need all of that self-control she had learned over the years as housekeeper to the gentry. Nor would she relish saying goodbye to Sir Andrew on Saturday morning when his leave was over. Such a fine young man Drew had grown into. Sir Giles would have been so proud of him.

Agnes Clitherow blinked away her tears, blowing her nose loudly. Packed carefully away was a silver-framed photograph of Drew she would treasure always; a memento of a fine young man who would come safely through this war, she knew it, and marry and have sons for Rowangarth. Oh please, God, he *must*!

Flight Sergeant Timothy Thomson was waiting outside the Plaza dance hall in Creesby when the Holdenby bus stopped outside.

'Tim!' Tatiana's cheeks flushed hotly. 'I said to meet me inside!'

'Oh, aye? So you think I'm mean, do you? Meet my girl inside so I don't have to pay her in?'

'I didn't think that at all!' She took a step away from him because she knew he was going to kiss her and it simply wouldn't do – not when someone from Holdenby might just be walking past. It was one of the awkward things about being a Sutton. So many people knew her. 'But I'm glad you could make it. Were you on ops. last night?'

'Aye, but it was only a milk run. Counts as an op. for all that. One more off my tour.'

'Your – *tour*?'

'Thirty bombing operations in a tour. Not a lot of air-crews make it to a full tour, but those that do are taken off flying for a while.'

'And how many have you done, Tim?'

'Last night was the eleventh, so it's fingers crossed for the next two. Crews seem to think that once they're over the thirteenth there's a good chance of making it. The first op., the thirteenth and the very last of the tour are the dicey ones. But the others have gone in and we're standing here blethering.'

They were wasting time when he needed so desperately to have her in his arms, to dance close so he could feel her breath soft on his cheek, smell the clean, sweet scent of her hair. And damned fool him, too, when he'd vowed never to get entangled with girls; to love them and leave them. Get the war over first, then concentrate on a decent degree. But now there was Tatiana and all he could do was think about her all day, then fall asleep hoping to dream about her all night. Soft in the head, he was.

'What's a milk run?' Tatiana asked when the first dance was over.

'It's an easy op. hen – easy as delivering milk. We didn't carry a bomb-load last night. Our lot did a diversionary run to draw their fighters away from the Dutch coast. That way, our main bomber force had a better chance of making it to the target – somewhere in the Ruhr, I think they went. You try to attract the German fighters, then climb like mad, out of their way . . .'

'Hmm. And 109s can't climb all that high, can they, and they can't stay airborne for very long; not like our Spits and Hurries.'

'So how come you know so much about Messerschmitts then?' He tweaked her nose playfully.

'Because I take a magazine called the *Spotter*. It's all about planes, gives silhouettes, too – both ours and theirs so you can recognize them in the air. I'm getting quite good at it.'

'There's more to you, lassie, than meets the eye!' He rose as a waltz was announced. He liked waltzing with her. The steps were slower, so he needed to hold her closer.

'Tim?' Tatiana moved her head so her lips were close to his ear. 'When we met tonight, you said you weren't so mean that you couldn't pay for your girl to go into the dance.'

'Aye, well – some Sassenachs think us Scots are mean.'

'I didn't mean that. You called me your girl. Am I your girl, Tim?'

Her eyes met his. Such big, brown, beseeching eyes.

'If you want to be.'

'That isn't what I asked.'

'Okay.' He lowered his voice to a whisper. 'Since you ask, Tatiana, you bowled me right over the minute I saw you. I haven't been able to get you out of my mind since – so what have you to say to that?'

She smiled, her eyes not leaving his. They were moving more slowly now; dancing on a sixpenny piece, she supposed. And all at once they were the only people in the world.

'Remember the night we met, Tim?'

'Every bit of it. Which particular minute are we talking about?'

'The one when I spoke to you in Russian.'

'I mind fine. You said you thought I was a good dancer, didn't you?'

'No, darling. What I really said was, "I think I am falling in love with you."'

'I see. So that makes two of us.' He said it very matter-of-factly. 'What are we going to do about it?'

'I don't know. I don't have much of a choice. I'm only eighteen, remember.'

'No chance of marrying me, then?'

'Not without Mother's permission and she'd never give it.' Her eyes pricked with tears.

'Then it's a pity you aren't Scottish. You'd be considered to have sense enough to marry at eighteen there.'

'I would? Is your law different, then?' Her heart began to thump uncomfortably.

'That part of it is.'

'But I'm English.'

'Then you'd need to live in Scotland for three weeks – become domiciled. You'd qualify then.'

The music stopped and the floor cleared, leaving just the two of them standing there, though it didn't matter because weren't they the only two people in the world, anyway, and in love?

'Then when you've flown your thirty raids, will you ask me to marry you, Tim?'

'I will, sweetheart.'

'And I shall say yes . . .'

They smiled into each other's eyes, then he took her hand and led her from the floor.

'Well!' Daisy gasped. 'Did you see Tim and Tatty? Standing there in the middle of the floor just the two of them, gazing into each other's eyes and not caring who sees them? She's supposed not to be here, you know.'

'I don't think she cares,' Gracie laughed. 'Nor him. Those two are smitten, if you ask me.'

'Lordy, I hope not,' Drew let out his breath in a slow whistle. 'But if they are, let's hope Aunt Anna doesn't find out about it. She'd hit the deck-head!'

'Oh, I wouldn't worry too much about her mother if I were Tatty,' Daisy said softly. 'But her grandmother is something else entirely. Grandma Petrovska would eat Tim Thomson alive.'

'Yes, and spit him out in very small pieces.' Drew was all at once uneasy. 'What are we going to do about it, Daiz?'

'Nothing,' said Daisy, who knew all about falling in love. 'Absolutely nothing. And the best of luck to them!'

8

'Well! Did you hear the six o'clock news?' Alice demanded hotly the minute Tom stepped through the kitchen door. 'Think they can do anything they want, just 'cause there's a war on!'

'They *can* do anything they want!' Tom kissed his wife's cheek. 'And I didn't hear the news, so you'd better tell me.'

'Income tax, that's what! It's going up to eight and sixpence in the pound in the New Year. That's more'n a third of what folk earn – and it's to be taken out of folks' pay packets *every week*. No more paying it twice a year!'

'Sort of pay it as you earn it,' Tom nodded. 'Seems fair enough to me. Mind, most folk don't pay anything at all but let's face it, somebody's got to pick up the bill for this war.'

'Well, I still don't think it's right! Legalized thieving, that's what it amounts to. It wouldn't surprise me, Tom, if both you and Daisy don't have to start paying tax come the New Year. And there's nothing funny about it, so you can wipe that smirk off your face!'

Alice tossed her head defiantly because to her way of thinking, taking tax out of folks' pay packets every week *was* thieving!

'Lass, lass! Daisy won't pay tax on the pound a week she earns.' He was careful not to mention how it would be for his daughter once she came into all that money. 'And as for me – well, it'll be heaven help a lot if I start paying income tax. Lady Helen and Mr Edward'll have to worry before I will.

'And talking about Mr Edward, I was having a word

with Pendenys' head keeper this afternoon. They haven't told him to go yet, but he's expecting to hear any day that the military want him off the estate. All the house staff have had to go to the Labour Exchange. They're expecting to be put on munitions, so talk has it.'

'Talk is cheap, Tom. What I'd like to know is what's going on at Pendenys.'

'And so would I! They've wasted no time if what I hear is true. Guard posts set up and sentries patrolling already. Barbed wire all over the place, an' all, and Mr Edward's only been gone five days.'

'It's for the King and Queen and the Princesses to come to, that's my belief,' Alice nodded, income tax forgotten. 'Just wait till they start *really* bombing London – and start they will before so very much longer! The government'll have the royal family out of Buckingham Palace quicker than you can say knife!'

'The royal family, Alice? Never! What have they ever done to deserve Pendenys? If I was the military I'd make it into a prison and lock up black marketeers in it!'

'We'll find out if we wait long enough.' Alice stuck the sharp point of a knife into a potato. 'Nearly ready. Away with you and take off your boots and leggings. Daisy'll be in soon. She'll want her supper smartish tonight. Off to spend the evening with Drew, seeing he's only got two more days left. Lady Helen asked especially for her to go over. Poor soul. Her ladyship's failing if you ask me, and no one to blame for it but Hitler! Oh, but I'd like just five minutes alone with that man!' Alice fumed because she would never, as long as she lived, forgive him for starting another war.

'You and a million other women! Now don't get yourself upset, love. Fretting and fratching will do you no good at all. And don't they say that nothing is ever as bad as we think it's going to be?'

'And who told you that?'

'Reuben, as a matter of fact.' And Reuben had reminded him not so very long ago that Alice was coming to the age when women were on a short fuse and had to be handled carefully. Women *that* age, Reuben warned, blew hot and blew cold at the dropping of a hat, then burst into tears over nothing at all. Queer cattle women were, so think on!

'He's entitled to his opinion!' Alice stirred the stew that thickened lazily on a low gas light then slammed back the lid. Jugged rabbit, stewed rabbit, savoury rabbit and rabbit roasted. Oh for a good thick rib of beef! 'Well, go and get into your slippers. That's Daisy's bus now at the lane end.'

Daisy. Still no letter from the Wrens. Happen they really had forgotten her.

'Pull up a chair, Daisy love, and have a cup. There's still a bit of life left in the teapot.' Polly Purvis set the kettle to boil.

Teapots were kept warm on the hob now, and hot water added to the leaves again and again until the liquid was almost too weak to come out of the spout. And she was luckier than most, Polly reckoned, having fifteen ration books to take to the shops each week. She had solved the egg problem and butter, lard and margarine she could just about manage on, but good red meat and sugar were a constant problem, especially when a land girl did the work of a man to her way of thinking, and needed a bit of packing inside her.

'You're all right, Polly? Not working too hard?'

'I'm fine. The girls are a good crowd. Always popping in for a chat – mostly about boyfriends. I was lucky to get taken on here, Daisy. Keeps me busy enough and keeps my mind off – well, *things*. And by the way, I had a letter from Keth this morning.'

'And?' Daisy raised an eyebrow, not needing to ask the one question that bothered them both.

'Not one word about *that*. I asked him outright last time

I wrote just what he was doing in Washington, but no straight answer. The job is fine is all I'm told and that he's saving money. Ought to be grateful for that, at least – our Keth with money in the bank! And he's obviously managed to get himself a work permit. His letters are cheerful enough and at least he's safe.'

'That's what I keep telling myself, Polly. Sometimes I wouldn't care if he stayed in America till the war is over. Not very patriotic of me, is it, when Drew's already in it?'

'I feel that way, too.' Polly stirred the tea thoughtfully. 'But folks hereabouts understand that he's stranded over there. I don't feel any shame that he isn't in the fighting. Wouldn't want him to suffer like his father did. My Dickon came back from the trenches a bitter man.'

'Don't worry.' Daisy reached for Polly's hand. 'One day it will all be over. Just think how marvellous it'll be! No more blackout, no more air raids and the shops full of things to buy.'

'And no more killing and wounding and men being blinded.'

'No more killing,' Daisy echoed sadly.

'But you'll give my best regards to Drew when you see him tonight, won't you?' Polly said, rallying. 'Wish him all the luck in the world from me and Keth?'

'I think he'll pop in for a word with you before he goes, but don't say goodbye to him, will you, Polly? He said sailors are very superstitious about it. You've got to say cheerio, or so long, or see you. I think Drew's going to be all right, though. Jinny Dobb told me he'd come to no harm; said he had a good aura around him. Jin's a clairvoyant, you know. She can see death in a face – and she isn't often wrong, either way.'

'Then I reckon I'd better ask her over for a cup of tea and she can read my cup – tell me when Keth's going to get himself back home. Mind, I'd settle for knowing just what he's up to and if he's getting enough to eat.'

'And I would give the earth just to speak to him for – oh, twenty seconds; ask him how he is.'

'Oh, for shame!' Polly laughed. 'You could do a lot better'n asking him how he is in twenty seconds! Now then, how about that cup of tea?' She began to pour, then laughed again. 'Oh, my goodness! Did I say *tea*?'

'Well, at least it's hot.' Daisy joined in the laughter because you had to laugh. If you didn't, then life would sometimes be simply unbearable.

'I won't come over tomorrow night, Drew. I think you should spend it with Aunt Julia and Lady Helen. I'll be there on Saturday, though, to wave you off.'

The July evening was warm and scented with a mix of honeysuckle and meadowsweet and the uncut hedge was thick with wild white roses. Beneath the trees, on the edge of the wild garden, tiny spotted orchids grew, and lady's-slipper and purple tufted vetch.

Drew reached for Daisy's hand, remembering scents and sounds and scenes, storing them in his mind so he might bring them out again some moment when he was in need of them.

'My ten days have gone very quickly. It seemed like for ever when I got on the train at Plymouth. I think Grandmother is feeling it. Her indigestion is playing her up again, but I'm not to tell Mother, she says. I think she's had it for quite a while. It's the war. I think she remembers the last one, and gets a bit afraid. You'll always pop over to see her, won't you, Daiz?'

'Of course I will. I love her a lot, and she was once Mam's mother-in-law and Mam loves her, too. We'll see she doesn't fret too much when you've gone back – and there'll be Mary's wedding in the afternoon to help take her mind off your going back.'

They skirted the wild garden and crossed the lawn to the linden walk. The leaves on the trees were still fresh with spring greenness and their newly opened flowers threw a sweet, heady perfume over them.

'Just smell the linden blossom, Daiz. I think I shall take it back with me to barracks – maybe think of it when I'm at sea in a gale, and being sick.'

'You won't be sick! Where do you think they'll send you?'

'Haven't a clue. They say big ships are more comfortable, but if I had a choice, I think I'd go for something small and more matey – perhaps a frigate. And having said that,' he grinned, 'I'll end up on an aircraft carrier, most likely. Wouldn't mind *Ark Royal*. There's always been an *Ark Royal* in the British Navy. There was one, even, in Henry Tudor's time.'

'Drew! Don't go for *Ark*! Every week, Lord Haw-Haw says the Germans have sunk her!'

'And every week we know they haven't. Still, I won't have a say in the matter. I'm a name and a number for the duration. I do as I'm told. Chiefie in signal school told us to keep our noses clean and our eyes down and we'd be all right. And that's what I shall do – and count the days to my next leave.'

'Drew – do you remember how it used to be?' They had reached the iron railings that separated Rowangarth land from the fields of Home Farm, and stopped to gaze at the shorthorn cows grazing in Fifteen-acre Meadow. 'It seems no time at all since that last Christmas the Clan was together. Remember? Aunt Julia took a snap of us all. Keth, me, Bas and Kitty and you and Tatty. In the conservatory. We'd all been dancing . . .'

'I remember. After that, Uncle Albert started getting a bit huffy about coming over from Kentucky twice a year, but that last summer we were all together was fun, wasn't it – except for Aunt Clemmy and the fire in Pendenys tower?'

'And Bas's hands getting burned. I'm glad Mr Edward

had that tower demolished – what was left of it.'

'Poor Aunt Clemmy. It was an awful way to die. I think, really, it was because she took to brandy after Uncle Elliot was killed. He was her favourite son, Grandmother said. She never got over it. Elliot was her whole life, I believe.'

'Yes, but I know Mam and Aunt Julia didn't like him. Even now, if ever his name is mentioned, your mother screws up her mouth like she's sucking on a lemon. I once heard her say he'd been a womanizer – but we shouldn't speak ill of the dead, should we, and Tatty hasn't grown up like him, Mam says. Tatty's okay.'

'Yes, but Tatty's going to have to watch it. You know how strict Aunt Anna can be and Tatty has really fallen for that air-gunner. She said she doesn't care what happens – nobody is going to stop her seeing him. She'll have to sneak out, tell lies.'

'Well, I'm on Tatty's side. Tim's a nice young man and someone should remind Tatty's mam that there's a war on and that young girls don't need chaperoning now!'

'But Tatty's so innocent, Daiz. She's always been fussed over and protected. And if Aunt Anna wasn't fussing, there was always Karl in the background to look after her.'

'Yes, and teach her to swear in Russian,' Daisy giggled. 'Don't worry about Tatty. She'll be all right. She's good fun – away from home. But oh, Drew, I could stand here for ever. It's all so beautiful I can't believe there's a war on.'

The distant sound of aero-engines at once took up her words and made a mockery of them. A bomber flew overhead, big and black and deadly.

'Looks as if they're going again tonight.' Daisy looked up, preparing to count. 'Take care, Tim,' she said softly as another aircraft roared over Brattocks Wood. 'Come home safely, all of you.'

*   *   *

Helen Sutton sat quietly in the conservatory, watching the sun set over the stable block. It tinted the wispy night clouds to salmon pink and shaded the darkening sky to red.

Red sky at night, sailors' delight . . .

Rowangarth's sailor had gone back to his barracks on the noon train from Holdenby. Soon now he should be in barracks, then where? She shivered as the short, sharp pain stabbed inside her chest. In yesterday's papers she had read that Somewhere in England – They always called a place Somewhere in England when it suited them not to name it – close-packed German bombers with fighter escorts had attacked harbours, fighter stations and naval bases on the south coast.

Naval bases. Plymouth and Portsmouth must surely have been targeted by the Luftwaffe. It was a part, Helen was sure, of the softening-up process so there would be less resistance when the tides were right – right for the Germans, that was. In September.

Where would Drew be then? At sea, Helen hoped fervently. He'd be safer at sea. How proud she had been today of the son Giles never lived to see, tall now, and straight and Sutton fair, with eyes grey as those of his grandfather John; like his great-uncle Edward's, too.

Drew would come back whole from this war. Fate could not be so fiendish as to take him. Besides, Helen had spoken to Jinny Dobb at the wedding this afternoon, with Jin asking why she was so sad; telling her she was not to fret over young Sir Andrew because his aura was healthy, she insisted, and was Jin Dobb ever wrong, she'd demanded.

'Take care of *yourself*, milady,' she'd urged. 'He'll come back safe to claim his own, just see if he doesn't.'

Dear Jin. Those words gave her brief comfort, Helen smiled, for sure enough, Jinny Dobb could see into the future and read palms and tarot cards – with which she, Helen, did not entirely hold. But this afternoon, at Mary's wedding, she snatched comfort from Jin's prophecies and smiled and waved and threw confetti when Will and Mary left Holdenby for a weekend honeymoon in quite a grand hotel in York.

Mary had looked beautiful. Blue certainly suited her and she and Tom walked solemnly down the aisle to where Will and Nathan waited. How nice, those cosy country weddings.

The door knob turned, squeaking, and Tilda walked softly to Helen's side.

'I've brought your milk and honey, milady. Miss Julia asked me not to forget it.'

'Tilda, you shouldn't have bothered, especially as you'll be managing alone until Mary gets back. You'll have all your work cut out –'

'Oh, milady, I'll be right as rain. There's only you and Miss Julia and the Reverend to see to and not one of you a bit of bother. It was a grand wedding, wasn't it, though I gave up thinking long ago that anyone'd ever get Will Stubbs down the aisle. But fair play, Mary managed it though no one can say those two rushed headlong into wedlock, now can they?'

'Tilda!' Helen scolded smilingly. Then raising her glass she took a sip from it. 'And here's wishing them all the happiness in the world!'

'Amen to that.' Tilda turned in the doorway. 'You'll think on, milady, not to forget and switch the light on?' An illuminated conservatory would fetch every German bomber on the Dutch coast zooming in over Rowangarth and would land them with a hefty fine and a severe telling-off from the police for doing such a stupid thing.

'I'll remember. I think you'd better remind me tomorrow to ask Nathan to take the light bulb out.' A conservatory was too big and awkward to black out effectively. Best take no chances. 'And don't wait up. Goodness knows when the pair of them will be back from Denniston. They have a key. You've had a long day – off to bed with you.'

And Tilda said she thought she could do with an early night, but that she would see to the doors and windows first, then check up on the blackouts.

'Good night, milady,' she smiled, closing the door softly behind her.

Dear Lady Helen. They would have to take good care of her for there were few left from the mould she'd been made from; precious few, indeed.

Tom Dwerryhouse hung up his army-issue gas mask, took off his glengarry cap, then leaned the rifle in the corner.

There had been an urgent parade of the Home Guard called for this evening and he and several others had had to leave the wedding early and put on their khaki for a seven o'clock muster.

It was a relief to be told that their rifles – ammunition, too – had arrived at last and he opened the long, wooden boxes only to sigh in disbelief. Those long-promised rifles – and he knew it the minute he laid eyes on them – were leftovers from the last war and had lain, it seemed, untouched and uncared for in some near-forgotten store.

He took the rifle, breaking it at the stock to squint again down the barrel. Filthy! It would take a long time to get the inside of that barrel to shine like it ought to. There would have to be a rifle inspection at every parade to let them know that Corporal Dwerryhouse wasn't going to allow any backsliding when it came to the care of rifles, old and near-useless though they were.

He snapped it shut, gazing at it, remembering against his will when last he fired such a rifle. It was something he would never forget. He knew the exact minute he took aim, awaiting the order to fire. And his finger had coldly, calmly, squeezed the trigger that Épernay morning.

It was the bullet from his own rifle, he knew it, that took the life of the eighteen-year-old boy. Aim at the white envelope pinned to the deserter's tunic to show them where his heart was, that firing squad had been told. But the other eleven men had been so uneasy, so shocked that he, Tom Dwerryhouse, took it upon himself to make sure the end would be quick and clean.

A sharpshooter, he had been, but an executioner they made him that day. Refuse to take part and he too would have been shot for insubordination and another, less squeamish, would have taken his place.

Then, directly afterwards, the shelling started and heaven took its revenge for the execution of an innocent and directed a scream of shells on to that killing field so the earth shook. That was when he fell, surrendering to a blackness he'd thought was death.

Rifleman Tom Dwerryhouse did not die in that Épernay dawn. He awoke to stumble dazed, in search of the army camp he did not know had been wiped out by the German barrage.

How long he walked he never remembered, but a farmer had taken him in and given him food and shelter and civilian clothes to work in. And Tom acted out the part of a shell-shocked French soldier, and those who came to the farm looked with pity at the *poilu* who was so shocked he uttered never a word.

The Army sent a letter to his mother, telling her he had been killed in action and his sister wrote to the hospital at Celverte, to tell Alice he was dead.

The night of that letter, Alice was taken in rape. She had not fought, she told him, because she too wanted to die, but instead she was left pregnant with the child who came to be known as Drew Sutton.

Now white-hot anger danced in front of Tom's eyes. He flung the rifle away as though it would contaminate him and it fell with a clatter to the stone floor.

He hoped with all his heart he had broken it.

9

Tom stood hidden, unmoving. To a gamekeeper, stealth was second nature. Such a man must move without the snapping of a twig underfoot, learn to sink into night shadows or merge into sunlight dapples. It was, in part, to ensure that young gamebirds were not disturbed nor frightened unduly, but mostly that inborn stealth helped outwit poachers, out to take pheasants or partridge.

The sudden clicking of a rifle bolt was a sound he remembered well. Breath indrawn, he awaited the command he knew would follow.

'Halt! Who goes there?'

'Friend,' Tom called clearly.

'We're armed. Step forward!' A pinpoint of light searched him out, swept him from head to feet. 'Put down that gun!'

'It isn't loaded.' Slowly, carefully, Tom laid his shotgun at his feet.

'You're on army property. What are you doing here?'

'I know I am. But it's been Pendenys land for a long time – I'd forgotten you lot.'

'That's as maybe, but I want to know why you're creeping around in the dark, and armed at that.'

'A gamekeeper usually carries a shotgun.' Tom had recovered his composure now. 'And they creep around because that's the best way to catch poachers. Meat's on the ration, and a brace of pheasants fetches thirty bob on the black market. And if I'm on Pendenys land it's because I often meet up with their keeper, doing his own night beat. I'm sorry. It won't happen again.'

'But how did you get in?' The soldiers lowered their rifles. 'This place is supposed to be secure.'

'It didn't keep me out. If it's security you're bothered about, I'd take a look at Brock Covert. It's the way I always come in at night. If you're interested, meet me in the daylight and I'll show it to you. Name's Tom Dwerry-house, by the way. I'm keeper on Rowangarth land, joining this. And I was a soldier myself once; was a marksman when you two were still messing your nappies. Could have put one through your cap badge at a hundred yards!'

'Ah, well. Got to be sure – and you shouldn't have been here.' The man reached into his pocket. 'We were just going to have a quick fag. Want one?'

'Don't smoke, thanks. Never did. Want a sup of tea?' Tom fished in his game bag for his vacuum flask.

'Thanks, mate. Name's Watson – corporal. And this one here's Johnny.'

'Which regiment – or shouldn't I ask?'

'Green Howards.'

'Ah.' Carefully, in the darkness, Tom filled the cap of the flask, passing it over. 'Yorkshire mob, eh? What's a regiment like the Greens doing here?'

'Buggered if I know.' They settled themselves comfort-ably, young soldiers and old soldier. 'They don't tell us anything.'

'Nothing changes. They never did.'

'It's my guess the CO doesn't know what's going on either though he makes out he does.'

Tom refilled the cap and handed it to the soldier called Johnny, knowing that if he didn't ask questions he would learn more.

'It isn't as if we're doing anything but guard duties. Flamin' boring, but the both of us were at Dunkirk so we aren't complaining. This posting would suit me nicely for the duration.'

'Reckon you both deserve a quiet number,' Tom

commiserated. 'Dunkirk couldn't have been a Sunday School outing, exactly.'

'It weren't. Ta.' Johnny gave back the flask top.

'Still, you'll be all right, here,' Tom directed his attention to the corporal, 'though I wouldn't fancy Pendenys as a billet. Great barn of a place.'

'A *billet*? We don't get nowhere near the place. Us lot are quartered in the stable block and the officers have been given the estate houses to kip down in. It's *them* that live in the big house.'

'Civilians.' Johnny lit another cigarette.

'You're guarding *civvies*?'

'We-e-ll, there's a few military amongst them, but what they are nobody knows. Not even our CO gets inside Pendenys.'

'There's women, too.' Johnny grunted derisively.

''S right. Fannies.'

'There were Fannies in France in my war,' Tom offered. First Aid Nursing Yeomanry. Brave lasses, they'd been. 'They drove ambulances. Went right up to the front line.'

'These lot don't drive nothin'. They throw a nasty hand grenade, though.'

'Fannies?' Tom frowned. 'Are you sure?'

'Johnny's seen 'em,' nodded the corporal. 'He'd nipped into the bushes for a Jimmy Riddle and a grenade landed not a hundred yards away. Live, it was. He got the hell out of it pretty sharpish. Could have done him a mischief.'

'Folk around these parts,' Tom said, 'reckon they're getting Pendenys Place ready for high-ups from London – when the bombing starts.'

'Nah.' The corporal said it was nothing like that. The King and Queen, in his opinion, would go to Balmoral if ever they left London.

'Then it's a rum do,' Tom frowned.

'Rum? It's bloody peculiar. Some of the civvies are foreigners – leastways one of our lads heard them talking foreign. And the military in the big house don't have any badges.'

'No regimental insignia?'

'Nothing at all to show which lot they belong to. But keep it shut, mate, or it's me for the glasshouse, and ta-ta to me stripes!'

'Not a word,' Tom assured him gravely. 'And if you'd like to give me a call one day – I live at Keeper's Cottage on the Rowangarth estate – I'll show you Brock Covert.'

'Ar. Thanks.' It would suit the corporal to be able to point out a breach in security where any old Tom, Dick or German could slip in. 'Might just do that. An' keep away from here, eh? Can't always guarantee that us two'll be on guard duty.'

'I will, and thanks. Good night, lads.'

Frowning, Tom made for Brock Covert. The Green Howards, a crack regiment, guarding civilians? And soldiers who wore no regimental badges? Fannies, an' all, who'd forsaken ambulances for grenade throwing. It was a rum do, all right.

In early August, the Luftwaffe flew over the south of England dropping not bombs, but leaflets. They fell in thick scatters and were eagerly gathered up. They detailed Adolf Hitler's proposals for peace between Great Britain and the Third Reich and were read with amazement.

Make peace with *that* one? Surrender – because that's what it would amount to – to an ex-corporal? Mad as a hatter, that's what he was and his leaflets a waste of good paper into the bargain.

On that day, too, Telegraphist Sutton was summoned to the Regulating Office and drafted to his first ship, and an envelope bearing the words 'On His Majesty's Service' dropped through the letterbox of Keeper's Cottage. With it was a pale blue air-mail letter, its American stamp franked clearly with a Washington postmark.

So it had come. Alice gazed at the manila envelope. The WRNS had not forgotten her daughter nor lost the application she filled in in a fit of pique almost seven weeks ago.

She swallowed hard and noisily, then placed the envelopes on the mantelpiece between the clock and the tea caddy. Oh, damn this war and damn Hitler! She gazed about her helplessly, then hurried into the passage to pick up the telephone.

'Hullo, Winnie,' she said to the operator. 'Give me Rowangarth, will you?' She stood, eyes closed, breathing deeply to fight the panic inside her. 'It's arrived, I think,' she said without preamble when her call was answered. 'An OHMS letter for Daisy. It'll be about her medical . . .'

'Put the kettle on,' said Julia Sutton. 'I'm coming over!'

'Where have you been, dear?' Helen Sutton laid aside the glove she was knitting in navy-blue wool.

'Popped over to Keeper's. Daisy's heard from the Wrens about her medical, Alice thinks. She and Tom were hoping they'd forgotten her.'

'I don't know why she had to volunteer. It's bad enough Drew having to go.'

'Dearest, don't worry. She might not pass the medical.'

'Of course she will!'

'Yes, she will. But they mightn't send for her for ages. And we've got to face it, women will all have to do war work before so very much longer and the young ones could well be sent into the Forces.'

'But they couldn't do that! Not to young girls. Is nothing sacred?'

'The way things are going, Mother, it seems not. I sometimes think I should be doing more.'

'But you and Alice go nights to the church canteen and you helped with the evacuees.'

'The evacuees have all gone home and serving cups of

tea to soldiers and airmen isn't doing a lot for the war effort.'

'You're the vicar's wife, Julia. Surely that's work of national importance?'

'Well I'm not so sure a vicar's wife would be exempt from war work. If push comes to shove – and it will, before so very much longer – they could have me emptying middens if they thought it would help with the war!'

'You *can't* mean it!' Helen picked up her needles and began knitting furiously.

'Of course not.' How could she be so stupid and her mother getting more frail and more afraid as each day passed? They were all afraid, but that was no excuse for upsetting her mother, who worried all the time about Drew. 'And if they did direct women into the Forces, it would only be as clerks and typists, or cooks. They wouldn't be in any danger, truly they wouldn't.'

'So when Daisy goes we shouldn't worry too much . . . ?'

'Daisy will be fine, and she hasn't gone yet.' Her mother adored Daisy; looked on her as an extension of Drew, which in reality she was. 'Now stop your worrying, dearest. I haven't seen the paper yet. Anything in it worth reading?'

'Nothing! They've shelled Dover – from across the Channel, Julia. Those poor people! And they've been bombing fighter stations on the south coast.'

'Don't believe all you read in the papers.' Julia wished she hadn't asked. 'Tune in to the BBC. They aren't scaremongers.'

'I did, and their news was just as bad, so it must be true. Our fighters were waiting for the German bombers, though. They were in the air before the Luftwaffe crossed our coastline. I wonder how we know they are coming, Julia?'

'Beats me. Probably we've got spies on the French coast – or something . . .'

Julia turned to gaze through the window, her thoughts

not to be given voice, for what she had feared all along was happening. We were being softened up for that September invasion. It made sense to knock out the fighter stations first. Hitler had to get here if he was to be complete master of Europe and the daily bombings signalled the start of it. The fight for Britain was on, it would seem.

'I shouldn't wonder if there isn't a letter from Drew soon, telling us he's got a ship. I've written a couple of letters but I'm not posting them until we get his new address. He'll be safer at sea, Mother, to my way of thinking. Plymouth has taken more than its fair share of the air raids.'

'You could be right.' Helen brightened visibly. 'I think I'll write to him, too.'

'You do that, dearest. Tell him all the nice things. He likes hearing about Rowangarth.' Home Farm starting the corn harvest, Jack Catchpole's anger at the newly-appeared molehills on the front lawn; Tilda bottling Victoria plums to store for winter puddings, Tom's bitch having a fine litter of puppies. 'I wouldn't mention the letter that came for Daisy this morning, though. She'll want to tell Drew about that herself.'

'Mm. And it mightn't be about her medical, you know. Maybe it's to tell her they've got enough Wrens for the time being.'

'You could well be right.'

Julia felt unease as she watched her mother walk away; not so straight, now, her steps slow and unsteady sometimes.

Dearest lovely Mother. Once you were so beautiful, so sure and brave. War took your sons from you yet you never wavered; you cared for the entire village, were always there to comfort when the death telegrams came.

We all leaned on you, drew strength from you. You were like a safe haven. You saw to it that the old always had logs to burn in winter and that no one went entirely hungry.

Yet now you are old yourself and have been called on

to face another war and what I'll do when you leave us, what Rowangarth and the whole of Holdenby will do, I don't dare think.

And, Mother, Daisy *will* have to go, sooner or later. We've got a long, terrible time ahead of us. We are on our own now, and women are going to have to help fight the war, whether we like it or not . . .

Daisy said, 'Hi, each!' looked up at the mantelpiece as she always did, faltered for just a second, then said, 'Well, what d'ya know? A letter from His Majesty.'

'Open it, love.' Alice could wait no longer. It had lain there all day, tormenting her so much that she had thought – only for a moment, mind – of taking the kettle to it and steaming it open.

'Albion Street, Leeds,' Daisy studied the stereotyped form. 'That's where I'm to go. On the twenty-ninth of August, at half-past three.'

'Two weeks away,' Alice frowned.

'So it is. If the date isn't convenient I'm to let them know at once, reusing the envelope and the enclosed label,' she grinned. 'There's economy for you!'

'It isn't funny,' Alice snapped, more than ever agitated now she knew that what she had feared all day was fact. 'And what do they mean – if it isn't convenient?'

'My period, I suppose. But I'll be all right.'

'Daisy!' Such talk, in front of her father!

'What's the matter, Mam – doesn't Dada know about the birds and the bees?'

'That'll do, lass.' Impudent young miss! Tom fought to keep the smile from his lips. 'What's Keth got to say for himself, then?'

'Don't ask.' Daisy took a knife from the table, carefully opening the envelope. 'That's between me and him – oooh, Mam, he's looking at rings! What do I want, he says.'

'Rings! I'd have thought he'd have better things to do

with his money than send a ring that'll likely end up torpedoed at the bottom of the Atlantic!'

'Well, since he's asking, I think I'd like a sapphire. It would go with my brooch.'

Would match the daisy-shaped brooch Aunt Julia had given her the day she was christened; petals of sapphires with a pearl at its centre. So valuable that she still had to ask Mam's permission to wear it.

'Your brooch, Daisy Dwerryhouse, would keep me in housekeeping for five years! Now where is Keth to find the money to match sapphires like those, will you tell me?'

'Don't know, Mam.' He still hadn't told anyone what his job was all about. 'But he said he's got money in the bank now. You should be pleased for him when he's had to live from hand to mouth most of his life – and had to take the Kentucky Suttons' charity.'

'Charity! You call saving Bas Sutton's life *charity*?' Alice lifted the potato pan from the stove top, walking with it to the yard to strain the water over the cobbles. Scalding saltwater killed the weeds, she insisted.

'Daisy love, don't rile your mother. She's all on edge these days and that letter of yours hasn't helped.'

'Sorry, Dada.' She was at once contrite. 'I'm not exactly pleased about it myself. But there's no going back now and at least it'll be better than working in a snobby shop. It'll help pass the time, I suppose, till Keth gets home. Anything I can do to help?' she asked as Alice returned.

'Please. Be a love and get the plates out of the oven.'

'Smells good. Stew, is it?'

'I suppose so, though it's more gravy than meat.'

Daisy sent her mother a smile across the table, realizing for the umpteenth time since the day she had filled in that application how much she was going to miss her if – *when* – her call-up papers came. She had such wonderful parents, such a lovely happy home; why, *why* had she been so stupid, so impulsive?

Because there's a war on, answered her conscience, and because you care very much about England and this precious, one-horse dump you live in. And because Drew has already gone to war and the sooner you do your bit, Daisy Dwerryhouse, to help win that war, the sooner Keth will be home.

More selfish, really, than patriotic she admitted with ruthless honesty.

'I think, Mam,' she said softly, 'that I really would like a sapphire engagement ring. But I'll tell Keth that if he gets one he's not to risk sending it.'

'You do that, love.' Alice was outwardly calm again. 'Like I said, we wouldn't want it to be sunk.'

Already the greedy Atlantic had claimed too much, a lot of which could never be replaced. The lives of young seamen, for instance . . .

'There's one from Drew, Mother!' Julia ripped open the envelope which, instead of a postage stamp, bore the red frank and scribbled initials of the censor. 'He's got a ship at last. Listen – I'll read it to you.

'Dearest Mother and Gran,

'When you get this I'll be en route to my ship. I won't give you the name for obvious reasons because this is to let you know we'll be stooging around, sweeping mines.

'I'll be based in home waters so I should get leave pretty regularly – at least they aren't sending me foreign. I'll let you have my official address when I get there.

'Just to let you know I'll soon be doing some sea-time, and glad to be out of barracks.

'In great haste, take care,

'Drew.

'Well now, isn't that good news, dearest?'

'Yes, but why hasn't he told us *which* ship?'

'Because he couldn't. He's let us know he's been drafted to a minesweeper based in home waters. If he'd given us the ship's name, too, the censor would have cut it out of his letter.'

'Censors! Such an invasion of privacy!' Helen said crossly. 'I'd be ashamed to be one of them, prying into people's private letters. How is a man to tell his wife he loves her – yes, and write about other intimate details, too?'

'Letters must be censored, Mother. If they got into enemy hands, even the most innocent remark could be a danger. One like, "I'll send you a picture of a camel when I get there" would be a giveaway; that such-and-such a regiment was being shipped to some place there was sand. Where else but North Africa – and before you know it, a troopship has been torpedoed. And it didn't stop Andrew and me in our war. We wrote the most passionate things to each other.'

'*Julia!*'

'But people in the censors' offices are human beings, too. They are only on the lookout for breaches of security. Love letters don't worry them one bit.'

'Well, I hope their cheeks are red, for all that!' Helen donned her spectacles, reaching for her grandson's letter. 'You haven't finished your breakfast. Where are you going?'

'To tell Alice.' Alice had a right to know.

'But can't you ring her up?'

'Best not. Got to be careful what you say on the phone. Never know who might be listening in.'

'But Winnie is the soul of discretion and so was her mother before her!'

Winnie Hallam, who manned Holdenby's tiny switch-board, never listened in!

'I know she is, Mother, but a German spy could climb a telegraph pole and tap in on any line he wanted. That's why telephones can be –'

Scrambled, she had been going to say, but her mother would never understand that vital war telephones were fitted with a device called a scrambler for just that very reason.

'That's why we have to be very careful what we say over the phone,' she amended.

'But I can't believe there are spies climbing up Holdenby's telegraph poles,' Helen frowned, her voice anxious.

'There aren't any. Holdenby isn't all that important. But if there were, Tom would soon spot them,' Julia comforted.

'Yes, of course he would.' Tom Dwerryhouse's presence was a great comfort to Helen, especially now that Drew was no longer here. Tom would take great pleasure peppering the behind of a telegraph-pole spy with gunshot. 'Well, off you go, dear, and tell Alice . . .'

'Won't be long.' Julia kissed her mother's cheek. 'And don't forget to let Nathan know where I am when he gets back from early communion.'

She closed the door of the breakfast room quietly, then leaned against it, eyes shut tightly.

Dear God, I know Mother is old now, and frail, but don't let her mind get old, too. I love her too much to let that happen.

Helen, Lady Sutton; always gracious and kind. Always her dearest mother. It would be too awful if her mind got old as well.

Please, God? I'd rather she died than went peculiar . . .

Guiltily, Julia shook such thoughts from her head, because the war was to blame! It was this awful war that caused so much worry, especially to the old. No one should have to live through one war, let alone two.

10

'Time to put the kettle on.' Gracie Fielding thrust her fork deep into the earth, then mopped her face and neck. They were digging the plot from which the early potato crop had been lifted, making it ready for replanting, and digging was hard work.

Yet already she felt as if she belonged here. It was as if she and Jack Catchpole were shut away from the war by the high, red-brick walls that enclosed the kitchen garden. Even on rainy days there was always something to do, something new to learn.

The tomato house she liked especially. Tomatoes were thirsty plants, Mr Catchpole said; needed more water than most. It had been a thrill to pick the first of the crop ready for the vegetable man who called each morning; tomatoes red-ripe and firm, with the scent of the greenhouse on them and not the sad, soft, ages-old things Mam had to queue half an hour for. Soon Gracie would be given a week of her annual leave and she would take home as many fresh vegetables and apples and pears as she could carry and maybe a rabbit, if she could sweetheart one out of Daisy's dad. People who lived in the country fared better for food than those who lived in towns and cities. Mam would be tickled pink to get a rabbit.

She filled the little kettle from the standtap outside the potting shed, stirred the fire in the iron grate, added twigs and wood choppings, then set it to boil on the sooty hob.

'Ready in about ten minutes.' She took up her fork again. 'Heard the early news, did you?' Everyone listened to news broadcasts and read the newspapers from cover to cover;

not because they wanted to but because it was their patriotic duty and anyway, people had to know the exact time blackout began each evening and when, in the morning, it ended. Since war came, newspapers were no longer allowed to print weather forecasts, nor were they read out at the end of news bulletins. It wouldn't do to let the enemy know when conditions would be best suited for their planes to come dropping bombs and incendiaries. Because mark his words, Mr Catchpole had said, there were those living amongst us pretending to be ordinary, normal English folk, who looked just the same as we did and spoke and acted as we did. But they were really spies and loyal to the Fatherland and had nasty, devious ways of getting weather forecasts back to Germany, and hanging would be too good for them when they were caught!

'News?' Jack Catchpole paused to lean on his fork. 'Makes you fair sickened. They're still bombing our fighter stations down south and we all know what for, don't we?'

'But we shot down sixty-seven of theirs.'

'And lost thirty-three of our own.' Never mind the Spitfires and Hurricanes. It was really thirty-three pilots we had lost, Catchpole considered angrily.

'The Air Ministry has confirmed that sixty-seven enemy aircraft were destroyed,' droned the newsreader, 'and thirty-three of our fighters failed to return . . .'

Thirty-three telegrams there'd be this morning. Regretting. And how many more telegrams before Europe came to its senses?

He drove his fork angrily into the earth, breaking down the clods with unnecessary force. Gracie noticed it at once but knew better than to ask what was bothering him.

'Think the kettle'll be just about on the boil,' she said, and headed for the potting shed. He was sitting on his upturned apple crate when she returned with two mugs, determined to cheer him up. 'Did you hear about Mussolini, Mr C.?'

'What's he been up to now?' Catchpole scowled.

'We-e-ll, you know he said that all British ports on the Mediterranean would be blockaded by Italian warships . . . ?'

'You mean the Eyetie Navy might actually put to sea?'

'Not exactly. They didn't get the chance. "Blockade us, will you?" said the Royal Navy, and sailed out there and then and sunk an Italian depot ship, a destroyer and one of their submarines!'

'And serve them right!' Mussolini was a strutting fool. No one took much notice of him. Talk had it that the Italian people hadn't wanted to go to war; that Mussolini only landed them in it to get on the right side of Hitler. But Hitler was a different kettle of fish. There was something unwholesome about him; the same wildness in his eyes you saw in the eyes of a mad dog before you had it put down. The evil in that face made Catchpole's flesh creep. 'But there'll be a nasty shock waiting for them Nazis if they try invading Yorkshire.'

'There will, Mr Catchpole?'

'Oh my word, yes! Now not a word to a soul about this, mind.' He tapped his nose with his forefinger and gave her one of his knowing nods. 'Us have been making 'em all week at the Home Guard. Petrol bombs!'

'But I thought petrol was on the ration, for cars.'

'So it is.' He'd thought much the same thing when two five-gallon cans had been delivered to their headquarters, petrol bombs for the use of. He had even gone so far as to wonder what those ten gallons would bring on the black market, but such thoughts were dismissed from his mind as he had seen himself hurling petrol bombs at a ruthless enemy, giving them a bit of their own back. 'So it is, lass, but it makes grand bombs, an' all. You get a bottle and half fill it with petrol. Then you stuffs rag down the bottle-neck.' So simple, he wondered why they had never been used in the last war. 'Then you wait till you see 'em coming, you light the rag and when it's burning you throw your bottle – and duck!'

Nor would there be a problem in the delivery of such missiles. Yorkshiremen were born cricketers, could throw anything from a ball to a bottle further than most!

'And it explodes, Mr C.?'

'It doesn't half!' And not only with a bang but with blazing petrol to add to the confusion. Would stop a tank, some said, but he had his doubts on that score. You would, he had worked out, have to lob one down the tank's turret to do any real harm and to do that would take a lot of luck. Still, petrol bombs would do very nicely until the long-promised hand grenades arrived.

'But are you sure they'll work?'

'Oh, they work all right! We had a dummy run up on Holdenby Pike.' They had thrown three, and so startling had been the effect that the entire platoon had wanted to throw one and the Reverend had been forced to point out that three was more than enough or where would they be when the time came with all the bombs used up? 'But not a word, mind.'

His good humour restored, Mr Catchpole blew hard on his tea then took a slurping swallow. Strange, he thought, that the Reverend was of the opinion there wouldn't be an invasion, though why he thought it he couldn't rightly explain. And no one wanted to be overrun like the French had been and especially himself, who would take badly to Germans goose-stepping all over his garden or even – and just to think of it made him shudder – throwing her lady-ship out of Rowangarth. There had been a Sutton at Rowangarth for more'n four hundred years and a Catch-pole had been head gardener here since Queen Victoria was a lass; four generations of them.

On the other hand, no one could blame him for wanting to throw a petrol bomb. Just one. Slap bang into the turret of a Nazi tank. He set down his mug and returned to his digging. And to his dreams of glory.

Tatiana heard the long, low whistle then ran towards it, arms wide.

'Tim! You're all right!' She always waited now in the shelter of the trees beside the crossroads, hoping he would come because it wasn't always possible for him to phone her after he had been flying nor dare she, sometimes, pick up the phone when he did.

'I'm fine,' he said when they had kissed, and kissed again.

'Were you on ops. last night? It wasn't Berlin?'

There was a tacit agreement that open cities were not to be bombed by either side, yet this morning's newsreader announced that 120 bombers had raided Berlin in retaliation for the bombs dropped two days ago on London.

'It was.' He pulled her close and they began to walk, arms tightly linked, thighs touching, towards Holdenby Pike. 'And for an open city, there was a heck of a lot of searchlights and flack.'

Open cities, Tatiana frowned, were supposed not to be of military importance and left unmolested; beautiful old places like Dresden, or York perhaps.

'They said it was a mistake – them bombing London, I mean. They'd been trying to bomb a fighter station, and got it wrong.'

'In broad daylight, henny? The RAF can fly in total darkness and get it right! No, they meant to do it. You can't mistake London for a fighter station.'

'It's getting worse for us, isn't it, Tim?'

'Hush your blethering.' He kissed her fiercely and she clung to him, eyes closed, lips parted, silently begging for more. She had loved Tim Thomson since first they met, but now she was *in love* with him and naked need flamed from him to her each time they touched.

Grandmother Petrovska had been wrong. It was a woman's duty to give her husband children, and a man, she said, liked making children. It was his nature. A woman, on the other hand, did her duty in the privacy of the bedroom, reminding herself that it was a small price to pay for a household of her own and the respect society gave to a married woman.

But this dizzy-making feeling could not be a part of duty but a need, and to have children with Tim would be a shivering delight. And why in the sanctimonious privacy of a bedroom? Why not here on the wide hilltop with the sun to bless them and little scuds of cloud to see them, then float by uncaring.

'Penny for them?'

'A penny won't buy them, Tim.' They had, to her reluctant relief, begun to walk again. 'I'll tell you if you want, but you mightn't like it.'

'Try me.'

'Remember I once said I thought I was falling in love with you?'

'Aye. You said it in Russian.'

'Well, I don't think any more.' She took a deep, steadying breath. 'I *know* I'm in love with you.' She looked down at the grass at her feet, cheeks blazing.

'Then that makes two of us. What are we going to do about it?'

'I can't marry you, Tim. My family wouldn't let me.'

'Because I'm a Scottish peasant, a Keir Hardie man, and you are landed gentry?'

'No, darling, *no!*' She wanted him to kiss her again but he walked on, chin high. 'All right – my mother was a countess, but countesses were two a penny in St Petersburg. And the Petrovskys aren't rich. The Bolsheviks took almost all they owned. What Mother and I have is because of the Suttons. It's their charity we live on!'

'Charity! You live in a big house with servants!'

'Only Karl, now, and Cook, and Maggie who comes twice a week. And Cook might have to do war work in a factory canteen, she says.'

'Aye, well, my mother works in a factory and glad of it, and my father works in the shipyards – unemployed for years till the war started – so I suppose that rules out marriage. And let's face it, your Grandmother Petrovska wouldn't take kindly to one of her enemies marrying into the family.'

'You're a Bolshevik?' He *couldn't* be!

'They call us Communists, now. And I'm not red. Just nicely pink around the edges. Before the war I wanted to go into politics – Labour, of course – try to help my own kind, because there are only two classes in this life, Tatiana: those who have and those who have not.'

'Then why do you love me when you despise my kind of people?' She was angry, now. Any minute she would round on him in Karl's earthy Russian.

'I don't know, God help me. But I do love you, Tatiana Sutton and I want you like I've never wanted a woman in my life.'

'And I think I want you, Tim. When you touch me and kiss me something goes *boing* inside me and I think how lovely it would be to make a baby with you.'

They had stopped walking again and she stepped away from him because all at once she knew that if he held her close, laid his mouth on hers, there would be no crying, 'No, Tim!' because she wouldn't want to say it.

'Make a baby! Are you mad? I could get killed any night and then where would you be?'

'Pregnant and alone, I suppose, and people would call me a tart.'

'And would you care?'

'Only that you were dead,' she said softly, sadly. 'But it doesn't arise because I wouldn't know what to do. I've never done it before . . .'

The pulsating need between them had passed now. They linked little fingers and began their upward climb and she didn't know whether to be sad or glad.

'I'd teach you, henny. And there wouldn't be any babies. No mistakes – I'd see to that. They tell you how to keep your nose clean in the RAF – if you don't already know, that is.'

'So you know how?' She felt mildly cheated. 'You've made love before, Tim?'

'Aye. It was offered, so I took it. It wasn't lovemaking though, because I didn't love her. It would be different with you, sweetheart. We'd be special together.'

'We wouldn't. I'd spoil it thinking about Grandmother Petrovska.'

'Not when I make love to you you won't!'

They scuffed the lately flowering heather as they walked, not looking at each other.

'So shall we, Tim . . . ?'

'Aye. When the mood is on us. It doesn't happen to order, you know – leastways not for a man.'

'And will I know when?'

'Oh, my lovely love – you'll know when.' He threw back his head and laughed. 'Darling lassie, we'll both know.'

'There, now.' Catchpole straightened up, hands in the small of his back. 'That's them seen to. Plenty for the house and for me and Lily, and two score extra for the vegetable man. Just got them in in nice time for the rain.'

'But how do you know it's going to rain?'

'A gardener alus knows, Gracie. Don't need no newspapers nor men on the wireless to tell me what the weather's going to be like. A drop of nice steady rain towards nightfall and them sprouts'll be standing up

130

straight as little soldiers in the morning. You'll learn, lass.'

'I hope so, Mr C. I like being here.' She liked everything about being a land girl except being away from Mam and Dad and Grandad. 'I had a letter from Drew this morning. He said he'd write, but I never expected him to.'

'Why not? Drew don't say things he don't mean.'

'I'm sure he doesn't, but he's a sir, and I come from mill folk.'

'He's a sailor and you'm a friend and sailors like getting letters. You write back to him and tell him about the garden and what we're doing, so he can see it all as if it was real.'

'But he didn't give me an address. He just put Somewhere in England and the date, because he's expecting to be sent to a ship, he says.'

'Then he'll send it later, or you can get it from Daisy Dwerryhouse. She'll have it, that's for sure, her being related.'

'Mmm. I know she's his half-sister, but how come?' Gracie concentrated on wiping clean her fork and spade before putting them away; one of Mr Catchpole's ten commandments. 'What I mean is – well, I know Mrs Dwerryhouse is Drew's real mother, but she's the gamekeeper's wife now, and you'd think the gentry wouldn't be so friendly with their servants – and I don't mean that in a snobby way,' she hastened.

'I know you didn't, lass. And to someone as don't know the history of the Suttons – *both* families – it might seem a bit peculiar. But Daisy's mam came to Rowangarth a bit of a lass nigh on thirty years ago. Worked as a housemaid till they realized she'd a talent with a needle and thread, and so made her sewing-maid.'

He rinsed his hands at the standtap then dried them on a piece of sacking with irritating slowness.

'And then, Mr Catchpole?'

'Well, one summer – before the Great War it was – Miss Julia went to London to stay at her Aunt Anne Lavinia's house. A maiden lady, Miss Anne Lavinia Sutton was and alus popping over to France, so her ladyship sent Alice with Miss Julia – Alice Hawthorn her was then. In them days, a young lady couldn't go out alone, not even to the shops. Alice was a sort of – of . . .'

'Chaperon?'

'That's the word! Any road, Alice went as chaperon and to see to Miss Julia's clothes and things, and there was all sorts of talk below stairs when the two of them got back. For one thing, they'd got themselves into a fight with London bobbies and for another, Miss Julia had met a young man and them not introduced neither.'

'So Daisy's mam wasn't very good at chaperoning?'

'Nay. Nothing like that. Miss Julia had fallen real hard for that young man and her mind was made up. Headstrong she's always been and not ten chaperons could have done much about it. A doctor that young man was, name of MacMalcolm. Was him seen to her when she got knocked out in the fight. That was the start of it.'

'But I can't imagine Mrs Sutton fighting, nor Mrs Dwerryhouse. What had they done?'

'Gone to a suffragette meeting, that's what. Those suffragettes were agitating for women to get a say in things. Women couldn't vote, in those days.' Jack Catchpole wasn't altogether sure that giving votes to women had been a wise move, though he'd never said so within his wife's hearing.

'So then what?'

'Then nothing, Gracie Fielding. It's a quarter to six and time us was off home. Lily'll have the supper on and her can't abide lateness.'

'But you'll tell me some more tomorrow?' The Sutton story had the makings of a love book about it, but unlike love stories it was real.

'Happen I will. But what's told within these walls isn't for blabbing around the hostel, remember!'

'Not a word. Hand on heart.' Besides, she liked Drew and Daisy too much to pass on scandal about them – if scandal there was to be.

'Right then, lass. We'll shut up shop for the night. See you in t'morning.'

Amicably they walked together to the ornate iron gates that Catchpole regarded as his drawbridge and portcullis both, though Gracie knew they would not be chained and padlocked until he had made his final evening rounds – just to be sure. On the lookout for cats an' things he'd assured her, but it was really, she supposed, to bid his garden good night.

'Wonder what'll be on the six o'clock news,' Gracie murmured. 'It's worrying, isn't it?'

'It is. All those German bombers coming day after day cheeky as you like in broad daylight!'

'But they aren't getting it all their own way!'

'No.' And thank God for a handful of young lads and their fighters and for young girls, an' all, that were in the thick of it. He wouldn't want a lass of his firing an anti-aircraft gun. If they'd had bairns, that was. Happen, he thought as he clanged shut the gates, if him and Lily had no family to laugh over then they had none to worry over now. It worked both ways. 'Good night, Gracie.'

''Night, Mr Catchpole. Take care.'

Reichmarshal Goering had sent a signal to his commanders that his Luftwaffe was to rid the skies of the Royal Air Force, though how the papers knew what Goering was saying to his underlings, or how our own fighter pilots knew the German bombers were on their way – as soon as they had taken off, almost – no one rightly knew. All the man in the street could be sure of – and the Ministry of Information could, sometimes, get it right – was that for every fighter we lost, the Luftwaffe paid three of their bombers for it. Talk even had it that one German bomber ace had asked Goering for a squadron of Spitfires to protect them on their raids over the south of England and that fat Hermann Goering hadn't been best pleased about the request!

Only talk, maybe, but it lifted people's hearts. Because we were not only going to put a stop to German air raids, Mr Churchill had growled in one of his broadcasts to the nation; we were going to win the war, as well! Even though we might have to fight on the beaches and in the streets we would never give in. And such was his confidence, his tenacity, his utter loathing for Hitler, that people believed him completely – about not surrendering, that was – though how we were going to win the war and when, took a little more time to digest. And as farmers and land girls cut wheat and barley and oats, battles raged in the sky above them – dogfights, with fields in the south littered with crippled German bombers. They became so familiar a sight that small boys stopped taking pieces as souvenirs and returned to more absorbing things such as searching for conkers, raiding apple orchards and queueing at the sweet shops when rumours of a delivery of gobstoppers circulated the streets.

Yet hadn't Mr Churchill warned, years ago, that Germany was becoming too strong and too arrogant and no one took a bit of notice of him, except to call him a warmonger? He'd been right, though, people reluctantly admitted.

So now the entire country listened to what he said and believed every word he uttered. We would win this war, no matter what, because good old Winston said so. One day, that was.

11

My darling Daisy,

Thank you for the birthday card. I did as you told me and didn't open it until the twelfth.

Once, we thought we would be together for my twenty-third birthday and the two of us house hunting and planning a wedding. Instead, you are going into the Forces and it seems immoral, almost, that I am away from it all and that we who need each other so much cannot be together. So I promise you this my lovely girl – somehow I will get home. There has got to be a way.

'Keth, no!' Daisy whispered. 'Don't do anything stupid – oh, *please.*'

She screwed up her eyes tightly, refusing to weep. There were thousands of women whose man had gone away and might never come home again; at least Keth was not in uniform and was safe in a neutral country, though Dada said it was a peculiar kind of neutrality that sent us tanks and guns and food and asked no payment in return. The Americans would get their fingers burned taking such risks, if anybody was interested in what he thought, and it would need only one incident at sea and before they knew it, America would be drawn into the war. Remember the *Lusitania* last time?

'But would it be such a bad thing for us to have an ally?' Mam had wanted to know, and Daisy supposed that for us, beleaguered as we were, to have someone on our side would be nothing short of a miracle.

But why should the United States become involved again? They had the wide span of the Atlantic between them and Europe. They were far enough away from Hitler so why should Bas, even though he was half-English, help fight our war?

Daisy jumped impatiently to her feet to stand at the wide-open window, gazing out into the August evening.

At least the weather was kind. There had been little rain for weeks. A farmer who hadn't got his harvest in wasn't trying, Dada said. And why, she demanded irritably, had she been so stupid; why was she leaving her home, her parents? Why had she lost her temper that dinnertime because an arrogant woman and her totally unimportant account upset her?

Because she was her father's daughter, Mam said; because she had the same stubborn streak in her and his quick temper, too.

Mam understood about being in love. Mam was silly and sentimental, too; had buttercups pressed in her Bible, still, just as her daughter pressed a daisychain between the pages of the Song of Solomon beside words written for a lover, by a lover. 'Rise up, my love, my fair one, and come away'; words about winter being past and flowers appearing and birds singing, yet now it sometimes seemed as if flowers had never bloomed and birds would never sing again. But nothing lasted, Mam said; neither bad times nor, sadly, good.

'Our time will come, Keth,' she whispered. 'We'll be together again, one day . . .'

The telephone began to ring, calling her back from her dreamings.

'For you,' Alice called. 'It's Tatiana.'

'Hi, Tatty,' Daisy smiled into the receiver. 'What's news?'

'The dance tomorrow night at Creesby – okay?' Tatiana Sutton's voice was low and husky as if she were whispering into the mouthpiece. 'I'm going with you and Gracie – all right?'

'But I'm not going.'

'That doesn't matter. I don't suppose Tim and I will be there, either. But if he isn't on ops. – and there's a good chance he won't be – I'll need an alibi.'

'But couldn't you just say you were coming over to Keeper's?'

'And have Mother ring me to check up? She might. She's getting suspicious.'

'Okay. It's Creesby, then. But be careful, Tatty – you know what I mean? 'Bye . . .'

'And what did Tatiana want, or shouldn't I ask?' Alice fixed her daughter with a stare, one eyebrow raised.

'No you shouldn't ask, Mam, but I'll tell you. She's meeting Tim Thomson and she wanted to know if I'll be at the Creesby dance on Wednesday. Her mother's a bit stuffy about her going there.'

'So she told her mother that you were going?'

'Yes.'

'But you aren't, Daisy. It's your medical the day after. Now you mustn't get drawn into things!'

'Mam, Tatty knows what she's doing. And I don't know why her mother tries to wrap her in cotton wool all the time.'

'Happen it's the way Russian mothers do it.'

'Well, it's stupid of her because Tatty's as English as I am! And Tim's a decent sort, though I don't suppose Grandmother Petrovska would approve of him.'

'What do you mean – approve?' Alice looked alarmed. 'Are things getting serious between them?'

'Don't think so, but you know what Tatty's like. If it's got anything to do with aeroplanes or aircrew, she's mad about it. And Tim's a good dancer, too.'

She turned to fidget with the cutlery on the table, straightening it, shifting the cruet so her mother should not see the flush that stained her cheeks. Mam knew she always went red when she told a lie, and Tatty *was* serious about Tim. Head over heels, truth known.

'I still think she's too young to be out alone.'

'She's eighteen, Mam!'

'Yes, but she's so – so *unworldly* to my way of thinking. They should have sent her to school instead of having that governess teach her; let her see how the other half lives!'

'There's nothing wrong with Tatty. And what's that? Smells good.' Deftly she steered the conversation into safer channels as her mother took a pie from the oven.

'Woolton pie. Again.' Once she'd have been ashamed to serve such a poor dish, but needs must these days. There had been a small piece of meat left over from Sunday dinner and a jug of good gravy, so a little meat, gravy, and a lot of vegetables were covered with a suet crust and heaven only knew what they would do if suet went on the ration! She glanced towards the window as the barking of dogs told her her husband was home. 'Get the plates out of the oven, there's a good girl, whilst I strain the carrots. And, Daisy – tell Tatiana to be careful. You know what I mean . . . ?'

'She *is* careful, Mam.'

'Yes – well that's as maybe.' Alice had not forgotten what it was like to be eighteen and in love. She offered her cheek, smiling, for Tom's kiss.

Come to think of it, she was still in love.

'Sorry I'm late, Mr Catchpole.' Gracie arrived, breathless, pulling her bounty behind her. 'Found it in Brattocks Wood. It looks good and dry – thought it would do for the fire. Hope it was all right to take it?'

'Course it was, as long as nobody saw you with it.' Jack regarded the branch of fallen wood. 'Get it stuck behind the shed and us'll get the saw to it later. And Miss Julia was asking for you.'

'I've seen her. Home Farm is letting her have six pullets so she's going into Creesby to the Food Office and getting their egg coupons changed to hen-meal coupons. Seems there's a shed at the back of Keeper's Cottage that no one uses. Said it needs a bit of repairing and she asked me to – er – mention it to you.'

'And I suppose her expects me to see to it? Well, I'm a gardener; no good with hammer and nails. You'd best see Will Stubbs – he's the handyman.' Jack shook his head mournfully. 'I mind the time when there was an estate carpenter here, but not any longer. And when you see Will Stubbs, tell him as how Miss Julia'll need chicken wire and posts for them birds. I suppose Alice Dwerryhouse doesn't mind having hens in the shed at the back?'

'Don't think so, Mr C. Mrs Sutton said that Daisy's mam would be saving her scraps and peelings for me.'

'And where are you goin' to boil the stuff for the hen mash, then?'

'We-e-ll – I did suggest the potting-shed fire, for the time being. After all,' she hastened, 'that would give you first refusal of the hen muck when I clean out the shed each week. Would only be fair,' she stressed.

'Fair.' Jack Catchpole coveted the droppings to make into liquid manure. When it came to fertilizers, hen droppings were in a class of their own. 'You got a pan for the fire, then?'

'No, but Mrs Sutton is sure there are old iron pans they used to use at Rowangarth before they got a gas stove. I'm to have a word with Cook about it. Tilda never throws anything away, I believe.'

'So it's all cut and dried, Gracie,' he murmured, relieved the hens would be housed well away from his garden.

'Almost. I'm really looking forward to having them.'

'Do you like it here, lass? Are you going to settle?'

'Oh, *yes*! I knew it the day I came. No complaints, I hope? I'm doing my best,' she added anxiously.

'Aye. You'm a trier, I'll say that for you, and as long as you see to it that I get that hen muck and don't let Tom Dwerryhouse get his hands on it, I won't grumble.'

Gracie let go a sigh of pure contentment. Of course she was going to settle at Rowangarth – for the duration, if she had anything to do with it. She loved living in the country; even in winter when it would be cold and wet and muddy she would still love it. She liked the land girls in the bothy, too, and the food was every bit as good as Mam's. And Daisy and Tatty were nice and Drew was lovely and not a bit snobby like she'd thought a sir would be. And then she felt a terrible sense of guilt.

'Oh dear, Mr C. I'm enjoying this war and I shouldn't be, should I?'

'Happen not, lass.' He gave her shoulder a brief, fatherly pat. 'But take my advice and make the most of the good days, 'cause for every good day, there could well be a bad one. Now get that branch out of sight like I told you and let's get on with some work. Have you ever clipped a box hedge, Gracie?'

'I haven't, Mr Catchpole.' Until she came to Rowangarth she hadn't even seen a box hedge.

'Then today, lass, you'm about to learn!'

'You aren't one bit interested in my medical, are you, Tatty? You're miles away.'

'No, Daisy, I'm not – not miles away, I mean. But they've been doing circuits and bumps all day at Holdenby Moor and you know what that means?'

'Mm.' Bombers taking off, doing two or three circuits of the aerodrome, then landing. Flight-testing the aircraft, which was always a giveaway that they'd be operational that night. 'But they mightn't go, Tatty.'

'They'll go, all right. There's no moon at all – not until

the new one on Tuesday. Perfect flying conditions.'

'Fine. They'll have good cover, then. Fighters won't find them so easily. Don't worry so, *please*. It's the Air Ministry's job to worry about flying conditions and it's yours to wish Tim luck every inch of the way; get him back safely. And Tatty – try not to get too involved.'

'Why? Because he's a tail-gunner and gunners get killed, even when the rest of the crew make it back? And why shouldn't I get involved? Why did you get involved with Keth?'

'Because I love him.' It was as simple as that.

'And I'm not capable of falling in love, is that what you're trying to say?'

'*No!* But I've known Keth all my life. He's always been there. When did you meet Tim? You hardly know him!'

'You know when I met him! I've known him thirty-seven days exactly. And I loved him the minute I saw him and now it's more serious than that.'

'Oh, my Lord – you haven't . . . ?'

'No we haven't, but we will, Daisy. It nearly happened on Wednesday night. We both of us know it will, one day soon. And don't look at me all holier than thou, as if I'm a common little tart! If you loved Keth as much as I love Tim, you'd understand.'

'Tatty! I'm not judging you – truly I'm not. And anyway, the pot doesn't call the kettle black!'

'You mean you and Keth – you've . . . ?'

'Been lovers? Yes. When Keth came home because he thought there was going to be a war – the summer of 'thirty-eight it was. It happened before he went back to America to college.'

'And was it marvellous? Was it worth it – all the worry? Because I know I shall worry – looking Mother in the face afterwards, I mean. Funnily enough, I'm not so bothered about getting pregnant because Tim says he wouldn't let it happen. And you didn't get pregnant, did you?'

'Tatiana Sutton! You are *so* innocent!'

'I suppose I am, but I trust Tim.'

'Oh, famous last words! Please, *please* be careful? And make sure Karl doesn't catch you out. You know he's always hovering.'

'Karl's getting old now. I can give him the slip any time I want to.'

They had come to the crossroads, to where a signpost once stood with 'Holdenby 1¼' on one arm and 'Creesby 5' on the other. Only signposts weren't allowed now, because of the invasion, nor names on railway stations.

'I'll be careful. Both of us will. And, Daisy – was it marvellous? If you were me – would you?'

'You'll be taking an awful risk, you know that? And I can't advise you now, can I? Your circumstances and Tim's – well, they're a whole lot different to ours. There's a war on now.'

'I know there is. And it wasn't fair of me to ask, was it?' She gave a little shrug of despair. 'Well – good night, then. Is tomorrow your half-day off, Daisy? Will I see you?'

'It is, but let's leave it? You'll probably be meeting Tim, anyway.'

'God, I hope so!'

'Of course you will! Tim will be just fine. And you don't know for sure he'll be on ops. tonight. Want me to walk to the gates with you?'

'No thanks. I'll be all right. I'm a big girl now – really I am.'

'Hmm.' Daisy watched her walk away into the twilight, shoulders drooping. Oh, damn this war and damn the stupid politicians who let it happen! Old men, all of them! Just declared war, they had, then expected the young men to fight it! 'Hey, Tatty!' she called.

'Yes?' Tatiana stopped, then turned slowly.

'It *was* marvellous! Good night, love.'

Tatiana smiled suddenly, brilliantly. Then she turned, head high, shoulders straight and walked with swinging stride towards the gates of Denniston House.

Good old Tatty, Daisy smiled. She still hadn't told her about the medical, but what the heck? Medicals were two a penny. And she had passed, anyway. She had known she would. Now all she had to do was wait until They sent for her.

She crossed the field where only yesterday sheaves of wheat had stood in stooks, drying. Today they had been piled high on carts and stored to await threshing after Christmas. She winced as the sharp stubble scratched her feet through her sandals then thankfully climbed the fence into Brattocks Wood. Here, in the shifting half-light, the wood was settling down for the night. She squinted at her watch but could not see the time. About ten o'clock, she supposed. Not a light was to be seen. Official blackout time tonight was 8.31, though it would not be completely dark for a little while. Yet despite the extra hour of daylight the nights were drawing in now. Soon the leaves would begin to yellow and then would follow the misty mornings, with swallows chattering on the telegraph wires, making ready to fly away.

Clever little birds. They came in May and left, suddenly, when they knew the time was right. The war made no difference to their migrations. Swallows didn't know about war.

A hunting owl screeched to frighten its prey into movement, and Daisy began to run towards Keeper's Cottage.

'Watch the blackout, lass,' Tom warned as she opened the kitchen door. 'Want to get us all locked up, do you?' He glanced pointedly at the mantel clock. 'And what time of night is this to be coming in?'

'Nearly half-past ten, Dada. The little hand is on ten and the big one on five,' she grinned mischievously. 'I've been with Tatty – just walking and talking . . .'

'Didn't you see your Aunt Julia? She's just this minute left.'

'No. I came across the field and through Brattocks.'

'And what have I told you about being in the wood alone at night? Anything could happen to you!'

'Dada! I know Brattocks like the back of my hand – even in the dark.'

'Happen you do, but you'll come home down the lane in future, especially now the nights are drawing in. I could tell you things about that wood –'

'What your dada means is that you could have been taken for a poacher,' Alice interrupted hastily. 'Or you could come across a tramp ... Your Aunt Julia came to tell us about Drew. Seems his ship is based in Liverpool, so he'll be nice and near when he gets leave. Only three hours by train to York. HMS *Penrose*, he's on. We have to write to him care of GPO London, so no one will know where the *Penrose* is.'

'But we do know, Mam, though I can't believe Drew would say a thing like that over the phone.'

'No. Seems the phone rang and Winnie on the exchange asked Julia if she would accept a trunk call, reversed charges. And it was Drew. Gave her his address and said they were tied up alongside, that was why he'd been able to ring, see? But he didn't say alongside *where*. Then the minute Julia put the phone down it rang again. "Did you get your trunk call all right?" Winnie asked. And when your Aunt Julia said she had, Winnie dropped her voice all dramatic, like, and whispered, "Well, it was from Liverpool, but not a word to a soul, mind."'

They all laughed, because it was good to hear from Drew and that he had sounded happy and sent his love and asked them all to write.

'But not a word about this!' Alice was all at once serious. 'We're family so we're entitled to know, but we don't shout all over the Riding where Drew's ship is and what he's doing. Drew has been lucky. He could have been sent all the way up to Scapa Flow – or even overseas. And the Germans haven't bombed Liverpool much, so far. Not like when he was in barracks. I'm glad he's left Plymouth.'

'Hmm. Wonder where I'll end up, Mam?'

'What do you mean, Daisy – end up? You've only just had your medical. They told you it might be quite a while before you get your call-up papers.'

And then Alice's blood ran cold and she wondered why she had never thought of it until now. Because they could well send Daisy down south where all the air raids were; where the fighter stations were being bombed and strafed day after day.

They could send her to Dover, which was being shelled from across the Channel every day, or to Plymouth or Portsmouth, where the invasion would be – if it came . . .

12

Julia unlocked the door of the room she had not entered for exactly a year. Next to it was the sewing-room where Alice once worked; the small back room in which they had shared secrets almost too long ago to remember. And this room – Julia slipped the key into her pocket – was Andrew's surgery. Major Andrew MacMalcolm of the Medical Corps, killed just six days before the conflict they called the Great War ended. In this room she had created a sentimental replica of Andrew's London surgery; a shrine, almost. Every piece of furniture, every book, pencil and instrument – even the grinning skeleton and the optical wall chart – had been brought here.

Once, she had found comfort from it; sat at his desk, picked up his stethoscope, willed him to walk through the door. Now she came here only once a year, on the last day of August.

She dusted the desktop, the chair, lifted the sheet that covered the skeleton then let it drop as she heard a footstep in the passage outside. Slowly, gently the door knob turned, then Nathan was standing there, eyes sad.

'Sorry, darling. I'm not prying . . .'

'Then why are you here?' Julia was angry, not only at the intrusion into her other life, but that Nathan should witness this rite of remembrance.

'I suppose because I thought you might need me. I do understand. Today would have been his birthday.'

'Yes.' The last day of August. Andrew had lived for just a little over thirty-one years. Today he would have been fifty-three and a consultant physician, maybe, or a surgeon;

a father, certainly – perhaps even a grandfather. One year older than Nathan, who had neither son nor grandson because he had loved a woman who clung stubbornly to the memory of another man. 'And very soon, Nathan, you and I will have been married for two years. I threw away a lot of happiness, didn't I, being bitter? Yet I can't forget Andrew. The part of me that remembers today loves him still. Does it hurt you to hear me say it?'

'No. Andrew was a part of your life. If I were him, I wouldn't want you to forget.'

'And would you have wanted me to marry again if you were dead and Andrew alive still?'

'Yes, I would. If I'd loved you as he loved you – and I do, sweetheart – then I would have wanted you not to be alone.'

'From heaven, would you have wanted it, Nathan?' she whispered, aware of the goodness of him and the compassion in his eyes.

'From that other place we have come to call heaven – yes,' he smiled.

'Then let me tell you – Julia MacMalcolm has gone.' She rose from the chair in which Andrew once sat and went to stand at her husband's side. 'I left her at a graveside at Étaples. And now I am Julia Sutton, who has been twice lucky in love; different loves, but each of them good. Can you accept that?'

'Easily, because you are you and headstrong and sentimental and honest. I wouldn't change what you are or what you were. And I shall go on loving you as long as I live, just as a young nurse will always love a young doctor. Nothing can turn back love, Julia, nor diminish it.'

'You're a good man, Nathan. Thank you for waiting all those years for me.'

She touched his cheek with gentle fingertips. She would not kiss him, not here in Andrew's surgery. Instead, she walked to the window, drawing across it the flimsy cotton curtains that once hung in a house in a London street called Little Britain. Then she took her husband's hand, leading him from the room, turning the key in the lock before placing it in his hand.

'I shall not open that door again. When Drew is next home, give the key to him, will you? He'll understand. And, Nathan – this woman I am now loves you very much, so will you kiss me, please?'

Alice took three plates from the dresser, trying to listen dispassionately to the early-evening news bulletin. For once, it seemed, the truth had not been held back. The Ministry of Information was actually admitting that fighter stations at Biggin Hill and Manston were so damaged by bombing that planes could no longer take off from them, nor land there. On this last day of August, Fighter Command lost thirty-eight planes. Usually, They, the faceless ones, never said how many, not the whole truth. But even They must admit it couldn't go on much longer because it wasn't how many planes were lost, Alice brooded. Spitfires and Hurricanes could be replaced; they were only money and man-hours in a factory. What was irreplaceable were those who flew them: straight, decent young men, driven almost beyond enduring, some of them younger than Drew, her son – her son, and Julia's. Nothing could replace such desperate courage. Drew had already gone to war and soon they would take Daisy.

Was her daughter to be called upon to face danger? Would Daisy, who was so beautiful, so in love, have to struggle on and on until she moved in a daze of exhaustion, fearful to ease off her shoes because if she did, even for one blessed minute, she could not put them on again because her feet were too swollen?

Would Daisy's kit lay ready packed beneath her bed because the sound of enemy guns was getting nearer and louder? Would Daisy ever know the stench of undignified death?

'No, no, *no*!' Alice raised the plates she held high above

her head, hurling them to the floor with all the anger that was in her. 'God! How dare You let it happen again!'

Then she sank to her knees amid a litter of broken white china. She was still there, sobbing quietly, when Tom came home for his supper.

'Lass, lass!' He reached for her hand, drawing her to her feet. 'Whatever happened? Are you hurt? Did you fall over? Don't take on so – it's only a few plates.'

'Only plates.' Plates could be replaced. 'And I didn't trip, or anything. I threw them, Tom.' She drew in a shuddering breath, tears spent now, all anger gone.

'And am I to know why?' His voice was gentle and he gathered her close and stroked her hair.

'Oh, it was the news that finally did it. All those fighters lost. The young ones, Tom, taking the brunt of it; fighting a war that our generation let happen. I think I'd been working up to it all day. I just exploded. Remind me never to go on about your temper after this, love?'

She took a brush and shovel and began to sweep. Daisy would be home, soon; she must not know about this.

'Building up to it all day, eh? Worrying about Daisy, were you?'

'N-no. Not this time. It was Andrew MacMalcolm on my mind. I almost phoned Julia, like I always used to . . .'

'Like on his birthday, you mean?'

'Should I ring her – let her know I haven't forgotten?'

'No you shouldn't.' He took the shovel from her hand. 'You should put the kettle on whilst I throw this lot on the rubbish heap. Remember she's Nathan Sutton's wife now, and happy again. Leave the past alone, bonny lass.'

'You're right.' She stood on tiptoe to kiss his cheek. 'I'm fine, now. Don't know why you put up with me, though.'

'Because you're a good cook.' He turned in the doorway to smile at her and she smiled back and whispered, 'I love you too, Tom Dwerryhouse.'

*   *   *

'Tim!' Tatiana stepped from behind the oak tree at the crossroads then threw back her head, laughing. 'What on earth . . . ?'

'Hi, henny! This beats Whitleys any day!' He wobbled to a stop, throwing a leg over the bicycle seat, leaning over the handlebars to kiss her. 'It only took a minute to get the hang of it again. Didn't have a bike of my own, so I'd cadge rides from the kids who did,' he grinned, pushing the dull olive-green cycle into the bushes beside the oak tree.

'But where did you get it?'

'I borrowed it – sort of. Was running late and didn't want to keep my girl waiting. Found it propped outside the Admin block. I'll give it back tonight.'

'Timothy Thomson, that's stealing!'

'No it isn't. All bikes at Holdenby Moor are Air Ministry property. There's a Nissen hut full of them – personnel for the use of. It's one heck of a walk from one end of that aerodrome to the other. First come, first served!'

'You are quite incorrigible,' she scolded, loving him more, were it possible, when he joked and smiled. When he smiled, something squirmed deliciously through her. 'And I haven't had a proper kiss yet.'

She clasped her arms around his neck, lifting her chin, closing her eyes, straining close to him and he placed his hands on her buttocks and drew her closer so she knew his need of her.

For just a moment, panic sliced through her and she wondered if this was the time. Then she closed her eyes again, searching for his mouth, relaxing against him.

'Tatiana . . .' His voice was low and husky and he drew away from her a little as if to break the contact of the electricity that sparked and crackled between them. His eyes looked directly into hers, asking the question his lips had no need to speak.

'I love you,' she whispered as if it were the answer to

all things, then stepped away from him, taking his hand in hers, holding it tightly because she couldn't bear not to touch him. 'Let's walk to the top of the pike.'

It would be quiet up there. Just the sky and almost always a breeze, even in summer. There would be no one there except other couples, who wouldn't care, anyway.

'The grass'll be damp.' He wondered why he was whispering.

'I don't suppose we'll notice it, Tim.'

All at once she felt shy of him because tonight, soon, would be the first time. And after tonight nothing could ever be the same again.

She glanced sideways so she might look at him without turning her head and he was staring ahead, because he knew it as well, didn't he?

And then, without shifting his gaze he said, 'I love you, Tatiana Sutton.'

Julia put down the telephone, then walked along the creaking passage to the library where her husband was most times to be found. When he wasn't baptizing or marrying or burying in Holdenby and the two other parishes he looked after, that was. And when he wasn't giving last rites, or comforting, or visiting the old and alone, she sighed. That he would one day inherit Pendenys Place and a half of his mother's fortune never entered his head, she was sure of it, and she too had become quite good at not dwelling too much upon it, because not for anything would she live in that vulgar barn of a place that looked like the product of a mating between the Houses of Parliament and Creesby Town Hall.

She dismissed it from her thoughts then stood behind her husband's chair, hands on his shoulders.

'Are you sermonizing? I need to talk, but I can come back later.'

'Just finished.' He replaced the cap of his fountain pen and laid it down, swivelling in his chair to face her.

'Giles always did that,' she said in a half-whisper. 'Swing round in that chair and smile, I mean. Just as you did, then.'

'I still miss him, Julia.'

'I know you do. You were twin cousins, sort of.'

'He was more a brother to me than – well, Elliot,' he said, at once regretting saying the name.

'What I want to know is can I have the parish hall for our wedding anniversary?' Deliberately, she made no reference to Elliot Sutton. 'I know it will mean slinging the canteen out, but it'll only be for one night.'

'For Aunt Helen's eightieth, you mean? Are you sure you want the hall? Wouldn't a little party here be better?'

'No. Mother would get wind of it and anyway, I want the entire village to come and I want there to be dancing. I've booked a band, provisionally.'

'But if you go round asking everyone, your mother will be bound to find out.'

'Not if I especially ask people to keep quiet about it. I think I'll be able to get beer, and lemonade for the children, and I can muster one drink apiece, I think, for the toast. But it'll have to be a bring-your-own-sandwiches-and-buns affair, I'm afraid.'

'They won't mind that, darling. Since rationing, it's been the done thing.'

'Yes – and a get-together and a dance can't do anything but good; help everybody forget bloody Hitler for a few hours.'

'There's a parish-council meeting tonight. I'll mention the hall then. I take it you've booked the band for the Saturday night and not for our actual date?'

'For Saturday, October the fifth, if that's all right?'

'It'll be fine.' He pushed back his chair, crossing the room to stand at her side as she gazed out of the window. 'Do you often think of Giles? I know I do.'

'Yes. Sometimes I'm angry still about his death; other times I wonder what would have happened if he'd lived.

Alice would still be Lady Sutton and she and Tom could never have married.'

'Nor Daisy been born. I suppose his death was a part of the order of things, though sometimes I resent it.'

'You resent God's will, and you a man of the Church?' She could not resist, sometimes, mocking God. There were times, still, that she blamed Him for Andrew's death.

'Priests can doubt. We are human, Julia – flesh and blood.'

'Yes, thank God.' She turned to gather him to her, kissing his mouth. 'And if I'm not mistaken, that was Mary with the tea tray. I'm dying for a cup. And could you remember to post these on your way to the meeting?' she smiled, picking up two envelopes. 'Letters to Drew. And, darling – could you remember to call in on Reuben, some time soon? Alice told me it was his birthday, yesterday. His ninety-fifth, I think, but even Alice isn't sure, so don't mention it. Whilst you are there, tell him about the party. I'd like it if he felt up to coming – Mother would like it, too. Just spread the word, will you, once you've agreed we can have the hall?'

'The old ones might not feel up to it. It'll be quite a long walk for some of them.'

'It will,' Julia frowned. 'I'll have to see if I can get a gallon of petrol on the black market, then I could run them there in the car. I suppose you couldn't spare a coupon, Nathan? You get more than I do.'

'My extra petrol is for parish work, and you know it! And what do you mean – on the black market?'

'We-e-ll, there are one or two hereabouts who seem to be able to get under-the-counter petrol, by all accounts.'

'Then let them, though their consciences can't be worth much if they stopped to think that seamen are being killed bringing it here.'

'Only kidding!' She smiled to picture the headlines in the *Yorkshire Post*: 'VICAR'S WIFE IN PETROL SCANDAL'.

'And ssh!' she commanded, opening the conservatory door, smiling in her mother's direction.

'Ah, there you are!' Helen Sutton returned the smile. 'I think, Nathan, that you can smell a teapot a mile away. Tilda's made us egg-and-cress sandwiches – dried egg, I suppose it is. I'll be glad when your hens start laying, Julia. Be a dear and pour, will you?'

'Of course.' There were days, Julia thought gratefully, when her mother was like the Helen of old; today was one of them. And she would enjoy the party, she really would. Her mother had always loved surprises. 'The hens should start laying very soon, Gracie says. Just a couple of weeks now and we'll have our own fresh eggs, at least a dozen a week.'

'Hmm. The land girl. She's doing very well, Catchpole said. It was so beautiful and sunny this morning that I went to the kitchen garden – did I tell you? I wanted to see the orchid house, really. One of the white ones is putting up late buds for some reason. Now do hurry and pour, Julia, before the tea gets cold . . .'

On that sixth day of September, fighter pilots along the south coast waited. Some lolled in chairs outside a makeshift mess; others lay, hands behind heads, on the grass, trying to relax. They had all existed on catnaps, hastily swallowed sandwiches and cups of strong sweet tea for weeks, jumping suddenly alert to their feet, running in a half-daze to their waiting fighters as klaxons blared or sirens wailed.

Now they walked and talked, even laughed sometimes, like automatons, trying not to notice that Johnny who snored and Mike who chain-smoked were no longer there.

Most times they took off in haphazard fashion, grouping their fighters into arrowhead formation once they were airborne and undercarriages up, their leader talking to them over the radio, calming nerves that twanged.

Sometimes a pilot they had thought killed would return, hands in pockets, his face split by an ear-to-ear grin.

'Bailed out,' he might say with studied nonchalance. 'Had to ditch and thought I'd bought it. But the rescue lads got to me. Bloody cold it was, in the drink. Wet, too!'

Such understatement really meant that a pilot had been shot down, had ejected and landed in the Channel. And when he had given up hope of ever being found, an air-sea rescue launch had picked him out of the water.

The sea shall not have them, was their motto. Neither the sea nor the Krauts! A pilot saved from the sea was a pilot airborne again within a week.

But often missing pilots did not return, and scarcely trained flyers with little more than twenty solo hours behind them came to take their places. It seemed that the future of Britain, of freedom itself, was held in the hands of a few unblooded youths, who hurled their anger and despair at everlasting formations of German planes set upon bombing them out of existence.

Obliterate the first line of defence; immobilize the fighters, then the rest would be easier. Soon, thought the German High Command, the tides would be high and full and right for the invasion of the arrogant little island that stood, bomb-happy, between them and total victory.

And so pilots waited in the early-morning sun of that sixth September day; waited uneasily until ten o'clock and eleven o'clock, and noon. The NAAFI van came with tea and bacon sandwiches and cigarettes as it always did, but not the Luftwaffe. And ground crews who cared for the planes, and aircraftwomen who stood around plots, ears strained for instructions that would tell them that the bombers were coming again, waited and waited but the sky above them was high and blue and empty.

On a day when it was stretched to the limit, when one more sortie would have been a sortie too many, Fighter Command, from its Air Chief Marshal to the lowest erk, asked with disbelief where the Dorniers and Stukas and Heinkels were, and what had happened that they seemed not to be coming.

And on that day, Hitler ordered the calling off of his squadrons, not knowing that two more days under pressure – perhaps even less – would have seen Fighter Command in disarray. It was the miracle Britain had been pleading for and it seemed that at last God had begun to listen to prayers spoken in the English tongue. Had Britain been given a reprieve – until next spring, maybe?

No one knew. None dared speak of his hopes. The men only knew that on that early-autumn day, neither klaxon nor siren nor the drone of enemy bombers broke the long, waiting silence.

One by one, exhausted pilots slipped into sleep. It had been a terrible and at times despairing summer, but for the moment the fight had been won. The youths who flew Hurricanes and Spitfires had earned the right to call themselves men. The September tides that would have carried an invasion fleet to England's shores flowed then ebbed again, and all along the French and Dutch coasts invasion barges lay unmoving.

Soon, winter seas and skies and gales would ensure that for six months at least, Britain would be safe from invaders. The battle for Great Britain, it seemed, had been won.

In a fury of frustration and rage, Hitler ordered his bombers over London and Manchester and Birmingham and Glasgow, and the war, which when it began people had said would be over in six months, entered its second year in deadly earnest.

No invasion, yet, but now it became the people's fight, with no one safe from bombing and civilians all at once in the front line. It would be a long-drawn-out war; every man and woman and child's war, and it would get worse before it got better. But at least, thought the man and woman in the street, we know now where we stand.

Somehow, just knowing that was a comfort.

13

'There now, Gracie Fielding, you've just witnessed a little bit of tradition.' Jack Catchpole pressed the flat of his boot against the soil around the little tree.

'I have? Well, I know we've planted four rowan trees and the house is called Rowangarth – so tell me.' Anything at all about the family who owned the lovely place she worked at fascinated her.

'You'll know the house was built more'n three hundred years ago, when folk believed in witches, and you'll know that rowan trees keep witches away?'

'I didn't, though I suppose people believed anything once.'

'Happen. But the Sutton that built Rowangarth must've believed in 'em, 'cause he planted rowan trees all round the estate at all points of the compass, so to speak. They'm bonny little trees; white flowers in summer and berries for the birds in winter, so it became the custom to plant the odd rowan from time to time, just to keep it going. My dad planted half a dozen before Sir John died – that cluster in the wild garden – and now it's my turn to do a bit of planting, an' all. Can't have a house called Rowangarth, and no rowan trees about, now can us? And you never know about witches – best be sure.

'Just a tip about when to plant trees, lass. Plant a tree around Michaelmas, the saying goes, and you can command it to thrive, but plant a tree at Candlemas and all you do for it won't ever come to much. It'll be a weakly thing alus.'

'When is Candlemas, then?'

'February, and the ground cold and unwelcoming. But those little rowans will do all right, 'cause it'll be Michaelmas in a couple of days.' He laid spade and fork in the wheelbarrow then shrugged on his jacket. 'Now didn't you say you had something for me at Keeper's?'

'I did, and you're welcome to it. Remember you gave me a sack? Well, it's half full of hen droppings now and starting to smell a bit. I don't want Daisy's mother to complain, so don't you think we should move it?'

'We'll collect it now, while we have the barrow with us,' he said eagerly. If it was starting to smell, then Tom Dwerryhouse might get wind of it, try to get hold of it for his own garden. 'Then I'll show you how to make the best liquid fertilizer known to man!'

'Have you heard about the party? All Rowangarth staff'll be there, so that'll include you. Supposed to be a bit of a do for the Reverend and Miss Julia's wedding anniversary, but really it's for her ladyship's eightieth. They're aiming for it to be a surprise for her. Reckon all the village'll go and there's to be dancing, an' all. But not a word, mind, about it being for Lady Helen or if she gets to hear about it she might say she doesn't want the fuss of it, and Miss Julia's set her heart on a party.'

It was a sad fact that the mistress was growing old, though considering the tribulations she'd had she had aged gracefully, Catchpole was bound to admit. And when her time came she would be sadly missed, because real ladies were few and far between these days.

'I thought she looked tired, t'other day, when she came to look at the plants.'

'Tired, Mr C.? If I look as good as she does when I'm her age, I won't complain.'

That day, Gracie recalled, Lady Helen had asked for her seat to be put in the orchid house. They kept a special green-painted folding chair in the small potting shed and Gracie had brought it for her and stayed to talk about the orchids and especially about the white one which seemed to be about to flower, when really it shouldn't be flowering.

'My dear John gave the original white plant to me – oh, more years ago than I care to remember, Gracie,' Lady Helen had said, her eyes all at once gentle with remembering. 'There are eight plants now, all taken from that first one. No one was to wear the white orchids but me, he said. They were to be mine alone, though Julia carried them at her wedding – her first wedding, that was.' She had touched that fat orchid bud as if it were the most precious thing she owned.

'Lady Helen seems very sentimental about the white orchids,' Gracie said now.

'Aye. Remind her of Sir John, young Drew's grandfather. Killed hisself speeding on the Brighton road in his new-fangled motor. Afore the Great War, that was, when I was a lad serving my time at Pendenys. Took it terrible bad. Wore black for three years for him. They don't wear black these days like they once did. For those three years her ladyship didn't receive callers nor socialize 'cause her was in mourning. Folk don't have the respect nowadays that they used to have.'

He sucked hard on his pipe, remembering the way it had been in Sir John's time.

'What are you thinking about, Mr Catchpole?'

'Oh, only about the way it used to be.'

'I wish you'd think out loud.'

'I will. Tomorrow, happen. What I'm more concerned about now is that sack you've got for me at the bottom of Alice's garden. Away over the stile and get it, there's a good lass. And go careful. Don't want to set the dogs barking.'

He smiled just to think of it. That hen muck was worth its weight in gold. Wouldn't do if it fell into the wrong hands!

* * *

Edward Sutton lounged in a comfortable basket chair in the conservatory at Denniston House, gazing out over the garden to the fields beyond and the trees, yellowing now to autumnal colours. Strange, he thought, that not since he married Clemmy so many years ago, and gone to live in Clemmy's house, had he been so contented.

It had always, come to think of it, been Clemmy's house, built for his only child by an indulgent father; always been Clemmy's money he lived on and their firstborn, Elliot, had been Clemmy's alone.

Now Clemmy was dead, and Elliot, too, and now Edward himself lived at Denniston House with Elliot's widow, Anna, and Tatiana, whom Clemmy had never forgiven for being a girl. Anna was charming and kind and Tatiana a delight of a child and he felt nothing but gratitude to the Army for commandeering Pendenys Place. They were welcome to it for as long as the fancy took them. He glanced up sharply as the door opened.

'Uncle Edward! Did I wake you up?'

'No, Julia. I wasn't asleep. I was just indulging an old man's privilege of remembering and do you know, my dear, when you get to my age you can dip into the past without any qualms of conscience or regret?'

Dear Julia. She still called him uncle, though for these two years past she had been his daughter-in-law. He offered his cheek for her kiss, smiling affectionately into her eyes.

'I know. I do it always when I come here to Denniston. And it doesn't trouble my conscience either, because now I am the parson's wife and middle-aged, and the girl who was once a nurse here is long gone.'

'Of course! You and Mrs Dwerryhouse did your training at Denniston in the last war.'

'And now Drew is in the thick of another one, and Daisy soon to join him.'

'Drew is a fine young man, Julia. How is he?'

'The last time we heard he was in port – tied up

alongside, he called it – having something done to his ship. He didn't say what, though. All I know is that the *Penrose* is part of a flotilla that keeps the Western Approaches free from mines. But we'll find out more when he gets leave. You know,' Julia reached out to touch the wooden table at her side, 'I have a good feeling about Drew. I know, somehow, that he'll make it home safely one day. But I've come with an invitation. I'll tell you both about it when Anna has finished phoning.'

'I already know about the secret party,' Edward chuckled. 'Tatiana brings me all the gossip and news. But Anna is always on the phone, lately, trying to get through to London. There is such a delay on calls – if you can get through at all, that is. Poor Miss Hallam on the exchange must be having a very trying time. And the delays have got worse. They say it's because of the bombing.'

Unable to break Fighter Command, Hitler had turned his hatred on London, swearing it would be bombed until it lay a smoking ruin. Night after night the Luftwaffe came. Poor, poor London.

'It must be. I booked a call to Montpelier Mews yesterday evening and I got it half an hour ago. It seems that Sparrow is coping with it all. When the sirens go she says she puts her box of important things in the gas oven, then takes her pillow and blankets and sleeps under the kitchen table.'

Mrs Emily Smith: Andrew's cockney sparrow. Once, in another life when Andrew lived in lodgings in Little Britain, Sparrow was his lady who did. Now she took care of the little mews house that once belonged to Aunt Anne Lavinia.

'Sparrow! I sometimes forget that Anne Lavinia left you her house, Julia. Is it all right? No bomb damage?'

'Not so far. I've told Sparrow she must lock it up and come to Rowangarth, but she won't hear of it. Hitler isn't going to drive her out of London, she says, and insists she's safer than most. It's the people in the East End who are taking the brunt of it, though the papers say that Buckingham Palace has been bombed. Everything's all right at Cheyne Walk, I suppose?'

'I suppose it is. Do you know, Julia, I'd forget all about that house if it wasn't for the fact that Anna's mother and brother live next door. It's been nothing but a nuisance. I could never understand why Clemmy insisted on buying it. I suppose some good did come out of it, though. Elliot and Anna met there.'

'Yes.' Julia had no wish to talk about Elliot nor even think about him and was glad when Anna came into the room. 'Did you manage to get through?'

'No, I didn't.' Anna and Julia touched cheeks in greeting. 'It seems Mama's number is unobtainable. What can it mean? Has Cheyne Walk been bombed, do you think? What am I to do?' Anna was clearly distressed. 'I asked Mama time and time again. "Come to me," I said. I warned her that London would be bombed but no – the Bolsheviks drove her from her home in Russia and Hitler wasn't going to drive her from this one, she said, poor though it was.'

'Poor? But the Cheyne Walk house is rather a nice one,' Julia protested.

'I know, I know!' Anna paced the floor in her agitation. 'But you know my mother, Julia. Always the Countess, always in black, mourning for her old way of life. She can be very stubborn. Do you think I should go down there?'

'No, I do *not*! All around the docks and a lot of central London seems to be in a mess. I doubt you'd be able to get on a bus, let alone find a taxi. It would be madness to go there at a time like this. Your mother has Igor to look after her and –'

'Not any longer! Igor is an air-raid warden now. Since the bombing started, he's hardly ever at home!'

'Anna, my dear.' Edward Sutton rose slowly to his feet to lay a comforting arm around his daughter-in-law's shoulders. 'No news is good news, don't they say? The

Countess will be in touch with you before so very much longer. Perhaps it's only a temporary thing. Leave it until morning and it's my guess you'll get through with no delay at all. Try not to worry. And Julia is here with an invitation for us.'

'Aunt Helen's party, you mean? We've already heard about it from Tatiana. Daisy told her.'

'Well, I'm here with the official invitation for the fifth. And don't forget, Anna, that it's our party – Nathan's and mine. And tell Tatty there'll be dancing, so she'll be sure to come.'

'I'll tell her.' Tatiana was so secretive these days. Always slipping out or hovering round the telephone. Anna frowned. A young man, of course, but why didn't she bring him home? 'She's in Harrogate this afternoon, collecting for the Red Cross. She said she would come home on the same bus as Daisy.'

'So it's settled. We'll all come. And here's tea,' Edward smiled as Karl, straight-backed and unsmiling, laid a silver tray on the table beside Anna.

'Where is the little one?' he demanded in his native tongue.

'Out, helping the Red Cross. She'll be all right . . .' Anna smiled apologetically as the door closed behind the tall, black-bearded Cossack. 'I'm sorry. He refuses to speak English. I've told him it isn't polite when we have guests, but he's so stubborn. And he does understand the language. I've heard him talking to Tatiana in English. I think it amuses him that people get the impression he doesn't know what they're saying.'

'He's a good servant, though,' Edward defended. 'So loyal, still, to the Czar and surely it's a comfort to you, Anna, that he's so protective of Tatiana. How old is he?'

'I don't know. He won't ever say.' Anna placed a cup and saucer at her father-in-law's side. 'But it's my guess he's about fifty-five. He'd been a Cossack for some time when he met up with us. We couldn't have got out of Russia without his help. He's been with us ever since.'

'He and Natasha, both. Didn't you pick up Natasha along the way, too?' Julia wanted to know.

'Sort of. She was the daughter of the woman who did our sewing,' Anna replied in clipped tones. 'When the unrest first started, she was delivering dresses to us at the farm at Peterhof – we'd gone there for safety. Mother insisted that Igor take her back to St Petersburg, but when they got there the rabble had taken over their house and her parents gone. What else could Igor do but bring her back to us?'

'Whatever became of her?' Julia persisted. 'She went back to London with you, didn't she, after – after –'

'After my son was born dead, you mean? Yes, but she didn't stay long at Cheyne Walk. She left Mama and went to France; Paris, I think it was. I can't remember. It was a long time ago. But do have a biscuit, Julia . . .'

'Positively not!' Biscuits were rationed and she and her mother would not eat other people's food. 'And those are homemade, too,' she sighed.

'Cook has a little sugar stored away.' Anna blushed guiltily because no one should have sugar stored away. 'But I think it will soon be used up,' she hastened.

'Mm. So has our cook. I think people who remember the last war quietly bought in a few things – just in case. I know Tilda has a secret stock of glacé cherries.' Julia had been quick to notice the tightening of Anna's mouth, the dropping of her eyes. Did she still mourn her stillborn baby or was it thoughts of the man who fathered it that brought the tension to her face because no one, not even the compliant Anna, could have been happy with Elliot Sutton.

'I think Tatiana is meeting Daisy in her lunch hour.' Deliberately Julia talked of other things. 'They'll spend most of it searching for cigarettes, I shouldn't wonder, though Tatiana told me the other day she was down to her last smear of lipstick, so perhaps they'll be looking for a lipstick queue.'

'I'll give her one of mine,' Anna smiled, all tension gone. 'Now won't you have just one biscuit?'

'Absolutely not, thanks. And did you see it in the papers this morning? When the new petrol coupons start in October, petrol is going up to two shillings a gallon!'

'Two shillings and a ha'penny, to be exact,' Edward smiled, 'and cheap at twice the price when you think of the lives it costs just getting it here.'

'Cheap,' Julia echoed, all at once thankful that exploding mines in the Western Approaches seemed safer by far than bringing crude oil to England. Seamen crewing a tanker deserved all the danger money they were paid when just one hit was enough to send the ship sky-high. There were no second chances on a tanker. Either men died mercifully quickly or perished horribly in a sea of blazing oil. 'And only the other day I was thinking about people who get petrol on the black market and wondering if I could come by the odd gallon. Very wrong of me, wasn't it?'

'Yes, but very human,' Edward said softly. 'You won't be tempted, will you, Julia?'

'Oh, I'll be tempted all right, Uncle, but I won't do it – promise. And I'll have to be going. Nathan is visiting the outlying parishes this afternoon and Mother is inclined to brood, if she's alone for too long – about Drew, you know.' She rose to her feet. 'Now mark it in your diaries: October the fifth. It's a Saturday. No big eats, I'm afraid, but it'll be a lot of fun. Sorry I can't stay longer.'

'That's all right. Give Aunt Helen my love,' Anna smiled as she closed the conservatory door behind them. 'And I think I'll ask the exchange to try Cheyne Walk just once more. She'll think I'm fussing, but I'm so worried, Julia. You honestly don't think anything awful has happened, do you?'

'No, I don't. Somewhere along the line, a telephone

exchange has been bombed. Even a telegraph pole getting knocked down could cause a lot of upset with the phones. You'd have heard something, by now if – well, if there was anything to tell.' She reached for Anna, hugging her close. 'Try not to worry too much if you don't get through, but either way, give me a quick ring, will you? 'Bye, Anna.'

'Grandfather will be so pleased with the tobacco,' Tatiana said. 'I know he's short. Last night he kept looking in his tobacco jar, then putting the lid back.'

'Dada's always short, poor pet. D'you know, Tatty, I nearly hit the roof when we got so near to the counter and then the man said, "Sorry. That's all, I'm afraid." And then he said, "Cigarettes all gone, for today. Only pipe tobacco left. Half an ounce to each customer." Imagine standing there for nearly half an hour for four slices of tobacco. I shall give two to Dada and two to Uncle Reuben. It's all Hitler's fault. I hate him.'

'Doesn't everybody?' The bus stopped at the crossroads and they got out, calling a good night to the remaining passengers. 'Shall I walk part of the way with you – stand at the fence till you're through the wood, Daisy?'

'No thanks. I'll be fine. It isn't dark yet. And I know Brattocks like the back of my hand – even in the blackout. I don't suppose you'll be going to the aerodrome dance tomorrow?'

'Not a lot of use. Tim's almost certainly on ops. tonight and as soon as he gets back he'll be off on leave to Greenock. I'll miss him, but at least I'll know that for seven days he'll be safe. I'm getting up early tomorrow. He's promised to ring the coin box in the village. Better than him ringing Denniston.'

'You'll have to set your alarm, and get out of the house without anyone hearing you. Wouldn't it have been better to get up early and wait by your own phone and pick it up the second it starts ringing? It's awful for you having to be so sneaky about Tim's calls.'

'I know, but I can't risk them finding out at home. Mother might say I wasn't to see Tim again and they'd watch everything I did, after that. Karl especially.'

'Listen, Tatty, I know I might be out of order, but Karl only watches over you because he's so fond of you. Haven't you ever thought of confiding in him – telling him about Tim? He might even be on your side, cover for you sometimes.'

'He won't. First and foremost he's loyal to Mother. She's still his little countess,' she sighed. 'I really couldn't risk it. I know I can get out of the house in the morning and it'll be worth the walk because there'll be no risk at all of anyone hearing what I say. I'll be able to tell him I love him loud and clear, and not whisper it down the phone like I'm ashamed to say it.'

'What time?' Daisy asked.

'About seven o'clock. He reckoned he'd be back and debriefed by then. The transport to take them to York station leaves at eight, so that'll give him time to get cleaned up and snatch some breakfast beforehand.

'The rest of his crew are going to Edinburgh, them being Canadians and not able to get home, poor loves. Tim's skipper said he was going to spend his entire leave hunting the shops for whisky, and sleeping. Oh, well – I'll give you a ring tomorrow night.'

She turned away abruptly because she was so miserable, so utterly lonely, and after tomorrow morning it would be worse. Tears filled her eyes and she let them flow unchecked.

Then she turned abruptly as Daisy called, 'Tatty – I do know what it's like. Remember I haven't seen Keth for two years.'

'Yes, of course. 'Night, Daisy . . .'

Daisy *didn't* know, she thought fiercely; not really.

Okay, so she hadn't seen Keth for ages but at least she knew he was going to survive the war. Keth was safe in America and tonight Tim would be flying over Germany, searching the sky for fighters. Tim was a tail-end Charlie and tomorrow morning, if Whitley *K-King* touched down safely, Tim would have flown his thirteenth op. – the dicey one.

She sniffed loudly and dabbed at her eyes. She would *not* cry. Tim would be all right. Her love would protect him because now they truly belonged. Now Tatiana Sutton was a living, breathing, pulsating woman who loved and was loved in return. No longer was she a cosseted only child, guilty for having been born a girl. She was one half of a perfect whole that was Tim and Tatiana. She existed, when alone, on a soft cushion of disbelief at the new creature she had become. Just to see a flower bud opening or a bird in graceful flight made her feel warm inside.

When the squadron took off from Holdenby Moor into a peachy early-evening sky, she was sick with despair and hugged their love to her like a child with a precious, familiar toy.

When they came together – really together – their first loving had been sweet and gentle and filled with the delight of belonging but the next time had been fierce and without inhibition and if, she thought through a haze of sadness, their last coupling had made a child, then so be it. And if one morning *K-King* did not come home, then she would have something belonging to him and she wouldn't care about Grandmother Petrovska nor a shocked Holdenby that would turn away from her and whisper behind her back that she was no better than she ought to be.

But she would never let them take Tim's child from her. Daisy would understand because Daisy and Keth had been lovers. And Uncle Nathan would help her because he was the kind of man who, if a child could choose its own father then she, Tatiana, would have chosen him.

She wondered if her own father had been kind, like his brother Nathan, and knew instinctively from things half remembered from a misty childhood that he had not.

She closed her eyes. She must not weep again because if she did, someone at home would ask her what was the matter. Instead, she squeezed her eyelids tightly shut.

'I love you so much, Tim,' she whispered. 'Take care tonight.'

'There, now! See how it's done, lass?' Jack Catchpole held aloft a broom handle from which was suspended the hessian sack of hen droppings. 'You tie the sack in the middle, then you tie it to your broom handle – or any suchlike piece of wood. Is the tub ready?'

'Ready, Mr C. Half full of rainwater, like you said.'

'Then that's all there is to it.' Catchpole regarded the zinc washtub his wife had discarded all of three years ago. Lily was alus throwing things away. Thank the good Lord he'd had the sense to rescue it from the rubbish tip. He had known he would find a use for it one day. 'You lay the broom handle across the top of the tub so the sack is covered with water, then every day you lift it up and down – give it a good ponching – and by next year, that liquid'll be food and drink to those little tomato plants.'

'Next *year*? But won't it smell, Mr Catchpole?'

'Smell? Oh my word yes, it'll smell.' He closed his eyes in utter bliss. 'There isn't a scent on God's earth, Gracie, like a tub of liquid hen manoor.' Unless it was the wonderful, spring-morning whiff from a well-rotted heap of farmyard manure. 'Next year's tomatoes'll wonder what hit 'em when they get a dose or two of that mixture. Tomatoes big as turnips we'll have!'

'But won't it attract flies – bluebottles and things?'

'Happen it could, and happen we might cover it up when the hot weather comes. But we'll worry about that next summer.' If they lived to see another summer, that was.

'And till then, I want you to see to the ponching. Every day. The hen manoor will be your responsibility, lass, so don't forget, will you?'

'Every day.' She closed her eyes briefly and shuddered inside her. Stuffed vegetable marrows were bad enough. Never would she eat one she had vowed, and now, just to think of tomatoes grown red and fat and juicy on hen muck made her towny soul writhe. 'I'll remember. And while I'm remembering – I won't be able to go to Lady Helen's party. Our forewoman told us this morning we're to go on leave in two lots. Now the corn harvest is in, she said, we'd all of us best take it whilst we could, because soon the farmers will be busy lifting potatoes and sugar beet. Sorry, Mr C. but we've got to do as we're told.'

She did so want to see her family again, tell them about Rowangarth and Mr Catchpole and all the things she was learning about gardening, yet it was a pity, for all that, to have to miss the party.

'Can't be helped, Gracie. I'll miss you, but a week isn't for ever. And them little hens are going to miss you, an' all. Who'll be looking after them?'

'Daisy said she and her mother would see they got a hot mash every day, and plenty of water, though I bet you anything you like they'll lay their first egg whilst I'm away,' she sighed.

She was fond of Mrs Sutton's six Rhode Island Red pullets, loved their placidity, the way they scratched industriously, their softly feathered bottoms wiggling this way and that. She had almost given each one a name until common sense told her she must not become too attached to them. But it really would be awful if Daisy were to find the first egg in one of the straw-lined nest boxes. In fact, Gracie was forced to admit, she was getting too contented with her new life in the kitchen garden, and seeing seeds she had helped to plant and pot on growing into fine cabbages and sprouts and leeks.

It was going to be awful going back to Rochdale. It would be unbearable were not Mum and Dad and Grandad there. In fact, the only thing good about leaving Rowangarth and Mr Catchpole would be the certain fact that the war was over.

'Now don't look so glum, lass. You look as if you've lost a shilling and found a penny. Cheer up. It might never happen.'

'No, Mr C. It mightn't.'

But it would happen. One day, one faraway day, the land girls and Waafs and the ATS girls would hand in their uniforms and go home and Gracie Fielding would take off her overalls for the last time and say goodbye to this beautiful garden.

It would be good that the war was over, but the wages office in Jonah Aykroyd's mill, she sighed, would never seem the same again.

14

'Mother!' Tatiana called. 'Where are you?' She ran up the stairs, pausing on the half-landing. 'Mo-*ther*!'

'Up here,' Anna called from the top of the narrow staircase that led to the attics. 'What is it? Who was that on the phone?'

'It was Grandmother. She's –'

'Mama! But why didn't you call me?'

'There wasn't time. The pips went.'

'Pips? She was in a call box? Did she say where? Is she all right?'

'She sounded fine.' And every bit as bossy! '"Thees is your grandmother end ay em at York station. I em kept waiting to be given this call end ay em very angry,"' Tatiana mimicked crossly, '"end cold end hungry! Please to collect me at once!" So you worried yourself silly for nothing, didn't you?'

'Thank God she's all right. But how *can* we collect her? And Tatiana, do *not* be disrespectful. Your grandmother must have had a terrible time in London.'

'Sorry.' But she wasn't sorry. London was a big place and it was the people who lived in the streets around the docks who had taken the brunt of the bombing; people with nowhere to go and nowhere to sleep now except in the Underground.

'*How*, will you tell me?' Nervously, Anna pushed back a strand of hair. 'The petrol, I mean . . .' York was all of twenty-four miles there and back and would use the best part of a petrol coupon. She hesitated only a moment before filial concern and fear of her mother's acid tongue combined to gain the upper hand. 'Quickly, dear. Ask Karl to get the car out. We'll go and meet her.'

'Think you'd be better without me. She'll have brought a lot of luggage.' Grandmother Petrovska always did. 'I'll stay here, help get her room ready.'

And damn and blast! she thought mutinously. Grandmother here soon and taking over the house; criticizing and running a forefinger over the furniture for dust. And that wouldn't be all! 'Bring me this!' and 'Bring me that, child!' Demanding attention and getting it, too! Nor did she miss a thing. How was she ever to get out now to meet Tim? Grandmother's eyes were everywhere and her nose permanently poked into everybody's business.

'Y-yes. Perhaps you'd better. Can you have a tea tray ready, too? And you'd better let your grandfather know, but don't waken him if he's asleep.'

'Mother – calm down! Go and powder your nose and I'll find Karl,' though what was wrong with the Holdenby train which would leave York in less than an hour, Tatiana did not know.

She ran down the kitchen stairs to where she knew she would find Karl, feeling all at once ashamed she could not share her mother's relief. Tatiana Sutton did not like her maternal grandmother though she had tried all her life to do so.

'Karl!' She opened the kitchen door so violently that the man who dozed in the chair at the fireside jumped startled to his feet.

'What is it, little one? Are the Germans coming?'

'No, nor the Bolsheviks either! Worse than that. Grandmother Petrovska is waiting at York station and you're to go with Mother to collect her!'

'Our Lady have mercy!' He crossed himself piously. 'Thanks be she is safe, but does she have to come here?'

'I'm afraid she does. And do hurry! She sounded really put out when she phoned. Sorry,' she whispered, all at once feeling the need to apologize, 'but there's nothing we can do about it.' Except keep out of her way, perhaps. 'And being bombed must be terrible. I suppose I shouldn't be so awful about her coming.'

'You shouldn't, but I understand,' he muttered, pulling on his boots. 'Pass me my jacket, there's a good child.'

Child? She watched the old soldier stump up the stairs. If only he knew she was no longer a child! *And oh, Tim my darling – hurry back!*

'Ooooh!' Wide-eyed, Tilda read out the label on the large package Julia had dumped triumphantly on the kitchen table; a food parcel from America. 'Two tins of butter, it says, miss; two tins of ham . . .' Of cream, of peaches in heavy syrup, cookies, candies, coffee and – would you believe it? – a whole boned chicken *in a tin*! The things they did in America! 'Oh miss, just imagine if the Germans had sunk it!' All that beautiful rationed food at the bottom of the Atlantic. It didn't bear thinking about, though food was of secondary importance, she admitted, when she thought of the lives risked getting it here.

'Well, they didn't sink it, Tilda, and Mother says it's to go into the store cupboard and we're all to share it.' Food parcels were all at once the fashion – those which arrived safely, that was! Kindly family and friends in the Dominions and America were convinced that poor besieged Britain was on the verge of starvation and determined to do all they could to help. 'Amelia is such a kind person. I miss her so much – and the children. We'll save the peaches for something special, Tilda – maybe for Mother's eighti-eth. I haven't seen a tin of peaches since Lord knows when.'

'It's the sugar,' Tilda sighed. Now the sugar ration had been savagely cut to eight ounces for each man, woman and child. Just about enough, each week, to fill a small sugar bowl and not a grain, she mourned, to spare for baking. 'And I don't think two tins of peaches are going to go far on Saturday night. There'll be all of fifty folk there. Best hang on to them for something extra special – like the end of the war.' Or young Drew's wedding breakfast, happen? 'Pity Sir Andrew can't be here.'

'It is, but the Navy doesn't give leave for something as frivolous as a party. It's got to be more serious than that, unfortunately. But we'll remember absent friends, won't we? Now I'm going to Creesby to the bank; mustn't miss the bus. Anything I can bring back for you?'

'Yes, miss. A keg of best butter, half a hundredweight of sugar and a whole fillet of steak!'

'Ha!' Julia had a feeling inside her that today she would find a cigarette queue. She had only one left which must be saved until tonight. If only she could give up smoking, life would be a lot easier. She should be ashamed, she knew, of the time she wasted hunting for cigarettes or standing in cigarette queues like a peasant with a begging bowl. Yet why she had promised Nathan she really would try to give them up in the New Year, she really didn't know!

'Hi, Grandpa. Did you think we'd forgotten you?' Tatiana sat on the stool at Edward Sutton's feet, arms clasped around her knees.

'Not exactly. I guessed something was going on,' he nodded, raising a questioning eyebrow.

'It is. It's Grandmother Petrovska. They've just gone to pick her up at York. Mother was in such a state. She asked me to come and tell you – if you weren't having a nap.'

'Well now, isn't that splendid? Anna was so worried about her.'

'Well, she's going to be more worried, because we've got her for the duration, if you ask me!'

'Your grandmother is an old lady,' Edward reproved mildly, 'and where else is she to come but here? Did she say how things were in London?'

'No. She only had three minutes on the phone and most

of them spent grumbling about how long it had taken her to get through.'

'She was probably tired and in need of sleep. Try to be kind to her.'

'Grandpa, you are such an old love. You find good in everyone. But I don't much like the Petrovska and if she says one word about the Czar-God-rest-him, I swear I'll scream!'

'You're upset, girlie; what is it?' Gently he stroked her hair. 'Missing your young man, are you?'

'My – how did you find out? Who told you?' She flung round to face him. 'Mother doesn't know, does she?'

'I'm not sure, though sometimes when you are in late, or when you slip out or hover within sound of the phone . . .'

'Hell! Was I that obvious? I thought I was being so careful. And if Mother knows, why hasn't she said anything? Is she hoping if she ignores him he'll go away – because he won't, Grandpa.'

'Your mother hasn't said anything to me because probably she doesn't know. Mothers are often the last to find out.'

'But *you* knew – well, suspected.'

'I'm an old man with a lot of time on my hands. And I wasn't prying nor spying, my dear – just observing, I suppose. Want to talk about him?'

'Grandpa, if only you knew how much I want to talk about him!' She reached for his hand, holding it to her cheek. 'But if I do, you'll not split on me, will you? Promise you won't tell?'

'Word of a Sutton I won't.'

'Then I'll tell you, but not now. I've got to help get Grandmother's room ready and they'll be back before long. Can we have a talk later, when there's no one about, I mean? But his name is Timothy – Tim – and he's an air gunner and he's on leave this week. Got to go now.' She jumped to her feet, then taking his face in her hands she kissed him gently. 'You're a darling and I love you very much!'

'Oh dear,' he whispered ruefully as his granddaughter ran up the stairs, 'that wasn't very clever of you, was it, Edward?'

Now he had become involved, lined himself up on Tatiana's side and promised to say not one word to Anna about the girl's secret. Dangerous ground he was treading on.

But it wasn't a lot of fun being eighteen these days. Not much for the young ones to look forward to when you thought about it – especially if, by all accounts, you were an air gunner.

He sighed, adjusted the cushion at his head, then closed his eyes. Being old sometimes had its compensations . . .

'I tell you, Edward, soon the Nazis will join forces with those Bolsheviks, and where shall we be then?'

Olga Petrovska pulled a forefinger across her throat dramatically, then closed her eyes, wincing, as a bomber flew low overhead.

'I wouldn't worry overmuch on that score, Countess. Fascists and Communists have little in common; they each dislike the other's doctrines.'

'You think so? Then be telling me why they have made this pact together! I tell you, they will overrun us! But I have lived too long. I should have died with the Czar-God-rest-him. The world I knew is gone!'

'And our young ones are fighting for what remains of the world that is left to us,' Edward admonished gently.

'Ha! The young generation doesn't care as we cared!' The Countess was astride her high horse and would not be silenced. 'And it is all right for you, here in the wilds. You do not know what war is. London is all hell. You should hear the stories Igor has to tell – when he is home, that is! Such devastation! London is finished!'

'London is *not* finished! You sound just like that

Kennedy man!' Tatiana could be silent no longer. 'He said Britain is finished, but we aren't!'

'I have never heard of him!'

'He's the US Ambassador to the Court of St James's, or was. He's gone back to America now.'

'And so would I go to America if I could. This England is no longer a safe place to be.'

'Then you should have gone there, shouldn't you, Grandmother, when the Commies kicked you out of Russia. You were glad enough to come to England not all that long ago!'

'Tatiana! You are being impudent! Your grandmother is upset by the bombing and a guest in our home!' Anna's cheeks flushed scarlet. 'Apologize at once, then go to your room!'

'I'm sorry,' Tatiana flung.

'Sorry? You do not sound it. And there goes another of those wretched planes!' The Countess sighed dramatically, lifting her eyes to the ceiling. 'You should complain, Edward; tell them at the aerodrome that their noise is upsetting and should not be allowed. But I suppose they do it to be devilish, see which of them can fly lowest, the hooligans!'

'Now that is *it*!' Tatiana jumped to her feet, slamming down her cup with such anger that coffee spilled over the arm of her chair. 'Do you realize, Grandmother, that those noisy hooligans risk their lives every time they leave the runway? Do you think they fly low just to annoy bad-tempered old women? No! It's called takeoff and they're all sick inside till they get airborne, I can tell you! They carry bombs and their wings are full of fuel and those planes are the very devil to get off the ground!

'And whilst I'm about it, you have been in this house only a few hours and all that time you have done nothing but complain and find fault, just because London isn't Leningrad and England isn't your precious Russia! You've never liked England because nobody here gives a damn about you and because England did away with serfdom years and years ago!'

'Tatiana! How *dare* you!' Anna, too, was on her feet. 'Have you gone completely mad? What is the matter with you these days? Do as I told you and go to your room!'

'Like hell I will!' She made for the door. 'I'm going out and don't ask me when I'll be back because I don't know and I don't care either!'

'Oh, my God!' Countess Petrovska's eyelids fluttered dramatically. 'I shall faint! Bring me my salts! That child should be smacked, Anna!'

'Should she, now? Well, the first one to try it will get smacked back, that I guarantee, Grandmother!'

The door banged with defiant fury and Tatiana ran down the front steps on angry feet.

So Tim was a hooligan! All those crews who went out night after night only did it to annoy a bloody-minded old woman who lived in the past! God, but it was awful being young; being treated like a child when there were children younger than she flying fighters and bombers.

She began to run, not knowing where, tears of anger running down her cheeks, her breath coming in harsh sobs.

Tim! How she missed him, needed him, wanted him, yet they couldn't meet until Saturday.

'I hate you, Grandmother Petrovska!' she choked, 'and I wish you *had* died with your precious Czar!'

She stopped, at once contrite. She mustn't wish anyone dead because ill wishes could rebound and then maybe something awful would happen to Tim.

'I didn't mean it, God! I'm sorry, truly I am!'

She dabbed at her eyes then blew her nose loudly. Better pull herself together because that was Daisy and Gracie ahead, waiting at the crossroads, and they had seen her and were waving. She took a deep, steadying breath then whispered, 'Did you hear me, God? I didn't mean it. I'm sorry.' Then she forced her lips into a smile and returned the wave.

'Hi, both!' she said.

'Hi,' Daisy said softly. 'You've been crying, Tatty.'

'Yes. Only Grandmother being Grandmother. She's arrived from London and she hasn't stopped complaining since she set foot in Denniston. She got me mad and I was cheeky. Mother said I was to apologize, then go to my room! I ask you! Go to bed like I'm a naughty little girl! So I told them the hell I would, and pushed off. I'll have to apologize, though, or life won't be worth living at home. And I'll say sorry to Grandfather, too, because he heard it all and I wouldn't upset him for anything. But I'm not going back yet. Think I'll go to Aunt Julia's.'

'Come to the dance at the aerodrome, why don't you?' Gracie comforted. 'The transport won't be long.'

'Better not. I look a mess . . .'

'You can borrow my lipstick and comb, Tatty.'

'No. Thanks all the same, Gracie. I think I want to be miserable tonight, truth known.'

'You're missing Tim,' Daisy soothed. 'Are you sure you won't come – help take your mind off things?'

'I don't want my mind taking off things. I'm just no use without Tim and that's the truth of it. Anyway, I couldn't bear the sergeants' mess and him not there.'

'Never mind, he'll be back on Saturday. Has he been in touch yet?'

'No. I told him not to and I can't ring him because his folks aren't on the phone. And I don't know what to do about Saturday. I'm expected at Aunt Helen's party.'

'Then take Tim along with you.'

'She's right, Tatty. Aunt Julia said that if any of the lads who normally use the canteen turn up on Saturday night they're to be asked to join in.'

'Problem solved,' Gracie smiled.

'No, it isn't. I couldn't risk Mother finding out – and she would, you know. More than one dance with Tim and she'd be suspicious. And wouldn't the Petrovska go to town on it? She'd be downright rude to him, especially as he isn't an officer. I know I'm awful about Grandmother, but she goes out of her way to upset people. She's living in the past with a great big chip on her shoulder. She even looked daggers at me because I called St Petersburg Leningrad – which it always has been as long as I can remember.'

'You really ought to tell your mother about Tim,' Gracie frowned. 'Not very nice for him, is it, knowing he's *persona non grata*?'

'I know, though he does understand, bless him. And even if Mother said I could take him home, I wouldn't risk it now; not with Grandmother there. I did tell Grandfather about him, though. He was ever so sweet; asked me if I was missing my boyfriend and I was so flabbergasted he'd found out that I told him yes, I was and that his name was Tim. And we're going to have a good chat about him when Mother and Grandmother aren't hovering. He won't snitch on me. But here's the transport. Have a good time, both of you.'

'We will.' Gracie gave a long, slow wink. 'And Tatty – it'll turn out just fine for you and Tim, I know it will.'

But would it, she brooded as she settled herself on the hard wooden seat. What did Grace Mary Fielding know about being in love; really in love like Daisy and Tatty?

Nothing, truth known, because she was canny and sensible and not for anything would she fall in love whilst there was a war on. She'd said it all along and she was right, too, when it was obvious how lonely Daisy was, and how miserable Tatty could be and how afraid when Tim was flying. Oh, no! Gracie Fielding wasn't going to wear her heart on her sleeve, risk getting it broken.

But what, she frowned, if it just did happen to her? Okay, so it was fine for Daisy. There'd never been anyone for her but Keth, never would be. Yet what if love found Gracie Fielding and hit her bang between the eyes like had happened to Tatty and Tim? What if one day she turned a corner and *he* was walking towards her and she knew, as Tatty had known, that it was love at first sight, and for ever?

The RAF transport lurched over a pothole and she clung to the wooden slats, all at once in charge of her emotions.

It would not happen. Not to her. Until the war was over she wouldn't let it. Absolutely not!

The train was early; actually early. It gave out two hoots as it always did before taking the incline that ran alongside Brattocks Wood, rounded the sweeping, curving bend of the track, then came to a stop almost four minutes before its designated time.

'Holdenby Halt!' called the stationmaster, jamming his pre-war stationmaster's hat on his head, taken completely unawares by events because the 12.15 was always one minute late. Always.

Gracie reached for her case and gas mask, then folded her jacket over her arm. All at once she felt a longing for Rochdale and Mam's kitchen and the smell of her grandad's pipe, though she knew that by the end of the week the only sadness she would feel was when she said goodbye to them. All else would be unimportant compared to the joy of pushing open the high iron gate of the kitchen garden again, gazing with affection at the little world she shared, all safe and shut away behind nine-feet-high walls.

Rowangarth was her life now, Tatty and Daisy her friends, and the noisy bothy her other home. She wasn't being disloyal to Rochdale; it was just that –

'Gracie! Hullo there!'

A familiar voice caused her to turn and gaze, laughing, into Tim Thomson's eyes.

'Hullo yourself! Thought it was Saturday you were due back. Did you have a good leave?'

'I did, and it should be. Came back a day early, sort of –'

'Missing Tatty, is that it?'

'Aye. Ah well, enjoy your own leave, Gracie. See you.'

'Tim! Don't go. Why don't I ring Denniston, tell Tatty

you're here? There's a few minutes yet before the train leaves.'

She reached for his hand, running to the bright red kiosk that stood outside the ticket barrier, reaching into her pocket for three pennies.

'Number, please?' The exchange answered the second, almost, Gracie lifted the receiver.

'Hullo, Miss Hallam. Can you give me Denniston, please?'

'Have three pennies ready.' The operator rarely exchanged pleasantries with public phone boxes. 'Your number is on the line, now.'

Automatically Gracie pushed three pennies into the slot, counting as they fell with a clatter, pressing the button marked A.

'Denniston House,' a voice said softly.

'Mrs Sutton? Good afternoon. It's Grace Fielding. Might I speak to Tatiana if she's in?'

'You might. She's beside me now.'

'Tatty?' Gracie breathed in reply to a querulous hullo. 'I'm at the station and guess who's here with me, back from his leave early? Hang on.'

She handed over the receiver with a grin then ran back to the platform just in case things got completely out of hand and the train left as it had arrived – early.

'Hullo?' The voice was apprehensive.

'Darling. I'm back early. Missed you. How about the crossroads at six?'

'Thanks, Gracie – yes. I'll pick it up later. Didn't realize I'd lost it . . .'

Why was her mother hovering? She always did it, Tatiana fumed silently, even though she knew it was Gracie on the phone. Why must she have to talk nonsense when she wanted to tell Tim she had missed him too and yes, she would meet him at six and need he ask?

'See you, then.' He dropped his voice to a whisper. 'Darling, I want you . . .'

'Oh, *yes*! Me, too. Have a good leave, Gracie.'

She made a small kissing sound into the mouthpiece, hoping Tim would hear it and that her mother would not.

'That was kind of her.' She said it automatically because her mother always expected an explanation. 'I left my purse at Keeper's. Daisy asked Gracie to let me know.'

'Wasn't that a little careless of you, dear? And why didn't Daisy phone?'

'Don't know,' Tatiana shrugged. 'Suppose she asked Gracie to, for some reason. Maybe she saw her this morning – when Gracie was feeding the hens at Keeper's, I mean. Does it matter?' Lies, and lies to cover lies. She was getting good at it and she didn't care. 'And yes, Mother, it was careless of me – I hadn't missed it, actually. I'll go over to Keeper's to collect it tonight when Daisy gets back from work. Now is there anything you want me to do?' All at once her heart was light.

'If you've made your bed and dusted your dressing table as I asked you to, you might try saying sorry to your grandmother. I know you *are* sorry but I'm sure she would like to hear a proper apology. You were very touchy last night.'

'Yes. Always the same when my period is due.' She said the first thing that came into her head then realized, amazingly, that it *was* due. Sunday, to be exact, though she could never be sure. Not these days; not when getting pregnant was a real worry, though she immediately forgot it the minute she was in Tim's arms. 'And I *will* say a proper sorry to Grandmother.'

It would hurt her pride to see the satisfied smugness on that face, but she wouldn't mean it. She would only be apologizing for the sake of peace and quiet and because nothing must happen to prevent her getting out tonight. And did it honestly matter? Tim was back a day earlier than she had expected and in five hours they would be touching and kissing and loving.

*   *   *

At a quarter to six Tatiana told her mother she was going to Keeper's and that she might go on from there to Rowangarth. She wasn't sure, she said, eyes on her shoes.

'And don't hold dinner for me. I'm trying to slim. Missing a meal will be good for me.'

'It will do you no good at all!' Anna admonished. 'Trying to slim, indeed! Whatever next!'

'Mother, I'm truly not hungry. You worry too much. See you,' she called, trying not to hurry, even though it would be almost six by the time she got to the crossroads.

She walked almost nonchalantly down the front steps and to the end of the drive, though once out of sight of the upstairs windows she began to run, taking a short cut across the paddock, pushing through the hedge. Then she saw him there, waiting beside the armless signpost and called, 'Tim!'

'I've missed you,' he said when they had kissed and kissed again.

His nearness almost overwhelmed her, and she wondered how she had endured almost a week without him.

'What did your family say?' she asked as they walked, hands clasped, towards the hill path that wound upwards to the flat top of Holdenby Pike. 'About coming back a day early, I mean. Didn't they wonder why?'

'No, because I'd told them about you, you see. My mother says I'm to take you home next leave I get. Maggie says you can share her bed.'

'She did?' Pleasure pinked Tatiana's cheeks though it would be futile to think she would be allowed to go. How could she be when up until now they didn't even know Tim existed – except Grandfather, that was.

'Aye. You'll be welcome, so how if you tell your folks about me? We're going steady, aren't we?'

'Tim, I'm only eighteen. Mother fusses. I couldn't risk her knowing. She'd watch me like a hawk and I'd never get out!'

'But sweetheart, this is 1940. Queen Victoria has been dead

an awful long time. There are Waafs at the aerodrome the same age as you are, and no one thinks anything about it!'

'I know, darling.' She didn't want to spoil this evening talking about how old-fashioned her mother could be. 'And if you'll give me time to get them used to my having a boyfriend I'm sure it'll come right for us. Grandfather Sutton has already guessed and I shall tell him about you as soon as I get the chance. Grandfather's a love, but Mother is altogether different.' She raised her eyes skywards. 'And as for Grandmother Petrovska . . .'

'Give you time? But time is the one thing you and me can't be sure of, darling. And I'm not your boyfriend, I'm your lover. We're married every way else but in name! Poor wee lassie. What am I to do with you?'

'Kiss me, please, then tell me what you told your family about me.'

'I told them,' he smiled, taking her into his arms, 'that you are a spoiled rich kid and your grandmother is a countess and that I'm after you for your money!'

'But I don't have any, Tim. Mother and I exist on handouts.'

'Some existence! Okay – I'm thinking about your expectations then.'

'No expectations either. When you think about it, I suppose, there are the Place Suttons, the Garth Suttons and the charity Suttons – that's us! Since my father died, all we have is what Pendenys allows us. If he hadn't been killed I suppose we'd have got Pendenys and most of the money, but as it is now, Uncle Nathan and Uncle Albert will get the money one day. But you didn't say those things about me, did you?'

'Course I didn't! I told them I'd met a lovely girl I'd like fine to take home with me, that's all, though Maggie kept asking about you. She wanted to know who gave you the Russian name and I said it was your Russian mother. She's intrigued, now. That's why she offered a share of her bed. My sister isn't usually so generous! And I wouldn't be so daft as to tell them I'd fallen for one of the upper classes! Dad would never hold up his head again at the Labour Club if it got out.'

'Wouldn't he, darling? It isn't my fault, being half-Russian and –'

'And well off by my standards? Of course it isn't; no more than it's my fault I was born into the working classes, so how if we stop blethering?' He drew her closer, kissing her hard and long.

Then he said, 'Y'know what, sweetheart? How about if I turn up at that party, tomorrow night? It would be a beginning, wouldn't it, and you did say anyone who uses the canteen would be made welcome. Why don't I just wander in – see how things go from there?'

'Tim! You wouldn't!' Fear took her. She had never considered taking him home just yet, much less letting him blunder into Aunt Helen's party. 'I mean – well, they'd know, wouldn't they, the minute they saw us together.'

'Don't worry. I won't let the cat out of the bag – yet. But your folks will have to know about us sooner or later. And I was only kidding about tomorrow night. I'll likely be on ops.'

'But you can't be! You're still officially on leave!'

'I *can* be. My leave ends at noon tomorrow.'

'And might you really be flying?' The worry was back again. For a week she had missed him until it hurt, the only comfort being that for seven days she need not worry about his safety.

'There's an even chance we will be, but if we aren't I'll know some time in the afternoon – about four. Can you be at the phone box so I can ring you?'

'You could ring Denniston tomorrow. Mother will be at Rowangarth, helping with the party.' She could get to the phone quicker than Grandmother if she sat beside the drawing-room door. 'And if I don't hear from you by . . . ?'

'By half-past four, say; if I haven't been in touch by then, you'll know we're on standby at least, and that I can't use the phone.'

She knew it. She had waited often enough, willing it to ring, knowing that when it did not the squadron at Holdenby Moor would be airborne that evening.

'Fingers crossed for tomorrow, then.'

'Aye. And after that, darling, we've got to think up ways and means. We can't go on like this, meeting secretly, always afraid to phone. I love you. I never thought I'd be fool enough even to think of marrying in wartime, but I hadn't met you then. If we were in Scotland, things would be different.'

'That's something we're going to have to consider, isn't it – my going to Scotland for three weeks – becoming domiciled, didn't you say it was?'

'They'd come after you, make you go home . . .'

'Not if I made sure they didn't find me.'

'You'd defy your family, Tatiana?'

'Try me!' She clasped her arms around his neck, need of him slicing through her, touching his lips, his closed eyelids, the tip of his nose with little whispering kisses, knowing all the time that nicely-brought-up young ladies didn't tease. Nicely-brought-up young ladies were expected to be virgins on their wedding night, too!

'Why are you smiling?' he asked huskily.

'Actually, I was thinking about you and me making love and me not being a virgin on our wedding night.'

'You won't mind?'

'Not a bit. What I *do* mind about is that we've been apart for a whole week.' She held out her hand to him, her eyes pleading and they began to walk again, up to the hilltop; to where wind-bent bushes would screen them from sight; to where they always made love now. 'Please, Tim – tonight? I need you so very much . . .'

15

The telephone did not ring at half-past four, nor had it by five o'clock. Yet determined still to try to reach Tim, Tatiana snatched up the receiver, not caring who might hear her.

'Can you give me Holdenby Moor, Winnie?' she whispered.

'Sorry. No calls in or out since three o'clock. Is that you, Tatiana?'

'It is.' Winnie wouldn't tell. She had sighed the Official Secrets Act. If Winnie Hallam let it out that Tatiana Sutton was forever ringing the aircrew mess, she could lose her job and the house that went with it.

'Looks as if they're on ops. tonight. Sorry, love.'

'Not your fault. Will I see you at the party?'

'You certainly will. I arranged a relief as soon as I heard about it. Lady Helen still doesn't suspect?'

'If she does she isn't letting on,' Tatiana smiled, glad Winnie knew – sort of knew – about Tim. 'See you then.'

So Tim's squadron was flying? She might have known that after last night, which had been so wonderful, the Fates wouldn't let them be together again. Not two nights running.

Why did she love him so much? And not just love him; why was she so in love with him, too? Why was she ordinary when they were apart only to come to exciting, pulsating life the moment they kissed? Had there ever been a love like theirs? Had Aunt Julia, Aunt Helen, her own mother, been so utterly besotted? Aunt Julia, perhaps, and maybe, in her own way, Aunt Helen too; but not her

mother, Tatiana thought sadly. Whenever she had tried to
talk about her father, her mother side-stepped the issue,
hinting that it hurt even yet to talk about the man to whom
she was once married.

But in which way did it hurt? Tatiana could never be
sure, because somewhere in the deeps of her remembering
was unhappiness and accusations and tears between her
parents.

No one ever actually talked about her father, Tatiana
frowned; not his own father nor his widow. Perhaps when
she was married and had children of her own, she and her
mother might grow closer and she would learn how it had
been, be told the whole truth of their marriage.

But she was always on edge when Tim was flying and
it was best she should go to her room, pin up her hair,
have a bath, then go through the motions of enjoying the
party, although all the time she would be straining to hear
the sound of the bombers taking off, counting each one
out so she could count them back in the early hours of the
morning.

'Take care, darling,' she whispered. What Tim had said
made sense. Sooner or later she must tell her mother about
him. Already her grandfather knew he existed and tonight
she would sit by his side at the party and tell him how
much she longed for Tim to be with them and how she
wished she had the courage to tell her mother about him.
At least it would be a beginning and if she and Tim could
not be together tonight, then talking about him would be
the next best thing!

'Poor Anna,' Julia sighed. 'Do you know, dearest, the more
I hear about mothers the more I know how lucky I am.'

'Flatterer,' Helen smiled. 'And what has the Countess
been up to now?'

'Nothing, really. It isn't what she does; more what she
says. Uncle Edward said there was a little petrol left in the

tank of the Rolls, so why didn't he use it in one glorious gesture before he puts it away for the duration.'

'It was Clemmy's car, remember? She did so love it.'

'Typical! She always had to have the biggest and the best! I can never believe she was Nathan's mother, you know – or that Elliot and Nathan were brothers. But let me tell you about Uncle Edward. He's going to drive the Rolls himself to the village and pick up Mrs Shaw, Reuben and Jinny Dobb on the way. There'll be an almost-full moon tonight so he'll be able to see just fine, he said.'

'And the Countess? Is he driving her to the party, too?'

'It seems not. She feels she will be indisposed. I rather think she'll have a headache tonight. Do you know, Mother, when Uncle Edward told her what he intended to do, her eyebrows hit her hairline. Then she closed her eyes and shuddered. She said not one word, but the look on her face said it all. *Mix with the rabble? The Countess Olga Maria Petrovska does not share a car with servants!*

'Uncle said he's really looking forward to having a chat with Reuben and Jin and Mrs Shaw. He's going to enjoy this evening and I'm glad old Petrovska won't be there. She'd only put a damper on things.'

Then, for absolutely no reason at all Julia bent to kiss Helen's cheek.

'Now – are you going to have a little rest, Mother? Mary has laid your things out; I'll give you a hand to dress later if you'd like.'

'I can manage quite well, thank you, dear. It is so nice seeing Mary happily married, at last, isn't it? I suppose, all things being equal, it's Tilda's turn next.'

'It could well be. Let's face it, we've never had so many unattached males in Holdenby,' Julia laughed. 'All the men at the aerodrome and Lord knows how many soldiers guarding Pendenys. It's turned into a spinster's paradise, around here. Now do you mind if I dash, Mother? A few last-minute jobs. If I don't wash my hair soon it won't be dry for tonight. Oh, trust Nathan to have a wedding, today of all days!'

'People *do* get married, dear, from time to time,' Helen murmured to her daughter's retreating back, 'and they do need a priest to marry them.'

Then she smiled, happy just to think how contented Julia was with Nathan. And not only contented. Recently, Helen was sure, Julia had ceased to feel guilty about her new happiness, her second chance. Now she rarely spoke about Andrew, and when she did there was a smile on her lips.

'We're going to have a lovely time tonight,' she whispered to John in the photograph at her side. 'I won't be dancing, of course.' Not as they danced that night they met. 'But it's ages since I saw Mrs Shaw and Reuben. We old ones will have quite a lot of catching-up to do.' Her eyelids drooped. Just a little nap, perhaps, before it was time to get ready. 'Such a lovely time, John dear . . .'

It was just as Julia gave a final tug to her husband's bow tie that the alert sounded.

'Nathan! It's the siren! Surely it can't be!'

They seldom had an air-raid warning in Holdenby. This one – if it really was one – was only the third of the war.

'Miss Julia?' Tilda clattered up the stairs. 'Can you hear it?'

'We can.' Nathan opened the bedroom door. 'Is it an alert, do you think?'

'Reckon it's got to be, Reverend. It's a lot of noise about nothing if it isn't. Trust that lot to start something tonight of all nights! I'll be in the kitchen if you want me, miss, or shall I pop along, see if her ladyship is all right?'

'Thanks, Tilda, but I'll go. And don't look so put out. It'll be nothing at all, like the others were. We'll get the all clear very soon. Probably a mistake . . .'

Julia walked catlike along the passage, ears straining, but all she heard as the last wail faded and died was a strange waiting silence; as if everyone, like herself, couldn't quite believe it.

'Julia! You heard it?' Helen stood there, clutching her dressing gown round her. 'Sssh! What was that?'

Sharp bursts of gunfire came from the direction of Holdenby Moor. Then more bursts, and louder. Our guns firing, was it? It had to be.

'Sounds like something's going on.' Nathan joined them, shrugging into his dinner jacket. 'I think we should go downstairs. You help Aunt Helen, I'll follow you. Best be sure.'

'Listen!' More firing. It wasn't nothing, this time. Julia reached for her mother's hand.

The shooting came from the aerodrome. This was going to be what had come to be known as a nuisance raid: enemy fighters flying in low, the moon behind them, firing at anything which took their fancy – sometimes at railway trains, sometimes firing down the beam of a probing searchlight or shooting up some small coastal village even, just for the hell of it. In and away again with such speed that most times there wasn't even time to sound the alert.

Tonight, Julia frowned, they had found Holdenby Moor and fear took her as she realized that perhaps the bombers there could already have had their bombs loaded, their guns fitted and primed, their wings filled with fuel. They could, even at this moment, be taxiing clumsily around the perimeter track to take off. Sitting ducks, and the runway already clearly marked by oil-filled gooseneck flares, not easily extinguished.

What a target for those marauding fighters, screaming in low and suddenly, guns spitting. Shoot up the runway and anything on it or near it, then up and out and away to their bases in Holland. So swift and vicious and deadly accurate that the aerodrome would hardly know what had hit it!

'Nathan,' she whispered, when they had negotiated the worn, twisting steps of the keeping cellar. 'What about your father? Hadn't you better ring Denniston – tell him not to leave just yet?'

'Think I'd better.' The aerodrome was the target, but there was nothing to stop the pilot of a Messerschmitt emptying his guns on the village. Strafing, it had come to be called, vindictive, senseless shooting, intended to bring terror to those who heard the scream of a low-flying fighter and the snarl and snap of tracers as they slammed into the earth, ricocheting wildly. A car, slowly driven along a country lane and clearly visible in the moonlight, would provide an ideal target, Nathan thought despairingly.

'Get me Denniston House, will you?' he asked when the exchange answered.

'Ringing them now. What's going on, Reverend? Looking for Holdenby Moor, are they?'

'Think they've found it. There's a lot of gunfire coming from that direction – oh hullo, Anna. It's Nathan. Are you all right? Did you hear the alert?'

'There's been a warning?' Fear sounded in her voice. 'But we didn't hear it. We're too far from Holdenby. When was it?'

'A couple of minutes ago. Has Father left yet? I think he should wait until the all clear. It's obviously the aerodrome they're after, but best be sure, will you tell him?'

'But, Nathan – he left about fifteen minutes ago. What shall I do? Will Karl go after him, bring him back? He'll be all right, won't he?'

'Sure to be. You'll know he was calling at the almshouses first. They'll have heard the siren,' Nathan said with an ease he far from felt. 'He'll be there by now. But keep your ears open, Anna. Any sound of trouble and you all go down to the cellar – okay?'

'We'll go now.' Anna was clearly agitated. 'Can you give us a ring when the all clear goes – just in case we don't hear it? And are you sure your father will be all right? I really think I should send Karl.'

'No! He'll be fine! Take care, Anna, and don't worry. It isn't the village they're interested in . . .'

Don't worry. But he *was* worried because in that instant there was an explosion so violent it could only mean that the aerodrome was not only being strafed, but bombed, too.

'Nathan!' Julia clattered up the stairs, eyes wide in a face drained of colour. 'What was that?'

'Go back down. Stay with Aunt Helen and Tilda. I'm going to the village. Father had already left Denniston, Anna said.'

'Darling!' Julia's cry was harsh with fear. 'Must you go?'

'Yes. I must.'

'Then take care. Please take care.'

'Of course I will.' Gently he kissed her lips. 'Back in no time!'

Helped by the moonlight Nathan ran urgently, making for the stile at the edge of the wild garden, then across Home Farm cow pasture to the lane that led to Holdenby.

Briefly he stopped, breathing deeply, ears straining. More strafing was that, or had our own guns joined in at last? But either way he thought, his mouth all at once dry, the firing wasn't coming from the aerodrome now – more from the direction of the village.

'*Damn!*' Sudden fear urged him on; quickly he reached the lane end then stopped again, horrified.

A dense cloud of smoke enveloped a building – God! not the parish hall! Then out of the drifting blackness came vicious leaping flames. Surely his father couldn't be in there, because if he was – and Jin and Reuben and Mrs Shaw – they'd all be trapped now, and injured. Or worse.

'Vicar!' The hand of an air-raid warden grasped Nathan's arm. 'Don't go any nearer! It's one of ours that's crashed over yonder. Its bombs have gone up, I reckon, but there's ammunition exploding all over the place! Keep well away. There's nothing you and me can do!'

'But my father could be under that lot, and more besides!'

'*No*, Mr Sutton. If they were in the hall then I don't rate their chances very highly. But are you sure? They'd have made for somewhere safer, surely, when the siren went?'

'Let's hope so! But are you sure it's the hall and not the church?' Rather the church, than his father.

A cloud covered the moon and the sudden darkness only served to intensify the leaping, raging flames.

'It could well be both! Any road, you're to go no nearer and that's an order! The fire engine's on its way and the ARP lot.' And ambulances, an' all, but best not tell the Reverend that! 'Like I said, there's nowt else I can do save keep folk away till we get a bit of help. Thank God nowhere else seems to have copped it.'

'All right.' Best do as the warden ordered. Nothing they could do, anyway, until the fire engines arrived.

'Anyway, my father and the others won't be in the church. I've just remembered. It's locked. The verger has the keys. We'll just have to hope and –'

Pray. He couldn't say the word. Prayers would be useless, anyway. It would take a miracle for anyone to be found alive in that inferno. He felt so helpless, so bewildered. Amazingly, he felt no anger. Just shock, he supposed, at the viciousness and the suddenness of it and his inability to think clearly.

As if to mock his thoughts, the all clear sounded; for a minute that long steady note would last and then the people of Holdenby would creep from their cellars and from beneath staircases or even from under a stout kitchen table. He hoped they would not go out, see if next door was all right. There was still danger, even though the night-fighters had gone, would be snarling now, low over the North Sea and back to base. But the fire still blazed furiously and there was danger yet from leaked fuel. Had anyone thought of that, he wondered.

A transport painted in the dull colours of camouflage arrived and steel-helmeted airmen jumped out, each of them carrying a rifle. Quickly they ringed round the fire, guarding it from intruders. It was followed by a fire truck that spewed foam into the heart of the blaze. By the time the fire engines arrived from Creesby, the well-ordered airmen had taken control.

'I'd not go inside, sir, if I were you,' ordered a sergeant. 'Never mind the all clear, Jerry often comes back, bombs on the fires. Leave us to take care of it . . .'

Nathan shook his head, trying not to accept what his reason told him to be true. Surely they'd had the sense to get out? But it had happened so suddenly, that fierce, vicious attack.

'Sir! I've already suggested you go to your home!' said the RAF sergeant. 'Now this time I'm *telling* you!'

'And I, Sergeant, think you should know that I am the vicar of this parish and I intend to stay!' Angrily he pulled off his bow tie and stuffed it in his pocket. 'It is almost certain there are people beneath that mess – my parishioners!'

'Then try not to get in the way, padre?' He spoke in the resigned tones used to placate the very young or the very stupid. 'We know what we're about and the ARP lot have arrived now. Leave it all to us, eh?'

'Very well.' His heart still thudded in his ears. He wished it would stop its noise so he could think clearly once more. It was, he supposed, the trenches all over again; his war was back only this was England, not faraway Flanders, and Holdenby was burning. But now the young lions had taken up the fight and had no time for do-gooders who got in the way.

All at once the pounding in his head stopped and his

mind was clear again. He knew that his father was dead; knew that the war would be long and bloody and that this time it would be the people's war, too.

'I shall stand at the road end,' he said softly, calmly. 'Have me called at once if anyone needs me – needs a priest – Sergeant.'

It was past ten o'clock when he closed Rowangarth's door behind him. Almost at once Julia appeared in the doorway of the winter parlour. She wore trousers and a sweater and old, scuffed shoes. Her face was indescribably sad.

'Nathan!' She held out her arms and he went to her, unspeaking. 'Bad, was it, love?' She fondled the back of his neck with gentle fingertips.

'Bad. Father, Reuben, Mrs Shaw and Jin. Sorry I'm late. Been to tell Anna. They've taken them to Creesby mortuary. I've already identified them.' It had not been easy. Fire left few traces. 'I think I got it right . . .'

'It's difficult with fire,' she said softly, and all at once he was glad she had been a nurse, learned to accept and live with death. 'I should have left Mother with Tilda – ought to have been there, in the village . . .'

'No. They'd have sent you back. The Air Force and the ARP lot have taken charge.'

'How did they take it, at Denniston?'

'Anna was – shocked. She cried a little, then seemed to pull herself together. It was Tatty who took it badly. She was fond of Father, closer than I realized. She went deathly white, started to shake. I thought she was going to faint. She didn't cry, though. Might have been better if she had. I felt so helpless . . .'

'Poor love. It's rotten, sometimes, being a parson. Would a snifter help?'

'Brandy? Do we have any?'

'A little.' For times such as this, that was. 'I loved Uncle Edward, you know – very much. He didn't have much of a life, come to think of it.' Her words were husky with unshed tears.

Nathan tilted the glass and the brandy sliced through the smoke and dust that clogged his throat.

'Alice came, briefly. Said Tom had been called out – the Home Guard, you know. She seemed to think the Germans shot down two of our bombers.'

'Yes. One crashed on to the village hall. They'd tried to release their bombs, it seems. The bomb-disposal lads found two of them unexploded in the field at the back of the church, but one of them went up. The other Whitley came down on Holdenby Pike. They've found it but they'll have to wait until daylight before they can do anything. I did hear that none of the crew was alive.'

'So much for the party. It's all my fault,' Julia said soberly, lips tight with shock. 'If I hadn't been determined to make a fuss about Mother's birthday . . .' Her voice trailed away into sadness.

'Nobody's fault, Julia. There'd have been a raid, those bombers would have crashed, party or not.'

'Yes, but Uncle Edward and Mrs Shaw and Jin and Reuben wouldn't have been there. Oh my God! Reuben! Do they know, at Keeper's?'

'Tom will know. He'll have told Alice. Leave it till morning, love.'

16

Alice stood numb with grief, gazing around Reuben's kitchen as if, somehow, she could push back time and he would walk in, dog at his heels. But he would never sit in the rocker by the fire again; never chuckle with Daisy at some shared private joke nor say, 'Nah then, lass,' when she took him a home-baked loaf.

Reuben was gone. Dead – that was the word. Three Messerschmitts had screamed in, wing cannons blazing, shooting up the runway at Holdenby Moor. Sitting ducks those bombers had been. One of them, Tom told her last night, had got its wheels up; was already airborne. The other had started takeoff and neither pilot could have known of the danger above them.

Had there been a celebration in that Luftwaffe fighter station when those marauders returned? Had there been drinks all round the mess to toast the wizard prang they'd had over an aerodrome in the north of England?

Neither Reuben nor Mr Edward nor Jin nor Mrs Shaw had been their enemies, though it would seem that now the war was being carried to Britain. The softening-up had started. Cities bombed, villages strafed – all in preparation for the spring tides and the invasion that would come next April.

'Damn you!' She closed her eyes and sent her hatred slicing through the air.

Reuben's labrador whimpered at her side, eyes beseeching, as she laid her hand on the back of the rocking chair; on the brightly knitted antimacassar where once Reuben rested his head. There was a hair on it, very white against the bright red splash of wool and just to see it brought the ache back to her throat.

She wished she could cry, that she was not so numbed by grief. But she was cold with fury, too, and there was no time yet for tears. Daisy must be comforted, and Tom, and there would be a funeral to endure with dignity. She must wish them goodbye. Dear Jin, with her fortune-telling and prophesying – why hadn't she known what was to happen? And Mrs Shaw, who had been kind to that thin, wide-eyed girl who came to Rowangarth from Aunt Bella's cold-comfort house. No one would ever bake cherry scones like Mabel Shaw.

Despair took Alice's heart and squeezed it with hard hands. She wished she had wept as Daisy wept, but tears eluded her. It was, she supposed, because she was empty and cold inside and tears were warm things that came from the heart and not the deeps of hatred.

The dog cried softly again and Alice took the lead from the nail behind the door. The creature would have been afraid last night and Reuben not there to comfort it. It would be hungry, too, and thirsty and pining already for a master who was gone.

She clasped on the lead, then turning in the doorway she whispered, 'Don't worry, Reuben. Tom will take good care of him for you.' She bent to fondle the dog's ears as Reuben had done, then locked the door behind her. 'Come on, old lad.' She took a deep, shuddering breath. 'Let's get you home, to Keeper's.'

And when, dear God, *when* would she weep?

'Mrs Dwerryhouse.' Tatiana was waiting on Keeper's Cottage doorstep, her face white, her eyes wide. 'I've come to –' She stopped, unsure.

'Come here, lovey.' Alice held wide her arms and Tatiana went into them gratefully. 'There, there now.' She laid her cheek against that of the young girl, patting her back, making shushing sounds against the sudden, jerking sobs.

'I'm sorry about Reuben,' Tatiana gasped, blowing her nose, dashing an impatient hand across her eyes. 'I came to tell you.'

'And I'm sorry about your grandpa, too.' Alice's voice was gentle. 'He was a lovely man, and do you know something? I'm sure he was really happy living with you at Denniston. But why don't you come in? Daisy's in need of a bit of comforting.'

'Could I? I'd like to see her anyway.'

'She'll be in her room I shouldn't wonder.' Alice opened the door to a deserted kitchen and a fire almost burned out. 'Go on up. She'll be glad to see you, love.'

Sighing, she filled a drinking bowl, carrying it to the doorstep, laying dog biscuits beside it, and the labrador drank thirstily, took the biscuits hungrily. Then it cried softly, its eyes begging her to take it home.

'Sorry, old lad.' She led it to the dog houses at the end of the yard, pushing it through the gate to the brick kennels in which it would sleep. 'Sorry, but Keeper's is where you belong, now . . .'

'Can I come in?' Tatiana pushed open the bedroom door.

'Oh, it's you.' Daisy turned her head away. 'I'm a mess. I've been crying.'

'So have I. I couldn't stand it at home. Can I stay for a while?'

'You know you can. Have you got through to the aerodrome yet?'

'No. Our phone is still out of order and the phone at the crossroads, too. Daisy – he'll be all right, won't he?'

'Of course he will, clot! They called off the op.'

'But one of them had taken off and another –'

'Yes. Dada said he heard it was a Rhodesian crew that came down in the village. Rotten, wasn't it, them coming all those miles from home to fight for us, then dying like they did. I hate this war, Tatty.'

'And do you think I don't? But what about the other Whitley – the one that crashed on the pike? I want to go up there, Daisy. Will you come with me?'

'Do you think we should?' She dabbed powder on her face but it did nothing to hide the redness of her nose and swollen eyelids. 'I believe they managed to get rid of their bombs – trying to get a bit of height, I suppose – but they didn't make it. Some of Dada's platoon went up there early this morning with the RAF bods, but that's all I know. They wouldn't let us near it, anyway . . .'

'I'm going to try!'

'No, Tatty. We'll keep lifting our phone – see if it's come on again and when it does you can ring Tim from here. The aerodrome will be off, too. Tim's probably wanting to get through to you, had you thought?'

'All right, then. I'll wait a while, till twelve, then I'm going up the pike!' She sat on the edge of the bed, meeting Daisy's eyes in the dressing-table mirror. 'And there's something else. I'm late.'

'What do you mean – *late*?' Daisy turned, eyes wide.

'You know what I mean. The curse. Should have come this morning, and it didn't.'

'Oh, for Pete's sake, girl – it's *still* this morning!'

'I know. But it's always there, regular, when I get out of bed – and it wasn't.'

'So just for once you're two and a half hours late? After what happened last night is there any wonder? You're worried sick about Tim and there's the shock of your grandfather, too.'

'I'm never late.' She set her lips stubbornly.

'Well this month you are! Now stop your worrying, Tatty, or it'll be even later.' She crossed the room to sit on the bed beside her friend, hugging her close. 'Lovey, you don't think – I mean, could you be . . . ?'

'Pregnant? Yes, I suppose I could.'

'Oh Lor'.' Imagine the scandal! A Sutton, getting herself into trouble! And what about Tatty's mam and they mustn't even *think* about the Petrovska! 'Do you suppose you might be? Have you been stupid?'

'Careless? I don't know. What I do know is that when I'm with Tim I want him. You don't say, "Hey! Hang on! You're not going to let anything happen, are you?" You just – well, *want* to, don't you?'

'I suppose so. But try not to worry too much.' All at once, she was afraid for Tatty, her own sorrow pushed behind her. 'Tell you what, I'll splash my face with cold water and then we'll see if they'll let us go up the pike – set your mind at rest about Tim.'

'But what if it's *K-King* when we get there?'

'It *won't* be. You know it won't be! Just give me a minute then we'll go – okay?'

'But won't your mother need you here? You ought to be with her.'

'Like you ought to be with yours? No, I think she wants to be on her own, Tatty. Maybe if we go out she can have a good cry – let it come. She needs to cry.'

'Bless you!' Tatiana began to sob again. 'I wish I had a sister. I wish you were my sister and your mother was my mother.'

'Hey! No more tears.' Daisy offered a handkerchief. 'Dry your eyes for heaven's sake, and then we'll go. And it won't be *K-King*; it *won't* be Tim's plane – okay?'

Oh, *please* it wouldn't. And anyway, why should it be?

'So. Four dead, and all of them dear to me. Why wasn't I told until now?' Helen Sutton whispered, her face ashen.

'Because you were asleep, dearest. It would have been unkind to –'

'You should have called me. Poor Edward. And Mrs Shaw and Reuben and Jinny Dobb. All my friends, Julia. Soon, there'll be no one left.'

She put a hand to her chest. The pain was bad this morning. She really ought to eat something. And she must stop feeling sorry for herself! In Creesby, on cold mortuary slabs, lay four people who would be glad to have her pain.

'Sssh. Try to eat, Mother. Some toast . . . ?'

'Just a piece then, and a little coffee. And where is Nathan? Has he had breakfast, yet?'

'Yes, and gone to Creesby to see about – *things*, though there won't be a lot he can do on a Sunday. And he wants to call on Jin's sister, and Alice.'

'I should have gone, Julia. It's my place to, but I can't face the village yet; can't look at what's happened to it, much less offer sympathy. It's good of Nathan, when his own father has been killed. How can he do it?'

'Because he's Nathan, I suppose; because he's good and kind.'

'Drew will have to be told!' Helen set down her cup with a clatter. 'Will they let him come home, do you think?'

'Maybe. If he isn't at sea, that is. Nathan is going to try to get through whilst he's in Creesby. The phones there are all right. He thought if he could get hold of the naval people at Liverpool, there might be some way of sending a message to Drew.'

'Good . . .' Helen gazed out of the window. The leaves of the lindens were yellowing. Soon they would fall and winter would be here again. Another dark winter with not a light to be seen. She dreaded the long hours of the blackout. In winter, night began at four in the afternoon and lasted for sixteen hours. 'Good,' she murmured again, then shifted her gaze from the window. 'Miss Clitherow! She should be told, too.'

'You're right, and I think I can get in touch with her,

once they've repaired the lines. Her cousin isn't on the phone but I've got a number I can ring if ever – well, if ever she were needed, she said.'

'Then will you do it, Julia? She would want to know.' And she, Helen, wanted her housekeeper to be here if she could manage to make the long journey south. Like Mrs Shaw, Agnes Clitherow had been a part of Rowangarth for so long; part of a life that had once been good and filled with contentment, and she wanted, *needed*, her to come. She pulled in her breath sharply then said, 'You *will* try?'

'Was that your pain again?' Julia demanded, all at once anxious.

'Just a little one, dear. It always goes when I've got something inside me. Now you promise to get through to Oban as soon as you can?'

'Only if you'll see Ewart Pryce when all this is over. Say you will, Mother, or I'll send for him – I mean it!'

'I'll see him. Word of a Sutton. How long do you think the phones will be off?'

'Not long. The postman told Tilda he saw a GPO van in the village this morning. Seems we could be in business again by evening. But I'll get off now, dearest.' She must go to the village, face up to it, do what she could. 'Promise you'll try to eat something, then take some magnesia. The bottle's on the sideboard.'

'I will.' Sighing, Helen picked up her coffee cup. It shocked her to see how much her hand shook.

Approaching Holdenby from Home Farm pasture and looking along the hedgerow to the first cottage garden, to Julia it seemed that nothing had changed. But then she turned the corner and stared with disbelief. It was as if some giant hand had wiped away the village hall in a sudden, vicious sweep, leaving a trail of devastation behind it. Or had some massive machine steam-rollered its way over it, crushing it, leaving a flat, empty swathe littered with burned-black debris.

'Morning, Mrs Sutton. It's a right carry-on, eh?' Holdenby's air-raid warden had been on duty all night. 'A miracle there wasn't more taken. Would have been, if all those bombs had gone up.'

'It doesn't bear thinking about. There'd have been nothing left of the village.' She clenched her hands, stuffing them into the pockets of her coat, trying to control the sudden shaking that had taken her. 'It's awful. Was anyone else hurt?'

'Nay. Shocked, happen, and not a house that hasn't had windows blown in or the roof damaged. Folks are grateful to be alive, I reckon.'

'Have you heard anything from the GPO men?'

'Yes, they aim to have the phones working by nightfall. And I'm right sorry about Mr Edward. Will you pass on our condolences to the Reverend – mine and the wife's?'

'I will, and thank you both. Is it all right if I walk down the street?'

'Aye. Only watch your step. There's been a lot of water about and it's slape underfoot. Morning, Mrs Sutton.'

He adjusted his helmet then walked importantly, hand held high, to halt a car filled with sightseers and send them back whence they came. Didn't know what the world was coming to! Watch a public hanging some folk would, never mind wasting their petrol coupons just to gawp at other folks' misfortunes!

'Line's still dead. I suppose we ought to go to church,' Daisy murmured, replacing the receiver of the phone box at the crossroads. 'Not that they'll have a proper service; just prayers, I think. Mam isn't going. Said she couldn't face people.'

'I said my prayers this morning.' Tatiana had said them in English and then again in Russian, her eyes on the Virgin on the icon above her bed, crossing herself devoutly just to be doubly sure. 'Sometimes I think God doesn't care.'

'Me, too. It's Hitler's lot getting all the favours these days. But never mind about them. We've got to try to make it to the plane and we're never going to get past that lot.' She nodded in the direction of the soldiers and the airmen from Holdenby Moor. They stood on guard, rifles on shoulders. There were trucks there too, one of them with a red cross on its side. Had anyone been found alive then, or did they always send an ambulance?

Tatiana saw it too, and her face drained of colour. 'Look at that thing over there,' she whispered. 'D'you know what the aircrews call ambulances? Meat waggons. How can they joke about it?'

'I know how to get up there.' Daisy shrugged away the question. 'If we cut back along the path then go through the woods round to the other side, we might make it. Well, they're Denniston woods, aren't they? They couldn't stop us.'

'They could. They can do anything they want. The military think they're Almighty God. But it's worth a try.' Deliberately she turned her back on the ambulance, running towards the wood. 'And, Daisy, if – *when* – we get up there, it won't be Tim, will it?'

'No, it won't! It's odds against it won't. And I'll bet you anything you like they'll not be operational tonight either. Not after what's happened. Tim will phone as soon as he can get through, and look, Tatty – over there.' She pointed to three deep craters in line ahead, a few hundred yards apart. 'That's where they jettisoned their bombs. They might have been able to make a belly-landing; might all be fine – just injured, I mean, or why the ambulance?'

'You know why,' Tatiana said dully, then, as if Tim's life depended on it, she reached for Daisy's hand and began to run.

There were no soldiers, no airmen guarding the far side

of Holdenby Pike when they got there. It would be a steeper climb but Daisy had been right, Tatiana thought gratefully. They would make it to the crashed aircraft. It would be terrible to see and she shouldn't feel grateful to find it was some other crew, yet she would be.

Please God, she prayed urgently, if You'll let Tim be all right I'll be grateful to You for the rest of my life and I won't ever moan or act like a brat again. And I'll be polite to Grandmother Petrovska, only let it not be Tim. It can't be Tim, God, when I love him so much.

Breathless, they reached the stricken plane, to find it was heavily guarded.

'Might have known it, but it seems all right, Tatty. Not like the one in the village.' Crouching almost double, they ran for the shelter of a clump of wind-bent trees and bushes. 'Can you see anything?'

'Not from here.' They were looking at the bomber head on, at the cockpit and propellers that almost touched the ground. 'But they did do a belly-landing. Can we get round the side – get a look at the fuselage?' That was where they would find it; the roundel of the Royal Air Force and the squadron markings, one of which would not be *K-King*. 'Come on. Don't let them see us.' Her mouth had gone dry, there was a thudding in her ears. Then the breath left her body. 'Oh, *Daisy . . .*'

They were looking at the rear gun turret, laying a little apart from the wreckage, torn off at impact. Men were working on it, removing a gun that could have been Tim's.

'Daisy! I've got to –' She cried out as a hand grasped her shoulder and she spun round to face an Air Force corporal.

'And what the hell do you think you're doing? Souvenir hunting, are you?'

'No we are not! What do think we are – ghouls?' Tatty flung, eyes defiant. 'And take your hand off me! We only –'

'Look, Corporal, we just want to find out about the

'crew,' Daisy intervened. 'One of them, you see –'

'Well, they were all killed. Gone. They took the last one down not so long ago.' He said it as if he were immune to all feeling. 'Him from in there, the tail-end Charlie.' He nodded in the direction of the gun turret.

'Please – if you'll just tell us.' Daisy reached for Tatiana's hand. 'We need to know.'

'Was the rear-gunner Sergeant Tim Thomson?' Tatty whispered, turning her back on the turret.

It hurt her to say it but she needed to ask. And why should it be Tim? She only wanted to know that it wasn't.

'Don't know. Didn't hear no names,' the corporal muttered uneasily. The dark-haired one had him worried, looked as if she'd pass out any minute and he'd got enough on his plate without fainting women. 'Just shove off, the pair of you. Get hold of the Adjutant at the aerodrome if there's anything you need to know.'

'We would have,' Daisy whispered, 'only the phones – Hey, Tatty!'

'Come back, you!' bellowed the corporal, but Tatty was too quick for him, had reached the bomber before they caught up with her.

For a moment she stood quite still, gazing at the long, thin fuselage. It blurred, then came sharply back into focus. It bore the station markings HM, the RAF roundel and the letter K. *K-King.*

She let go a cry, then crumpled, eyes closed, into a pathetic heap at the corporal's feet.

'Tatty, love – try to make it? Just a little further.' Their feet crunched on the gravel of Denniston House drive, sometimes slipping unsteadily as Daisy supported the softly moaning girl leaning heavily against her. 'Soon home now, Tatty.'

'Don't want to go home.' She didn't want to go any-where, only to the crossroads to wait for Tim, but Tim was dead. Tim's beautiful body, battered and broken. They'd have put it in a coffin by now. They did things quickly, always. Already Tim's bedspace would have been cleared, his locker emptied. Tomorrow night a new gunner would sleep in his bed. It was the way it had to be. His family would know by now and she ought to send her love and thoughts to them, but there was no love in her. Only despair and disbelief and a hard, cold ache where her heart should have been. And hatred. White-hot, vicious hatred for an unknown Messerschmitt pilot.

'Tatiana!' Her mother was running to meet them. 'What is it? Has she been hurt?' she demanded of Daisy. 'Where have you been?'

'We – I'm sorry, Mrs Sutton,' Daisy whispered. 'We went up the pike to –'

'To the crash? How could you? Who knows what awful things you might have seen?'

All at once Tatiana straightened her shoulders, tilted her chin and gazed at her mother with pity.

'How right you are,' she said softly, too softly. 'You never know *what* you might see.'

Without a backward glance she walked to the house, flinging wide the door, clinging to the banister rail as she walked wearily up the stairs.

'Tatiana! What is this?' Countess Petrovska stood in the hall, looking up. 'I was watching you from the window. How dare you come home in this state? And look at me, girl, when I speak to you!'

At the head of the staircase Tatiana paused, then turned slowly to look into the irate face.

'Go to hell, Grandmother,' she said softly, then, with all the venom she could muster, slammed the door of her bedroom behind her.

17

'All over, love,' Julia said softly, settling herself on the floor at her husband's feet. 'Mother is asleep, now. I had a brief word with Doc Pryce at the churchyard. He said he'd call in tomorrow afternoon and have a look at her. How do you feel now?' She reached for the hand that rested on her shoulder, holding it to her cheek.

'Drained. Glad I asked the bishop. Good of him to come. I couldn't have done it . . .'

'No.' People sometimes forgot, Julia frowned, that priests had feelings, too. 'There was great respect this afternoon. All the village there, and more besides. I should have been more help, I know, but I was worried about Mother.'

'She shouldn't have been there, Julia.' It had been cold in church, colder still in the churchyard. They had laid his father next to Elliot in the Sutton plot. His mother insisted, long before she died, that that was the way it should be. Elliot between them; just as he'd always come between them in life. He closed down his thoughts. *Think no ill of the dead.*

There was a small tap on the door, then Agnes Clitherow stood hesitantly on the threshold.

'I'm going to bed now, Mrs Sutton. They were making tea downstairs so I thought I would bring you a pot on my way up.'

'Bless you.' Julia rose to take the tray. 'It's lovely to have you back, Miss Clitherow, sad though it's been. But you'll stay a few more days – make the journey worthwhile?'

'I wouldn't not have come and I'd like to stay for a

while.' The words came eagerly. 'If I wouldn't be in the way, that is.'

'Not you,' Nathan smiled. 'You're part and parcel of Rowangarth. It's as if you've never been away.'

'Yes. Oh, dear.' The housekeeper turned, murmuring, 'Thank you. Most kind. Good night, Mrs Sutton, Reverend . . .'

'There were tears in her eyes, poor old love.' Quietly Julia closed the door. 'Do you think she misses us, darling?'

'Like I said, this family was part of her life for a long time. She's bound to miss it sometimes.'

'But do you think she's happy in Scotland?' Julia persisted.

'I couldn't say. It was her decision to leave, remember.'

'I suppose so. And look – Tilda has baked scones. Probably used the last of her precious cherry hoard, too. Oh, Nathan – hasn't this been a sad day and isn't everyone so kind?'

'Come here, woman.' Gently he patted the tears that brimmed in her eyes with his handkerchief. 'I love you, sweetheart. And thanks for everything.'

'Everything?'

'Well, that cup of tea if ever I'm going to get it!'

'By the way, Vicar dear,' smiling she picked up the pot, 'I'm rather fond of you, too.'

'Well, best be getting off home. Will's going to be wondering where I've got to.' Mary rose reluctantly to her feet. Today had been upsetting and to be sitting here late in Rowangarth kitchen gave her comfort. 'I'm glad you baked cherry scones, Tilda. Mrs Shaw would have wanted you to.'

'Aye. That's what I thought.'

'Will I see to the fire for you, before I go?'

'Leave it, thanks all the same. Think I'll let it go out – give the flues a bit of a clean in the morning. And the coal ration's getting low; no more due till November. The fire is cheery, but I'll have to start using the gas stove a bit more.'

Tilda did not like the gas stove, even though it gave her not one bit of bother; not like the big, black range, with its side hotplate and two ovens and temperamental flues. It was greedy on coal, too, but for all its faults she liked it, had learned to cook on it and knew it in all its moods.

'Good night, Mary love,' she smiled. 'I'll just have a little sit, then I'll be off up. I'm glad this day is over. Take care on the cobbles in the dark.'

She laid back her head and closed her eyes, thinking of the day past. At least there had been a clear sky and a little sun. Laying folk to rest was kinder when the sun shone.

Her ladyship had taken it badly. Never before had she seen her break down. Keeping a hold on her feelings was a part of her nature, her upbringing, yet today she had clung to Miss Julia, eyes closed, as they lowered Mr Edward's coffin, and she had not bent to take a handful of earth when the bishop said the ashes to ashes bit. Real badly, she'd looked. Shouldn't have been there in that cold churchyard, not to stand through four buryings.

It was when they had stood beside Mrs Shaw's coffin that her ladyship turned her face away, holding a handkerchief to her eyes. That was when Miss Julia led her to the church porch, and the poor lady walking all bent and defeated, like; not straight and proud like once she'd been. Poor Lady Helen. Two wars in anybody's lifetime wasn't fair.

She rose to riddle the poker through the coals, pull out the damper to get the benefit of what remained of the fire for the hot water. Sighing, she placed the fireguard in place. Best she get herself off to bed. No point sitting alone, watching the fire go out.

An image of a long-ago kitchen danced through her thoughts. Once there had been Alice, Mary, Bess and Mrs

Shaw to say good night to when she, Tilda, was nobbut a kitchenmaid; aye, and straight-laced Miss Clitherow, too. Yet now she was cook and middle-aged and unwed and the only live-in member of staff.

In the doorway she turned, her eyes on the rocker that once was indisputably Mrs Shaw's; where many a time the elderly cook had pulled her white apron over her face and wept.

'Good night, Mrs Shaw,' Tilda whispered. 'God bless.'

Alice kneeled on the hearth rug in Reuben's kitchen, grateful for the warmth of the fire. Tom wanted to be with her, but she had asked him not to stay. There was coal in a bucket beside the hearth and a basket of logs and kindling, so he had lit a fire for her, then kissed her gently, telling her not to get too upset.

'I'll be fine, Tom.'

'Sure you'll be all right on your own – it's black dark outside.'

'I'll come to no harm in Reuben's house, love. But come about ten and walk me back home.'

So he had kissed her again and told her he would, leaving reluctantly, telling her to bolt the door when he had gone and to think on, and wait until he came.

He'd be remembering the night in Brattocks Wood, she thought, when Elliot Sutton had first tried to harm her. But Elliot Sutton had taken Drew's secret to the grave with him. Drew was safe, now; safe from *him*, that was. She clutched Reuben's tin cash box to her, closing her eyes, whispering, 'Please, God, be good to Reuben and take care of Drew.'

Drew had not come home for the funerals. His ship was at sea and by the time it docked, it would have been too late. And it was as Tom said: they didn't give compassionate leave for great-uncles, only near kin. The fact that it had all happened in Drew's village and that three of the dead were in Drew's care, in a manner of speaking, made little difference to Them, the faceless ones. So maybe it was as well that HMS *Penrose* was out mine hunting, she thought, reaching for the tiny key she knew she would find beneath the vase to the left of the mantelpiece.

All he owned was hers, Reuben had once said, and she had admonished him sternly and told him he would live to be a hundred. But still he insisted on making it legal. Didn't want her Aunt Bella – who was closer kin than Alice, truth known – to turn up on his doorstep like a black crow, and take the lot. Reuben had not cared overmuch for Aunt Bella.

She turned the key in the lock and lifted the lid. On top lay an envelope, addressed in Reuben's thin, shaky writing, to Mrs Alice Dwerryhouse. Beneath it lay his bankbook, his birth certificate and marriage lines and a faded photograph of a young Reuben and a woman she did not recognize. Turning it over she read 'Wedding Day'. Just that. No date.

She held the photograph to the light. Reuben's wife had been bonny, had died after twenty years of childless marriage. He rarely spoke of her, yet she must have been dear to him, or why had he put the photograph in the cash box with his precious things?

He had not sealed the envelope. Gently she laid it to her cheek then took out the folded sheet she knew to be Reuben's Will. It was dated, and began,

This is the only Will and Testament of Reuben Pickering, widower, of 2 Almshouse Cottages, Ings Lane, Holdenby in the County of York.

I wish it to be known that Alice Dwerryhouse née Hawthorn is my dearest if not my nearest and I would like her to see to things when I am gone.

I leave my dog and my guns and my gold pocket watch to Thomas Dwerryhouse.

Oh, dear God! He always wore that watch on special occasions. He'd have been wearing it last Saturday and fire was no respecter of precious things.

All else I own is to go to Alice Dwerryhouse for being a grand lass and she may give a keepsake of me to Jinny Dobb and Percy Catchpole for their neighbour-liness.

Neighbourliness. That was a big word for Reuben, Alice smiled sadly. Had Percy helped him spell it?

My funeral is to be paid for out of my bankbook and I would take it kindly if folk did not send flowers.

That was it. Reuben's Will, signed by him and the names of Jane Dobb, Servant, and Percy Catchpole, Retired head gardener, added to bear witness.

Dear Reuben who was her only blood kin, save for Aunt Bella and she'd rather not think about Aunt Bella. Reuben, who had been friend and father to her, and kept her secret.

Then she read the three lines at the bottom of the sheet and the cold ache inside her was all at once gone. They came, then, the tears she had been unable to shed on his death and at his graveside; warm tears that washed away the pain in her throat and came in great sobs from the deeps of her heart.

To Daisy Julia Dwerryhouse, the granddaughter I never had, twenty pounds to be paid to her from my bankbook on her wedding day if I am not here to see it.

'Oh, Reuben, Reuben . . .' Alice rocked to and fro on her knees, hands covering her face, weeping the hurt from her and the anger and remembering only an elderly gamekeeper who had claimed her for his own.

The sobbing eased, then ceased, but still she knelt there because all at once she knew a great feeling of love and gratitude and it was as if she could hear his voice, feel his arms around her once more and a hand patting her back. *There, there, lass. Don't take on so. I'm not all that far away* . . .

'Reuben?' She rose stiffly to her feet, looking around the room, wanting – *needing* – him to be there. But she heard only the echo of a chuckle and the crackling of the logs in the grate.

Yet now she knew he had not completely left her; that she only had to call to him with her heart and he would hear her.

She closed and locked the cash box, slipping the key into her purse. Then she pushed in the fire damper and placed the guard over the grate. In half an hour, Tom would be here to take her home.

She sat in the chair to wait, eyes closed, head resting on the brightly worked antimacassar, and let the stillness wash away her bitterness.

'Goodbye, Reuben. We shall never forget you . . .'

'Tatiana?' Anna Sutton pushed open the bedroom door. 'Are you awake?'

'Leave me alone, please.'

'I came to check your blackout.'

'No you didn't!' She sat up in bed, reaching for the light pull. 'You've come to give me a telling-off for going up the pike!'

'I think it was foolish of you.' Anna seated herself at the foot of the bed, trying not to notice her daughter's swollen eyelids. 'But what I'd like to know is why didn't you come down for supper?'

'Because I wasn't hungry.' Because she never wanted to

eat again. She wanted to die and not eating was the only way she knew how – without violence, that was.

'Hush, now. Try not to let it upset you; try to forget it.' Anna smoothed back a straying strand of hair from her daughter's face. 'Is it the time of the month, perhaps?'

'No, it isn't!' Oh God, Mother, if only you knew! 'All I want is to be left alone!'

'But why, dear? It's a terrible thing for those young men to have died so dreadfully, but what really happened up the pike to upset you so much?'

'You want to know? You really want me to tell you?'

'If it would help, dear.' She reached for Tatiana's hand, but it was snatched away.

'Help? Mother of God, there's no one can help! And you want to know what I saw? All right, I'll tell you! There were three damned great craters up there. They'd let their bombs go – trying to get a bit of height. But they didn't make it. The tail end was torn off from the fuselage when they crash-landed, but they didn't go on fire like the one in the village. The crew didn't burn!'

'Stop it, child!' Hands on her daughter's shoulders, Anna shook them roughly. 'Pull yourself together! Calm down. You're acting like a – a –'

'Like a peasant, Mother; a serf? Acting like a Petrovska shouldn't act? Well, do you know that someone I loved was killed up there? He was the tail-gunner and his name was Tim. He came from Greenock and they'll have taken him home now to his family. But I can't be with them to say goodbye to him because I'm a Pendenys Sutton and my mother's mother is a jumped-up Russian countess. *That's* why I'm upset!'

'But, darling – you should have told me about him.'

'Why? So you could stop us meeting?'

'No. But as it turns out it wasn't very wise of you, now was it?'

'Not wise to fall in love when there's a war on?' Her

eyes were wide and brown in an ashen face. She wanted to hurt her mother; hurt the whole world.

'Tatiana!' Anna jumped to her feet and began to pace the floor. 'I'm so sorry for the young man – for all of them. And I'm not being unfeeling. It must be terrible to lose someone you love.'

'*Must* be?' She flung aside the bedclothes to face her mother, eyes glinting, chin jutting. '*Must* be, Mother? Don't you know, then? Didn't you feel as I feel when my father was killed? Or didn't you love him? Did you marry him for his money – in return for the son you never gave him! Is that how it was?'

'How dare you!' Anna lifted her hand, catching Tatiana's cheek with a swingeing slap. 'How – *dare* – you!'

'So that's the truth of it?' Tatiana took the force of her mother's anger with hardly a flicker of emotion. 'You didn't love him. Even when he was still alive I think I knew it!'

'Oh, Tatiana.' Anna closed her eyes, shaking her head, anger spent. 'You didn't know. You couldn't have. You were too young . . .' She walked across the room, opening the door, turning to face the distraught girl. 'I'm sorry I hit you. I shouldn't have done it. Tomorrow, when you are feeling a little better, we'll have a talk, you and I.'

'There's nothing to talk about; nothing you or Grandmother would understand, anyway!' She reached for the light switch, plunging the room into darkness. 'Go away, Mother. Leave me alone. *Just leave me alone.*'

Anna closed her eyes, leaning shaking against the closed door, bewildered at the violence of Tatiana's outburst, but fear warned her not to probe further – not tonight.

And how could Tatiana have known about the tension surrounding Nicholas's birth? Someone must have told her; someone who knew.

She ran quickly downstairs and lifted the phone, forgetting for a moment that the lines were down, then surprised when a familiar voice asked, 'Number, please.'

'Miss Hallam – you're back! Can you give me Rowan-garth, please?'

They must talk tomorrow. She must ask, carefully, how much Julia knew about what had happened all those years ago. Anna had unburdened herself to Nathan, not as a brother-in-law but as a priest, and the confessional was sacrosanct. Tomorrow, as soon as possible, she and Julia must meet!

'And how are you feeling, this morning?' Julia sat beside her mother's bed, relieved she looked more rested. 'You got yourself chilled through yesterday. You must stay in bed and not get up until Doc Pryce has been.'

'Julia! It is going to be a lovely day.' Helen nodded towards the window. 'An Indian-summer day, and I shall not waste it in bed. I have made up my mind to go to the kitchen garden. There was a white orchid budding – remember? It should be opening now and I want to go and see it. It will be pleasant to sit in the orchid house. You know how I enjoy it.'

Her mother had latched on to the unseasonally flowering orchid, Julia brooded, as if it were a comfort sent by Pa. So be it. If it would help wipe the last awful week from her mother's mind, then who was Julia Sutton to gainsay her?

'A good idea, dearest. And you are right about it being a nice day. I tapped the glass this morning and the needle shot over to fair. I'll come back and give you a hand when you are ready to get up, then I'll take you to see Catchpole.'

'You will take me nowhere! I am well able to walk to the garden alone. Miss Clitherow brought my tray in and she will give me any help I need. It's so good to see her again. She told me you suggested she stays for a few days and I think she will.'

'Good. Nathan's got an appointment at Carvers. You

realize he's saddled with Pendenys now? Thank God he won't have to worry about it till the Army has done with it. But there's still the estate, and the money, of course, to be seen to,' she shrugged. 'Anyway, Anna is coming this morning. I rather think she wants a talk.'

'Splendid. Then I shall take my stick and make my way entirely under my own steam,' Helen smiled, 'and have a look at your pa's orchid. Off you go, now, and see if there's any post.'

There was no letter from Drew; had there been one, Miss Clitherow would have put it on the breakfast tray. But at least her mother looked better this morning and this afternoon, Ewart Pryce would get to the bottom of that niggling pain. And yesterday – awful, awful yesterday was behind them. From today things could only get better.

As if to mock her optimism, a bomber from Holdenby Moor flew low overhead to remind her they could not. Indeed, things would get a whole lot worse before they got better. Any fool knew that.

Grace Fielding had returned from leave to find the hostel deserted. Some were still at work; others, on their rest day, had gone to York. It was Polly who told her, surprised she had not known. Yet how could she? It had not been reported in the papers nor read on the news bulletins on the wireless. The shooting down of two bombers was enemy action so it was censored by the Ministry of Information. There were a lot of things that lot in London didn't tell folk.

'Dreadful, it was. They were taking off, those bombers, and they didn't stand a chance. Was a wonder all Holdenby didn't go up, Gracie. A terrible mess.'

'I didn't see it, Mrs Purvis. I hitched a lift from York on an army lorry. They dropped me off at the crossroads.'

'Then you're in for a shock. Village hall just gone as if it had never been, and nobody without windows blown in or tiles off. Never thought the war would come to Holdenby.

'There are times I'd give ten years of my life just to see Keth, but when things like that happen, I'm glad he's in America, though he'll get a bit of stick for avoiding the call-up when it's all over and he can get back home. Not that it'll worry me, though it hurt to think of those young lads and their mothers. Mostly from Canada and Rhodesia, they were. Sad, them being all that way from home.'

'I'll go and see Daisy. She'll be upset about Mr Pickering.'

Gracie had been looking forward to seeing the hens again, wondering if any of them had started to lay whilst she was away. Now it didn't seem all that important, especially when Daisy told her about Tim and how terrible it had been for Tatty, finding out about it the way she did. Cruel, that's what.

She shook away her thoughts, stirring the tea leaves in the tiny pot, then set it beside the little iron grate to gather strength; to mash, as people in these parts called it.

'Tea up in one minute.' Gracie opened the door of the greenhouse where Jack Catchpole worked, pulling up the tomato plants, sorting the last of the crop into two piles – red and green. The last few ripe ones he would take to Tilda Tewk; the green ones, now there was little sun to ripen them, would be wrapped in newspaper and placed in the warmth of his fireside cupboard to take pot luck and maybe come red in time for Christmas. Once, there was a demand for green tomatoes for chutney, but no one could get sultanas nor spices these days and if they had sugar to spare for such things, then they were getting it on the black market and deserved to be caught. He straightened his back and looked up, smiling.

'Well, if it isn't her ladyship come to call on us.'

'Oh dear. What will I say to her – about Mr Edward, I mean.'

'Best say nowt, lass. Just go and meet her, friendly like,

and don't proffer any help unless she asks for it. Off you go whilst I wash my hands.'

Smiling, Gracie called, 'Good morning, your ladyship.'

Gracie was learning. When first you met Lady Sutton you gave her respect, acknowledged her station in life. Then after that you called her Lady Helen. It was like if you met the Queen; first you would call her Your Majesty, and then it was Ma'am. And you never knew when you would meet the Queen. She was always popping in at odd times, especially to call on the people in London who had been bombed.

'Oooh, it's lovely to see you. Isn't this a grand day? I bet I know why you're here.'

'Do you now?' Helen was glad of the smiling eyes, the happy face. 'Then tell me?'

'You've come, Lady Helen,' Gracie fell into slow step beside her, 'to see the white orchid that oughtn't to be flowering, but is. And did you know there are three of the flowers out already and ever so many nearly open. There'll be eleven blooms on that one stalk. They're beautiful.'

'They are, Gracie, and special. And I *have* come to see them, so will you be a good girl and bring my little folding chair to the orchid house? And then, if Catchpole can spare you, perhaps he'll allow you to come and sit with me for a while, so I can tell you about them.'

'That would be lovely.' Gracie knew about the white orchids; had the importance of those eight plants explained to her when first she came to Rowangarth. But she was fond of Lady Helen who Mum had said sounded like a *real* lady, and she liked to talk to her, listen to the beautiful voice, wish she could learn to speak like her. 'I'll just pop off. Mr Catchpole's been seeing to the tomatoes and he's just washing the green off his hands. Would you like a drop of tea? It'll run to another cup if I squeeze the pot.'

'No, thank you. Just bring my chair then go and see to

Mr Catchpole's tea – perhaps he would let you bring yours to the orchid house?'

He would, Gracie was sure of it, and ran to bring the little green chair.

Gracie was happy; glad to be back at Rowangarth again – well, as happy as anyone had the right to be after what had happened in the village. Smiling, she sped off in search of the chair.

'We won't be disturbed?' Anna was clearly agitated.

'I'm sure not. Nathan is with the solicitors in Creesby and Mother has taken herself off to the garden to sit in the orchid house. She's looking better, this morning. We're out of coffee, but can run to a cup of tea. Sit by the fire and I'll bring a pot.'

'No, thank you.' Anna Sutton made it a rule not to take other people's rations in any shape or form. 'And this is – well, delicate. I know I shouldn't ask it, but when the baby was stillborn, Nathan was very kind to me, you see. He baptized the little soul, then laid him with the Suttons. It gave me a lot of comfort.'

'Yes?' Julia prompted softly, sitting in the armchair opposite.

'I was almost out of my mind. Things happened. Elliot was upset – no, *angry* – about the baby being stillborn. He threatened to divorce me. It was important to him to have a son, you see – but you would know that?'

'I did.'

'But what I came for is to ask how much you know about it? Were you told?'

'Told about what, Anna? How can I answer a question like that? Look – something is bothering you and I can't help you till I know what it is.'

'All right, then.' She took a shuddering gulp of air. 'At the time I told – well – *certain things* to Nathan. How much did he tell you, Julia?'

'I don't know. Did you talk to him as a brother-in-law or as a priest?'

'I blamed myself for the baby's death. In the absence of an Orthodox priest, I asked Nathan to hear my confession.'

'In that case he would have told me nothing. Things like that aren't talked about to anyone in our Church. But something is clearly wrong, Anna. I'm not prying, but if it would help to talk to me, then I think you'll find I'm a good listener in spite of my bossy ways. Anything you say will be between you and me. Not even Nathan will know, if that is what you want.'

'I do want it and yes, I'll tell you, and ask your advice, too.' Anna relaxed visibly, taking off her hat, shaking free her hair. 'It happened last night. Tatiana was distraught. She said things to me that I'd rather not have heard. But it all started nearly fourteen years ago when the baby was born dead, so I suppose I'd better start there.'

And so Anna told her, her lips sometimes rigid with distaste; sometimes her cheeks red with the shame of things remembered. Bitterness flowed from her lips in an ice-cold torrent until finally she whispered, 'Well, that's just about it. All the dirty washing in the open and somehow I feel Tatiana knows about it.'

'No, Anna, you *think* she knows. Maybe from way back, little things flit in and out of her mind. She's unhappy and in shock. What she said last night probably came from that unhappiness. You mustn't blame yourself that the babe was stillborn. So you flew at Elliot like a wild cat when you found out about Natasha Yurovska, but so would I have done.'

'Maybe so, but I'd already miscarried two children and my rage killed my son. I went into early labour next day. But it was awful to hear them together in that bedroom. It was as if I were listening outside the door of a brothel. Elliot would sneer about her, you know – call her the servant in black – but for all that, he had to have her.

'So perhaps Tatiana *did* hear servants' gossip. The night I caught Elliot sneaking out of Natasha's room, I screamed obscenities at him. They'd have heard the row going on, below stairs. I wouldn't be surprised if they'd heard it in Holdenby, too.'

'Elliot got what he asked for. I disliked him always.'

'Why, Julia?'

'Oh – you know.' She felt her cheeks redden, realizing she had almost gone too far. 'He was a brat of a child. Spoiled rotten. It was he who sent Giles three white feathers. People did that in the last war; three white feathers, the badge of cowardice. Giles wasn't a coward; he just refused to kill. He went to the war, but as a stretcher-bearer. Yet Elliot never went near the fighting, though he liked people to think he was in France. And so he was, but at a desk in Paris, did you know, Anna? He was never near the trenches. Aunt Clemmy must have had friends in high places. It's surprising what money can do.'

'So you believe me, Julia? And you can understand why I wasn't grief-stricken when Elliot died?'

'I'd believe anything you told me of that one. Sometimes I marvel how unalike brothers can be. There were others, Anna. One of them was a Creesby girl – a butcher's daughter. There were ugly rumours about that little affair until Aunt Clemmy stepped in. Natasha wasn't the only one.'

'I realize that. But there's more.' Anna jumped to her feet to stand staring rigidly out of the window. 'What I haven't told you is that Elliot not only slept with Natasha – he got her pregnant, too. It could only have been him, she told me, and I believed her.'

'The bastard!' Julia hissed.

'I believe I too called him that – and a few choice words in Russian no lady should know! Elliot's mother was never told about Natasha's baby. Only my mother knew, and Nathan, of course. Mother took Natasha back to London with her, said she would look after her. And after all, she was our responsibility.'

'And what happened?'

'I don't know. I wouldn't have been told, even if I'd asked. Natasha left Cheyne Walk, and afterwards the baby was adopted.'

'So somewhere,' Julia whispered, 'Tatiana has a half-brother – or -sister!' *Another* half-brother or -sister . . .

'Yes. And just a few months younger than Nicholas, had he lived. And now Tatiana is almost out of her mind because of one of the airmen who was killed. Did you know about him, Julia?'

'I knew she went dancing with an airman,' Julia said warily. 'I believe Drew and Daisy and our land girl were there when first they met. I didn't know how serious it was, though.'

'So you knew – and Drew and Daisy and Gracie. Seems everyone knew but me.'

'Sometimes, Anna, mothers are the last to hear things.'

'That's true. Mothers and wives. What a mess it all is. There was such wickedness in Elliot. Do you think it is coming out in Tatiana?'

'For heaven's sake why? Just because she had a boyfriend she didn't tell you about? Just because she rounded on you last night in a rage? But mightn't the things she said have come from grief? Perhaps she truly loved him – or thought she did. He was probably her first love. First love can be very precious, you know.'

'So I must go home and make it up with Tatiana. And I'll pray to the Virgin every night on my knees, Julia, that none of Elliot's badness is in his daughter.'

'It won't be, love.' There was none of his evil in Drew, could she but tell her. 'Don't worry. Just be kind to Tatty. She's a sweet girl, and right now she's in desperate need of your love.'

'You are a good soul, Julia. You should have had children of your own.'

'I should. Andrew and I planned at least four, but it wasn't to be. And Drew was born to comfort me and now I've got Nathan. I'd like to have given him a child but I'm too old.'

'I'm sorry.' Anna reached for Julia, folding her in her arms, laying her cheek close. 'Thank you for listening to me, and please believe me when I say how sorry I am that I thought even for one moment that Nathan might have betrayed a confidence. I think perhaps what Tatiana said to me last night was only to hurt, that she couldn't have known how very near the truth it was. I'll go, now. I feel like walking. There won't be many more good days like this. Bless you, Julia, and give my love to Aunt Helen and Nathan. Y'know, there are times – even in spite of Elliot – that I'm glad to be a Sutton. 'Bye, my dear.'

18

'There now – that's Mr Catchpole's tea seen to.' Gracie settled herself at Helen's feet, hands round knees. 'I know I shouldn't ask, but will you tell me about the white orchid – why it's so special?'

'Shouldn't ask? If only you knew how we old ones love to talk about when we were young! Where would you like me to start?'

'When you and Sir John first met, please. Was it romantic?'

'I suppose it was.' Helen glanced at the orchid and it seemed to smile encouragement. 'I was seventeen – a debutante. Do you know, we were taken straight out of the schoolroom, told to put up our hair, then pitchforked into life – with a capital L,' Helen smiled. 'In my day, a girl was often married and a mother long before she came of age. But where was I? Ah, yes. My first ball. I was chaperoned by my grandmother Lady Stormont – such a dragon. We girls used to hope our chaperons would drink rather too much wine at supper and nod off so we could flirt a little.'

'And did you?' Gracie giggled.

'Goodness, no! There was this man, you see; he put paid to any ideas I might have had about flirting! So tall and fair, and when he came over to ask for my dance card, the first thing I noticed were his eyes, big and grey – or were they green? I can remember not being sure. However, he presented himself to Grandmother, then took my card and –'

'Sorry – but what is a dance card?'

'Things of the past now, Gracie, but in those days – and Queen Victoria was still on the throne, remember – young ladies always carried a dance card. Each dance was listed on it and a young man would write his name or initials beside one of them, reserving it, sort of.

'We all worried in case no men wrote in a dance – so shaming it would have been – but this young man put his name beside three of mine, would you believe? The next dance, the supper dance and the last waltz. No more than three dances were allowed on first acquaintance, you see – not considered proper. I was ready to faint with delight, I was so in love!'

'But you hardly knew him! How long – two minutes?' Daisy teased.

'Two minutes was long enough. He was the man for me! It happened just the same to Julia with Andrew. I think it must run in the family. I wouldn't be at all surprised it if doesn't happen to Drew, too. He'll see her, and that will be it!' She clicked her fingers. 'In love for life!'

Dreamily she touched the wax-white orchid, a smile tilting the corners of her mouth.

Gracie coughed politely. 'The ball, Lady Helen . . .'

'Ah, yes. The ball. Well, this young man offered his arm for our first dance. It was a Viennese waltz. I was dressed in blue that night. We hardly spoke and I was glad because I was so besotted I don't think I was capable of speech.'

'So do you know when you've fallen in love,' Gracie frowned, 'or does it kind of grow on you?'

'Sometimes you know at once; sometimes it just grows on you – that's what is so nice about falling in love. It can hit you *bang*! or it can steal up on you unawares.'

'And you wore blue that night, and white orchids?'

'No. Blue, and white roses. The orchids came later. In those days a bridegroom provided his bride's flowers. It arrived on my wedding morning – a bouquet of white orchids, with a sprig of white heather tucked in it. When we returned to Rowangarth from our honeymoon, a plant of white orchids had already been delivered to the head gardener. They were to be grown especially for me and worn by no one but me, John said – but Julia carried them to her wedding.'

'But how did you manage to meet if you were always chaperoned?'

'Oh, those things could be arranged,' Helen smiled, tapping her nose with a forefinger. 'I remember the conversation after John returned me to my grandmother after that first dance. She read his name on my dance card then said, "John Sutton, eh? Anything to do with the Rowangarth Suttons?" and I said yes, I thought he was. "Hmm," she said, "I believe his father is Gilbert Sutton."' Helen mimicked the stern tones of her grandmother. '"Married a Whitecliffe, if I'm not mistaken – the eldest son, I think." My grandmother had sorted through John's pedigree in less than a minute. Thank heaven he was acceptable. I don't know what we'd have done had he not been. Run away together, I suppose, and shamed both families!' Helen laughed with delight. 'But away you go, Gracie, or Catchpole will come looking for you. We'll talk again – and thank you for listening to an old lady's ramblings.'

'Not ramblings. Rememberings. And when the war is over and I fall in love, I hope my young man will be tall and fair and have grey – or maybe green – eyes.' She placed a hand lovingly over Helen's. The old lady's was frail and white, with veins that showed blue through the transparent skin and it caused silly little tears to prick Gracie's eyes. 'Thank you for telling me, Lady Helen. You'll be all right?'

'I'll be fine. It is so nice and warm in here. I shall have a little chat now to John's orchid. Goodbye, my dear.'

Smiling, she watched the land girl go, shifting her position, wishing she had brought a cushion. She would like to sit here all day. Pity she had ever agreed to see the young doctor. Today, she felt so much better.

'John, dear.' She reached out to the stem of orchids, touching a flower with gentle fingertips. 'You'll know about what happened; so sad, but Edward will be with you now.' Helen believed implicitly in the hereafter. Had she not done so, the years after her husband's death would have been unbearable. John was waiting for her, so she did not fear to die. Once, there were times when she had longed to, until Fate stepped in – and always with comfort.

Andrew MacMalcolm, for instance. Julia's first love. His eyes were so like John's; looked directly into hers when he spoke to her just as John had done. Dear Andrew. And then Alice had given them Drew: Sutton fair, and again with John's eyes. Drew became her *raison d'être*. No more grieving when there was a young Sutton to be reared.

Only now They had taken Drew and sometimes she was so tired, especially when the pain came. Perhaps it was as well Dr Pryce was calling. There were so many clever things, these days, for pain.

'John?' She touched the flower again. 'Drew is at sea, but you'll know that, too. Julia says he will come home safely, but you'll watch over him for all that, won't you?'

Yet why, she frowned, had this particular orchid bloomed now? What was John trying to tell her? Once old Catchpole forced a plant into flower in time for Julia's wedding in November. He had grumbled about it and said it wasn't natural, but, secretly triumphant, he was able to produce three sprays for a wartime bride.

Yet young Catchpole had been surprised to find the fat bud a month ago. Interesting, he said, but sometimes nature would play a trick like that just to confound them.

'Interesting, but why *now*, John? Did you make the orchid flower because you already knew about the bomber and that Edward would die and Mrs Shaw and Jin and Reuben and that I would be so very sad? Is the orchid to comfort me?'

She shifted uneasily again on the chair. Her bones were

getting too frail for sitting on wooden seats. And that annoying indigestion was back again and bad this time, really bad.

She rose to her feet, hand pressing her side. It was getting worse! Awful! *Awful!* 'Aaaagh!' The breath left her body and she lunged forward. The green chair skittered then fell over with a clatter.

From the door of the potting shed, Jack Catchpole heard the noise. Frowning, he made his way to the orchid house.

'Lady Helen . . . ?'

He saw the upended chair and her ladyship face-down, a hand flung wide to rest beside the orchid in the terracotta pot.

'Gracie!' he yelled. *'Gracie!'*

She heard the urgency in his voice, the outrage, the disbelief. Fear took her and she ran.

'What is it?'

Jack Catchpole stood at the door of the orchid house, eyes wide. 'What has her done?' he whispered.

'Oh, dear God!' She pushed past him, flinging aside the chair. 'Your ladyship!' She dropped to her knees. 'Oh please, Lady Helen . . . ?'

She reached for the hand, lifting it gently. A single orchid flower fell to the floor as she searched for a pulse. Frowning, she tried again, then slowly rose to her feet, pulling her tongue round lips gone suddenly dry.

'Mr Catchpole – I think she's – she's real poorly.'

'Nay!' He took a step nearer. 'Let's have a look at her.'

'No! Don't touch her. Don't move her!'

'I'll go and fetch Miss Julia!' He was shaking all over. 'Miss Julia'll know what to do!'

'Stay with her. I'll go.' She could run the faster. 'And *don't* move her!'

She ran swiftly, flinging open the gate, flying across the wild garden.

God, please, don't let Mrs Sutton be out. Let someone be there.

'Mrs Sutton!' She and the doctor were walking across the lawn. They were smiling. They hadn't heard Gracie. She stopped running and took in a gulp of air to steady her heaving lungs. 'Mrs Sutton!' she cried. 'Come quick! In the orchid house! It's Lady Helen . . . !'

Julia began to run, followed by the doctor. 'Gracie – what is it?'

'It's Lady Helen! Fallen on the floor. Mr Catchpole's with her. I told him not to move her.'

'Quite right!' Ewart Pryce flung, following Julia who ran with panic at her heels.

Gracie watched them go, still gasping for breath, marvelling that just when they needed him, Dr Pryce had been there.

Slowly she retraced her steps, reluctant to return. She didn't want to be there when they told Mrs Sutton her mother was dead.

Daisy shook the crumbs from the greaseproof paper in which her sandwiches had been wrapped, then folded it carefully into four. Paper was a material of war now, and precious. Shops no longer used paper bags. You took your own much-used, very crumpled bags to the grocer's or the butcher's shop, and almost always Mam slipped a plate into her shopping bag when she went to Creesby, just in case she came across a fish queue. Fish was still unrationed; fish queues could stretch almost fifty yards, and fishmongers had no bags either. Most things were wrapped in old newspapers, now; even fish and chips.

Daisy slipped the folded paper into her jacket pocket and pulled out Keth's letter. Today was special. Today the sun shone far more brightly than it ought to in October and there had been a letter from America this morning. Usually, she had to wait until evening before glancing up at the mantelpiece but today the postman was early, had handed her the pale blue air-mail envelope just as the bus rounded the corner.

She read Keth's letter three times on the journey to work; now she would read it once more, try yet again to discover what might be written between the lines. Because you had to write between lines or the hawk-eyed, suspicious-minded censor would take his razor blade to any offending word or sentence and a letter could end up looking like a paper doily.

Keth, she sighed, would soon know about the two bombers, if the censor allowed it. It had been a sad letter to write and Keth would be sad to read it. Would it make him want to come home more than ever, she frowned, because he was in Washington and safe, whilst old people were being killed at Holdenby? Reuben, Mam said, had been ninety-five, though you'd never have known it.

But she must try to write more cheerful letters. She supposed she would if there was anything cheerful to write about. She always wrote that she loved him, though, and missed and wanted him. And she almost always told him to stay where he was, though he wouldn't like it, she knew, when her call-up papers came and she was in uniform.

When those papers came, of course. The invasion would have been and gone before the Navy sent for her. You would have thought, she reasoned, that since we were in such a mess, backs to the wall and all that, that They would be only too glad of a bit more help.

'JOIN THE WRNS AND FREE A MAN FOR THE FLEET' urged the poster on the bus-station wall. Rather a nice poster with a Wren on it looking slim and smart in her uniform and a proper services-issue respirator on her left shoulder.

But she supposed they didn't have men shorthand-typists in the Navy, so Daisy Dwerryhouse's contribution wasn't going to free anyone.

Did she really want to go, yet did she want to spend one day more than she had to in that shop? Being a typist-dogsbody at Morris and Page wasn't doing much to help the war effort. Selling cashmere twinsets and bespoke shoes and expensive make-up – when such things were available for sale, of course – to people who had more money than patriotism sometimes made her want to puke. She opened Keth's letter.

My dearest girl,
I love you, love you, love you . . .

Her cheeks pinked. She loved him, too; wanted him so much that she could blush for shame at her wanton thoughts. Sometimes she wished they had never been lovers because what you'd never had you never missed, people said.

Could his work in Washington be important or secret? The United States wasn't at war, even though an entire squadron of Americans had arrived in England, already trained as pilots and eager to wear the uniform of the Royal Air Force. And so pleased was the Government that they had given them those uniforms, with American shoulder-flashes on them and given them fighters to fly and called them the Eagle Squadron.

Those young Eagles had somehow made it across the Atlantic and maybe Keth was even now trying to do the same. Was he, the stupid love, so intent upon getting back home that he, too, was making plans? Did he intend crossing over into Canada and volunteering for the Canadian Forces? Canada was a part of the Commonwealth; had joined in our war from the very first day. Yet it would be useless to tell him not to do anything foolish. If there was a way to get home, Keth would find it.

Daisy's eyes scanned the page, searching again for those between-the-line sentences.

I love you so much, my darling, want you more than you know. Just keep wanting me and thinking about me and we may be together sooner than you think.

Was he trying to make her believe, then, that the war would soon be over, or would he try again to find a merchant ship in need of spare crew? Why was he such an idiot and why did she have to love him so much?

Sighing, she got to her feet, unwilling to return to the counting house at Morris and Page. But let one, *just one*, customer complain about her account today and the snooty madam would get the full force of the Dwerryhouse temper!

Keth, where are you? She sent her thoughts winging high and wide. *And oh, my darling, why do I want you so much I could die of it?*

'Ewart, do they *have* to take her away?'

They stood on the front steps, watching the ambulance disappear round the sweep of the drive.

'I'm afraid so.' His arm rested on Julia's shoulder and he could feel the trembling that shook her. 'Your mother hasn't seen a doctor since Richard James' time. There'll have to be a post-mortem.'

'But I don't want them to – to touch her. They didn't do post-mortems when the bomber crashed.'

'That was because the cause of death was certain. Enemy action. With Lady Helen,' Ewart Pryce said gently, 'I'm as certain as I can be they'll find she had a massive coronary. Now, how about a cup of tea – or something stronger, if you've got it? I'll stay with you until Nathan gets back.'

'He won't be long. Miss Clitherow phoned the solicitors and asked them to tell him. Thank goodness she hasn't gone back to Scotland yet. She's taking it badly, though she wouldn't for the world show it.'

'And you, Julia – no tears?'

'No tears. Not yet. I suppose I'm holding them back till Nathan gets home. All I can feel now is anger, with myself; angry because she died alone and I can't get it out of my mind. Did she call for me, and I wasn't there . . . ?'

'No, she did not. If what I think happened, there would just be one pain, then – nothing. She wouldn't know it was the end. It would be blessedly quick.'

'Mother looked peaceful, didn't she, Ewart?' Desperately Julia sought comfort.

'She did. It would be gentle for her.'

'Yet lonely, for all that. But I think a cup of tea is a good idea. We still get tea sent from Shillong. We were lucky. It got through this year. But come inside; it's cold out here.'

She hugged her cardigan around her and he knew it was not the mild October afternoon that chilled her. He would be glad when Nathan got back. Julia needed to weep.

There was no smell of cooking when Daisy opened the door of Keeper's Cottage, no pans bubbling on the stove.

'Daisy, love . . .' Tom rose to his feet, his face pale, his eyes serious and sad.

'Dada – what is it?' Fear took her. 'Where's Mam?'

'Gone to be with your Aunt Julia. There's something I've got to tell you.'

'Not Drew, Dada?' Oh please, not Drew?

'Drew's fine, though he'll be coming home I shouldn't wonder. His gran, you see. Lady Helen died this morning about eleven. A heart attack, they're almost sure.'

'*Dada!*'

She went into his arms and he stroked her hair and said, 'Hush now, lovey,' just as he'd always done when sobs took her and shook her.

'Those damned Germans!'

'No, Daisy. Wasn't anything like that. She just passed on quiet, like, in the garden. Jack Catchpole found her.

She'd been talking right as rain to Gracie not ten minutes before. She went kindly, lass. Don't fret overmuch.'

'But I *am* fretting. And it *was* their fault. What happened when the bombers were shot down was a terrible shock to her. Didn't you see her at the funerals? Bloody, *bloody* Hitler!'

'Now then – try to pull yourself together for Mam's sake, eh? Her and Lady Helen were always close. Be brave for Mam? Her ladyship would want you to be.'

'Yes.' She took a shuddering breath, sniffed loudly, then pulled a hand across her eyes. 'Better see to something to eat for us. Will cheese sandwiches do?'

'Reckon not. Mam's clean out of cheese till she collects the rations. But come and see what I've got in the pantry.' He pointed to six eggs, round and brown and newly laid.

'Dada! You didn't get them on the black market?'

'Course I didn't. Been clearing the rabbits for Home Farm. Getting to be a nuisance, they were, so those were a kind of thank you. How about having poached eggs for tea?'

Her mother would enjoy that, Daisy thought. Mam said that rationed eggs from the grocer weren't fresh at all. Reckoned they were all of three weeks old when you got them; had to break them into a cup first, and sniff them before you used them. And it wasn't any use trying to think about eggs because Lady Helen was dead and not all the fresh eggs in the world would bring her back.

'I'm going to miss her. She was such a love. I can't even try to imagine Rowangarth and her not there. And as for Drew . . .' Tears, more gentle now, came again.

'We'll all miss her, and that's a fact. She was a lady. They don't make them like her any more.'

Daisy dabbed at her eyes again. 'Best set the table and put the plates to warm. Mam'll be home soon, I shouldn't wonder.'

Mam was going to need a lot of fussing over – and love.

* * *

They used the little winter parlour at Rowangarth all the time now. It was less trouble to keep clean and easier to keep warm in winter now that coal was in short supply. Julia sat at Nathan's feet, arms clasped round her knees, staring into the fire.

'You know, darling, it seems that ever since I can remember, life has been stealing from me. Pa, my brothers, Andrew and Uncle Edward. And now Mother. And what really hurts, what is more awful than that even, is that I never said goodbye to any of them. Oh, I accept that Mother has gone, yet wherever I look, everything I touch she has seen and touched.' Like the way she always trailed her left hand up the banister rail as she walked upstairs; the way she held her head, when thinking; the big bow window where she liked to stand and look down the length of the linden walk, a small smile lifting the corners of her mouth. Julia turned to him, eyes beseeching. 'Don't ever leave me, Nathan? Be there for me always? I couldn't bear it if they took you away from me, too.'

'Listen to me, woman.' He took her face gently in his hands, so she had to look up into his eyes. 'I waited half a lifetime for you and I'm not going anywhere.'

He dropped a teasing kiss on the tip of her nose. He wanted to kiss her mouth, her closed eyelids, the little hollow at her neck. She had a beautiful neck. Everything about her was beautiful. He wanted to turn the key in the door, switch off the lamp, make love to her here and now in the fireglow.

But this was not the time for passion. He knew her so well that he too felt the pain that coursed through her. Tonight she needed to talk some of that pain out of her and, please God, to weep. 'Anyway, how could I leave you? Who in her right mind would want a middle-aged parson?'

'I'm going to let it all come soon.' She reached for his hand, laying it to her cheek. 'I'm going to weep and scream and slam doors and be a thorough bitch!'

'No, my darling, you are not. She wouldn't have wanted you to do that. But when you need me, I'll be there.'

They turned as the door opened slowly, quietly.

'It's the land girl – says her name is Grace Fielding,' Miss Clitherow said, 'and can you spare her just one minute? If you can't, she'll understand, she says.'

'Of course I'll see her.' Julia rose to her feet, glancing at her husband as she did so to see his nod of approval.

Gracie was the last person to see her mother alive and Julia needed to talk to her, ask her how it had been and how her mother had seemed.

'Come in, Gracie,' she said warmly.

'I'm sorry, Mrs Sutton.' Nervously she cleared her throat. 'I only work here and I know I shouldn't intrude on family grief, but –'

'Sit down, Gracie.' Rising to his feet, Nathan indicated a chair. 'It's kind of you to come; we're both glad you did.'

'Yes – well – I thought that perhaps there might be something you wanted to ask me and I came, too, to say how sorry I am. She was a lovely lady. I could have sat in that orchid house all day, just listening to the way she spoke.'

'You had a talk, Gracie? She seemed all right?'

'She was fine.' Gracie sat on her hands, balancing on the edge of the chair. 'She asked me to bring her little green chair from the potting shed, then I took my tea in and sat with her. We had a lovely chat. I wanted her to tell me about the white orchid and why it was so special, but she said she'd start from the beginning – from where she and Sir John met.'

'She told you about the ball?'

'Oooh, yes. Blue, she wore, and white roses in her hair. And she told me about her dance card and about Lady Stormont chaperoning her. We had a bit of a giggle. She said all the young ladies used to hope their chaperons would drink a drop too much wine at supper and – oh, dear.' She stopped, blushing bright red. 'I shouldn't have said that, should I, and you so sad, Mrs Sutton.'

'Of course I'm sad but of course you must tell me, Gracie – everything you talked about. Mother didn't seem in pain at all?'

'Bless you, no. Like I said, I could have sat there all day with her but she said Mr Catchpole would be wanting me and that we could have another chat soon.

'We'd got to the part where Sir John said that only she was to wear the white orchids – because of her wedding bouquet, you see – then she thanked me for listening to an old lady's ramblings and I said they weren't ramblings. I really was looking forward to the next bit. It was better than a love story. Then I asked her if she was all right – before I left her, that was.'

'And up until then she *was* all right?'

'Seemed so. She said she'd be fine. "It's so nice and warm here," she said. "I shall have a little chat now to John's orchid." Then she said goodbye to me.'

'Did you hear that, Nathan? She was happy right up until the end. A chat to Pa's orchid, would you believe?'

'Yes, I *would* believe it. I think that one plant flowered when it shouldn't have especially for her, and I think it was beautiful that she died beside it, Julia.'

'And I was worrying.' Tears trembled on Julia's words and she swallowed hard on them and forced her lips into a smile. 'Worrying because I thought Mother died alone, and perhaps calling out for us. Bless you for coming, Gracie. You've helped me a lot.'

'But that isn't all. I won't keep you a minute.' Gracie reached into her pocket, carefully bringing out a handkerchief. 'When everyone had – well, when there was no one in the orchid house – I went back there. I wanted to take her little chair back and to say a proper goodbye to her. Then I remembered. When Mr Catchpole called me, I found Lady Helen – well – just like she was when you and the doctor got there. It was as if, when she'd fallen, she'd reached out. One hand was touching the orchid pot and when I took it to feel her pulse, something fell out of it. It didn't mean anything at the time, but then I thought about it and all of a sudden I knew it was important. It was why I went back, I suppose.' She opened the handkerchief carefully to show the single orchid bloom. 'I thought you would want to have it.'

'She'd been holding it?' Eagerly Julia took the white flower, cupping it in her hands, lifting it to her cheek. 'And I was worried that she'd been alone – but she wasn't! Pa was with her. Pa did it, to let us know . . .'

The tears came then. They fell into her hands and on to the little white flower; tears of relief and love – healing tears.

'Oh dear. I'm sorry, Reverend. I shouldn't have done that. I shouldn't have said –' Gracie backed to the door.

'But Gracie, you should have. And you said *exactly* the right things,' Nathan smiled, gathering Julia to him. 'How right, I don't think you'll ever know. Mrs Sutton will be fine, now. Good night, my dear. Bless you.'

Then, tilting Julia's chin he whispered softly, 'And now, my doubting Thomasina, are you ready to believe, just a little, in that heaven I'm always going on about? And might you, one day, accept that perhaps after all, little miracles do happen?'

'Like little white orchids, you mean?' she whispered tremulously. 'Y'know, I thought I was going to stay awake all night, worrying about where they'd taken her, not wanting her to be alone in some cold, strange place. But now it's all right because the part of her that matters is with Pa. And will you hold me tightly, my darling, and let me weep all over you, and have you got a handkerchief, please?'

'I have, as it happens. I always carry a spare in my left pocket. Conscientious parsons always do. And Julia,' he said softly, tenderly, 'I love you so much. Don't ever leave me, either?'

'I won't,' she sobbed on to his clean, carefully starched white shirt. 'Never, I promise . . .'

Much later, Julia stared into the dying fire, determined that when the last flame flickered and was gone she would force herself to her feet and go to bed. But for all her resolve, it was a softly spoken 'Miss Julia?' that put an end to her aloneness.

'Miss Clitherow – come in, do. I was just debating the merits of going to bed or sitting here all night thinking.'

'Has Mr Nathan –'

'Gone to bed, poor love. He's whacked. I suppose I should go too, but –'

'Then I won't keep you. It's nothing that won't wait, really.'

'No – please come in and close the door. If I go to bed I shall only toss and turn and wake Nathan. I'm afraid the fire is almost out.'

'Then in that case . . .' Agnes Clitherow sank slowly to her knees, searching in the log basket for small pieces of wood, laying them on the embers, blowing them softly. 'There now, that's got it going.' She placed logs on the blaze then, hand on the chair arm, pulled herself upright, straightened her back and lifted her chin. 'If you are sure?'

'I'm sure. Truth known I'm glad you came. I think Mother must have sent you because I was just going to have another weep. And do sit down. Would you like a glass of sherry? Mother always enjoyed a glass before bedtime.'

'So she did. It helped her to sleep. Then tonight I think that perhaps we might.'

'Having said that, I don't know how we're fixed. Think there was a little left last time I saw the bottle.'

'If you'll permit me, the last time *I* saw it was yesterday evening. I gave one to Lady Helen. There is a little left. It's in the cupboard. Shall I pour for us?'

'Please.'

Carefully Agnes Clitherow filled the glasses; as she had always done, she placed them on a small silver tray then carried them to the hearth.

'To my mother.' Solemnly Julia lifted her glass.

'To her ladyship; to my dear Lady Helen.' The elderly voice faltered, then she straightened her shoulders, extended a little finger and sipped genteelly.

'There now – there's something you want to tell me?' Julia hoped there was. Some small, seemingly insignificant happening perhaps, from which she might find comfort.

'To ask, really. And maybe this isn't quite the time.'

'If it concerns Mother then it is, Miss Clitherow. Did you perhaps want to ask for a keepsake to take back with you?'

'No! Oh no, I wouldn't presume!'

'Well, I know she has left you one in her Will; something you particularly like. So tell me?'

'It's really something Lady Helen and I talked about – when I was about to leave Rowangarth to live in Scotland with Margaret. I felt so sad I almost relented, asked to be allowed to stay and wait until one of the almshouses came vacant. And her ladyship must have read my thoughts because she told me that if ever I found I was missing Rowangarth too much, then I was to let her know at once and I would be more than welcome to return. What she really meant, though she would never have dreamed of saying it, was that if Margaret and I couldn't get on together I was to come back. I was on the point of deciding against leaving when a bomber flew over, very low, to remind me.'

'One from Holdenby Moor, you mean? But what did it remind you of, Miss Clitherow?'

'It reminded me –' she took another sip then said in a rush, 'reminded me that I'd always felt that one of those bombers would crash somewhere hereabouts. I spoke of it – in an unguarded moment, you'll understand – to Jinny Dobb and she agreed with me. "Mark my words, Miss Clitherow," she said. "One day, one of them – er – *those* things is going to do a mischief around these parts."'

'So Jin knew,' Julia said softly. 'Pity she didn't know where.'

'She was a fatalist, Miss Julia. Perhaps she did know, and accepted it.'

'So you were well out of it in Oban.'

'Yes. I deserted Rowangarth where I'd hoped to end my days. I could have been in the village hall at that time, though I very much doubt it. All I know is that I should not have left. The country around Margaret's house is so beautiful and never a bomber flying over, but here is where I belong, and I'm asking –'

'You want to come back? But the bombers . . . ?'

'I have taken all that into consideration and decided that if you'll have me, my first duty is to Rowangarth. Being safe isn't everything. And besides,' she fidgeted with the stem of her glass, 'Cousin Margaret can be a little, well – bossy. Oh, she is good-hearted, but in my position as housekeeper to the gentry, Miss Julia, it was I who gave the orders. Does that sound presumptuous?'

'No it doesn't,' Julia smiled, 'but it sounds very much like Miss Clitherow.'

She set down her glass on the low table between them. Then she removed that of the elderly woman, placing it beside her own.

'Miss Clitherow; dear, straight-laced, lovely Miss Clitherow.' She took the old hands in her own. 'Would you like your old rooms back, or would you like an almshouse of your own? Sadly, you now have the choice of all three.'

'I may come back? Then in that case, might I have my old rooms back? Her ladyship managed the stairs and so will I. And I wouldn't expect my position back. I have my old-age pension and a little money saved. I can work for my keep – polishing the silver, perhaps, and the furniture. And another ration book will help . . .'

'Ssssh.' Julia lifted a forefinger, then passed back the sherry glass. 'I have felt so sad. Not for Mother – she's with Pa now, and I *will* learn to accept it. But I was sad for myself, because lately so many people who have been a part of my life seem to be slipping away from me.' Smiling softly, she lifted her glass. 'Thank you for coming back to us, Miss Clitherow. Welcome home.'

'Oh my word, Miss Julia.' It was all she was capable of saying and she turned her head away, groping for her handkerchief.

It was the first time in her entire life that Julia had seen Miss Clitherow weep.

Alice awakened with an ache in the pit of her stomach. The day, the awful day, had come. At two o'clock, in the church dedicated to souls departed, they would pray for the soul of Helen Mary Sutton, then bid her goodbye. Alice turned on her pillow to see Tom, carrying two cups of tea.

'Been in to look at Daisy. Still asleep, so I didn't wake her.'

'Best not. She was tossing and turning half the night.' And weeping, too. 'Leave her be. Stay with me for a while, Tom?'

'Bad is it, bonny lass?' Tom took the cup he had filled for Daisy then sat beside his wife.

'Worse than bad. Lady Helen meant a lot to me.'

'Aye. She was both mistress and mother-in-law to you, and I know how you cared for her.'

'I loved her very much. She made me one of the family. Imagine the upset if Mrs Clementina had been presented with a sewing-maid for a daughter-in-law.'

'Then thank God she wasn't! And it's only right that you should be with the Suttons today. Julia and the Reverend want it and I reckon you should do it.'

'But I was family for only a year. I'm the keeper's wife now.' Gently she laid a hand on his.

'You're Sir Andrew's mother. He wants you there, an' all. And you are Julia's closest friend. You've always been there for each other in times of need. She'll want you beside her this afternoon.'

'She'll have Nathan. He isn't taking the service.'

'She'll still want you, and our Daisy, too. Daisy's blood kin to Drew. You two must be with the family today, Alice.'

The family. The Kentucky Suttons not able to come. Only Nathan and Julia and young Drew – and Mrs Anna and Tatiana. Precious few of them left now. Only right that Alice and Daisy should ride in the funeral cars, an' all.

'I suppose there'll be no getting out of it, Tom, no matter what the village might think.'

'The village knows you are Drew's mother, for heaven's sake. There's no one going to think Alice Dwerryhouse is trying to get above herself. It's Lady Helen they'll be bothering about.'

'You're right. You usually are. And, Tom, take Reuben's back-door key and look in the top drawer of his chest for his black tie. That one of yours is dropping to bits. It isn't fit to be seen. Reuben would want you to wear his for Lady Helen. Off you go now. It's nigh on eight o'clock and Julia's expecting me at Rowangarth. They're bringing her ladyship home this morning.' She threw back the bedclothes, feeling with her toes for her slippers. 'And mind you lock his door behind you!' she called after him.

Life must go on, people said, but oh, she would be glad when this day was over.

*　　*　　*

It was accepted around Holdenby that there were few who could hold a candle to Jack Catchpole when it came to the making of wreaths and floral tributes. As a gardener, time-served in the traditional manner, it was part and parcel of his calling, yet he had reason to be glad when Miss Julia had not asked that the stem of white orchids be included in the family wreath. A pity to cut it, she had said; that while it flowered there they could keep her mother for just a little while longer. It was known that a stem of orchids remained in bloom for a month, but her ladyship's last orchid would stay fresh longer than that, or he wasn't the best head gardener in the North Riding!

'What is it, lass?' He turned as Gracie hesitated in the doorway. 'And shut that door, or we won't have a plant left!' The Government considered it unpatriotic to use coal to heat greenhouses now.

'I'm a bit bothered, Mr Catchpole. Are you sure I should be with you this afternoon? I'm only the land girl.'

'You'm Rowangarth's land girl, so that makes you staff. You'll walk with the rest of staff, like proper. You've got the right and it's your duty, Gracie Fielding. Bear in mind you were the last soul to speak to her ladyship.'

'Yes. But won't Holdenby folk think I'm being a bit pushy?'

'Bugger what the village thinks!'

The matter was closed.

'Can I come in?' Tatiana pushed open the bedroom door.

'Hecky! You gave me a fright, creeping about like that!'

'Sorry, Daisy. There was no one downstairs.'

'Well, there wouldn't be. Dada's doing the rounds with the dogs and Mam's at Rowangarth.'

'I've been up for ages. Couldn't stand it at home,' Tatiana whispered.

'I'm usually up early, too, but I don't think I got to sleep till three. Suppose Mam left me, since I'm not going to work today. And sorry I snapped. It's just that I can't think of anything else but this afternoon. How are you?'

'If you mean am I pregnant, then I'm not. It came, this morning. If you're asking how much I hurt inside – well . . .'

'Come here and have a hug.' Daisy held wide her arms. 'It's just a week, isn't it, since –'

'Yes, and it seems like it's all my life.' Tatiana stepped back. She didn't want to be hugged.

'Try to take it one day at a time, love.' Daisy shrugged into her dressing gown, padding across the room to where her friend stood at the window, staring out, seeing nothing. 'And at least be glad you aren't going to have a baby.'

'I suppose I should be, but honestly, I didn't care, though it'll save a lot of trouble. Imagine the talk in Holdenby?'

'Talk is cheap. Come downstairs and we'll have a cup of tea.' Daisy didn't usually offer tea, but today tea rationing was the least of their worries. 'Dad is walking with staff, but Mam and me are to join the Suttons, did you know?'

'Yes, and I'm glad. Will you stay by me, Daisy? If things get bad, can I grab your hand, so I can hang on? Grandmother Petrovska will be there and she doesn't allow tears in public. But it's going to be awful. I'll be thinking about Tim, you see, as well as Aunt Helen.'

'I know you will and we'll stay together,' Daisy said softly. 'Now, let's get the kettle on. Want a piece of toast? There isn't any butter, but we'll run to jam.'

'No thanks. Just a drink. I had something before I came out.' She hadn't. Toast and jam, potatoes, porridge, rabbit stew – they all tasted like cardboard in her mouth. 'A drink would be fine.'

'When did you last eat?' Daisy demanded.

'Lord knows. Yesterday, I think.'

'I thought you said you'd had something this morning.'

'Did I? Oh, do give over. You sound just like my mother!'

'Right! That's it! Put the kettle on and I'll make us some

toast. And you'll eat some! You'll eat it, Tatty, if I have to hold your nose and make you!'

'If you say so.' More cardboard. 'If I do, can I stay here with you for a while – until Mother gets back from Aunt Julia's, I mean? Karl's gone to Creesby and there's only Grandmother at Denniston.'

'Stay as long as you like, love.'

'Thanks.' She pulled out a chair, then sat at the kitchen table, chin on hands. 'Y'know, Daisy, I was going to tell Grandfather Sutton about Tim at Aunt Helen's party. I wish I'd been with him the night it happened. I wish I was dead, too . . .'

19

On the twelfth day of October, in the early morning, Helen
Sutton came home to Rowangarth for the last time. They
laid her coffin on the narrow refectory table in the hall
with candles flickering at her head and feet. From the greenhouses, Jack Catchpole had selected the very best of his
potted chrysanthemum blooms.

'She loved flowers, Gracie.' He had shaken his head
sadly. 'Make sure those plantpots are clean and then us'll
take them to the house, ready for when she comes home.'
And more the pity it wasn't summer. They could have
surrounded her with sweet-smelling roses and orange blossom and lilacs, because chrysanthemums weren't really her.
Lady Helen was a summer-day person and chrysanths, he
brooded, were overformal and not in keeping. But they
were all he could muster in October, save Michaelmas
daisies; especially with a war on and it not considered
proper to grow flowers at all.

'We'll take these pots in the barrow up to the house,
Gracie. I'll push, you walk alongside to steady them.' Chrysanthemum blooms with heads big as mops were all very well
provided you were after a prize at the Autumn Flower Show,
but they were so top-heavy that they snapped off at the least
provocation, he warned. 'I reckon there's eight pots that's
fit to be seen.' Nothing but the very best for her ladyship.
'And then you can fill the stone jugs with Michaelmas
daisies. Reckon they'll look well standing in the hearth.'

And so her flowers were waiting for her, that autumn
morning.

* * *

'She looks very beautiful in the candlelight,' Drew whispered to Julia.

The hall was dark, save for the candles and a beam of light that slanted down from the window on the half-landing. Rooms were always darkened in times of bereavement; curtains drawn across front windows and not pulled back until after the funeral. It was an inconvenience to be endured, a mark of respect to the dead and a warning to callers not to intrude upon family grief.

'You don't have to whisper,' Julia said.

'I suppose not. But it's as if she's asleep and not – not –' He didn't want to say the word.

'She's at peace. She's with Pa, you know.'

'Do you believe that, Mother?' He was not so sure. He wanted to believe in God and in heaven. When there was a war on you had to believe in someone. There had to be a place where the buck stopped; some higher authority of which he could ask, 'Let me see this day through' – or this night or this duty-watch. 'And if my name is on the next torpedo, don't let me know it's running. Let it be quick.' Already he had seen sailors dying in a sea of blazing oil. 'Do you believe there's a heaven, Mother, though I suppose that's an awful thing to ask a vicar's wife.'

'Once, Drew, I didn't.' She took his hand, holding it tightly because really they shouldn't be saying such things beside the open coffin of one whose faith had never wavered. 'When Andrew was killed, I hated God for letting me think he'd come through that war. And I hated the world because there were people in it who were happy – actually happy. And I saw such sights when I was nursing that I screamed inside me at a God who could let such terrible things happen. For a time I turned my back on Him.

'But over all the years I'm beginning to think, to hope, that there is someone and somewhere. Just little things make me wonder.' Like the small, precious white flower

Gracie had brought when she was in such desperate need of comfort. 'Catchpole has done Mother proud, hasn't he? He and Will Stubbs are going to take all these flowers to the church later; just before the –'

'Before the service, Mother,' Drew finished gently.

'Yes. Y'know, Drew, I'd like it if we said our goodbyes to her here, not in the churchyard; our own personal ones, I mean.'

'Yes. And I think those close would want to see her. Death can be so awful, Mother, but Gran looks so beautiful that I want everyone to feel she's truly at peace. I know Tilda wants to, and Catchpole, and on my way home last night I saw Ellen at Home Farm and she would like to, she told me. Would you mind? Just us, and staff, I mean.'

'I think it would be lovely. And she would want it, you know – to say goodbye to them, too, because she's here, Drew; she's really here in this house. That's why I won't weep and make a fuss this afternoon, because I know she won't ever leave us. Some part of her will always be at Rowangarth to look after it. If I weep, you see, it will be for myself and my own loss when I know I should be glad she's with Pa again. She loved him so much – just as I loved Andrew.'

'But you love Uncle Nathan, don't you?'

'Yes, I do. I love him very much, but differently, Drew. One day you'll understand. Mother wanted you to marry and be as happy as she was. You *do* want to get married?'

'Of course I do, but there hasn't been anyone, yet.' He looked down and smiled as if he wanted his grandmother to hear him. 'But I shall know when I meet her – just as you knew, and Grandmother knew. It'll be a typical hook, line and sinker job, I shouldn't wonder.' He bent to touch the sleeping face with gentle fingertips; touch her because he loved her and because he wanted to be sure she knew that one day, if his name, rank and number weren't on a torpedo or a shell, he would have sons for Rowangarth. 'I think we should leave her for a little while. Mary is bringing up tea soon, and I'll tell her that anyone who would like to can say goodbye to Gran, shall I?'

'Yes, please.' Julia gazed tenderly down at the much-loved face. 'I'm only now beginning to realize how very lucky I've been to have kept her for so long, Drew. Alice never even knew her mother . . .'

It's me, milady, come to pay respects and bid you goodbye.

Jack Catchpole gazed at the dancing candle flames that cast a pale golden glow on the stark whiteness of the massed chrysanthemums and hoped she liked the flowers.

There won't be another Catchpole at Rowangarth, milady. He had neither son nor nephew to follow him. A pity, when you thought about it.

But I'll see to your garden as long as I'm able and to your flowers. Her special flowers, that was. *I'll make sure they're always taken care of, never fear.*

He didn't know what else she should know. He was a gardener and not one for fancy thoughts, so he tipped his forelock as he had never done since he was a garden apprentice at Pendenys Place, then shook out his carefully folded handkerchief, blowing his nose loudly because it was very cold here in this lofty hall.

And I'll see these flowers is arranged all nice for you in the church this afternoon. God bless you, milady . . .

Grace Fielding, dressed in her best breeches and jacket, stood beside Jack Catchpole, not at all sure she should be here. It wasn't that she was afraid to look on death. She had seen her grandmother; been relieved to find her looking so nice – as if she hadn't been one bit bothered about dying.

Just as her ladyship looked now. Contented, like. Having a little gentle nap, dreaming perhaps of a girl of seventeen in a blue ball gown and who wore white roses in her hair.

Goodbye, lovely Lady Helen. I knew you for so short a time but I'll remember you always.

Ellen, who was parlourmaid in Sir John's time and taught Mary Strong – beg her pardon, *Stubbs* – all she knew about parlourmaiding, smiled gently as she touched the gleaming oak of the coffin.

Once, she was proud to be a part of Rowangarth; now, she was the mother of two and soon to be a grandmother, the mistress of Home Farm kitchen and in marriage still a part of Rowangarth in a roundabout way.

Her ladyship looked so beautiful. Eighty, didn't folk say? Nay, never! But then Lady Helen had always done everything beautifully; even the way she died.

'Goodbye, milady,' she said softly. 'God love you.'

And because she was Ellen who remembered the way it had been when there were ten house staff and as many outdoors, she bobbed a final curtsy to the mistress of Rowangarth.

Then she walked away, head high.

Tilda and Mary stood beside Lady Helen, holding hands, weeping softly and unashamedly, filled with so overpowering a sense of love and loss that they could only whisper, 'Goodbye, milady.'

They had cried so many tears since it happened that it were best they leave quickly before they really broke down and acted in a manner not becoming to Rowangarth's cook and parlourmaid, and got a stare from Miss Clitherow, for it.

In the doorway Tilda turned, hesitated, then walked away. She ought to have told her ladyship she had baked cherry scones for Drew's homecoming, but thought better of it and followed Mary disconsolately down the kitchen staircase.

There was plenty to be done to keep their thoughts

occupied, thanks be, though the usual high tea that followed a Yorkshire funeral could not take place because of food being rationed. Folk who called at Rowangarth after the burial would expect nothing more than a cup of tea.

Miss Clitherow had suggested they use the best china, of course. Giving orders already and her not back in the housekeeper's sitting room for more'n five minutes.

'I'll be glad, Mary,' she muttered, 'when this day is over!'

Will Stubbs, wearing his grey wedding suit and a carefully knotted black silk tie, wondered where on earth his wife had got to. Said she'd be here to pay her last respects with him, but she was nowhere to be seen.

He took a step towards the long narrow table and the woman who lay there. Refined, she was. Always the lady. Never once had he heard her raise her voice.

The years slipped from him and he remembered the day – in the last war it was and not so long after Miss Julia's wedding to the doctor – when the Army had come with a veterinary in tow and taken Rowangarth's carriage horses without so much as a by-your-leave. Needed for the Front, they'd said, and the Government would pay compensation later.

He hadn't been best pleased and had said so in no uncertain terms and Miss Julia had gone off like a firecracker and ordered them off the premises. Yet Lady Helen achieved more with one glance of disapproval as the army rider rode those horses away. Breeding, that's what. It took years of it to glance as disapproving as her ladyship could and not lose dignity.

He stood, cap folded in his hands, looking down, saying not a word. Then he walked away unsteadily in search of Mary, knowing she would be in need of comforting. And it would give him the time he needed to pull himself together, for men could not weep, even at a time like this.

* * *

Agnes Clitherow, who had flitted in and out of the great hall for most of the morning, came to stand at Helen Sutton's right hand.

'How peaceful you look,' she whispered.

She had thought when all had been and gone that she and her ladyship could have time together and alone, thinking of times past, good and bad. Yet now the moment to part had come, she knew she did not have the courage and that all her memories would be spent this afternoon in the church. She would fill her heart and her mind with them, shutting out the words of the service.

This she must do or she would break down and weep and she had learned well from Lady Helen and did not weep in public. This afternoon she would stare at the crucifix picked out in glass on the east window and would think her thoughts and smile a little in her heart to remember the happy times; of Sir John bringing home his beautiful young bride – only nineteen, she had been; and of the birth of two sons and a daughter, and being there to watch them grow up.

This afternoon she would fill her heart with happiness. The sad times she would remember in the privacy of her room when there would be no witness to her tears.

Lady Sutton had never held with curtsying yet she, Agnes Clitherow, had always given her her due and bent her knee to her each night before climbing the stairs to her bed. Now, she did it again, deeply and with dignity and for the last time.

'Good night, dear Lady Helen. Sleep well,' she whispered.

Tom Dwerryhouse had put on his best tweed keeping suit and his brown leggings and boots because that was what a keeper wore on such occasions. He was ready dressed for the funeral by eleven o'clock, though he wished that this afternoon he could be miles away.

He had good reason to be grateful to her ladyship for she had known about him, and though the war had taken her sons and Dr Andrew, too, yet still she did not condemn him for walking away from that war, for being a deserter. And afterwards, when Sir Giles died, she sent Alice to him with her blessing.

Thank you, milady, for everything you have done for me, and for mine. I'll always be there for young Drew, be sure of that, should he ever need me.

A hand, cold and slight, slipped into his and he turned to smile at Alice. She was dressed in black and her hair done up tightly so she could wear her funeral hat with dignity.

'Hullo, lass. Is Daisy all right?'

'She's with Tatty in the winter parlour. I'll see they don't get too upset this afternoon.'

'And how are you, Alice?'

'I'm fine, Tom, and Julia too. Said goodbye to her ladyship, have you?'

'Aye. And you?'

'No. Not really, though I've been popping in and out all morning. She looks so contented, doesn't she – as if she were relieved, sort of, to go. It's like Julia said; if we make a fuss at the church, then it'll only be for ourselves and not for her.' She was glad Drew managed to get home, though he'd have to be away first thing in the morning. Lucky they'd got a few days in dock – getting something done to their gun barrels, he said. 'And I'm trying to be brave, Tom, for her sake, yet all I want is for you to hold me – tight . . .'

'Come here.' He laid an arm across her shoulders and his nearness gave her the courage she had been seeking all morning.

'Goodbye, dearest.' She bent to kiss the forehead of the woman who, for so short a time, had been her mother-in-law. 'Thank you for being such a lovely lady.' Then she turned to her husband. 'I really came to find Miss Clitherow, but I'm glad I found you instead. The undertaker has come, you see, and Jack and Will are waiting outside to take the plants to the church. I'd best go, Tom.'

'Aye.' He took her face in his hands, kissing her mouth gently, tenderly. 'Chin up, Alice. No tears, mind, at the church. Remember that once you were a Sutton, an' all.'

'Yes, but a long time ago.' She smiled gently into his eyes, her heart filled with gratitude for his understanding. 'Do you know how much I love you, Tom Dwerryhouse?' she asked softly. 'Do you?'

The little breeze had plucked the yellowing linden leaves then dropped them like tears as Helen Sutton left Rowangarth. Now that breeze took the fat white cloud that hid the sun and puffed it away.

At the graveside, Julia stood with Drew, looking down at the coffin and the sprinkling of rich Holdenby earth a young sailor had thrown gently upon it glad that this, their last goodbye, was touched with sunlight.

At a distance, hidden behind the clump of yew trees that stood at the crossing of the churchyard paths, the grave digger waited. Nathan, Alice, Anna and all the others had left.

'Come home now, Mother?' Drew took Julia's arm.

'No. Give us a minute alone? I won't be long.'

'Only if you're sure you won't get upset.'

He didn't want to leave her. She had been so brave, so calm through it all that surely, soon, she must give way to tears.

'I'll be fine. There's just something I want her to have.'

'I'll wait at the gates, then.' He took a last, lingering look, then turned abruptly, jamming his cap on his head as he walked away.

'Mother – I want to say thank you,' Julia whispered. 'Thanks for oh, *everything*, but especially for leaving me this.' She reached into the pocket of her coat then, slipping to her knees, she let the flower fall gently from her fingers. It came to rest on the coffin plate inscribed,

Helen Mary Sutton
10.8.1860–9.10.1940

'I thought you'd want it back – Pa's orchid, I mean.' The flower was still fresh, still creamy white and perfect. It seemed small and fragile lying there, but it was where it belonged. 'I love you very much. Goodbye, dearest.'

Smiling softly, she rose to her feet, then she lifted her chin and set off at a brisk walk, pausing beside the yew trees to nod to the grave digger and whisper, 'Thank you. I'll be back before dark to arrange the flowers.' Then she walked to the gates, where Drew waited.

'You weren't long.' Anxiously his eyes sought hers.

'I said I wouldn't be. Now suppose you escort your mother home – there'll be people waiting at Rowangarth.'

And Drew smiled, saluted smartly, then offered her his arm.

'I love you, Mother,' he smiled.

'Do you know, that's what I've just said to mine. And don't worry about her, Drew. She's with Pa again. She's happy.'

20

'Remember the two soldiers I ran into in Pendenys woods a while back?' Tom leaned his Home Guard rifle in a corner of the kitchen and unfastened his battledress top. 'I met one of 'em tonight in the village. Name of Johnny, as I recall.'

'So?' Alice set the teapot to warm in the hearth. 'And did you find out what's going on at Pendenys, then?'

'No, but the lad looked real pleased with himself. He's going back to civvy street for at least six months, he told me. Seems a lot of joiners and roofers and bricklayers are being released from the military to help repair bomb damage. The lad was a bricklayer before he was called into the militia.'

'Was he, now? Well, if you ask me, he's safer guarding Pendenys than working in London.'

'But he isn't going to London. Tomorrow afternoon, he said, he'll be walking down Lime Street and –'

'Lime Street?' Alice's eyes narrowed. 'That's Liverpool!'

'Aye. There's been a lot of bombing there. More'n two hundred raids, he told me. Liverpool is where he comes from.'

'But it's never been in the papers or on the news that there'd been that many. Mind, the Government can't keep it quiet about what's happening to London, but how much is really being kept from us, Tom?'

'Quite a bit, I shouldn't wonder. Stands to reason, doesn't it? Hitler's lot can tune in to our news broadcasts like we can tune in to theirs. Government's got to be careful what it gives out. Johnny managed to get through on the phone last week and his dad told him Jerry had had a go at Liverpool docks the night before. Four ships sunk and one of them a navy ship. That wasn't in the papers either, now was it?'

'Tom! Shut up! Haven't you thought that Drew is based in Liverpool?'

'*Hell!*' Why hadn't he thought on? 'Well yes, love – but Liverpool's a big place,' he hastened, 'and there's miles and miles of docks.'

'Been there, have you, Tom Dwerryhouse? Seen them?'

Her mouth was set tight; her watch-what-you-say mouth. Round, like a red button.

'I'm sorry, bonny lass. Just didn't think. Well –' he hesitated at the staircase door, 'reckon I'll nip upstairs and get out of this daft uniform . . .'

Frowning, he hung the khaki trousers and the battledress top with two stripes on each sleeve on a hanger.

Bloody fool, him. Drew meant a lot to Alice but he hadn't been thinking of HMS *Penrose* when he'd gone on about Liverpool dockland. His thoughts had been nearer home; had been for Daisy, safe asleep in her bed.

Soon the Wrens could send for her and she would be drafted to where there were sailors and ships. Ports. And the Luftwaffe was knocking hell out of our ports and the Government trying to hide it.

Trouble was that Alice hadn't yet tumbled to the fact that Daisy might be sent into danger. Alice, stubborn as a pot mule when the mood was on her, hadn't even allowed herself to accept that maybe soon an OHMS envelope would arrive at Keeper's Cottage or if she had, he frowned, she was doing a good job of keeping it to herself.

'It doesn't seem like November, does it, Tatty?' They were standing in the queue at the picture house in Creesby. 'Strange, there being no Guy Fawkes' Night.' Bonfires after dark were against the law and no fireworks could be made, even if they had been allowed, because makers of fireworks were turning out things more deadly now than Catherine wheels and Roman candles. 'Mind, Mam never made a fuss about it. She only let me have sparklers when I was little because that was when Dr MacMalcolm was killed, you see. November the – oh God, Tatty, I'm sorry!'

'It's okay.'

'No, it isn't!' Daisy reached for her friend's hand. 'I'm stupid. I don't think before I open my mouth.'

'The world doesn't stop spinning just because of what happened to Tim. Did you know that he died not fifty yards from where we used to make love – those bushes at the top of the pike?'

'Stop it!' Daisy hissed. 'I said I was sorry. Don't go on, *please*. It's as if you're trying to torture yourself on purpose.'

'You're right. I am. It's my Russian soul. It wants to be miserable. I thought, you see, that if I made myself think about Tim all the time and cried a lot and raged inside about it that I'd get the hurt out of me. But it isn't like that. It's worse than ever. Every time I hear a bomber fly over, it's hell. Still – what about Coventry, last night?' Abruptly the subject was changed. 'They couldn't keep a raid like that quiet.' It had been given out on the morning news bulletin.

'I know – just terrible. That beautiful city and the cathedral, built all those hundreds of years ago, just wiped out. Senseless, but that's the Hun in them. And all those people killed – how many?'

'Over a thousand, They said. I'm surprised They told us so soon after, though something like that can't be kept quiet – just as They can't keep it quiet about London.'

The queue began to move. The first showing was over, the picture house was emptying. Soon they would sit in the cushioned warmth, gazing at another world in glorious Technicolored make-believe. *The Wizard of Oz* would help them forget their war for a little while and there might even be saccharin-sweet ice cream on sale during the interval – if they were lucky.

All through gloomy December the bombing of London raged with unbelievable savagery. A bomb damaged the high altar at St Paul's; water was so scarce that often there was none to drink, let alone to put out fires.

Londoners continued to sleep in the Underground. They reserved their spaces early and then, when the last train had passed through, lay on the platforms to sleep, hoping they would awaken next morning. Safest of all places was the Tube, yet rumours persisted that some strange new German bomb had penetrated an Underground station, killing many. By unspoken consent, though, no one delved too deeply into the incident and the Ministry of Information offered nothing. There was bad news enough, decided the new breed of troglodytes, without looking for more.

But for all that, what the Ministry of Information did release was the grave news that more than six thousand civilians had been killed in air raids and eight thousand injured. That was what They said. Double that figure, said the man in the street, and you'd be nearer the mark.

Yet for all London's anguish, nightingales still sang in Berkeley Square. Strange but true, said those stoic Londoners. They heard them every night. And if the nightingales could put up with the bombing, then so could they!

That second Christmas of the war, the Ministry of Food announced that extra tea and sugar was to be given for one week during the festive season, and ration books marked accordingly by the grocer.

On the dark side, Britain was told that no more bananas were to be imported. Bananas took up too much cargo space and were not essential to the war effort, yet what incensed housewives was the news, sneaked in briefly in only one bulletin and scantily mentioned in the newspapers, that from February the ration of lard, butter and margarine was to be cut by half.

And a merry Christmas to one and all!

There was no watchnight service at All Souls'. Churches with their high, wide windows were near-impossible to black out and in the dark months, Evensong was held at three in the afternoon because of it.

Yet Jack Catchpole let in the New Year of 1941 at Rowangarth, bearing salt and bread and coal as he had done these many years past. And this year it was Julia who handed him a carefully hoarded tot of whisky and received his good wishes on behalf of one and all.

Then Miss Clitherow handed round sherry as she had always done – as if she had never been away, really – though the glasses were only half filled. And they raised a toast to those they loved who were no longer with them, and to Drew and to all men and women who were away fighting.

Nathan saw the sudden tears that filled his wife's eyes and walked to her side, pulling her close.

'May God keep our dear ones safe,' he said softly, 'and His love be with them *all* . . .'

'I still think,' said Daisy, when the National Anthem had been played at the end of the film, 'that Mrs Danvers was an all-time bitch.'

The film of *Rebecca* had proved so popular that the Odeon retained it for a further week and Tatiana and Daisy had watched it a second time.

'Then Mrs de Winter should've stood up to her, showed her who was mistress of Manderley. I would have. They're in for a nasty shock at Denniston, you know. I didn't tell you where I've been today, did I?'

'No, but you're going to.'

'Then I'm not! Not until I've told them at home – that I know, that is.'

'Know *what*, for heaven's sake?'

'What they told me this morning, at Carvers.'

'The solicitors?'

'Yes. Oh, Mother knows about it – seems she always has done – but it's going to be a bit of an eye-opener when she and Grandmother find out that I know, too. Especially for the Petrovska! I'm going to enjoy seeing her face when I tell them. But there's one thing I *will* tell you now.' She nodded in the direction of the poster pinned to the wall of the dimly lit foyer. It showed the head and shoulders of a smart, very beautiful young girl in army uniform and beneath her the words, 'Join the ATS.'

'Tatty, you can't! You aren't twenty-one yet!'

'If you can sign your father's name then I can sign my mother's. I'm sick of being at home. What I'll do when your call-up papers come, I don't know. That's why I'm going to York on Monday. I'm going to join up!'

'You've decided on the ATS, then?' Sighing, Daisy buttoned up her coat, wound her muffler round her neck, then stepped into the dark street, blinking her eyes to help them focus on shapes.

'I don't know yet. But I want out of Holdenby, so whichever is the quickest way, I'll take.'

'You know you're acting like an idiot?' She linked Tatty's arm. It was the safest way to walk in the blackout.

'Aren't we both? Now hurry up, do, or we won't get a seat on the train.'

The once-a-week Saturday-night train ran from Harrogate to Holdenby. It was always full of servicemen and women, sitting close, kissing, whispering, knowing they could not be easily recognized in the light of the blue twenty-five-watt bulb that faintly illuminated the compartment. And at Holdenby station, Karl would be waiting with his bicycle to ride home with them. Much as she cared for Karl it would be bliss, Tatiana yearned, to do something, go somewhere without first being closely questioned by grown-ups and sometimes even followed closely by Karl. It was one of the reasons she was going to York on Monday.

Tatiana shifted her position, then sat on her hands. The bench was very uncomfortable and she had waited over an hour just to be seen. Now at last, it would be her turn next – unless the woman behind the desk decided to take her tea break which, rumour had it, could last half an hour in the case of civil servants.

She thought about breakfast and mutinous anger surged right through her, ending in her toes so she had to tap them impatiently.

'York, darling?' her mother said when she had told them. 'But why go all the way to York for a trim when Dorothy in Creesby cuts your hair so nicely?'

'It doesn't need cutting, if you want my opinion,' said Countess Petrovska. 'A young lady should wear her hair long and put it up only for formal occasions.'

'There are no formal occasions now, Grandmother,' Tatiana reasoned. 'No one wears ball gowns any longer.' And nobody wanted her opinion!

'Then more is the pity! Ah, in the St Petersburg of my day, girls going to their first ball looked like sweet young angels.'

'Well, most of the sweet young angels in the North Riding are busy helping with the war and if you'll remember, St Petersburg – Petrograd – has been called Leningrad for the past twenty years!'

'Don't be impudent, miss! You are not too grown up to be spanked!'

'Mother. Grandmother. I am going to York on the 9.15 train tomorrow,' she sighed. 'I shall have my hair cut and maybe have a shampoo and set if they can fit me in. Then

I shall go to the British Restaurant and have some lunch and maybe, afterwards, I shall window shop.'

'The British Restaurant! A soup kitchen! But you are being provocative to annoy me!' Olga Petrovska shook with anger.

'No. I am taking a trip out. It is you, Grandmother, who is being provocative. And British Restaurants are *not* soup kitchens. They are clean cafés, run by the Government, where I can get a decent meal off the ration for one and sixpence! And if my eating with the rabble upsets you, then I'm sorry.'

She had walked from the room calmly and slowly, closing the door quietly, whilst all the time the anger inside her made her want to storm out, slam the door so it rocked on its hinges, then yell, 'Just wait, that's all! You'll be in for a shock tonight, Grandmother!' For two shocks, come to think of it.

Now it was she who waited. She could, she knew, get up and walk out but the longer she waited on the uncomfortable bench in the Labour Exchange, the more sure she was that for once in her pampered, protected life, she would do what *she* wanted!

'Miss Sutton?' The voice jerked her back from her wanderings. 'Will you come to the desk, please?'

'Yes – oh, sorry . . .' She jumped to her feet, flustered, then taking a calming gulp of air, sat down opposite the young woman who had called her name.

'Tatiana Sutton?' she smiled, reading from the form Tatiana had already filled in. 'Of Denniston House, Holdenby?'

'That's me.' She was shocked to find that her voice trembled.

'And you want to find employment? Could I please see your identity card?'

Tatiana offered it at once because it had been ready in her pocket. You couldn't change your mind these days without producing your identity card.

The woman was young and pretty. Her wedding ring was very new and on the left lapel of her blouse she wore a pilot's wings brooch made in silver. Just to see it made Tatiana's stomach contract.

'And I don't want employment really. What I want to do is war work, if you've got any.'

'We've got a lot.' The smile was still there. 'What had you in mind?'

'Oh – anything . . .'

'Then tell me – what can you do? What is your present employment?' This one, decided the clerk, was just a bit uppity. Munitions, maybe, would knock a few of the corners off her!

'I can't do anything and I've never been employed.'

'Whyever not – been employed, I mean?'

'Because there didn't seem a lot of point in it. I suppose Mother wouldn't have wanted me to work and Grandmother would have forbidden it if I'd even mentioned it.'

'I see.' Very uppity. And languid and spoiled if she was any judge of character. Most definitely a candidate for munitions. The new factory at Thorpe Arch was crying out for them! 'Then would you like to train for something? Or perhaps you can drive?'

'Sorry. Can't drive, either, but I'd like to have a go at learning something – perhaps in the women's Forces?'

'The Forces.' They were getting somewhere. And perhaps the Forces would be better than pointing her in the direction of munitions. A good drill sergeant behind her and – She shut down her thoughts. She wasn't really being very nice, and the kid couldn't help being a brat. 'The Wrens, perhaps?'

'No, thank you. My friend had her medical for the Wrens ages ago and they still haven't sent for her.'

'Then had you considered the WAAF? Are you good at figures or –'

'No! Not the Air Force! I couldn't – I mean, isn't there something else?'

All at once, the disinterest was gone. Now she was a wide-eyed, sad-eyed girl protesting vehemently that the Women's Auxiliary Air Force would not do.

'Tell me why not.' The voice was gentle again.

'Because Tim – my boyfriend – was aircrew, a rear-gunner. He was killed in October. If you don't mind, I'd like to get away as quickly as possible from the sound and sight of bombers.' Her eyes brimmed with tears and impatiently she wiped them away. 'Sorry,' she choked. 'I'm just a bit raw round the edges still, you see . . .'

'I do understand.' A hand reached out for hers and squeezed it tightly. 'My husband is a pilot in Coastal Command, in Scotland.'

'Scotland is an awful long way away,' Tatiana whispered. 'Why don't you pack all this in and go to him? I would!'

'Because he's applied for a posting in England. We don't want to cross in transit, sort of. Now let's find something for you to do. You realize you are still a minor?'

'Yes – and that if I go into the ATS my mother will have to give her signed consent. I know about that. But what could I do in the Army? I suppose I couldn't be a part of a gun crew – learn to fire an ack-ack gun?'

'You could be crew, but you could only learn to aim the gun. Only men are allowed to fire them.'

'Pity. I'd like to shoot one of that lot down. Oh, hell! Looks as if I'm pretty useless, doesn't it?'

'Not at all. How did you do when you took your school certificate? How many subjects did you get?'

'None. I didn't take it. I never went to school.' Her cheeks burned. The pilot's wife would think she was no better than a parasite.

'So you were taught at home? A governess?'

'Mam'selle. I'm not very good at arithmetic, but at least

I can speak French. Fluently. When Mam'selle had a mood on her, nothing but French was allowed all day.'

'Good!' But a pity, for all that. Plenty of grammar-school leavers had fluent French, too. 'Any other language?' One despairing last try. 'German, perhaps?'

'Only Russian.'

'You speak it well?'

'Yes. I speak my mother's very correct Russian and I speak Karl's too. Karl uses what he calls proper Russian. He's a Georgian and was once a Cossack. I can read Russian, too, but I'm not quite so good at writing it. It's a very peculiar alphabet, you know. And I don't suppose it'll help at all, but I swear fluently in Georgian. It comes in very handy sometimes.' A smile briefly lifted the corners of her mouth, then was gone. 'Please find me something to do and something, if you wouldn't mind, that gets me away from home. Can you? Please . . . ?'

'Up until a couple of minutes ago I couldn't have been so sure, but yes – I think I've got just the job for you. How do you feel about being a translator? If you were to join the ATS, it would be considered a responsible enough job to carry a bit of rank with it – not that you're old enough yet to be a commissioned officer. If you wanted to stay a civilian, though, there could well be an opening at the War Office. Either would rate as war work. Is London far enough away for you?' All at once, she felt a strange pity for the sad-eyed girl on the opposite side of her desk. 'Mind, I'm not promising anything and they would want to interview you and you'd have to take tests. It would involve secret work, I shouldn't wonder, so they'd want to check up on your background. Can you leave it with me for a while?'

'It won't take a long time, will it? It's bad enough now, but when Daisy – she's my friend who's going into the Wrens – when she goes, it's going to be murder. I'll work hard, I promise.'

'I think, dear, that we can have an initial interview arranged for you in about a week, though you'd possibly have to go to London for it, and with all the bombing –'

'I'd be all right. The people of London have to put up with it.'

'But you might have to work in London, too. Could you cope with it, do you think?'

'Tim coped with flying, yet I know he was often afraid.'

'Yes.' A hand went up to touch the silver wings. 'I think they often are. Now – give me your phone number and I'll be in touch.'

'It's Holdenby 147. And who will be ringing me – your name, that is?'

'I'm Mary Smith. An easy one to remember, isn't it?'

'Yes.' Tatiana returned the smile. 'And if I don't answer, will you tell whoever it is that it's my bank speaking – not the Labour Exchange – the National Provincial it is.'

'I'll do that if you want me to, but why the secrecy? Your parents will have to know because you aren't twenty-one, remember.'

'My father is dead, but if I go into the Army, my mother's signature will be no problem. It's Grandmother Petrovska. She'd try to stop me leaving home. She interferes a lot.'

'Very well. Let's say, then, that I'll be in touch as soon as I can.' She held out a hand as Tatiana got up to leave. 'And, Miss Sutton, I'm so very sorry . . .'

'Yes. Thanks for understanding – and for being so kind.'

The tears came again because she wasn't used to kindness from a stranger; not real, caring kindness.

Head down, she ran from the room.

On the third Wednesday in February, Stuart Hibberd announced over the wireless in clipped, unemotional tones, that the proposed cut in the lard, margarine and butter rations was to take effect immediately.

'Cut by half!' Alice stormed. 'Down to two ounces now!'

Angrily she switched off the set. She was tired of doom and gloom and the unusually cold weather; was sick of trying to feed her family on meagre rations and of worrying, always, about the invasion. Then she looked at the sailor who smiled down from the mantelpiece.

'Sorry, Drew love. It's worse for you, isn't it? I'll bet it's awful at sea in this weather.'

She sent him her love in great warm waves. She must not grumble. She had Tom and Daisy, and even in spite of the aerodrome so close by, they were safer here than in most places.

She smiled at her other child on the opposite side of the mantelpiece, marvelling that people as ordinary as she and Tom could have made such a beautiful creature.

Daisy would be getting on the bus now at the crossroads and in a few minutes the postman might bring a letter from Keth. There had been no letters from Washington for a week. All letters came by sea now. Had Keth's letters been sunk? More importantly, had the ship carrying them been sunk? Even Mr Churchill admitted the seriousness of the sinkings and the loss in shipping. We must win the battle of the Atlantic before we can win the war, he had said. Yet to her way of thinking, Alice frowned, it wasn't shipping and cargoes we were losing though the dear Himself must know how serious that was. But not *ships*. It was the men we were losing; sailors like Drew. Sons, brothers, husbands, fathers.

She jumped, startled, as the knocker came down with a bang on the front door and the letterbox snapped. Letters for Daisy! They hadn't been sunk. No seamen had been killed, bringing them to her. Thank you, God.

She walked quickly into the passage. No pale blue airmail envelopes; nothing, again, from Keth. Just a brown envelope, face-down. Alice looked at it for several seconds before picking it up.

It was addressed to Miss D. J. Dwerryhouse. It bore no

stamp and across the top, written black and importantly, were the words 'On His Majesty's Service'.

Daisy's call-up papers had come.

'So, Tatiana,' said the Countess at breakfast, 'it is obvious you did not visit the hairdresser. I want to know why you told lies and who you met in York!'

'Do you, Grandmother? But perhaps I might not want to tell you.'

'Impudent miss!' The cheeks flushed an angry red. 'Your daughter, Anna Petrovska, is insolent. Tell her to apologize at once!'

'Mama, dear – oh, Tatiana, why must you be so – so provocative?' Anna pleaded.

'She is meeting a man in secret! I know it! I have not lived all these years not to know it!' The Countess had regained her composure. 'I think you have been sneaking out and meeting this man for some time now. Who is he? You met him in York, didn't you?'

'No, Grandmother, I did not.' Slowly, deliberately, so that she should keep absolutely calm, Tatiana laid her knife and fork on her plate, folded her serviette precisely into four, rolled it and pushed it into its silver ring. Then she took a deep, slow breath. 'I met no one in York, though I wish I might have. But you are right. I *have* been sneaking out as you call it, and meeting a man. Surely Mother told you? He was aircrew at Holdenby Moor and he was killed in the bomber that crashed on the pike. I wish with all my heart I could have been going to York to meet him. I would crawl there and back on my hands and knees just to be able to say goodbye to him.'

She gazed from her mother's eyes to those of her grandmother. Neither woman spoke. The silence in the room was absolute because neither had seen Tatiana so calm, so much in control.

'But I *will* tell you what I did in York and I'm sorry for

saying I was going there to get my hair done – sorry, that is, that I had to lie because I knew my mother and my grandmother would forbid me out of hand to go.

'And no; don't interrupt me!' she said softly as the Countess opened her mouth, made a feeble, protesting sound then closed it again. 'I went to the Labour Exchange in York to try to find some war work to do. I had thought to volunteer for the ATS, but I was told that –'

'Tatiana! I won't let you! You are still under age!' Anna cried.

'I'll grant you that, Mother, though I'd have been willing to write your name on the consent form. I would even have used your fountain pen to do it. But that won't be necessary. I think there will be work for me as a translator in London, and if they will have me I shall go there. You can't stop me working, especially when there's a war on!'

'No, but we will have you made a ward of court!' the elder woman flung triumphantly. 'I know all about your English laws. You will *not* leave home, miss!'

'But I *will*, Grandmother! I am no longer the child you think I am. Both you and Mother were married when you were my age. Very soon now I shall be nineteen, so please remember it. I shall go to London and live at Cheyne Walk with Uncle Igor. Surely I can be trusted to him!'

'Then I forbid it! For one thing, your Uncle Igor is too busy with the ARP and the bombing to be bothered with the responsibility of a young girl and for another, you forget that the Cheyne Walk house belongs to *me* and you may not stay in it! Now, what have you to say to that!'

'I would say that perhaps Uncle Nathan might let me use the house next door, then. No one lives there. It's his house now and I'm sure he'd like to have someone in it. But whilst we are talking about whose house belongs to whom, I wonder why I was never told that Denniston House is mine – or will be, in two years' time. I had always thought it was yours, Mother, but Carvers have told me differently.'

'Carvers? You've been there, asking question?' Anna gasped.

'Poking and prying! I said your child was deceitful, Anna Petrovska!'

'No deceit. Young Mr Carver asked me to call in. It was about the money Grandfather Sutton left me. I can have the interest from it twice a year, and it will be wholly mine when I am twenty-one. That is when I was told that Denniston House will be mine, too. It seems it was left to me. But nothing need change, Mother. It will be your home for as long as you want to live in it – for ever, I hope.

'But what *must* change is your attitude towards me, Grandmother.' She fixed the older woman with a steady gaze. 'It will be better for us all if you could remember, just sometimes, that you are a guest in *my* house and that if you carry on being rude to everyone, then I think it would be better if you were to return to *your* house in Cheyne Walk.'

Very calmly, Tatiana walked to the sideboard and picked up a small, ornate bottle, placing it on the table in front of the woman who gasped in anger for breath.

'Here are your smelling salts, Grandmother, and might I ask you that if a Mrs Mary Smith telephones you try very hard to be polite to her. That is all I have to say,' she finished, as quietly and as firmly as she had begun.

Then she opened the door and closed it gently behind her, shaking all over, yet exulting inside that she had challenged her grandmother and won. For once, Olga Maria Petrovska was speechless!

21

As soon as she opened the kitchen door and followed her mother's eyes to the mantelpiece, she knew.

'Here!' Alice thrust the letter into Daisy's hand. It had mocked her all day and she wanted it opened.

'Well, now – another letter from the King!' The studied nonchalance failed dismally because her mouth had gone suddenly dry.

'Open it,' Alice said, though it sounded more like an order.

'Okay. No hurry.' It was surprising what a fumble it was to get the letter out. 'Dunfermline, it says . . .'

'When?'

'Take a look.' Daisy passed the letter over. 'Read it out loud so Dada can hear it, too.'

'You're to go to Robertson House, Dunfermline on the twenty-eighth. Travel warrant is enclosed, it says.' Tears blurred Alice's eyes and she pushed the envelope at Tom. 'Oh, read the dratted thing for yourself!'

'Don't take on, Mam. We all knew it would be coming. I'm to take sufficient clothes for two weeks – for my initial training period, it says. Seems I won't be asked to sign on the dotted line for two weeks. If I don't fancy the Wrens, I can say so, and come home. By that same token, if I don't fit the bill they'll tell me to go.'

'So it isn't all cut and dried, then?' Relief washed through Alice and ended in two bright patches, high on her cheeks. 'You never said.'

'I didn't know. If they think I'm stupid or if I give cheek, maybe, or if I'm just not acceptable, they can –'

'*Stupid?* You're a bright lass, and as for not being accept-able, I don't suppose there'll be many at that Robertson House who'll be as well-heeled as you!'

In Tom's eyes, his daughter was completely perfect and if that lot at Dunfermline saw fit to think otherwise, then more fool they!

'It isn't a question of money, Dada. It will be if I can pass my tests. They'll have to find out what I can do and anyway, they might not like my Yorkshire accent.' She tried to say it lightly, even though her voice was wobbly still.

'What do you mean – your Yorkshire accent? You speak real nice, our Daisy. And you're a Yorkshire lass, aren't you?'

'Born in Hampshire, Dada?' She went to stand behind his chair, bending to lay a cheek on his head. 'And don't get yourself upset. I'm not.'

Not upset? Oh, but she was! Soon, she was to leave Keeper's Cottage and Mam and Dada and Brattocks, and everything that was sane and safe and lovely.

'But, lovey – don't you see?' Alice's heart bumped with hope. 'If it's a sort of probation thing, then you can write, can't you, and tell them you've changed your mind – not bother going? I'm sure they won't mind.'

'Maybe I could, but I'm not going to. Drew didn't have any choice – do you think I'd do a thing like that?'

'I don't see why not!'

'No, Mam. I'll give it a try and besides, I might like it. I was talking to Will Stubbs the other day and he says there's nothing so certain than that before long women are going to have to do war work whether they like it or not. And the young ones like me will probably be sent into the Forces – no choice. Might as well go now, while I still have a say in the matter.'

'Ha! Will Stubbs *says!* Will Stubbs was always a know-all,' Alice flung. 'For two pins I'd box his ears!'

'You'd have Mary to reckon with.' Daisy managed a smile.

'And who's bothered about *her*?'

'Oh lass, bonny lass . . .' Tom rose to his feet, taking Alice into his arms. 'Don't upset yourself. Happen for once Will Stubbs might just be right! And you did the same daft thing, didn't you, when you were Daisy's age?'

'I wanted to get to you, Tom Dwerryhouse, more fool me! But there's no chance at all that Daisy will end up anywhere near Keth, now is there?'

'Happen not, but it's still Daisy's decision.'

'But she isn't twenty-one yet. You could still stop her going, Tom.'

'Mam, I'm as near of age as makes no matter. Just four months.'

Four months, then she and Keth should have been getting married yet now it could be four years – *fourteen* years! Tears filled her eyes and ran unchecked down her cheeks.

'Daisy love, don't take on so. You don't have to go if you don't want to. I'm sure if you wrote them a nice letter, explaining . . .'

'Mam, I'm going, and there's an end to it.' She dried her tears and took a deep breath. 'It wasn't the Wrens made me cry. It's the thought of how long before Keth can get back home. Will Stubbs said this war could last as long as your war did!'

'Ooooh! If I hear one more word about *him*, I'll explode!' All at once, Alice was angry. 'Now listen, the pair of you! Anything Will Stubbs says, I don't want to hear about. From this very minute, his name and any of his daft prophecies are banned from my kitchen – is that clear? Now put that letter away, Daisy Dwerryhouse, and give me a hand with the vegetables. Those potatoes'll be boiled to a mush! And when we've had our supper I'll show you something that'll happen put a smile on your face!'

'What, Mam? Tell me.'

'The potatoes!' Alice ordered. 'Your dada's off Home Guarding tonight and it wouldn't do for Corporal Dwerryhouse to be late, now would it?' All at once, she was in control again but oh, Scotland was such a long way away. 'And then, when I've shown you, you'd better go and see your Aunt Julia. She'll have to be told about Dunfermline, you know!'

'Well now, talk of angels,' Julia smiled as Nathan opened the door of the winter parlour. 'They've just been asking where you are. Finished sermonizing, darling?'

'More or less. It just needs a bit of polishing. I heard the doorbell, though, and decided to investigate. Hullo, you two.'

'Hi, Uncle Nathan. We've come with news,' Tatiana beamed.

'Both of us,' said Daisy.

'Daisy and I met up near the bothy. Karl left me there. He'll be calling to take me home at ten,' Tatiana sighed. 'He's a grumpy old love but I wish, just sometimes, I didn't have to be escorted everywhere.'

'Karl is right,' Nathan admonished, though not too sternly. 'You never know what might happen in the blackout.'

'Well, I'm going to have to learn to look after myself if things work out for me. I've come to tell you both.' She slipped off her shoes, pulling her feet beneath her, and explained about her interview in York and the prospect of working at the War Office.

'She went and did it!' Daisy exulted. 'Good for you, Tatty! What did your Grandma say?'

'Threatened to have me made a ward of court! She was really awful and it isn't any business of hers, is it?'

'You are her only grandchild.' Nathan was wholly on the side of his niece, though not for the world would he say so. 'She's bound to be concerned.'

'It's nothing to do with feelings, Uncle. She's just plain bossy. Anyway, I might soon be going to London for an interview and Grandmother says Uncle Igor is too busy to have me, so might I stay the night at your house? It *is* your house now, isn't it?'

'Well – yes.' He hadn't given the matter a lot of thought, truth known. 'Your Grandmother Sutton left it to Father for his lifetime, and then to me. That's something else I'll have to talk to Carvers about, though why Mother ever needed a London house, I'll never know.'

'But can I stay the night there – when I go for my interview? *If* I go!'

'I'm not sure, poppet. Everything is dust-sheeted, and the beds won't be aired. Don't you think it might be better to stay the night at a hotel? I wouldn't like to think of you alone in that house.'

'Uncle Igor would be next door,' Tatiana protested. 'And of course it would be better if I stayed at a hotel, but I'm not all that well off. I haven't got any of Grandfather's money yet and I know Mother won't help out with expenses because she's against my going.'

'Your mother is probably worried about you being alone in London. There's been no let-up in the bombing,' Nathan reasoned. 'Are you absolutely set on this job?'

'Absolutely. I've got to get away from Denniston. Mother fusses all the time and the Petrovska's always trying to stir up trouble. I wish she'd go back to her precious St Petersburg. I wish she'd never left it.'

'If she hadn't,' Julia laughed, 'you wouldn't be here now, trying to inveigle your uncle into opening up the Cheyne Walk house. Well, you are *not* going to stay there, young woman. If you are set on this interview, then you'll stay at Montpelier Mews with Sparrow.'

'Aunt Julia, can I? I hadn't thought about Montpelier. You're sure? You won't change your mind if Mother gets on to you?'

'Word of a Sutton I won't. But Sparrow would be responsible for you so you'd have to do as you were told, you realize that? And Sparrow can be every bit as bossy as your grandmother.'

'I know, but she's twice as nice.' Tatiana went to sit beside Julia on the hearth rug, snuggling up to her, smiling contentment. 'I won't be a bit of bother, I promise.'

'You better hadn't be. Sometimes I feel Sparrow shouldn't be there alone, but she refuses to move out. And I suppose she's safer there than a lot of people in London.'

'I shall look forward to it. Wish they'd get a move on at the Labour Exchange.'

'Tatty! It was only yesterday you went to see them. Maybe the Wrens will send me to London and then you and I can meet and visit Sparrow whenever we can. She tells some awful stories about goings-on in London,' Daisy giggled.

'Whether or not,' Julia said sternly, 'one thing she won't tell you is her age. I once asked her and she snapped my head off. Told me to mind my own bleedin' business!'

'Then I'll be careful not to ask. I do so want to go to London to work.'

'Are you sure?' Nathan said softly. 'Couldn't it be that you just want to get away from Denniston? London isn't a very safe place to be at the moment.'

'Okay, then – I want to get away from home. But why shouldn't I go to London? The Londoners are putting up with the blitz. The royal family is still there so why must I be different? What's so special about me? Mother was married when she was nineteen, had you realized that?'

'Yes.' Julia closed her mouth, traplike.

'You are your mother's only chick,' Nathan soothed. 'You're all she's got. Try to understand. And life hasn't been kind to your grandmother, either. She's a stranger, still, in a strange country.'

'Mother has got used to England – why can't *she*?

Anyway, we had words, this morning. I'm still in disgrace. I – I'm afraid I told them I knew about Denniston House being mine when I'm twenty-one. Mr Carver told me. Seems Grandmother Sutton left it to me – I suppose blood is thicker than water. But no one thought to tell me. I told the Petrovska she'd have to stop being rude to everybody or she'd better go back to Cheyne Walk!'

'Which wasn't very polite,' Julia reproved.

'No. I suppose, really, it was a bit childish of me. But she gets on my nerves, sometimes. She's unhappy, you see, and she wants everybody else to be miserable. I'll say I'm sorry, though – just for peace and quiet. And thanks for letting me stay at Montpelier, Aunt Julia, though why they need Russian translators, heaven only knows. I'd have thought German would have been a lot more use. After all, the Communists aren't fighting us yet –'

'*Yet.* Doesn't that answer your question, Tatty?' Daisy interrupted. 'Now can I tell my news – *please?*'

'Your call-up?' Julia whispered.

'Dunfermline, on the twenty-eighth. I'll be on two weeks' probation. Mam's tickled pink about that. She thought it was a *fait accompli*, sort of. But I've got to give it a try. Sometimes I get so impatient with everything – wanting Keth home, you see, that I feel like giving things a bit of a push.'

'So now is your chance,' Nathan smiled. 'You'll look rather smart in uniform. We shall have two sailors in the family.'

'I won't get a uniform right away. I'll have to pass out first. They sent me a rail ticket – a *single* one – and I'm to take sufficient clothes for two weeks. And a pair of walking shoes, my gas mask, my ration book and identity card. I feel a bit peculiar inside. It's Mam I'm sorry for, but Dada said she'd done exactly the same thing when she was less than my age. But there's something else! It's so lovely, I've got to tell you. I got a bit weepy – about Keth and me, I suppose. There hasn't been a letter for over a week now, and I'd been so sure there'd be one waiting for me when I got home tonight. But instead, it was my call-up papers.

'Anyway, Mam took me upstairs after supper and guess what? You'll never believe what she had there, all rolled up carefully inside a pillow case. She produced it with a flourish, sort of, then told me to get hold of one end of it, whilst she unfolded it. I had to keep walking backwards. It stretched right across the bedroom and through the door and on to the landing. Ten yards of lovely silk, Aunt Julia, for my wedding dress! Mam said it would cheer me up just to see it. It's beautiful!'

'You lucky girl. You can't get silk for love nor money now. Wherever did she get it?'

'She's had it ages. When she went to the warehouse at Leeds for blackout material, she bought it on an impulse because she was so miserable about there being another war. An act of faith, she said. And she had my confirmation veil there, too, rolled round a piece of cardboard. "War or no war; shortages or not, you'll walk down the aisle like a real bride, Daisy Dwerryhouse," she said. I could have hugged her to pieces. It's all there – except a bride-groom,' she added tremulously.

'So we wrapped it up again, carefully. Mam wanted to change the folds, because you've got to be careful with silk, she says. But somehow it made me feel good just to touch it. It seemed like a good omen.'

'Then I think we should drink a toast, wish you both all the luck in the world,' Julia smiled, 'if we've got anything, that is. I know we're out of sherry – the last of it went on New Year's Eve.'

'And no whisky, nor gin,' Nathan grinned, 'though I'm almost certain there's the odd bottle or two of Madeira in the cellar, from Pendenys. Shall we go mad?'

'Let's all get tiddly,' Tatiana grinned.

'We'll have a hard job,' Julia said, 'on one bottle! But what the heck? Let's live dangerously!'

When Karl arrived at ten and had taken Daisy and Tatiana home, Julia said, 'It was good to see Tatty smile. Lately she's been so sad. But good for her – standing up for herself, I mean. Seems the worm has not only turned, it's bitten!'

'But should you have offered Montpelier?' Nathan frowned. 'Should we have interfered?'

'Taken sides, you mean? But, darling, if Tatty gets the interview she'll be better staying the night with Sparrow than anywhere. Where she'll live if she does land a job in London is really up to Anna, but I reckon that now Tatty has got the bit between her teeth, she's going to take some stopping.'

Tatty seemed determined to get away from Denniston House. Or did she, perhaps, want to escape from a memory? The signs were there; Julia could recognize them easily. Tatiana's strangeness and sadness started at the time the bombers crashed. A dead lover, was it? Julia hoped they had been lovers; hoped Tatty had something to cling to.

'Well, let's keep our fingers crossed the war work doesn't fall through. And with Daisy away, the poor child will be half out of her mind if it does.' She crossed the room to sit beside her husband on the old, sagging settee. 'But had you thought, that will be my Clan all gone? Drew and Daisy in the Navy, Keth and Kitty and Bas on the other side of the Atlantic and Tatty probably in London. I watched them all grow up; used to pretend they were mine. And now the war has got them and I wish Hitler had never been born!' She covered her face with her hands and began to cry softly, despairingly. 'Everyone gone. Even Mother! Nathan – you'll look after yourself, won't you? Don't do anything heroic? Don't ever leave me?'

'Never.' He dried her tears and kissed her gently. 'Never, and that's a promise. Word of a Sutton.'

22

'Come in, Tatty. We've got the place to ourselves.' Daisy closed the back door, pulled the blackout curtain across it, then switched on the light. 'Dada's Home Guarding again. They've got their ammunition, now, but he wants to check it over. He says their rifles are museum pieces and the ammunition is probably left over from the last war, as well.

'He's been playing merry hell about Whitehall. Says they are all probably old blimps left over from the last war, too, and nobody's thought to tell them the Kaiser signed the Armistice,' Daisy grinned. 'Mam said if he was going to go on and on about them not getting new rifles she was going out. She's at the bothy with Polly. But sit down. Did you come alone?'

Outside, the blackness was thick and complete. No stars, no moon and a new one not due for three more nights.

'Karl brought me, wouldn't you know? I'm to ring home when I'm ready to leave and he'll come and meet me – if I can use your phone? But talking about blimps, there was a letter from the War Office this morning. I've got an interview at half-past ten on Friday. Read it for yourself.'

'That's the day I go to Dunfermline. They haven't wasted any time. I'll have to tell Dada that some of his blimps are actually awake.' She handed back the letter. 'Are you pleased, Tatty?'

'Slightly nervous but glad about it, really. I'll have to travel down the day before – stay the night at Montpelier Mews. Mother insists I get there before the bombing starts so I'll be catching an early train from York. And I'm to come back as soon as I've had the interview and not hang around London looking at the shops – if any are open, that is.

'She's in an awful state about it. She's only going along with it because she thinks I'll make a mess of it and come home with my tail between my legs, I know it. But what's going to happen if they give me a job? Can you imagine the fuss? The Petrovska will write to Hitler, demanding he stops bombing London. And had you thought that after Thursday we won't see each other for ages? But what's your news? Any letters?' she ended breathlessly.

'Not a word, but I'm not worrying too much. Keth's letters have probably been sunk on the way over. But there *is* news. I gave in my notice today. The counting-house manager's face dropped a mile. "Five days isn't a great deal of notice, Miss Dwerryhouse. Not very thoughtful, is it?" And then he said that if my probation didn't work out, he very much doubted my position would be there for me when I got back! Well, he knows what he can do with my position! If it doesn't work out at Dunfermline, I won't be going back to Morris and Page, that's for sure!' She glanced up as a bomber flew low overhead. 'That's them going again,' she whispered. 'Look – how if I make us a drink? Cocoa?' Cocoa – when you could get it – was not rationed yet, nor milk. 'Let's drink to the twenty-eighth, shall we?'

'I'll drink to anything that's going to get me away from Denniston and from the sight and sound of *those*.' Tatiana lifted her eyes briefly to the ceiling as another bomber flew over. 'What is this?' She picked up a small tin box.

'That's going to be my housewife. It's one of the things I have to take with me. A mending kit, really. Dada had one in his war. Said they called it a *hussif*. It's a pretty little tin, isn't it? I got it in my stocking the Christmas before we left Hampshire. Half a pound of toffees in it; I'd never had so many sweeties all at once in my life. I kept it because the picture on the front reminded me of Willow End.'

On the lid of the little tin was a cottage with roses growing round the door, a garden filled with flowers and birds flying over.

'Isn't Willow End where Keth used to live? Did his house really look like that? Did it have a thatch?'

'It really did, but a lot of houses down there have thatches. We lived at one end of Beck Lane in the gamekeeper's cottage and Keth and Polly and Dickon – that was his father's name – lived at the other end. It was like our own little world, all shut away amongst beech trees.

'Mam filled the tin with things she thinks I'll need.' She tipped the contents on to the table top: white shirt buttons, black thread and white thread, a packet of needles, a sheet of pins, a tape measure, scissors and safety pins. 'Just seeing it makes it all seem so near. Less than a week, then that'll be it. No more Holdenby for three or four months. I wonder where I'll end up – if I pass out, that is.'

'Wonder what'll happen to me, too, on the twenty-eighth. It's exciting and worrying all at the same time. Last night in bed I got all panicky, but I *am* going to try to get away, Daisy. There's been an awful atmosphere at home since I was cheeky to Grandmother.'

'I thought you'd said you were sorry?'

'I did. Trouble was I didn't *sound* sorry and now Grandmother's going round looking badly done to and Mother's all weepy and keeps wanting to know why I'm being so stubborn about a job and that there's still time to change my mind. But I won't!'

'We're a couple of barm pots, aren't we?' Daisy sighed. 'Mam's upset about Friday and Dada's like a bear with a sore head. He'll be finding fault with that ammunition tonight, though he's been grumbling for ages about them having rifles and nothing to fire. It's because I'm going, I suppose.

'And I know how you feel about being excited and worried. It sort of bubbles up in my throat, and then I think about Drew. Being in the Navy isn't all that bad, he says, though I suppose it'll be a bit choppy on a small fishing boat in this weather.'

'Drew is on a minesweeper, now. When he was home for Aunt Helen's funeral he told me the *Maggie* was once a deep-sea trawler before the Navy took it – *her*. Said they are tough little boats. I suppose they'd have to be when they used to fish in Icelandic waters. He said he'd rather be on a small ship – more friendly with only a crew of fifteen. Do you suppose they might send you to Liverpool when you've done your training, or would it be too much of a coincidence to get near Drew?'

'Haven't a clue. I don't much care, either, though it might be better to go some place where there isn't too much bombing, if only for Mam's sake. And talking about bombing,' her eyes swept the ceiling again, 'I wonder where they are going tonight. They're taking off pretty early, aren't they?'

'That's because they'll be going on a long one; Berlin, maybe. I hope they all get back.' She bit hard on her lip, tilting her chin. 'Hell but it hurts, you know. Wanting Tim, I mean, and knowing I won't ever see him again.' She stirred her drink absently. 'It was all such a waste. He should've been in university, but instead he volunteered for aircrew in a fit of pique – just as you did – because he was mad about the Clydeside bombing. And look what happened . . .'

'I know, love.' Daisy reached out, taking Tatiana's hand across the table top. 'I know just a little bit how awful it is wanting someone and them not being there. And okay – Keth will be back one day,' she hastened, 'though when, I'd give a lot to know. I worry, sometimes, that the longer we're apart, the more apart we might grow. And I worry because he might meet a girl out there. American girls are very attractive and they can get make-up and perfume, too.' She sighed deeply, then forced her lips into a smile. 'Let's switch the dance music on. It's better since Mam moved the wireless here into the kitchen.' Once, they had used the sitting room every night, but not any more when you didn't know, Mam said, where the next piece of coal was coming from. 'Or would you like to listen to Tommy Handley?' Perhaps not the dance music when every tune was one Tatty and Tim had danced to together.

'Tommy Handley, please. And, Daisy, I *am* leaving home. If my Russian isn't good enough, I'll find something else to do. For Tim's sake, I've got to!'

They sat on either side of the fire in the little kitchen with its white, brass-handled cupboards and a red tiled floor, polished to such a shine that it seemed a sin to walk across it. The fire in the iron grate burned brightly and as yet the air-raid siren had not sounded. Tatiana felt a rare contentment.

'Drew told me,' she said to Sparrow, 'that you and he used to toast bread at that fire when he stayed with you. When he was little, I mean.'

'That we did. And now he's fighting for his country. Not five minutes since Drew and Mrs MacMalcolm as was used to come here to stay and him only a toddler. Life slips away, Tatiana girl. You got to make the most of it while you got it. Sparrow knows . . .'

'So you think I did right, leaving home?'

'You ain't left yet. Depends on tomorrer, don't it, and how well you speak your Russian? And there'll be Daisy, sleeping for the last time in her own bed. She'll be orf to war in the morning and Alice all upset about it. That Hitler has a lot to answer for. I'd give him –' She stopped, breath indrawn, eyes sliding left and right. 'Sssssssh . . .'

'I can't hear anything,' Tatiana whispered.

'No.' You only heard the silence – or did you feel it

perhaps? That brooding stillness just before an alert sounded. 'There she goes, Wailing Winnie! Come on – let's see to the shelter then.' Sparrow sprang to her feet, positioning the guard in front of the fire. 'Give us a hand with the table. Just lift it to one side so I can shift the rug. And move yourself, girl, or he'll be dropping 'em before we've got ourselves ready!' she urged, as Tatiana sat there, incapable of movement.

This was the night of the hit-and-run raid all over again; the night Tim died. There hadn't been an alert at Holdenby since and the sound of this one sent Tatiana's blood running cold.

'I'm sorry.' Quickly she was across the kitchen, taking the end of the table, helping move it. 'What on earth is that?' she demanded, as Sparrow rolled up the rug on which the table had stood.

'That's an inspection pit. Tell you about it later. Just get hold of the ring at your end and give it a heave with me. It's a lot easier to shift when there's two of us. Just move it to the side. Now then.' She stood, hands on hips, looking down. 'Where is there a better little bolt hole, will you tell me, this side of Hyde Park?'

As the last low notes of the siren hung quivering on the air, Tatiana looked down. On the floor of the pit lay a rug and on it a three-legged stool and several cushions.

'Now give us a lift back with the table and then we're ready in case the bombs get near. We upends it, see, then we pull it over the pit when we gets in.'

Sparrow did not take cover until the very last minute and was adept at judging when that minute was.

'But why don't we get in, then pull the pit cover back over us?'

'Because for one thing we'd suffocate.' Sparrow fixed her with a glance reserved for idiots. 'And for another, it wouldn't be easy to do it from below – far too heavy.

'No, we pull the table top over us and leave just enough

space for air, then if we catch one and they come looking for people, they'll see the table and they'll know we're under it – see?' She nodded to the underside of the table top on which the word 'HELP' was painted in bright red.

'When they gets into a bomb-damaged house, Tatiana girl, those ARP rescue lot knows where to look. Some people have got their kitchen tables made into little shelters. They gets under 'em. Surprising what protection a good solid table gives. Some go in the cupboard under the stairs. The rescue boys know to look there, too. Mind, the lucky ones has cellars, but this little house has got a pit. Now don't stand there gawping. Get yourself in there and I'll pass the stuff down so we'll be ready when the time comes.'

'Do I jump – it's quite deep.'

'No!' Sparrow clucked impatiently. 'You uses that stool as a step. And get a move on. We want to be ready – just in case.' She handed down a torch and a tin marked 'Biscuits'. 'And this 'ere has my important papers in it, so be careful of it.' Down came a stout, brass-bound box. 'Now get yourself out and we'll have a cup of tea and fill the Thermos while we're waiting.'

'Wouldn't it be best if we got in now?' Tatiana's tongue made little dry clicking sounds as she spoke.

'Nah! We're luckier around here. It'll be the docks and the East End that get it first, poor sods. We'll hear 'em. Jerry hasn't started yet. Tell you what – switch off the light and come to the door. There's a couple of ack-ack guns over yonder in the park and a searchlight battery. Them guns'll be all ready to fire now, and when they do, that searchlight'll be turned on and sweep the sky so the guns know where to aim. When the searchlight goes on, then we'll go down into our hole – if we don't hear the bombs for ourselves, that is.'

Sparrow considered the anti-aircraft guns and the search-light with pride. There were guns and searchlights all over London, but those near at hand in Hyde Park were her own special protectors. She always gave a cheery wave to the soldiers and ATS girls when she walked past and they always called back, 'Hullo, Ma!' which pleased her because she was old enough to be their grandmother. And as for those ATS girls – if they'd been anything to do with her, they'd be safe at home with their mothers, the foolish, brave young things!

'But why is there an inspection pit in the kitchen?' Tatiana was less nervous now, and turned her attention to the hole in the kitchen floor. 'I thought they were things you had in garages.' Less afraid, though her heart still beat much too quickly.

'Because this little house was once a garage. It was built as stables really, for one of the big houses over yonder.' She nodded in the direction of Montpelier Square. 'Then the motors came and the toffs got rid of their horses and carriages and got rid of the groom that lived in the loft above as well. Then somebody thought to make little town houses of all the garages.'

'But if we just did get bombed,' Tatiana asked as they closed the door because Sparrow said that if she came to live in London she would have plenty of chances to see the searchlight and anyway, they were letting the heat out, 'if we *did* get hit, would they really come looking for us?'

'Oh my word, yes. Our local rescue boys know about my pit, be sure of it. Now let's see to that tea, and then we'll sit quiet and listen so we'll know when to shift ourselves sharpish, like.'

'And then?' Tatiana was still apprehensive, though she was pleased to see that her hands no longer shook.

'And then when we hears the first ones, we'll sit up and take notice and weigh the situation up. They'll be over the East End, like always. When they drop 'em – far away, that is – it's more like a cross between a thud and a crunch. That's when you know some poor bleeder's home has gorn up in smoke and you says a quick prayer.'

'Why, Sparrow?'

'Cause you're sorry for 'em and you're thankful – or you ought to be – that it ain't your own house them bastards has hit! Now are we going to get that tea made?'

'I'll do it.' Tatiana wanted to because all at once she felt quite brave. 'And, Sparrow, if they offer me a job can I come and live with you? I wouldn't be any trouble and an extra ration book would come in handy, wouldn't it? And I could stand in queues for you when I had time off work. Could I stay? Please?'

'If your Aunt Julia says it's all right, then it's all right by Sparrow. But wait and see what tomorrer brings, eh?'

Poor young thing. Hadn't had enough love, it was plain to see. And always anxious and jumpy, but that was because of her being half-foreign. Yet for all that, it might be nice, Sparrow considered, to have someone to fuss over and give a bit of love to.

'I'd like you to stay here,' she nodded. 'And now let's have hush . . .'

So they sat unspeaking, listening to the brooding silence, waiting for the sound of that first, faraway bomb. Sparrow hoped the gunners and the searchlight crew in the park would get one of Goering's lot and that those ATS girls had their warm scarves on because it was a bitterly cold night.

And Tatiana thought about how calm she suddenly felt and about Daisy, sleeping for the last time at Keeper's and sent love and good wishes to her. Then gently she said good night in her heart to Tim.

She did not think about Denniston House at all.

Daisy had said her goodbyes. Yesterday, she had gone to the churchyard and taken some chrysanthemums to Reuben, then said goodbye to Jin and Mrs Shaw and Mr Edward, too.

The earth had settled now on Lady Helen's grave, the

headstone replaced. Now, carved there in stone, she was 'Helen Mary his wife'. Sir John's wife, that was, who had been killed thirty years ago. And beneath their names the word 'Reunited'.

'I miss you, Lady Helen,' Daisy whispered. It had been like losing a grandmother.

Daisy whispered her goodbye then walked back across Home Farm cow pasture and cut into Brattocks Wood where the elm trees stood and the rooks nested. Then leaning her back against the trunk of the tallest tree, placing her hands behind her, palms against the rough bark, she sent her thoughts upwards.

Rooks, it's Daisy from Keeper's. I'm going to be a Wren, tomorrow. I don't really want to leave Rowangarth, but I hate this war and I'm sick and tired of waiting for Keth to come home.

Mam and Dada are going to be upset and I'm sorry about that, and I suppose tomorrow Mam will be coming to tell you I've gone. So don't leave Brattocks Wood, will you? I don't want any harm to come to Rowangarth and that includes Drew especially . . .

If ever the rooks left Brattocks, so the old ones had it, tragedy would come to Rowangarth. Once, the rooks had left; just upped and off, Reuben told her, and that was when Doctor Andrew was killed and Sir Giles died and Drew was such a sickly baby that Aunt Julia had worried herself half to death that he would die, too.

Then for no reason at all, the rooks returned to Rowangarth's elms and things got better again. It was a fact, Reuben said. At the end of 1918 it happened.

So don't you go flying off, remember? And I'll come and see you when I'm home on leave . . .

As she walked home through Brattocks Wood for the last time for many, many weeks, all at once Daisy wished she were not going and yet she wanted it to be tomorrow so she could go. Leaving Mam and Dada would be the worst part. After that, when the train had left York, she wouldn't feel quite so bad – would she?

Tom heaved the case on to the luggage rack, giving it a shove to make sure it didn't fall.

'You'll have to ask someone to give you a lift down with that,' he said, 'when you get to Edinburgh.'

The London-to-Edinburgh express had been an hour late arriving in York. Trouble on the line, which usually meant that somewhere along the way, railwaymen had probably worked through the night repairing track damaged by bombing.

Daisy put her folded coat and gas mask on the seat to reserve it, then went to stand on the platform with Alice and Tom. There didn't seem anything to say except 'See you. Take care. I love you both,' so she said instead, 'I was lucky getting a seat, wasn't I?'

The stationmaster and the assistant stationmaster and an elderly porter were already walking the length of the train, slamming doors so those who stood on the platform snatching a last-minute kiss – maybe even a last kiss – should shape themselves and get aboard.

'Best be getting on, love.' The words were hard for Tom to say. He pulled her into his arms, hugging her close. 'So long, our lass. Take care. Let's know you've got there all right.'

'I will, Dada.' It was awful, trying to smile when your lips wanted to tremble and give way to sobs.

'God bless, sweetheart.' Alice kissed her daughter. 'Just get yourself settled, then we'll go . . .' You didn't wait, if you had any sense, for that last awful moment of parting. You said, 'Be seeing you,' or, 'Cheerio.' You never said goodbye and you never turned round for one last wave. To do that was bad luck. Alice knew how it was from her own war. 'Take care, Daisy love.' No more words would come.

'And you take care, too, and don't worry. I'll write. I love you both . . .'

She took her seat, then closed her eyes against sudden despairing tears. When she opened them again, her parents had gone and the train was slowly heaving and hissing and clanking out of the station. She was leaving York, leaving Yorkshire, leaving England. She was going to war!

That was when the tears came. Big, warm, silent ones; was when a hand took hers and squeezed it so that she had to mop her face and blow her nose very loudly and look into friendly eyes.

'It can be awful the first time,' said the young woman in air-force-blue uniform. 'Joining up, are you?'

'Mm.' Daisy sniffed inelegantly. 'The Wrens. Going to Dunfermline.'

'Well, what d'you know, so am I – well, ten miles the other side of Dunfermline. On leave.'

See you, Daisy whispered inside her to the Minster as it slipped away. It had stood there for hundreds of years, guarding York. When next she saw it she would only be minutes away from the station and half an hour away, on the little local train, from Holdenby. When she came on leave, that was.

After that, it became almost bearable. 'Did you feel like this when you joined up – all funny inside, I mean?' she asked of the aircraftwoman beside her.

'Actually – no. I joined in 'thirty-nine. It was a very daring thing to do so I felt really excited. And anyway, the war was going to be over by Christmas, if you remember? But for a week afterwards, I awoke every morning with a rather soggy pillow,' she laughed. 'Most girls have a weep. The sooner you get it over with, the better.' She reached into her pocket, bringing out a chocolate bar. 'Want some?'

It was chocolate cream and Daisy's absolute favourite but she said, 'No, thanks. Kind of you, but I couldn't take yours.' She had joined the queue at many a sweet shop but hadn't so much as glimpsed a chocolate cream bar since the war began.

'It's okay. We get them in the NAAFI. One of the perks, I suppose.' She snapped the bar into two. 'You're welcome, chum.'

Chum. That one word all at once established that Daisy Dwerryhouse was one of the special ones now. She belonged, like Drew and Gracie and Tim Thomson and the WAAF corporal at her side, to His Majesty's Armed Forces and she wouldn't be opting out at the end of her probation – unless asked to, that was.

There would be times, she knew, when she would hate it and long to be home again, but there would be times – like this shared chocolate bar – when she would be glad she had joined, especially if anything she could do helped shorten the war by just one day.

'If you're sure, then thanks – chum.'

'So, Tatiana, tell us about London,' Countess Petrovska demanded.

'Please, Grandmother, I've only just got in.'

The interview had been longer than she had ever supposed, and thorough, and she had caught the two o'clock train to York by only seconds. They advised her to take the Tube to King's Cross because buses were very slow-moving and streets blocked with rubble or cut off by signs warning 'DANGER. UNEXPLODED BOMB.' But because she was Tatiana and very stupid, she had got lost on the Underground and passed the station at which she should have changed trains. This had caused trouble because she realized for the first time that there were no footbridges in the Underground.

The train to York was crowded and hot because windows could not be opened, and it was dusty because there were not enough women now to clean trains and it stopped three times on the way for no reason at all except, she supposed, to give priority to an ammunition train or to one carrying troops. Not that she would have admitted such irritations for the world; not to invite a look of I-told-you-so triumph on her grandmother's face.

'Mama dear, do let's have our cup of tea first. Are you hungry?' Anna asked solicitously, supposing that the look of utter fatigue on her face was one of disappointment that the War Office had no use for her services and not because she had been forced to stand for the better part of the journey.

'Hungry? Not particularly, thanks. Sparrow gave me sandwiches and an apple. What I want is a drink, really. A cup of tea would be fine.'

'And what did the man in London have to say?' the Countess pressed. 'Was he a Bolshevik?'

'I didn't ask about his politics, Grandmother, especially as he was English. And I didn't go to the War Office, exactly. I went to a sort of annexe nearby. I saw two men, actually, and one lady. The lady didn't say anything – just sat there taking notes.'

'And did you tell them that your grandfather was Count Peter Petrovsky, who died in the service of his Czar?'

'No I didn't, because I'd always thought that he and Uncle Basil were killed trying to get some of their belongings out of the St Petersburg house.'

'Your trip to London has not improved your manners! And what did you do when the bombing started, eh, because there was a another raid last night! Your poor mother was beside herself when she heard the news, this morning. Were you not afraid?'

'Not really. Actually, it was the dockland and the people living around who caught the worst of it. Aunt Julia's house is near Hyde Park and some way away. We didn't even get into the pit – er – Sparrow's air-raid shelter, under the kitchen floor,' she hastened on seeing the look of disbelief on the old woman's face. 'Aunt Julia's little house was once a stable, you see, and then it became a garage when cars got popular. That's why there is an inspection pit there. Very handy, too. Just enough room in it for two.'

'A stable? Your father's aunt converted a *stable* to live in!'

'Yes, Grandmother. They do it a lot in London now, you know they do, and that they call them mews houses. It's in a select part,' she hastened, because if Grandmother thought a converted stable was not fit for a Petrovska to live in, there would be no end of trouble getting away to London, even supposing the War Office gave her a job.

'It's a dear little house, Mama,' Anna urged. 'I have seen it for myself. And Sparrow – er – Mrs Emily Smith, is a very dependable lady and a stickler for discipline.'

'Ha!' jerked the Countess, wondering why, all at once, her daughter seemed to be siding with the child. 'But we are bothering ourselves over nothing. We will decide where Tatiana is to live – if, that is, she is offered a position and *if* we decide she is to be allowed to accept it!'

'Yes. And if you'll excuse me,' Tatiana said flatly, 'I'd like a bath. Is there any hot water, Mother?'

'Of course – if you don't take too much. And I'll come up and see you later, dear. Grandmother and I want to listen to the nine o'clock news, first. Up you go!'

She gave her daughter a small smile, knowing it were better if she waited until Tatiana was ready to admit that things had not gone entirely as she would have wished and that London, in spite of her nonchalance about the raid, was a very dangerous place in which to be. It was obvious Tatiana's little rebellion was over. Soon, things would return to normal at Denniston House.

'I don't want to listen to the late news, Tom, if you don't mind.' The war had taken its toll of Alice's emotions this day and she wanted nothing more than to sit, staring into the fire, thinking about her daughter and where she was and what she was doing and if there was a telephone close by. She hoped there would be no air raids there, tonight, but it was Glasgow and the Clydebank shipyards that lately had been taking the brunt of the bombing. She should be glad, Alice brooded, that Daisy was travelling by way of Edinburgh, although Dunfermline was very near the Forth Bridge and it could only be a matter of time before the Luftwaffe had a go at that, damn their arrogance!

'Lass – give over.' Tom's words cut into her thoughts. 'Oh, I know how it is, but did you give a thought to danger when you were Daisy's age? Didn't you tell me that when you and Julia arrived at Celverte, the gunfire from the Front was so near you could hear it and you and me not twenty miles apart, did we but know it? And were you frightened?'

'N-no. Just excited that you were quite near and maybe I'd turn a street corner one day and . . .' Her voice whispered away. She hurt all over. Her only child had gone to war and nothing from the past would change that. 'It's different for Daisy. Keth is safe in Kentucky and there was no need at all for her to go!'

'Not even if she believes she's helping to shorten the war?'

'To get Keth home one day sooner, you mean?'

'In our war, lass, *in one day*, ten thousand men were killed.'

'I know.' She shifted her eyes to the mantelpiece. This morning when they got back from York, there were letters from Keth, six of them, and not sunk as Daisy feared. Yet tonight Daisy did not open the kitchen door and reach for them with a cry of delight. Those pale blue envelopes stood there all day between the clock and the tea caddy, to remind them that Daisy had gone.

'I'll put Keth's letters in a big envelope tomorrow, ready for when we get her address, Tom.'

'You do that, bonny lass. And she'll have posted the card, by now.'

Daisy had a postcard, ready addressed and stamped in her handbag to pop into the pillar box when she reached Dunfermline station. On it was written, *Arrived safely. D.* There was a posting box in almost every railway station and the card was considered a good idea in case no telephone kiosk was near. And there would, they had considered, be at least a three-hour delay on a trunk call. You booked your long-distance number these days, then hung around waiting, whilst the overworked telephonists tried their best to deal with them all.

It was the fault of the armed forces, really. Air Force, Navy and Army numbers were given priority and civilian calls came very low in the pecking order when it came to trunk calls.

'Maybe we'll get it tomorrow – the postcard, I mean.'

'Sure to, and there's still time for a phone call tonight, Alice love.'

Alice transferred her brooding gaze back to the fire.

'I want to go to bed, Tom.'

'Oh . . . ?'

'No, not that!' *That* was the furthest thing from her mind tonight. 'I just want you to hold me tight because I'm in such a shake inside that it's as if I'm about to explode. Come upstairs, Tom – unless you want a drink and a bite, that is?'

'No.' Even a slice of hot drippinged toast would take a bit of swallowing tonight. 'Best if you have a good old cry, bonny lass; let it all come.'

He was right. Tom understood about the writhe of tears in her throat and that she needed to weep them out of her.

'Leave the bedroom door,' Alice whispered as she undressed. 'Prop it open so we'll hear it if the phone rings . . .'

304

23

'Hullo, Mr Catchpole.' They met at the kitchen-garden gate. 'Mind if I have a word with Gracie?'

'Take all the time you want, Tatiana lass. I'm off for a bite of dinner. Be back at one o'clock sharp.'

Which really meant, Tatiana considered, that all the time she wanted spanned the duration of dinner break. She pushed open the door of the potting shed where the land girl sat beside the little firegrate on an upturned box.

'Hi, Tatty. I've just made a brew. Grab yourself a mug – the top shelf beside the bottle marked poison. What's news?'

'About London?' What other news could there be?

'Mm. And what your grandma said about it.' Gracie was partial to a smidgen of drama.

'No one has said anything. I didn't get home till late. The train kept stopping and I had to stand until Newark. I was dead beat. Trouble was, I think they imagined I was quiet because the interview had gone wrong and I was too upset to tell them. Grandmother must have had a hard job keeping the gloat off her face. Anyway, I went to bed and left them to it and I still haven't told them.'

'Told them what?' Gracie offered a sandwich. 'Have one. Polly gave me too many. Now, *what happened*? Nothing went wrong?'

'No, but I was so nervous I thought I'd made a mess of it like I make a mess of most things, but the man I went to see – he'd been a Professor of Russian at some university before the War Office recruited him – spoke impeccable Russian to me, but *too* impeccable, sort of. That was when

I stopped worrying because that far I'd got it right. I was just uncrossing my fingers when in walked this man who flung the lot at me and do you know, Gracie, it was exactly as if I'd been speaking to Karl. The second man was a real Russian; could have been a Georgian. I even expected the odd swear word, but it didn't come, though if they'd said I was no good I think they'd have had a few from me for good measure.'

'But they didn't say you were no good, did they?'

'They didn't!' Tatiana took another sandwich. 'As a matter of fact, they sort of hinted that once they'd had time to think things over, I'd be hearing from them. The professor asked me that if everything went to plan, when could I start work – oh, I forgot! They gave me a book; just opened it and I had to read the page out loud then translate it into English.

'It was a walkover. Tolstoy – *War and Peace*. I started reading that when I was twelve, though it took me a year, almost, to get through it. But how about that for luck?'

'Great! But if you were that good, Tatty, what is there to think over?'

'Nothing, hopefully. What they'll do now is go into my background – make sure I'm trustworthy, you see. Because they told me that if I worked there, the work would be highly confidential and I would have to sign the Official Secrets Act and to put it bluntly, I'd be in trouble if ever I broke it. Careless talk, you know.'

'Trouble?' Gracie laughed. 'Write out one hundred times, *I must not blab about state secrets*?'

'Worse than that. Prison, actually. For a long time.'

'Oh, Lordy. You'll have to learn to keep your mouth shut.'

'Yes, and I'm not going to tell them at home about any of it until I get official confirmation about going to London. And I'm as certain as I can be they'll give me a job. What I don't understand, though, is that they didn't seem very interested in my French. It was only Russian they seemed keen on and we aren't at war with Russia. But I think they'll give me some sort of war work to do.'

'And will you live with your uncle at Cheyne Walk?'

'Not if I can help it! As a matter of fact, I'm going to give them time to get lunch over with at Rowangarth, then I'm going to ask Aunt Julia if I can live at Montpelier Mews with Sparrow. Sparrow is a love, and I think Aunt Julia will let me, even if it's only so Sparrow won't be on her own in the bombing.'

'So everything seems set fair? I'm glad for you, though I'll miss you. First Daisy and now you. It won't be the same at Rowangarth. You'll get leave, though?'

'Yes. I'll be entitled to two weeks' annual leave, plus seven days' sick leave, whatever that might mean.'

'So how soon will you know? Weeks? Months?'

'Pretty soon, let's hope. The more I see of the outside world the more I realize what a lily of the field I am. London was in a terrible mess, you know, and people trying their best to carry on and get to work when everything is almost at a standstill. I was ashamed how useless I've always been.'

'Don't be a clot. Actually, getting away from Denniston might be the best thing that could happen, though I'll hate it when you go.'

'*Hope* to go.' She crossed her fingers. 'And, Gracie, if I go to London, will you do something for me? Will you go up the pike, sometimes, and say hullo to Tim for me? I've asked Daisy to as well – when she's home on leave.'

'Of course I will – and perhaps getting away will help you forget what happened.'

'Happened to Tim, you mean? But I don't want to forget.'

'Of course you don't and that isn't what I meant. I was trying to say that getting away from around here might help the hurt go sooner – so you can remember happily.'

'And what do you know about being in love, Gracie Fielding; you who's always saying she won't get entangled until the war is over? But here comes Catchpole; I'd better be on my way, see if Aunt Julia is in. And come over to Denniston any time you want, Gracie. I wish you would, especially now that Daisy has gone.'

'I will. Promise. I wonder what she's doing right now, and if they've heard from her yet at Keeper's. Might just call in on the way home tonight. I'll walk to the gate with you, then it's back to digging for victory! Take care, Tatty, and good luck. Let me know the minute you've got news?'

And Tatiana said she would, then went in search of Julia.

There had been no mail that morning. No word from Daisy; nothing from Keth, even, and Alice spent the entire morning wondering about her daughter and what she was doing and if it was colder in Scotland than it was at Holdenby and if her bed was properly aired.

She'd had no stomach for the morning paper because her world was bleak enough and to read such news as the Ministry of Information chose to release would do nothing to help.

Tom had gone out at first light, after seeing the Post Office van pass without stopping. He was, he said, going to walk the beat and take a look at his snares. Tom was restless, too, and Alice wondered how she would survive this war without Daisy. Then at once she felt ashamed of her self-pity and reminded herself that there would be many other mothers wondering how things were going this morning at a faraway place called Robertson House.

Yet for all that, she could concentrate on nothing and decided to waste the morning entirely, tidying drawers and maybe looking through photograph albums. Almost at once she decided against the photographs because, quite honestly, she wouldn't be brave enough to do it without weeping.

She reached for the photograph that stood on the right of the mantelshelf. 'Take care, Daisy love,' she smiled, then closed her eyes tightly as tears pricked.

'Oh damn you, Hitler, you evil man!' she cried. '*Damn* you!'

Later, when she had splashed her face with cold water and combed her hair and powdered her red nose and taken several deep breaths which she had always found to have a calming effect, she heard Tom's whistle as he crossed the yard to kennel the dogs.

'Dinner's just ready,' she called. 'Seen anyone?'

'Saw young Tatty on her way to Rowangarth.'

'Anyone else? You didn't see –'

'Didn't see the postman? Well since you mention it, I did. Now where did I put that postcard?'

'Tom! Give it to me!'

'Here you are – and another from Keth.'

Sighing tremulously, Alice peered at the postmark: Dunfermline 6 p.m. or was it an eight? It didn't matter. Turning it over, though she knew already what was written on it, she read the message Daisy had written in this very kitchen the night before she left. 'Arrived safely. D.' and below it, written in pencil, 'Pro-Wren Dwerryhouse D., Cabin 3, Robertson House, HMS *Cochrane II*, c/o GPO London.'

'She's given us her address! She didn't post this at the station, then?'

'Seems not, and look –' Tom turned the card sideways as Alice reached for her reading glasses. Squeezed in the margin were the words 'I love you both.'

'There now.' Alice hugged the card to her. 'I'll send her Keth's letters and write her a few lines from us both. They'll catch the half-past five collection if I shift myself. She'll want letters from home.' Letters were important. Alice knew. She smiled brilliantly, all at once briefly happy, wondering how Tatiana had fared in London, making a mental note to remember to ask Julia when next she saw her. 'Come on, then! Get your hands washed while I dish up.'

She wanted dinner over quickly. She had a letter to write to her daughter in the armed forces!

'Hullo, darling.' Julia hugged Tatiana tightly. 'Himself's over in the far parish; got a quickie wedding – a special-licence job. A soldier on seven days' embarkation leave, it seems, and no time to read the banns. I suppose we'll have to get used to that now. So tell me – how was London?'

'London itself was awful.' Tatiana pushed off her shoes, then curled up in her favourite chair. 'You wouldn't believe the devastation, and so many killed and injured . . .'

'I would. I once went to war, remember.'

'Sorry. Of course you did. Anyway, London's in a mess. Houses just wiped out or sliced in two; you can see staircases just hanging there, and firegrates on bedroom walls. I wondered who had once slept in those rooms, and if they were still alive. And in one wrecked house there was just one wall standing and a picture hanging, all crooked, on its nail. There are whole streets blocked off because of the danger of falling masonry or unexploded bombs and the air smells dusty – *nasty* dusty, I mean – and there's the stink hanging over everything of burning wood that's been doused with water.'

She paused, sighing dramatically.

'Sparrow keeps the kettle always filled and a bucketful under the sink, just in case the water gets cut off – which it often is, she says.

'It wasn't quite so awful at Montpelier, though the area around King's Cross station was dreadful to look at. I was glad to get down into the Tube!'

All at once, she wondered about the bombs *K-King* had dropped on Germany and if any of them had killed women and frightened children and then she closed her mind to it because Hitler had started the war, not us.

'And Sparrow? How is she managing on one ration book? Do you think she's getting enough to eat?'

'She's fine, she says. There's a barrow boy comes round twice a week and he saves her a few things. He let her have a pound of apples the other day. I felt guilty when I opened my sandwiches on the train; she'd put one of them in for me.'

'I worry about her being alone, Tatty. Is the shelter very near?'

'Shelter, Aunt Julia? But she's got one of her own!' Tatiana laughed. 'The pit – remember?'

'*Pit?* Y-yes . . .' Aunt Sutton had said something about a hole under the kitchen floor. 'Tell me.'

'It's an inspection pit, really. Sparrow has cleaned it out and it's very snug though we didn't use it the night I was there.' She went on to explain Sparrow's air-raid drill, and how they had heard bombs falling away over dockland and the East End streets. 'She was really brave. If I get a job, I hope you'll let me stay with her. I asked Sparrow and she said she was willing, if you were. Can I live at Montpelier, Aunt Julia – *please?*'

'Of course you can, if your mother will let you and *if* you are offered a job. But are you sure about going to London? It isn't the safest place to be, right now.'

'I'm sure. If the Londoners can put up with it, then so can I. D'you know, thousands of them sleep in the Underground. It's the only place they've got. Their houses have been bombed so they stay in rest centres during the day and go down the Tube at night before the bombing starts and find a space on the platform to sleep. They'll never give in to Hitler, you know. I'm very proud of my English half, Aunt Julia. I hope I hear from the War Office soon.'

'But your mother seemed to think things hadn't gone all that well at the interview. She was on the phone just before you got here and said you seemed very quiet last night when you got home and hadn't mentioned London at all, this morning.'

'Mother couldn't be more wrong. I think things went well, only I don't want to say anything till I know one way or the other because I couldn't bear Grandmother Petrovska's smugness if it all went wrong.'

'Then if doing war work means so much to you, Tatty, I hope you'll have good news soon. And it would take a worry off my mind if you were to stay with Sparrow, though I wouldn't say anything to your mother about it yet, or she might think that I was –' She stopped, red-cheeked.

'That we were conniving? Don't worry, Aunt Julia. I'll be very tactful about staying at Montpelier. And if the Petrovska gets uppity about it, I shall remind her that she said Uncle Igor was so busy with the bombing that he couldn't have the bother of me. And anyway, who would want to stay with him, will you tell me? He still hopes there'll be a Romanov back on the Russian throne one day. He's living in cloud-cuckoo-land.'

'But I won't keep you. I want to call in at Keeper's and tell Mrs Dwerryhouse about London. She and Sparrow are quite old friends, I believe. And I want to know if there's been word yet from Daisy.'

'There has, but I'll leave it for Alice to tell you. She'd be glad to see you, I know.'

'Good. We can have a chat.' A long chat, she hoped. The kitchen at Keeper's Cottage was one of the nicest places Tatiana knew. 'It's going to seem funny without Daisy around.' Sighing, she gave voice to her thoughts. 'But never mind – I might soon be away myself.'

'You might. I'll say one for you . . .'

'Thanks. 'Bye, Aunt Julia. I'll see myself out. And give my love to Uncle Nathan and tell him he mustn't say anything at Denniston until I hear from London.'

'I'll *ask* him not to and be off with you, you terrible child!' Julia laughed.

Yet why was she feeling so happy when always, now, at the back of her mind was the certainty that the last of her Clan might soon be away? Before so very much longer there would be no young ones about the place but Gracie.

Grace Fielding, Julia pondered, raising a hand to wave as Tatiana sped past the window, making for the wild-garden stile that led to Brattocks Wood. Gracie was such a nice girl. Drew liked her, too. Indeed, their land girl with the warm Lancashire accent had become rather special, for Gracie it had been who last saw her mother alive; Gracie who last listened to an elderly lady's rememberings about a long-ago ball. And Gracie had found the orchid.

Cabin 3, Robertson House, HMS *Cochrane*. Julia picked up the paper on which she had written Daisy's address. Daisy was almost a Wren now, yet only five minutes ago Julia had stood godmother for a tiny baby who cried angrily at her christening.

Why did the years seem to slip past so quickly? Julia frowned. When you reached forty, why did they?

The noise was like a hundred alarm clocks, each of them screaming inside her head. Daisy sat up in bed, blinking in the sudden glare of light. Was this an air raid and if it was, what was she doing in this place?

'Good morning, girls! Wakey-wakey!'

How could anyone be so brash and blithe this early on so cold a morning? And *this place* was Robertson House, wasn't it, and Leading-Wren Anderson was awakening them and how *dare* she?

'Aaaagh . . .' came a half-awake groan from the top bunk. 'Go 'way.'

Daisy looked up at the bouncing bulge in the mattress above her as its occupant settled down to sleep again; then she gazed at the cream-painted glossy walls, damp with condensation. It had been a shock last night, finding out just where she was going.

'Robertson House?' the minister smiled when she asked directions of him on the station platform. 'Well, I'll walk with you, lassie, and give you a hand with that case. I live at the manse close by. You'll forgive my hesitation when you asked. It hasn't all that long been called by that name. It's not so many months ago that Robertson House was a workhouse, you see. Bleak old place. I believe the Navy has made it a wee bit more cheery now, so don't look so dismayed.'

A *workhouse*. She was to be billeted in a workhouse where people went as a last resort, Mam once told her. Widows without support; unmarried girls who'd got themselves into trouble, turned out of respectable homes and pointed in the direction of the workhouse master.

There was one at home, on the York road, where a man tramping the highways could find a bed for the night and a breakfast of porridge and bread and dripping before he was sent on his way to tramp to the next workhouse, begging at doors as he went. Daisy looked again at the glossy wall and wondered how much misery was steeped into it.

'Come along now, girls! Show a leg! Breakfast at 7.15 sharp and I want all beds properly made and the floor mopped and polished by then!'

The door slammed, the awful ringing sounded again, further down the passage. Cabin 4 was being called now.

'Go to hell!' grunted another as one brave spirit lowered herself half awake from the opposite top bunk, wincing as her feet touched an icy floor, reaching hastily for her slippers and fluffy dressing gown.

Probationer-Wren Dwerryhouse swung her feet to the floor, reached for her soapbag and towel and walked in a daze to the bathroom.

There would be a leaping, crackling fire at Keeper's and Mam would be slicing bread for toast. And Keeper's Cottage kitchen was the dearest, warmest, most faraway haven in the entire world and Mam, in the white apron she always wore for cooking, was the dearest, warmest, most faraway mother in the whole of creation and for two pins Daisy Dwerryhouse would have packed her case and left. Trouble was, no one was offering pins, this dark, cold morning.

Oh Mam, Dada, what on earth am I doing here . . . ?

24

All things considered, February had been a bad month and even colder than it should have been, Tom brooded. There were no shoots now, at Rowangarth. He still raised gamebirds, but not for sport. For one thing, cartridges for shotguns were in short supply and for another, pheasants, partridge, wood pigeons and rabbits now helped eke out the paltry meat ration and all he could catch was sent to shops in Creesby and York.

Yet reading between the drear February lines, no one could ignore the fact that the Atlantic was a seethe of hunters and hunted and the bad weather no protection for our merchant ships. German battleships still attacked convoys, then returned to Dutch ports or the safety of some Norwegian fjord. And day and night U-boats stalked convoys like packs of slavering wolves. Always there. Always ready to strike and kill.

It must be a terrible thing to see a ship die, Tom pondered; not only the taking of good lives, but the actual killing of a beautiful creation with turbines and boilers and engines that throbbed like the heart of a woman, for a ship was always a she and never, Drew said, an *it*.

Tom bent to push in a knocked-over snare peg, wondering where Drew was now. Damned awful weather for small ships to be at sea. Drew's little *Maggie* helped keep the Western Approaches free from mines. It must be a sad thing for a merchant ship to make it safely across the Atlantic, only to hit a mine almost within sight of home.

Drew's war was nothing like Rifleman Dwerryhouse's war had been. Drew's war, Daisy's war, Tom frowned, was not to be fought by the old rules. This time around it was kill or be killed; sink or be sunk; bomb or be bombed. Happen it was better that way, he shrugged, turning his thoughts to Daisy who had been gone for three days now. He supposed there would be a letter by the midday post. He hoped so for Alice's sake, because this far there had only been two hastily written postcards.

He climbed the gate into Home Farm pasture, empty now of milk cows, the grass brown and coarse and not a sign of spring growth to be seen. Neither had he seen a daffodil in bloom. Tomorrow would be St David's day and on the first day of March folk might have expected daffodils to nod to them that winter was almost past. Yet their buds were still tightly closed and hardly a flower to be seen, save for a few celandines, small and golden and braving the cold with the last of the snowdrops. Surely now that March was around the corner, spring couldn't be all that far behind.

For no reason at all Tom thought about Tatiana Sutton. Young Tatty, Elliot Sutton's only child – only *legitimate* child. Now the lass was agitating to be off, an' all. Not that you could blame her. That old Russian woman at Denniston was a bit of a martinet, by all accounts.

He looked at his watch, decided he had time to check the hedgerow and pick up any snared rabbits before he made for Keeper's and the warmth of Alice's kitchen. Vegetable broth, thick with pearl barley they'd doubtless be having, and vegetable pie with maybe the odd scrap of leftover meat and gravy in it.

It amazed him how women managed to feed a family on such paltry rations, especially a family with growing lads in it. But it was simple, really. The mothers of growing lads went without – until their sons had grown old enough and strong enough to be called into the armed forces.

Stupid. Bloody stupid. Deliberately he turned off his brooding lest he get himself into a fratching mood, and thought instead about Alice and Keeper's kitchen and the fire crackling with logs. And maybe a letter on the mantelpiece, from Daisy.

'Thank you. Thank you very much.'

Tatiana replaced the receiver, letting go a huff of breath, thinking that by no means had the phone call put an end to her worries. Far from it. Her worries were only now about to begin.

'Tatiana! Who was telephoning you?' came the voice of her grandmother who, once the phone began to ring, had crept quietly across the drawing room to stand, breath indrawn, within hearing distance.

'Only the War Office.' Tatiana tilted her chin.

'The War Office, dear?' Anna put down the khaki scarf she was knitting. 'I thought we'd heard the last of London.'

'Why did you think that, Mother?'

'Because – well, you'd have said, wouldn't you, if –'

'No, I wouldn't – didn't. You and Grandmother thought that because I said nothing, then nothing had happened. Well, it has. That was them, offering me a job. A letter of confirmation is in the post, the professor said. I told him I would accept, and thanked him.'

'So! In spite of all we said, you have defied us! What kind of work is it?' Olga Petrovska was angry. 'More to the point, what on earth can you *do*?'

'Speak fluent Russian it would seem.'

'So you will be working with *them*, with the scum who killed the Czar-God-rest-him.' She closed her eyes, crossing herself devoutly, then returned to the attack. 'Don't you realize that any day those Bolsheviks could declare war on this country and then where will you be? And where will I, the Countess Petrovska, be? Hunted down, then shot in a cellar like our Czar! Where is your loyalty to *my* Russia? Don't you care that all we owned was stolen by the Bolsheviks?'

'Grandmother, I shall be working as a translator at the

War Office. I haven't the faintest idea what I shall be asked to do, or who I will meet. But the Secrets Act I shall sign will forbid me telling you – even if I wanted to.

'And I owe no loyalty to your Russia. England is where I was born and English is what I am. I shall be doing war work for my King and Queen and I wish you would remember, just sometimes, that your Czar died almost twenty-three years ago!'

'Tatiana! How *could* you?' Anna was on her feet in an instant. 'Say you are sorry! At once!'

'No, Mother, I am not sorry and I will not say so. And in case either of you is interested, I shall almost certainly be starting work on March the seventeenth. The letter will confirm it.'

Slowly, with an aplomb she never knew she possessed, Tatiana walked to the door, then hand on knob, she turned.

'I am going to Rowangarth now, to tell Aunt Julia and ask her if I can live with Sparrow at Montpelier Mews.'

She closed the door gently, wondering at her calmness, her control. Indeed, so absolute was her resolve that if Tim were still alive she would have used her new-found courage to pick up the phone and beg him to marry her, just as soon as Scottish law allowed it.

But Tim was dead and instead she was going to London and not her grandmother, nor a whole regiment of grand-mothers exactly like her, would be allowed to stand in her way!

'By heck, lass, it's sharpish outside still!' Tom hung up his cap, unwound his muffler. 'Saw the GPO van over at Home Farm – was there anything for us?'

'There was.' Alice dipped into her pinafore pocket. 'Sit you by the fire and read it. Dinner won't be a minute.'

'Now this is a bit more like it!' Tom felt the thickness of the letter. 'There'll be a bit more news in this one.' Postcards were little comfort when they needed to know all that was taking place. 'The lass is settling down now, happen.'

'Happen she is. It's me won't settle till I get her home for good.'

'But when it's all over she'll be marrying Keth and you'll lose her all over again.'

'Oh, no!' Alice lifted a pie from the oven. 'Married or not, you never lose daughters. But read it while I dish up.'

Tom smiled, savouring the moment. Three sheets, back and front in Daisy's small, neat writing.

Dear Mam and Dada,

At last a minute to myself. PO gave us a make-and-mend this afternoon and we are all busy catching our breath, washing our undies and writing letters.

The train was only an hour late arriving here and a very nice minister gave me a hand to Robertson House. But would you believe it – your daughter has ended up in the workhouse! It's a barn of a place and the only fire allowed is in the common room.

There are four cabins with three double bunks in each. (I sleep in a bottom bunk – not so far to fall!) Twenty-four girls started last Friday and already three have had to remuster because they failed the typing test.

I am to be a teleprinter-operator and if I pass I will wear crossed flags on my right arm because I will be in Signals.

Leading-Wren Alderson is our quarters assistant and wakens us at six each morning. Petty Officer Green is our instructor and we have been divided into two watches, port and starboard.

Cabins 3 and 4 are on starboard.

'She's on starboard watch,' Tom smiled as Alice set down his plate.

'Yes. I've read it.' Three times, truth known.

'Hmm.' Tom spread the letter on the table beside him, then picked up his knife and fork.

In the teleprinter room are twelve machines, so we take it morning and afternoon about. When one watch teleprints, the other does squad drill and helps clean the hostel.

The teleprinters have a mind of their own. You can't hit the keys like you can on a typewriter and you must learn to keep an even rhythm or they make funny noises and print out gobbledegook. I thought I would never get the touch, but this afternoon I got the hang of it and PO said, 'Very good, Dwerry-house,' which was praise indeed because she doesn't half give us the runaround.

'This pie is good, love.' Tom turned over another sheet. 'What's in it?'

'I shudder to think. Bits of this, bits of that. But do you think she's managing, Tom? Do you reckon she's homesick and won't admit it?'

'I doubt she'll have time to be homesick; the runaround she says they're getting. They do that, y'know. They reckon that if they can't break your heart in the first two weeks, then you'll do. Things get better after that.'

The food is good, though not as good as yours, Mam. We have porridge and something on toast for breakfast, bread and jam and cocoa for standeasy, then dinner and supper which are quite good, then standeasy before lights out. (Standeasy is the naval word for a break for tea or cocoa or a cigarette.)

We have to use naval terms, now. The yard where we do our drill is called the quarterdeck, the floor is the deck and the ceiling is the deck-head.

A male petty officer comes from the dockyard each day to drill us. He says we are the worst lot he's ever had and that we march like left-footed camels. I wasn't keen on squad drill at first but I'm getting the hang of it and learning a few manoeuvres. This morning we did right wheeling and left wheeling. The PO said we all flounced about like a crowd of chorus girls. One girl only brought high heels with her which are useless for marching in. She had to go to sick bay this morning to get her blisters seen to. I don't think she's going to last the fortnight out.

I will try to phone you as soon as we are allowed out, which won't be until next week.

No uniforms as yet, but we have been given armbands with WRNS on them to wear next week when we'll be given a late pass so that any of us whose feet have survived the squad drill will be going into Dunmfermline to the dance at the ice rink.

The packet of Keth's letters arrived by the afternoon delivery and two from you, Mam. Wheeeee!

Don't worry about me. Just take care of yourselves because I love you both very much.

Tea and rock buns will be coming up soon from the gallery and if you don't get there smartly the gannets scoff the lot so will sign off with an AR. That's signal jargon for 'end of message'. God bless,
Daisy.

'Well now,' Tom smiled. 'She seems to be managing fine. What's a make-and-mend?'

'Time off. Drew told me. It started in Nelson's day when sailors were excused duties to mend their kit. Make-do and mend, they called it. Mind, what a gannet is, I don't know,' Alice laughed.

'Now there I can help you.' It was good to hear Alice laugh. 'A gannet is a greedy seabird – one with a liking for rock buns, it would seem.' Tom laid down his knife and fork, reaching for Alice's hand. 'Now tell me you feel better, bonny lass. Tell me you won't worry so much about her?'

'Happen I won't, Tom, but when we'd got our war over with, we were so sure there would be no more. Our war was the one to end all wars, yet now our own girl has gone.'

'Just as her mother did. Two stubborn, self-willed women I landed myself with,' he teased, 'and do you know what? I'm right proud of them both.'

'Flatterer! Get your dinner finished. I want the place tidy. Julia's coming over for a chat this afternoon.'

'Is she, now?' And no prizes for guessing what they would be on about.

'Hi, Uncle Nathan! Got something to tell you. Where is Aunt Julia?'

'Gone over to Keeper's, Tatiana. There's news from Daisy, too. She's going to be a teleprinter-operator.'

'And I have got myself a job! I've *got* to tell someone, and Mother and the Petrovska aren't best pleased about it. Are you busy, or can I stay?'

'I suppose so, you troublesome miss! We'll go into the winter parlour. The fire is laid – I'll just put a match to it. And why are you looking at me like that?'

'Like what?'

'Quizzical, sort of.'

'If you must know, I was wishing you'd been my father.' She walked quickly ahead of him, settling herself on the sagging, chintz-covered settee.

'Were you, now?' Her wide-eyed gaze, so like that of her mother, made him feel uneasy. 'Well, I'm glad I'm not – for obvious reasons, if you see what I mean?'

'I don't mean *that*.' She turned to watch the crackling leap of the kindling in the firegrate, eyes brooding. 'You'd have been a better father, though. I'm sorry you and Aunt Julia didn't have children. You should have had heaps and I could have been one of them. I didn't like my father, you know.'

'Tatiana Sutton – you never knew him!'

'Didn't I? Well, I knew a lot of things nobody knows about.'

'But you were only a tot when he died.'

'I know. But there were – *things*. I think I must have sensed them. Unhappiness, my mother crying. Perhaps it's my Russian soul that picks things out of the air so it can suffer.'

'Away with your imaginings!' *Imaginings?* 'And you are a Sutton, never forget, and as English as the rest of us. Now tell me about that job because I'm going to throw you out at three. I've a call to make on a parishioner.'

He crossed the room to sit beside her, laying an arm on her shoulder, and she snuggled close.

'Then I'd better tell you. I start work in London on the seventeenth. It's official. I came to tell you both and to make sure it's still okay for me to stay with Sparrow.'

'That's splendid news!' he smiled. 'And I'm sure Julia's offer is still open, though it's really up to your mother, you realize that?'

He hoped there would be no objections from Denniston House and wondered if Anna really knew how much her daughter needed to get away, be allowed to live her own life.

'Sadly, yes. If they had their own way they'd forbid it. But I won't let them stop me going, Uncle Nathan. But let me tell you all about it . . .'

'There were two letters from Drew this morning. He sends his love.' Julia gazed at the photograph of the young sailor on the mantelpiece at Keeper's Cottage, returning his smile. 'His letters seem to come in twos and threes; suppose they get posted when the *Maggie* comes alongside.'

'Why,' clucked Alice, 'must he call his boat the *Maggie*?'

'The entire crew does it. The *Margaret Penrose* was once a fishing trawler called after the owner's mother. At least the Navy kept most of the name. There's an old sepia photograph hanging on the bulkhead outside the ward-room door, Drew says, of Mrs Penrose herself. Seems it always hung there when the *Margaret Penrose* fished for cod and the owner insisted it stayed there, because his mother had always watched over the fishermen and she would have no objection, he was sure, to watching over a few naval lads.'

'Now isn't that nice? So between the good Lord and Mrs Penrose, Drew is in good hands. Don't know about Daisy, though. I used to tell her she'd end up in the workhouse when she was little because she couldn't spend her pocket money quickly enough. And now she has – ended up in a workhouse, I mean,' Alice smiled, 'though it'll only be till she's trained for teleprinting, whatever that might be. She hasn't got a uniform yet,' she added, ever hopeful that Daisy wouldn't like the Wrens or the Wrens wouldn't like Daisy and send her back home. 'She'll get that when – *if* – she passes out. At the moment, all she has is an armband.'

'She'll pass! I know you don't want her to, but aren't you proud of her, deep down?'

'Suppose I am,' Alice admitted. 'D'you know where I was when you arrived? Upstairs, about to have a look at my precious things, and likely have a weep. I'm glad you came early.'

'Precious like what?'

'Oh, silly little things like the butterfly Keth gave Daisy when he was no more'n three – still there in its matchbox. You'd have thought it would have crumbled to dust by now. And there's Daisy's first tooth and the birthday card she made me when she was in infant school when we lived at Windrush. And there's Drew's first tooth . . .'

'No there isn't. I got his first one. You got the second one he wiggled out! Oh, Alice, whoever would have thought we'd come to this? It isn't five minutes since we lived in fear and dread of Sister Carbolic, though that staff nurse at York Military Hospital came a close second!' Julia handed back Daisy's letter then rose to leave. 'Got to go. Want to make a call in the village before dark.' She hugged Alice close, then whispered, 'And don't worry about Daisy, nor Drew. Mother is watching over them, too. They'll both come home to us one day. I know it.'

Tatiana decided to walk the long way home because the more time it took, the better. She was not looking forward to facing her grandmother's renewed probings and her mother's look of hurt, because her mother had big brown eyes that couldn't half look hurt when she wanted them to.

She hurried past the great yawning hole where once the village hall stood and turned her head sharply to look towards the churchyard.

'Hi, Aunt Julia!' she called, running away from the bomb crater because it reminded her too much of Tim.

'Hullo, Tatty. Were you looking for me?'

'Not exactly. I expected you to be at Keeper's. I was dawdling, I suppose.'

'I've not long left there. Daisy seems fine, by the way. You've got her address?'

'Yes, and I'll write now there's something to tell her. I got the job in London, Aunt Julia.'

'Then well done you!'

'So you don't think I'm a fool, running away from home?'

'Since you ask, I do – well, running away to London, that is. It isn't a very safe place to be at the moment. But I did exactly the same thing and ran away to France, which was in no way a rest cure. Foolhardiness must run in the Sutton females, I think.'

'Mm. Did you come here to have a word with Aunt Helen?'

'I did. I like to come every day if I can, and see that your grandfather is all right, too, and Reuben and Cook and Jinny Dobb.' She bent to lift withered flowers from the grave. 'That flash frost must have got at these last night. I'll have to see if Catchpole has anything decent left. Trouble is, the daffodils aren't out yet and I think I've had the last of his chrysanths.' She trailed her fingers over her parents' headstone then asked, 'How are things with you now, Tatty?'

'*Things*, Aunt Julia?'

'Your mother told me about your young man – not a lot, mind.'

'Did she tell you that I loved him very much or did she mention my girlish crush in passing?' Pain darkened her eyes and she bit hard on her lip.

'Your mother wasn't being unkind, dear. She just said you'd told them you'd known one of the crew who were – well – the plane on the pike . . .'

'That's Mother all over. She dismisses Tim in a few sentences. It's the Petrovska in her. Well, it wasn't like that at all. I got in a rage and told them both about him. Everything. I wasn't going to, ever, but it all came out. I was hurting so badly, you see, and I wanted to hurt them, too.'

'I know, Tatty. I really do know.'

'Do you? Tim wasn't just my young man. We were lovers, Aunt Julia. When he was killed, my period was late. I thought for just a little while that I was pregnant, and I didn't care. Do you think I'm common?'

'No, sweetheart. I used to ache all over for Andrew. I'd have done anything, gone anywhere, just to be with him for an hour, in bed.'

'Thank you for understanding.' Tatiana reached for Julia's hand, holding it tightly. 'But the awful thing is the loneliness. It seems to stretch ahead for the rest of my life. Having Tim, even for so little a time, has spoiled me for anyone else. It's sad to think of always being alone – can you understand that, too?'

'Oh, yes. But I was luckier than you, Tatty. I did have Drew to love. I'd have gone out of my mind without that little baby to fight for. But come with me to Jinny's grave, and let me tell you what she said to me – oh, years and years ago.'

'Jin Dobb used to tell fortunes, didn't she? She told Daisy's mother's fortune and it all came true.'

'Yes, and one night I went down to Rowangarth kitchen. If I remember rightly, it was to tell them that Alice and Tom had been married – you'd know that Alice was first married to my brother Giles? – and that they'd just had a little girl.'

'That would be Daisy.'

'Daisy Julia Dwerryhouse, as ever was! Anyway, it was then Jin told me. She said that one day I would love again, but I wouldn't listen, of course. She told me there was first love and last love and all shapes and sizes of loving in between, so I hadn't to shut my heart to love when I chanced on it. Dear old Jin.' She traced the simple inscription on the simple gravestone with tender fingers. 'She was a no-nonsense soul. I think she would have approved of what they've put there for her. "Jane Dobb, Spinster. 4.11.1866–5.10.1940 RIP." Rest in peace, Jin . . .'

'You were a long time chancing on Uncle Nathan, though.'

'Eighteen years after Andrew. He waited for me all that time. He'd always loved me, you see. He's a dear, good man, Tatty. One day, when the hurt goes, will you remember I told you here beside Jin's grave that one day you'll meet your last love?' She gathered the sad-eyed girl to her, laying a cheek on hers. 'And you will, darling, I promise.'

'Aunt Julia – can I tell you something? I told Uncle Nathan I wished he'd been my father. I told him I wished you and he had had lots of children and that I had been one of them. And I really mean it. I wish you were my mother, too. I do!'

'Gracious, child – and what has poor Anna done to deserve this? Your mother is a dear person, Tatty. Try to understand that she –'

'That she's completely under Grandmother Petrovska's thumb and that she and my father weren't happy? They weren't, you know.'

'And whoever told you that?' Julia demanded warily.

'No one told me and it's true. I was only little, but I knew, even then. Small children aren't as stupid as grown-ups imagine. It was something I must have sensed; something I picked out of the atmosphere. And it became a part of me, that hatred between them.'

'Tatiana Sutton, what am I to do with you?' Julia held the troubled girl from her, smoothing back her tousled hair. 'And I suppose what you really want to ask me,' she smiled, though the smile came hard to her lips, 'is whether you can live at Montpelier Mews when you go to London to work?'

The question she asked was the only way she knew to avoid talking about how it had been at Denniston when Elliot – oh, *damn* Elliot!

'I do, and can I, please?'

'As far as I'm concerned, yes. Mind, it would be subject to Sparrow's rules and regulations and if your mother agrees.'

'Bless you. I shall like being at Montpelier. And you just asked me whatever were you to do with me. Well, will you keep loving me, you and Uncle Nathan?'

'You know we will. Always. And will you do something for me? Will you come here in the morning and help me tidy the Sutton graves? There are so many of them, and

Catchpole has neither the time nor the staff to do it. I'd be so glad if you would.'

'I'd like that. I'll do Grandfather Sutton's and Jin Dobb's and Mrs Shaw's, too. Mind, Daisy's mother sees to Reuben's grave, so we'd better not do his, had we?' And she didn't want to tidy her father's grave nor that of her Grandmother Clementina. Neither of them had loved her; she knew it from the hurt that was hard and deep inside her and made her wish all the more she had been born a Rowangarth Sutton. It was wicked to think such a thing here, only feet from where they both lay, but the hardness and hurt they had both helped put there made her feel not too guilty. 'And do you promise me that the loneliness will go one day? And you don't think I'm stupid for loving Tim so much, when I'd known him for such a little time?'

'It isn't stupid to love. I fell in love with Andrew the minute I saw him and your Aunt Helen fell in love with my pa in just the same way. That's another female Sutton trait. We fall in love too instantly and too well. Now let's be off. It's starting to get dark and your mother will be wondering where you are. Oh, don't you just ache for summer and the long, light nights?'

'I do.' Tatiana really did. In the summer she would be in London, away from her grandmother and from the reproach in her mother's eyes. Away, too, from the sight and sound of bombers she thought, as one flew over. 'I can't wait.'

At the end of the village street, where it met the lane that led to Home Farm and the crossroads beyond, she turned and waved, calling, ''Bye. See you in the morning!' Then she was gone, her long, dark curls lifting and falling as she ran.

Julia watched her go. Tatiana would find happiness again. Her need to love and be loved was too great for her to remain too long alone. Only she must not fall in love with Drew. He and Tatty could not love, just as Drew and Daisy could never have loved.

Julia remembered the night in long-ago Hampshire when they told Daisy and Drew they were brother and sister. Yet they could never tell Drew and Tatiana that the man who had fathered them both was Elliot Sutton.

'Don't ever fall in love with Drew, Tatty?' she whispered. 'Because if you do your heart will be broken again and Drew will hate me, too.'

And that, she could not bear.

25

The intake of twenty-four at Robertson House dwindled to nineteen. Three had left for London to remuster to another category, High Heels and her aching feet had declined to accept the King's shilling, and The Flaming Red as she had been dubbed because of her carroty hair and Communist leanings declared she would never tip her cap to anyone and They knew what They could do with their saluting and their yes ma'am, no ma'am, three-bags-full-ma'am!

So Petty Officer Green suggested they might both be better off in other occupations, arranged for a third-class travel warrant and a packet of sandwiches to be made available to each on the following day, then sighed with relief because they had both caused her more trouble than either was ever likely to be worth.

It was about that time that Daisy began to lose her fear of teleprinters. She had learned to whisper her fingertips over the keys and was pleased that a flick of the little finger, right hand, could return the carriage without effort. And better still, a teleprinter had only three rows of keys, not four like typewriters. Figures, on the top line, were easier to reach.

Now she could forgive the typing teacher who insisted on the wearing of eye masks so that touch-typing might be exactly that, and feeling for typewriter keys instead of peeping at them became second nature. Because she could send pretend signals without taking her eyes from the copy in front of her, she had passed out with an amazing eighty-two per cent and an A mark for general efficiency.

Glowing pinkly from her instructor's seldom-given

praise, Daisy joined the intake climbing into the back of a naval truck to be taken to Rosyth Dockyard by a Wren driver with a death wish, but PO Green, who had driven with her many times before and always came back alive, emerged unruffled from the front of the truck, formed her probationers into a squad, then marched them to a large building which could only be described as a warehouse.

'*Squaaaad* – stand at ease!'

They relaxed, feet twelve inches apart, hands behind backs, heads now free to move.

'I will now explain your joining-ship routine. First you will have your final medical checks and a dental examination. You will receive the usual inoculation and those in need of vaccination, if any, will be vaccinated. And if any of you are afraid of jabs, then you'd better go home to your mothers now!'

She paused meaningfully, then told them their height and weight and physical features would be recorded and a photograph taken, during which process they were not to smile.

Only when they had taken an oath of allegiance to their sovereign would they be given a paybook which must be kept at all times in the inside right pocket of their jackets and which they would guard with their lives. There followed another meaningful pause.

'Try, if you can, to remember any birthmarks, operation scars, moles or blemishes, et cetera, so as not to waste time. You will start at one end of the building and by the time you have progressed the length of it you will be a member of the Women's Royal Naval Service and nothing on the face of this earth will get you out, save ill health or death, an act of treason, or pregnancy – is that understood?'

The entire intake murmured, with only slight hesitation, that it was; the petty officer, her joining-ship piece recited called, 'Right, then! *Squaaad* – atten-*shun*!'

They came to attention with an efficiency that would have warmed the heart of the drill instructor who called them a flouncing chorus line not two weeks before.

'*Squaaaad* – dis-*miss*!'

They turned as one, swivelling on right feet, bringing left feet down with a stamp. Then they took one step, right-footed, and that was it. They were all very good at dismissing. It was the best part of squad drill.

'Now follow me! And no chattering and no speaking unless spoken to!'

They followed the small, grey-haired woman into an echoing place of cathedral-like proportions to begin their initiation into the Women's Royal Naval Service. Some felt elation. Others felt an inside churning. All followed the pointing arrow on which was painted 'Medical Officer'.

'PO – will I have to strip off?' came a worried whisper. 'I've got the curse.'

'And that makes you unique, does it?' PO could be very cutting when she set her mind to it. It came of having twenty-four ewe lambs foisted upon her every two weeks of the year. 'I am quite sure the MO and nursing sister know all about menstrual periods!'

'Sorry I spoke!'

'*Say again!*'

'I said I'm quite sure they are, PO.'

'That's better! Right, then. First stop the MO. Give your particulars to the writer as and if they are asked for. She does *not* want your family medical history, remember!'

The writer, who, had she been a civilian would have been called a clerk, murmured, 'First one – surname, please,' and Daisy wished, not for the first time, that her name had been Sutton or Smith because she would be asked to spell out Dwerryhouse. She always was.

'Here we go then,' someone whispered. 'There's one born every minute . . .'

*　　*　　*

By the time Daisy reached the exit of the building cubicled into departments, it had been established she was fit enough to serve in the WRNS, her date of birth and religious demonination noted together with her home address, and that her father, Thomas Dwerryhouse of the same address, was her next of kin. She had been asked to spell her surname six times during the progression from civilian to Wren and she longed for the day when to marry Keth would free her from it.

It was also recorded that her height was five feet five inches, that her chest measurement – they didn't have busts, it seemed, in Nelson's day – was thirty-four inches, that her eyes were blue, her complexion fresh and her hair was fair. In that dockside warehouse they had not heard of blonde, Titian, mousy or raven's wing; only down-to-earth colours like fair, red, medium and dark. And because they were becoming used, as they passed from one department to the next, to having their souls stripped bare almost, and because everyone seemed to have something to be noted under the heading Distinguishing Scars, Marks, etc, Daisy blushingly volunteered her own and was at once sorry that she had.

'I have a mole, Chief, on my – er – left bust.'

'Mole on left breast!' yelled the Chief to his writer so it seemed all eyes in the whole of the building swivelled to that part of her anatomy as though she were some kind of freak.

'Why do you need to know such things?' she demanded crossly and unwisely, wondering why he couldn't have called it a bust, too, and why he seemed to delight in letting the whole of the dockyard know about the very small mole – on her *breast*.

'Because if yer 'ead gets blown orf, we'll know that the torso with a mole on its port-side titty could be that of Wren Dwerryhouse D. J. – orlright?'

'Yes, Chief.' Red-faced and defeated, she hurried to catch

up with the remainder of the flagging group who by now had reached the final hurdle and were being told that the period of their engagement would be for the duration of hostilities, be it long or short. *For the duration*: words to strike awe into the heart of all recruits.

'All we need now is your National Identity number,' said PO Green. 'You will each keep your civilian identity card until tomorrow when you go to St Leonards to be kitted out. You will then exchange your identity card for your naval paybook and an identity disc, and after that . . .'

She left the remainder of her oft-repeated monologue hanging on the air, to be interpreted as her listeners wished.

For her own part, Daisy murmured, 'Identity number KRMA 127/3.' It was all, she realized, that remained of Daisy Julia Dwerryhouse. From tomorrow on she would be Dwerryhouse D. J., plus a number. For the duration.

What *had* she done?

'Wasn't that Chiefie at the dockyard ghoulish? If our heads are blown off, indeed! Who the hell would care? I mean, when your head has been blown off you *can't* care, can you?'

'I need a filling! Got to report to the dental surgeon when I arrive at my new base.'

'They used a blunt needle for my jab,' sighed another. 'Why did you need a vaccination as well, Dwerryhouse? No one else did. I thought it was the law that all babies must be vaccinated before they were three months old. Why weren't you?'

'I was. Seems not even one of them took so the doctor said I was immune, Mam said, like the cows they get the vaccine from.'

'Lucky so-and-so. You should see my vaccination scars!'

'I told the MO about mine not taking and he said, "This one will," all nasty, sort of. And he said I was to keep it dry.'

Only one vaccination was given, Daisy thought thankfully, and was forced to admit the medical officer would probably be right because already, beneath the plaster Sister stuck over it, there was a distinct tingling.

'How soon will we know where we're being sent?'

'I'm not sure. But we'll have to sew our flags on our greatcoats and jackets. And we'll have to put on our hat ribbons,' offered one whose sister was already a Wren and who could be told nothing about naval procedure, Admiralty Instructions or any item of Wrens' clothing, and who knew all the fiddles about late passes, though she wasn't going to tell! 'I think it'll be the day after tomorrow when we get our draft chits.' Daisy had christened her Know-All.

'I hope they don't send me to Glasgow,' mourned another. 'That's where I live and I only joined up to get away from my daddy. He's a narrow-minded old booger! It's fingers crossed for a draft to England for me! How soon can I volunteer for overseas?' The further away, the better!

'As soon as you like,' Know-All supplied promptly. 'My sister says the best foreign draft any of the women's Forces can get is Gibraltar. They all try for Gib. but nobody seems to know anyone who gets it.

'And don't forget we'll have to pack our civilian clothes and post them home tomorrow. They'll give us sheets of paper and sticky tape and they'll be sent home OHMS, so we won't have to pay the postage.'

Cabin 3 was charged with nervous chatter, apprehension and second thoughts, and Daisy calculated that there were only twelve hours left in which to change her mind. And she wouldn't. She was stubborn, like Mam, and like Mam she was sticking it out for the duration. But it still hurt just to think of Keeper's Cottage and Brattocks Wood and Rowangarth. And especially it hurt to think of Mam and Dada and how much she loved them. She glanced at the letter she had been trying to write for the past hour.

Darling Keth,

Soon I will be able to send you a permanent address and you can stop sending your letters to Keeper's. This is my last night as a civilian and I feel all peculiar inside. Tomorrow I will get my uniform, paybook and an official number. Everything here is chaotic; everything at the double.

Just got time to say I love you, love you, love you and I want you to hold me and touch me and kiss me so much that it hurts.

Take care, my darling.

Your Daisy.

'So that's where you're hiding!' Tom stood in the doorway, looking at his wife who was kneeling in the corner of the bedroom. 'You haven't been crying, lass? Daisy is going to be fine.'

'Happen. But she shouldn't have gone; not till they brought in conscription for women.' *If* they ever brought it in, that was. 'And it wasn't thinking of Daisy that made me sniffy. I got the idea to wrap her christening mug in tissue paper and put it away. I've tried all the shops I know and I can't get a tin of silver polish for love nor money, so the sooner this is somewhere dark, the better.'

'I see.' Memories of Daisy's christening mug, given to her by Mr Hillier, nigh on twenty-one years ago. Memories of Daisy being christened and Julia standing godmother for her and he and Alice so thankful there would be no more wars. If anything was certain in their world, it was that. 'And you've been going through the precious box, I suppose.'

'Yes.' What else was there to do now, when knitting wool had all but disappeared from the shops and yardage was in short supply and expensive, even when you chanced on it. Nothing to knit with; nothing to sew with and no daughter to welcome home each night.

'I was looking at Daisy's christening brooch that Julia gave her. It must have been worth a pretty penny, even then.'

'Didn't it come from the Whitecliffes?'

Not only valuable, but old. It might be nice, Alice thought, for Daisy to wear it at her wedding. It would take care of the something old, something blue requirements. Her wedding dress would be new, of course . . .

'Hm. Something borrowed?' she whispered to which Tom asked, 'Something *what*?' and to which Alice replied, 'Oh, nothing. Just thinking out loud.'

She closed the lid of the box of precious things, slipped it into its hiding place, eased the loose floorboard over it, then laid back the linoleum, pressing it down firmly. She had looked at Tom's buttercups and Daisy's butterfly, checked that her pearl eardrops were still there and her marriage lines and bankbook and Daisy's bankbook. The six ten-shilling notes, too, always kept in the house in case of dire emergency – like sending Daisy her fare home, which didn't seem to be going to happen, now.

'She hasn't rung. Not once, in the entire fortnight.'

'Happen she tried, and couldn't get through. You know the way it is with trunk calls these days. Or maybe she hasn't been allowed to. We'll be hearing soon. There'll be a letter or a call letting us know where she's landed up. And look what I've been given for the lass.' He dipped into his pocket to bring out a pair of navy-blue woollen gloves. 'Will Stubbs' auntie knitted them for her. The old lady isn't managing over well on one ration book. I've been slipping her a rabbit from time to time to help eke out the meat and these are by way of a thank you. When you send them to the lass, tell her to be sure to write to the old lady. She'd be tickled pink to get a letter.'

'I will, Tom.' Daisy would need no reminding. 'I hope she'll be able to wear gloves that aren't official issue. She did say in one of her letters that they can't wear jewellery

– only an engagement ring or wedding ring. They can't wear earrings either, and they have to wear their hair short so it doesn't touch their jacket collars. Let's hope she got herself a decent haircut in Dunfermline.'

'The lass is capable of getting her hair trimmed,' Tom sniffed. 'And is a man who has worked all day and is off Home Guarding all night to get his supper, do you think?'

He frowned as he followed Alice down the stairs. She was too quiet these days. Julia had had to get used to Drew being called up and Alice would have to do the same, or she'd make herself badly.

Trouble was, though, that Daisy hadn't needed to go. She had volunteered in a fit of pique and there lay the cause of Alice's unhappiness. Daisy could be stubborn and self-willed and if Alice thought that maybe tomorrow there would be a phone call to say it hadn't worked out at Robertson House and she was on her way home, then Alice had better think again.

'Something smells good,' he smiled, even though he knew it was rabbit. Again. 'And had you thought it won't be many more months before Daisy'll have to get herself off to Winchester? She gets that money in June, don't forget.'

'I hadn't forgotten. It'll be Sir Maxwell she'll have to see, won't it, but whether the Wrens will give her time off to go down and sign things, I'm not so sure. Maybe it's going to have to wait till she has leave – unless they send her somewhere near there. But whatever put that idea into your head?'

'Can't for the life of me tell you. But it proves, doesn't it, how quickly time passes. Seems only yesterday we were worried out of our minds, wondering what having all that money was going to do to Daisy. Only goes to show that before you know it, she'll be home on leave.'

But Alice only smiled in a vague kind of way and wondered if she would ever get used to the ache she felt inside her every time she thought how far away Daisy was, and wondered for the thousandth time what her daughter was doing now.

'No one,' said Petty Officer Green, 'is allowed to walk up that staircase.'

The staircase was extremely wide and beautiful and highly polished; a reminder of long-ago craftsmen who knew about proportions and how to match the grain in wood, and who were proud to have fashioned a sweeping staircase made from the wood of holly trees.

'Then how do they manage, PO – to get upstairs, I mean?'

'They use the back stairs, which we will all do.' PO Green would be glad to see the back of this intake. For one thing they asked too many questions and had, with only a few exceptions, made the transition from typewriter to teleprinter extremely reluctantly. And what was more, five of them had slipped her net.

'Which toffs lived here before the Navy swiped the place, PO?'

'I'm sure I don't know. I only know this was once a school for young ladies – St Leonards – before it was requisitioned by the Navy. I have no time to pry into the history of the place nor am I interested.' And the sooner she got this lot on their separate ways, the better pleased would she be. 'Now follow me! And I want no nonsense in Slops. This is not a fashion house and you will take what is given to you. Give your hip and bust sizes clearly and distinctly or you'll get brassieres which don't fit and knickers, too. And hurry!' she clucked. 'There *is* a war on, you know!'

The clothing store, known affectionately as Slops, they found in a large, high room which once could have been an assembly hall in the house's days as a school, or the great hall when once a family lived in it. Now it was filled with shelf upon shelf and row upon row of WRNS uniforms.

When Daisy's turn came, a leading-wren eyed her up and down and quickly handed her a jacket. 'Try it,' she was ordered and when she put it on, fumbling with the black, anchor-embossed buttons, she was forced to agree it wasn't a bad fit for a first guess, though Mam would have tutted a bit that it seemed too big over the hips.

'Can I try a size smaller?' she ventured. 'It's a bit loose on –'

'Next!' called the leading-wren, handing Daisy a second jacket of the same size, indicating with a sideways nod of her head that that was what she was getting. Two skirts were then thrust at her and she was elbowed further along the line.

A heavy top coat was offered. 'Try this. On *top* of your jacket, idiot! And put your other things down. Stand back. Let's have a look at it for length . . .'

Daisy fastened the top and bottom greatcoat buttons then took a step backwards, turning obligingly round only to be ordered to stand still.

'Hmm. Fourteen inches from the floor you know it's got to be. You'll have to have that taken up a couple of inches. Next, please!'

A raincoat was added to the pile, by which time Daisy had decided to walk the length of the line and take what was given to her and remember that this was not indeed a fashion house, though Mam wouldn't like the roughness of the navy-blue serge material at all. She wasn't over enamoured of it herself.

It was as the girl from Glasgow remarked later when apprehensively they put on their uniforms for the first time in Cabin 3, 'I'll admit that considering the way this lot was thrown at us, they haven't made a bad job of it.'

'Not made a bad job of it?' wailed Know-All. 'Just look at these bloody knickers!' Dramatically she stood centre stage, exactly as Kitty would have done Daisy thought achingly, white shirt tails flapping and the navy, rayon-knit

Directoire knickers reaching down to her knees. 'This isn't on, you know.'

'Oh, they aren't so bad. I think those are just a tiny bit big – by about two sizes!' Someone getting her own back for Know-All's bossy ways. 'Why don't you cut twelve inches off the legs!'

'But I can't! It isn't allowed!'

'Who says not? Is somebody going to lift your skirt and take a look at your knickers, then?'

Daisy regarded the pile of uniform on her bunk. She had taken off her civilian clothes, put on her pyjamas and dressing gown, then folded the clothing she would not wear again until heaven only knew when. Carefully she filled the cardboard box provided for the purpose, wrapped it round with the large sheet of brown paper, then wrote Keeper's address front and back in large, clear capitals. And all the time a cold hand squeezed her heart, not only because she was packing almost twenty-one years of being Daisy Dwerryhouse into a cardboard box but more because of what Mam would think when she unpacked it.

First, she would have a little weep just as she, Daisy, wanted to weep now. Then she would shake out the skirts and the coat and put them on hangers, sorting what was left into piles, ready for wash day. Mam was like that. Very systematic.

Daisy blinked away the tears that threatened at a vision of Mam washing and mangling her clothes and hanging them out to dry at the bottom of the garden near Gracie's hens. And the hens made her forget the tears for a moment and think how Gracie must have felt the day she first put on her own uniform. Lucky Gracie, to be living in the bothy and being looked after by Polly and working in Rowangarth kitchen garden.

But Gracie liked being in the Land Army, didn't she, and if Gracie could like her service then so could Daisy Dwerryhouse.

'We'll have to get our flags sewn on and our hat ribbon fixed before tomorrow,' said the girl in the top bunk. 'We're going to look like a squad of penguins, all black and white. And the *hats*! I mean, they're just like my school hat, except they're in gaberdine. They're a bit Great War, aren't they? The army girls have far nicer caps.'

'I know. And we all look so *new*. It's going to take for ever, wearing the fluff off these uniforms. And as for the stockings! I thought I'd said goodbye to black woollen stockings the day I left school! As soon as they let us out, I shall buy silk ones.'

'Black silk stockings aren't allowed, nor lisle ones – not officially,' said Know-All, 'but my sister says they all wear them when they go on dates and to dances. I've already got a couple of pairs with me,' she added smugly. 'And do you all realize that everything, absolutely *everything*, has to be marked with our name and number?'

'Which we can't do,' snapped the girl from Glasgow, 'until tomorrow!' She was still worried that her drafting orders, when given to her, would bear the destination Flag Officer in Chief, Port of Glasgow.

Daisy contemplated all the naming and numbering. One greatcoat, still to be shortened; one raincoat – rather nice, the raincoat – also to be shortened. Two jackets and skirts in need of attention. One hat, one pair of woollen gloves, two pairs of black lace-up shoes. How did you name and number shoes, for Pete's sake?

Three brassieres in pink cotton – no problem, there – two suspender belts, three pairs of stockings size nine; a money-belt in webbing. The money-belt was a good idea, since handbags – even shoulder bags – were not allowed. Three pairs of knickers, two pairs of brushed-cotton pyjamas. Three white shirts, six collars and back and front collar studs. Dad was always losing his collar studs. She must buy a spare pair!

And vests! Mam would be pleased about the vests. You

needed them, she said, especially in winter and had been much put out when Daisy had refused any longer to wear hers, saying that vests and liberty bodices belonged to schooldays and oh, how she wished she were wearing her vest and liberty bodice again and suspendering her long black school stockings to it and that Keth would be waiting at the gate, to walk with her to the school bus.

Tears threatened again. She wanted Keth, wanted the blessed warmth of Keeper's Cottage kitchen, but most of all she wanted Mam.

'I'm going to get a bath,' she announced to no one in particular because only in the bath could she weep – unless someone came in to use the bath alongside. There was no privacy at Robertson House. Only in the lavatory. It surprised her that the lavatories were not in long lines, too. Yet only in the unprivate bath, she had discovered, could she feel really warm in this stone-floored, cold-comfort billet.

Bathing at Keeper's had been different. Once, when there was plenty of coal, the washboiler in the back kitchen was filled with water and a fire lit beneath it every day. Then Mam had taken the large zinc bath off the hook on the wall and placed it beside the boiler fire and ladled hot steamy water into it.

Baths at Keeper's were cosy affairs, even if you had to ladle all the water into a bucket when you'd finished, and tip it down the back kitchen sink.

That was when she remembered she couldn't have a bath. Her left arm reminded her because now it throbbed and had hurt a lot when she was trying on her uniform. On an impulse she took off her pyjama jacket then eased back the plaster and gauze that was becoming frayed and grubby-looking.

'Ooooh,' said Know-All, who missed nothing, 'your arm is in a mess, isn't it? I think it's gone poisoned. You should let Leading-Wren see it. She'll send you to sick bay, I shouldn't wonder.'

'Well, you can wonder all you like, because I'm not going to sick bay with a vaccination that's gone a bit red,' Daisy snapped.

'Sorry, I'm sure.' Know-All took her spongebag and towel and flounced off to the bathroom. That she was able to take a bath made Daisy dislike her all the more and she sat on her bunk with an angry bounce which made Top-Bunk lean over and ask her if she was all right.

'Thanks, but I'm *not* all right! My vaccination hurts like mad. I need a bath and I can't have one because I've got to keep my arm dry and you can't have a bath without getting your arm wet, can you? And this place is like an icehouse and oh, roll on my draft chit!'

She really meant it. The sooner she was out of this workhouse, the better. And how she needed Mam and Dada. Especially she needed Dada to hold her and hush her and tell her it would all come right; tell her, too, that the war had never happened and that Keth would be back from America on the very next liner to dock at Liverpool.

She gave way, then, to the tears she had been fighting for the past two weeks; let them flow unhindered and did nothing to muffle the sobs that came from deep inside her.

'I think,' said Know-All, who had returned from the bathroom because all the hot water had been used, 'that you should have got your tears over and done with long before this. Are you quite sure you're going to be suited to life in the Armed Forces?'

'Oh, go to hell!' Daisy stormed, and wept some more.

The intake of 28 February stood straight and still for Petty Officer Green's inspection and Daisy wondered if they all felt as bemused as she did.

They had pulled up their skirts to the regulation fourteen inches from the floor, tucking them into the wide, webbing belts until such time as they could be properly shortened, or in one case, lengthened. They had all experienced a great deal of bother with collars and ties. Collars were attached to the back of the shirt by a back stud and fastened at the front by another, larger stud. Then, when secured, the tie had to be slid in and knotted to PO's satisfaction. Knots must be neither too small nor too large so they were tied again and again that morning until nineteen knots were the same size and nineteen heavily starched white collars looked less pristine than they had done earlier.

Civilian gas masks in their small, square cardboard boxes had already been exchanged for large, Forces-issue respirators in khaki holders. They were to be worn to the left, over the hip so as to leave the right arm and hand free and unimpeded for saluting.

Jackets must be worn at all times and only removed in extreme cases. Should removal be necessary, then shirt sleeves must be rolled up level with the elbow, which was roughly three folds of the width of the cuff.

Cuff links may not be worn, except by commissioned officers; earrings may not be worn. Hair *must* be worn off the collar on all occasions. Civilian underwear must not be worn beneath uniforms and perfume was not, repeat *not* allowed.

The latter remark had caused a raising of eyebrows and a mild snigger in the ranks because who, repeat *who*, had so much as glimpsed a bottle of decent perfume these last twelve months?

Perhaps those lucky ones, maybe, with family in the Merchant Navy who could buy all the perfume and face creams they wanted when ashore in New York. The only drawback to that, of course, was that women would rather do without such things for ever than have the worry of a man who sailed the Atlantic with only an even chance of ever crossing it safely.

'Right! I think you'll do, though I have to say you are the worst intake it has ever been my burden to instruct!'

'I bet you say that to every intake, PO!'

'Qui-*et*! No talking in the ranks! Now get yourselves on to the transport and watch it! First Officer will be there for the oath-taking and I don't wany any cock-ups!'

Nineteen Wrens, having exchanged their civilian identity cards for naval paybooks which they placed in the right inside pockets of their new fluffy jackets, and having received their new identification discs, stood dry-mouthed in two lines in a large, white-painted room at St Leonards, eyes toward the blackboard on which the Oath of Allegiance was written in white chalk.

Daisy slid her eyes to the right to where the Union Jack hung and to the left to the White Ensign, then again to the front where a very smart, very beautiful First Officer stood ready to bear witness to it all.

As one, nineteen trembling voices recited the words then on the command, turned half-right to smartly salute their country's flag. And then, to PO Green's delight and relief, they made an immaculate turn-to-front, right arms returning to sides as one.

The beautiful First Officer thanked them, smilingly welcomed them to the Women's Royal Naval Service, then left the room.

It was over. They were in. For the duration. Now, they were to attend standeasy after which they would muster at 15.30 hours outside the drafting office, each to learn her destination.

Wren Dwerryhouse D. J. whose official number, written inside her paybook and on her identification disc, was 44455, wished her arm did not throb so much and that everyone who passed her did not seem intent upon bumping into it. Treble four, double five. An easy number to remember.

She held back from the scramble for tea and rock buns lest her arm be bumped again and when she was able to reach the table in comparative safety the teapot was empty and the buns gone.

She eased a finger round the inside of her collar. PO had pulled her tie too tight at final inspection and the collar was rubbing her neck.

She sighed deeply. Rock buns aside, she would have given almost anything for a cup of tea and two aspirins. Disconsolately she made her way to the drafting office where a line had already formed outside the door.

She went to stand beside Glasgow Girl, whose real name was Jeanette and whose eyes were closed because she was praying for a draft to England.

'Attention, please!' Petty Officer Green again. 'You will enter the room singly. Do not salute the officer as she will be sitting down and unable to return your salute. Come to attention on reaching the desk and say, "Ma'am." And it's ma'am as in jam, don't forget.'

They came automatically to attention as a Wren officer walked along the corridor and into the drafting office, then stood at ease to await their separate fates. Jeanette, who had manoeuvred a space up the queue, stood with eyes still closed. Daisy closed her eyes and sent up her own brief supplication.

God, it's Dwerryhouse 44455 and if there isn't a draft to Washington I don't really care where they send me. She really didn't care. She only wanted her arm to stop hurting and her head to stop throbbing. And she still wanted Dada to hold her, and Mam to tell her that of course she wasn't in the Wrens – for the duration.

The girl from Glasgow left the drafting office with a smile on her face like the sun on a spring morning.

'Appleacre,' she whispered. 'I'm away to NOIC Appleacre.'

'Where is that . . . ?'

'Devon!' Her travel warrant was made out to Bideford

and they didn't come any further away from Glasgow and her booger of a father than Bideford! 'Oh, jings!'

'Quiet!' hissed PO. 'Go on then, Dwerryhouse!'

Daisy walked smartly to the table, came to attention and said, 'Ma'am! Dwerryhouse D. 44455!'

'Ah, yes. You are to report to Wrens' Quarters, Hellas House. It's Liverpool. Good luck – er – Dwerryhouse.' She smiled whilst at the same time inclining her head to her right to indicate that the interview was over.

'Dwerryhouse,' said the petty officer at the table alongside. 'Sorry, but we can't tell you a lot about where you'll be going. Here's your travel warrant. Dunfermline to Lime Street, Liverpool. Change at Edinburgh. Report to the RTO's office on arrival. He'll tell you how to get to Hellas House.'

'And where will I be working, PO?'

'That I don't know. Somewhere new, I think. Not at Flag Officer's, that's for sure. Here's your warrant. Best you get the overnight train. Next, please!'

Liverpool. To somewhere new. So new, it would seem, that no one knew a great deal about it. Well, at least she'd been told she would be sleeping in a place called Hellas House tomorrow night, though where it was she had yet to learn from the Railway Transport Officer at Lime Street station.

'Where to, Dwerryhouse?' The girl from Glasgow grinned like the Cheshire cat.

'Liverpool. That's all I know.'

'A bit dicey, that. Air raids, I mean.'

'There are raids at most ports,' Daisy shrugged. 'And at least it isn't all that far from York. I'll be able to make it home on a forty-eight-hour pass. And my brother is based there. I'll be able to see Drew.'

'I didn't know you had a brother. You said you were an only child.'

'I am. Drew's my half-brother. Mam married twice.'

'I see.' The girl from Glasgow continued to smile. She would still be smiling, Daisy decided, when she reported to the Naval Officer in Charge at Appleacre. And as for Liverpool – well, what did it matter? All she wanted was to see Keth again.

Keth, I want you so much and we could be apart for years and years. Don't ever stop loving me? Please?

26

Goodbye Robertson House with its workhouse chill; good-bye Petty Officer Green and Leading-Wren with her early-morning breeziness. When the train hissed and clattered south across the Forth Bridge, Daisy had thrown a sixpenny piece through the window as people said she should, and wished; wished with all her heart for the touch of Keth's mouth on hers, gently unbelieving at first after so long apart, then urgently to show his need of her: kisses to close her eyes to – remind her how it had been one faraway summer when an old, bewildered man said there would be no war with Germany, that it was peace in our time. Almost three years ago, their daisychain summer; three years since she and Keth had kissed and touched. And loved.

She stared into the rushing blackness. The compartment was hot and smelled of dust, and the lavatory in the corridor outside had no door to it and no water in the pan which was the cause of the smell because a water closet should have water in it and lavatories not used as a dumping ground for cases and respirators and kitbags. Trains now were mostly filled with servicemen and -women, and the few civilians who ignored the posters demanding to know if their journey was really necessary travelled at their own discomfort. There was a war on, so trains were no longer for civilians but for service personnel going on leave or returning from leave or being taken to a port of embarkation. And trains were sometimes for the wounded. There had been a great many hospital trains after Dunkirk.

Daisy shifted in her seat. The sailor who had made room for her to squash six into a seat intended for four when passenger trains were for the sole comfort of passengers, looked at her sideways.

'You all right, Jenny?'

'Fine, thanks. Just tired, I suppose.'

Tired and uncomfortable in a cardboard-stiff collar and black itchy stockings, and hungry and thirsty and wanting Mam and Dada. And *please* for her head to stop aching? She was hot, too, but that was surely because none of the train's windows opened, and the crowd of bodies in this small, dirty compartment. She would feel better at Edinburgh. With luck she could spend the hour-long wait on an icy platform and cool her blazing cheeks and hot, throbbing head.

'If you're sure . . . ?' He didn't want her to be sick; not here. Very messy, if she was sick. 'Going far?'

'Edinburgh – then to Liverpool.'

'Been in long?'

'Liverpool is my first base.' She wished he wouldn't talk to her. He was probably only trying to be kind, but she wished he wouldn't. 'It's my arm, you see.' Perhaps if she told him he would leave her alone. 'I think my vaccination has gone funny.'

'Nasty things, vaccinations,' he nodded, glad at least she wasn't likely to be sick. Vaccinations didn't usually make you throw up. 'I'll give you a hand at Edinburgh, if you like.'

She said that would be very kind of him, hoping all the time he wasn't trying to pick her up.

'Want one?' He ripped the Cellophane wrapping from a packet of cigarettes and she watched, bemused. She hadn't seen a Cellophane-wrapped packet of twenty in months. 'Go on. We get a pack a day on board. Duty-free. For sixpence.'

She shook her head, thinking yearningly of Aunt Julia who would kill for a crackly-wrapped packet of twenty.

She closed her eyes to shut out the sailor; shut out

everything so she could think of Aunt Julia and Mam and Dada and Keeper's Cottage; Keeper's all quiet and still because they would have gone to bed. She would not think about Keth because if she did she would weep and that wouldn't do. She had to get on with the war as best she could and hope that if the invasion came – April, people said it would be, on the spring tides – she would be brave and not want Mam and Dada because they would have enough on their plates; Mam worrying about her, and Dada with his Home Guarding. She wondered if Dada's platoon would be called up into the real army if the Germans came.

The train began to judder and slow. She squinted out of the window but saw only a blackness with not even the denser black associated with buildings or solid things.

A soldier in the uniform of a Gordon Highlander stretched his legs as if to give notice he was about to move and upset the close-packed balance of the compartment, the look on his face one of pure joy.

'Auld Reekie,' he said. 'Home, for seven days.'

'Edinburgh, soon,' said the sailor. 'Lucky for some. I'll see you on to your train, Jenny . . .'

'It won't leave for an hour. Wouldn't want you to miss your own connection,' she said half-heartedly, because it would be bliss for someone to carry her case so her right arm could cope with all the other bits and her left arm could get on with its throbbing unhindered.

Poisoned, Know-All had said. Perhaps it was and where the poison would end up . . . Tears filled her eyes and she dashed them away with the back of her glove because they were packed thigh to thigh, and she couldn't dip into her pocket for her handkerchief.

'I'll see you on to your platform at least,' he said firmly. The poor kid looked bad. 'And mind you report sick as soon as you get to Liverpool – okay?'

'I will – and thanks.'

The train began straining against its brakes, letting off steam in loud hisses. From the window now she could see the blue-lit dimness of Waverley station.

The Gordon Highlander reached up for his kitbag, his respirator and greatcoat. Daisy wondered if his girl would be there to meet him. She hoped so and envied them both as her cheeks burned more hotly and her head throbbed in unison with her arm.

'*I hate you!*' She sent her thoughts winging high and wide and venomously to the Medical Officer at Rosyth and hoped he knew how right he had been. The vaccination *had* taken!

The train hit the buffers and sent the compartment into disarray. Then they regained their balance and went on with the business of pushing and heaving and shoving their way on to the platform.

Next stop Liverpool and Hellas House and a bunk with clean sheets on it. And she didn't give a damn about what the Medical Officer had said about keeping her arm dry. If there was any hot water she would have a bath or soon she would start to smell like the toilets in the corridor.

'Come on then, Jenny. Let's get you on to that train.' The sailor picked up her case, shouldering his kitbag as if they were no weight at all. Obediently, gratefully, Daisy followed him.

Getting to Hellas House had been nothing less than a nightmare. At the RTO's office at Lime Street station, the help she expected was reluctantly and meanly given. The duty writer, having been up all night, was in no mood to worry overmuch about a Wren who shouldn't have joined if she couldn't get from A to B without the use of navy transport.

'You get the tram outside the station to the Pierhead then you take the overhead railway to the end – the *south* end – all the way. Get off at the Dingle. You'll 'ave to, 'cos that's where it ends. From there it isn't far . . .'

'But I can't –' She stood desolate, fighting tears of weariness.

'You'll 'ave to. 'Aren't you got the fare? Didn't they give it to you?'

'Yes, but it's –' It wasn't any use. He disliked Wrens and went out of his way to show it.

'On your way then, Jenny. Some of us have work to do!'

He picked up the insistently ringing telephone on the desk, giving it his full attention, indicating the interview was over. Daisy picked up her case, blocked open the door with it, then manhandled the rest of her kit outside, letting the door go with a loud bang. A feeble protest, really, when all she wanted to do was to sit on that case beneath the big station clock and weep. A little civility and maybe even the offer of a mug of tea – there had been a kettle and tea caddy on the table behind him – would have been bliss and she wondered if all sailors were as rude and horrible. Then she remembered the sailor on the train and Drew, and to think of Drew made her bite hard on her lip and sniff back her tears.

She glanced around. The station was unusually quiet for one so big and important, even so early in the morning. It was littered with rubbish, too, and so dimly lit it was almost frightening. She hoped the rest of this city wasn't like it or life here would be unbearable, especially after the safeness of Keeper's and Brattocks and Rowangarth and the beautiful gardens where Gracie worked. Lucky Gracie Fielding, so far away from Liverpool.

Three women, laughing loudly, came into the station. They were shabbily dressed, headscarves only half covering their curlers. One of them was smoking; all wore pinafores beneath their coats and held brown paper carrier bags.

'Excuse me, please?' Daisy rose to address her plea to the one with peroxided hair and large, motherly breasts. 'Can you tell me where I can get a tram? I'm afraid I'm –'

'Lost, are yer, queen? Fed up and far from 'ome, eh? Ar

hey, look at the kid,' she murmured. 'Ought to be at 'ome with her mammy.' She glanced indignantly at the station clock which pointed, dimly, to six. 'What's to do with the Navy, then, dumping you here at this hour?'

Her concern brought fresh tears to Daisy's eyes and she could only sniff loudly in reply.

'Now if you tell us which tram, and where . . . ?'

The motherly one drew deeply on the last of her cigarette, threw it to the ground then flattened it beneath her shoe.

'The sailor in the RTO's office said I was to get a tram to the Pierhead then take the overhead railway to the Dingle.'

'Oh, *him*! A right misery guts he is! Wouldn't smile, that one, not if Hitler caught his willie in the mangle! No, yer best bet is to get the green Corpy bus to Lark Lane – if it's Sevvy Park you're goin' to.'

'It's Hellas House, Aigburth Drive, and I'd manage, truly I would, but my left arm is pretty useless – vaccination gone wrong, I think.'

'Ar. One of the toffs' houses on the Drive, it'll be. Nice, out at Sevvy Park. Not like 'ere. And you do look a bit off colour.' She laid a cold hand on Daisy's forehead. 'Well, will you feel that?' she clucked. 'Runnin' a fever, she is. When are they expectin' you at your billet, luv?'

'I don't know if they're expecting me at all,' Daisy choked, 'and right now I don't much care.' She didn't. She wanted a bath and her own bed at Keeper's and Mam telling her it would be all right because Mam had been a nurse and would know what to do about her arm. And if she didn't know, Dr Pryce would. 'I feel like taking the next train home.'

'Now you couldn't do that, queen. That'd be deserting, wouldn't it, and they'd only find you and throw you in the glasshouse.'

'If they had mugs of tea in their glasshouse, I wouldn't care at all!'

'Well, if they aren't expectin' you and it's tea you want, we're in business. Us girls is cleaners, see, and the first thing we do is made a brew. You'd be welcome, if you don't mind dried milk.'

'Bless you. That would be wonderful. And if you had a couple of aspirins . . .'

'Granted soon as asked. Come on then, girl. Too cold to be hangin' about in this draughty hole!' By unspoken consent they picked up her kit, carrying it between them. 'Soon have the kettle on!'

Bemused, Daisy trailed behind, pushing away all thoughts of Keeper's. Of her own free will she had joined the war and ended up in Liverpool, which seemed bawdy and dirty and had received more than its fair share of bombs. But if the people of Liverpool were all as kind and caring as the three cleaning ladies who called her *gayle* and *kweeen*, then it wasn't going to be half bad – when her arm stopped hurting, that was. And Liverpool was where Drew's minesweeper was based. It could, she admitted, be a whole lot worse.

'Here we are, then.' They stopped at a door marked 'Cleaners'. 'Take your coat and hat off while Teresa finds the azpreens. An' when you've had a cuppa, we'll see you on to the Lark Lane bus – now how would that suit you?'

Daisy said it was very kind of them and would suit her nicely. And she would never forget the kindness of Teresa and her cleaning ladies, she vowed, all at once feeling amongst friends. Not ever.

Hellas House was large and built of red brick. It had a basement area and six balustraded steps which led up to an important-looking front door. To the left, a windowed tower ran from top to bottom of the building; everything about the place, in fact, assured her it was not another workhouse.

The steps were scrubbed and she left her kit at the foot

of them then jabbed her finger on the bell with the brightly polished brass surround, then jabbed it again, in case it hadn't worked first time.

'All right! What's your hurry?' rapped the steward who answered. 'Aren't you capable of letting yourself in? And shift yourself. Bring your stuff in!' Then opening a door to her left she called, 'There's a new one here, Ailsa. Better come and see to her,' she added meaningfully.

'Dammit! The one from *Cochrane*. I'd forgotten her!'

Daisy had dropped her kit in a litter around her and was standing in the middle of it, determined not to move a step further when quarters assistant Ailsa Seaton found her.

'Dwerryhouse, is it? From *Cochrane*?'

'From teleprinter school, Dunfermline.' Daisy flopped into a chair.

'From teleprinter school, *Leading-Wren*!' came the sharp rebuke. 'And stand up when you speak to me!'

Daisy closed her eyes and remained seated. Leading-Wren Seaton, who wasn't a quarters assistant for nothing, noticed the too-flushed cheeks and laid a hand on the new arrival's forehead.

'You're running a temperature. Feel a bit off, do you?' Her voice was all at once gentle. 'Flu, is it?'

'Vaccination, I think. My arm – hasn't done it a lot of good, heaving my kit about. Could I go to bed, Leading-Wren – please?' Daisy got to her feet with the greatest reluctance.

'You aren't going anywhere till I've had a look at that arm. Come into the regulating office.' She closed the door behind them. 'Take off your jacket and shirt . . .'

One-handed, Daisy unbuttoned her jacket then tugged at her tie. Leading-Wren Seaton, who by now had decided the new kid was genuinely out of sorts, gave help. Then, 'Bloody hell!' she jerked and picked up the phone on her desk, nodding to Daisy to sit down. 'Sister's going to need to have a look at that,' she said as she waited for her call to be answered. 'She might want you over at Meadowbank – that's the other side of the park, where sick bay is. Get your shirt on, then.

'Hullo, Sister. Seaton here, Hellas House. I've got an arm here needs looking at. Vaccination playing up. Can do? Will I send her over?'

She listened, unspeaking, then putting down the phone smiled apologetically.

'Sorry, Sister *can't* do – can't take you into sick quarters, that is. One ward is closed – measles, would you believe, at *that* age – and the other is chock-a-block with flu. She says it's best if you keep out of contact with either. You're to go to bed here and she'll come over to see you as soon as she can. Meantime, plenty of water and two aspirins every four hours. I'm to take your temperature and let her know what it is. Poor Sister. Run off her feet.' She rummaged in a box marked 'First Aid', stuck a thermometer in Daisy's mouth, ordered, 'Stay here. I'll take your stuff upstairs for you,' and disappeared.

'You're in Cabin 4A,' she said when she returned to remove the thermometer. 'D-watch. They're on duty, now – earlies. You'll get a bit of peace till one o'clock. Gracious – you're 102! Let's get you into bed. C'mon. This way.'

The stairs were wide. On a half-landing Daisy vaguely noticed a low table on which stood a vase of chrysanthemums. Flowers. One step up at least from the workhouse. And there was a telephone, on the wall . . .

'You're in the dressing room off Cabin 4 – we call it the cubbyhole. Bottom bunk. Unpack your kit later. The bed's made up. Feel like anything to eat? Toast?'

Daisy shook her head. 'Just water, if you don't mind.' She felt awful. She wanted Mam. Tears rolled down her cheeks and she sniffed inelegantly. Ailsa Seaton disappeared to return with a length of toilet paper.

'Here – blow!'

'Sorry,' Daisy sniffed. 'Don't usually –'

'That's okay, but weeping won't help get your temperature down. You've got a dose of the fed-up-and-far-from-homes, as well, and the long journey won't have helped. You'll be fine in a couple of days,' she said briskly, as if arms swollen like red balloons were commonplace. 'I'll bring you up a drink and a couple of aspirins. Sister will be over soon. And don't worry. You aren't going to kick the bucket!'

'Right now I don't really care, Leading-Wren.'

'Well tough luck. You'll be on watch just as soon as you're back to normal,' she said with irritating cheerfulness, breezing from the room, banging the door behind her.

With difficulty, Daisy took off her uniform and got naked into bed. Her pyjamas were in her case and there they would have to stay. The sheets were cool, the pillows soft. She wished she could have a bath but her spongebag was in her case, too, and anyway she didn't really care.

She lay, staring up at the underside of the bunk above, wondering who slept in it, knowing only that she was on duty, somewhere, with D-watch.

Her head had stopped thudding and her arm seemed a little less painful, except when she moved it. Her raging thirst had returned but nowhere could she see a tap in this small room which held a two-tier bunk, a four-drawer chest with a mirror above it and two wooden chairs. And her kit, of course, littering the remaining floor space. She hoped Top-Bunk would not fall over it when she came in, but she didn't much care.

From the vague distance came sounds of occupancy. One watch would be sleeping, she supposed, after night duty; another would take over from D-watch around midday, maybe, which meant that the ones making the noise would probably take 'lates' – the one before the night watch. That was how Know-All had explained it and it seemed reasonable to assume that for once she had been right.

From now on, Wren Dwerryhouse would live from leave to leave and exist, between times, on a four-watch system. Like clockwork, really, and if she allowed them to, the Women's Royal Naval Service would probably do her thinking for her as well. For the duration.

She moved her left arm to look wincingly at her watch, but to no avail. She supposed, in the darkness, it could be about ten in the morning and that she would remain, thus forgotten, until D-watch returned from duty.

The door knob turned quietly. Ailsa Seaton whispered, 'Awake? Here's Sister.'

'What time is it?' It was all Daisy could think of to say.

'A little after eleven. Have you slept?'

'Dozed, I think . . .'

'Hullo,' smiled the nurse. 'Sorry to take so long. Ease yourself up so I can take a look at you.'

A pillow was placed at her head as Daisy offered her arm. Sister tutted at the state of the dressing, removed it deftly then said, 'Open . . .'

Daisy juggled the thermometer under her tongue, listened intently as Sister pronounced that her arm was scabbing over, thank goodness, and that her temperature was 101.

'Going down nicely. Don't worry. You'll soon be fit for duty.' She applied a fresh dressing, which hardly hurt at all. 'Aspirin and plenty of fluids.' She addressed her last remark to the quarters assistant. 'Sorry to saddle you with more work, but I can't take her into sick bay at the moment. Just watch her temperature.'

'No bother.' The smile was wide and genuine, as if she didn't mind at all being saddled with a sorry-for-herself Wren. Seaton's smile really was something, Daisy was forced to admit. Her teeth could advertise toothpaste any day of the week. 'I'll bring you water and a glass. The lav's to the left, outside the door, by the way. And cheer up, Dwerryhouse! You're on the mend!'

'You really are,' Sister nodded. 'I won't be calling again. Leading-Wren can cope with you. As soon as you feel you want to eat you can get up and mooch around, but no duties until your temperature has been back to normal for twenty-four hours. Okay?' Thus dismissed was she who not so long ago had stood at death's door.

Daisy lay down again, heartened at the drop in her temperature, wondering what Top-Bunk would be like; hoping she would not be a restless sleeper.

Leading-Wren Seaton returned with a glass, a white enamelled jug of water and two aspirins. Daisy swallowed them at a gulp then gratefully drank the glass empty.

'Don't knock that over or you're in trouble!' She placed the jug on the floor beside the bunk then drew the curtains again. 'And try to get some sleep.'

'Welcome to the Wrens, Dwerryhouse,' Daisy whispered to the darkened room.

Then she closed her eyes. Her arm *wasn't* poisoned and she *wasn't* going to die was her last thought as she drifted dizzily into sleep.

'Sorry. Didn't mean to waken you. Ailsa says you aren't too good. Mind if I open the curtains?'

'No. And it's me who should be sorry – all the mess, I mean.' Daisy sat up, pulled the sheet over her nakedness then reached for the glass.

'Here – let me.' Top-Bunk poured water and Daisy smiled her thanks, eyeing the young woman who draped her jacket over one of the chairs.

She was beautiful; very beautiful. Her hair was auburn – no, lighter; the colour of a conker when you broke open its green case and it lay on your hand, all chestnutty and shiny. She had freckles, but not too many, and her cheekbones were high and fine, like Rita Hayworth's.

'Carmichael,' she smiled into the mirror, catching Daisy's eyes without turning.

363

'Sorry. I was gawping, wasn't I, but your hair really is so –'

'Carroty?'

'No. It's lovely. I'm Dwerryhouse, by the way.'

'Nice to meet you. Hope we'll get on. We'll have to in this little hole. It was a dressing room when this was a real home. The last Bottom-Bunk was a snooty piece but she's gone now, for her commission, thank God. You aren't rich and snooty, are you?'

'No – truly.' Maybe rich – soon – but no need to mention that.

'Great! I'm going downstairs for something to eat now. Shall I bring you something up? It's liver and onions today and bread-and-butter pudding. Don't recommend the liver. It'll have been kept warm since first lunch – not invalid diet. The pudding might slip down all right, though. Do you like custard?' She was gone before Daisy could say she did.

She poured more water, sipping it slowly, looking at her arm which seemed less swollen and had toned down from turkey red to a more seemly vermilion. She was relieved that to think of a dish of bread pudding didn't make her want to puke. And then she thought of Mam and getting to the telephone on the wall downstairs, and when Top-Bunk returned with the pudding which really did slip down all right, Daisy asked, 'Is there any drill about using the phone and can you pass my raincoat, please? I've *got* to go to the lav!'

'Here – cover up with this.' A pale green fluffy dressing gown was thrust at her. 'I'll tell you about phoning out when you get back. You know where the bog is . . . ?'

Afterwards, when she was sitting up in bed, her head almost touching the bottom of the bunk above, the pale green dressing gown around her shoulders, Daisy said, 'Are we allowed to use Christian names? In training school we didn't, but –'

'Well, this isn't training school, thank God, and

364

Christian names are used – of course they are. What's yours?'

'Daisy. Daisy Julia Dwerryhouse.'

'Mm. Suits you, the Daisy bit. I'm Lyndis Carmichael. "L-y-n-d-i-s." ' She spelled it out. 'And before you say anything it's supposed to be Welsh, though knowing my mother, I think she made it up. Anyway, people call me Lyn.'

'But Lyndis is a beautiful name – all sort of Court of King Arthur and Guinevere-ish.'

'That's as maybe, but it's Lyn, if you don't mind. Now then – Seaton gave me these for you.' She dropped two aspirins into Daisy's palm. 'She's coming up later to take your temperature, but I told her I'd look after you. I'm not doing anything this afternoon – what say I unpack for you, then we'll be able to move around in here? It's a bit cramped, but I like it better than in the main cabin. They're a noisy lot, through there – go round in a gang. And this cubbyhole is warmer in winter though it can get a bit pongy in summer if you don't keep the window open. I take it you have no objection to fresh air?'

'Sorry about the mess and the fresh air is fine by me. Where I live, it comes at you in great gusts.'

'And you don't smoke? You don't smell as if you do. It isn't allowed in cabins, but that lot in 4 smoke all the time. It's really why I pulled the chest of drawers over the connecting door. They used to use this room as a passage, you know.'

'I don't smoke, Lyn, and if I smell it's because I have to keep my arm dry. I haven't had a bath for four days and I stink of the train as well – sorry.'

'Don't keep saying sorry! Let's get ourselves organized. You'd better phone home first, then we'll unpack you, get your pyjamas and soapbag out, then how if I help you into the bath?'

'Would it be possible? Oh, heck,' she said ruefully, 'do I smell *that* awful?'

'Actually, no. But I reckon if we wrap a big handkerchief round your vaccination and you let your arm hang over the side of the bath, it'll be just fine. And anyway, we're only allowed six inches of bathwater – hardly covers your bum. You can't do a lot of damage with six inches, now can you?'

'Not a lot.' She liked Lyn Carmichael, really liked her. 'And thanks a lot. You don't have to, you know – be this kind, I mean.'

'I know I don't, but I'm so thankful Snooty Piece has gone that I want to be, so no arguing. Now put my dressing gown on and I'll help you with the phone. And don't forget your money. Let's hope that we get through. Sometimes there's a terrible wait for trunk calls, so fingers crossed!'

'I tell you, Tom, something is wrong! Surely she could have got in touch somehow. Her last letter said –'

'I know, bonny lass. It said she was leaving Dunfermline as soon as she'd been given her drafting orders and we weren't to send any more letters to Robertson House – that's all.'

'But it was dated three days ago. Where on earth has she got to?'

'There'll be a phone call tonight – or a letter, midday post, just see if there isn't.'

'Second post has been, ages ago. And you're taking it all a little too calmly, Tom Dwerryhouse, because I think they've sent her abroad!'

'They wouldn't send a raw recruit abroad!'

'They sent plenty of raw recruits to France in our war!'

'But she isn't twenty-one. She'd need my permission for something as daft as that.'

'She joined up without your permission, didn't she? But she was always headstrong, just like you!' Alice's voice wobbled with threatening tears.

'Aye.' Their daughter had all her father's vices and all

her mother's virtues when the mood was on Alice. Best not argue. And truth known he was worried, too. Only called in in passing to collect the dogs, he'd said, but it was really to see if –

The telephone rang with an amazing urgency as if Winnie at the exchange was giving the handle a good old turning. Alice was out of the kitchen in a second and Tom let go his indrawn breath in a puff of relief, knowing without doubt that when she lifted the receiver, Daisy would be there.

'Mam! It's me! Hi!'

'Daisy Dwerryhouse, where on earth have you been?'

'Getting here, and I'm at Liverpool. Mam, have you a pencil handy? I'll give you my address.'

Alice had a pencil waiting there beside a notepad for just such an occasion.

'Liverpool?' Alice could not keep the disappointment from her voice until she remembered the *Maggie*. 'We-e-ll, at least you'll be near Drew. Now are you sure you're all right? Anything you want?'

'No, Mam. I'm fine – and there go the pips!' The operator on trunks was interrupting to tell them their three minutes was up. 'Mam – listen! Ring me on Liverpool Lark Lane 1322 – Lark Lane, got it? 1322 . . .'

The line went dead. That Liverpool operator had been very stingy with her time, but they would try to get through again tonight. Alice frowned. Winnie on the switchboard would give them longer than the three minutes they were allowed for a trunk call, especially when she knew it was Daisy they were ringing.

'Well!' Alice turned to Tom who hovered there, relieved they knew at least where the lass had landed up. 'That was short and sweet if you like. Liverpool, eh?'

'Near Drew, when his boat docks. We'll give her a ring later on tonight, eh, and be blowed to the expense.'

'Tom! What a good idea,' Alice beamed as if she hadn't

already thought of it. 'Now away with you and get the dogs. I'll just give Julia a quick ring – let her have Daisy's address and phone number.'

Tom closed the kitchen door behind him, whistling cheerfully as he walked down the garden path to the dog houses. Alice was herself again. Her lost chick had been found, alive and well in Liverpool. Life could happen return to normal now. Well, *almost* to normal.

'They're fine,' Daisy said a little weepily. 'Mam didn't sound too pleased about it being Liverpool; I think she wanted somewhere safer. Then she realized I'd be able to see Drew quite a bit – my brother, that is. He's a telegraphist on a minesweeper.'

'Lucky you – not being an only child, I mean. What's he like, your Drew? Tall, dark and handsome?'

'Tall, fair and handsome. And he's my half-brother, really. Mam married twice. Drew is called Sutton and he's got their looks. Sutton fair, they call it. I favour Dada . . .'

'I don't look a bit like either of mine. Wouldn't be a bit surprised if Mother told me I wasn't Dad's.'

'Lyn!' Daisy giggled.

'No, honestly. They're a peculiar pair, my parents. They're in Kenya, living off the fat of the land and thankful they can't get a passage home. I was already here at boarding school when the war started, so I can't get back – wouldn't go even if I could!'

'So where do you spend your leaves?' Daisy was genuinely concerned.

'With Auntie Blod, near Llangollen. I had all my school holidays with her. Mother never thought to send the fare so she could see me and I was glad. Auntie Blod is far nicer than Mother. You'd never think they were twins. Blodwen and Myfanwy. Blod and Fan – only mother calls herself Margot, the silly thing. She doesn't like me much and I don't like her. Dad's not so bad, mind, but I'd swop the pair of them just to belong to Auntie Blod. Do you think that's awful of me, Daisy D.?'

'N-no.' Lyn was nothing if not direct. 'But are you sure you don't like your parents? Not even a little bit? Mine are just – well – *wonderful.*'

'Then you're lucky. It's Mother, really,' Lyn shrugged. 'Got such grandiose ideas. I think Dad goes along with them just for peace and quiet and more fool he.

'But hop back into bed, and I'll get you unpacked. Give me your case key then I'll make a start. I've told that lot outside that you've arrived but you aren't well and not to disturb you. I kind of hinted it might be catching, so they're keeping well away.'

'But that's awful,' Daisy laughed. 'I'm feeling a lot better.' She fumbled in the pocket of her money-belt for the key. 'And I appreciate all you are doing for me – truly I do.'

She was going to really like Lyndis Carmichael and it had been lovely to know, when Leading-Wren had taken her temperature not long ago, that it had dropped to below 100.

Tomorrow, she would feel like writing to Keth and Mam, and perhaps the day after she would begin her war. With D-watch.

Darling Mam and Dada,

Thanks for your letter and for sending Keth's two. Yesterday, I did my first watch. We were taken in by bus with a driver called Tommy. All the Wrens like him.

I shall be working on a four-watch system and after doing a week of nights, D-watch will get forty-eight hours off duty and it seems if I were to travel on my sleeping day it would mean I could get a couple of days at home. Fingers crossed that I will see you in about two weeks.

> I can't tell you a lot about where I work – at least
> not in a letter. There is nothing extraordinary about
> what I do but it is a secret place and we need a pass
> even to get past the sentries.

Daisy read contemplatively what she had written. No, she
must *not* say she worked for the Commander-in-Chief,
Western Approaches, nor that the Wrens and Waafs in a
place called Epsom House were virtually troglodytes
because there was no Epsom House, really. Their headquarters was a hole in the ground; a massive, three-floors-
deep cavity, hastily portioned off into rooms and offices
and canteens, with a two-floors-deep Operations Room
where a massive plot showed every convoy and ship in the
Atlantic – enemy ships, too.

And there were dormitories for men and women, ready
should they be needed, she had learned, and some of the
offices so secret than an armed marine stood guard outside
each door.

The rooms and corridors were a maze to Daisy this far.
Would she ever learn her way around? Lyn was only just
getting the hang of it, she said, because the place had only
been operational a month. Commander-in-Chief and his
staff had arrived in a bit of a panic, so the buzz had it –
bombed out of Plymouth.

> Our Petty Officer is called Marjorie Roberts. She is
> very pretty and everyone calls her Marjie. She doesn't
> give orders – rather she asks you to do things. She
> has a lovely smile.

Marjie had just got engaged. Her fiancé proposed to her
in a rose garden, which was very romantic, really, except
that he'd had to go back to his regiment next day. Marjie
wore a diamond-and-ruby ring and had been very kind
when Lyn deposited the new Wren in her ill-fitting uniform

at the door of the teleprinter room, then scurried off down a dark, narrow passage to the telephone switchboard at which she worked.

'Dwerryhouse, is it? Are you sure you are better?' PO had asked of Daisy when she reported for duty three days late. 'It gets so hot in here. If it gets too much, just sing out. We are allowed to go up to street level for a gulp of air,' she smiled. 'Twenty printers constantly running create their own heat – without the other . . .'

The other, Daisy was soon to learn, had been the over-looking of a ventilating system when the massive hole was being converted at breakneck speed into a war machine, and the makeshift ducting added almost as an afterthought did not function as well as it might have and thus, sadly, situated as it was at the lowest level, the teleprinter room got less than its fair share of air. Yet of far more interest was one teleprinter standing apart from the rest.

'Why is this machine different, PO – its colour, I mean?' Grey, when all others were black. 'It is newer?'

'No, but it *is* different. It's our direct line to America, you see, and only ever used when necessary. Its signals sort of run along the floor of the Atlantic on the submarine cable. Only the quickest and most accurate operators send out on it. Speed is essential, you see. Whilst that cable is in use, the Germans could home in on it. They'd give a lot to find it.'

'And destroy it?'

'Oh, no! They could listen, then, to our signals.'

'Even signals in code?' Daisy was intrigued.

'Codes can be broken. We do it all the time, I believe. But now you know why the line to Washington is so important.'

'Washington?' Where Keth was! She gazed at the silent machine, her mind running riot. Imagine – just *imagine* – if she were to sit at that special teleprinter and Keth could be there, at the other end of it!

I love you, love you, love you, Keth Purvis, she could type, *and when are you coming home to me?* And he could read her words; read them in a city which wasn't blacked out nor bombed and had lipsticks in the shops and cigarettes and cream chocolate bars and loads of food. But America – and Keth – were a whole world away.

'Washington? Why do we have a line to them, PO? America isn't at war.'

'No, but we have more in Washington than you or I know about.' PO had tapped her nose. 'Secret, of course. Not to be talked about.'

'Sorry. I only asked because my boyfriend is in Washington. He's got a job there. I've asked him what he's doing, but he seems determined I won't find out.'

'Like I said, Dwerryhouse, we've got more going for us in Washington – in America, even – than most people imagine. But secret, don't forget.'

'You mean my boyfriend might be working for us British out there – maybe even at our Embassy?'

'He could be . . .'

'Well, imagine that!' Daisy nodded in the direction of the teleprinter which had its other end in a city in which Keth worked; perhaps even *where* Keth worked.

She began to write again.

I forgot to tell you when I rang that I share a little cabin with a telephonist called Lyndis. This is a very grand house. Marble fireplaces in the downstairs rooms, red silk wallpaper in the mess – and rough old blackout curtains and brown linoleum, just to spoil the poshness! Even so, Hellas House is quite an improvement on the last hostel and we don't have to do everything at the double now.

She laid down her pen and rubbed the palms of her hands together. They made a rasping sound, because after only four days at Epsom House, her hands were dry and rough because of the mortar dust that still hung around in the air and whitened everything it fell on. The first thing each incoming watchkeeper did was to dust her machine, desk and chair. Marjie said it could be weeks before they finally got rid of the stuff the builders had left behind them. It meant they had to wash their hair a lot, too, which wasn't on, Lyn said, when decent shampoos were as scarce in the shops as hens' teeth.

Yet for all their discomfort, they would be safer than most should Liverpool be blitzed as London was. Three floors down and three feet of reinforced concrete above them. Lucky, really.

I am fine. Don't worry about me. I have written to Drew and when his boat docks he will have my address and phone number. I miss you both so much, but just to know I might see Drew, or be home sooner than I ever hoped, makes everything a whole lot better.
I love you both,
Daisy.

Her eyes blurred and she forced herself to think of York station and hurrying across the footbridge to where the little slow train to Holdenby Halt would be standing. And come to think of it, being drafted to Liverpool might turn out to be a good move, air raids apart. In fact, now that her arm hardly hurt at all and she was getting good at taking a bath and keeping it dry, things were improving. And any day now, Drew might ring her from a dockside phone.

If only Keth could ring or even, crazily, be at the other end of that direct line to Washington so she could type out that she loved him, life, for the duration of hostilities, could become almost bearable.

In her mind she trailed her fingers across the grey, aloof teleprinter and it was as if she were reaching out and touching Keth. And in her heart she whispered, *Good night, my love* . . .

27

Daisy settled into the teleprinter-room routine with amazing ease, though she had not, this far, so much as glimpsed the Commander-in-Chief. Her final acceptance of her new, strange life was in part due to an arm which no longer ached and a pink and complete vaccination scar. Mam would have called it counting her blessings, because the joy of a phone call at the exact moment she was changing the On Watch disc beneath her name for one marked In Quarters, gave yet another blessing for the counting.

'Drew!' she cried with such delight that D-watch heads turned and eyebrows shot upwards. 'Drew, where are you?'

'We just tied up alongside and collected our mail. Wasn't sure I'd be able to get hold of you – and there you are, at the end of the phone!'

'Just coming off watch and happened to be passing it. How are you?' she sighed ecstatically.

'Same as always. Can we meet, Daiz?'

'You bet! When? I'll have to be in by half-past ten, though.'

'Then how about five-ish? Shall I pick you up?'

'No. I'll be in town, anyway. We're – oh, damn! I'd arranged to go to Liverpool with Lyndis Carmichael – try to find a lipstick queue. She's my cabin-mate; she'll understand if I explain that –'

'Bring her along, if she can put up with Rowangarth gossip, that is. I'll treat you both to supper. Is she nice, your Lyndis?'

'She is, Drew. And she's good fun and very forthright.

She was an absolute love when I was running a temperature.'

'You've been ill? Sure you're okay now?'

'Just fine! But if you're taking the overhead railway from the dock, why don't we meet at the Pierhead? Five is just fine.'

'Then it's a date. It'll be great to see you, Daiz.'

'You're invited too, Lyn,' she said as they ate their kept-warm lunch. 'It's lucky we are on earlies. We can do the rounds of the shops, see if anywhere's got a lipstick, and still be in good time to meet Drew. It's ages since I saw him. We've got so much catching-up to do.'

'Sure I won't be in the way? Wouldn't want to play gooseberry or anything.'

'Lyn! He's my brother, not my lover!'

'That's okay then.' Lyn pushed aside her plate. 'Think I'll give the pudding a miss. It looks a bit off.'

With the best will in the world, cook's jam roly-poly could only be classed as fair-to-middling; cook's jam roly-poly kept warm from early lunch degenerated into a suety sog only fit for the pig-swill-for-victory bucket.

It was not until they were sitting on the clanking overhead railway, Liverpool-bound, that Daisy all at once realized how completely changed her life was. She had never had a close female friend before this. Tatty was family, almost, and in summer and at Christmas there had been Kitty, who blew into everyone's life like a gust of notice-me wind, then returned to Kentucky; and lately there had been Gracie, to go dancing with. But living in a Rowangarth house and apart from the village, her whole life had revolved around Rowangarth and Mam and Dada and Aunt Julia.

'What is he like, this brother of yours?' Lyn broke into Daisy's thoughts. 'You haven't shown me his photo.'

'Haven't got one with me.' Of her own choice she had not packed anything to remind her of Keeper's. She had not known then if bedside photographs were allowed and anyway, she would have burst into tears every time she looked at them.

Now she no longer wept for home; just felt a brief achy pain when she saw Liverpool's bomb-shattered streets and desolate, rubble-piled spaces where once office blocks, shops and houses had been. Yet now the worst was over and because in little more than two weeks she would see Mam and Dada and Rowangarth again, being in the Wrens had become bearable. Given time she could even enjoy it – air raids apart – and if she could begin to hope that by some almost unbelievable miracle, the war would soon be over and Keth could get home . . .

'On your feet!' Lyn reached for her respirator, hung it from her left shoulder and not properly slanted as they were instructed at Dunfermline, straightened her hat, then ran her hand across the front of it to emphasize the rakish curve of the brim. 'Pierhead. We're here!'

They clattered down the wooden stairs to the road below, then made for the shops.

'Where to?' This was Daisy's first outing; her first run ashore.

'We'll try Lewis's first. They're pretty good with their cosmetics when they get a quota.' Lewis's, said Lyn, sold their stuff the minute it came in and didn't hide it under the counter for the favoured few. 'We'll soon know if there's a queue forming.' Lyn Carmichael prided herself on her ability to sniff out a queue. 'Then we'll do the other department stores, then the chemists. By the way, is he good-looking, your Drew?'

'I suppose he is.' Daisy fell into step. It seemed the natural thing to do now. 'At least if you like fair-haired men with grey eyes.' She would bring photographs back with her. She was brave enough now to cope with them. 'Anyway, you'll meet him soon. Have you got a boyfriend, Lyn – a steady one, I mean?'

'No – but I'll know the right man when he happens along. Till then I get by very nicely on a love-'em-and-leave-'em basis. Now let's get a move on and see if we can't pick something up – lipsticks, I mean!' She threw back her head and laughed.

Drew Sutton turned from where he stood at the foot of the stairs leading to the overhead railway. The Pierhead at five, Daisy had said, but best be early. He checked the time on the Liver Building clock then glanced up Water Street to see two Wrens, running, hands on hats, towards him, past him.

'Daiz!' he yelled.

The fair-haired one stopped, then cried, '*Drew!*' Arms wide, she threw herself on him with such joy that she sent his cap flying. 'Drew, it's so good to see you,' she laughed as he swung her round, feet flying.

'Daisy Dwerryhouse, you look just – just *awful*!' he laughed. 'You look like Orphan Annie! Wait till Lady sees you!'

'I don't look *that* bad? I know it only fits where it touches but –'

'It's fine. Only teasing. A bit of a shock, though, seeing you in uniform.'

'Yours I believe, sailor?'

The tall, slim Wren with Titian hair spun his cap on her forefinger then threw it for him to catch.

'Thanks,' he smiled, settling it on his head, holding out his hand. 'You've got to be Lyndis.'

'No, but call me Lyn and I'll answer. Hullo, Drew.' She smiled up at him and hoped he could dance. 'And Dwerryhouse will look just fine when she's worn the fluff off her uniform, if you get my meaning.'

Drew said he did. It was accepted that once a sailor or a Wren had worn their uniform into a more acceptable smoothness, they knew what life in the Royal Navy was all about; in short, that they had Got Some In – got some service in, that was!

'Are we late? We ran like mad. Lunch was uneatable and we're both starving.' Lyndis Carmichael never stood on ceremony. 'If we cut along sharpish, we'll catch the British Restaurant before it closes.'

'No. Let's celebrate. How about the Adelphi?'

'There's posh! Are you rich or something?'

'No, but there isn't a lot to spend your pay on when you're at sea and I haven't seen Daiz for ages. We can sit and talk for as long as we like there. I'm due long leave soon, by the way,' he said to Daisy.

'Me too, Drew. Well, not leave exactly but it seems we can fiddle seventy-two hours off after night watches. We might make it home together.'

'Mother and Lady would like that – you and me home at the same time, I mean,' Drew said absently as they sat in the hotel foyer, studying a menu that was mindboggling in its inventiveness. 'I suppose the game pie is really rabbit and pigeon; think I'll go for the fish.' They couldn't disguise fish.

He liked this hotel because although food rationing had struck it like a mortal blow, it still tried, short of staff though it was, to offer the same old-fashioned service of pre-war days, when cotton brokers and ship owners and Grand National winners had thrown lavish parties there. Sometimes he spent one of his nights ashore here, luxuriated in a hot bath and slept in a real bed which didn't tilt with every movement of the ship.

'Mother and Lady – who are they?' Lyn sipped her bitter beer shandy because the hotel, regretfully, was completely out of aperitifs of any kind until their next quota was due, sadly not for two more weeks.

'Mother is *my* mother – though she's really my Aunt Julia and Lady is Daisy's mother – mine, too, though she didn't bring me up,' Drew offered, laughing. 'When Lady married again she went to Hampshire and left me behind with the Suttons, if you see what I mean?'

'Drew. It's short for Andrew, isn't it?' All at once, she needed to know more about Daisy's half-brother.

'Andrew Robert Giles Sutton,' Daisy supplied, determined to break the eye-to-eye gaze. 'And Aunt Julia isn't my aunt, really, but she's Mam's best friend,' Daisy finished breathlessly.

'You're a complicated lot, aren't you? And I'd like the game pie, please.' Smiling, Lyn handed the menu back to Drew. 'By the way, it's pay day tomorrow and I've still got a ten-bob note in my pocket. I think we should go Dutch. And do you dance, Drew Sutton?' she added without the batting of an eyelid.

'I've been wondering much the same about you,' he smiled. 'Yes, I like dancing and no, we won't go Dutch, thanks all the same.'

'Then if you aren't at sea, how about coming to the Wrennery dance two weeks today? Daisy and I will be on nights so we'll be there for most of it.'

'If we're alongside, it's a date,' he laughed. 'I'll let Daiz know if I can make it.'

'You could even try ringing me,' Lyn said softly.

'I could.' Drew met the challenge in her gaze. 'Okay, I'll do that . . .'

Even when Drew had seen them both safely on to the Lark Lane Corporation bus and promised to do his best to get ashore tomorrow afternoon – Lyn had told him that tomorrow they began a week of late watches which meant being on duty from six in the evening until midnight – Daisy was not a little put out that far from not being included in the Sutton talk, Lyn had engineered the entire evening so she sat nearest to Drew, talked to Drew about things Daisy knew nothing about and generally made *her* feel the gooseberry.

They were walking back to Hellas House under a star-sprinkled sky when Lyn said, 'You're quiet, Daisy. Anything wrong? Feeling okay?'

'No I'm not and since you ask, didn't you realize that Drew was *my* date, is *my* brother, and that I hadn't seen him for ages?'

'Sorry, sweetie. I did monopolize him, didn't I? You should have warned me how good-looking he is – *and* he dances.'

'Monopolize him!' Daisy snapped. 'The two of you talked all night. You haven't fallen for him, have you? You were flirting like mad.'

'Was I? It wasn't intentional, honestly. But he really is quite something, your Drew.'

'I asked if you've fallen for him!'

'D'you know, I rather think I might have. Hell! Don't tell me he's got a girl?'

'He hasn't as it happens and – Hey! Look out!'

The warning came too late and Lyn Carmichael walked into a lamppost with a sickening crack, so bemused was she with the sudden realization that not only did she find Drew Sutton attractive, but it seemed it had the makings, on her part at least, of a hook, line and sinker job unless firmly checked. And there wasn't, she said afterwards as she held cold cloths to her swollen, bleeding nose, anything like a good, solid Liverpool lamppost for bringing a Wren down to earth – with a nasty bump.

'I've negotiated that lamppost dozens of times before in the blackout,' she wailed. 'Why tonight, of all times, do I have to walk into it?'

'Because your mind was on other things, Carmichael. And do you know that tomorrow, when we meet Drew, you're going to have one heck of a black eye?'

Daisy wondered why she felt so smug about her friend's misfortune, then realized she didn't want Drew to fall in love with her, maybe to get hurt.

'Oh, here – give me that flannel and I'll hold it under the tap for you.' All at once she felt ashamed of her uncharitable thoughts. And maybe Lyn wouldn't get a black eye. A swollen nose, Daisy decided, would suffice.

Daisy eased herself gently from her bunk, gathered up her uniform and shoes then walked softly into the bathroom to wash and dress. Tonight would be her last night watch. Awful, awful too-hot nights, when the war seemed to slow down around three in the morning, but not for long enough to let her fold her arms on the teleprinter top, lay her head on them, and sleep. The minute anyone did that, the silent printer would start up with a shocking clatter to banish all hope of a ten-minute doze.

The early hours, Marjie said, were the godless hours; when time seemed suspended between living and limbo and your brain didn't respond half quickly enough to the chatter of your printer and you had to think, quite hard sometimes, what your initials were and transcribe the figures on the wall clock into naval time before typing a receipt for an incoming signal.

Ma'am insisted, Daisy admitted as she knotted her tie, that watchkeepers must remain in bed until four in the afternoon after a night duty but she had awakened, pulled aside the blackout curtain to find it was already three o'clock on a bright afternoon and that she had only to cross the road and the wide expanse of Sefton Park was there to pretend in.

Sevvy Park, the cleaning lady had called it that dismal morning of Daisy's arrival. Sometimes she found things in it to remind her of Brattocks Wood. Yet there were no clumps of elm trees, no rooks; no startled pheasants scurrying with a *kaaaark* of alarm into cover. But tomorrow she would see Brattocks again, wallow in the bliss of being home for three nights and two days.

She walked towards the Palm House, wondering how it

would be tomorrow. You paid your own fare, Lyn said, for a crafty weekend and hoped like mad a naval patrol didn't stop you and demand to see your leave pass. Crafty because their forty-eight hours off duty was really intended as a rest break from the rigours of seven nights of acute discomfort and not meant to be converted into leave. Yet their motherly quarters officer, whose husband had been killed at Dunkirk, turned a blind eye to the disc which indicated that a Wren was sleeping when in fact she was almost certainly homeward-bound.

Daisy stopped, delighted to see a clump of primroses to remind her that winter was almost over and that tomorrow, at this very time, she would find wild violets and wind-flowers in Brattocks Wood and primroses, of course, on the edges of the wild garden.

Tomorrow. Just to think of it brought a lump to her throat; not a knot of tears like most times, but a great lovely dollop of indescribable joy.

The early-spring sunshine glinted on the great glass expanse under which tropical plants sheltered and made her think of English elm trees and a beautiful, creaky old house called Rowangarth. And tomorrow she would see them again. Lovely, lovely tomorrow.

Daisy had the choice of two early-morning trains out of Liverpool. One from Lime Street station which would take her to Harrogate and another which started at Exchange station and ran to Edinburgh by way of York.

She had already decided on Exchange station, partly because it was within walking distance of Epsom House, but really, even had it not been so convenient, because that was the way it had been in her dreamings: pulling into York station, crossing the wide footbridge from which she could see the Minster, then on to the side platform where the Hold-enby train would wait especially for Daisy Dwerryhouse, ready to start the moment she heaved her case aboard.

Then the unhurried journey to Holdenby Halt, which would seem to take ages, and the engine straining as it took the incline that ran past the far end of Brattocks Wood and, sometimes in her imaginings, Dada standing there, gun over his arm, waving.

She had no idea how she would carry her case from Holdenby to Keeper's but that was the least of her worries. What she really looked forward to was the three hoots the engine driver always gave just before they rounded the curving track to the station, half a mile ahead. That was when the train would begin to slow in great, off-balancing shudders.

'Could you get this off?' Daisy looked up to see her petty officer beside her, a signal in her hand. 'A long one, I'm afraid and in code, but it's a rush-immediate . . .' Two pages of a signal pad in figures arranged into groups of four. 'Just sing out when you've finished, and I'll check it with you – okay?'

'Sure, Marjie.' Tonight, everything was okay. Only don't let there be an air raid tonight to louse everything up, God. Oh, they were safe enough down here. Epsom House was just about the best place in Liverpool to be when bombs were falling, but tonight there was a moon, high and full and bright; a bomber's moon.

The signal was to the Royal Air Force at Valley and repeated to RAF Wood Vale, and though she was transmitting in code, Daisy knew it was a request for fighter protection.

A slow-moving convoy of merchant ships rounding the southern tip of Ireland, maybe, and within smell if not sight, of land. There would be a couple of destroyers already at sea, steaming to meet it; the hawk-eyed nightfighter pilots soon to be scrambled to give it air cover. Our fighter pilots could see in the dark. Heaven only knew how, but even the Germans accepted they could.

She flicked over the first of the pages, pausing to regain

her rhythm, to glance briefly at the wall clock. Six minutes past midnight. Already it was tomorrow and *today* she was going home. Lovely, lovely today!

Suitcase at her side, twelve shillings and sixpence in her hand, Daisy asked at the booking office for a Forces' return to Holdenby Halt. Last night there had been no air raid and today she was going home to Brattocks and Mam and Dada and Keeper's Cottage. Maybe even to Drew. She glanced around for sight of a naval patrol. You couldn't miss them. Big lads, all of them, bell-bottoms tucked into gaiters and Naval Police armbands on their sleeves. Crushers, they had come to be called, and you kept clear of them if, like Daisy this morning, you were up to no good; about to become absent without the Royal Navy's permission.

For Lyn, travelling light to Llangollen, it would be easy. Lyn had merely removed her respirator from its khaki case, then crammed the empty holder with shirts and underwear to be washed and ironed when she got to Auntie Blod's, and hitchhiking all the way into the bargain. But she, Daisy, had uniform to be altered; a case, though necessary, drew attention to her.

She held her head high as if she had a pocketful of leave passes signed by the Commander-in-Chief Western Approaches himself, and walked to the barrier, ticket at the ready. Without comment, the collector punched it and nodded her through. He looked tired as if he, too, had been on duty all night. He hardly glanced at her.

The train waited at platform two and was still only half full. Kneeing her case in front of her, she walked its length to find an empty window seat. A soldier opposite lifted her case with ease, jamming it on the rack above her.

'Going on leave, Jenny?'

'Sort of. A crafty seventy-two hours,' she confided. 'If the naval patrol comes down the train, I'm finished.'

385

'They won't do that,' he said comfortably, sitting down again, folding his arms over his chest, preparing to sleep. 'They'll be at the RTO's office this time of the morning, guzzling tea. Nip out of the door, if you hear them coming, then get on again, further down the train.'

It seemed the soldier knew all the dodges; she had an ally. In twenty minutes the train would have filled up and she would be on her way home.

Home. The loveliest, weepiest, most wonderful word in the world.

She had luck with her all the way. The train left on time and was only half an hour late into York, a little miracle in itself. And across the wide footbridge, as if it were waiting especially for her, the train to Holdenby Halt stood at the side platform as she knew it would be, letting go little puffs of steam as if impatient to be on its way. These, the last few miles, were the longest, happiest part of her journey. She took off her hat, slipped her respirator over her head and laid them on the seat beside her.

The compartment was empty and she was glad. She didn't want anyone she knew – and she knew everyone in Holdenby – to get in and talk to her. All she wanted was to gaze out of the window for every bit of the way, pretending she had never left home and would never leave it again; passing the Minster, leaving York behind, seeing fields and trees waking up from winter. There would be daffodils out in sheltered corners and windflowers and a few late snowdrops. And primroses, of course, and the weeping willow on the edge of the wild garden should be bursting into leaf. The willow always greened first, even before the sycamores.

A whistle blew; the train juddered, buffers clanked along its length. The engine heaved and pulled; the train slipped from the platform. Dry-mouthed, Daisy settled chin on hand at the window to wallow in every wonderful minute.

In half an hour from now she would hear the three hoots from the engine, pass the far end of Brattocks Wood, then step out on to the platform at Holdenby Halt. In a little less than an hour, even if she carried her case every bit of the way, she would be standing on the doorstep of Keeper's Cottage.

Dear, sweet heaven, life was so *good* . . .

Alice glimpsed her daughter as she rounded the bend in the lane beside the bothy and flew to meet her.

'Oh, give me that case, child. Surely you haven't lugged it all the way from the station?' This between hugs and kisses and, 'Let me look at you! You're tired out! Are they working you too hard?'

'No, Mam. I've had a week on night watch. I should be sleeping now, that's all. And I hitched a lift to the crossroads.'

'Nights?' Alice knew all about night work. 'Then it's up the stairs with you, the minute you've had a cup of tea!'

'No! I'll go early tonight. Promise. And Mam, my uniform is an awful fit. Could you alter one skirt and jacket and maybe take up my raincoat – just to be going on with?'

'You know I can. Your eyes are younger than mine – if you'll do the unpicking I'll see to the lot if you've brought it with you.' And judging from the weight of the case, Alice thought happily, her daughter had. 'That jacket fits fine on the shoulders but you've moved the buttons, haven't you?'

'Had to. It was so baggy.'

'Well, that isn't the way. I'll put the buttons back to where they ought to be and take it in on the hips. No trouble. And that skirt! Whyever didn't you try it on first? And did you see your dada? He said he'd be at the waving place, if he could and oh, Daisy love, it's good to have you home. Drew's home too, did you know?' Alice draped the offending jacket over a chairback. 'Came two days ago.

And you'll know that Tatty's gone. No one's seen hide nor hair of her since!'

'Sssssh!' Daisy laid a gentle finger to her mother's lips. 'Yes, I saw Dada and waved, and I didn't know Drew was home but I hoped he might be. I'll be able to meet him in Liverpool every time the *Maggie* docks, you know.' She spun round as the door opened.

'Now then, our lass . . .'

'Dada!' She was in his arms, cheek against his chest, holding him tightly, not speaking. There was no need for words between them. This, too, had been a part of her yearnings; the size and safeness of him; the tweedy, out-doors game-keepery smell of him.

He kissed her forehead, pushing her gently from him, smiling across at Alice, still pink-cheeked and fussing with the teapot; a mother hen who had found her lost chick.

'If you're mashing tea I'll stop for a sup, love. Be in at the usual time for a bite of dinner.'

'Mam – I'm sorry. This leave is unofficial, sort of. They know we all do it after a week of nights and turn a blind eye, but they don't give us a travel warrant nor a ration card. I'll be eating your food, I'm afraid.'

'Of course you'll be eating our food! Whose ever else would you eat? And if I can't spare my own daughter a spoonful of sugar or a scrape of butter, then it's a poor carry-on! And there's a pheasant and a rabbit in the pantry.'

'Dada. For shame! Taking pheasants out of season!' Daisy teased, feeling better about the rations.

'A young cock,' Tom grinned. 'Happened to get in the way when I took a shot at a rabbit!'

They settled themselves at Mam's table in Mam's kitchen and it was as if she had never been away and Dunfermline nor her arm nor Epsom House had ever happened. And when they had had their tea and Mam had hugged her yet again, she would take off her uniform and put on trousers and her thick blue jumper and go in search of Polly and Drew and Aunt Julia – and maybe Gracie. But first she would walk the length of Brattocks Wood, breathing in the earthy, woody-green springtime scent of it.

And she would tell the rooks she was home.

Back to Hellas House and Cabin 4A and the noisy crowd on the other side of the door; back to the fugginess of Epsom House and chattering teleprinters and sometimes to air raids, too, though this far the bombs had dropped on the docks and city centre. This far, those not on watch had only once to collect pillows and blankets and take shelter, suddenly apprehensive, in the cold, cobwebby cellars of Hellas House.

Returning to Liverpool had not been as awful as Daisy feared because she knew now that Keeper's would always be there, safe and unchanging, to come home to. And there would be long leave in June to count the days to.

'I must admit,' said Lyn, 'that you look a bit more presentable now – like you've got some in, I mean.' She eyed Daisy's perfectly fitting uniform. 'Your mother must be good at sewing.'

'Of course she is. She was sewing-maid once, for Drew's gran. She's going to make a start on my wedding dress, she says; have it ready for a first fitting when I get my long leave. She's had the material for ages. There's no silk in the shops, now, so it's as well she bought it when she did. I asked her not to tempt fate, but war or no war, I'm going down the aisle dressed like a proper bride, she says.'

'Did you see Drew?' Lyn had no wish to talk about a wedding that this far lacked a bridegroom; one trapped for the duration in Washington.

'Of course I saw him. He came to the station to see me off. I said goodbye to everyone, then he and I hitched a lift on the back of Home Farm's tractor into Holdenby.

Best, that way.' She hadn't wanted Mam and Dada to see her off, at the station.

'And how was Drew?'

'Same as when we last saw him at the Wrennery dance. He sent his regards, by the way.'

'Regards?'

'Yes. Said he'd enjoyed dancing with you.' Regards wasn't quite true. Give his *love* to Lyn, he'd said, though only in passing when her name had been mentioned. She still felt vague unease about her cabin-mate's interest in her brother, because interested she was and had been right from the start.

But no one, not even someone as nice as Lyn, could be allowed to hurt Drew, and Lyn had admitted to a love-them-and-leave-them outlook on life. 'I'm looking forward to my long leave, by the way. In June, it should be. Suit me nicely; I'll be able to have my twenty-first at home.'

And get married, or so they had planned. Strange that Polly mentioned it, Daisy frowned – or maybe the way she had actually said it had been strange. The land girls had long gone to work. It was Polly's quiet time, when she allowed herself the luxury of a cup of tea and a slice of toast. Daisy had arrived then, hugging Polly to her.

'My, but you've lost weight! Sit you down, my lovely, and I'll do an extra slice of toast.' And butter, Polly thought mutinously. The Land Army rations would stretch to a smear of butter for a member of His Majesty's Forces. 'What news of Keth, then?' she asked as they settled themselves at the table. 'And don't look so guilty about a slice of buttered toast 'cos no one's going to find out.'

'I heard four days ago. The letters seem to arrive in twos and threes. There'll be a couple waiting when I get back, I shouldn't wonder. When did you last hear, Polly?'

'Yesterday morning.' As if she had known Daisy would call, she dipped her fingers into the pocket of her pinafore.

'I'm supposed to tell no one – not even you – but I reckon you should know what the daft young fool is up to. Here – read it.'

Daisy read the short letter through then read it again before the words made any kind of sense.

> . . . I had thought to be stuck here, sitting the war out in safety, doing well for myself. But that isn't for me and now there's a chance – a slight one – of a passage home.

'Polly, he *can't*! Oh, I want him home, heaven knows, but not working his passage again on a merchant ship! I know better than most now how dangerous it would be.'

'Can't is a word Keth don't acknowledge – you should know that, Daisy love.'

'Then I'll write to him at once, tell him –'

'No you won't, girl. You're supposed not to be told, remember, and you'll respect my confidence,' Polly said sternly. 'And you know deep down that you want him home as much as I do. But I shall write back and tell him we don't want any heroics.'

'I agree, Polly. This war is going to drag on for years – maybe as long as the last one did – but I'd still rather wait than have him come home for the Army to take.'

'Maybe he feels bad,' Polly shrugged, 'that his girl is in uniform and him safe over there.'

'Then he shouldn't! I wouldn't care if he said he was a conscientious objector if it meant him staying alive. I want Keth and me to be married, Polly, and I'll wait as long as it takes. So please tell him, *beg* him, to stay where he is and not do anything stupid. And tell him you are sure I would agree with you. Tell him I'm fine, won't you?'

'Even though you're getting bombed at Liverpool?'

'Even though. And where I work is pretty safe and I'm billeted well away from the docks and the city centre.

That's where the bombs are dropping. Liverpool is a big place,' she comforted.

'So is London, but that don't stop the Germans.'

'London is getting blitzed, God help them. It's not so bad where I am.' Not yet, though the full fury of the Luftwaffe could still be turned on Liverpool. She had only to look at the miles of docks and the hundreds of ships there, to know it could happen. 'So don't worry, Polly, and don't let Mam worry either – promise?'

'If you'll promise not to let on to Keth that you've seen that daft letter.'

'I won't tell him – and I'm glad you're going to be my mother-in-law, Polly. You don't think,' she frowned, 'that Keth will get tired of waiting?'

'Away with your bother! Keth has loved you for as long as I can remember. Now where are you away to, this lovely morning?'

'Off to the churchyard to see Reuben and Lady Helen, then I'm going to help Mam. Drew and I are going to pick up Gracie tonight. There's a dance at the aerodrome so we'll pop in and see you when we call.'

She kissed Polly's cheek then said, almost as an afterthought, 'There's a teleprinter where I work connected directly to Washington. I'm not allowed to use it yet, but the other night PO said I had the makings of a good operator and that I'd soon be able to send out on it. Do you think that's an omen?'

'Hey!' Lyn passed a hand in front of Daisy's face. 'Come down to earth. You were miles away!'

'Sorry. I was in Washington.'

'Well, we were talking about Drew, sending me his regards. How did he seem?'

'Just fine. He and I and Gracie went to the aerodrome dance.'

'*Gracie?*'

'Grace Fielding. She's Rowangarth's land girl. Didn't I tell you?'

'No, you didn't. I thought Rowangarth was a house where Drew lived.'

'It is, but houses can have land girls, especially when there's a huge kitchen garden on war work, kind of. Rowangarth sends a lot of fruit and vegetables to the shops; they're entitled to help.'

'Then it must be one heck of a garden.'

'It is. Rowangarth is one heck of a house. I told you Mam once worked there.'

'Yes, you did.' But there was a lot she *hadn't* told her, Lyn frowned, which was a pity, really, because she had admitted to Auntie Blod that she thought – *thought*, mind – that she could find Drew Sutton very attractive if she didn't keep a hold on her feelings.

'Tell me, Daisy, is Drew fond of this land girl?' Lyn persisted.

'Of course he is.'

'And her? Is she gone on him?'

'No, but she likes him and they dance together well. I once asked Drew if he was interested in Gracie and he said no – only as a dancing partner, and I know she has no intentions of falling for anyone till the war is over. A very level-headed Rochdale lass is our Gracie,' Daisy added, almost by way of mitigation because she *had* been a bit peevish about Lyn's interest in Drew. 'Tell you what – I'll show you some photographs when I unpack. I've brought a few with me. Will I be able to put them on my locker?'

'Sure you will. You just put them out of sight at Captain's Rounds. That's when a bod from HQ does an inspection of the Wrennery about once a month. Bags of bull, before Rounds. Everything as per King's Regulations, then back to normal again as soon as he's gone. But show me now.'

It was only afterwards, when Daisy had arranged the

photographs on her locker top that Lyn almost wished she had not been so eager to probe the charmed life of a place called Rowangarth.

The Clan. Four Suttons and Daisy and her Keth. All of them close and belonging to another, faraway world, their picture taken in the conservatory of a big, old house with a glimpse of a gracious room behind them, and a Christmas tree. A world that warned intruders to keep out. An almost smug world. And she whose parents didn't want her, whose father wasn't really her father, truth known, had fallen in love with one who was a part of that tightly-knit group.

'Tell me about the day that photograph was taken,' she said, because Lyn Carmichael was a fighter and prepared to take on the entire Clan if she had to. Come to think of it, her mother in Kenya, her snobbish, social-climbing mother, might even approve of such a setup.

Not that Auntie Blod would be impressed. She would take it all in her stride and say, 'Well, there's posh eh, girl?' and laugh her lovely laugh and think it was no end of a joke. It was what Auntie Blod made of it that counted, Lyn acknowledged soberly; she was the only one who mattered, because she was the nearest she would ever get to a real flesh-and-blood mother.

'The day it was taken? We-e-ll, I suppose it was just about the last time the Clan was together – all six of us, I mean. Bas and Kitty were over for Christmas. Aunt Julia's brother-in-law married an American lady – Drew's Aunt Amelia. She loves England. They used to come over on one of the liners every summer and for a month over Christmas and the New Year. They have a stud in Kentucky. Bas is a vet now, and works there, too.'

'And your boyfriend – he's with them?'

'Not now. Only sometimes. He went back with them in 'thirty-seven. He couldn't get a scholarship to university so Mrs Amelia paid for him to get his degree in America. He went to Princeton with Bas.'

'But why on earth should she?' People, in Lyn's world, didn't do things like that.

'Because she felt she owed it to Keth. He got Bas out of a burning house, you see – but it's a long story. I'll tell you some other time. That's Kitty beside me and Keth,' she pointed, 'and Bas is really Sebastian.'

She lapsed into remembering. Aunt Julia had called them her Clan, the children she had never had. Lovely, long-ago days and Kitty always the exhibitionist, teaching them to dance the Tango, that day the way they did it in France.

'Tell me about that one.' Lyn's finger jabbed.

'That's Tatiana. She was a bit of a spoiled brat, but she's okay now. We call her Tatty. Her grandmother is a Russian countess. No money, of course, but I think they must have been rich once. They had a town house in St Petersburg – Leningrad, I mean – and an estate at Peterhof, out in the country. Tatty can't bear her grandmother. She cleared off to London to be a translator. I never thought she had it in her. She's grown up really beautiful – like her mother.'

'Are you coming downstairs? It's time for standeasy.' Abruptly Lyn shut out the Sutton clan and their charmed world, admitting that the sailor she found so attractive had another life – a good life, if she wasn't mistaken – in which there were other girls and all of them attractive to look at. Kitty and Tatiana and now, it seemed, a land girl he took dancing. 'We'll have to get ourselves to bed, soon. Remember we'll have to be up for earlies.'

Yet she wasn't giving in without a fight and she didn't care if there were a dozen good-looking girls in Drew's life. All was fair in love and war, didn't they say? She wanted Drew Sutton by whatever means it took. It was as simple as that.

Daisy lay unsleeping, trying not to toss and turn too much because it wasn't on when there was someone in the top bunk and every movement transferred to the sleeper above.

She did a mental addition to June. The Navy allowed her four travel vouchers a year and four one-week leaves. Added to that, she was entitled – crafty weekends apart – to two forty-eight-hour leaves which could be added on to her long leaves. So in June, it might be politic to ask for ten days because, Lyn said, you always *asked* for leave. Leave was a privilege, and not theirs by right, not their due, though they were seldom refused it. A pity, Daisy brooded, that almost half of her first real leave would be spent in travelling. Dada had reminded her about it.

'You'll know the time has come, lass?' He had referred, of course, to her money; her mythical money, because up until now it hadn't been hers, really – only for special things like grammar-school fees, and even then the faceless trustees had had to approve them.

Ten thousand pounds, Mr Hillier had left her. He had never married to have children of his own. A rich, lonely man he'd been, and Dada's employer. Only now the shrewdly invested money had almost doubled itself and would buy Rowangarth and Home Farm and all Holdenby village and there would still be lots to spare. When she eventually told Keth about it he was very angry because he'd wanted to better himself, he said, and buy Daisy and their children all the things he had never had. Her money was the only thing they ever quarrelled about.

Sad that Keth's father had to die so Daisy Dwerryhouse could be rich, she sighed. Dickon and Mr Hillier were drowned one late-November afternoon, trying to rescue a retriever from a swollen river. Beth, she was called; a labrador bitch and trained by Dickon into a near-perfect gun dog.

Daisy's family all left Hampshire, then – Polly and Keth, too – and came home to Rowangarth and Polly had never been able to see her husband's grave since. And before the furniture vans came, Daisy remembered, she and Keth had stood beside the little marker beneath which Beth lay with

Morgan, Mam's old spaniel. Dada had bought the stone so people would always respect the dogs' grave beneath the beech trees in Beck Lane. 'B & M 1926' was all there had been room for the stonemason to carve on it.

She sighed, staring up into the darkness, willing sleep to come. But thoughts of Keth tumbled inside her head and would not go away.

'It's all right,' he had comforted when they said their goodbye at the little grave in Beck Lane, fifteen long years ago. 'Beth and Morgan have each other. They won't be lonely when we're gone. And when we get to Yorkshire and see the bluebells, we'll remember them especially, and know the bluebells in Beck Lane will be chiming for them.'

Dear, lovely Keth. Always there to comfort her, care for her, ever since she could remember, and she remembered now that she had turned angrily upon him, telling him that bluebells did not chime.

'They do, Daisy,' he'd said earnestly, his dark eyes filled with pain because he had been saying goodbye to his father, too. 'Humans can't hear them, but dogs can.'

'For God's sake, Dwerryhouse, will you stop your tossing and turning and sighing and let me get to sleep?' Lyn hissed angrily.

'Sorry . . .' Daisy had taken her handkerchief from beneath her pillow where she always kept it, because she knew that soon she was going to weep for childhood days at Windrush, when there was never going to be another war and the most awful thing that could happen to her was to stand beside the little grave where bluebells chimed and whisper a last goodbye to Beth and dear old Morgan. Only now there *was* another war and Keth was in America and trying to get back to England and he mustn't, oh, please, he mustn't.

She wanted Keth, needed to feel him, touch him, have him take her in love. But she wanted him to stay safe, too, and that was a foolish thing to think when need of him throbbed inside her like an exquisite pain.

The tears came then, big and salty and she let them trickle down her cheeks and into her ears and on to her pillow. And she tried hard not to move nor even to sniff until she was sure Lyn was asleep. And then she would creep into the lavatory and weep until there were no tears left in her because all at once she was afraid for Keth.

All at once, she was certain she would never see him again.

28

Three letters from Keth had awaited Daisy when she returned to Hellas House, each of them full of love and longing yet not one word to hint at a passage home.

Common sense briefly replaced the niggling apprehension and she found comfort in insisting that passages home were not so easily come by, and the knowledge that by now Keth would have received Polly's letter, begging him to think and think again about taking such a risk.

A week of early watches slipped by and Daisy plucked two more pale blue envelopes from the crisscrossed tape of the letter board. They told her that five days ago, Keth was no longer in Washington but staying with Kitty and Bas at the Kentucky stud. And there, Daisy was sure, their mother would insist he did nothing so foolish as try to cross the Atlantic. Keth liked and respected Mrs Sutton, would listen to what she said. His letter said:

Spending a few days with Bas and Co. Everyone sends best love to you and Drew. Nothing changes here. Kitty and Mrs Sutton are busy collecting things to send over there. Bundles for Britain, they call them. Kitty says she should insist on her right to a British passport so she can come over and join the Navy with you and Drew, but her father said he would spank her bottom if she ever mentioned such a thing again.

Kitty does not change. She is finished with drama school, now, and taking dancing and singing lessons, still determined to go on the stage. Mrs Sutton says she should be thinking about getting herself a steady beau but there is still a lot of the old Kitty in her; still a show-off – in the nicest possible way, of course, and she has grown very attractive.

Daisy had felt her cheeks blaze then. He must not find Kitty attractive. Keth loved *her*. He said so in every letter.

I miss you, my darling Daisy. Why are we so far apart and why does needing you hurt so?

Keth must not get tired of waiting, must not fall in love with Kitty whose eyes sparked mischief, whose smile was sudden and perfect and whose black, Mary Anne Pendennis curls framed the perfect oval of her face. And now, it would seem, she had grown even more beautiful.

'I'm going for a bath,' Daisy said to Lyn, 'before all the hot water gets used up. Coming?'

'No, ta. Got letters to write.'

She hadn't, of course, but it was obvious her cabin-mate wanted time alone. Ever since that first brief leave there were moments when Dwerryhouse was in another world – usually when letters arrived from America, Lyn frowned. She had once asked if anything were wrong.

'Of course it isn't! Why should anything be wrong!'

'Sorry I spoke,' she had murmured, determined never to pry again, reasoning that if she and Drew were in the same position, if Drew loved her as she loved him, then she would feel exactly the same. Frustrated, to say the least!

Telegraphist Drew Sutton. Lyn picked up the picture of the Clan. Now, like most other young people, he was a name and number who, for the duration of hostilities, had lost the right to call even his soul his own. Yet Andrew Robert Giles Sutton lived in a very old house with all the trappings of wealth and a kitchen garden so big it needed a gardener and a land girl to work it. And Drew had a close and loving family – small wonder the young Suttons were called the Clan.

Why did she find him so attractive, she who had so little to offer by way of family? Only Auntie Blod really.

Mrs *Margot* Carmichael didn't accept Auntie Blod; had rarely replied to the letters she wrote so often. It was only, Lyn frowned, when her parents decided an English education would be best for their child that her mother had asked her sister to act *in loco parentis* for the daughter they found an encumbrance and sometimes, because of her plain-speaking, a downright embarrassment. Her father, Lyn recalled, had been reluctant even to show her affection, though she had realized from a very early age why that was so. She wasn't her father's child. Somewhere, in her mother's past, there had been a lover. There must have been or why did she resemble neither parent and from whom had come the colour of her hair?

'Beautiful,' her ayah had sighed as she brushed and stroked the carroty hair she, Lyn, so disliked. 'Like gold touched by the sunset . . .'

Then they sent her ayah away with never the time for even a goodbye because Lyn was going to school in England, they told her, and would spend her holidays with Aunt Blodwen because it would be better that way. At the age of thirteen they had virtually abandoned her because since the day they placed her in the care of the ship's nurse and waved her goodbye at Mombasa, she had never returned, even briefly, to Kenya. And Auntie Blod had clasped her to her big, soft bosom and gave her the attention and affection she had longed for ever since she could remember, Lyn smiled. And her parents became faraway people who had vanished from her life – apart from the twice-yearly allowance paid to Auntie Blod, that was.

Soon she would see again the little cottage and the river with its big, flat stones they could sit on in the summer when the water was low; after her week of night duties, that was, on Friday, May 9. She would take the ferry across the River Mersey, then jab her thumb at the roadside to hitch a lift to Chester or maybe, if she really got lucky, in the direction of Wrexham.

She would be at Blod's place by noon, in good time to hear her say, 'Come on in, girl, and take off that old uniform. Dinner's nearly ready. It's tired you look, *cariad*. Dratted old war!'

Lovely Auntie Blod. Many's the time Lyn had wished she were her mother; many's the time more she had wondered how two women so unalike could have shared a birth and a growing-up together.

She replaced the photograph, wondering if Daisy would ever ask her to spend one of their weekends at Rowangarth, knowing she would not, of course. Rowangarth – Daisy's other life – was jealously guarded against all comers and if Lyn was ever to glimpse that tightly-knit, enchanted world it would be at Drew's invitation. Many times, in her dreamings, Drew had said, 'Come home with me, Lyn? Meet the folks?' He said it, usually, when they were dancing. Only he wouldn't say *exactly* that. More likely she would be asked to meet his family – something altogether different – because those Suttons over in Yorkshire were something rather special; a family in their own right, Lyn was sure. And Lyndis Carmichael had a mother who denied her grass roots – even the name she was born with – a father who wasn't her father, truth known, and a Welsh aunt who was as earthy and lovely as they came.

'Fancy sleeping the night with him?' Auntie Blod asked all matter-of-fact when they had talked about Drew, and she had said that yes, maybe she would – *if* he asked her.

Only there was no *maybe* about it. Of course she would let him make love to her and sod what people said about nice girls who *didn't*. It was all a matter of how much you wanted your man; whether you were determined to wait for the blessing of the Church and the complete approval of society, or if you were prepared to be labelled a tart, and take the consequences. Her own mother had been no angel, surely? Did it run in the blood, then? Was she no better than the mother she so disliked and would she give a damn about losing her virginity, provided she lost it to Drew Sutton?

'You bet your sweet life I wouldn't,' she said to the empty room. 'Not a single damn . . .'

The nights were lighter. Last October the clocks were not put back to their proper time and now they had been pushed forward another unnatural hour so that soon the nights would be light until almost eleven, which not only saved a lot of electricity for the war effort but made it less easy for the Luftwaffe to bomb London. They were not so brave when silhouetted against the brightness of a sinking sun and perfect targets for a snarl of Spitfires whose pilots could see in the dark.

Lyn and Daisy walked in the park which ought to have been closed at sundown each night or 8 p.m., whichever was earlier. But the iron railings around it had been taken away and all the sets of high, ornate gates, because they were needed to melt down into munitions of war, so no one took one iota of notice of the faded, painted board on the granite gatepost and walked there as late as they wished.

'So tell me, when is Drew going to be ashore again?' asked Lyn.

'Your guess is as good as mine. We'd know better if we worked in the Ops. Room and could get a look at the Plot.'

'Are minesweepers shown on the Plot? They aren't very big, are they? Not like a clonking great convoy.'

'Suppose not.' Daisy knew nothing of what went on in Western Approaches Operations Room nor had she as much as glimpsed the Plot, though the Wren messenger, who went in and out all watch long with signals, said it was thirty feet high.

'I'm bored.' Petulantly, Lyn kicked a stone. 'And tomorrow we start a week of late watches. I hate lates. What if Drew came in unexpectedly? We couldn't go out with him.'

'Even supposing he were to ask us,' Daisy said pointedly, staring ahead.

'Well, he usually asks us both . . .'

Daisy admitted that he did. 'It's pay parade tomorrow,' she said hopefully. 'You're only bored because you're broke and you wouldn't be broke if you hadn't bought three pairs of silk stockings.' To buy two pairs was economical; to buy three was extravagance.

'So it's pay parade in the morning and at six we're on lates. Doesn't give us a lot of time to do anything, does it?'

'No, but when we start nights we can begin counting them off one by one. Just think – this time next week we'll both be on countdown! And it's nearly four – we'd best get back.'

Supper, for those on the six-until-midnight watch, was at five sharp, an inconvenient time to eat though as Lyn pointed out, at least they got first cooking. Those they relieved would have to eat kept-warms which were pretty awful, with the gravy on the plates gone leathery and the mashed potatoes brown around the edges.

'If Drew's *Maggie* is alongside next Friday, I'll ask him if he wants to come to Llangollen. You could come too,' Lyn added. 'Auntie Blod would love to meet you.'

'I'm sure she would, but what would she do with three of us landed on her for two days? How would she feed us on one ration book? And anyway, when Drew gets a night's shore leave he likes to stop over at the Adelphi – you know he does.'

'Yes, and bed and breakfast there costs the earth. How

can an ordinary telegraphist afford it? But you Suttons are all well-heeled, aren't you? Drew is slumming below decks. With an accent like his he could get a commission any time he wanted one – so why hasn't he?'

'To answer your questions if I must,' Daisy said, far too quietly, '*we* Suttons, even if you count me as one, are not all well-heeled, and if Drew prefers to be lower decks and not apply for a commission it's his business and no one else's. And I didn't know you were a snob.'

'Sorry.' She *had* sounded snobby – just like her mother – and she didn't really mean to. If Drew Sutton swept the streets it wouldn't bother her one iota.

''S okay. And, Lyn, don't set your hopes too high – I'm talking about Drew and the way you feel about him. I know he likes you but he takes out a lot of girls and I don't want you to get the wrong idea. He and Gracie go dancing all the time when he's on leave, but she knows there's nothing in it.'

'Then ten out of ten for the land girl! And, okay, so he takes a lot of girls out? So maybe I'm happy to wait in the queue?'

'And what good will that do you, for heaven's sake?'

'Lord knows. But I'll have the satisfaction of knowing I tried, and didn't take too much notice of his sister who always seems to be warning me off! You do it all the time, Dwerryhouse. Did you know?'

'I'm not *always* warning you off. You'd think I were jealous, or something. All I want you to realize is that Drew doesn't seem to want to settle down yet.'

'So I'll be around, if I wait long enough, when he *is* ready. And after that if I get hurt, then I've only myself to blame, haven't I?'

'Okay. I tried. Now let's shift ourselves!' Late watches were trouble enough. Late watch and no supper was unthinkable.

'Tcha!' Lyn stared ahead, chin jutting. 'Oh, damn this war!'

'I wouldn't say that if I were you,' Daisy smiled, good humour restored. 'You wouldn't have met Drew, would you, if it hadn't happened?'

On the last of their late watches, at about ten o'clock at night, Marjie, who came down from street level where she had gone for a breath of cool air, came down to tell them the siren had sounded.

'We're in for a raid. I stood a while, listening, and they dropped a stick of bombs – quite a way off, it seemed, but there was an awful explosion and a blinding flash. The sentry told me to get downstairs where it was safe, but something went up with a big bang. It's like daylight up top. A full moon – they know when to come,' she said distastefully. 'Oh well, we're safe enough down here.' PO always felt guilty that they should all be so safe, so protected.

'So if it's going to be a big one,' someone asked, 'how will A-watch relieve us, at midnight? They'll not let them drive through an air raid, will they?'

'And we'd none of us expect them to, would we?' Marjie reasoned. 'If the all clear doesn't go soon, then we'll have to carry on here regardless and do the night watch as well. Agreed?'

They said okay, though it had never happened before.

'Well, it has now,' PO said. 'And let's face it, this place has only been going for three months. Looks like tonight might be a dummy run, watchwise. And if it is, it'll be up to the bods in Staff Office to worry about it – not us. Now – who's for a mug of tea and a sticky bun? And who'll volunteer to go to the canteen for them? Did I hear Dwerryhouse saying she would?'

There was a sickening thud, high above them. Not an explosion. No real noise. Just a shaking of the earth beneath them and around them as if some massive iron fist had slammed into it.

'I reckon we're in for a long watch,' someone whispered. 'Here you are, Daisy. Sixpence for tea and two buns, since you're offering to go.'

Daisy sucked hard on her breath then collected pennies and sixpences, making a mental note of teas and buns. And they *were* in for a long night because now there were more bombs, and not so very far away, either.

She had a brief picture in her mind of Mam, turning on the wireless tomorrow morning for the news and the funereal voice of the announcer: 'Last night, the port of Liverpool suffered a heavy air raid.' Poor Mam.

'Okay,' she called. 'Has everybody ordered – and paid!'

Twelve teas and fourteen jam buns and please, *please* God, don't let me be afraid – not when it's so much worse for the people up top . . .

The all clear sounded at half-past one in the morning. D-watch had felt the air raid rather than experienced it at first hand. That no relief watch had arrived did not seem to matter. They were safe in their deep hole, they acknowledged thankfully and guiltily, and only when A-watch came to take over would they see for themselves the devastation above them in the city.

'It's a big one up there,' Lyn had said when they met in the canteen queue. 'Must be. Half the phone lines are useless. The switchboards are in chaos.'

It was the Wren messenger who told them about the all clear, but it wasn't for two more hours that their reliefs arrived, pale-faced from a night spent in cellars, shocked by what they had seen on the journey from the suburbs to the city.

'Three hours adrift,' someone quipped. 'What kept you?'

'Listen, smarty-pants – just wait till you see it, that's

all! How we got through I'll never know. Looks like all Liverpool is on fire!'

The relief watch had witnessed the worst air raid of the war and wondered if now it was Liverpool's turn to experience night-after-night bombing such as London had endured for so long. Blitzkrieg, Hermann Goering called it. A systematic bombing into submission of Britain.

'Right, you lot!' Marjie held up a hand for silence. 'A-watch carry on. D-watch – sorry! No one is going back to quarters till daylight. Seems it's pretty grim up there. It was touch and go whether A-watch could make it through.'

'Make it through! That transport went up and down side streets like crazy. Walls falling, unexploded bombs, gas mains gone up – you name it . . . Reckon they'd have turned us back if we hadn't been a bus load of Wrens going on duty.' The Leading-Wren of A-watch was cold with shock. 'If I'd been Tommy I'd have refused to take that bus out. He doesn't have to take orders, he's a civilian!'

'So that bears out what I just said. D-watch to the dormitory; grab yourselves a bed. If the morning watch gets through, you'll go back to quarters on the transport. Someone will give you a shake,' Marjie smiled. 'Now off you go. Strip off and kip down and the first one to say she wants clean sheets is in the rattle!'

Disconsolately the teleprinter-operators of D-watch joined coders and plotters and typists, too tired to sleep – to complain, even. They had wondered about the dormitories on the first floor down: doors marked 'Men' and 'Women' and rows of beds and bunks, close-packed. There, in case they were needed, was the only explanation Authority offered for the apparent waste of space. Yet for once, it seemed that Authority had got something right first time. Now those beds *were* needed, Daisy frowned, looking for Lyn, not finding her.

There was a peg beside each bed. Slowly she stripped

down to brassiere and knickers. Best keep something on – you never knew . . .

There were no sheets. Someone said, 'These blankets are disgusting!' then pulled them over her face, wriggling herself comfortable with a creaking of bed irons.

''Night, everybody,' came a forlorn whisper from halfway down the long, windowless room. 'Sleep tight.'

But no one answered. No one slept.

'Julia?' Alice gasped into the phone. 'I'm coming over!'

'You've heard it on the news, then?'

Alice had heard it. The eight o'clock news bulletin had dropped like a bomb right in the middle of her kitchen.

'. . . Last evening, Liverpool suffered its heaviest air raid of the war. Bombing, which was widespread, was carried out by an estimated one hundred planes. Incendiaries were also dropped and it is feared there were heavy casualties . . .'

Alice had reached out, then, to turn off the set and because Tom had already left for the game cover on the far side of the estate, she rushed shaking to the phone to ask for Rowangarth.

'I've just booked a call to Liverpool, but Winnie says trunks just haven't got a line. She's going to keep trying, but I don't hold out a lot of hope. It must have been bad there last night, Julia.'

'Look – just get yourself over here. I'll tell the exchange that if the call comes through and Keeper's doesn't answer, you'll be at Rowangarth and to shove it through here – okay?'

'Oh, Julia . . .'

'Sssssh. I'll have a pot of tea ready. Just come – or shall I come to you?'

'No!' Rowangarth was the best place to be in times of trouble. 'Bless you, love . . .'

'I'm so worried,' Alice whispered when they were settled in the small parlour. 'Why did she have to join up? There was no need!'

'But Daisy *did* join up so there's nothing we can do about it now. And didn't she say the place she works in is pretty safe?'

'Yes, but she mightn't have been at work! And I know I'm not the only woman with a daughter or son away at the war, but she's all I've got and I'm worried sick.'

'I know, love. I worry about Drew and about Daisy and Tatty, too. Tatty's had a lot of bombing to put up with in London, you know. But don't forget that Mother is watching over them all. I know it.'

'Drew's little *Maggie* could have been in port last night. They bomb the docks, don't they?'

'Sometimes. It's at times like this I hope he's at sea. I reckon he's safer out there. And that wasn't the right thing to say, now was it? But you'll soon hear that Daisy's just fine. And whilst you are talking to her, ask her if Drew's ship is in. She's sure to know. Now let's have that cup of tea. And try not to worry? Mother *is* watching over them, Alice. I promise she is.'

The May Blitz as it was already called, lasted for nine awful nights. On that tenth night Liverpool waited; gun crews, searchlights and barrage-balloon crews at the ready, nerves stretched. On rooftops and from church towers, fire-watchers and spotters searched the sky with weary eyes and in Air-Raid Precautions centres, men and women checked their watches and thought that tonight they were late coming.

The trek to safer parts had begun early, with women whose husbands were away at the war leaving with their children in search of a bed with friends or relations who lived outside the city.

'They're late.' If it was said once it was said, in hope, a thousand times on the tenth night of May. Then, almost in disbelief, people wondered – because you didn't say a thing like that out loud for fear of tempting Fate – that perhaps tonight they weren't coming after all. Perhaps the bomber crews were fearful of the barrage snarling up from a defiant, bomb-happy city; from anti-aircraft guns, warships anchored in the river and from gun sites. Or maybe those who sent them had counted the cost and found it too high. But for whatever reason, all was quiet along the banks of the Mersey that tenth night when the moon was on the wane.

'I'll have to try, somehow, to phone home. They'll be out of their minds with worry,' Daisy said to Lyn as their transport picked its way through shattered Liverpool streets to Epsom House. No telephones, little public transport and of the three railway stations, one bombed to smithereens and the other two damaged.

Night watch left quarters early now to beat the alert, because whatever else, the sirens did not start their wailing until almost dark. Around ten o'clock it had usually been. The Luftwaffe was nothing if not predictable.

So each night the watch were at their stations before it all started and the outgoing watch borne back to their billets in time to snatch a sandwich, then claim their bed-space in the cold, cobwebby cellars and wait for yet another wailing alert.

At midnight, when the Wren messenger collected signals from the out-trays in the teleprinter room, she told them, fingers crossed, that so far there had been no alert. Not that she had needed to tell them because safe as they were, they could feel the shuddering of the earth above them and knew when, if not where, the bombs were dropping. And tonight, this far, all above them had been quiet, though it was reassuring to hear it at first hand.

At a little before six in the morning, for the first time in ten days, early watch arrived on time to relieve those who had listened and waited all night for the raid which had not come.

'We'll just grab a bite to eat, then we'll be off,' Lyn said as, disbelieving, they made their way to the canteen. Their week of night watches was over. Now came their two precious rest days. They had decided, nights ago, that for Daisy to try to reach York would be near impossible. Train timetables had been disrupted by the nightly bombing, trains cancelled, and those which made it into and out of the city were hours late arriving and departing.

Late-arriving trains were acceptable, they had reasoned, provided a Wren had a leave-pass the Railway Transport Officer could endorse with his all-important rubber stamp, but a Wren late back on duty and without permission to travel in the first place, would be pushing her luck.

'Best we hitchhike to Auntie Blod's,' Lyn said. 'You'll never make it home and back by train and you know it, Dwerryhouse.'

'But I haven't been able to get them on the phone. They'll know about the bombing and they'll have been trying to ring me, too. Can you imagine how they'll be worrying? And you know the main post office got a direct hit – how can I be sure my letters got through?'

'I still say you can't get home and back by train and you can't thumb a lift, either, all that way. If you come with me to Auntie Blod's, you'll be able to ring home from there. I'd take bets you could. We've hardly slept all week – at least it's quiet in Wales. Of course, you could always spend your rest days in quarters, if that's what you want.'

Daisy did not want to spend her days off at Hellas House. She wanted away from Liverpool; from the water-soaked, shattered streets and the stench of destruction; needed to fill her lungs with air not tainted by the stink of water on burning timber; forget, for two days, the awful reminders of maiming and killing.

Rescue teams still dug frantically in the rubble for bodies, dead or alive; twisted tramlines still defied repair; hospitals were filled with casualties.

Many of the dead were laid in long, straight lines and buried in mass graves; frantic men and women went from one rest centre to the other, calling out the names of missing relations and friends. Only after that did they visit the makeshift mortuaries set up in almost every other street.

Daisy wanted time away from all that. On Monday they would wait outside Hellas House for the transport that would take them to a week of early watches, but until then she needed desperately to sleep, to wash her hair and lie in a warm bath, because water had been in short supply since the bombing started – water in taps, that was. During the last few days and nights, any water which did not gush from bomb-shattered mains had been needed to put out fires. But more than sleep, Daisy needed to forget.

'Okay. I'll come with you.' Finally she surrendered to the pressure of Lyn's common sense. Best not to risk the journey to York.

'I think we should walk down to the Pierhead – take the ferry over to the other side. No use relying on buses or the Underground,' Lyn brooded.

'Whatever you say.' Daisy had so desperately needed to see Keeper's after the nightmare week, but Lyn was right. Making it home was one thing; getting back again would be altogether another if the bombing started again. Hitching a lift to North Wales was by far the most sensible, especially when, virtually, they were going absent without leave. 'But I shouldn't be turning up uninvited, and what's your aunt going to do about rations? We can't eat her food, now can we?'

'She's got jam on the pantry shelves and bread isn't rationed, nor fish and chips. We'll manage. For goodness' sake, Dwerryhouse, just be glad we're leaving it all behind us for a couple of nights! And you'll be going on long leave pretty soon, don't forget.'

'In six weeks.' More than forty days and nights still to live through with part of that leave spent travelling to Winchester. At least two days wasted, though it would be nice to be rich, she supposed. If she lived that long! Right now, keeping alive seemed more important than the money.

'Then for Pete's sake, snap out of it! Okay – so you can't make it home this time, but it isn't the end of the world.'

'No. It isn't.' Daisy hitched her respirator on to her left shoulder, pulled on her hat and followed Lyn up the winding stairs and out into the street.

Not the end of the world. Up here, in the devastated, rubble-strewn streets, though, it looked like it.

The minute they jumped down from the cab of the Milk Marketing Board lorry and called their thanks to the driver who collected churns of milk from outlying farms, Blodwen Meredith appeared at her front door, called a joyful 'Coo-eeee!' then ran to meet them.

'Worried, I've been! Are you all right, our Lyndis? Heard those Germans flying over every night!' She hugged her niece fiercely. 'And who's this, then?' Daisy, in her turn, was grasped tightly to Auntie Blod's bosom.

'She's Daisy Dwerryhouse. We room together. She can't get home this weekend – trains in a mess. Thought it'd be okay if I brought her. We need to sleep . . .'

'Of course it's okay! Where else would you bring your friends but here? You look tired out, the pair of you. Dinner's nearly ready. Take off that dratted uniform – and you, too, Daisy. Lyndis will find you something of hers to wear. Those shirts look as if you've slept in them for a week! Soon have them washed, and dried. And I'll do your underwear whilst I'm about it!'

'She's lovely, isn't she?' Daisy wriggled into trousers and found they fitted perfectly. 'Can I borrow the green jumper, Lyn? And are you sure your aunt won't mind washing my stuff?'

'Mind? She loves having someone to fuss over. I suppose it's because I'm all she's got – really got, I mean. But let's try ringing up your folks. Auntie Blod isn't on the phone but she has the use of next door's. You'll have a better chance of getting through, from here.'

'I hope so. Mam must be desperate.'

'Look – the telephone exchanges around here haven't been bombed. The sooner we book the call the quicker it's going to come through. Won't be a minute, Auntie Blod,' she called through the kitchen door. 'Just going to see if we can get through to Daisy's folks.'

'Then don't be too long!' She knew how Next Door loved to gossip. 'Ten minutes, and it's on the table!'

This little village near Llangollen, Daisy thought as she closed the garden gate carefully behind her, must seem a million miles away from the war – if it wasn't for the German bombers they had heard each night, flying over on their way to Liverpool.

'Lyn!' From the open doorway, Blodwen Meredith gesticulated frantically. 'Come you here and listen to this! You'll never believe it! Hess – he's landed in Scotland. It's on the news, now!'

They stood, disbelieving whilst the announcer read on.

'. . . and that is the end of the special communiqué issued at noon by the Ministry of Information. Our next news broadcast will be at five o'clock. This has been Stuart Hibberd speaking to you.'

'Well! What was all that about?'

'Hess – Hitler's right-hand man, I tell you! Seems he took off in a German fighter and landed in Scotland. Said he was looking for the Duke of Hamilton.'

'But where is he now?' They found it very hard to believe; a pre-invasion hoax.

'Dunno. Got him locked up somewhere, I hope. Wants his head looking at, coming here, and us getting bombed all ways. Must be a bit gaga. Suppose the Home Guard is out now, having a good look round in case Hitler's come, an' all!'

'I don't believe it,' Lyn gasped. 'It's a send-up.'

'Can't be. Was read out proper, on the BBC. Ah, well – let's get our dinner. Toad-in-the-hole. I told the butcher you'd likely be here this weekend, our Lyndis, so he let me have half a pound of sausages. Wish I'd known you were coming, Daisy girl. I'd have sweethearted a couple more out of him. But never mind. There's plenty of gravy . . .'

All at once, Daisy felt very normal and contented and safe; just as she had felt at Keeper's before she joined up. And all at once she was certain that before so very much longer, Next Door would call over the fence that her trunk call to Holdenby had come through.

'Auntie Blod,' she sniffed, because there were tears in her eyes, though she was smiling in spite of them, 'I'm so glad I came.'

'So are you happy now, Dwerryhouse?'

'Mm.' Daisy gazed out of the open window into the early-evening sky. 'Nice, isn't it, not having blackout curtains?'

'Auntie Blod sees no need for them.'

Electricity had not yet reached the little huddle of stone-built cottages. Downstairs rooms were lit by paraffin lamps; upstairs, since only candles were used, it was economical and far nicer not to have to hang thick black curtains at the windows. Nasty, depressing things Blodwen Meredith said they were and after all, she reasoned, you couldn't accidentally switch on a wax candle, now could you?

'I shall sleep and sleep now that Mam knows I'm all right. You should have heard her! Nearly burst my eardrum she let out such a shout. Told her I was safe in North Wales and that there wasn't any bombing at Liverpool last night. She said that London must have had Liverpool's bombs. The worst raid of the war on London on Thursday, it seems. Poor Tatty . . .'

'But your folks are happy, now they've heard?'

'They are, and I especially told Mam to tell Aunt Julia that as far as we knew, Drew's *Maggie* was safely out of it, at sea. They hadn't had my letters, by the way. I was right. Somewhere along the line, they must have got bombed.'

She lapsed into thinking how comfortable the big fat feather-filled mattress was. It reminded her of the one she had when she was little and lived in Hampshire. She remembered snuggling into it on winter nights. Pity Mam had gone all modern and bought her a hard one . . .

'Daisy?'

Asleep already. Smiling softly, Lyn plumped her pillows and wriggled into a nest of feathers to think about Drew.

Where are you now, Drew Sutton? What are you doing and who are you thinking about? Take care. Please take care.

29

'That,' said Tatiana to Sparrow, 'was Mother on the phone. Frantic. And then the Petrovska snatched it off her and demanded I come home at once. Seems they saw it in the papers about the big raid, the night before last.'

'Saw it! A wonder they never heard it, the noise that went on. You told her you was all right, that Sparrow's looking after you?'

'I did, though she thinks I left home just to be awkward and that the joke's over, now, and I ought to consider her feelings. Act like a responsible adult, she says, and go back. All at once I'm an adult, Sparrow. Not so very long ago I was a child who didn't know my own mind!'

'But didn't you, though? Didn't you get a job down here to spite them?'

'Not really. I realized what a mess my life was in and that I'd better do something about it before it was too late. It was awful, at Denniston – Grandmother acting the countess, still, and Mother nursing a secret sorrow – over my father, I think. It's nothing I can put my finger on, but things weren't right between them. Things you sort of sense from way back. Not memories, exactly. Just – well –'

'*Things*,' Sparrow nodded. 'Like you're always saying, it's your Russian soul as wants to suffer – as if there isn't suffering enough in the world.'

The ferocity of the bombing of the last two nights had caused even the imperturbable Sparrow to climb into her pit.

'I ought to go to Cheyne Walk – see Uncle Igor. Grandmother said she hasn't heard from him. Doesn't she know that half the phones in London are out of order?'

'He mightn't be in, girl.'

'Exactly.' Probably he would be in and decide not to open the door to her. Uncle Igor, too, had disliked her father. 'I'll write a note and take it with me – put it through the letterbox if he doesn't answer. At least I can say, then, that I tried.'

'You watch yourself, mind.' It made Sparrow shudder just to think of the state her city was in. 'You should get yourself a nice young man, Tatty Sutton, to look after you.'

'I suppose I ought, but nice young men are very transitory these days. And they get killed, Sparrow.' She would like to get married when she was twenty-one, if only to fling defiance at her grandmother; marry the man she herself chose, but there couldn't be two Tim Thomsons. 'The one I wanted was shot down by some bastard German.'

'Language!' Sparrow clucked. 'What about that nice young feller from the Embassy, then?'

'*Him?*' She hadn't said he was nice; had mentioned him only in passing. 'Vladimir, you mean?' She only remembered his name because he said he'd been called after Lenin.

'You see quite a lot of him, don't you?'

'Only because he brings things from the Russian Embassy and because it's me he usually gives them to.' And because he had asked her not to speak to him in Russian, they sometimes chatted – '*In the English, plis, so I may better learn . . .*'

'Has he asked you out, then?'

'Of course he hasn't. He wouldn't dare. They're watched, you know. The Communists don't trust anybody – not even their own.'

'Then why is that Vladimir bringing things to our lot when his lot are thick with Hitler? The Ruskies and the Krauts 'ave a pact, don't they?'

'Hitler's pacts aren't worth the ink they're signed with.

Stalin must know that. And you mustn't mention anything of what I say about where I work.' Especially her grandmother must never know she had spoken to a despised Communist.

'As if I would!' Sparrow knew that walls had ears and careless talk cost lives. 'And when are you going to Cheyne Walk? I want to know when to make Sunday dinner.'

Sunday dinner was every bit as ordinary as Monday dinner or Friday dinner but each Sunday, Sparrow set the table with the best tablecloth and napkins and silver, and used wine goblets for the water, to make it a little more special.

'I'll get dressed, then go right away. I suppose there's no hot water for a bath?'

'Not till tonight. You'll have to make do with a lick and a promise.' Water was in short supply, ran sluggishly from the taps since the bombing started. It was unpatriotic to waste it and what was more, it needed coal to heat it; even to heat the six inches of bathwater people were morally bound to use, now. 'We'll have a bath tonight.' Sparrow preferred evening ablutions, reasoning that if they were bombed in the night and she had to be carted off in the ambulance, at least she would be clean underneath when they took off her clothes. Sparrow had explored the timing of baths with great thought.

She gazed after the sad-eyed girl. Poor young thing. Not much of a growing-up for her generation, was it? Been real fond of that young flyer, truth known, but that was what war did to the young ones.

The phone began to ring, and she picked it up.

'Just a quick one to see if you're both managing, Sparrow. The papers say you're still having a bad time, down there.'

'Why, Mrs MacMalcolm dear! Me and Miss Tatty are as right as rain, though it's good of you to concern yourself. And we haven't had our phone lines bombed yet as you'll have discovered. Tatty's upstairs, getting ready to visit her uncle. Shall I call her down?'

'No, don't bother. Just give her our love, will you? I'll let her mother know she's all right.'

'Her mother has just been on, fussing . . .'

It was not until the pips warned them their three minutes were spent and she had gently replaced the receiver, that Sparrow realized she had called Miss Julia by the doctor's name and him dead these twenty years past and her Mrs Nathan Sutton for three of them. She hoped she hadn't caused distress, but maybe her slip into the past hadn't been noticed.

'That was your Aunt Julia,' she called up the stairs. 'I told her you were fine, and they're all right up in Yorkshire. Did you hear me, girl?'

'I heard you, Sparrow. Thanks . . .'

What a way to spend a day off, Tatiana sighed. Loveless, and going to see an uncle who didn't like you very much. But come to think of it, Uncle Igor didn't like anyone very much. Like Grandmother Petrovska, he still lived in the past in St Petersburg, in a big house overlooking the river; still waited for a Romanov to rule again. The Petrovskys were all peculiar, though. Even her mother took a bit of understanding, sometimes.

It made Tatiana very glad she was half-English.

'Will you listen to Mam's letter!' Daisy laughed. 'She says she was relieved to hear from me and of course she understood that I couldn't have got home. Good of Auntie Blod to have me. And then she says,

'. . . Poor lady. However did she manage for rations, and her living on her own with only one book. Your dada says we ought to send her a brace of pheasants, even though they are out of season. He said that before the war, you could send them them by post.

You just tied a label round their necks, stuck stamps on it, and the Post Office would deliver them. He's going to enquire when next he's in Creesby if it's still possible to do it.

'Imagine the postman! "Here you are, Miss Meredith. Two dead birds for you. Funny sense of humour the English have!" But seriously, Lyn, it was lovely in Wales. Didn't know how strung up and tired we were. And have you noticed – Mam's letter hasn't taken all that long? Things must be getting back to normal here.'

'There was no trouble on watch this morning. The switchboard is working just fine – but I suppose Epsom House would get priority, repair-wise. Don't know how long the poor civilians will have to wait, though, to get their phones seen to.'

They had seen again the devastation that was Liverpool. Streets of houses wiped out; a dock near-obliterated because an ammunition ship tied up there had taken a direct hit; a match factory gone up in such a blaze it had lit the streets around and directed yet more bombs on to the area. Four thousand people killed, the evening paper said; maybe more.

What had amused Lyn – if the expression on her face could be called one of amusement – was the fact that amongst the carnage that had once been the centre of the city, the statue of Queen Victoria stood aloof and unscathed.

'Just look at the old girl. Looking down her nose at it all with her We-are-not-amused expression as if she can't believe her beloved Albert's lot could do such a thing.'

'Never mind. Her Albert's lot are going to get some of the same – one day.'

'You hope! I'll tell you something for nothing, Dwerry-house. This war is going to go on and on and Lord knows how old we'll be before they let us out of this mob!'

'Oh, do shut up!' Daisy had been angry if only because Lyn was right. She and Keth would be strangers before it all ended.

'Sorry, old love. Didn't mean to rub it in.'

'Okay. Since you're sorry, you can read this. It was stuck in the board with my letter.'

. She handed over a scrap of paper and watched as Lyn's face pinked with pleasure. 'Dwerryhouse – 4A. Drew Sutton phoned. Will ring again at 2.30.'

'The *Maggie*'s in dock, then.' Lyn handed back the note, hoping her voice sounded as unconcerned as she meant it to be. 'He'll be – er –'

'Taking us both out, I shouldn't wonder – that's if you haven't got anything better to do?'

'You know I haven't! And thanks, Daisy. It's good of you to ask me along – you know what I mean?'

'Think nothing of it.' She knew exactly what Lyn meant. She was getting used to playing gooseberry, in fact. And she was learning to keep her opinions to herself. If Lyn was determined to rush headlong into heartbreak, then it was her own affair. In future, what happened was up to Lyn – and Drew! 'Come on! Let's get something to eat. Hell, I hate kept-warms. Let's hope we do meet Drew. At least he'll buy us a decent meal!'

Slowly, warily, Liverpool was getting over the shock of the nine-night fury. Water mains and gas mains were being repaired, trams began to run again and unexploded bombs – those which had been found – were made harmless by disposal squads with steady hands and nerves of iron.

New-fangled machines with giant scoops – bulldozers, they were called – shoved the rubble of houses into bomb craters so traffic might move freely again. Daisy wondered how the cleaning ladies from Lime Street station had fared, and if their homes had escaped.

I went through a blitzkrieg with them, Daisy thought

fondly; it made her almost one of them and in years to come she could tell her children about it and how –

But to have children was impossible when the man you wanted to have them with was on the other side of the Atlantic and only God knew when they would meet and touch and kiss. And make children. Perhaps, as Lyn said, the war would last for ever and she would be old and dried up like Miss Clitherow before it ended.

Stop it! Tomorrow would see the first day of June. Three weeks more to the longest day; three weeks to her long leave. She wanted to go to Winchester if only to turn the knife in the wound of her longing; wanted, if she could, to see again the gamekeeper's cottage in which she was born; walk down Beck Lane to Willow End and pretend she had only to knock on the door for Keth to appear, ready to go with her the mile to school. And she wanted to find the little marker beneath which Beth and Morgan lay.

'It might be possible,' she brooded out loud.

'*What* might be possible?' Lyn laid aside the magazine she was reading.

'We-e-ll, you know I have to go to Winchester . . .'

'Yes, but you've never said why. What's so important in Winchester?'

'A firm of solicitors called Briggs and Partners. They are holding money of mine. When I was little, someone left me some.' It all came out in a rush. 'I couldn't have it till I was twenty-one, though the Trustees let Dada have some for grammar-school fees and uniform.'

'Money? You lucky so-and-so! You kept quiet about it, didn't you? How much – or shouldn't I ask?' Lyn leaned to stare down from the top of the bunk.

'It isn't a lot and like I said, we've had some of it already. But it'll have made a bit of interest, I suppose.'

'*How much*, Dwerryhouse?'

'Only a thousand pounds.' Her cheeks flushed red at the

424

ease with which the lie slipped out. 'And like I said, we've already had –'

'*Only* a thousand pounds! I'd route march to Winchester for that much! You and Keth will be able to buy a decent house *and* a car! Why didn't you tell me? If I had that sort of money coming to me I could buy Auntie Blod's cottage for her and the one next door and still have some left!'

'As a matter of fact, Carmichael, I try not to think about it because Keth was angry when I told him. Said *he* wanted to provide for me; said I'd better invest it for our children.'

'Typical male stupidity!'

'All the same, I can understand his point of view. Anyway, I don't want it to get around, so you won't tell anyone at all, will you?' Lies, lies, lies. If Lyn really knew how much! Fifteen thousand by now, most likely. Enough to buy not twenty but *thirty* newly-built semi-detached houses. If the war hadn't put an end to the building of houses, that was. 'Promise you won't say anything – not even to Drew?'

'Of course I won't, idiot.' She returned to her magazine. 'But a thousand quid! Cor! Some people make me sick! Oh, and by the way!' She closed her magazine again. '*What* might be possible?'

'Winchester, like I said. I've been working it out. I'm twenty-one on the twentieth of June and we'll be finishing a week of nights on the morning of the nineteenth.'

'Yes. A Thursday.'

'Well, that means I can not only get ten days' leave, but I could travel down south on my sleeping day. Do you suppose they would date my travel warrant and leave pass for the nineteenth?'

'Don't see why not. Everyone tries to wangle leave to include a sleeping day. They turn a blind eye to it in Regulating Office. What time would you get there?'

'Don't know. I'll have to ask at the station. I should

think I'll be able to see the solicitors some time in the late afternoon. Maybe I can get a through train to Southampton; at a pinch I could hitch a lift from there to Winchester. What I had in mind was to get a bed there for the Thursday night, otherwise I'm going to have to travel back overnight and that's going to be two nights without sleep. What do you think, Lyn?'

'Sensible, I'd say. Once you've got your hands on the loot you can look for a hotel, get yourself a hot bath and a meal then get your head down. If it were me, that's what I would do.'

'That's settled, then. I'll check on the train times, then fill in a request form for leave.'

'You'd best do it at least a week beforehand. They work wondrous slow in the Regulating Office.'

'I'll remember. When is your long leave, Lyn?'

'A week after you come back. I'll go to Auntie Blod's and sleep and sleep and wash my hair in rainwater. Can't wait!'

She might miss seeing Drew, of course. On the other hand, though, with Daisy away for eleven days, she might fall lucky and get him all to herself! Now wouldn't that be just something? Smiling, she looked down at her watch. In fifteen more minutes he would be ringing.

'By the way, Dwerryhouse, have you hung up your In Quarters disc? Don't want them to think you're out, when Drew rings.' Oh, my word no!

'Will you look at this, Tom! The *cheek* of it!' Alice thrust the Sunday paper at her husband, her face bright pink. 'And the sneakiness of it! Announcing it on a Sunday so no one can go to the shops and buy anything – stockings, I mean, and shoes and –'

'Hush your bother, bonny lass.' He reached for his reading glasses. 'What's all the commotion about?'

'Clothes, that's what! The stupid Government is

426

rationing *clothes*! How are they to do that, will you tell me, because I'm blowed if I know?'

Clothing had been in short supply; knitting wool and yardage hard to find and a winter coat had doubled in price since manufacturers adapted their production lines to the making of uniforms rather than clothes for civilians.

'If you'll let me digest what it says, then happen I'll be able to tell you.'

'Well thank goodness I got that silk for Daisy's wedding dress, that's all I can say! According to the paper, those ten yards of silk would set me back twenty clothing coupons, and that's most of what we are to get to last us for *six months*! The deviousness of it!'

Clothing rationed. What next, Tom frowned. Bread, happen? Or fish and chips? Surely they couldn't ration fish and chips when they were all a woman could turn to when hard pressed to find the next meal.

'It says here we've got to take our ration books to the council offices and there'll be folk there who'll give us our clothing coupons. And, lass, do you realize that a pair of shoes is going to take up five of them and a pair of silk stockings another two?'

'Of course I do!' Alice had already thought it out. One brush with a thorn then *ping*! went a stocking and a coupon. There would be a lot of bare legs, she thought sadly, from now on.

'I suppose there'll be folk,' Tom considered, 'who'll sell their clothing coupons.'

'*Sell* them and only sixty-six to last for a year? Had you thought, you great softie, that your working boots are going to use up seven, that three pairs of socks will cost nine and if you add trousers and a shirt, then that's more than half of your coupons gone for a Burton!'

Yet poor people with large families and clothes to hand down might do well to sell coupons they had no use for – illegal or not. There would always be the rich and greedy

427

who would pay well for the means to buy a winter coat.

'I reckon there'll be a good trade in second-hand clothes. Seems they don't come under the regulations.'

'Hm!' Alice had clothes in her wardrobe too good to send to the village jumble sale; perhaps, she reasoned, they could be unpicked, the pieces washed and pressed, then sewn up into other garments. Hand-knitted jumpers could be unravelled, too. Women like herself who knew what they were about could manage, just about, to stay reasonably smart.

But two coupons just for a pair of silk stockings! It was awful just to think of it. And as for bare legs – whatever next!

June blazed and the Wrens on D-watch longed for the freedom of sandals and bare legs and cotton dresses. An air of blitzkrieg still hung over Liverpool but in the park opposite quarters, the grass was green and if you didn't look at the Palm House with most of its panes of glass shattered during those awful May nights, you could almost believe the bombers were never coming back.

'Sad about the Palm House.' Daisy turned from the window, then drew the long black curtains across it. 'They'll never be able to get enough glass to repair it – even if they could find the men to do it. All those beautiful tropical plants – they'll die, when winter comes.'

It made her think of Rowangarth and Mr Catchpole's rage if the orchid house were damaged, then she smiled, just to think that on Friday she would be home for a week. Seven days of bare legs and cotton dresses and no watchkeeping. And Mam and Dada, and Brattocks. No Tatty, of course, but there would still be Gracie.

The days were long, now. Blackout curtains hung undrawn until almost eleven at night. In Brattocks Wood, at this very minute, there would be long dark shadows and the scent of evening greenness and a late-singing blackbird, maybe, on the topmost branch of the very old oak tree. And soon she would see it all and smell it and hug it, precious, to her.

'Ready, then? Got everything?' Lyn asked.

'All packed. And my leave pass and travel warrant are okay.' Slipped inside her paybook for safe-keeping. 'And I've checked on the train. I just hope it isn't too late getting there. The solicitor said in his letter that he works late Thursday and Friday nights, so he'll wait until eight o'clock for me.'

'Surely you won't be *that* late. Marjie's letting you leave early tomorrow morning, isn't she, to get the six o'clock train? How far is it from Southampton to Winchester, do you suppose?'

'Not too far.' About fifteen miles, if she remembered rightly. 'There'll be loads of military traffic about – I'm not worrying overmuch about thumbing a lift. Just want to get it all over and done with so I can be home in time for my birthday.'

'Imagine – spending the best part of your twenty-first birthday on a train,' Lyn shrugged. 'But at least you'll be able to think of that lovely money all the way home.'

'With luck I should be home a little after six. Mam has planned a bit of a party on Sunday and Aunt Julia is bringing champagne. I haven't heard from Keth for more than a week, did you know? He knows I hoped to be home, though. I think he'll have sent a card and a letter to Keeper's.'

It would be nice, having his letters waiting for her. On the mantelpiece they would be, between the clock and the tea caddy.

'Okay, then. We'd best be getting downstairs. Lord, how I hate nights! It'll be like an oven, down there. Can't wait to get to Auntie Blod's.' Lyn pulled on her hat, reached for her respirator, the case of which contained not what it

429

should, but her spongebag and as many dirty shirts as she could cram into it.

It would be hot in the teleprinter room, too. There were promises, of course, to improve the ventilation, but nothing had happened. The air was as stale and dusty-smelling as ever. Only by climbing up three flights of stairs to stand beside the sentry at the sandbagged entrance and taking deep breaths of cool night air could they find relief.

'Can you manage?'

'Fine. My case isn't heavy. Nothing much in it but dirty washing and my slippers and dressing gown.' She glanced round the small cabin, saying a mental goodbye to it, telling it she would be back in ten days.

'I must say,' Lyn dropped her voice to a whisper as they walked downstairs, 'that for someone who's going to come back off leave a whole lot richer, you're being a bit offhand.'

'Not really.' Not if you *really* knew how much, Lyndis Carmichael! 'I've known about it since I was little; had time to get used to it.'

Lyn opened the front door, holding it with her foot as Daisy manhandled her case through it. Then they walked down the front steps to stand on the path, waiting with the rest of D-watch for the bus with blacked-out windows to take them to Epsom House. The sun had set, now, and a reluctant twilight gentled outlines and softened trees to deep purple.

'I expect you'll see Drew. The *Maggie*'s due in any day now.' It stood to sense; small ships could not stay at sea for long periods of time. 'And be warned, Carmichael, don't take liberties with my brother!'

'I should be so lucky!' Lyn scanned the sky. It was something they all did now; wondering if at any moment, the air would vibrate with the wails of sirens and long fingers of light from searchlights would, all at once, sweep the skies. 'Let's hope that –'

The front door opened. The duty Wren called, 'Dwerry-house! Phone. And shift yourself, I think it's long-distance.'

'Oh, Lordy . . .' And the transport due, any minute!

Lyn, hoping it was Drew, closed the door behind her.

'Dwerryhouse,' Daisy smiled into the receiver. Mam, with last-minute instructions about Winchester.

'Wren Daisy Dwerryhouse?' asked a female voice.

'Y-yes . . .'

'Hold the line. I have a call for you. There you are, sir. Go ahead.'

'Daisy? Darling . . . ?'

'Who's that?' Her voice was sharp.

'Who else calls you darling, then?'

All at once her mouth went dry, her heart started to bump. If she hadn't known better she would have thought it was –

'Darling – are you there? Sweetheart, it's me – Keth!'

'*No.*' Her voice was little more than a whisper because someone was playing a joke; a nasty, spiteful joke and it wasn't fair. 'I have to go. The transport's coming.'

'Daisy, listen! It *is* me. It's Keth. I'm home and I love you!'

'*Home?*' Her throat hurt and any minute now she was going to burst into tears because he couldn't be home. She wanted him to be but it just wasn't possible! 'Please – I don't understand . . .'

'I made it back, all in one piece. Tell me you love me?'

'You know I love you, but where are you, and *why*?'

'To see you, of course.'

'I'm going on leave in the morning, to Winchester – about the money. Where are you, Keth?'

'Oh, Somewhere in England, as they say. What time are you seeing the solicitor?'

'I don't know. It'll depend on the train and how late it is. I'm hoping to get there about four-ish, though. Keth – if it *is* you – where are you?' Her hands shook, her voice sounded strange and harsh.

'Can't tell you – not over the phone. But what say we meet in Beck Lane? Remember that place where bluebells chime?'

'Morgan and Beth's grave? You're somewhere near there?'

It had to be Keth. Only Keth knew about Beck Lane.

'Near enough. How soon can you be there?'

'But that's just it – *I don't know!* It'll all depend.' Her heart thumped with agitation because it was Keth, it *was*! And she had waited so long to see him yet all she could say now was that it would depend.

'Darling! I won't go to the solicitor's. Can you meet me at Southampton – the railway station?'

'No. Meet me in Beck Lane.' His voice was so soft she could hear the love in it. 'I'll be there at six and I'll wait till you come.'

'I'm not dreaming, am I? Please be there. Promise you'll be there?'

'Only if you'll say "I love you".'

'I love you! You know I love you!'

'Then you aren't dreaming, Daisy Dwerryhouse. See you tomorrow. I'll be there at six.'

'Will you hurry up and get off that phone! The transport's waiting!' Lyn stood in the doorway. 'I've put your case on for you. What's the matter? Why are you crying? Daisy – has something happened?'

'I'm not crying. It's just that –' She climbed on to the darkened bus, feeling for her seat, blowing her nose loudly. 'Lyn, that was Keth. He's home. I don't know where he is, but it *was* him!'

The tears came afresh, even though she was smiling. She had thought it was someone playing a horrid joke, but only Keth could have known about Beck Lane and the little grave marker where once he had promised her the bluebells would chime for Beth and Morgan.

'Keth! Back from America? But how come? Where is he?'

'I don't know. He said he couldn't tell me. But he's somewhere near enough to Winchester to meet me, can you believe?'

'Listen, old love, I don't want to be a wet blanket, but isn't it a bit peculiar that he's not only home, but within spitting distance of where you'll be tomorrow? I mean, well – talk about the long arm of coincidence . . .'

'I know. Things like that don't happen, but it *was* Keth and he *did* know things about the place we're meeting that no one else could know! Don't spoil it, Lyn. It's such a lovely dream I don't want to wake up from it.'

She leaned back, closing her eyes, breathing deeply to calm the turmoil inside her because of course it hadn't been Keth. Keth was in Washington where he would stay till the war was over and it had all been a lovely, lovely dream even though whoever it was on the other end of that phone had spoken with Keth's voice and said he loved her the way Keth always said it.

'Will you tell me, Lyn,' she whispered, 'how I'm going to get through the night and most of tomorrow? How am I to endure eighteen hours until I see him? Because the more I think about it, the more I'm sure. It was Keth. It really *was* him.'

'Then if I were you, old love, I'd spend the time just wallowing in it and thinking how it's going to be when you do meet. How long has it been? Three years, almost? So what's a few more hours, will you tell me?'

'An eternity, that's what.'

And how you lived through an eternity, she did not know.

30

Alice very quickly put the upset of clothes rationing behind her. The day it was announced in the Sunday papers, people had been amazed by the suddenness of it – and the slyness, too – but on reflection, Alice decided it was fair if not generous because very soon after had come the news of utility clothing; fixed-price blouses and skirts and under-wear and coats. Shoes, too. A blouse, she had discovered, could cost no more than fourteen shillings and sevenpence – not that she couldn't make one for less – but though ordinary in quality and not too generously cut, utility cloth-ing would enable people on low incomes – and heaven knew there were plenty! – to buy clothes.

Now Alice accepted the rationing of clothing as a chal-lenge. She was one of the lucky ones who could sew and besides, she had better things to think about, for wasn't Daisy coming home on Friday? For a week she could pre-tend her daughter had never gone off to join the Wrens; it would be like old times again for just a little while.

Not so long ago she had been worried out of her mind when Liverpool was bombed night after night, but now the raids had stopped; even the ferocity of the London bombing had lessened.

She sighed with pure pleasure to think of the week ahead. Tomorrow morning, Daisy would leave for Winchester and on the day after she would be home, twenty-one years old.

She glanced at the mantel clock. Time to set the veg-etables to boil for supper. Tom would be home soon, and tonight there was no parade of the Home Guard. Tom could sit in his chair, read the evening paper or perhaps talk with her about how it would be when Daisy came home on leave. The day after tomorrow!

There was a knock on the back door. The sneck clicked then Polly stood there, cheeks flushed, eyes wide.

'Alice! Such news!'

'What is it, Polly? You look as if you've run all the way here. Why didn't you think to use the phone?'

'Because the minute I put it down, someone picked it up. You know what it's like – twelve girls and all of them ringing their young men the minute they get back from work! But that doesn't matter – not when our Keth's home. He rang me, Alice, not five minutes ago! He's back in England!'

'Keth *home*? But when, Polly?'

'I don't know. All he said was that he'll be here on the twenty-third – that's Monday – and with that, the three minutes were up! And anyway, I was too flummoxed to think to ask him. But I knew he'd do it, the young fool! Told me he was going to try to get home, and I wrote back and told him not to be so stupid. Well, he's back, bless the lad and stupid or not, Alice, I can't wait to see him, though heaven knows where he'll stay. He'll not be able to sleep at the bothy, now it's full of young women. But we'll worry about that when the time comes.'

'And what about Daisy? Does she know? Has he phoned her?' Alice demanded, setting the kettle to boil because if ever a women was in need of a cup of strong, sweet tea, it was Polly Purvis.

'Happen she'll know by now. He was trying to get through to her, he said. But it'll likely be the same in Liverpool. A hostel full of young lasses and the phone always engaged! But Alice, just think! Daisy and Keth both home at the same time! And if you're putting the kettle on for me, thanks, but I can't stay. Got the girls' supper to see to! Happen I'll pop over again later.'

And with that she was through the door and running

up the lane like a slip of a girl. Amazing, Alice, thought, what a bit of good news could do. But Keth home! How had he managed it and more to the point, *why*?

Luck was with Daisy all the way. The train was only half an hour late into Southampton and from outside the station the driver of an army truck told her to hop on if it was Winchester she was making for.

At ten minutes before four o'clock she brought the palm of her hand down sharply on a bell beside which stood a notice saying Please Ring.

A door opened. A tired-looking man looked over the top of his spectacles and murmured, 'Miss Dwerryhouse?' It had been as simple as that.

'Mr Miller?' Daisy held out her hand. 'I made better time than I'd hoped. I've been waiting so long to meet you and Sir Maxwell.'

'But didn't you know? Sir Maxwell died two months ago. Sad he couldn't be here, today.' He opened the door of the inner office and motioned her to a chair. 'I'm sorry to seem in such disorder. What with Sir Maxwell's death and our junior partner being called up into the Army, it's a little difficult to manage sometimes.' He smiled and straightened his shoulders. 'But enough of my worries. You must be a very excited young lady. And I appreciate you'll be eager to get on with your leave, so I have pre-dated all the documents. They have today's date on them but it's only,' he glanced at his watch, 'a matter of eight hours. Everything is ready to be signed. I have asked the two ladies in the offices next door to witness your signatures. But first let me explain what I have done – and entirely as Sir Maxwell would have wished, I might add.'

'Of course,' Daisy nodded, wriggling on the hard chair.

'Firstly, I have opened two bank accounts in your name; one a current account with a cheque book and the other a deposit account, the interest on which will be transferred twice yearly to your day-to-day account, to keep it solvent. The bank requires specimen signatures, but that is quickly done. Also, I have arranged for the dividends on your investments to be paid into your deposit account so you will always be comfortably placed financially. The bank manager agreed to let me have the cheque book – in lieu of your signature, naturally.'

'It all sounds very complicated,' Daisy frowned. 'I'm afraid I'm not very good with money – not with a lot of money, I mean.'

'It's quite simple, really. Sir Maxwell had a flair for investments. Take ship-building, for instance. When you came into your bequest, the shipyards were at an all-time low, so he bought shares cheaply. Now, of course, they are booming. Ships, ships and more ships. Those shares alone would show a very tidy profit, though I hope you won't sell them yet. Sir Maxwell got together a very astute portfolio for you; could I suggest you leave it with Briggs and Partners?'

'I don't see why not.' No reason to change things. 'I know Mr Hillier left me ten thousand pounds; could you tell me what it has grown into?'

'I can indeed! Of course, your father as one of your Trustees has been kept regularly informed . . .'

'Yes, but somehow it seemed like figures, not money. And certainly not my money. The last time I saw a statement of account it showed about fifteen thousand pounds.'

'And Sir Maxwell, as I said, was an astute gentleman because now you are even richer, by five thousand pounds!'

'Good grief!' *Forty houses!* 'Thank you – and Sir Maxwell too, of course – for looking after it so well. I'll be glad to leave things in your hands, Mr Miller.'

'Then let's get down to the real business. I'll just give the ladies a ring, then I'll explain everything as we go along,' he smiled, gratified. 'I have some knowledge of share dealing – all gained from Sir Maxwell. You can be sure I shall keep a keen eye on your investments and send the usual yearly statement of account – less my fee, of course – though now it will come to you and not to your father.'

The afternoon sun glinted through the tall window; a fly buzzed angrily against it. Footsteps. The ladies coming up the stairs to bear witness to her wealth. Because as from tomorrow, she was very rich; forty houses rich, yet all she could think of was Beck Lane and Keth waiting there. Since he called her she had thought of little else, blowing hot, blowing cold; believing it then insisting the phone call had never happened.

The last of the night watches had dragged, with Keth hardly out of her mind and with every hiss and clack of the wheels of the train all she could think was that every second took her nearer to him; not to a fortune, but to Keth. If it really had been him on the other end of the line.

Going-to-Keth-going-to-Keth beat the steady rhythm of the train. Darling, she had sighed inside for the hundredth time, why did you do it? And oh, I'm so glad you did . . .

'Miss Dwerryhouse?' The mild voice caused her to start, guiltily.

'I'm so sorry. When I was little, all that money was a shock to me. Now, I'm having to come to terms with so very much more. Please forgive me? And I will be sensible with it, I promise you.'

She would have little choice, for what was she to spend it on? Clothes were rationed and members of the armed forces were not given clothing coupons. Jewellery had all but disappeared from the shops; even wedding rings, now, could only be made of nine-carat gold. And there was little make-up to be had, nor perfume, and property, because of the war, was a bad investment.

Nothing for it, she supposed, but to leave her money in the careful hands of Briggs and Partners' Mr Miller. What

438

did money matter when there was a war on, when Hitler might still invade Britain. Some good her stocks and shares and bank accounts would be then.

'Right! Your current account and cheque book. First we'll have your specimen signatures – in duplicate, please.'

Daisy looked at the clock on the wall. Already she had been here almost half an hour with the solicitor insisting on explaining every small detail of every document. And even when it was all done, she still had to get to West Welby and from there, walk the mile to Beck Lane where Keth waited. At the place where bluebells chime. At six.

Oh, please, *please* let me not have dreamed it. Let him be there.

It had seemed to take for ever at the solicitor's, yet it was only little past five o'clock when Daisy set off, almost at a run, in the direction of the Romsey road. It was hot and the case was nothing but a nuisance. Why hadn't she travelled light as Lyn always did?

She fished inside the pocket of her money-belt for the tiny key and unlocked the case. Then she pushed her respirator inside it and taking off her jacket, folding it, laid that in, too. Pity she couldn't take off her hat and her thick, woollen stockings! She was rolling up her shirt sleeves – as King's Regulations and Admiralty Instructions demanded on the removal of a jacket – when a lorry stopped beside her.

'Going far, miss? Want a lift?'

'Oh, *please*. I'm trying to get to Romsey.'

'I'm going to Wimborne to pick up a load. If it's on your way, sling your case in the back and hop on.'

She heaved the case up and over. Not only was it on her way, but the route took them beyond Romsey and past the crossroads that led to West Welby.

She explained to the driver how very convenient it was and she would tell him – because now there were no

439

signposts – where exactly she would like him to stop. After all the years, she had not forgotten.

It would be only three miles, then, to the village and another mile down the narrow road to Keeper's Cottage and Willow End and the little grave marker she had thought never to see again.

She was lugging her case along the Welby road with the fingers of her watch pointing to a quarter to six, when she heard the sound of a tractor behind her. Standing in the middle of the road, she jabbed her thumb over her shoulder and smiled sweetly. Lyn always smiled and it had never failed them. And anyway, it would have to stop, or run her over!

The tractor was driven by a land girl who smiled sweetly back and said, 'Where to, chum?'

'I'm trying to make West Welby – a little beyond there, actually – in time for six o'clock.'

'On the Shepfield road, is it? That's where I'm going. Will that be any use?'

'Couldn't be better!' Daisy laughed out loud. The Shepfield road crossed Beck Lane! Only a few hundred yards to walk, after that.

'Okay, then. Sling your case in the trailer. You'll have to travel on the tow bar behind me – the trailer stinks of manure. Put your arms round me and hang on. Okay? Keep tight hold and try not to mind the smell!'

'I'm a country girl. A spot of muck doesn't worry me,' Daisy offered when they started, at a crawl, on the last, the longest part of her journey.

'Six o'clock? We'll just about make it. Got a heavy date?'

'You bet! My boyfriend. Haven't seen him since the summer of 'thirty-eight. He rang me last night. I still can't believe it.'

'So you haven't seen him for three years?' the land girl asked over her shoulder. 'Oooooh! Bags of passion, eh?'

'Hope so,' Daisy laughed. 'But it's all happened so suddenly that I still wonder if I didn't imagine that phone call.'

'Which mob is he in?'

'None of them. He's a civilian. Been in America, at university. Never thought he had a chance of making it home. I still don't know how he did it.' She had to shout above the noise of the tractor.

'Don't suppose you care much?'

She was right. Daisy didn't care. Keth was home, he really was. In her state of utter elation, she supposed she didn't care if he walked on water all the way across. All she was certain of was that she was living in a dream. In her case was a cheque book she could begin to use tomorrow and a large envelope containing statements showing her how rich she was. She had never written a cheque in her life. Just to think of it gave her a peculiar feeling.

Yet even more peculiar, more wonderful, was that in minutes and just a few hundred yards, Keth would be waiting at the place where, long ago, two children stood hand in hand to say goodbye to Morgan and Beth; a place where bluebells would chime for them so they shouldn't feel lonely, Keth had comforted.

They were bumping through West Welby, now; past the little school she and Keth had walked to every day, past the post office, and the church where Mam and Dada were married, and the graveyard where Keth's father lay, the stone Polly could ill afford at his head.

'We'll come up to the crossroads soon,' Daisy called, feeling so choked inside that her voice sounded strange. 'Can you put me down there?'

'Sure. That's where I turn off for Shepfield. Hold on.'

They swung sharp right in the narrow lane, bumping over the grass verges. To her left was the wood of beeches and oak trees and hidden amongst them Beck Lane with

Keeper's Cottage at the top of it and Willow End at the bottom.

'Thanks, chum.' Daisy reached for her case, not caring that it smelled of manure. 'I made it!'

'You're a lucky so-and-so. My husband's in Singapore with the Air Force. Still, I'm glad, really, that it's pretty safe out there. Anyway, all the best. Don't do anything I wouldn't do!'

The tractor started with a roar and a belch of fumes. Daisy held up her hand in an answering wave. Now she had only to walk a hundred yards, then turn the corner into Beck Lane.

Her stomach was making noises, her mouth was dry, too, and if anyone had told her that meeting Keth after so long would be like this, she wouldn't have believed them.

She took off her hat, pulled her fingers through her hair, then began to walk slowly; deliberately slowly because she wanted to spin out the last few seconds of her waiting. Ahead, she could see the chimney stack of Keeper's Cottage and it made her want to laugh and cry, all at the same time. She ran her tongue round lips gone dry, trying to remember what it was like to feel Keth's mouth on hers.

Then she was looking at the house in which she had been born, its windows dust-covered, the path weed-choked. She wondered if she called, would Morgan come lolloping to meet her.

She looked down the lane at Willow End. Its windows met her gaze then returned it like blank, uncaring eyes. Beck Lane was deserted. Keth had not come.

Leaving her case at the gate, she walked up the path to the front door. Bending down she pushed open the letter-box, her eyes drawn the length of the passage and through the open door of the kitchen to the window beyond. Mam's kitchen. She must never tell her how neglected it had become.

She turned to her left and walked to the back yard and the

pump, once green-painted, that now stood rotting. And there was the shed where Dada had kept his snares and traps and nets and mixed food for pheasant chicks. Its door was chained and padlocked and Dada wasn't there.

She walked back to the gate, hurting inside. At that gate, Drew once waited for her and Keth to come home from school when he and Aunt Julia came to stay.

Tears rose in her throat in a hard lump. This was her childhood and Keth's and Drew's. She wished she had not seen it all mouldered and sad, for now those years would be tarnished in her remembering.

Shrugging off the hurt she walked down the lane. The beeches beneath which Morgan and Beth had been buried were grown taller and thicker, but saplings grew into trees, didn't they, in fifteen years?

She looked down. At her feet was the little marker with B & M chiselled on it and the date, 1926, below. The tall grass around it had been pulled away and thrown aside. Had Keth been – and gone? Had she somehow got it wrong, last night? Time had been short and half the call wasted not believing it was him.

She dropped to her knees. This was the place where bluebells chime although now they had flowered and withered, their stalks standing straight and tall with fat, bright green seed heads to tell her she was too late; fifteen years too late.

She remembered the evening they buried Morgan at this spot. Mam and Dada and Keth had been there. It was a very beautiful service. They sang 'All Things Bright and Beautiful' for him, then said, 'Our Father . . .' because Dada said dogs always got into heaven. Lovely Dada, who always understood.

The tears she had been fighting blurred her eyes and when she turned to look down the lane again she had to blink them away and pull the back of her hand across her face, because someone was standing there, outside Willow

End gate. A soldier. Just standing, cap in hand, looking at her. And he was dark like Keth and tall, too, and she blinked again to see if the soldier were real and not something she had imagined.

He began to walk towards her and she knew Keth had come. She stood without moving, taking in every detail of him; his slimness and straightness and the way he looked at her, not speaking; loving her with his eyes.

Then they were so close she could have touched him had she been able to reach out to him. But she was incapable of speech, of movement, of breathing, almost.

Softly he said, 'Hullo, you . . .'

'You're late,' she whispered, her tongue making little clicking sounds because her mouth was so dry.

'Only ten minutes.'

'A *year* and ten minutes!'

'Yes. The summer of 'forty, we said.'

Their eyes met. She had been weeping. Just like always, her long lashes clung together when she cried. And just like always, he had thought her beautiful, but now she was slimmer, the high bones of her cheeks more defined, her eyes more blue than ever he remembered. Now she was exquisite. And she was his.

He held wide his arms as he had always done and with a little cry she went into them, holding him to her, laying her cheek against his, letting the wonder of it flow over her, leaving her suffocated with love of him.

They did not speak, nor kiss. Sufficient that they were together and clinging fiercely as if each were afraid that Fate would reach out and tear them apart with a malicious hand.

'I love you, Daisy Dwerryhouse,' he whispered, lips against her ear.

'And I love you, Keth.' She pulled a little away from him. 'Will you kiss me, please?'

And when they had kissed and kissed again Daisy said,

'Oh, my goodness,' and gave a breathless little laugh, because all at once she was shy of the soldier who spoke with a faint Kentucky accent. 'Let's find somewhere to sit.'

The grass was dry, and warm still. He took off his tunic and laid it with his cap on the ground at his side. Daisy picked up her hat from where it had fallen and tossed it beside Keth's. They looked good together, his cap and her hat.

He reached for her fingers, twining them in his own then tucked her arm beneath his, afraid to let her go.

She laid her head on his shoulder, then whispered, 'I'm in a dream today. I can't believe all this – that I'm touching you and holding you and,' she reached up, brushing his lips with her own, 'and kissing you. I'm afraid it's all just a bubble and soon it's going to float away from me, and burst. You and me back at Windrush, I mean, and seeing Keeper's Cottage and Willow End, all deserted. It's like they've been waiting all these years for us to come back – Beth and Morgan, too.'

'I went to the village to see Dad's grave – took a snap of it, for Mum. I brought a camera over with me. They've got colour films in America, now. That's why I was late. I met one of the ladies from the Mothers' Union. They've kept the grave tidy all these years. I wanted to thank her.'

'Polly will be glad about that, but what is she going to say when she sees you in uniform? Does she know?'

'No. When I rang her I just said I was back and that I'd be home early Monday evening. She was so flabbergasted she didn't ask any questions.'

'So tell me, Keth – why did you join up?'

'Didn't have a lot of choice. This British Army guy came into the cipher room – you knew I worked at the British Embassy?'

'No, I didn't. I kept hinting in letters, but you never told me.'

'No. Best I shouldn't, I guess. Anyway, this guy put it

to me that the Army could use me, but back in the UK. I'd be given rank, he said, and a flight over. It was the passage that clinched it – and a spot of conscience, I suppose, that Dad didn't have a choice in his war. Besides, there was this Wren, back home in England . . .'

He bent to kiss the tip of her nose and she closed her eyes and parted her lips to let him know it was all of a minute since they had kissed.

'So you're in Signals, now, and did you know I'm supposed to salute you?' she smiled.

'That's something I'm going to have to learn about – army procedure,' Keth grinned. 'Going on a crash course tomorrow.'

'Tomorrow? You *can't*! I'm on leave!'

'And so will I be, starting Monday, till next Sunday. Got to go first, though, to see what makes the Army tick – learn about being an officer and being saluted by Wrens and all that guff. Then I'll virtually be a back-room boy – a boffin.'

'You mean you'll not be fighting?'

'No. Seems I'm more use to them doing other things. The army rank is just a cover, I suppose. Listen, darling – don't ever ask what I'll be working on and forget that I've told you I'll be code-breaking.'

'But we have coders and cipherers at Epsom House. There's nothing too secret about that.'

'They'll be coding up and decoding. I'll be working on code-*breaking*. There's a whole lot of difference.'

'Enemy codes, you mean?'

'That's it. Let's leave it there, shall we? And I haven't come all this way to talk shop when I haven't seen you for three years.'

'So tell me – have you been unfaithful?' she teased.

'Oh, sure. With every chick on the campus. What about you?'

'Working my way nicely through the lower decks,' she

grinned. Then all at once serious she said, 'Are we going to have time to get married? We could make it. Nathan Sutton would fix a special licence with the bishop.'

'Do we have to, just yet?'

'You mean you don't want to?' she gasped.

'Idiot. We *are* married. Can we get the approval of the church in about six months' time, do you think?'

'If that's what you want,' she murmured. And of course they were married. She could wait a little longer to use Keth's name. And there was no urgency. Back-room boys didn't get shot at. 'I'd like a ring, though. Just a little one. I'm sick of calling you my boyfriend.'

'Dammit! I'd forgotten.' He reached for his jacket, fishing into the pocket, bringing out a small velvet box. 'Got you this in Washington. Went broke to do it, but I saw it in a shop window and knew I had to have it for you.' He flicked open the box, then gave it to her.

'*Keth!*'

On a bed of velvet lay a sapphire ring, its stones arranged to form the petals of a flower, at its centre a diamond.

'I thought it would match the daisy brooch your Aunt Julia gave you when you were christened. Do you like it?'

'It's the most beautiful ring I ever saw.' She held out her left hand, eyes bright with silly, happy little tears. 'Put it on for me, please. And will you tell me why, since I got your phone call, I seem always to be weeping?'

'You always did weep. I remember you here, at Morgan's funeral.'

'Mm.' She brushed the ring with her lips. 'If you'd told me that fifteen years on I'd be sitting here with you, a ring on my finger . . .'

'I bought a wedding ring, as well.'

'Then let me have it, please? I'll wear it on the chain round my neck with my dog tag and St Christopher. Mam did that, you know – wore her mother's wedding ring with the locket and chain Dada gave her. She married

447

Sir Giles with it – and afterwards Dada put it on her finger again.' She turned from him, lowering her head. 'Can you fish down the back of my collar, unfasten the chain?'

'No, darling. Not yet.' He took her face in his hands so she had to look at him. 'I don't have to be back until tomorrow.'

'You've got a sleeping-out pass?'

'Sort of, except that I don't have to ask, exactly, for permission. When do they expect you at Keeper's?'

'Not until tomorrow. They know I planned to stay the night here. Shall we . . . ?' she whispered.

'I think,' he said gravely, 'that since we once planned to be married tomorrow, we should at least allow ourselves a wedding night. And I'm paying for the hotel.'

'You've booked us a room already?'

'Yes. In Winchester.'

'There's nothing a girl likes more,' she said softly, 'than being taken for granted.' She took off the sapphire ring, then held out her hand again. 'Well, I suppose you'd better make an honest woman of me – put my wedding ring on,' she smiled. 'And isn't it customary for the groom to kiss the bride?'

'It is.' And when he had kissed her hard and long he said teasingly, 'By the way, I'm glad you've got a case with you.'

'How come?' She traced the outline of his face with the first finger of her left hand because all at once the two rings made that hand top-heavy.

'We-e-ll, they're inclined to be a bit suspicious if you turn up at a hotel without luggage.'

'Well, we've got the wedding ring and the case, so what are we waiting for?' she murmured throatily.

'You're right. I think we'd better go.' He got to his feet, holding out his hand, helping her up. 'Because if we don't, we're going to –'

'Yes. I know how you feel. And it wouldn't seem right, would it; not here in Beck Lane? But kiss me – just once more.'

'Do you know how much I love you, Daisy Dwerryhouse?' he whispered, taking her into his arms.

'Yes.' She lifted her lips to his. 'I do know, my darling.'

Daisy opened her eyes, stretched lazily in a strangely large, strangely soft bed then turned to gaze at the empty pillow beside her; Keth's pillow.

'Good morning.' He stood beside the bed, a towel round his waist.

'Good morning yourself.' She held out her arms to him and he went to her, his hair wet and tousled. 'You smell gorgeous,' she murmured, kissing his throat, his newly shaven chin, his mouth.

'And you smell of sleep, and kisses. Happy birthday, darling. Congratulations! How does it feel to be your own woman?'

'You could've fooled me. I thought I was your woman.' She clasped her arms tightly around his neck. 'Get into bed – please?'

There was a knock on the door. Keth jumped to his feet; Daisy slithered down on her pillows, pulling the sheet over her nakedness.

Keth opened the door, said, 'Thank you very much – and yes, we are awake,' then walked to the bedside.

'Saved by the tray,' he grinned, 'and anyway, I've got to get you to the station, don't forget. I asked them for an early call . . .'

'So you prefer breakfast to me?' she pouted.

'Right now, yes. I've got you a birthday present, by the way, but you can't have it till I see you on Monday.'

'Why not? Darling, let me have it – *please*.'

'Absolutely not. Have you forgotten we aren't supposed to have met? And before you get home, you'd better take off your rings. It's a bit underhand, I know, but it's best you should.'

'You're right. Downright deceitful, in fact, but we can't let the folks know we've spent the night together unwed. They'd hardly approve.'

'Hardly,' he smiled. 'Sit up and I'll put the tray on your knees. It's just toast and marmalade.'

'Will it always be like this when we're properly married?' she whispered, closing her eyes, offering her mouth to be kissed.

'No! I shall expect you to be out of bed and dressed and breakfast on the table! Pour me a cup of tea, uh, whilst I put some clothes on.'

'Do you have to? I'm still willing to do without breakfast. Do you know how good you look, Keth Purvis, from here?'

'Tea!' he grinned, banging the bathroom door behind him. Their own private bathroom, Daisy sighed. Pure luxury. It made her think about her rings and how much they must have cost, and her birthday present, too. She wondered how well fixed Keth was for money, but money was the last thing she wanted to talk about. Nor had she mentioned by so much as a word what had gone on at Briggs and Partners simply because Keth had not asked. Once, he and Polly had been desperately poor. Now, it seemed, he'd had a good job in Washington and would have his army pay at least to live on. They would have to talk about her money, but not until he came on leave.

'Do you take sugar, darling?' she called, mischievously.

'Someone,' he smiled, accepting the teacup she offered, 'is asking to have her bottom spanked!'

'Ooooh – *please*.'

'Do you know how absolutely gorgeous you look?' He took a step back from the bedside. 'All tousled and sleepy and loved. And your eyes –'

'What you see in my eyes, Lieutenant Purvis, sir, is

unladylike lust, so keep your distance. And by the way, just where are you stationed?' She threw the question, to catch him in an unguarded moment.

'Where I am doesn't matter. I'll know where I'll end up when I've done the weekend course. I'll know then where they'll be sending me.'

'To which back room?' she asked, anxiously.

'That's it. I'm not at all sure now they've got me that they know quite what they're going to do with me. But I won't be in the Army proper, thank God. Does that sound cowardly, sweetheart?'

'The words of a sane and truthful man, I'd say. No one wants to get shot at – and you could have stayed over there for the duration, don't forget. Come to think of it, you should have, but I'm glad you didn't.'

'That makes two of us. Take off your rings before we forget, and slip them on the chain.'

'Ah, well.' She removed them reluctantly. 'It was nice being Mrs Purvis – if only for a night.'

'You'll get the engagement ring back on Monday. I'll put it on again in Brattocks – under the elm trees so your precious rooks will know,' he teased. 'Now get yourself up and dressed! You've got a train to catch!'

'I'd be home quicker going via London.'

'No!' He had seen London on his return. The bombing had shocked him, made him even more sure he had been right to grasp the offer of a ticket home – even if it meant joining the Army to do it. 'The Southampton–York train, like we said. London's in one hell of a mess.'

'What do you know about London?' she demanded, instantly alert. 'You never said you'd been in London.'

'There were better things to talk about. You and me, for instance.'

'You're determined not to tell me, aren't you? What am I to say to people when they ask me what my fiancé is doing?'

'You tell them I'm in Signals, in the Army. That should cover it.'

'It's very secret, isn't it? You really can't tell me,' she accepted, defeated.

'No. But I can tell you I love you and that in about six months we'll be married. As far as I'm concerned, that's all that matters.'

'I love you, too,' she whispered, swinging her feet to the floor. 'And it isn't dangerous, is it? Promise me that, at least?'

'It isn't dangerous. Just very secret. Now are you going to get dressed?'

'You're very bossy with that uniform on, Keth Purvis.'

She reached up, clasping her arms around his neck, drawing him close so he could feel her nakedness and her need. Slowly, he drew his hands down the length of her body then laughing, administered a smart slap to her buttocks.

'You've been asking for that all morning!'

'I love you even more when you beat me,' she called from the bathroom.

'And I love you, Daisy Julia Dwerryhouse,' he whispered to the empty room. So much, that it would take a whole lifetime, just to begin to tell her.

God, but she was good to look at – even in those dreadful navy-blue knickers!

31

Daisy smiled when the engine driver let go his customary hoots as the train slowed at the incline that ran alongside Brattocks Wood. Once around the long sweeping curve the train would begin to slow in a series of shudders and judders then come to a protesting, squealing stop at Holdenby Halt.

Home. For seven days and nights; home to spend the last few hours of this, her coming-of-age day, with Mam and Dada; tell them about Mr Miller at Briggs and Partners and show them her cheque book. She wanted to tell them about the money and how she felt; needed them to reassure her she would be able to cope with being rich. Yesterday, she had not been able to tell Keth. It was as if he didn't want to talk about it, didn't want it to intrude on the specialness of their meeting, so she remained silent because yesterday and last night and awakening this morning with Keth beside her wiped out three years of being alone and was all that seemed important.

'In case I'm not able to phone, I'll almost certainly be at Holdenby on the six o'clock. You'll be there, won't you?'

'You know I will. And you'll put my ring on again, so I can surprise Mam with it.' She would have to watch every word she said. Keth had phoned his mother; Mam would know he was back in England and she, Daisy, could tell them that Keth had phoned Liverpool just before she went on night watch, and that yes, she knew he would be home some time on Monday. But about her sapphire ring, and Keth being in army uniform and about their night in Winchester she must not, dare not, say a word.

The squealing of brakes told her she was at Holdenby Halt. In the station yard, a car, camouflaged in black and green and khaki waited, the driver beside it.

An army officer, who must have travelled on the same train, acknowledged the driver's salute, then turning to Daisy, who was behind him at the ticket barrier, said, 'Are you looking for a lift, little lady?'

'Yes, sir.' He had red flashes on his uniform. She wasn't quite sure about army rank but the flashes looked important.

'Where to?'

'As near to Rowangarth as possible. If you're passing the crossroads, sir . . . ?'

She sensed they would be. The only army people around were the secretive lot at Pendenys. She wasn't surprised when he said, 'Hop in, then.'

She sat beside the driver, her case wedged between her knees, staring straight ahead, knowing she must not speak unless spoken to.

'A spot of leave, eh?'

'Yes, sir. Seven days.'

'Good show!'

For the rest of the journey, no one spoke. She wondered, when she got out at the crossroads, if she should salute him – after all, he did have rank up – but decided against it, him sitting in the back and it being awkward, really, to return it. So she gave him a brilliant smile of thanks then stood for a while, watching the car disappear in the direction of Pendenys Place.

'And rather you than me,' she grimaced, grateful, nevertheless, for a lift in a staff car.

Her case seemed no weight at all and she strode out, heart thudding with pleasure, towards Brattocks Wood and the path that wound through it to Keeper's Cottage.

*　　*　　*

Alice saw her as she turned the bothy corner and came running up the lane, arms wide, gathering her close, kissing her.

'Daisy love, it's good to see you. And give us another kiss for your birthday! Fancy spending your twenty-first on an old train, but congratulations all the same!'

Tears filled Alice's eyes and she mopped them with the corner of her pinafore.

'Is Dada home yet?'

'No, he's Home Guarding. A shooting contest with the Creesby lot. He wasn't for going, but I told him it could be quite late when you got home – and he enjoys it, really, him being a good shot.

'And what about Keth, then? You'll know, of course. He'll have been in touch? He told Polly he'd been trying to ring you but your number seemed engaged all the time. He managed to get through, though?'

'He did, Mam. Just as I was waiting for the transport to go on watch. Another couple of minutes, and he'd have missed me. He's coming home on Monday, he told me.' That much, at least, she could say. 'He said he'd try to let me know when.' Lie number one. She knew, almost certainly, which train he would be on; knew about him being in the Army; knew, but couldn't say.

'You'll be tickled pink. What was it like, hearing him on the phone?' Alice opened the kitchen door, then flopped into a chair.

'I couldn't believe it. I wasted half the call, just making sure it really was him.'

'Well, it's right enough. Polly had a call, as well. She's been going round in a daze ever since. Ready for some supper? The vegetables are done. We'll have ours, shall we? I'll keep your dada's warm between two plates.'

'I haven't eaten since this morning. I'm ravenous!'

'You'll know,' Alice chattered happily on, 'that Keth won't be able to sleep at the bothy – not with it being a hostel for land girls, now. A pity – for Polly, I mean. He'll be able to visit all he likes, but not to sleep.'

'So he's having our spare room,' Daisy supplied.

'He is! The bed is made up, and aired. Oh, lass, who'd have thought the pair of you would be home for your twenty-first?'

'He'll miss my party . . .'

'Afraid so. But when we planned it, we didn't know he'd be back. And Sunday is a good day for Polly – her afternoon off. Now away and wash your hands whilst I dish up, then when you've had a bite to eat, you're to take off that old uniform and I don't want to see you in it again till you go back!'

'Something smells good.' Daisy sat down at the table.

'It's rabbit again, wouldn't you know? But at least it was a nice young one, so I stuffed it with thyme and parsley and roasted it. Can't tell roast rabbit from chicken, really. I shouldn't wonder if half the chicken they serve in posh cafés isn't rabbit. And listen to me going on and on! But it's so good to have you home, and twenty-one! And Keth home, too. I tell you, me and Polly both have been having palpitations since the night Keth phoned. I'm so excited!'

'So am I.' She went to stand beside Alice's chair, kissing her warmly. 'That's to say thank you.'

'Whatever for, our Daisy?'

'For being you and for having me and for twenty-one lovely years . . .' *And Mam, I don't like myself for deceiving you and telling lies about me and Keth, but it's best you don't know.* '. . . and right now, I love you so much I think I could burst out crying!'

'Cry? On your twenty-first birthday? You'll do no such thing! Now away with your soft-soaping and get that supper eaten!'

Alice cupped her flushed cheeks in her hands. Her bairn was home and soon, too, would Keth be. What was around the corner for both of them no one could tell, but tomorrow and Monday would be special days, so what was around the corner wasn't all that important – for just a little while.

With the discipline learned in all of four months in the Women's Royal Naval Serice, Daisy hung her skirt and jacket on a hanger, took off her tie, collar and shirt and stuffed them in the dirty-linen bag hanging behind the bedroom door. Then she stood, contemplating herself in the wardrobe mirror, and the navy-blue Wren-issue bloomers, the legs of which reached almost to her knees.

'Oh, Daisy! Those knickers!' Alice said from the bedroom doorway.

'Aren't they awful? Whoever decided on them should be shot at dawn! I don't suppose you could cut an inch or two off the legs?'

Alice said she could, and with the greatest of pleasure. Even she wouldn't wear knickers like those! And would Daisy mind, before she got into something cooler, trying *this* on?

'What do you think to it, then?' Alice held up the bodice of Daisy's wedding dress. 'It's only tacked together, so mind how you go. A low V-neck, fitted bodice and long, narrow sleeves with six buttons to the wrist. Can't beat a simple line.' Alice didn't like fussy wedding dresses. 'There's nearly eight yards left for the skirt and train . . .' She liked voluminous skirts. Such a lovely swish they made, going down the aisle. 'Funny that I got the urge to make a start on your dress. Must have known about Keth. Careful, now . . .'

Daisy held back her arms, then shrugged on the bodice, the silk soft and sensuous against her skin. Keth was home and the day on which she would wear her dress no longer a distant dream.

'Right, then. Turn round and let's see if the sleeves are sitting right. Looks like –' Alice stopped, drawing in her breath, then frowning she reached for the chain that hung around her daughter's neck. 'What are these, then?' The two rings lay on the palm of her hand with the St Christopher medallion and identity disc. 'Did you buy them with some of your new money? Where did they come from? That wedding ring isn't nine-carat gold and there are no engagement rings like that one in the shops now.' A glance at Daisy's blazing cheeks prompted her to ask, 'Did Keth send them – and if he did, why didn't you think to mention it?'

'If I said yes, he did – sent them ages ago, I mean – would you believe me, Mam?'

It seemed an age before Alice whispered, 'No, I wouldn't, so happen you'd better tell me.'

Daisy stood in the tacked-up bodice of the dress and a pair of long, baggy knickers. She should, Alice thought, have burst out laughing at the woebegone sight of her, but she couldn't.

'Tell you that Keth and I met yesterday? All right – so we did – in Beck Lane after I'd seen the solicitor. Keth is down there. Quite a coincidence – though he couldn't tell me exactly where.'

'Why not?' Alice's eyes were still fixed on the rings.

'Because he's in the Army now, though you're not to tell Polly. She'll find out soon enough when he comes home. But he's got some kind of a job in the Signals Corps that carries rank with it. He's a lieutenant.'

She pulled her tongue round her lips, fearing what was to come.

'Take off that top,' Alice whispered, 'and put your dressing gown on.' They had to talk, and before Tom got home. 'You stayed the night down there, didn't you, at Winchester?'

'Yes, Mam.' She shrugged into her dressing gown, avoiding her mother's eyes.

'And you spent it with Keth. He brought you those rings from America and –'

458

'Yes. And I wore them last night!' Defiantly, Daisy lifted her head. 'We always planned for this to be our wedding day. On my twenty-first we'd hoped it would be.'

'So you jumped the gun?' The angry flush was gone from Alice's cheeks. Now, her face was very white.

'Yes, though put like that, you make me feel like a tart. Well, you're not to blame Keth. It takes two people to do that. He didn't have to ask me twice. And why was it so wrong of us, Mam? Have you forgotten how it was between you and Dada?'

'No, I haven't. I'm just disappointed in you, that's all. Me and your dada didn't spend the night together in a hotel!'

'No. It happened in Brattocks Wood, didn't it?' Daisy said softly. 'Does *where* it happens make any difference?'

'Happen not. And no pot has the right to call a kettle black, I suppose.' Then the tension left her face and what could have been the smallest of smiles briefly lifted the corners of her mouth. 'Anyway, your dada couldn't have afforded a hotel.' With studied care she returned the creamy silk bodice to its hanger and walked to the door. Then she turned. 'Well, all I can say is that I hope you haven't landed yourself with a baby!'

She left the room, sighing. No use, she reasoned, condemning the girl for something she had done herself; no use blaming Keth, either. And she was glad she had held on to her temper when her instinct had been to tell Daisy she was a fool, and deceitful into the bargain. She had bitten on her words because today her lass and Tom's had come of age and not for anything must they quarrel on this special day. And she must remember, when she had counted to ten, then counted to ten again, to tell Daisy that her dada must not know about the meeting in Beck Lane. Best he should think, as Daisy had intended them to, that last night had never happened. As from this day, Daisy was her own woman and in charge of her own life and she, Alice, must never forget what it was like to love a soldier. And Keth, it would seem, was a soldier now.

She turned, walking back into the bedroom where Daisy sat disconsolately on the bed.

'You didn't say,' she said gently, 'if you liked it.'

'The dress? Yes, I do. It's going to look beautiful. And Mam – I'm sorry. Not about last night. I can't be ashamed about that. But I'm sorry if what me and Keth did has hurt you.'

'Aye, lass. Well, happen I understand more than you give me credit for, though I'll admit it came as a bit of a shock. And think on not to say anything to your dada. It had better be between you and me, eh?'

'You and me,' Daisy smiled, relief washing over her. 'And Mam – I love you very much.'

'Oh, away with your bother,' Alice flung. 'Just get those dreadful knickers off, and let me have a go at those legs!'

'Daisy! How lovely to see you!' Daisy walked into the bothy as Gracie walked out. 'Such news about Keth. Polly is tickled pink. Is it to be wedding bells, then?'

'I'm not sure. I'll know more when Keth gets home tomorrow. You can't plan a lot on a three-minute phone call, you know.'

She was not to be caught again. Not to anyone, especially to Polly and Dada, when he got home, would she betray by as much as a word that she and Keth had already met. And been lovers.

'Going to see Polly? I don't suppose it's any use asking if you want to come to the Creesby dance?'

'Best not on my first night home, Gracie – and my twenty-first birthday.'

'But of course! Congratulations! Y'know, I thought I'd feel different once I was twenty-one, but I didn't. Just a year older, that was all. You'll not have got used to it yet?'

'No, but I'm working on it,' Daisy laughed. And as for

460

not feeling different – well, that wasn't entirely true. Her coming of age had brought riches with it that she shuddered, sometimes, to think about.

Her new money, Mam had called it and she hoped that money wouldn't cause bother between herself and Keth. After last night, she loved Keth so much that she would give it away before she would let that happen.

'Will Drew be coming home for your party?'

'I don't think so. His ship had just gone back to sea when I left Liverpool, but we'll have a bit of a celebration together when I get back from leave.' She and Drew – and Lyn, of course.

'Okay, then. See you around. I've got the offer of a lift from the crossroads – best press on. You'll call in on us at the garden, you and Keth? I'm looking forward to meeting him.'

Daisy said of course she would, then pushed open the kitchen door where Polly was cleaning the last of the pans.

'Daisy!' She spun round, holding out her arms, hugging her tightly. 'Well, isn't this just something? You and Keth, back together at last!'

'I can't believe it, Polly. When he rang me it took ages for it to sink in.'

'What time do you think he'll be home? He'll be coming from down south, I think; maybe from London.'

'I hope he'll be on the six o'clock train into Holdenby. Shall we go to meet him?'

'No, lovey. You go. You'll have things to say to each other and as for me – well, it'll give me time to get washed and changed before he arrives. And it's good of your mam to put Keth up. I hope it won't be too much work for her. Mind, Keth will be eating here in the kitchen with me.'

'It won't be any trouble at all. His bed is made up, already. She can't wait to see him.'

'Nor me, though he took not a blind bit of notice about what I said in my letter about not coming home. Why do you think he did it, and how did he manage it? And what is he doing now?'

'Your guess is as good as mine.' Daisy's cheeks pinked. 'I only know I still can't believe any of it,' she said warily.

Watching every word you said took a bit of doing, especially when you were as high as a kite. But already she had made up her mind not to tell Keth that Mam knew. It would embarrass him to face her. She had said as much to Mam.

'I suppose you're right. Best not complicate the issue,' Mam had reluctantly agreed.

'I usually make myself a little pot of tea when I've got supper over and done with.' Polly dried her hands and took off her pinafore. 'Was going to ask you to have a cup with me, but look – that's your dada back from his shooting. Run after him. Let him know you're back. And come and see me again in the morning.'

'I'll do that.' She hugged Polly and kissed her then ran, feet pounding, down the path and into the lane.

'*Dada!*' she yelled. 'Dada, I'm home!'

Tom turned, pleasure warming his face. Then he lay down his rifle and held his arms wide, hugging her to him, swinging her off her feet.

'Lass! It's good to see you. You look tired. Been dashing around Winchester, have you?'

They linked arms and walked towards Keeper's Cottage and she smiled up at him and said, 'I missed sleep on the way down. Nothing wrong with me that a night in my own bed won't put right. Mam's keeping your supper warm. I'll tell you both about Winchester whilst you're eating it. It's an awful lot of money, Dada. I'm going to have to make sure it doesn't mess up my life – mine and Keth's, I mean. And I've got my own cheque book now.'

'Well, don't be writing too many cheques, that's all,' Tom cautioned. 'And I don't think Keth's going to be over-worried about it. He's a man of letters now, don't forget.

He'll be able to get himself a good job – if the Army doesn't get him first!'

Daisy was saved from answering by Alice, standing on the doorstep, demanding to know what had kept him and had he been to the pub instead of getting himself home?

'You know I've been in the pub, lass.' No use denying it. Alice had a nose like a bloodhound. 'For one thing, we were celebrating winning the contest and for another, I was buying a round to drink our Daisy's health.' He laid his arm on his daughter's shoulder, his voice all at once husky with emotion. 'And congratulations. Your mam and me are right proud of our lass.'

'No regrets then, Dada?'

'Only that we didn't have a couple more bairns as good. Now then, Alice love – is a man to get his supper, then?'

From her seat on the brass stool by the fireside, Daisy smiled contentment.

Countess Petrovska sat erect, staring ahead, waiting for the one o'clock news to begin. This far there had only been snippets and unconfirmed reports; not the plain, unvarnished facts from the Ministry of Information that the entire country was waiting for. Now, soon, she thought grimly, they would know the truth of it.

'There go the pips, Mama.' Anna sat opposite, white-faced, fingers clasped tightly to stop their shaking. 'Now perhaps they will tell us.' She reached to turn up the sound, then swallowed noisily.

'Here is the one o'clock news,' said the unemotional voice of the announcer, 'and this is Alvar Lidell reading it.

'An official communiqué from the Ministry of Information has stated that early this morning, at about three a.m., German forces attacked the Soviet Union on a front of two thousand miles from the Black Sea to the Baltic. One hundred and fifty-one divisions, about three million men, took part in the attack supported by tanks, planes and guns. This attack on a country with whom Hitler signed a pact of non-aggression, was codenamed Barbarossa and appears to have taken the Russian nation by surprise. It is thought that Nazi forces have advanced swiftly and with very little opposition. Several towns and cities have been bombed, causing heavy casualties. General mobilization has been ordered by the Soviet Supreme Council. It has been announced from Number 10 Downing Street that Mr Churchill will broadcast to the nation at nine o'clock tonight.'

'Turn it off,' the Countess ordered harshly. 'I have heard enough. Is there no end to that man's madness?'

'But they are attacking the Communists,' Anna whispered. 'I thought it would make you happy.'

'Then you are wrong! Hitler is attacking my country, my Russia. Like London, it will be bombed and blasted and left in ruins. The Bolsheviks, it would seem, have no stomach for a fight – cannot defend the country they presumed to rule.'

'But they were taken by surprise. Those bombers would find their targets easily with lights to guide them. There was no blackout there. Russia trusted Germany.'

'First a revolution and now this.' Olga Petrovska's voice shook with emotion. 'What will be left of my Russia for you and Igor to go home to? What would you find where our house once stood? And what will happen to Peterhof?'

'Houses don't matter. At least we are safe here, Mama. It's the people who stayed behind when we left who will suffer.'

'The peasants, you mean? Yes, I fear they will, may God help them.'

Piously she crossed herself, head bent. It was the first time Anna had ever known her mother to sympathize with the masses who had connived at the ousting of the Czar. Once, they had been beneath her contempt. Now they were her fellow countrymen, called upon to face the terror of invasion.

'Perhaps all we suffered after the uprising was meant to be,' Anna whispered. 'Think – it might have been this country the Nazis invaded. We were sure it would be. "Britain will be next," you said, yet for some reason Hitler has turned on Russia.'

'So he has.' The Countess rose wearily to her feet, lips tight. 'I think I will go to my room,' she whispered. 'This day is too much to bear.'

'Will you go to bed, have a rest? Shall I sit with you?'

'I thank you – no. I would like to be alone. I shall pray for Russia, for it is still my country.'

'As you wish, Mama.' The stern, uncompromising Countess did not show her feelings in public but behind her locked door, Anna knew, she would sink to her knees before the icon that hung over her bed, and weep for Mother Russia.

Daisy rose to her feet as the six o'clock train rounded the bend. On time again and with luck, Keth would be the first off.

She had cycled to the station because with a bicycle it would be impossible for them to hitch a lift and she wanted time alone with Keth. The walk back to Keeper's Cottage would provide it.

She had always loved the arrival of a train. When she was little, just to stand on the platform, eyes closed in anticipation of the hissing, clanking monster that would fill her head with thunder, always sent a strange thrill through her. It still did, doubly so when this train was bringing Keth back to her.

Brakes screeched, doors banged open. From the middle carriage of three Keth stepped down, case in hand, respirator over his shoulder. The uniform made him even more handsome if that were possible. She smiled as he walked towards her. No, she did not regret the night they spent together. Eyes closed, she lifted her lips to be kissed, whispering his name softly.

'I missed you. Say you missed me?'

'You know I did.' He stood, gazing around him. 'I wonder if you realize how many times I have imagined all this – the train, Holdenby Halt, and you waiting for me.'

He twined her fingers in his own, walking to the barrier, smiling down at her. It was the smile of a lover; of one sure of her love. He was so sure, Daisy thought wonderingly, that he could wait another six months to marry her.

'I came on my bike. Put your case on the seat, and I'll push.'

'It'll take an age.'

'That's why I did it. I want us to talk. Will the Russian invasion make any difference to things?'

'To you and me, you mean?'

'Well, Tatty's going to be a whole lot busier now the Soviets are on our side. Will you be busier – and will you still be a boffin?'

'I don't suppose anything will change,' he shrugged. 'It was a shock, all the same. Hitler must be mad.'

'Even though his lot are advancing almost without opposition?'

'Napoleon tried it, don't forget and they made mincemeat of him. But I'm home. I'm with my girl. Let's forget the war for a few days?'

'Sorry.' That was when she should have told him that Mam knew about Winchester, but she bit on the words. Mam had said Dada mustn't know. Best leave it. 'And talking about being your girl – will you put my ring on again, please? I want to walk into Keeper's, wearing it.' She leaned the cycle against a gate, then hooked a finger round the chain at her neck, unfastening it, slipping the ring into his hand. 'Put it on again – I've missed it.'

'How was your party?' he asked when they had kissed, and kissed again.

'Not the big do Mam always wanted – I think she'd originally had it in her mind to combine it with our wedding. But it was great. Aunt Julia gave me pearl earrings – *real* pearls. She gave earrings to Mam when she was twenty-one, and she wanted me to have some, too. They were her Grandmother Whitecliffe's. And your mum gave me a set of saucepans. They were the last in the shop. There'll be no more pans, the assistant told her, till the war is over.'

'Good old Mum. Ever practical,' Keth smiled fondly. 'What else did you get?'

'Mam and Dada gave me two suitcases. They got them ages ago and kept them hidden. And a good job they did, because –'

'Like the saucepans there'll be no more in the shops for the duration,' Keth finished, smiling. 'Y'know, darling, the shortages are going to take a bit of getting used to. In America, the shops are full. You wouldn't think there was a war on.'

'There isn't over there. Is Mr Sutton against getting caught up in our war?'

'Of course he is. Wouldn't you be if you had a son and daughter who'd have to fight in it? This war has nothing to do with America and most Americans want no truck with Europe. They got themselves into the last one and they don't want it to happen again. I suppose they are as relieved as we are, really, that Germany has attacked Russia.'

They were back to the invasion again, which wasn't surprising since just about everyone was talking about it.

'Dada says it's going to make a lot of difference to us. He says there won't be so many planes to bomb us, now that Hitler's going to need all the clout he can muster to

467

knock the Russians out. And he says that Hitler isn't going to be bothered invading Britain now he's got bigger fish to fry. The Germans are only a couple of days away from Leningrad, according to this morning's papers. Tatty's gran and mother are really cut up about what's happening. I almost felt sorry for the Countess when I saw her. She looked dreadful. "Where next," she says. "America – or us?"'

'Hitler is going nowhere till he's knocked Russia out and got his hands on Russian oil.'

'So you don't think Hitler will polish them off quickly, then turn on us?'

'Not a chance!'

'You're not just saying it, Keth?'

'No I'm not, so stop worrying. And no more war talk! Tell me you love me. Now that *is* important!'

'I won't come in. You and Polly will want time to your-selves,' Daisy said when they were in sight of the bothy. 'And anyway, you'll be sleeping at Keeper's. I'll see you later.'

'No. Give us a couple of hours, then pop in. I'll need your support because what Mum is going to say when she sees me in khaki, heaven only knows. Come over about half-past eight? She's sure to want to know when we're getting married.'

'And when *are* we getting married, Keth?'

'Next spring, like we said.'

'But why not now? Why not this week? We could get a special licence in three days.'

'And cheat the mothers out of a proper wedding?' he smiled, tilting her chin, kissing her.

'I see. There's no hurry now, is that it?' Angrily Daisy jerked away her head. 'Men don't run after a bus, once they've caught it, do they?'

'What a stupid, utterly childish thing to say!' Keth's cheeks flushed. 'Of course we'll be married, but properly.

And before you say it, I *know* there's a war on and big weddings aren't possible but I want you to have your white wedding and so do the mothers.'

'White, eh – even though I'm not a virgin? And had you forgotten that clothes are rationed now? That's another shortage you'll have to get used to after the good life in America!'

'Daisy Dwerryhouse, you haven't changed,' he laughed. 'Still ready to fly off the handle at the drop of a hat!'

'*Ooooooh!*' He was laughing at her! How *dare* he laugh at her? 'All right, then – what if I'm pregnant? Next spring is going to be a bit late, isn't it?'

'Sweetheart!' He leaned the bicycle against the hedge. Then he gathered her into his arms and kissed her hard. And because she loved him so much and had missed him so desperately, she relaxed against him.

'That's better,' he whispered, lips close. 'They aren't sending me to the trenches, thank God. We can wait. And you are *not* pregnant.'

'All right. If you say so . . .' And she really did want a proper wedding, wanted to walk down the aisle in a swish of silk. And wasn't she being stupid when less than a week ago, if the Angel Gabriel himself had told her she would be standing here with Keth, she wouldn't have believed him. 'And you are right. We can wait – well, to be married, that is . . .' They must not quarrel, spoil these precious days. 'Give me just one more kiss, then off you go to your mum.'

'See you later.' He turned at the bothy gate to watch her walk away and wondered how he had endured three years without her. Hell, but she was beautiful – why was instinct warning him off marrying her this very week? Was it because, he frowned, it had all been too easy? Codebreaking he had been offered and army rank to cover the secrecy of it. He had rushed in blindly, grasping the chance because it was the only way to get home – and to ease his conscience about not being in his country's war when his girl was in uniform, getting bombed.

The door of the bothy opened and his mother stood there. Just to see her cleared his mind of all doubts and suspicions. Whatever those doubts, he had been right to come home.

'Mum,' he said softly and she went into his arms with a cry of joy.

'Keth, it *is* you!' She seemed not to notice he was wearing army uniform. 'You're home, son, at last!'

32

'Sssssh,' Daisy warned softly and the dogs did not bark as she closed the garden gate behind her. She had awakened to birdsong and reached from her bed to pull aside the blackout curtain.

Brightness streamed into the room; five o'clock on a June morning and June mornings such as this were rare; something to be stored in the deeps of her memory and taken out and lived again in dark November.

She had pulled on trousers and a jumper then, sandals in her hand, walked gently past the closed door of her parents' bedroom and the one behind which Keth slept, creeping downstairs, avoiding the fourth-from-the-top stair which creaked loudly.

The morning was such that she wanted to hug it to her; demand of God how He could create something so wondrous yet let a war happen. In the distance, Rowan-garth's linden trees rose dove-grey from a dove-grey mist, whilst from the east the sun, rising low and morning-pale, slanted through the trees of Brattocks Wood to throw long, dark shadows.

The early air was cool – it almost always was in Brat-tocks – and green-scented and woody. She trod the moss at the side of the path and little squelches of dew wet her toes through the straps of her sandals.

She smiled fondly at the elms on the far edge of the wood, just because they were there, and enduring. They were there long before she was born and would be there, older and taller, when she was long gone. But this morning she was gloriously, wonderfully alive and in love and Keth was home from Kentucky, sleeping in the little back bedroom.

She leaned her back against the trunk of the tallest elm, touching each side with the palms of her hands to embrace the rough bark. The rooks would be nesting again, their first brood already flown and the size of blackbirds now. Rooks did not know about war. They might have wondered, once, about the monsters that flew low over their nests, but by now they had ceased even to be startled by them. Daisy closed her eyes and sent her thoughts to the treetops.

Rooks, it's Daisy. I'm home on leave. It was awful in Liverpool during the bombing, but I'm fine. Drew is at sea – you'll know that because Mam will have told you already. Stay there in the elm trees, won't you, then nothing can happen to Drew?

You'll know Keth is home. We haven't talked about my money yet – you'll remember about my money? I've got it now and it's going to be a bit of a worry till Keth and I come to an understanding about it.

Keth and I are engaged. It's official. He brought a sapphire ring back with him. Keth is in the Army but he's doing a safe job though I'm not sure what. But look after Keth, too, just in case?

Tatty is in London and getting bombed, though not as badly now. Tatty is very unhappy still about Tim. I wish something good could happen to her . . .

Then she promised that she and Keth would pay them another visit before his leave was up, even though he thought it odd to tell things to the rooks.

But Mam believed; told things to the rooks all the time. They wouldn't, Daisy realized, have been one bit surprised that she was here, this moring. They would be expecting her because Mam would have told them already about her birthday and her leave.

She turned to face the tree, smiling up into the dense

472

greenness, then climbed the fence and made for the pike.

When she reached the top she sat down and closed her eyes, calling out softly with her mind and her heart.

Tim – if you can hear me, it's Daisy. I promised Tatty I would come whilst she's in London and bring you her love. And she does love you. She'll always love you. I know, because it's the way I love Keth. It's a once-and-forever thing and Tatty will never love anyone the way she loved you, Tim . . .

There was a silence around her so complete that just to breathe in and breathe out disturbed it. And then the sun rose over the far side of the pike and sent more shadows, throwing them on the scrubby bushes in the lee of the hill, sheltered from winter winds that blew from the east because they grew just a few yards from the summit. It was there, Tatty once said, that she and Tim loved together. And Tim's bomber crashed beside those bushes, yet now there was no sign that it had ever lain there. The Air Force had taken it away and the small pieces left behind had been snatched up as souvenirs by children and people who came to gawp. Now Tim was gone; it was as if his love and Tatty's had never been.

And then, high above her, a curlew called and she squinted into the sky to see it descending, burbling out as it sank to its mate, nesting in the rough moorland grass. Seagulls, someone said, were really the souls of sailors, killed at sea. Did that bird, then, have Tim's soul in its keeping and was it calling to let her know it was glad she had come to bring Tatty's love? It was a comforting thought and she wanted to believe it. And it was half-past seven and Mam would be tutting because she had taken herself off without leaving a note on the kitchen table.

Someone was shouting, waving. Below her, Keth ran up the steep slope. She waved back, then ran, feet slithering on the still-damp grass and went laughing into his arms.

'Darling – what are you doing up here?'

'Just wanted to come, I suppose. How did you know where I'd be?'

'You weren't in Brattocks, so I thought this was where I'd find you.' He filled his lungs with air, closing his eyes, letting it go in little huffs. 'There's no place on earth quite like the top of the pike, is there? I often thought about it, when I was away.'

'Mm. I came up here because I'm so happy, Keth; a pilgrimage of thanks, I suppose, to say hullo to Tim. I promised Tatty I'd come up here sometimes; give him her love. Tim was her boyfriend, you know. This was where he was shot down.'

'And you think –'

'Think that some part of him is still here? Yes, Keth, I do. And Tatty thinks so, too.'

'But *how*, darling?' Keth was a mathematician; things had to be proved.

'I just know, that's all. A touch of the Jinny Dobbses, I suppose.' No need to tell him about the curlew. Tatty would understand but Keth wouldn't, because men were different. She held out her hand to him. 'We are so lucky, you and I. Always take care, won't you?'

'I will. I promise.'

'I love you.' She closed her eyes and lifted her lips to be kissed and the curlew called once more.

'Bye, Tim. I'll come again . . .

When they came to the gentler slope and were able to walk without slipping and sliding, Daisy said, 'We've got to talk, Keth – about the money, I mean. We keep putting it off and we can't change it, you know. It's there, twenty thousand pounds; that's how much it has grown into. The solicitor at Winchester said I should make a Will, but I couldn't do it. It would have been like spitting into the wind, I suppose; asking for trouble.' She stopped, holding tightly to his hand so he had to stop, too, and turn and face her. 'Keth, I'm trying to talk to you and you don't want to listen!'

'Why talk about it? We can't change anything by talking. I try not to think about it, especially when Dad had to die so Mam had enough money to buy my uniform for grammar school.'

'So that's it! You think that because your dad died – and Mr Hillier, too – I got rich? But I didn't know he was going to leave me all that money. And Mr Hillier didn't know he was going to die, that day; didn't know Beth would get into trouble in the river. And he didn't want your dad to drown, helping him to get her out! You knew he left your dad a hundred pounds in his Will, like all the other estate workers, but did you know that he'd left Beth to him, too? He loved that bitch and your dad would have been proud to think that Mr Hillier wanted him to have her.'

'I know, Daisy. I'll come to understand it – just give me time?'

'Then till you do, remember there's a war on, Keth. Not so long ago Liverpool was blitzed and thousands were killed. I could have been one of them, and twenty *million* pounds wouldn't have bought back my life! *Please* understand. I've just been to where Tim was killed. He was only a little older than me. If this war hadn't happened he'd be alive and at university; if those fighters hadn't shot up the aerodrome, even, he might still be alive. He and Tatty used to go up the pike to be on their own, be lovers, and now there's nothing left of him but an echo. For God's sake, Keth, get that chip off your shoulder!' She stopped, white-faced with anger, her breath coming in sharp gasps, her eyes clouded with despair.

'I'm trying, Daisy . . .'

Was this then, Keth thought, what he had come home for? He had been eager, grasped at the chance to get back to her. Not to his mother nor to England nor to fight in the war but to Daisy, the girl he had loved since ever he could remember.

Yet after so short a time together, her money already stood between them; money left to a little girl who once lived in the gamekeeper's cottage at Windrush. And she could do nothing about it; it was fact. Twenty thousand poundsworth of fact!

'I didn't mean to say that – about Dad's money,' he said softly. 'Dad dying, Mr Hillier leaving a small fortune to you – none of it was your fault. I'm sorry, sweetheart. I should be man enough to accept it.'

'No, Keth! Damn the money! You should be man enough to accept that I love you *in spite* of the money! Can't you see that? Is it to spoil things between you and me for the rest of our lives?'

'No, Daisy, it isn't. I won't let it.'

'I see.' She was calmer, now. 'So instead you'll work and work and think of nothing else but getting as rich as I am – is that it?'

'No. I just said I won't let it spoil things for us, and I meant it. All I ask is that you don't spoil our kids – give them everything they ask for.'

'Children! So you'll give me children, then?'

'Try and stop me!' He was smiling again. 'And I'll tell you something else! If we were both in uniform, I might just put you on a charge for back-chatting an officer!'

'Hey! I hadn't noticed. Where did you get those civvy togs from? You look great, Keth!' Talk of ships and shoes. Talk of anything but money . . .

'Bought them in Washington when I started earning a bit of money. I've grown some, in three years.' Forget the money. Civvies were safer ground. 'Mam and I were looking at the clothes I left behind. We had a good laugh about it. I must have been a skinny kid.'

'You were – or so Mam said. She always wanted to feed you up when you were little – give you dripping toast.'

'And sugar butties. I remember!' He threw back his head, laughing, then held wide his arms. 'And I'd have given ten years of my life, two months ago, to be here with you. To hell with that money!'

'Agreed!' She went to him, hugging him close. 'I won't ever mention it again, Keth.'

'But you must, sweetheart. It's got to be talked about. You were right. It's fact. It isn't going to go away – only we'll not quarrel about it.'

'Agreed.' She took a deep, calming breath then reached for his hand as they walked back to the crossroads. 'I've decided we're to tell no one else – not even your mother – about it. And I accept that sometimes it might make difficulties, but at least we'll be able to start off in a house of our own and we won't have to pinch pennies to get a car and have a phone.'

'When the war is over, that is . . .'

'Yes.' And damn the war, too! It was spoiling everybody's lives. 'But we've got to think of the future. It's the only way we can keep going. One day, this war *will* be over.'

'And then?'

'Then that money is ours, Keth. *Ours*, not mine. And we'll say nothing about it so people will think that all we have has been provided by you.'

'Even though I know it hasn't?'

'Even though. I'm sorry, Keth, but that's the way it'll have to be. You take me as I am – money and all!'

'We-e-ll – I suppose our kids can have ponies and go to fancy schools . . .'

'No, they can't! They'll have their pocket money, and anything else they want they'll have to do jobs for. You had a newspaper round for years!'

'Mm. Two bob a week – and sixpence pocket money from Mam. Half a crown was a lot of money, in those days.'

'And it still is, when you've had to work for it! And there'll be no fancy schools, either. Our kids aren't going to be sent away, boarding. They'll go to grammar school, like we did.'

'You've got it all worked out – might I know how many you plan we'll have?'

'Heaven only knows! The way I feel about you now, we'll have lots. And I didn't get pregnant at Winchester, so I think we'll be able to wait till spring to get married.'

'When did you know?' He was laughing now.

'Last night. I'm afraid we'll have a very celibate leave!'

'Looks like it, but you'll have to organize our honeymoon better!'

Then she began to laugh with him because Keth was gloriously alive and not the echo of a cry in the air above her and she was the luckiest, most loved woman that ever was or ever would be.

'I love you, Keth Purvis.' She reached for him, twining her arms around his neck, lifting her mouth to his. 'I'll always love you. And, darling, we did have Winchester.'

'We did. And it was wonderful. We'll wait till spring?'

'Mm. Will an Easter wedding suit you, Lieutenant?'

'It will suit me very nicely,' he said, then kissed her again. Very thoroughly.

At Hellas House, one of the noisy lot from Cabin 4 flung open the door of 4A without ceremony and called, 'Phone for you, Carmichael. Chop chop! It's a bloke!'

Lyn picked up the receiver and took a long, calming breath. 'Carmichael,' she said not too steadily.

'Lyn! Hi, it's Drew.'

'Hi yourself! Daisy's on leave.'

'Yes, I know.'

'But did you know that Keth's back in England?'

'Keth – *back home*! How come?'

'Haven't a clue. I only know he rang just as we were

going on night watch and that he was meeting her somewhere Winchester way. She had to go there, you see.'

'Yes. She used to live there, once.' Best be careful what he said. Daisy was still a bit touchy about her inheritance. Maybe she hadn't even told Lyn. 'But it was you I wanted to speak to. I've been trying to work out your watches. You're on earlies?'

'Right first time!'

'So how about coming dancing? Or would you like a meal?'

'Both, please,' Lyn laughed. 'When and where?'

'Get the Overhead and I'll meet you at the Pierhead stop – okay?'

He liked Lyn Carmichael. She was straight and to the point and didn't flutter her eyelashes. She was good to look at, too.

'It's a date! Five o'clock on the dot suit you?'

He said it would and replaced the receiver, smiling.

Yes, Lyn really was good to look at and her hair . . . He had only ever seen her with it rolled up round her head. She did it that way, she once said, because she refused to have it cut short as most women in the armed forces did. It was a beautiful colour, Drew thought, wondering what it was like when she took the pins out of it and let it fall to her shoulders.

He fished in the pocket of his belt, bringing out sixpenny pieces. He always made sure he had some for the dockside phone. He probably wouldn't be lucky but if he couldn't get Rowangarth he could always try again tonight, when he had seen Lyn back to the Wrennery. He had already booked a room for the night at the Adelphi and thought with pleasure about shaving standing on a floor that didn't tilt, and a long, hot bath before meeting Lyn.

But Keth, home? How had he managed it and what was he up to? But perhaps they would know about it at

Rowangarth. He felt good as he picked up the phone and asked for Holdenby 102.

The operator told him to replace the receiver and have one and sixpence ready. By coincidence, she had an open line to trunks, she said. Could he wait outside the phone box and she would ring him back?

Drew thanked her, then smiled broadly. Keth back, a date with the lovely Lyndis and a phone call home with hardly any delay. Things were looking up!

'Tell you what,' Lyn said when they met on the dot of five at the Pierhead, 'let's go to Charlie's and grab ourselves a wad and a mug of tea – not waste time, eating?'

'I thought you'd be hungry,' Drew laughed. 'You always are.' He usually kissed her, too, when they met, but usually Daisy was there and you couldn't kiss your sister's cheek without kissing that of her friend. Tonight, circumstances had changed. He and Lyn were alone, a real date; different, sort of.

'Of course I'm hungry, but a sandwich at Charlie's will be quicker.' Charlie served tea and sandwiches from a battered van near the landing stage at the Pierhead. He was a favourite with dockers and all who liked their bread cut thickly and tea so strong you could stand a spoon up in it – if Charlie trusted you with his spoon, that was! People wondered how he could make so strong a brew of tea on the miserable rations allowed by the Ministry of Food to people like him – but no one asked and if they had they would have been met with a blank stare.

'Why quicker?'

'Because then we can get to the dance before the floor gets crowded and the place gets hot. When the pubs chuck out we can leave. Will you be doing escort duty, tonight – deliver me safely to the Wrennery door?'

Drew said of course he was; that he wouldn't dream of letting her go back alone, since Daisy wasn't there.

'It's strange, isn't it,' he frowned, 'without Daiz?'

'You'd rather she were here?'

'I like seeing her. I like seeing you both,' he hastened. 'It's just funny without her, that's all.'

'Well, I'm glad she's on leave. At least I might get a proper good-night kiss from you and not a brotherly peck. And by the way, if we got off the tram at the top of Lark Lane, there's a smashing chip shop nearby. They'll be open tonight. What say we get some and eat them on the way back to quarters?'

Fish and chips wrapped in newspaper, liberally salted and vinegared – it was the only way to eat them. Fingers, Lyn said, were made long before forks. Besides, she liked the way the vinegar dripped out of the corner of the paper, so was it to be fish and chips – later?

'Yes to leaving the dance early and escort duty; yes to kissing you good night.'

'Properly, Drew?'

'Yes to a proper good-night kiss, but couldn't we land ourselves in bother, eating fish and chips in uniform in the street?'

'We could, but only if we get caught. There are very few naval patrols around Sefton Park. The crushers have all their work cut out at the dockyard gates.'

'Then let's live dangerously!' Yes, he *did* like Lyn and looked forward to kissing her at the Wrennery gate.

'Bet Daiz is on cloud nine.' He took Lyn's elbow, guiding her across the road in search of tea and a cheese sandwich. 'Smashing for her, having Keth back. I phoned home this morning. Mother was full of it. Keth came home on Monday night till Sunday and he brought an engagement ring for Daisy with him. They're hoping to get married in spring, she said. Oh, and she said Keth was in the Army – something to do with Signals, but she didn't quite know what. Anyway, he's got rank up. She said I'd have to salute him when next we meet. Quite a laugh, really.'

'What is? Keth having a commission, you mean? Why shouldn't he have a commission?'

'No. Saluting him. I'll do it, just for a lark!'

'You'll do it, Drew Sutton, because his uniform demands it!' Lyn admonished. 'Just because it seems Keth has made it the hard way and you are Lord of the Manor –'

'Who said I was Lord of the Manor?' Now it was Drew's turn to be sharp. 'What has Daisy told you?'

'Nothing as such, but I've gathered you live in a big place, and you haven't a father so it stands to reason that the place is yours. Doesn't take much working out.'

'I suppose it *is* mine,' Drew frowned. 'It was mine, technically, less than an hour after I was born. But somehow I never bothered much about it. Whilst my grandmother was alive, you see, people always still looked on Rowangarth as hers. She died, not so long ago, in the orchid house. Gracie found her.'

'Gracie is the land girl, isn't she?' Lyn felt a pang of jealousy that everyone seemed bound up in the place called Rowangarth, except herself.

'Yes. She and Daisy and Tatty used to go around together, mostly to the dances.'

'So you're not a snooty crowd, then? You hobnob with land girls, and all that?'

'Of course – why not?' Drew laughed. 'Whatever must you think of us?'

Us. That little word said it all and what was more, Lyn frowned, she wanted to be a part of it. Well, she had Drew all to herself tonight so it was up to her, wasn't it? With Daisy on leave, there was no telling what might happen.

'Okay, then. I'll buy the sandwiches; you buy the fish and chips tonight,' she laughed. 'And get a move on, or he'll have sold out!'

They took hands and ran towards the rusty van. Also against King's Regulations, of course. Men and women in uniform should not hold hands nor link arms; should walk smartly at all times when in public.

Thank goodness for the eleventh commandment, Lyn sighed: Thou shalt not get caught! And thank goodness, too, that King's Regulations and Admiralty Instructions did not have a section dealing with what you shouldn't get caught doing, though given time, their lordships probably would.

She turned to smile brilliantly into Drew's eyes. Tonight she was very, very happy.

'Ah, now that's more like it,' Sparrow beamed when Tatiana arrived home at Montpelier Mews earlier than ever before. 'No raid last night, see.'

For the first time in many weeks, London had heard no air-raid siren. There had been a strained, waiting quiet, for all that, which was accepted eventually with something akin to disbelief.

'I got a lift part of the way, Sparrow. Can you believe it – no sirens last night. The Russians are starting to fight back, now – maybe that accounted for it. Maybe the Luftwaffe has been switched to the Russian Front. They haven't got Leningrad yet.'

Poor St Petersburg; poor Grandmother Petrovska. Tatiana could almost feel pity for her. To have your home taken from you by Bolsheviks was one thing; to have it bombed into destruction was altogether another. Sometimes, she had spoken about the house near the banks of the River Neva. Only sometimes, of course, but when she did, her face softened and her eyes took on a faraway look as if she could see it there, distantly through the window. Tatiana had felt hatred for what the Luftwaffe had done to Tim; now they were doing it, indirectly, to her grandmother's memories.

'No. Let's hope those Ruskies put up more of a fight of it than they did in the last war. Anyway, girl, wash your hands and get your supper. It's cold, tonight.' It was often cold because Sparrow never quite knew when Tatiana would be home. 'And there's a letter for you from York-shire.' Sparrow always scrutinized the postmarks.

'What's for supper?' Tatiana pulled up a chair.

'Egg salad, and stewed apples and custard. There's bread, if you want to cut yourself a slice, but no butter nor marg. Not till tomorrow.' Sparrow always collected the rations every Friday morning. If something was used up before then, they just did without. 'Aren't you going to read your letter?'

'If you don't mind?' Reading at the table had never been allowed at Denniston House.

'Course I don't mind. Open it up then. From Daisy, isn't it?'

'Yes. She's on leave. Oh . . .' All at once the smile left her face and she looked up, cheeks flushed, eyes wide. Then the smile was back as she whispered, 'Keth is home. He's back from America.'

'There now, girl. Don't take on. It's hard, I know, but you're happy for Daisy, now aren't you?'

'Yes. Yes, I truly am. I'm glad for her, only just for a second I wished it could have been me.' She often had fantasies about Tim; that he hadn't been shot down and that his crew had been reported missing on operations. Missing wasn't so final as killed in action. She would pre-tend, sometimes, there was hope that one day she would hear from his mother, telling her there had been a letter from the Air Ministry and Tim was in a prisoner-of-war camp, somewhere in Germany.

Sometimes she believed it so strongly that she went to sleep believing it and dreamed about the day the war was over and all the prisoners came home. And then she awoke and knew it had all been make-believe.

'I'm glad, Sparrow. It's just that sometimes –' A tear ran down her cheek and she forced her lips into a smile. 'You didn't seem surprised when I told you Keth was home. Did you know?'

'Your Aunt Julia phoned yesterday, late on. You'd gone to bed. It was then she told me and I'm sorry, but I didn't have the heart to mention it.'

'Well, you should have, because most times I accept that Tim has gone and that I'll never see him again. Everyone does it – tries to protect me – but I'm tougher than you think, Sparrow.'

She tilted her chin, biting hard on her lip and Sparrow reached over and gently wiped away the tear.

'Yes, girl, you are,' she said softly, 'and I'm proud of you.'

Drew squinted at his watch in the gathering darkness. Soon it would be eleven o'clock and official blackout time. And at eleven, too, Lyn's late pass expired and she would run up the steps of Hellas House, say 'Carmichael, 4A,' to the duty-Wren who would then tick off her name on the late-pass list.

'Made it in time,' Drew smiled. 'Just five minutes to go.'

They had laughed and danced, and eaten supper with their fingers, still laughing. Lyn was fun to be with, Drew thought, wondering what it would be like to kiss her good night properly, and knowing he would enjoy it.

'On second thoughts, I don't think you should kiss me,' Lyn whispered, breaking uncannily into his thoughts.

'Whyever not?' He had been looking forward to it.

'Because I smell of fish and chips and salt and vinegar, none of which is very romantic. There should be the scent of roses, for our first kiss, and a nightingale singing –'

'Or the blackbird that sings late at the top of the old oak in Brattocks Wood, and the scent of linden blossom,' Drew said softly. 'The lindens at Rowangarth will be flowering soon. It's lovely at night to sit on the seat in the linden walk and smell them. It's one of the things I especially remember about home.'

'And shall I ever smell linden blossom?' Lyn whispered. 'With you, I mean, at Rowangarth?'

'You might, if you get yourself into quarters on time like a good little Wren.'

'Ha! Hasn't anyone told you, Drew Sutton, that *good* little Wrens don't have any fun?' She stepped closer, twining her arms around his neck. 'Are we going to meet tomorrow? Can you make it ashore again?'

'Don't see why not. We don't keep wireless watch when we're tied up alongside. Same place, same time? If our sailing orders change, I'll try to ring you. But it should be okay.'

'Mm. Nice . . .' She tilted her chin, closing her eyes, parting her lips, and he kissed her gently.

Her lips were exactly as he'd imagined they would be; warm and full and firm, so he kissed her again. And again.

It was five minutes past eleven when she opened the inner door of the hostel and murmured, 'Carmichael – 4A. Late pass.'

'Hmm,' said the duty-Wren, looking pointedly at her watch, putting a tick beside the last of the late passes, saying nothing. It wouldn't have made one iota of difference if she had, she realized, because Carmichael was walking upstairs in a dream, her hat askew and her lipstick all over the place. Lucky for some, she thought, snapping shut the roster, tapping on the door of the Regulating Office.

'Everyone in,' she smiled to the quarters assistant who stood at the filing cabinet. 'Blackouts all checked.'

'Fine.' Ailsa Seaton was well pleased that at last the victualling account had balanced and shown enough on the credit side to warrant another Wrennery dance. 'Think I'll hit the hay myself. G'night . . .'

On the half-landing she passed a Wren wearing a dressing gown and carrying a spongebag and towel.

'Night, Lyn,' she smiled. 'If you're going for a bath you're too late. No hot water left.'

But Wren Carmichael smiled dreamily and floated down on her soft, pale-pink cloud to the basement baths.

Hot, tepid, cold? What did it matter when you were in love?

Tatiana groped in the darkness for the flashlight at her bedside and read once again the last page of Daisy's letter.

> . . . and I sat there, sort of calling out to Tim with my thoughts and sending him your love. It was very quiet and the sun just coming up over Brattocks.
>
> Then a curlew called. Not the sad, winter cry, but the lovely burbling summer mating-sound – their love call. It was as if Tim knew I was there. I thought you would want to know about the curlew . . .

Tatiana switched off the light, smiling sadly into the darkness, chiding herself for thinking she had lost Tim when all the time she had not. Tim was there, still, at the top of Holdenby Pike.

He would always be there for her.

33

Keth passed the church in Smith Square almost at a run, looking at his watch yet again. He had thought that to travel to London on the overnight train from York would leave him ample time for his ten o'clock appointment. But he had little knowledge of wartime Britain and less still of the overburdened railways and had not allowed at least two hours for stoppages, shuntings into sidings or giving right of way on the track to trains more important than those carrying passengers.

He arrived at King's Cross a little before nine – almost two hours late – shaved in cold water in the station toilets, then stood in a taxi queue, remembering how, in Washington, he would only have had to raise his hand to call a passing cab to the kerbside. Now, he had five minutes in which to find the offices he had been directed to and, more important, to locate Major G. A. Bruce, MC.

He would be late, which was a black mark with which to start his army career, but when he arrived at a door marked 'Knock and Enter', he was told by a smiling ATS corporal that the major had been called away not ten minutes ago.

'He's expecting you, sir. If you'd like to wait, I'm sure he won't keep you long.'

Keth sat down heavily, glad of a respite in which to regain his composure and his breath. Trouble was that at the quarters near Winchester to which he had first reported, he was told very little, save that in the considered opinion of the medical officer who gave him an examination he was fit enough to be a boffin and that as soon as transport

488

was available he would be driven to Andover to be kitted out as befitted his rank, sign the Official Secrets Act and swear allegiance to King and country. After which, his time was more or less his own until Monday, 30 June, when he would report to a Major Bruce at the address given at 10.00 hours.

Nothing, yet, made sense, save that it would seem he had been of far more use in the Embassy in Washington, and now They had got him here, he would take bets They hadn't the slightest idea what to do with him. But whatever happened was worth it all, just seeing Daisy again and holding and touching and kissing her; making sure she was not a figment of his longing. The night in Winchester she had been real and so wonderful to love that right now, if he awoke in his one-room apartment in Washington and realized the last two weeks had been one great big, beautiful dream, then just to have dreamed it so vividly would be worth the disappointment. Since he could remember he had loved her; now he worshipped her and she wore his ring.

He heard an inner door banging and was at once alert, straightening his back, reaching for his respirator and cap, wondering if he should put it on and salute the major.

A bell rang on the corporal's desk and she looked up and smiled again.

'You're to go in now.' She rose to open the communicating door for him. 'Lieutenant Purvis, sir,' she announced to the thin-faced man who sat behind the desk.

'Sir!' It was all Keth could think of to say.

'Sit down, Mr Purvis.' His voice, he knew, was brusque from pain but the pills the medical officer had just given him usually eased it. 'Sorry to keep you. Leg playing up a bit. Dunkirk.'

'Sorry, sir.' Keth deduced he had been wounded at Dunkirk. He unlocked a drawer and took out a file marked Purvis K.

'Right! Born Cornwall, 12 July 1917. Parents, Richard and Mary Purvis, née Pendennis. What were they better known as?'

'Known as?' Keth frowned. 'Dickon and Polly, I suppose.'

'Hm. Father died 4 November at West Welby, Hampshire. Mother –'

'Look, sir – with respect – what has my parents' history got to do with all this?'

'A great deal, because their history is your history. And it *is* Keth – not Keith?'

'K-e-t-h,' he spelled it out, 'the older form of Keith, I believe. But is all this important? Someone, somewhere in England decided I had the ability to do something they wanted doing and I grabbed the chance because I wanted to get home. I thought there was a job for me, code-breaking – er – sir.'

'There is, now. Thought it was a *fait accompli*, did you? Well, for the job, as you call it, we need to know if you can be trusted and every detail about you and yours.'

'And you do, sir?'

'Practically. Present address, The Bothy, Rowangarth, Holdenby, North Yorkshire. Mother a warden.'

'No. She's a cook.' Trying to trip him up, was he?

'Of course.' He adjusted his spectacles then continued to read. 'Educated at Creesby Grammar School and Princeton University, New Jersey. Graduated with honours in 1940. Employed at the British Embassy, Washington –'

'In the cipher room. I take size-nine shoes and I'm engaged to Daisy Dwerryhouse of Keeper's Cottage, Rowangarth.'

'Daisy *Julia* Dwerryhouse,' the major corrected. 'At present with the Women's Royal Naval Service at Commander-in-Chief Western Approaches. What is her official number?' He flung the question without warning.

'It's 44455. But surely this has nothing to do with my fiancée?'

'It's all right, Purvis. Don't be so damn' aggressive. You've been cleared, anyway. It's just that we had to know. It's all here.' He pushed the file across the desk. 'Want to take a look?'

'No thank you, sir.'

'Don't get shirty, man. You aren't the first we've checked out for Bletchley and I dare say you won't be the last.' The pain in his leg was easing, now. 'They all go through the same procedure. Your file is and will remain completely confidential.'

'Bletchley? What place is that?'

'It's a house, about forty miles north of here. In Buckinghamshire. That's all you need to know. Got all your kit with you?'

'Yes, sir.'

'Then you'd best be on your way. My corporal will ring for a car for you. Wait at reception.'

'And is that all you can tell me, sir?'

'That's what you came here to find out, wasn't it – that you're posted to Bletchley. It's all I can tell you. And no sly postcards in pillar boxes on the way there. From now on, all – and I mean *all* – your mail will be censored.' He rose awkwardly, then held out his hand. 'Good luck, young man. And get rid of that chip on your shoulder, eh?'

'Chip, sir? Is that in my file, too?'

'No, it isn't. No need. It sticks out a mile for all to see. On your way, Purvis.'

'Thank you, sir.' He reached for his cap and respirator. Then, thinking that perhaps some parting gesture was required of him, he turned in the doorway. 'And good luck to you too, sir.'

The older man nodded, unspeaking. The interview was over.

'You're to wait downstairs, Lieutenant Purvis,' the

corporal told Keth. 'Your driver will be Sergeant Walker. He knows where you are going. Goodbye. Good luck, sir.'

Keth gazed out of the window as the driver picked his way through the traffic, thinking about the brief, strange interview, wishing he'd had the cheek to take the man up on his offer and read exactly what was written about him in the file.

The sight of London still shocked him: whole blocks of offices and shops and houses bombed into rubble; gangs of men, and women, even, clearing the streets. He wondered how many bodies still lay there undiscovered. And was Liverpool like this; Liverpool, where Daisy was stationed? She would be back in her billet soon. The Wrennery, she called it. Daisy's war began whilst Keth Purvis was still safe in America. Had she been afraid, poor love, in the bombing?

He tried to think about Washington where no bombs had fallen and where lights still shone brightly, and about Kentucky and Kitty and Bas; Kitty, rehearsing for her first ever show, Bas content to be with his beloved horses.

Why had he come back to this, he demanded of his common sense and then his mouth lifted into the smallest of smiles. The reason was plain. She was called Daisy and he loved her to distraction.

'Soon be out of the mess,' said the driver over his shoulder. 'Won't take us long, after that.'

'Thanks.' Keth leaned back, closing his eyes. He had seen enough of the devastation that was London. He hoped this Bletchley Park place would be all right, when he got to it. Daisy would be at York station now, waiting for the Liverpool train. *His* Daisy. How had he endured so long without her?

Take care, my darling. I love you so much . . .

* * *

'Well, hi!' Lyndis, back from watch, threw her hat, jacket and respirator on the top bunk. 'You've had it, chum, you've had it, never mind . . .' she teased. People always sang that to someone just back from leave. 'So how was it, then, or more to the point, how was the gorgeous Keth?'

'Gorgeous, of course.' Daisy smiled smugly, mysteriously. 'He got leave as well, you know.'

'Yes, I did know. And I know he's a lieutenant in Signals and that he brought a ring back from America!'

'You did? Lyn – you've seen Drew!'

'Mm. Twice. The *Maggie*'s back at sea now, but that's okay. I'll be on leave myself on Friday. And before you ask, no, we didn't miss you. As a matter of fact, we got on rather well without little sister tagging along! But let me see your ring and have a wish on it.'

'There!' Triumphantly Daisy held out her left hand, wiggling her fingers. 'And if you'd told me two weeks ago I'd be wearing an engagement ring, I wouldn't have believed you.'

'Dwerryhouse! It's *beautiful*, you lucky dog! You couldn't get one like that here for love nor money now. Let me put it on, have my wish?'

'So what are you going to wish for – one like it?'

'I'm not supposed to tell.' She slipped the ring on her finger, turning it three times, closing her eyes. 'Or it won't come true – not that you don't know already.'

'That you'd like one of your own, preferably put there by Drew?'

'Whoever puts one there, it won't be anything like yours!' Lyn sidestepped the question. 'You know there's a waiting list at jewellers' shops and when they get their quota in they're only diamond chippings.'

'It isn't the ring, it's the thought that counts and besides, if it's Drew you've got in mind, well – the girl he marries will most likely get a choice from about half a dozen rings. Aunt Julia inherited her Grandmother Whitecliffe's

493

jewellery and *when* Drew gets engaged, I shouldn't wonder if Aunt Julia doesn't offer his fiancée one of the Whitecliffe rings. It would be silly for Drew to buy a wartime engagement ring when there's a boxful available – well, at least six.'

'I suppose they're all clonking great diamonds,' Lyn sighed, knowing she would accept the ring that fell out of a Christmas cracker if Drew were to offer it.

'I haven't seen them. They're mostly kept at the bank.' Daisy slipped the sapphire flower back on her finger. 'Oh, and Keth bought me a white leather case just *full* of make-up for my twenty-first. There's no shortages of things like that in Washington.'

'Ooooh! Show me.'

'Can't. I left it at home just in case I was tempted to start using it and I want to keep it for my honeymoon.'

'Well, I hope he's got the colours right.'

'He has. He told the girl on the cosmetic counter that I was a blue-eyed blonde, and left it to her. But let's get down to supper quick, or all the gravy will have gone.'

'It'll have gone anyway. Leathery! You're not on leave now, Daisy D. Half-past-six supper is kept-warms, remember. Like I said – you've had it chum!'

But Daisy, happy to be wearing Keth's ring and knowing that even though he was in uniform there was little chance he would be posted abroad, was still in her own special dream world. Back-room boys worked in secret places, and usually in the British Isles. Keth would be just fine. He *would*. And next spring they would be married and she would wear white silk and a circlet of flowers on her head instead of a veil.

'Had it? Suppose I have, but Keth should get leave like anyone else, he said, even though he didn't know where he'd be posted to when he went back last night.'

'Where did he go, then?'

'Oh, to see some bod in London for instructions. And I'm

ravenous, even for kept-warms, so do hurry, Carmichael!'

Hungry, and so crazily in love that even gravy dried leathery and peas gone hard as little bullets couldn't dim it. Trouble was, she thought, briefly apprehensive, no one had the right to be this happy. Not when there was a war on.

'So that's the two of them gone back to the war.' Polly often visited Keeper's Cottage when supper was over at the bothy and she knew Tom to be busy with his Home Guarding. 'Keth told me he's made an allotment to me out of his army pay so that if anything happened to him, I'd get a pension.'

'Polly! You don't think it would – happen, I mean!'

'No. As far as Keth is aware, he'll be doing something secret to do with ciphering, or suchlike. At least they'll not send him to be shot at, like his father. I think, really, it was his way of making sure I had a bit of extra behind me, though since I came to Rowangarth, I've been able to save. Imagine that – Polly Purvis with money in the bank!'

'And why not, pray? And isn't it good to think we can look forward to a wedding, next year? Daisy promised, hand on heart, that where she works is real safe; three feet of reinforced concrete above them. I suppose I'll not worry so much, now, if they start bombing Liverpool again – except for the poor souls who haven't got three feet of reinforced concrete above them!'

'The bombing is easing off all round. Hitler's throwing all he's got at the Russians now. Did you hear it on the wireless, Alice? Stalin said the Germans are to get nothing but scorched earth. Says that if the soldiers retreat, then people are to leave their homes and retreat with them and every house and barn is to be blown up or set alight. Oil wells, too! Imagine having to do that to lovely old Rowangarth!' Polly dipped into her pinafore pocket, taking out a twist of paper. 'Here you are. I've brought us a spoonful of tea; just enough for your little pot. Think I've got time for a cup, if that's the kettle you're putting on.'

'Thought reader,' Alice smiled. They had so much to be thankful for, she and Polly, and best of all, a wedding to look forward to. She had sewn up the bodice of Daisy's dress and was busy making small silk buttons for the sleeves and neckline. And she had masses of material left to make into a swishing, rustling skirt and train. 'Just imagine – Keth bringing home films for the camera, in *colour*. Amazing what they've got, in America.'

'It'll be nice, them being snapped in colours when they're wed. Won't they make a lovely couple? Dickon would've been proud to think of his son, an officer.'

'We're all proud of him.' Alice swirled water round the pot to warm it, then tipped in Polly's offering. 'And by the way, Daisy told me she wants Tatty to be her bridesmaid. It seems Tatty has got ball gowns I could make over into a bridesmaid dress for her, so that's one coupon worry solved. And don't forget to keep an eye open for some nice material for your own dress, Polly. We'll go into York as soon as you can get a bit of time off and choose a pattern and once we've settled on the colour we should get a hat for you whilst there are still some in the shops.' Amazingly, hats could still be bought without clothing coupons. 'Now let's have that drink. Daisy said she'd try to get through on the phone – let me know she's got back all right. And had you thought Keth might even be able to ring you, Polly, now there isn't the Atlantic between you?'

'Aye. I think things are getting better.' Sitting in Alice's kitchen, making plans, Polly felt a strange contentment. 'I really do . . .'

'You're quiet,' Lyn said softly into the darkness. 'Asleep?'

'No. Just thinking.'

'About Keth?'

'Mm. Wondering where he is and how he is and when

496

he'll be able to ring me. I can't get used to the idea – Keth being able to phone, I mean. And his letters won't take days and days to get to me now. Am I too happy, Lyn?'

'No. We all get what we deserve – I hope. Only with you, it all happened so suddenly.'

'Suppose I'm still in a state of shock.'

'Or unwilling to come down off your pretty pink cloud, more like. By the way, Dwerryhouse, did you know that Drew is still a virgin?'

'*Wha-a-a-t?*' Daisy sat up so quickly that her head bumped the bottom of the bunk above her. 'What do you mean – still a virgin? And why shouldn't he be? Drew isn't like some men – out for all they can get. But how did you know, anyway? Go on.' She reached to thump the sagging springs above her. 'Tell me!'

'I know because that's what he said. I told him I was, too. I've had a few hairy moments, mind, but some of us haven't gone the whole hog, Dwerryhouse!'

'Then you could have fooled me.' Angrily Daisy threw back the bedclothes, groping her way to the door, switching on the light. 'Now look here – this is my brother you're talking about and you'd better explain yourself! Have you been trying it on with him? Intend having a bit of a fling do you? Loving him then leaving him like you say you do with the rest? Well, I'm warning you that if –'

'Hey! Hold on! And switch that light off!' Lyn blinked, 'or Seaton's going to see it under the door and we'll be in the rattle. And keep your voice down – it's nearly midnight. Some people want to sleep.' She indicated the door that led into Cabin 4 with a nod of her head. 'Go on, Dwerryhouse, get back into bed, there's an old love. You know I wouldn't do anything to hurt Drew. You know how I feel about him.'

'Oh, all right.' Daisy put out the light, then got back into her bunk with an exaggerated bouncing of bedsprings.

'But I think you should tell me what's been going on between you whilst I've been away.'

'Oh, you do? Well, what went on is my business and Drew's, but I'll tell you for all that! We had two dates and no way was I trying to seduce him!'

'I should hope not! So tell, Lyn.'

'There isn't anything to tell. It was just that I got a proper good-night kiss instead of the peck on the cheek reserved for sisters. He's a smashing kisser, by the way!'

'So what got you on to the subject of Drew's virginity?'

'Oh, just talk. We got a bit confidential, I suppose. Anyway, he said he never had and I told him it was the same for me, too.'

'I don't believe you!'

'Please yourself, but I haven't ever gone all the way. Anyway, we talked about it – had a bit of a giggle, too. We agreed it might be a bit of a fumble first time, and that you'd have to like the girl you fumbled, sort of – or words to that effect. Honestly, Daisy, you'd think I was a scarlet woman with designs on him and I'm not – well, not a scarlet woman. But I like Drew a lot. No, dammit, I'm nuts about him!'

'And Drew?'

'I don't know how he feels about me. But we had a great time. We danced and laughed a lot – and ate fish and chips . . .'

'And had a few heavy petting sessions?' Daisy's sarcasm was not to be disguised.

'And what's so wrong in that? Think that was when we started to talk about – well, you know . . .'

'Virginity?'

'Yes. And before you go any further, Dwerryhouse, I think you should think twice before you call the kettle black!'

'Keth and I are engaged. It's different for us.'

'But not for Drew and me? Well, I don't know how you

can be so smug because I'll bet you anything you like you and Keth spent the night together when you went to Winchester to see about your money! And don't say you didn't, because I wouldn't believe you!'

There was a long, marked silence punctuated only by a sigh of pure contentment from the bottom bunk.

'So you did!' Lyn hissed. 'I knew it!'

'Look – do you blame us? We hadn't seen each other for three years. And if the war hadn't come, it would have been our wedding night.'

Another silence. Then: 'Lyn? I didn't mean to sound smug – only don't hurt Drew, will you?'

'I won't. I promise. Drew is the last person I'd want to hurt.' She pulled the blankets around her chin. 'Now pipe down! Good night, Dwerryhouse. God bless.'

''Night . . .'

Lyn lay unmoving, staring into the darkness. From the bunk below came the deep, even breathing of one asleep. Yet sleep eluded Lyn Carmichael because she was thinking back to how it had really been.

True, it started with good-night kisses, but it had been she who stepped back from Drew; she who broke the spell.

'No, Drew, no! We mustn't!'

And he had let go his breath in a big, long gasp and said, 'Why not?'

'Because it's something we can't rush into and anyway, I haven't ever – not before . . .'

They were standing apart, then, leaning against the wall and he reached out and took her hand in his.

'Neither have I, Lyn. A lot of blokes I know have, but I never wanted to – not until now. I'm not pansy or anything, only it hasn't cropped up before.'

'It has for me, Drew, but like tonight –'

'You were the one to call a halt?'

'Yes.'

499

'Why, Lyn?'

'Because girls who have – y'know, done it – say the first time is a bit of a fumble, if you see what I mean?'

'Yes, I do see. And you'd have to think a great deal about the girl you fumbled, sort of, or it would be a disaster. Mind, I know about being careful. We got all that guff in barracks when I was a rookie. I wouldn't – *couldn't* – have been careful tonight.'

'There you are, then!' she laughed shakily. 'Female intuition!'

'Oh, Lyn!' They began to laugh and he gathered her close again and kissed her gently, all tension gone.

'Time you were in! Thanks for tonight.'

'You'll be away tomorrow?'

'First light.'

'Then take care, Drew.' She lifted her mouth to his. 'I love you.'

He had kissed her back, she sighed, but he hadn't said 'I love you, too.' Instead, he steered her to the foot of the Wrennery steps, gave her bottom a gentle pat and said, 'Take care, yourself. See you.'

He walked away then, and it wasn't fair because she loved him, *really* loved him and she wouldn't have cared at all about them being careful. Being careful shouldn't come into it when you were both in love and realizing for the first time that you wanted each other.

But he *would* tell her! One day he would say the words oh, please, he would?

'Good night, Drew Sutton. Have a good patrol and a safe landfall.' She whispered the words like a prayer.

Drew, Drew, Drew . . . She closed her eyes, determined to go to sleep thinking about him because if she did, she might dream about him.

And dreams knew no bounds.

34

'So!' said Jack Catchpole to his land girl, his face severe, 'you've comed back. And a right fuss I had to make at the bothy an' all, to get you!'

'I'm back.' Grace Fielding's smile was one of relief. 'Sorry, but the forewoman sent me to help with the hay at Home Farm. Short-handed, it seems, and you've got to cut hay while the sun shines, they say.'

'Aye, and that's when you've got to pick strawberries! Any road, I made my position plain to that boss lady of yours, and here you are!'

What Catchpole had uttered to the forewoman had been terse and much to the point: that Miss Fielding was Rowangarth's land girl and he wanted an assurance that there would be no more shunting her this way and that as the mood suited. He was aware that haytime was important, but so was the gathering of strawberries, blackcurrants and raspberries in his kitchen garden and if necessary he would get Miss Julia to send the strongest protest not only to their member of parliament, but to the Ministry of Agriculture and Fisheries, an' all, and heads would roll if the Ag and Fish got to hear about fruit that was rotting for want of a land girl to pick it! And Catchpole, sucking angrily on his pipe and making the most alarming noises, had finally convinced the forewoman at the bothy that he would tolerate no more intrusions into the smooth running of Rowangarth kitchen garden!

'Here I am!' Gracie had missed the warm relationship that existed between them and the way they had come to understand each other's ways. She had even missed the planting out of their second crop of runner beans which had become very special to her since she had had complete control of the tiny plants, each being nursed in its own pot ready to be planted beside the canes she herself had tied up in readiness. 'I see you've planted my runner beans . . .'

'Couldn't wait, Gracie. I know you'd got fond of 'em, but us have to have succession if the shops are to rely on us.' Like hay, beans couldn't wait. 'Sorry, lass,' he added guiltily because they could have waited another day or two. 'Just go and give 'em a good watering and see as I've planted 'em to your satisfaction, then us'll shift the nets and start picking those berries.' He had laid out large shallow trays and lined them with cabbage leaves in readiness, and now that his assistant was back and not likely to be purloined again, he felt near contentment. 'Tea as usual, at ten.'

'As usual, Mr Catchpole.' She squinted up into the July sky, wondering how, when the war was over, she could ever bring herself to work in an office again. Then she dipped the watering can into the rainwater butt and carried it to the newly planted beans, regarding them with near-motherly affection.

'Hullo,' she whispered softly so that Mr Catchpole should not hear her. 'I'm back . . .'

'So!' said Olga, Countess Petrovska, shaking the newspaper violently in her anger, 'those Nazis continue to advance and Stalin's soldiers continue to run. The Cossacks would have charged into battle bravely!'

'Mama, the Cossacks were horse soldiers! They'd have stood little chance against tanks and armoured cars and dive bombers.'

'They would have advanced for all that! Are these papers never to print any good news?'

'But there have been fewer air raids since Russia was

invaded. Surely that is good news?' London had not been bombed for many weeks. 'At least we needn't worry so much about Tatiana.'

'Tatiana should not have gone to London. She did it to annoy, you know. And had you thought, Aleksandrina Anastasia Petrovska, that when you were her age you were wedded and bedded and two months gone!'

'I try not to – to think, I mean.' As the first clod of earth fell on her husband's coffin, she had known nothing but relief. To her shame, of course, and she had prayed devoutly for his soul and that she might, in time, find the grace to mourn him. Yet she had only become more certain that she would hold tightly to her widowhood and trust no man again.

'You are still young and fertile. Have you never thought to marry again?'

'Never, Mama.' Not ever! Elliot had seen to that! 'And will you excuse me? I think I heard Cook arriving and I want to talk to her about tonight's dinner.'

'Cook!' exploded the Countess when the door closed firmly behind her daughter. A woman from the village who obliged, more like! Denniston's real cook had left six months ago, the ungrateful hussy, and their housekeeper, too. The one to work in a factory canteen for three times the money and fewer hours she had said; the other to manage a hostel for munition workers. And where would the pair of them be when the war and the big money it paid to some was over? Cap in hand at Denniston House again, asking for their situations back!

Oh, for the old days when servants had known their place and worked long hours for little money. They had had ten at the St Petersburg house.

The Countess closed her eyes in anguish. Her beloved St Petersburg was surrounded by the German Army. It had survived the revolution only now to be destroyed, street by beautiful street by Nazis! And by winter, they would be goose-stepping around the squares of Moscow, too! It did not bear thinking about. A common corporal, a house painter, presuming to rule Mother Russia!

She closed her eyes tightly, saving her tears for bedtime when she would kneel before the Blessed Virgin and pray that famine and pestilence should strike down the invaders of her country – or at least that the snows would come early this year. The Nazis had yet to experience a Russian winter!

The thought was sufficient to make her forget her anger for a little while.

'I tell you, Cook, I think things are going a little better for us, at last!'

'*Better*, Miss Clitherow?' Better, when the fat ration had been cut again and never a piece of under-the-counter suet from the butcher in weeks?

'Why, yes. That Man has other fish to fry, now; other places to drop his bombs on. Mr Hitler has bitten off more than he can chew, if you ask me!'

Tilda sipped daintily from the rosebud china cup the housekeeper brought out on special occasions when she entertained in her own sitting room. Once, that privilege had been accorded only to Mrs Shaw, but now Matilda Tewk was the recipient of that honour; she who once had scrubbed carrots and peeled potatoes and scoured pans in the brown sinkstone in the scullery kitchen.

She smiled, then said with the directness that had never completely left her, 'What made you come back from Oban, Miss Clitherow? Us all thought you'd retired to a life of ease, yet here you are back again in your own domain as if you'd never been gone.'

'Ah, yes. But Rowangarth called, Cook. And the danger was past, then.'

'Danger?'

'The aerodrome, of course. RAF Holdenby Moor. Now

you mustn't repeat this to a soul, Cook, but I always knew that accident would happen. Sometimes the feeling was so strong I trembled just to think of it. I regret to say I succumbed to my cousin Margaret's offer of a home mainly because of it. And then the bomber crashed and I knew my place was back here, with her ladyship.'

'Even though it could happen again?'

'Even though. But lightning rarely strikes in the same place twice, you know.'

Tilda nodded, knowing full well that cousin Margaret had been a mite too bossy for one used to giving orders all her life. 'And you think us'll be safe around these parts, now?'

'I think so. Please God I shall live to see another Armistice, then be laid to rest not far from her ladyship.'

'I'm sure you will,' Tilda soothed. Poor old lass. She still played the housekeeper, even though she did little, now, save polish the silver and arrange flowers and answer the door when the mood was on her. But Miss Julia could afford to keep her. 'I only hope, Miss Clitherow, that when this war is over and the Army gives back Pendenys, us won't be expected to up sticks and live there. I couldn't abide that place. Folk say as how Mrs Clementina haunts it!'

'Not haunts, exactly, though the memory of her will always be there, I am sure. And perhaps Miss Julia *will* take up residence in Pendenys, one day. After all, it rightfully belongs to the Reverend, and young Sir Andrew will be living here at Rowangarth once the Navy has no use for him. Sir Andrew will marry, be sure of it, and carry on the Sutton line.'

For once, Tilda did not offer a reply because she had always thought of Sir Andrew as young Drew and never once imagined him wed with bairns of his own. And happen, him being such a catch, with an estate and a title to offer, it wouldn't be long before some Wren got her claws in him! A new mistress of Rowangarth; and new brooms often swept clean. What would happen, then, to Tilda Tewk?

'I don't suppose,' she said quite shocked, 'that there would be another cup in that pot – if you were to squeeze it, happen?'

'I don't suppose I could borrow the car, Mother?' Drew hazarded.

'But of course you can. Mind, the petrol is quite another matter!'

'Hell – sorry. I'll wait for the bus. It's just that my number ones and my greatcoat need cleaning. The shop at Creesby guarantees to have them back in five days for members of the Forces.'

'Then take the car – I'm due August petrol coupons in a couple of days, anyway – but only if you take Nathan's sports coat to the cleaners, too. And call and see Tom. He's got rabbits and pigeons he wants dropping off at MacFisheries. And ask Alice if she wants anything collecting whilst you're about it.'

'You certainly get value for your petrol, Mother,' Drew grinned. 'I was calling in on Lady, anyway.'

'Oh, away with you!' She could deny him nothing; not even her last gallon of petrol. 'And take it gently. Keep your foot off the accelerator and coast down hills . . .'

She watched him go. Drew, Alice's son. Alice and Giles's. Never did she forget for a minute he was Giles's.

Drew stopped the car outside Keeper's Cottage, called, 'Hi, there! The fleet's in!' to Gracie who was watering the hens at the bottom of the garden, then whistled loudly as he opened the kitchen door.

'Lady!' He lifted Alice off her feet, kissing her soundly.

'Drew, love! My, but it's good to see you! Seven days, have you got? Now then, are you going to stop for a cup of tea – tell me about Daisy?'

'No tea, thanks, but Mother said Tom has stuff to take into Creesby.'

'Aye. It's hanging up in the shed. The shop usually settles up at the end of the month, so just drop them off. They'll be glad of them.'

'Can you spare a minute? There's something I want to talk to you about, Lady; something I don't really want to mention to Mother. She'd get ideas, if I did.'

'Serious, is it?' Alice sat down at the kitchen table, indicating the chair opposite.

'Not so much serious as personal. There's this Wren, you see. Daisy's friend.'

'Oh, *yes*?'

'Now there you go too, Lady – getting ideas!'

'No. I promise I'm not. But you'll be talking about Lyndis? By all accounts she's a nice girl.'

'She is, and very good-looking. She's a good dancer, too, and fun to be with. When Keth was home and Daisy on leave, Lyn and I went out alone instead of in a threesome as we usually do. I'm afraid things got a bit out of hand without little sister being there.'

'You took – *liberties*?' Alice tried to keep her voice even.

'No, but I wanted to – I think. I can't be sure, you see, not having had – well . . .'

'Not ever having made love to a girl, you mean? Well, there's nothing wrong in that. Better than sowing your wild oats all over the place, like some do.'

'So I shouldn't, if it were offered, sort of – which it hasn't been – take advantage . . . ?'

'I'd rather you didn't, since you're asking, Drew. Tom and I did – just the once,' Alice said frankly, 'but we were both a bit sorry afterwards and Tom said there must be no more, till we were wed. Mind, in those days lovemaking was a hit-and-miss thing. We could've landed up in a real mess and wouldn't the village have had something to gossip about, then!'

'There are ways and means now, Lady. They tell you about it when you join up, how to avoid – well, all sorts of things. Sorry. Am I being a bit personal?'

'You can't shock someone who was once a nurse, Drew Sutton! And I know there's a war on and men and women thrown together and a lot of those women little more than young girls who don't know much of the facts of life. But having said all that, I suppose it's understandable – if you're taken with Lyndis.'

'I am.'

'And do you intend asking her to marry you?'

'Lord, no! But I think she'd marry me – does that sound a bit big-headed? She told me she loved me, but I'm not sure how much I love her. I really like her, though.'

'Liking isn't loving.' Alice sucked in a deep breath, then said, 'Don't take advantage of the girl unless you're real serious about her – and then think twice, and carefully, before you let anything happen. Would you like someone to play fast and loose with Daisy?'

'No, I wouldn't!'

'Then think on. Take it easy. Seems to me you haven't met the right one yet.'

'You think not? Will I know when I do, do you think?'

'Well, put it this way. The minute I met Tom I knew, and the minute your mother opened her eyes and saw the doctor she was smitten likewise. And Lady Helen, an' all. Mind, love does sometimes grow gently, like your mother's second loving, but when you meet a girl you can't get out of your mind, then she's the one. And when you meet her, let's hope she's right for you, because you'll not listen to reason, whether or no, once you want her!'

'I was right, then.' Drew pushed back his chair. 'Last time the *Maggie* was in, I asked both Daisy and Lyn out as I usually do. I think if I'd wanted just to be with Lyn, Daiz would have understood.'

'Then you did the right thing. Don't mess about with

the girl's feelings till you're sure. And Drew – any time you want a bit of a talk . . .'

'I'll remember. And you'll not say anything to Mother?'

'Not a word. Now off with you and collect those rabbits and things. And put a newspaper down on the seat. Don't want a mess in Julia's car!'

'I forgot! Mother said to ask if you wanted anything from Creesby.'

'No thanks – unless you can light on a pound of sirloin steak and a leg of lamb on your travels – and a couple of pounds of butter!' Alice laughed. 'Come and see me again, soon.'

'Thanks – for listening, I mean. I feel I've got the measure of it now.' He bent to kiss her cheek, then smiled. 'You know, if you can't have a father, having two mothers is almost as good.'

She watched him go, the child she had hated when he moved inside her, the child she was glad there was no milk for in her breasts. She had left him with Julia to be brought up a Sutton and she and Tom made Daisy together – a child of love.

Then one day a small boy looked up at her with Giles's eyes and she knew he had been born a true Sutton and would never be dark as the man who fathered him in rape had been.

'Take care, son,' she whispered.

Darling one,
    Now I can give you an address to write to. Just name, rank and number, c/o BX3, GPO London. I miss you already.

Keth lay down his pen, frowning, gazing round the small, bare room he shared with Flight Lieutenant Robinson – Robby. He was still shaken by events, especially by his interview with a colonel whose name had not been offered.

I had a good journey here and share a room and a
batman with Robby Robinson. I'm going to be bored
out of my mind at this place. Washington all over
again, but with the blackout!

Best make light of it, get used to the fact that there was
no glamour at Bletchley Park. Hard work, sometimes frustrating work but above all, work so secret that he must
never, ever, let out one word of what he had come here
to do.

'There is just one warning I will give you,' the colonel
had said. 'What we do here is so important that to let slip
just one word about this place will be considered an act
of treason and you know what happens very swiftly and
thoroughly to traitors.'

The colonel had gone on to say that now, knowing what
was demanded of him, was the time to opt out and the
interview and the house in which it had taken place erased
completely from his mind. That was when Keth said he
chose to stay.

But at least I am near you, sweetheart, and when I
know more about things and how the system works,
I will be able to start looking forward to my next
leave. I believe that wives and fiancées are allowed
leave with their men; let's hope we can arrange ours
together.

He read through what he had written and his words
sounded stilted. But he was still in a state of complete
bewilderment at the little he had already learned.

'This place,' said the colonel, 'is where we spy on Germany. Codes, as you already know, are easily gathered,
easily broken, but here at Bletchley we have a machine
which Hitler, in his stupidity, thinks is an impenetrable
puzzle.'

British Intelligence, it would seem, had been handed it on a plate because a vigilant Polish customs official warned Polish Intelligence about a strange machine in transit from Berlin to the German Embassy in Warsaw. And so astute had the Poles been that before their Customs released the cumbersome package, it had been photographed, measured and studied in great detail. And before being carefully repacked, copies were made of the instruction manual that went with it.

'And may heaven reward Poland, young man, because they handed Enigma to us just days before Germany invaded them. And the beauty of it is that it is widely used by the German Army, Air Force and Navy. Because of it, we were able to tell Fighter Command where the main attacks would be when the Luftwaffe were trying to bomb the daylights out of us last summer. And because of Enigma, Mr Churchill warned of the invasion of Russia, though stupidly Stalin gave it little credence.

'All that and more, because later a German, greedy for a lifestyle he couldn't afford, sold updated instruction manuals and code settings to the French.'

I have had no letters from you as yet and I don't know when I will be able to phone you, but now that I am in my quarters and settling into my new and very boring routine things will improve. At least now there is no Atlantic between us.

Had it been better, Keth fretted, when he lived with the almost certain knowledge that for as long as the war lasted he and Daisy must remain apart, or would this dreadful responsibility for which he had exchanged a passage back to England be worth it? He shrugged, then smiled down at the notepad in front of him as if it could carry that smile to Daisy.

Of course it would be worth it – once he had learned to

accept that here at Bletchley Park were assembled some of the most brilliant brains in the country. And that, apart from the worry of careless talk that must forever hang over him like Damocles' sword, he should be proud to be one of them.

'You will be rooming and working closely with Flight Lieutenant Robinson,' the colonel said. 'Like you he is an honours graduate. We got him just in time. He had already joined the RAF and got his wings up. Would've been piloting a bomber, now, but for us. Robinson will show you around and give you the benefit of his knowledge – such as it is. It doesn't do, here, to let left hands know what right hands are doing . . .'

> I have unpacked and settled in. Our room is spartan. Black iron beds, lino on the floor and the inevitable blackout curtains. In one corner is a wash-hand basin; in the other a little table with Robby's gramophone on it. He's dance-band crazy.

All at once Keth gasped with frustration. This was a letter he would write to his mother, not to the girl he loved so much she filled most of his thoughts.

> I miss you, my lovely love. I need to hold you, love you. Just to think of our night together will keep me sane.

And be damned to the censor who would read every word of what he was writing!

> To have had that night makes me realize all the more how much I adore you. Easter can't come too soon for me. Once we are married, every night, I promise, will be like the one we stole in Winchester . . .

Think of me always. Write to me soon. Take care of yourself, sweetheart.

He was just about to seal the envelope when a voice called, 'Hey, old chum! No can do! That letter has got to be read by the censor, don't forget!'

'As if I could,' Keth grinned, 'though it's a bit much, isn't it – having someone read everything you write to your girl.'

'Couldn't care less, old sport. My popsy would go raving mad if I didn't write her the odd spot of passion now and again. To tell you the truth, Purvis, sometimes I lay it on really thick, just to make the censor's toes curl up! Think nothing of it!'

'But who is it, around here, who does the censoring?'

'Haven't a clue. Nobody knows. Best, that way.'

'So what do I do with letters?'

'You leave them, unsealed, in the basket at the top of the passage to be collected. And don't look so sheepish. It's the same for all of us. And don't stamp it. Censored letters don't need stamps. So are you happy in your work?'

'Are you?' Keth begged the question. 'With the Official Secrets Act hanging over us, I mean.'

'I'm happy enough now. The work can be deadly boring. You can work for hours and count yourself lucky just to break one letter or figure. Then some other bod breaks another, and so on, *ad infinitum*.

'Reckon I've come to accept that if I hadn't come here I'd have gone for a Burton, by now, or at best been in a prisoner-of-war camp. No fun, really, being a bomber boy. Nearly as bad as being in the Merchant Navy. Between you and me and the gatepost, our convoys are taking a real mauling.'

'I know. My girl said things weren't too good in that direction. She's a Wren at Western Approaches HQ. But if this Enigma thing is so good, why don't we home in on the U-boat signals?'

'We do. Seems our lot pick up thousands of signals but the Krauts change their codes every day and we can only break the naval code one day in four, which isn't so good. The Enigma machine the U-boat packs use is different, you see, to the one the Army and Air Force use. When we can crack that, our Merchant Navy bods will be a whole lot safer.

'But how about your little Wren applying for a draft here? Nice to have your girl around – provided you didn't let the powers that be know, of course. Close relationships aren't allowed here – officially, that is. What does she do?'

'She's a teleprinter-operator.'

'Couldn't be better! We've got 'em here.'

'Yes.' Keth had seen Wrens, ATS girls and Waafs on his conducted tour, earlier in the day. 'And she stays where she is! I don't want her to have hell and damnation hanging over her just for one slip of the tongue.'

'Why not? All the women here accept the nature of the work and sign the Official Secrets Act.'

'But I was led to believe that we could face treason charges if we stepped out of line.'

'So we could, so we keep to the straight and narrow.'

'But women, too? That's awful!'

'Listen, old chum, the women who work here are absolute bricks. They put up with long hours and are treated like the rest of us – except they wouldn't be accused of treason. Probably, if they let anything slip and were found out, they'd be certified insane and locked away for the duration.'

'You can't mean it!' Keth was horrified.

'Course I don't, you stupid clot! Leastways, I don't think I do! But go and pop your love letter into the basket then forget codes and ciphers and adding and subtracting and

I'll let you hear my *pièce de résistance*. Ever heard of Glenn Miller? He's very big in the States, I believe.'

'Heard of him!' Keth grinned. 'A month ago I was in the States. Got my degree there. I've got all his records. Managed to bring about twenty over in my trunk. Next time I'm home, I'll bring some back with me. And you *were* kidding about, well, you know what?'

'What the colonel said about back-room boys who can't keep their mouths shut, you mean? Well, put it this way – the worst nightmare I ever had was one in which I got as tight as a tick, stood in Piccadilly Circus and yelled out at the top of my voice all I know about Bletchley Park and Enigma and about how we're trying to crack Hitler's personal code, too. All I can say is that I was bloody glad to wake up!'

'Think I'll just get rid of this letter,' Keth said soberly.

'You do that, then I'll play you some music. And Purvis,' Robby added, his face all at once serious, 'you get to learn to live with it – you really do . . .'

But would he, Keth frowned as he went in search of the basket. And thank heaven Daisy wasn't working under such stress; that she was miles away in Liverpool with three feet of reinforced concrete over her when she was on watch.

He closed his eyes and sent his thoughts high and wide.

I love you, love you, love you, Daisy Dwerryhouse. Take care, sweetheart.

The dreaded week of night watches had come round again and only to be endured because at the end of it came a rest period.

'That teleprinter room gets hotter every watch,' Daisy grumbled. 'I'll swear the air in it hasn't been changed since the day it was built.'

The promised air conditioning had not been installed so now, when the temperature reached 80°, operators were allowed to take off their stiff collars and ties and open the top two buttons on their shirts.

'Shall you go home on Friday, Daisy?'

'You bet! Tatty said she might apply for a weekend off, so there'll be half of the Clan at Rowangarth because Drew is on leave, too.' Then she bit hard on her words, annoyed Drew's name had slipped out. 'Sorry, Lyn. Look – I'd ask you home with me but I –'

'But you don't think it wise,' Lyn said bitterly. 'And don't look so sheepish. If Drew had wanted me at Rowangarth he knew he had only to ask and I'd have gone like a shot. It's my own fault. I all but threw myself at him when you were on leave and he and I were on our own, yet next time the *Maggie* docked, we were back to the old threesome. He couldn't have made it plainer!'

'Lyn – I did offer not to come when I knew you and he had got on so well, but he insisted.'

'I know. I'm not blaming you – just my own stupidity. Suppose it all boils down to the fact that he doesn't want me as much as I want him. I suppose he'll be taking that land girl out while he's on leave?'

'Well, yes, he will. He usually does. He takes Tatty out, too, and me.'

'You're his sister. You don't count. Are you sure he's not sweet on the land girl?'

'If you mean has he had any petting sessions with Gracie like you and he had, then I'm pretty certain he hasn't – nor with Tatty.'

'Well, he wouldn't with her, would he?' Lyn let go a sigh of pure frustration. 'She *is* his cousin.'

'Hey! Cousins can marry. Aunt Julia married Nathan. But you can count Tatty out. She'll be a long time – if ever – getting over Tim Thomson,' Daisy soothed. 'But if you want my opinion –'

'Which I don't!'

'My opinion, Carmichael, for what it's worth, is that

Drew is more attracted to you than any other girl he's taken out. Just don't rush your fences, that's all. Drew was always a serious little boy – never went headlong in, as I did. It's my bet he'll weigh things up very carefully before he asks any girl to marry him. But he *will* marry, Lyn, and when he does he'll be a loving, protective husband. And he would want children, too. He's always felt sad, deep down, about not ever knowing his father. Perhaps he doesn't intend marrying till the war is over and he can give all his attention to his wife and family – and to Rowangarth, of course.'

'Ha!' Lyn slipped down from her bunk and reached for her towel. 'Seems that Rowangarth is a pretty important place.'

'Not really. But it's very special if you're a Sutton.'

'Oh, heck!' Not only did she have to compete with a land girl, Lyn mourned, but with a house, as well. 'I'm going down to the basement for a bath before all the hot water goes. Coming?'

'Suppose I'd better – and chin up, love. Drew might not have gone down on his bendeds yet, but I'd say you're the front runner.'

'You reckon?' She brightened visibly. 'Well, I hope you're right, because I'm mad about him!'

'Like I said – give it time.'

'But do we have time, Daisy? There *is* a war on, remember?'

35

1942

'I suppose,' said Daisy as their blacked-out transport made its slow way through bomb-damaged, blacked-out Liverpool, 'they'll have seen in the New Year by the time we get back to quarters.'

'They won't have waited. It's well past midnight,' Lyndis shrugged. 'I suppose we might look in on the party, though – see if there's anything left to eat and grab a couple of dances.'

A-watch arrived five minutes before midnight to take over and Daisy called, 'Happy New Year, girls!' as the second hand on the teleprinter-room clock jerked into 1942. Then she ran up and up the winding stairs into the cold, still night.

'Watch ashore will have wolfed all the sandwiches,' Lyndis grumbled.

Bread was still unrationed, but sandwich fillings presented a grave problem to the cook when providing refreshments for the Hellas House dances. But tonight, because the victualling officer allowed the quarters assistant extra rations for the festive season, Ailsa Seaton had made a half-pound block of margarine and six eggs available for the quarters' New Year dance, and so adept was leading-cook at making a little go a long way on such occasions that she had long ago earned forgiveness for the leathery gravy on kept-warm meals.

'Wonder what Drew is doing,' Lyn murmured a mite too casually.

'The usual, I shouldn't wonder.' Daisy winged her love

to a minesweeper somewhere in the Western Approaches. Four hours on duty, four hours off around the clock when on patrol; listening out for four hours, eating and sleeping as best he could for the following four. Watch-about, Drew called it and was happy enough with the arrangement. On HMS *Penrose*, life was as good as might be expected. Serving on small ships was a muddled, matey existence and they didn't come much smaller than the sturdy *Maggie*. 'Hope he got my birthday card before they sailed.'

'I sent him one too,' Lyn said defiantly. 'Hope you don't mind.'

'Now why on earth should I mind?' Then she laughed. 'By the way, happy New Year, Lyn!'

Frowning, Amelia Sutton stirred her coffee. The war she so dreaded had come to America. Without warning, Japanese bombers wiped out the fleet at Pearl Harbor. The announcement on all radio stations was listened to with a stunned disbelief which quickly flared into white-hot rage. Who did those Japs think they were! How dare they wipe out the entire Pacific Fleet with a cunning that dispensed with a declaration of war!

America, enraged, demanded vengeance. In the time it took to say Pearl Harbor, neutrality was forgotten and young men flocked to enlist.

'What is it, dear?' Gently, Albert wiped her tears.

'Do I have to tell you?'

'No.' He reached for her hand. 'But this war won't be like the last one,' he comforted. There would be no dangerous, degrading trench warfare.

'Young men will be killed, for all that!' Amelia reached for her cup, willing her hand not to shake. 'Do you love me, Bertie?'

'Of course I do!' He did. He had married Amelia Newton – older than himself – when he had no expectations and she had wealth enough for the two of them. Loving her had happened almost without him knowing it. 'You know I do!'

'And I love you, my dear.' She placed cup and saucer on the table beside her, straightened her drooping shoulders and lifted her chin. 'If it were all to end tomorrow, you have made me very happy and I'm grateful, Bertie.'

'End, Amelia? Why on earth should it end?'

She took his hand, turning it to leave a kiss in the upturned palm, shaking her head, refusing to answer.

'It will already be another year, now, in England,' she said instead. 'Remember our New Years over there?'

She would give a great deal to be able to cross the Atlantic in the pampered comfort of a luxury liner with the clock turned back and Bas and Kitty children again.

Yet now war had reached out and drawn America into the madness, and Amelia's son had volunteered for the Army Air Corps in a haze of patriotism. Not to be outdone, madcap Kitty announced her intention of getting to England any way she could, since she was half English, wasn't she, and had as much right to fight for England as Daisy and Drew.

'You'd have thought Bas and Kitty would have had the consideration to stay home, tonight,' Albert said gruffly. This, he conceded, could be their last New Year as a family for a long time to come, though he took good care not to say it.

'Leave them, dear. They're young and it's New Year – or will be in a few more hours. Let them have their fun.'

Let them enjoy their young lives, she thought despairingly, as apprehension niggled through her. Next year at this time, they could both be thousands of miles away and in great danger. She closed her eyes, sending a silent prayer winging.

Dear God, whatever they do, whereever they go, please watch over Bas and Kitty for us, and send them safely home.

* * *

Keth checked his new, 1942 diary, satisfying himself he had pencilled in, as far as he could calculate, the different times of Daisy's watches. Phoning her, he had come to accept, was a hit-and-miss thing, with long delays. The overburdened telephone exchanges were not equipped for the flood of official demands made on them and private calls went to the bottom of the queue. It made him wonder how demanding Winnie Hallam's life had become at Holdenby's little telephone exchange. Talk had it, his mother said, that she had asked the GPO for an assistant, so often was she awakened from her sleep.

'If you try now, you might just get through to her,' he said out loud to the empty room. By his reckoning she should just be coming off watch.

He wanted so desperately to speak to her. In America he had accepted that to hear her voice would be nothing short of a miracle; now he was in England again, the temptation to pick up any available phone was always with him, if only to hear her say that she loved him.

He was bored tonight, and restless. Robby had contrived to be home in Norfolk on New Year leave and the silence in the bare little room was irritating. Keth needed, after a particularly hectic day, to talk to someone about anything but codes and ciphers and clicking, rotating *bombes*. Work here could be soul-destroying. The frustration of finding a break after hours of comparing and shifting columns of letters and figures only to arrive at a dead end, often left him irritable and depressed.

It would have helped, he brooded, if he'd had even an inkling of the German language. His French, excellent though it had become with Tatty's help in his school years, was of little use here. Tatty spoke French with a Normandy accent – her governess had been born at Lisieux.

He rose from his bed, padded along the corridor on stockinged feet to the wall telephone.

'You couldn't be an absolute angel, and get me through

to my girl in the next half-hour – before she goes to bed, I mean. She'll just have come off watch. It's Liverpool, Lark Lane 1322.' And because the telephonist had just managed – at great risk of landing herself in trouble – to snatch three minutes with her own boyfriend stationed in faraway Lerwick, she promised she would do what she could, only the switchboard was going mad tonight and he would understand, wouldn't he, that she could only do her best to get him through at all, never mind within the next half-hour.

He thanked her, wished her a happy New Year, then returned to his room, propping open the door with a shoe so he might hear the ringing of the phone. Then he reached for his writing pad and pen.

Dear Mum,
    A happy New Year to you. Are you well, and not working too hard? I'm fine, though life can get a bit boring here.

He must, he frowned, be very careful in letters. He must be even more careful when someone in a public house asked what they did up there at the Park.

'It's a signal school. We teach men and women morse, principally,' was Keth's reply.

The deception seemed to satisfy curiosity, especially since he wore the insignia of the Royal Corps of Signals on his uniform. It was accepted more readily than, 'I can't tell you. It's highly secret.'

The phone at the end of the corridor began to ring and he ran to pick it up.

'I've got your Liverpool call on the line, sir.'

'Bless you. Thanks a lot. Hullo? Can I speak to Daisy Dwerryhouse, please? Cabin 4A,' he asked.

There was the noise of a party in the background and the unmistakable boom-boom of a conga chain.

'Dwerryhouse!' he heard. 'Call for you!' which meant she hadn't gone to bed.

'Darling? Keth, is it you?'

'It is. Happy New Year, sweetheart. Had you realized we're getting married *this year*?'

'I had! I'm counting the days!'

'Tell me?'

'I love you, Keth. Love you, love you!' she yelled without inhibition above the din.

'I love you too! Desperately! Do you realize how much I want you?'

All at once life was good. This year, he and Daisy *would* be married.

Olga Petrovska yawned inelegantly, reached for the handbag beside her chair and announced her intention of going to bed. Indeed, she didn't know why she should have been so foolish as to stay up to see in a year she knew would be no better than the one which had, hardly an hour before, slipped into history.

'I should have gone long ago,' she fretted, 'had I known your daughter would not ring.'

'Your *granddaughter*, Mama, has probably been trying to get through to us, just as we have been trying to get through to her. There *is* a war on, you know.'

'She is probably out enjoying herself. The young are very selfish. They have no thought for their elders. And I do know there is a war on, Anna Petrovska. My war began in 1917 and I fight it still, inside me!' First the Bolsheviks and now the Nazis. What would be left of Mother Russia but scorched earth?

'Mama, your war is best forgotten. We can't turn back the clock. We were lucky to escape alive from Peterhof. How many that we knew were killed?'

'Ah, yes.' People of their own kind, of course, and loyal to the Czar. Yet what a time they once had in Petersburg each New Year. Dinners, balls, bonfires shooting flames and sparks into a star-bright, frosty sky; firework displays. Then the great bell of St Basil's booming out the start of another year; a year that would be kind to Peter Petrovsky and his wife and three children.

Yet now the Nazis were closing in on St Petersburg. Rumour had it amongst London's White Russians that the Romanov treasure had, for a second time, been taken from the Hermitage and carried secretly into hiding to where it would be safe, please God, from Nazi looters.

And God, she acknowledged reluctantly, had seen fit to send the first snow of winter early this year. Time would soon tell, she silently exulted, how well prepared for a Russian winter Hitler's soldiers were!

Of course, now Japan had entered the war and taken Hong Kong on Christmas Day. *Christmas Day*, mark you – but what could you expect of an unchristian country? The Czar-God-rest-him had never trusted the Japanese Emperor and how right he had been!

'I read in today's paper, Anna, that Hitler can't use his tanks because they are frozen up by cold. I hope Stalin has the good sense to counter-attack whilst the Germans are still wondering what to do, but likely he will not!' Stalin was a peasant in Olga Petrovska's estimation.

'He will do what he thinks best for Russia, Mama. The German advance has been slowed. As I said, we are lucky to be alive. There will be many in Russia tonight who will have lost their homes; many who have nowhere to sleep.'

'Then they should have kept their Czar. The Kaiser dared not have sent his armies into Russia then – and besides, the Czar was his cousin.'

'I think,' said Anna, knowing that if they continued to talk about Russia in general, and St Petersburg and Peterhof in particular, her mother would either dissolve into unstoppable tears, or rant and rave and curse Stalin and Hitler until she brought on one of her headaches, 'that if my call to London doesn't come through by one o'clock, I shall give up and go to bed. As you say, Tatiana just might be enjoying herself and who,' she rushed on so her mother might not remark again upon the selfishness of the young, 'can blame the child? She deserves to enjoy herself after all that dreadful bombing.'

'And that bombing can start again, and then where will Tatiana be? She should never have left home. What could she have been thinking about to desert her mother in her time of need?'

'Need? I am not in need and am not in any way unhappy with my life – except for the war, that is. Tatiana is young and the young live differently now. Don't condemn her out of hand. In my opinion, she has grown up a credit to us all.'

'You are entitled to your opinion, Anna Petrovska.' The Countess turned, hand on the door knob. 'After all, you are mistress of this house.'

'Oh, no. Denniston belongs to Tatiana. You know it was willed to her by her Grandmother Sutton and you and I live here by Tatiana's favour. We would both do well to remember that! And I wish you a happy New Year. Sleep well, Mama.'

The door closed without comment from the Countess. But then her mother was, Anna sighed, determined not to be happy, even at New Year. Her mother would be unhappy for the rest of her days unless, of course, she ended those days in St Petersburg.

It was then the telephone began to ring and Anna ran to answer it.

'It's your call to London, Mrs Sutton – and a happy New Year!'

'A happy New Year to you too, Winnie,' Anna laughed, glad of a friendly greeting. 'Hullo? Tatiana?'

'Mother! Would you believe it, I've just this minute got

in – haven't even taken off my coat! Happy New Year, darling!'

'And the same to you from your grandmother and me. I'm glad you were out enjoying yourself. A party, was it?'

'N-no. Not exactly. But I remembered you once told me that in Russia on New Year's Eve, no one refuses to answer the door to a caller, so I tried it and it worked. I called on Uncle Igor. I thought he would be at Cheyne Walk, there being no air raids for him to go out to. Luckily he was in – and he opened the door to me!'

'And how is he?' Anna's voice was apprehensive.

'He's well.' Well for Uncle Igor, that was, though she had the good sense not to give voice to her thoughts.

'And what did you find to talk about?'

'Oh, lots of things – but mainly about things past. Well, you do, don't you, on New Year's Eve?'

'Things like . . . ?' There was an edge to Anna's voice.

'Like how it was in St Petersburg at New Year when he and Uncle Basil were cadets at the Academy and put on their dress uniforms and escorted young ladies to balls – and how it was when he returned to the St Petersburg house and the farm at Peterhof after the Revolution and found the Bolsheviks living in both of them. And he said I could call again!'

And call again she would, Tatiana thought, if only to hear more about her father and about her mother's unhappiness and why, as she suspected, her uncle disliked her father to the point of loathing. Given patience and a little cunning, she would get the entire story out of her mother's brother.

'But how is Holdenby? And how are you and Grandmother? Is she in bed? You'll wish her a happy New Year from me, won't you?'

'Yes, she is in bed, but I'll pass on your good wishes in the morning. And, darling – are you sure you are all right? I worry about you and if the bombing will start again.

Couldn't you find war work back here, at home?'

'Mother! There is little use for the Russian language in the North Riding, and besides, I am quite comfortable here. Sparrow is a dear and I like spending money I have earned myself.' *And there are no RAF bombers flying overhead here to remind me.*

'But you have money of your own, Tatiana. Your Grandfather Sutton saw to it you would never want for anything. There is no need for you ever to have to work.'

'There is, Mother. There's a war on, don't forget.' And Tim had been killed so she had to do her bit because that was what he would have wanted. 'I want to be in the war just as Daisy and Drew are.'

'Yes, of course you do.' Tatiana was as English as Daisy and Drew. 'But promise me you'll always take care, darling? And come home just as soon as you can get time off work?'

'I will – take care, I mean. And I'm planning to come home for a long weekend very soon now.'

'You are! When, dear?'

'As soon as I can make it.' As soon as her uncle had told her what she wanted to know! 'And you take care, too, Mother. There go the pips! 'Bye . . .'

'Goodbye, Tatiana. God bless you.'

The line went dead and Anna replaced the receiver, glancing as she did so to the rails on the upstairs landing at which her mother stood.

'Was that Tatiana?'

'Yes, Mother.' She knew it was Tatiana. She had been listening all the time! 'And she wishes you a happy New Year. She spent the evening with Igor.'

'Ha! Igor!' Her son had not telephoned tonight. Preferred to spend his time with his niece, it would seem. She turned abruptly, then slammed her bedroom door behind her. Igor, indeed! She hoped her younger son had not drunk vodka this evening to loosen his tongue and release his inhibitions. Especially she hoped it in view of Tatiana's visit.

Strange, wasn't it, how often the ghost of Elliot Sutton still manifested itself, may his soul rot in hell!

'Alice! At last! I've been trying to get you for ages! Happy New Year!'

'And to you and Nathan, Julia, from Tom and me. The phone's been going all night. First Daisy from Liverpool, then Keth from goodness only knows where, for Polly.'

'Polly's with you?'

'She is, as usual. Was tickled pink to hear from Keth. Tom's just walking her back to the bothy. Jack Catchpole let in the New Year for us, after he'd been to your place. Wonder what 1942 will bring?'

'Wish I knew. But I think it's going to be a better year for us all. There'll be Daisy's wedding and maybe I shouldn't say this, but what if Bas lands up in England? The Americans came over last time. Wouldn't it be wonderful to see Bas again?'

'The Americans came over last time because they were fighting the Kaiser. But America's quarrel is with Japan, this time. I think Bas's war will be in the Far East.'

'You're right, Alice. You usually are. It's the only thing I can't stand about you – you're always so common-sensically *right*! But let's forget the war for a little while? You'll be having a word with the rooks as soon as it's light, no doubt?'

'I will.' Alice could hear the laughter in her voice. 'And, Julia – I don't want to bring back unhappy memories, but do you know who it was I first thought about when the midnight pips came over the wireless?'

'Tell me?' Julia whispered, though she already knew.

'Well, I – I thought about her ladyship. I thought, dear, lovely Mother-in-law, this is a strange New Year without you. She was always there in my life, right from when I first came to Rowangarth. And she was so kind to me.'

'I thought of her, too, but I can't be sad, Alice. Mother is where she wants to be – with Pa. And we haven't lost her. She's still with us. She was with us tonight, when Nathan opened the door to Jack Catchpole to bring in the bread and coal and salt like always.'

'Mm. I'll pop over to the churchyard tomorrow, and have a word with her, take her a few flowers. Well, best be off. All the very best to you all at Rowangarth.'

'And to you, my very dear Alice, and Tom. I might just call in on you in the morning. Nathan's going out with the shoot, though he won't hit anything. I think it's only the exercise he's going for – and maybe to take a pot at the odd carrion. Ah, well. 'Night, Alice – and thanks.'

'Thanks? For what?'

'For being you, I suppose. And for being there all the years when I needed you. You'll always be there, Alice? Don't ever go away again?'

'You know I won't. 'Night, Julia. God bless.'

She smiled, and put down the phone. She was still smiling when Tom walked into the kitchen, hurrying to the fire.

'My, but it's a cold 'un tonight! Julia's been on, then? You gave her my love?'

'She has, and I did. She sent hers to you.'

'Well, then. Everybody's been in touch that matters. Daisy, Keth, Julia. Reckon we can have a sup of tea, lass, then be away to bed. I'll have to be up good and early in the morning, don't forget.'

'You missed someone out,' Alice smiled as she set the kettle to boil. 'People who matter, I mean.' Gently she took his face in her hands; softly she laid her lips to his.

'Will I tell you something? Once, a long time ago when I was carrying Drew and Julia had come back from France bitter with grief, it seemed that all the world was grey and cold; seemed like the sun would never shine again. If anyone had told me then that Julia and I would ever be happy again, I'd not have believed them. So thank you for coming back, Tom, when I thought you were gone from me for ever and thank you for Daisy and all the lovely years. Happy New Year, Tom Dwerryhouse. I love you very much and don't ever forget it.'

'So,' Nathan smiled as Julia settled herself on the floor beside his chair, leaning close. 'That's all your calls made, Mrs Sutton.'

'Not quite all. I couldn't speak to Drew, but I sent him my love at midnight. He'll be fine, you know. Whenever I start to worry about him, I hear Mother's voice telling me not to. And Nathan.' She turned to face him, kneeling, tilting her chin so he would know she needed him to kiss her. 'Thank you for the last three and a bit years, my dear, and for waiting all that time. I didn't deserve it.'

'No, you didn't,' he smiled, bending to kiss her gently. 'I nearly gave up. But did I see a drop of whisky in the bottom of the decanter? What say we polish it off – drink to absent ones?'

'Mm.' Julia rose to her feet. 'Mind, you know that's the last of the Scotch and Lord only knows when we'll get another bottle. But when we raise our glasses, I'm going to wish that Drew soon meets a nice girl. He really ought to be married. I've earned the right to be a grandmother.'

'Julia! Drew is only just twenty-four. There's time enough. He's perfectly normal – takes girls out all the time. He's just studying form, that's all. And didn't you say he seems taken with Daisy's friend?'

'Lyndis? I suppose he is, but he doesn't bring her home, does he, and she and Daisy both have time off after their stretch on night duties. Why doesn't he, Nathan?'

'Because it's my opinion that when he does bring a girl home she'll be the one. When is he due leave again?'

'Some time in February. The *Maggie* usually comes in for supplies and to take on drinking water, but last time he wrote, remember, he said it seemed ages since they'd been alongside and that they had victualled at sea from a supply ship.

'But, Nathan, do you think we might be winning the war now – just a little? Do you suppose it might be a good thing to do as Mother always did on New Year's Eve, and count our blessings?'

'Well, on the debit side, poor little Malta is still being bombed a lot, and after the attack on Pearl Harbor the Japs seem so near to Australia. I think we should send all the Australians back home. They should be looking after their own country now, not ours. Mind, talking about Australian troops, at least Tobruk is still holding out and we are getting supplies to them by sea, so that's one in the eye for Rommel. And Leningrad hasn't given in, nor Moscow. The Russians have pushed the Germans back from Moscow, don't forget.'

'Yes, but that's because of the terrible cold there. What will happen when spring comes and the freeze-up ends?'

'I think by then that Stalin will have got himself organized and they'll really start fighting back. Russia is so vast. Hitler must have been mad to think he could take on a country that size. Tom always said that the best thing that could happen was for Hitler to attack Russia.'

'Not very nice, though, for the people who live there.'

'No, but since it's happened, Julia, we've got to be grateful that the best part of the Luftwaffe is at the Russian Front and we aren't getting so many air raids. And there's little chance we'll be invaded now. So that's another blessing, though I'd take bets that Albert and Amelia are very worried tonight.'

'Mm. Bas volunteering, you mean, and Kitty agitating to get into the war, too, the silly young thing. But do you really think we're winning the war at last, because we ought to drink to it,' she smiled, settling herself on the hearth rug again, leaning against the arm of his chair.

'All right, then! Maybe we aren't winning exactly, but here's to a lovely little light at the end of the tunnel!'

They raised their glasses, each smiling into the other's eyes and as they did so, Julia knew with absolute certainty, that love can happen twice.

'And can we drink,' she smiled, 'to Drew and Daisy and Keth and Tatty and Bas and Kitty? Now that it seems the whole world is at war, dare we hope they'll all come safely through it?'

'We can. We must.' Solemnly, Nathan clinked his glass with hers. 'To your beloved Clan, God keep them. And, Julia – I love you very much . . .'

36

The week of night watches, which followed the weeks of earlies, afternoons and lates as surely as day followed night, was with them again.

'Like a monthly period,' Lyn grumbled.

'But nights aren't as bad as they were.' Not now that another attempt at ventilation had produced a little more air. 'And we *do* get time off after nights and you *are* coming to Holdenby with me.'

'Shouldn't grumble, I suppose.' Lyn shrugged expressively. 'And I really am looking forward to meeting your folks and Drew's folks.' Especially, if she were to be scrupulously honest, to meeting Drew's mother and seeing for herself the old house that seemed to have a hold over those who knew it. 'Sure it'll be okay with your mother – the food, I mean.'

'Your Auntie Blod fed me when I stayed with her, didn't she? Mam said it was all right for you to come, so don't worry. Besides, we don't do too badly in the country.'

Few alerts, even fewer air raids – and country people were able to grow their own vegetables, keep a few hens and a pig, even. And Dada could always provide something for the table when the meat ration ran out; rabbits, of course, and sometimes wild pigeons or a pheasant.

'We might miss Drew, had you thought?'

'If the *Maggie* comes in, you mean? Yes, I suppose we might. But I'm sure you won't pine and die, Lyn, for want of seeing him – and you'll meet his mother and his Uncle Nathan and see where he lives, so that'll be some compensation. We just might go up the pike so you can get a look down at Pendenys Place the Army has taken over. We might even go to Denniston so you can meet Tatty's mother and her gran, though on second thoughts, maybe we won't. The Petrovska's face frightens the horses, you know. On a bad day, it's been known to turn milk sour!'

'You're kidding? Is she really that awful? Think we'll give Denniston a miss.' And after all, it was Tatiana Sutton she was interested to meet; she who was a part of the hallowed Clan. And Tatiana was in London.

'Okay – but you'll have to meet Gracie. If there's a dance at the aerodrome, we'll go with her. She's good fun.'

'Yes. You said.' Lyn knew she would have to meet Gracie, and when she did, if she was as pretty and as good to be with as Daisy said, then she would spit feathers! 'Is Gracie *really* pretty?'

'I think so. And she's got lovely teeth, just like you see on the toothpaste adverts.'

'Thanks a lot! You really do know how to make a girl feel good. When he goes on leave, I shall just *love* thinking about Drew and that land girl!'

'Lyn – I've told you before! Drew likes you, I know he does. And you can bet your next long leave that he wouldn't mess about with any girl's feelings if he wasn't serious about her. So just be content with the way things are. If it's any comfort, he's shown more interest in you than any other girl I know.'

'Even Gracie?'

'Even Gracie, if what you told me is true about your petting sessions. But I've got some dhobeying to do and a letter to write to Keth. Are you coming to the wash house?'

Hellas House had an assortment of brick outbuildings, one of which was a wash house. In it were deep terracotta glazed sinks, hot running water, a mangle and several lines strung along its length for drying. And of far more importance, it housed the hot-water boiler which made it a much-sought-after place for lovers' meetings on cold, wet, winter nights.

'Okay.' Lyn took her dirty-clothes bag from the peg behind the door. 'Got a few smalls to see to. Might as well do them.'

Just to think of missing Drew if the *Maggie* came alongside was misery-making enough; to see that sapphire ring set smugly on Dwerryhouse's third finger left hand and the wedding ring that hung on the chain around her neck made her want to spit something more deadly than feathers. Indeed, there were times, Lyn sighed, when she wished she had never met Drew Sutton. And tonight, just to rub salt in, they began a week of lousy night watches!

'Do you think, Mr Catchpole, I could leave a little earlier tomorrow night?' Gracie asked. 'Some of us are going to Creesby to the pictures. We want to catch the first house, so we'll have to get the half-past-five bus from the crossroads.'

'Something special, is it?' Jack Catchpole blew on his tea, sipping it carefully.

'It's *Target for Tonight*. One of the girls saw it when she was on leave and says it's marvellous. It's a real film, taken on a bomber on an actual raid – a Wellington – and it gets hit by flack over the target then manages to get home to land in fog.'

'Seems there isn't much sense in going since you know what it's all about. Is there any lovey-dovey in it?'

'*No*, Mr Catchpole! It's a very serious film, though I don't suppose Tatty will ever go to see it. Well, she wouldn't want to, would she?'

Now the new Wellington bombers were replacing the outdated Whitleys Tim had flown, and the squadron was still flying operations over Germany in spite of the bitterly cold weather. It made Rowangarth's land girl all the more certain she would never, if she could help it, love as completely as Tatty had loved – not until the war was over, that was. Though come to think of it, the way the war was dragging on even with Russia and America in it now, on our side, she was going to be a middle-aged matron before it was over. And who would want a middle-aged matron except a middle-aged man!

'Penny for 'em, lass.'

'I – oh – I was thinking how beautiful everything looked this morning when I came to work; most of the trees and bushes were silvered all over by the frost.'

'Ar. And tomorrow morning when you come to work, you'll find it's raining.'

'And how do you work that one out, Mr Catchpole?'

'Well, this morning was the third heavy frost in a row, and three hard frosts is alus followed by rain, depend on it. And you can leave early provided,' he added sternly, 'you make up the time!'

'Oh, I will, and thanks. And did you know Daisy is coming home at the weekend and bringing a friend from the Wrens with her? Mrs Dwerryhouse was telling me about it this morning. I'm looking forward to seeing Daisy again.' She rose to her feet. 'Just going round the back for some logs – best we keep the fire going. Anything special you want doing, Mr Catchpole?'

There seemed little to do in the garden. Either the ground was too wet or too frozen for digging. She broke the thin layer of ice on the water butt by the potting-shed door, rinsed out their mugs then placed them on the shelf beside the bottle marked poison.

'Aye, lass. You can sort out a few cooking apples and take them to Tilda. And dig up a few leeks for her, will you? Take 'em out careful.'

Gracie brightened visibly. She liked going to Rowangarth kitchen and today especially she hoped she would see Mrs Sutton and tell her the hens were coming out of their winter moult and feathering up nicely. Soon, they would start laying eggs again – with plenty of good hot mash inside

536

them, that was, and shelter from the biting winds that blew, Gracie was convinced, straight from Siberia.

She sighed contentment. She was happy and she shouldn't be. No one should be enjoying this war and it made her feel ashamed and determined to work even harder just to make up for it.

'Won't be long, Mr Catchpole!' She shrugged into her thick, working jacket.

'An' you'd better not be, lass! There's a war on, don't forget!'

'I won't!' She wasn't likely to. If only the killing and wounding could stop and husbands come home to their children, then she wouldn't mind if the war went on until she was a middle-aged matron.

Provided our side won, of course!

Lyn sat on the brass stool by Keeper's Cottage kitchen fire, wearing Daisy's second-best skirt and twinset, her feet snugly slippered. She liked Mrs Dwerryhouse the minute she had been hugged and kissed and told she was welcome. And she liked Daisy's father, too. It was easy to see where Daisy's so-blue eyes came from and her silver-fair hair. Now, with Mr Dwerryhouse out on Home Guard duty, they were free to indulge themselves in women's talk and to oh! and ah! over the wedding dress.

On the fire hob, the kettle began to boil and Alice said, 'Be a love, Lyndis, and make the cocoa.'

It was another thing Lyn liked about Daisy's mother. She treated her not as a guest but more an extension of Daisy and it made her feel wanted, just as Auntie Blod made her feel wanted. But for all that she felt guilty about the food she would be eating, and said so.

'Oh, for goodness' sake!' Alice removed the pins from her mouth. 'Cocoa isn't on the ration and Ellen at Home Farm sees me all right for milk. And your auntie fed Daisy, didn't she, for a weekend? Stop your worrying, lass, and tell me what you think to this dress, then Daisy can take it off. We don't want cocoa spilled on it.'

'I think it's really lovely. Doesn't it make you feel good, Mrs Dwerryhouse, being able to make something so beautiful?'

'We-e-ll, it's what I'm best at,' Alice smiled modestly, though her cheeks pinked at the sincere compliment. 'Now tell me, do you think the waist is right? You'd better make up your mind, Daisy, because I'm going to stitch it tonight when you two have gone to bed.'

'I like the waistline where it is, Mam. I really do.'

'Mm. Her hips are very slim. She can get away with a dropped waistline,' Lyn nodded her agreement. 'And that skirt! It's so full and – and *romantic*,' she sighed.

'There's almost six yards in it and a couple left for the train. Now if you're absolutely sure . . . ?'

'I'm sure. It's perfect and you were a clever mam to buy the silk when you did. Now all I need is a bridegroom.'

'Hmm,' Alice frowned. 'Y'know, it does surprise me that Keth hasn't had any leave before this. Drew gets a week every three months, yet it was last June when Keth was home. You don't suppose they've sent him abroad? After all, he couldn't tell you if they had, all his letters having to pass the censor, I mean.'

'No. He's still in England doing whatever it is he can't tell me about. I know, because sometimes he rings me. He's been going on courses and things. Seems they're always sending him on courses. Maybe that's why he's had no leave. But I'm just grateful he's on this side of the Atlantic and safer than most men in uniform. He'll get leave soon, I'm sure of it.'

'Well, it's a good job you can take it all so calmly. Now be careful when you take that dress off – the skirt is only tacked on. And before you go back I shall want you to stand on the table in it so I can see how it hangs and pin up the hem.

'And by the way, Mrs Anna came over the other day and left me two ball gowns – one of hers and one of Tatty's. She said you were welcome to them since nobody goes to balls, now. I'm to alter them about a bit and make them look more like bridesmaids' dresses, she said. Tatty is going to be bridesmaid, Lyn, and I want everything seen to just in case Keth springs some leave on us unexpectedly. I was saying only the other day that I ought to have a word with Nathan about getting the banns called so we don't have to go rushing off to get a special licence from the bishop if we get caught on the hop.'

'You're enjoying this wedding, aren't you, Mrs Dwerry-house?'

'I am, Lyn. My first marrying was in a little chapel in France, and me in my nurse's uniform and Nathan, bless him, marrying us – me and Drew's father, that was. And then my Tom came back from the dead, and me a widow – well, I got married the second time in my best grey costume. Maybe that's why I want Daisy to have a white wedding, even if there is a war on and clothes rationed.

'But I'll take this dress upstairs out of harm's way and bring down those ball gowns. Good job we've got them. Tatty wouldn't want to use her precious coupons for a dress she's only likely to wear once. It's a crying shame, clothes being rationed.'

'Your mother is a love,' Lyn smiled as the silk wedding dress swished out of the kitchen on Alice's arm. 'Do you suppose she would let me try on those ball gowns – I've never had one, you see.'

'Nor me – well, nothing like the Suttons wore. But be a love and see to the cocoa, then you can help me decide which of them we'll use.'

Alice rustled in again with two satin ball gowns over her arm. One was in dusky rose, the other was sky-blue. Carefully she draped them over chairs.

'Oh, what absolutely gorgeous dresses. Can I try them on – *please*?' Lyn gasped.

'Try the blue, first,' Alice smiled. 'You'd look lovely in it with white flowers in your hair and a bouquet to match. And Daisy! Why didn't we think of it before? We've got two dresses for me to remake – Mrs Anna said to keep them both – so why don't you have two bridesmaids? Oh, I do so like a flutter of bridesmaids! Why not Lyn, too?'

'Why not? What do you say, Lyn?'

'If I can get leave, then yes please. I'd love to.' She flushed with pleasure. 'And thanks, Mrs Dwerryhouse, for being so nice. It's lovely being part of a family. I can see now why Daisy loves Rowangarth so much.'

'But you've got a family?' Alice frowned.

'Two people in Kenya who sent me to school in England and who I haven't seen since – if that's what you call family. If it wasn't for Auntie Blod . . .'

'It was good of Miss Meredith to have Daisy after that awful bombing. She said you just slept and slept. 'And talking about sleeping! You two worked all night and spent the best part of half a day getting here. You look tired out. Now what about you both drinking that cocoa then getting off to bed? You can try the dresses on tomorrow, Lyn.'

'But I haven't said good night to Dada. Do parades go on so late, Mam?'

'Of course they don't! But it's Friday night, isn't it, and they'll have got their quota of beer in at the pub.' It was Alice's guess that the entire platoon would be fighting the war over pints of bitter at this very moment. 'So, off to bed the pair of you! I've put your hot-water bottles in. Five minutes I'll give you, then I'll be up to tuck you in!'

This was, Lyn thought as she lay snuggled, tucked in and kissed good night, quite the nicest place to be; almost as nice as Auntie Blod's. Mind, she'd had a bit of a shock; three shocks, really.

The first one had been on meeting Grace Fielding. Nice, Daisy said she was, with a smile that could sell toothpaste. Well, Rowangarth's land girl *was* nice and her smile lit up the whole of her face. She even smiled with her eyes! But nice was the wrong word, because Grace Fielding was head-turning attractive and thank heaven that Drew had not, this far, fallen head over heels for her because she looked stunning in old dungarees and a thick, working jacket and her nose red from the cold. What she looked like all dressed up with silk-stockinged legs and her hair swinging free instead tied up in a turban, just didn't bear thinking about!

But Gracie, Daisy had said afterwards, was determined to remain heart-whole for the duration and that being so, it was hardly likely she would be giving Drew overmuch encouragement.

Drew. Now there had been the second shock. Telegraphist Drew Sutton was not what he seemed because when Mr Catchpole, who had invited them to share the fire in the potting shed asked of Daisy how young Sir Andrew had been when she last saw him, Daisy said, 'Just fine, wasn't he, Lyn?'

'Sir Andrew?' Lyn had frowned.

'Aye. Sir Andrew Robert Giles Sutton. Our Drew. Daisy's brother – well, half so.'

'You mean Drew's a *sir*,' Lyn squeaked.

'He is. Was a baronet afore he was hardly an hour old.' Jack Catchpole was enjoying Lyn's consternation.

'You go dancing with him!' She turned, wide-eyed, to Gracie. 'So what do you call him, then?'

'Drew. What else?'

'Ar. Us gives him his due when first we meet. "Good morning, Sir Andrew," we say, then after that it's just Drew. Mind, once he's wed we'll have to watch ourselves.

'Won't be right, then, treating him like the lad we've watched grow up.' The gardener clamped his pipe between his teeth, wishing he had tobacco to fill it with.

'So your mother was . . . ?'

'Lady Sutton,' Daisy supplied. 'Sir Giles – Drew's father – caught flu. I told you. There was an epidemic after the war. He died of it just about an hour after Drew was born. Aunt Julia said it was as if he'd been waiting to know that Rowangarth had a son. He was still weak from his war wounds, you see. He didn't have the stamina to fight the infection.'

'And then your father came back from being a prisoner? Wasn't that how it was?'

'That's it. I told you before. And he and Mam were married and lived at Windrush. Mam left Drew with Aunt Julia to be brought up a Sutton. Best that she should because Rowangarth was already his – well, technically. That's why he calls his Aunt Julia Mother and Mam, who's his real mother, he calls Lady.'

'And thanks be she had him. We all wanted that bairn to be a lad or the title would've sidestepped to Mr Edward at Pendenys Place and then to that cocky young Elliot, and that would never have done,' Catchpole remarked.

'It's like a novel,' Lyn laughed. 'But why didn't Drew tell me?'

'About his title, you mean? Why should he?' Daisy defended. 'Come to think of it, he'd take a bit of ribbing from the lower decks on the *Maggie* if ever they found out, so don't you ever say a word, Lyn – especially in front of any of the *Maggie*'s crew when they come to the Wrennery dances. But if you want some real romance, then come with me and meet Aunt Julia, and Rowangarth. Rowangarth is just – well, it's just –'

'Magic,' Gracie supplied, smiling at the disbelief that had left Lyn bewildered.

And magic Rowangarth had been, Lyn admitted as she

snuggled into her pillows. Rowangarth was as if the war had never happened. The minute they walked through the tall iron gates of the kitchen garden and saw the cupola rising through the trees ahead and the linden walk, its branches bare and black and shiny in the winter sun, she drew in her breath. And that late-afternoon sun, all winter-red, touched its old bricks and stones and the crisscrossed mullioned windows and made a picture she would never forget.

And how now would Lyn Carmichael fare? she thought, staring at the little cracks and bumps on the ceiling. Drew would marry – nothing was so certain. There had been a Sutton at Rowangarth, it seemed, since before Elizabeth Tudor died and James Stuart, on his triumphant procession south to claim his English throne, had slept in the best bedchamber that now Daisy's Aunt Julia and the Reverend used.

Did people like Drew Sutton marry people like Lyndis Carmichael? Did people like Lyndis Carmichael, whose parents did not like her and whose lovely Auntie Blod lived in a little stone cottage in Wales, marry into the aristocracy?

And the answer, she realized as she blew out the bedside candle was yes, because Daisy's mother married Drew's father. Mrs Dwerryhouse was once a sewing-maid and she had given Rowangarth a son.

I love you, Drew Sutton. From the hazy edges of sleep she sent her thoughts to him. *I shall always love you and I think that one day you will come to love me, too. Only don't let Rowangarth come between us? Please . . . ?'*

Lyn and Daisy, greatcoat collars pulled high against the cold, hands thrust deep into pockets, waited at the cross-roads with Gracie and a cluster of land girls for the transport that would take them to the dance at RAF Holdenby Moor.

Tonight, all wore uniforms. Pretty, summery frocks were all well and good, but on nights such as this and when no one had the coupons with which to buy silk stockings, bare legs mottled blue with cold were not a pretty sight.

Gracie glanced up at a sky void of stars or moon, from which icy rain blew on an icy wind to play havoc with their carefully curled hair.

'At least there'll be plenty of partners in the aircrew mess,' she remarked. 'They aren't flying ops. tonight.'

'How do you know?' Lyn demanded. She could not help liking Grace Fielding.

'No circuits and bumps this morning, you see. Which means no taking off, circuiting the aerodrome then landing. No test flights, no ops,' Daisy explained.

'Mm.' Lyn would rather dance with a naval telegraphist than all the glamorous aircrews with wings on their tunics, she thought as she recalled this morning, and trying on the sky-blue ball gown.

It had been lovely; such a voluminous skirt, so daring a neckline. Daisy's mother had said they would have to do something about that plunge or the whole village would be talking, but Lyn had only imagined floating down the wide staircase at Rowangarth and into Drew's waiting arms. Not that she ever would, of course, but at least there was a good chance Drew would see her dressed in her bridesmaid's finery because surely he would be given leave for his sister's wedding. If the *Maggie* was not at sea, that was. And she must try to persuade Daisy's mother not to change the neckline too much. Perhaps if she were to suggest that a large flower would serve to cover the offending four inches of cleavage she would leave it as it was.

'It's coming!' The call invaded Lyn's thoughts and though no lights were to be seen approaching, the sound of the transport could be clearly heard. It made Lyn glad she was a telephonist and not a driver. People said you could recognize drivers in HM Forces; they all had eyes that stood out like chapel hat pegs!

A Waaf corporal wound down her window, called, 'Hi, you lot! All aboard the love bus, then! And shift yourselves. I haven't got all night!'

Then they were off into the darkness, and Lyn, sitting on the low wooden bench and clinging, eyes closed to the side of the truck, reaffirmed her belief that to drive a large vehicle without headlights on icy roads in the blackout was not for her.

'It'll be a good night,' Daisy said. 'They've got a really great dance band at Holdenby Moor. I did hear that Joe Loss's drummer is in it.'

But Lyn only murmured, 'Really?' and closed her eyes because she was still wearing the sky-blue ball gown with the plunging neckline and she was dancing with Drew. And through the open windows – because in her dreamings there was no war and no blackout – came the scent of roses and honeysuckle and a nightingale sang beneath a full, August moon.

'Really?' she breathed again.

They heard the hoots the Holdenby train always gave out as it approached the bend, half a mile down the track.

'It's coming,' Daisy said. 'Goodbye, Holdenby, for another four weeks.' She shivered, turning her back to the wind. 'I'd forgotten how the wind blows here, in winter. Glad we persuaded Mam not to come and see us off.' Or even stand at the waving place as their train passed the far end of Brattocks Wood. 'Have you had a good time, Lyn? What do you think to the North Riding – apart from the cold, that is?'

'It's every bit as nice as North Wales and every bit as cold,' Lyndis laughed. She had thanked Daisy's mother prettily and begged to be asked to come again and Alice had said of course she must come; would have to, anyway, for the trying-on of the sky-blue bridesmaid's dress. 'Your mother makes marvellous gravy,' she added, remembering the roast pheasant they had eaten for Sunday dinner.

'You've got a thing about gravy.'

'I know. What time will we be back at Hellas House, d'you think?'

'Well, this train is almost always on time, so we'll get the 3.30 from York – be in Liverpool about seven, provided there aren't too many holdups on the way. Reckon we'll be in the Wrennery by about eight – given luck.'

The signal fell with a clatter, the York to Holdenby train juddered and shuddered to a hissing halt and Daisy closed her eyes to savour, as she always did, the heady train smell of hot grease and coal-smoke and steam. And when she opened them, a sailor was standing there and Lyn was calling, 'Drew!' and running down the platform to meet him.

'Drew!' Daisy picked up their overnight bags and followed her cabin-mate, who was being hugged very thoroughly. 'Well, fancy meeting you!' She offered her cheek for a chaste, brotherly kiss. 'Why didn't you let us know you were coming?'

She threw their bags through the open door of the compartment, because the train would start its journey back to York almost at once.

'I didn't tell Mother I was coming because she'd have come to meet me and wasted her precious petrol. And I tried to get in touch with you two but they were pretty cagey at the Wrennery; said you weren't about, at the moment.'

'That would be because they knew that most of D-watch was AWOL on a crafty weekend,' Daisy smiled, wishing Lyn would let go of Drew's hand and get herself on the train, because much as she loved her brother and was sad they couldn't stay longer together, she was aware that the train was the only one into and out of Holdenby, a concession only allowed because there was a war on. Once, Sunday trains would not even have been considered. 'Hurry up, Carmichael.'

The stationmaster was closing carriage doors with loud bangs because the sooner the train was away the sooner he could eat his Sunday dinner.

'All aboard, please!' He unfurled his green flag to let Sir Andrew and the two ladies know he meant business.

Lyn reluctantly stepped aboard and slammed shut the door, letting down the window, leaning out. 'And, Drew, guess what? I'm going to be bridesmaid for Daisy with Tatiana. Isn't it just brilliant?'

'It is,' Drew smiled indulgently, 'especially as I'll almost certainly be best man.' He winked suggestively, then kissed her once more. Kissed her on the mouth, Daisy noticed as the train heaved and shuddered on its way.

'Tell Mam we got the train okay,' she called, determined to get a word in. 'See you, Drew. Have a good leave!'

They leaned precariously out of the window, waving until the train had taken the bend and the station was lost from sight.

Then Daisy said, 'Of all the rotten luck! Why couldn't he have started his leave earlier? It would have been fun, all of us together – and Gracie, too,' she sighed.

Gracie. Grace Fielding. The name hissed round Lyn's brain. Drew was home for seven days and she would have him all to herself!

She took off her greatcoat and hat and sat down with a bump. Then she hissed, 'Damn, damn, *damn*!' and closed her eyes and folded her arms and didn't speak one word until they reached York.

'Thought I'd call, Lady,' Drew smiled. 'Got a message from two Wrens. They wanted you to know they got the train all right.'

'Come you in out of the cold. Tom's walking the rounds

– poachers, you know – and I'm all on my own. There's such a quiet over the place after all the giggling and chattering that's been going on.' She reached on tiptoe to kiss him then smiled affectionately. 'I know it isn't the thing to say, but every time you come home I'd swear you've got taller and broader. Must be all that sea air. Now sit you by the fire and I'll put the kettle on. How did you think Daisy looked, Drew?'

'She looked fine.'

'Not tired? They were dead beat when they got here.'

'She was fine,' Drew stressed. 'But what about you, Lady? Up to the eyes in sewing, Mother says.'

'Well yes, I suppose I am. Daisy had her second fitting for the wedding dress, though there's still the hem to see to, and I've got ideas about the two frocks your Aunt Anna gave me – how to make them a bit more bridesmaidy, that is. Sad that young women can't have a decent wedding, these days, nor a wedding cake. Brides' dresses ought not to be on coupons. I'm only thankful I bought that silk when I did.'

'Hope I'm not at sea when the big day comes.'

'*If* it comes!' Alice clucked. 'Do you know, Keth hasn't had one day's leave since the end of last June. Seven months! Mind, it's like Daisy says: at least he isn't in danger and he isn't likely to get shot at nor find himself in the thick of any fighting. He's one of those back-room boys, though what he does with his time beats me. Highly secret is all I know and that uniform of his only a cover so people think he's in the Signals. But there's more to it than that, if you ask me.' Alice tapped her nose with a forefinger, then took cups and saucers from the dresser. 'But tell me, Drew – how are things on HMS *Penrose*? Winning the war for us, are you?'

'We're doing our best but we're still losing ships. The *Maggie* helps sweep a safe channel for vessels coming into Liverpool and sometimes I hear what has been done to those convoys. Our lookout spotted a periscope the other day. We reported it to Flag Officer, but it would be away before they could do much about it. A German U-boat, it was. Usually they hunt in packs. The Coastal Command boys flew over not long after – probably scared it off. We don't often see one. Usually, they don't come so near inshore. Getting arrogant with it . . .'

'Don't say things like that, Drew.' Frowning, Alice covered the teapot and set it in the hearth to brew. 'I'd got it into my head you were fairly safe in home waters.'

'I am. That submarine was probably laying mines in Liverpool Bay, not after minesweepers. They usually try to keep out of our way – don't like to advertise they've left a few for us to blow up, so stop your worrying!

'And I'll tell you something to put a smile on your face, Lady. When I was getting the train, Lime Street station was really buzzing – with American soldiers! The dough-boys have arrived. Must have disembarked at Liverpool, though I don't know where the train was taking them. But isn't that great news? We've got somebody on our side at last!'

'It's good news for us, though I doubt mothers in America will be overpleased about it. And Amelia certainly won't be! Had you thought, Drew, Bas could end up in England and all the time me and your mother thought he'd be sent to fight the Japs? After all, it was the Japanese brought America into the war.'

'Then we'd better hope that if he's got to be sent overseas it's England he ends up in. It would be great if the Clan could get together again – a good omen, sort of.'

'What, and young Kitty, an' all! Now how would she get over here from Kentucky?' Alice frowned.

'Your guess is as good as mine, but you know my dotty cousin. If Bas gets here, she'll find a way, too; bet you anything you like she will!'

'Keth brought some films over with him that take snaps

in colour,' Alice brooded. 'Now wouldn't it be grand if Julia could get a picture of you all again in the conservatory, like she did that Christmas you were all young?' And there was never, ever, going to be another war, even though a man called Herr Hitler was making a nuisance of himself.

'Just grand. What a reunion,' Drew laughed. 'And why are you looking at me like that, Lady? Peculiar, sort of.'

'Well, if you must know – and I have the right to my own thoughts about you, now don't I? – I was thinking that when Tom wasn't much older than you, him and me were married.'

'And is that a hint?'

'N-no. But haven't you –' she turned to face him, then, chin defiantly high, 'ever met any nice young ladies you'd like to take home to Rowangarth?'

'Five or six,' he teased. 'Well – you know what sailors are. But seriously, Lady, girls get the wrong idea if you take them home to meet your folks!'

'I'm being serious, Drew. You can't go on loving them and leaving them for ever.'

'No, but I intend to till the war is over. Gracie agrees with me on that point.'

'So you and Gracie have talked?'

'Not about marriage. More about *not* getting married.'

'And you don't like Lyn either? You seem to take her out a lot when your ship docks.'

'Yes, I do. And if you're determined to pin me down, Lady, I'd say Lyn is my best girl this far. I like her a lot.'

'But not enough to get serious?'

'No, though she's great to be with. No sugar for me, thanks,' he said as Alice filled his cup.

'I hadn't forgotten,' she said flatly. 'Lyndis thinks a lot about you, Drew, so what's holding you back? And don't tell me it's none of my business because you *are* my business, Drew Sutton!'

Now that she had come this far, Alice was determined

to have her say, because if he was to search for a month of wet Sundays he would never find a bonnier – no, nor a nicer – girl than Lyndis Carmichael.

'I know I am and I care for you very much, Lady. And of course you and Mother want to see me married, but since we're talking about it, I'm not sure – about Lyn, that is. There's just something – and I don't for the life of me know what it is – that's holding me back.

'But maybe it will grow between us or maybe, like it happened to Mother with Andrew, I shall turn a corner and there she'll be. The right one; the one I'm maybe waiting for.'

'Well, your mother didn't turn a corner, exactly.' Alice knew it was time to let the matter rest. 'And I won't ask again, Drew; I won't pry. But don't turn your back on falling in love, just because there's a war on. I didn't, and your mother didn't.'

'Yes – and look what happened to Mother.'

'I know. But she had *some* happiness with the doctor.'

'I suppose so. But I'll tell you one thing – *both* my mothers will be the first to know just as soon as I meet the right girl – now does that suit you?'

'The day it happens, I'll be very well suited Drew, but think on, and don't leave it too long!'

And with that, Alice had to be content.

37

Keth looked at his watch. Again. A porter had told him the train from York would arrive at platform five and yes, he hoped it would be on time – well, as on-time as could be expected, allowing there was a war on.

Keth thanked him, calculating he had ten more minutes to wait. He was fast learning that trains could be hours late and almost always made a mockery of timetables.

Lately, now the Russians were taking the brunt of the Luftwaffe's bombing, blitzed railway stations were being repaired, as far as building restrictions allowed, and damaged tracks given urgent attention by gangs of overworked men.

It was an age, he thought, since he had seen Daisy and held her and kissed her. Six months, which was nothing, really, compared to the three years apart they had endured. But it was still six months too long and the offer, yesterday, of a forty-eight-hour leave pass surprised him. He had accepted with grateful disbelief and was on his way to Euston station before Authority had time to change its mind.

Daisy didn't know about the courses he had been on – not their exact nature. He wore the uniform of a soldier, Keth reasoned, and must be expected to have a basic knowledge of pistols. He had not told them his father was once a gamekeeper who had taught him to use a shotgun from the day he was old enough to be trusted with one, because a four-day course away from the eternal click-clicking of the *bombes* was something to be looked forward to.

The rifle course, too, was a welcome break in routine

and after that, the small-arms course. He had accepted, too, that a man wearing khaki should be able to throw a hand grenade but what he could not equate with code-breaking in secret back rooms, was being required to make his first – and last, as it happened – parachute jump. The parachute course really started him thinking.

He shrugged and went to stand beneath a dim, paper-shaded light to check his watch yet again. There was a very large clock in the centre of the station but its face was not illuminated because of blackout restrictions, so it was of little use at night.

Five more minutes and then she should be here. Five more minutes to ponder the need to be able to leave a plane on the end of a parachute.

As it happened he had made such a mess of it, had landed so badly that the instructor told him – with respect – that the severe bruising to his back and shoulder were as nothing compared to what might have happened, *sir*!, and that in his considered opinion – and he'd made more jumps than sir had had hot dinners – sir should forget parachuting and concentrate on signals which obviously he was better at!

In great discomfort, Keth returned to Bletchley and the clicking of the *bombes* seemed all at once not to irritate him so much, nor the sheer frustration of failing to find a match for just one vowel or consonant. Jumping from an aircraft – no, being literally thrown out of the damn thing – figured now in most of his worst unguarded moments. Pitching into nothingness, praying the ripcord would work and feeling a jerk that nearly broke his back when it did, was the stuff bad dreams were made of and the remark of the sergeant-instructor that he would never be any good at it, he hoped would reach the ears of those in authority at Bletchley.

So now, when they had tried to show him what soldiering was all about, he hoped he could return to the code-breaking that was his real contribution to the war effort. There were worse things than the job they had brought him from America to do, the more so when he had been given a forty-eight-hour leave pass.

Activity at platform five cleared his mind of brooding. A ticket collector arrived to stand at the barrier, switching on the torch attached to the lapel of his jacket. Keth heard the approach of the train though in the darkness he could not see it. Then it came slowly, huffing and hissing to a squealing stop. Not ten yards from him was the dark outline of the York-to-Liverpool express from which Daisy would alight.

Doors banged open. The platform began to fill with dim shapes, then all at once Daisy was at the barrier, and through it.

He called her name but she did not hear him. She began to walk away and he ran after her, and the Wren at her side. It was quieter, now, away from train noises so he whistled the way he always did; low and warbling – a whistle only she knew.

He saw her stop and he whistled again.

'*Keth?*' She turned to fling herself into his waiting arms. 'Darling, it *is* you! How did you know I'd be here?'

Their lips met and she closed her eyes, relaxing against him, her fingertips gentling his cheek.

'I rang the Wrennery. They said you weren't about. So I put in a call to Mum. When I got through she told me I'd just missed you; that you were on the 3.30 from York. By the way, I love you!'

'I love you, too. How long have you got?'

'Forty-eight hours and I've used eight of them already!'

'Keth! After six months, all they give you is *two days*! But better than nothing, I suppose. Oh, and this is my cabin-mate. Lyndis Carmichael, Keth Purvis.'

'So what have you got fixed up?' Daisy asked of Keth

when he and Lyn had shaken hands and said how nice it was to meet each other at last.

'Nothing. I thought I'd wait until I saw you. Any suggestions?'

'Now see here,' Lyn laughed, 'do you want me to stand at a discreet distance whilst you sort out your sleeping plans or shall I push off?'

'You'd better push off,' Daisy replied with equal directness. 'See you later, old love!'

'Okay. And don't be late in, Wren Dwerryhouse. I shall be waiting,' she mimicked Ailsa Seaton's Scottish accent, 'at the Regulating Office door with a stopwatch! Well, 'bye, you two. Nice to have met you, Keth.'

She disappeared into the darkness and they stood, listening as the sound of her footsteps grew fainter.

'Will she be all right alone?' Keth frowned.

'Of course she will. She knows not to speak to strange men.'

'You've changed, Daisy Dwerryhouse.' He gathered her to him, kissing her again.

'I haven't, really; just grown up a bit. I still love you and that's all that matters. Shall I put in for a sleeping-out pass for tomorrow night, then?'

'I'd like that, darling, but aren't you on early watch?'

'Yes, but we can ask the hotel for a very early call.'

'In that case, we'd have to go to bed very early, wouldn't we?'

'Just as you say, and with respect, sir,' she lifted her head so their lips were almost touching, 'you haven't kissed me for a whole minute.'

She said, several kisses later, that she was hungry. 'Look – we aren't far from the Adelphi – let's eat there? They put on a decent meal, all things considered. Drew sometimes takes us there. I'll pay. I've got a cheque book now, and I haven't written a cheque yet. There's nothing in the shops to spend it on.' She thought briefly, longingly, of

Morris and Page where once she worked, and an imp of mischief made her want to go there and buy something – anything – and charge it to her account.

'The Adelphi it is – but I'll pay. If you think I'm sitting there while you fork out for my meal, you can think again!'

'I adore you when you're bossy.' She shaped her mouth into a moue, then blew him a kiss. And because it was very dark and no one could see them, she slipped her arm through his and they kissed as they walked. And it was so wonderful that she forgot it was six months since last they had met and touched and loved and that only thirty-six more hours were left to them; forgot, because there was a war on and you lived for the moment.

'Will they give you a sleeping-out pass, darling?'

'No reason why not. Ma'am is a bit sticky about them, but I haven't asked for one before so I should be okay.'

'But what if –'

'If she says no, then I'll slip out after last rounds. Lyn will lock the back door after me. And I think that tonight I'd better play it by the book and get in on time.'

'I love you,' he said softly. 'I want to marry you now.'

'We'll talk weddings when we've ordered. Mam wants to get the banns called now so we won't get caught on the hop if you get unexpected leave, though I must say they're a bit stingy with it at your place.'

'I've been messing around on courses and things. It'll all settle down now, and surely they can't refuse me marriage leave?'

'They can, you know! Leave, haven't they told you, is a privilege, and not a right! And do you think we're awful? Not for sleeping out, but for not feeling guilty about it, I mean.'

'Guilty? Not when there's a war on, though I often wonder what would happen if the parents found out.'

'Doesn't bear thinking about,' she said soberly, grateful for the darkness that hid the flush to her cheeks. 'And let's get inside and grab a table or all the food will have gone and I'm –'

'Ravenous!' Keth finished. 'Come to think of it, Daisy Dwerryhouse, you haven't changed all that much.'

'Grab me a plate, Lyn,' Daisy asked when D-watch came off early duty. 'I want to go to the Regulating Office and see if my sleeping-out pass is okay.'

'Come in!' Ailsa Seaton called in answer to her knock. 'Oh, it's you, Dwerryhouse. You're to see Ma'am.'

'*Me*? What about?' There was a distinct squeakiness to her voice.

'About your SOP.'

'You mean I can't have one?'

'I mean you've got to see Ma'am and you'd better be quick about it. She's just going to have her lunch.'

'Hell!' Daisy straightened her tie, rubbed her shoe toes against the backs of her legs, then tapped on the wardroom door. Ma'am couldn't say no. She *couldn't*!

'Ah, Dwerryhouse. Won't keep you long.' The quarters officer glanced meaningfully at the tray on the table at her side. 'About your pass – I suppose you know I'm not very happy about my girls sleeping out without very good reason.'

'Yes, Ma'am.' Daisy took a deep breath. 'It's my brother, you see. His ship is in dock. I don't see him often and – and it's his birthday. You can check, Ma'am. HMS *Penrose*.'

Lies, lies, lies!

'I didn't know you had a brother, Dwerryhouse.'

'My half-brother, Ma'am. Drew Sutton. My mother's first husband died in the last war.'

That, at least, was true. But if Ma'am really checked, they would tell her Telegraphist Sutton was on leave and his birthday, according to his record sheet, wasn't until December! But she wouldn't check? She couldn't be *that* petty!

'It's all right, Dwerryhouse.' The quarters officer picked up her pen, initialling Daisy's request. 'I'm sure your brother will take good care of you. I have to check, you see, since I'm *in loco parentis*, so to speak. Where will you be staying?'

'I'm not quite sure, Ma'am. Drew sometimes stays a night at the Adelphi when his ship is in dock. I suppose it will be there.'

'Very well. You may go.'

'Yes, Ma'am. Thank you, Ma'am.'

When she had returned the requests book to the Regulating Office and gone to sit beside Lyn who had collected a dinner plate for her, Daisy whispered, 'Ma'am wanted to know who I'd be staying with tonight.'

'Oh my Lord! What did you say?'

'That I'd be with Drew; that his ship was in dock and she could check.'

'Bet you were worried.'

'Not half! Oh, not about sleeping with Keth but I did feel awful telling all those lies, especially when Ma'am is such a decent sort. She wanted to know where I'd be staying and I said I thought it would be the Adelphi.'

'So the Adelphi will be out, then?'

'It'll have to be now. Anyway, she signed my pass, but it seems a bit – well, *tainted*, if you know what I mean.'

'No. I don't. I've never slept – well, you know – though if Drew asked me to spend the night with him, I would,' Lyn said defiantly. 'And while we're on the subject of Drew, I feel a bit miffed that he's at Rowangarth and I'm here.'

'Well, you shouldn't be. He deserves his leave – if only because I've just used him shamelessly.'

'Yes – but leave Drew to me and worry about your own date. You're meeting Keth at the Pierhead at three, so get a move on, Dwerryhouse!'

*   *   *

When Daisy had washed, and cleaned her teeth, and was laying out clean clothes, Lyn said, 'I wonder what Drew is doing now.'

Daisy looked at her watch. 'He'll have had his lunch – they have dinner at night at Rowangarth – and he might have gone to Keeper's, or maybe he'll be walking the game covers with Dada. They'll probably have a shotgun apiece over their arms and the dogs will be with them. Rowangarth is beautiful, even in winter when everything is bare and asleep.'

'Yes. I've just seen it, don't forget, though I'd like to see it in summer. Imagine a summer wedding at Rowangarth – all those lawns and climbing roses, and trees . . .'

'Keth and I will have our wedding reception there. Aunt Julia insisted on it and I must say it'll be pretty marvellous. Even if it's wet, there'll be loads of room inside.'

'I know exactly what you mean.' Lyn lay back on her bunk, hands behind head. 'I'd marry Drew just to have a Rowangarth wedding.'

'Kitty said once,' Daisy said as she buttoned her shirt, 'that she would marry Drew just to get her hands on Rowangarth.'

'Kitty?' Lyn sat bolt-upright. 'Kitty Sutton from Kentucky, you mean?'

'Mm. She loves England, though she's more likely to end up at Pendenys.'

'You never told me about Kitty being sweet on Drew.'

'You never asked, and I don't think she ever was. Kitty has always been a drama-drawers. And it was only kid's talk. She hasn't seen Drew for – oh, for five years.'

'So what about Pendenys Place, then? Who will she marry to get her hands on that?'

'No one. And don't get all hot round the collar, Carmichael. Kitty likes Pendenys almost as much as she likes Rowangarth and if it has anything to do with her brother he'll give it to her – lock, stock and barrel. If the Army doesn't blow it up, meantime, which I'm pretty certain Bas would like them to.'

'Bas?' Another of those well-heeled Suttons!

'Pendenys will come to Bas one day, nothing is more sure.'

'And Bas doesn't want it?'

'He does *not*!' Daisy made a face in the mirror as she knotted her tie. 'I think he really will give it to Kitty.'

'If she doesn't get her hands on Rowangarth, that is – and Drew,' Lyn said sourly.

'Listen! Kitty was just kidding about getting hold of Rowangarth. There's nothing between her and Drew. Last time she saw him was in 'thirty-seven. She was only sixteen. You *have* got it bad, Carmichael!'

'I know,' came the reluctant admission. 'But then, I've never tried to deny it, have I? I wish it were me spending the night with Drew. I'd be hoping like mad I'd get pregnant.'

There really had been no reply to that remark, Daisy thought as she sat on the rocking, racketing overhead railway – except of course to feel sorry for Lyn, because she hadn't realized until now how very much in love with Drew Lyn was. Sorry, because Lyn would be laying on her bunk now, staring at the ceiling and worrying not only about Drew taking Gracie dancing most nights of his leave, but about Kitty, too. She felt guilty, as well, because in just a few more minutes she would offer her mouth for Keth to kiss. And tonight she would sleep in his arms.

Take care, Lyn. Don't wear your heart on your sleeve. Don't get hurt.

Tatiana Sutton left the Underground at Knightsbridge and turned into Brompton Road, hands in pockets, head down against the cold. Soon, she thought, she would be twenty-one. On the first of March, actually, when Denniston House would be legally hers and she need no longer see the solicitors and have Mr Carver countersign any cheque she might need to write. On her coming of age, the money Grandfather had left her would be completely hers, though she would be responsible for the upkeep of Denniston House and perhaps other things she had once taken for granted and which Carver-the-young would doubtless explain to her in great detail.

And why she was thinking about the money or even about being twenty-one, she didn't know, because the money meant little to her. She would give it all away, and Denniston House, too, if that was what God wanted in return for Tim's life. And being of age and able to marry without anyone's permission meant nothing at all since there was no one she wanted to marry. Not now. Not ever.

Yet she knew, really, why she was thinking about being twenty-one. She could have thought of other things – how cold and dark and joyless this night was and how her footsteps echoed in the empty darkness and how she wasn't one bit afraid being out alone because she really didn't care what might happen to her in the blackout; didn't care about anything, save that she would never see Tim again – and about what Uncle Igor had told her tonight in the kitchen of the house in Cheyne Walk.

Uncle Igor lived now in the semi-basement with the curtains drawn on the other windows and each room locked. He had become a recluse, she supposed, except that recluses didn't ever go out and Uncle Igor, at least, had joined the ARP and went out all the time in his navy-blue uniform with 'Warden' on the shoulder of his battledress top and his steel helmet with 'ARP' on it.

Since New Year's Eve, Tatiana had gone to the house in Cheyne Walk on three Sundays and been invited in. Uncle Igor, she had thought, was mellowing, and she was pleased about it because life hadn't been very kind to him, she was forced to admit. Losing almost everything you had was bad enough, without having the Petrovska for a mother. Yet tonight she discovered that her uncle was bitter, still, not only about losing everything, but about –

No! She *wouldn't* think about it! Not yet. Not until she was in bed and could weep if she wanted to, without anyone knowing. And what he had told her would make a saint weep!

Her eyes were accustomed to the darkness now, and she could make out the outline of the house on the corner of Montpelier Square. Soon she would be back to the little mews cottage and the warmth of Sparrow's welcome. Sparrow at least liked her. Just to think of it made her eyes prick with tears and she had to bite on her bottom lip and sniff loudly to stop them from running down her cheeks because she must not weep over what Uncle Igor had said. Not yet.

Daisy hung up her greatcoat and hat, took off her jacket and unfastened the third button down of her shirt, fishing for the chain that hung there.

'Put my ring on, please?' She liked to wear the wedding ring Keth had brought back from America. It seemed so right with the daisy of sapphires and she ached for the day when he would put it on her finger in All Souls' and she need never take it off again.

He did as she asked, then upturned her hand to place a kiss in its palm.

'I'm afraid this is all I could get. It isn't much of a room, but most places were full. Seems the Americans are in town.'

'It certainly isn't like the one in Winchester,' she smiled, 'but that was our honeymoon, don't forget.'

The bedroom was small, the bed large and the blackout hidden by cornflower- and poppy-patterned curtains that matched the quilt. The bathroom and lavatory were at the end of the passage to the left of their door.

'Sorry, darling.' Keth dropped to his knees to feed the electric meter with shillings. 'It'll soon be warm.'

'It's a lovely room,' she said softly, kneeling beside him. 'We are so lucky, Keth.'

The single bar of the fire began to glow red and she held out her hands to it.

'I wish we were married. I was stupid to think we could wait until spring.'

'But soon it *will* be spring. Easter, we said, when you get long leave. Not so long ago I didn't know when I would see you. Years and years more, I used to think. Yet here you are, here *we* are, together. After tonight, we can wait a few more weeks and anyway, I wouldn't mind a summer wedding. Lyn and I were talking about Rowangarth. I think she was quite envious that we'll be having our reception there. She's really in love with Drew and of course I had to put my foot in it.'

'But is Drew serious about Lyn? Oh, she's a good-looker, no doubt about it. She could tweak her little finger and have most fellows she wanted.'

'She's beautiful and she looks even better in civvies, with her hair down. But I said something like, "Kitty would marry Drew just to get Rowangarth," and you could've cut the air with a knife afterwards.'

'Do you reckon Kitty would marry Drew?'

'Of course not. I was only joking, but Lyn's got it pretty bad and she can't make a lot of headway with Drew because whenever he's ashore he takes me out, too. Always a threesome. I suppose, really, I ought to say I've got a headache, or something – give them time on their own – but Drew seems to want to see me and I want to see him, too.'

'I think that if he wanted to be alone with her he'd tell you, Daisy. But I wouldn't worry too much about it.' He rose to his feet, holding out his hand, pulling her into his arms. 'It's turned five. Shall we find somewhere to eat?'

'N-no.' She began to unbutton his jacket with shaking fingers. 'I'm not hungry. There'll be time to eat later.'

'I was hoping you'd say that.' He loosened his tie, taking off his shirt.

'Food, when I haven't seen you for six months?' Then her head jerked up. 'Keth! What are those bruises? What have you done!'

'They're on my back, too.' Best she should see them.

'But how did you get them?'

'I fell downstairs.' He had already decided on an explanation and the lie came easily. 'The light on the landing didn't work. I missed my footing. Sober as a judge, honestly.' Instinct had warned him she must not know about the parachute jump. 'I'll be more careful, next time. I had the light bulb replaced.'

'I'll kiss it better, if you like.' She gentled the angry bruises with her lips.

'Fine by me,' he said huskily, turning the key in the lock. 'Come to bed . . . ?'

Tatiana said she didn't want any supper, thanks all the same.

'You had something to eat at Cheyne Walk then?'

'No. Uncle Igor has only one ration book.' It wouldn't have been fair to take his food, even had he offered. 'But I'd like a cup of cocoa, if you don't mind, then I'll go to bed. I'm tired, tonight.'

'Hm. You do look a bit peaky. Your visitor due, is it?'

Tatty said it was – which was the truth, as it happened – and Sparrow was satisfied.

'Well, the milkman let me have a little drop extra, so we'll both have a cup. I've put your hot-water bottle in.'

'Thanks. You're a darling.' She liked Sparrow; liked the way she fussed because it was nice being fussed over. No one had ever done it before, not even her dimly remembered nanny.

She thought about nanny when she switched off her bedside light. Nanny was in the past – or had been, until this evening. Now, all at once, nanny was very real and she, Tatiana, was a small girl again and her mother weeping and her father shouting. And just because tonight, she had mentioned the fighting in Russia. One thing had led to another.

'Stalin is doing a little better now, Uncle,' she had said. 'He's holding the Wehrmacht – even pushing them back in places. We should be glad.'

'I suppose we must be. And speak in Russian, child. I like to hear my own tongue.'

'Grandmother Petrovska's rule is only English to be spoken until there is a Romanov on the throne again. Russian used only on saints' days.'

'Well, your grandmother isn't here now!'

'No,' she conceded, because her uncle seemed to be in a bad mood tonight. But perhaps he hadn't wanted her to come? 'Do you think if Stalin beats the Germans that things will get better in Russia when the war is over – that people like us will be allowed back, perhaps to visit?'

'Visit? Who would want to see what has been done there? Stalin and Hitler – a clash of monsters and whichever monster wins, Russia will suffer. St Petersburg is under siege, still holding out and thousands starving. Our house there could be a heap of bomb rubble now. And the Nazis have advanced far beyond Peterhof. There will be nothing left of our farm. Scorched earth, Stalin ordered. Peterhof will have burned. I hold the title deeds to two ruins!'

'Was it a lovely farm, Uncle?' She was eager to offer comfort and talking about St Petersburg and Peterhof almost always gave comfort to Grandmother Petrovska.

'It wasn't a farm, really. It was our summer house. We went there when Petersburg became too hot. Even though we had no use for it in winter, we still had servants there so they paid for their keep by farming some of the land – keeping a couple of house cows, a few hens, and pigs. And of course, there were always horses to be looked after.

Carriage horses, and saddle horses. It pleased us to call it a farm. We ran barefoot, there, as children.'

He stared moodily into the fire, his mouth working in small, angry movements as if to talk about his other life distressed him.

'I suppose I am lucky having Denniston House left to me, and money, too. It was kind of him,' she ventured.

'Kind? It was the least she could do, after what your mother endured!'

'Endured? Losing the baby, you mean? Or giving up her religion?' she pressed. Grandmother Petrovska was still strictly Orthodox, though now her daughter worshipped regularly and devoutly in the Anglican church.

'She has not given it up entirely. She will call for a priest of her own church on her deathbed.'

Tatiana nodded. There was still an icon above her mother's bed. She had always known that sometimes she prayed to the Virgin and Child in the old way.

'Will you tell me something, Uncle Igor? My mother has never remarried. Did she love my father very much?'

'Once, she did. She was like someone possessed, for want of him. I told her. I told your grandmother, but neither would listen.' He stopped, mouth clamped tight.

'And?' Tatiana coaxed.

'You don't want to hear. And anyway, it is a long time ago. I forget.'

'Yet you don't forget St Petersburg nor Peterhof nor the Military Academy and dancing with young ladies at balls.'

'Some things are best forgotten – especially concerning your father!'

'No, Uncle! You must tell me! I remember, you see – *things*. You said my mother once loved my father. What happened to them?'

'You are determined to know, aren't you? But you are stubborn. You defied your grandmother and left home for

566

London when you had no need at all to work. When I was young, in Russia, a girl obeyed her parents.'

'And then a girl married and obeyed her husband, didn't she? I've heard it all before! In Russia! In Russia! Always in Russia! But I am half-English!'

As if to defy him, she lapsed into English again, holding her head defiantly, pacing the hearth.

'Yes, and your English blood is not to be commended, young woman. But your grandmother Clementina Sutton wanted a title in the family and she wanted a brood mare to give sons to Pendenys. Your mother was ideal. She was – *is* – a countess.'

'Brood mare? That isn't very kind!' Her cheeks flushed crimson, her eyes sparked anger.

'The truth is often unkind.' Igor Petrovsky allowed himself the smallest smile because there was some of the Russian fire, it would seem, in his English-sired, English-born niece. 'Oh, Tatiana Petrovska Sutton, I am tempted to tell you!'

'Then I wish you would. Perhaps then I could understand why there is no happiness at Denniston House, nor ever was at Pendenys; not like at Rowangarth, I mean.'

'Simple. There is breeding – *gentility* – at Rowangarth. The English have a saying about it. You cannot, they insist, make a silk purse from a sow's ear and your mother married into a family that wouldn't recognize a silk purse if it saw one, even though there is Rowangarth blood in them.'

'From Grandfather Edward, you mean?'

'Yes. And Nathan Sutton is a gentleman, too, I'll grant him that.'

'So tell me?' She settled herself on the floor at his feet, feeling easy in his company for the first time. 'There is something my Russian half should be told, isn't there? I know it. I remember tears and screaming and loud voices.'

'You were too young to remember anything. Your father died when you were little more than a babe.'

'But I *do* remember! Half a story is no use to me. I want to know all of it. I'll be twenty-one, soon; I earn my own living. Tell me?' she pleaded.

'Very well.' He reached for his tobacco jar. 'Would you mind if I smoke?'

She was so taken aback at his request that she said, 'No, of course not,' and fished into her handbag for her cigarette case. 'Would you mind if I did?'

'It isn't ladylike.'

'But everyone smokes these days.' Cigarettes, when you could get them, soothed frayed nerve ends. She took a spill from the hearth, lit it at the fire and passed it to him. Then she flicked her lighter and drew deeply on her cigarette. 'Tell me?'

'Even though it might not make pretty hearing?'

'Yes.'

'Well, as I said, Pendenys wanted an heir; Clementina Sutton wanted Elliot to settle down and provide it. She chose your mother with great care.'

'*Chose* her? But I thought that after the last war, arranged marriages didn't happen.'

'Oh, but they did and especially so since your mother wanted the marriage. Elliot Sutton was handsome and attentive and from your Grandmother Petrovska's point of view, he was rich – or would be, one day.'

'But my mother didn't sell herself like a tart! She loved him!'

'She did. She came back from their expensive honeymoon pregnant with you – and already a sadder, wiser young woman, I suspected.'

'And I was not a son. Poor mother; poor me.'

'No. I think you were lucky to be born a girl. Had you not, you would have been given everything you wanted by a doting Clementina – just as she spoiled your father. She would have ruined you as she ruined him.

'But then your mother slipped two babies – miscarried.

568

Two in two years, and before she was hardly over the second miscarriage, she was pregnant again. It made me sick to think of the way she was being used.'

'Used, Uncle? But she loved him.'

'Yes. She couldn't see he was an arrogant womanizer.'

'So when did all the upset start? Because something awful happened – I know it!'

'The upset, as you call it, was when your mother was in her fourth pregnancy; four in four years. She was happy she had carried it full term; was looking forward to giving her husband the so-important son. Then she found him in bed with a servant, and went berserk. She told me afterwards that she forgot all that was expected of a lady and screamed and kicked like a fishwife. Her pregnancy had two weeks to run but she started her labour next day. She had a difficult birth. She blamed herself for the child's death.'

'But she shouldn't have! My father was as much to blame!'

'Oh, no! It was entirely Anna's fault, your father said to me. Even when the doctor said that for the good of Anna's health she must not get pregnant for another year, Elliot still insisted Anna must do her duty, as he called it, or he would divorce her for refusing him his rights! It didn't seem to matter to him that another conceiving so soon after could have killed her.'

'I can't believe any man could be such a beast.' Tatiana threw the end of her cigarette into the fire and reached for another with shaking hands. Tim had been a sweet lover, and gentle . . .

'I told you it wouldn't make pretty hearing. And there is more. The servant was pregnant. Her child was your father's, there was no doubt about it. Your grandmother Petrovska brought her back to London out of harm's way and for once, your mother listened to reason and came back here to Cheyne Walk, too.'

'She left my father? Then I'm glad!'

'She left only for the good of her health. She would have gone back to him, fool that she was; tried to give him his son. I warned your father that if he so much as attempted to get her back to Denniston House until she was fully recovered, he would have me to answer to. I told him, too, that when she did return, Karl would return with her, as her personal servant. Had Elliot Sutton harmed your mother in any way, Karl would have let me know – maybe even have dealt with it himself. Karl had always been protective towards her. Two days after your mother left for London, he died. He had been drinking – had probably been with a whore. He was seen with a woman, I believe, but no one knew who she was.'

'What you would call poetic justice, Uncle?'

'I suppose so. Your mother didn't shed a tear at his funeral. I don't think anyone did.'

'Not even his mother?'

'Clementina Sutton was too ill to attend. Perhaps she did weep for him, though I believe she was given drugs to calm her.' He tapped out his pipe on the corner of the firegrate and sighed deeply, feeling almost sorry for the venomous outburst. But the child had to know; make sure she didn't make a similar mistake. 'Are you shocked, Tatiana?'

'Not shocked. More disgusted. I feel as if I want to brush my teeth – clean my mouth out. You were right: it didn't make pretty hearing.' She got to her feet stiffly. 'At least, though, I'll be able to understand why Mother seems so distant, sometimes. It must be awful to love someone and have it thrown back in your face.'

'Perhaps she is not so much unhappy as angry. What do they say? Heaven has not rage like love to hatred turned, nor hell a fury like a woman scorned. Something like that, I believe. I think your mother was not so much scorned as betrayed.'

'I think you're right. And I won't tell anyone about tonight, and what we have talked about.'

'No. Better you should not. And you'll come again? Ring first, though, to make sure I'm in.'

'I'll do that.' She reached up to kiss his cheek and he did not shrink from her touch as she had thought he would. Instead he took her coat and held it for her to put on. Then, at the bottom of the area steps that led up to street level she turned and said, 'What happened to the servant? What was she called? I'd like to know because somewhere I have a brother, or a sister.'

'Natasha Yurovska, her name was, and she was very beautiful. I think the baby was adopted but my mother will never discuss it, so never ask.'

'I won't. I can't, or they would know you and I had been talking about things. But somewhere there is someone who half belongs to me – how old will they be?'

'About sixteen, I would say. But I trust you to keep what I have said tonight a secret.'

'I will, Uncle. Word of a Sutton, as Aunt Julia says.' She had touched his cheek with gentle fingertips, then walked up the steps and away into the darkness.

She wished, as she pulled the blankets up to her nose and reached with her toes for the hot-water bottle, that she had told Uncle Igor about Tim and how much she loved him. Perhaps she would next time she visited.

She closed her eyes and from the edge of sleep her thoughts were not of what she had learned of her past, nor of Tim, but that somewhere she had a half-brother, or -sister.

Keth leaned back in his seat, eyes closed. One of the advantages of being an officer, he acknowledged, was that his travel warrants entitled him to a first-class seat, though it seemed unfair on the corporals and privates who were crammed into third-class compartments with hardly room to move. He wondered what his father would have made of it all and smiled gently to remember him as last he saw him; dressed in Daisy's father's second-best keeper's suit, limping away in his highly polished boots and leggings, the bitch at his heels. What would a man who endured the filth of the trenches and wounding in another war have made of his officer son? A son who worked in secrecy, breaking enemy codes and never once getting his soft, officer-issue boots muddy?

Sorry, Dad . . .

He stretched his legs and thought instead of Daisy and the softness and sweetness of her; of her silver-blonde hair and eyes so blue you had to notice them.

She was his. He knew intimately every beautiful inch of her body. Naked, she had lain close to his nakedness. There were no inhibitions between them, no feeling of the shame society demanded they should feel by being lovers without the blessing of the Church.

There had been times, at college, when the talk was frank and often bawdy. Women figured hugely in their discussions.

Some women, talk had it, would and some wouldn't; some could, and some couldn't, and nice girls, of course, *didn't*. Well, Daisy was a nice girl, and she *did*, but only with him. She belonged. She was his, his, *his*!

A feeling of love of her and protection for her washed over him, and in the fierceness of those feelings he knew he could kill for her.

The train hooted, then plunged into the blackness of a tunnel, making a different, hollow sound. He looked at his lonely reflection in the dark of the window, wondering if it was really only four hours since they had kissed, briefly, then said, 'See you. I love you. Take care . . .'

She had asked him, sleepy from loving, why he never answered her questions; why his letters must be censored and sent to a GPO number and not to his billet or his workplace and he had answered, 'Because . . .' then kissed her hard to stop her questioning.

The train came noisily out of the tunnel and clattered over a bridge. If it stopped at a station on the way, would there be a WVS tea trolley on the platform? He and Daisy had had no time for breakfast. There might have been time, after their early call, but they had made love instead, then ran hand in hand through the dark morning to ask of the Marine sentries outside the sandbagged entrance of Epsom House if the watches had changed, yet; relieved to be told they had not.

Five more minutes together to stand sheltered by the complete blackness of a winter morning; to kiss and whisper lovers' promises until the bus with its blacked-out windows drew up and a sleepy D-watch stumbled out of it.

'Take care, darling,' Daisy whispered. 'Don't volunteer for anything.'

'Of course I'll be careful,' he said, kissing the tip of her nose. 'You be careful, too. You're so precious, and I don't want to leave you.'

Whilst she was standing close in the shelter of his arms, nothing had mattered but the sixty seconds of that minute together that might be their last for a long time. Yet surely, now that the business of the courses was over, life would slip into a more orderly routine and he could hope to be given leave as Daisy and Drew were given it.

A vague resentment sliced through him. He wanted Daisy; needed her. Tonight he would have a few beers in the Mess with Robby and hope to get so relaxed that the pain of leaving her became bearable. But even drinking was discouraged. Drinking loosened tongues.

He shifted restlessly and the discomfort he still felt in his bruised back reminded him of that parachute jump last week and made him silently demand *Why?*

He closed his eyes to shut it out and to try to sleep, but the anguish of wanting Daisy would not let him.

38

For once, when someone banged on the communicating door between the cabins, Lyn Carmichael did not yell back, 'For Pete's sake stop your noise, you lot!' because something in the urgency of the voice that called, 'Quick, you two!' made her turn the key and fling open the door.

'What is it?'

'Ssssh! Listen!' demanded the Wren who had her own wireless set. 'It's *awful*!'

'. . . and that is the end of the special bulletin. Mr Churchill will speak to the nation this evening at nine o'clock.'

'So what was the special bulletin?' Daisy's mouth had gone so dry that her tongue made little hissing sounds as she spoke. 'What did we miss?'

'Singapore, that's all! They've taken it, the slant-eyed little sods!'

'But Singapore is untouchable – or so we always believed,' Lyn protested. 'So how did they do it?'

'Everybody expected an attack would come from the sea, so all the heavy guns were sited to fire seawards. My cousin is with the Fleet out there. I just hope they up anchor and get the hell out of it before the kamikaze pilots have a go at them!'

'And?' Lyn urged.

'Well, the Japs just walked in by the back door, so to speak. Across the Strait from Malaya – that's all! But we'll have to wait till tonight, I suppose, to hear what really happened.'

'Well, at least old Winston never wraps it up.'

'Had you thought – that's both Hong Kong and Singapore they've got their hands on. Where next?'

'Can we listen to Mr Churchill on your set tonight?' Lyn asked, for once willing to fraternize with the noisy crowd on the other side of the door.

'Sure. Makes you think, though – where are they going to stop? Having to fight the Krauts was bad enough, but now we've got the Japs as well! And it's only two months since Pearl Harbor, yet they seem to be everywhere!' Funny, short-sighted little blokes who were funny no longer.

'See you, then.' Lyn closed the communicating door, remembering to lock it again despite the bad news. 'Well, what do you know, Dwerryhouse? First soap rationing, then Singapore; bad news always comes in threes, don't they say? What next, do you suppose?'

'Don't know,' Daisy shrugged, recalling the two coupons she had been given at pay parade. Each coupon represented two ounces of soap – the ration for one week. Two ounces of toilet soap or of soap powder or soap flakes. 'I managed to get some toilet soap just before it went on the ration; it'll last me until next payday, if I'm careful. I think I'll buy four ounces of soap flakes, with this fortnight's coupons, and keep them in a jam jar.'

'Never mind about soap flakes! What about Singapore?'

'You're right. It *is* awful and, Lyn, do you remember when I was going to meet Keth in Beck Lane and I got a lift on the back of a tractor? Well, that land girl's husband was in Singapore with the RAF she told me. She thought herself lucky because he'd got a nice safe posting.' Her heart went out to a girl whose name she did not know, because Keth was back in England and the threat of invasion receding – for the time being, that was. 'This is a swine of a war, isn't it?'

'Tell me what's new, Dwerryhouse. It might be the three Ss. Soap, Singapore – and Stalingrad? Maybe Stalingrad will be next?'

But even as she said it, she knew that defiant, besieged Stalingrad would hold out – until the snows melted, at least. And that would not be until April.

'It's a pity,' Tilda sighed as she weighed an ounce of rice, 'that when this is used up, there'll be no more rice puddings for the duration.'

The Japanese had occupied every rice-growing country except India and India needed all it could grow for itself. And even had there been rice for puddings, Tilda sighed yet again, there was little sugar to spare, and no sultanas nor currants nor raisins to be had for love nor money. And, by far the worst, no glacé cherries. No cherry scones! Things, foodwise, she had to admit, had come to a pretty pass and would get worse before they got better.

Even the flour she used in cooking was no longer white! The sight of the National wholemeal flour had dismayed Tilda, even though the newspapers said it was every bit as good as the pure white variety and every bit as nutritious. Tilda had her doubts on both points. Pastry made from puggy flour did not look as good nor taste as good as white pastry, gently browned, and as for those little brown bits They seemed determined to leave in – well, healthy or not, little brown bits could do a lot of harm, in her opinion, to people's insides!

'I said it won't be long before rice puddings are a thing of the past,' Tilda said again, to which Mary, who was reading in her magazine about pulling out hand-knitted jumpers and winding the wool into skeins and washing it and hanging it out to dry so it was almost like new wool again and saved clothing coupons, replied, 'Puddings! It's fine for them to tell us how to save coupons pulling out old jumpers,' she grumbled, 'and say we must wash it in nice, soapy suds, but it isn't going to be all that easy now, is it, when me and Will only get four ounces of soap between us for the week! It isn't sanitary, rationing soap.

There'll be germs all over the place, Will says, just see if there isn't!'

'I'll bet small boys are glad about it, though.' Tilda remembered her young brother to whom the sight of a bar of soap had been a fearsome experience.

For no reason at all, she thought about the young Suttons and wondered, as she placed the brown-glazed pudding dish on to the bottom shelf of the fire oven, how long it would be – if ever – before the Clan was together again. Eating cherry scones.

The third piece of bad news Lyn had predicted arrived a week later. It was nothing to do with soap nor Singapore but came from Kenya in the form of a pale blue air-mail envelope. It was, Daisy thought as she took it from the letter rack along with her own, the first time since she had known Lyn there had been a letter with a Kenyan stamp on it.

'It's my father's writing,' Lyn said. It was usually he who wrote. 'Must've got my birthday wrong.' She slit open the envelope with her thumb.

'Will you go back to Kenya, when the war is over?' Daisy asked, hanging up her jacket and hat.

'What do you think?' Lyn smiled obliquely, eyebrow raised. 'Even supposing they wanted me back . . .'

'Drew, you mean?'

'Drew. I want to be around,' she said, her eyes taking on the faraway look they always did when she spoke about him, 'when *he* gets around to thinking of holy wedlock. Come to think of it, though, I just want to be around. The way I feel now, I'd settle for less than marriage.'

'But Drew isn't like that, Lyn. It'll be all or nothing, with him. But what about your letter?'

'I'll read it when we've eaten. It smelled like macaroni cheese when we came in. What's your letter? One from Somewhere in England, c/o GPO London?'

'It is,' Daisy smiled, already halfway through the second reading. 'And guess what? The guy still loves me!'

When Daisy came back from the pillar box on the corner of the road, Lyn was sitting on her bunk, bewilderment in her eyes, the letter beside her.

'So how are things, then, at home?'

'My mother's dead.' Lyn's voice was toneless.

'*Wha-a-t!*'

'In her car. She'd been out. When she didn't get back my father went looking for her. He found the car in a ditch, skid marks on the road. He didn't say so, but I suppose she'd been drinking.'

'Lyn! Are you all right?' She was so matter-of-fact and she shouldn't be. Just imagine Dada writing from a long way away, telling her that Mam had been killed!

'My father thought a letter was the kindest way, he said,' Lyn whispered, staring at the floor. 'A cable would have been a bit brusque, I suppose. The funeral was a week ago. I'm to tell Auntie Blod. Seems he doesn't feel like writing to her – well, she and mother were twins. Dad was always fond of Blod, you know.'

'Are you going to ring Llangollen, or write?'

'No. I'll go there if I can. Surely they'll let me have time off? It *is* a bereavement . . .'

'Look – I don't understand you.' Daisy sat down beside her. Lyn was too calm. 'Shall I nip down to the galley, see if I can get you a cup of tea or something?'

'No thanks.' Lyn rose to her feet. 'I haven't seen my mother for almost ten years. We weren't ever close, you know. Dad was fond of me, in his own way,' she shrugged. 'It was almost always Dad who wrote – remembered my birthday. But thinking back, I don't think my mother liked me overmuch, in spite of what Auntie Blod says.'

What do you mean, merchi? Your mother does love you. Don't ever say no one cares about you!

578

'All right – so maybe my mother loves – *loved* – me; so why did she send me to England to school, foist me on to Auntie Blod? And why didn't she get me back to Kenya while there was still time when everyone knew there was going to be a war?'

'I don't know. Maybe some mothers aren't very maternal, can't show affection even though they feel it,' Daisy comforted. 'Why don't you have a word with Seaton – ask her if you can see Ma'am. And I'm sorry about your mother, Lyn . . .'

'Are you?' Her face was slablike as she turned, hand on the door knob. 'That's funny, because I can't feel anything, except maybe for my father. I've just had a letter, Dwerryhouse, telling me someone I once knew has died in another country, that's all. It's Auntie Blod I'm more worried about. She and my mother grew up together, then suddenly went their different ways. But she's bound to be hurt because they were twins, you know.' She took a deep, steadying breath, avoiding Daisy's eyes. 'I'm going to the Regulating Office to find Seaton. Won't be long.'

Daisy shook her head. So that, she thought, was that! Your mother dies and nothing changes. What, in heaven's name was the matter with Carmichael, because no one could be that unmoved – well, not without good reason. You couldn't not love your mother.

She closed her eyes, sighing deeply, glad beyond all reason that she loved Mam a lot, yes, and Dada, too. And that they loved her.

Lyn thanked the driver of the red Post Office van who had given her a lift, then set off down the lane to Blodwen Meredith's cottage.

It had been easier than she thought. Leading-Wren Seaton, unbelievably sympathetic, had at once sought the help of the quarters officer.

579

'I'm so very sorry, Carmichael, and of course I'll try to help, even allowing that –'

'Allowing that I couldn't have gone to my mother's funeral, anyway? Yes, Ma'am, I accept that, but I've been in my aunt's care since I came to England to school. When war started, I'd first left school, so I joined up instead of going back,' she lied without a qualm of conscience, because you couldn't say, really, that your Auntie Blod was far nicer than your real mother who hadn't exactly fallen over herself to send her a one-way sailing ticket back to safety.

'And your aunt . . . ?'

'She's my mother's twin. My father thought it would be kinder if I broke the news to her personally, sort of. You can read the letter, Ma'am, if you'd like.' She held out the envelope.

'No. That's all right.' She believed Wren Carmichael, felt sorry for her. And it was natural she should want to be with someone close at a time like this. 'I'd be grateful, Ma'am, if you could put in a word for a pass for me. It would only be a matter of getting a relief for one watch. I could be there and back in twenty-four hours.'

'I'll do what I can. And, Carmichael, if there's anything I can do or say to help, come and talk to me?'

'Thanks, Ma'am. It's kind of you. But all I want is to see my aunt. She and my mother were very close . . .'

That had been another lie, she thought as she turned the bend in the lane to see the little stone cottage ahead, but she had needed the comfort of Auntie Blod's arms and her help to sort out the cold, hard feeling inside her and the turmoil of hurt; hurt not for her mother but for a child, waving goodbye at the rails of a liner bound for England.

'Well then, our Lyndis!' Auntie Blod called and waved from the bedroom window. 'And what are you doing here? More leave, is it, or have you run away from sea?' The window closed with a bang, then she was there, arms wide at the front door. 'Come you here, *merchi*, and give us a kiss!'

'Oh, Auntie Blod!' From the middle of the cocoon of love and warmth, Lyn whispered, 'I've got forty-eight hours – compassionate.'

'And why is that? But come in and shut the door. We're letting all the warmth out. *Compassionate*, did you say?'

'Yes. I've come to tell you.' She dipped into the pocket of her greatcoat for the letter, handing it over. 'You'd better read it.'

Blodwen Meredith recognized the bold, black handwriting, 'From your dad, is it?'

'Yes and Mother is –' There was no other way to say it, except straight out. 'Mother's dead. It was a fortnight ago. Her car skidded off the road.'

'Ooooh . . .' She closed her eyes and screwed up her mouth, fighting tears, handing back the envelope. 'You read it, Lyndis. Don't know where my glasses are.' She dabbed at her eyes, then blew her nose loudly. 'And it won't sound so bad, coming from you. Poor Fan.' She whispered the pet name she had always used for her sister. Fan. Short for Myfanwy and not for the name Margot her sister had assumed. 'Go on, then. Read it to me?'

She settled herself beside the fire, handkerchief in her hand in a tight ball, gazing out of the window at the greyness of a February day, wondering if the sun was shining, all those miles away on her sister's grave and maybe on Jack, her husband, because no matter how toffee-nosed and social-climbing her sister had been, she sighed inside her, there had been some feeling between them. Once. A long time ago . . .

'So that's how it was,' Lyndis said softly, returning the letter to her pocket. 'And I'm very sorry, Auntie Blod. I know you were fond of her.' Very fond, though her mother had never treated her twin with anything like affection or respect. Blodwen Meredith was a fool to herself, her mother had said more than once. Not at all bad-looking, mind, yet she had chosen not to marry and to live in near-poverty, never trying to get on in the world as she, Margot Carmichael, had done! 'Don't cry, Auntie Blod? Please don't cry. I said I was sorry . . .'

'Sorry for who, our Lyndis? Aren't you sorry for yourself, then?'

'I don't know. I don't think I liked Mother all that much. It's so long since I've seen her, you see,' she finished lamely when her aunt's head jerked upward.

'That's a fine way to speak of the dead, then. Have you no respect, girl?'

'Respect, yes, and sadness for my father and for you, but for myself – well, I don't know how I feel, Auntie Blod. She didn't like me, you know. I could feel it, even as a child. There was a coldness between us. It was almost as if I were in the way – a nuisance. And yes, I know! I've said this all before and always you've said my mother loves me. But I'll never understand her and I really don't believe she loved me. Children are like animals. They know when people like them so don't ask me to believe she cared. She didn't, and you can say it as many times as you want, but I'll never believe you!'

'Lyndis Carmichael – listen you here! Your mother *does* love you! She always has, from the minute you were born only she was never allowed to show it as a mother should.'

'Show it? What do you mean?' Now it was Lyndis who sat bolt-upright in her chair, senses tingling. 'Who didn't allow her? Not my father, surely? When she wasn't around, Dad wasn't half bad. He liked me, I knew that instinctively, too, as much as he was allowed, that is, because when *she* was around, liking me wasn't on!'

'Oh, *merchi*! I didn't know it was that bad for you. I tried extra hard to be nice to you when you were on holiday from school because I thought you'd be missing your mam.

582

But it seems you weren't. Why didn't you tell me all this before?'

'Because it didn't arise, I suppose. Things were just as I wanted them to be. School was bearable and I knew that I'd be coming home to you when the holidays came round. You loved me more than she ever did, Auntie Blod. I wish you had been my mother!'

'Do you now? Oh, come you here, girl, and sit beside me. I don't suppose Fan will mind, now, my telling you. They say there's no ill feeling in heaven. And if there isn't a heaven,' she frowned, 'then I suppose it doesn't matter, anyway. Now sit you on a cushion and snuggle up, eh?'

So Lyn sat on the floor on the fat feather cushion with the patchwork cover and leaned against her aunt's chair, reaching up to clasp her hand.

'So what won't she mind about?' She tried to say it lightly and was surprised her words sounded normal, almost, and didn't betray the apprehension that all at once niggled through her.

'Won't mind if I tell you. And I hope Jack won't mind, either, him being a party to it – to the deception, I mean. But your mother did – *does* – love you, only when she got you she wasn't married and that was a terrible thing to happen in the little village we were brought up in. Strong chapel, see? If a girl got into trouble then she had to take herself off before she was showing!'

'It's still like that, now,' Lyn whispered. 'And the man usually gets off scot-free. It's a man's world, Auntie Blod. But my mother – getting pregnant! I can't believe it. She was so very correct. And I must have been Dad's, or why did he marry her? To make it respectable, was it?'

'Well, no. Not exactly. Oh dear, I'm not very good at things like this, *merchi*. I should have said it outright.'

'Then say it outright, for heaven's sake! Tell me, Auntie Blod! Okay, so I'm illegitimate – or conceived out of wedlock. But I can't help that, now can I?'

'No, lovely girl, you can't.'

'And that's why she didn't like me – because she and Dad had their bit of fun then found they had to get married in a hurry! Bet she didn't like you knowing, because she always looked down on you – well, said you could have made more of yourself. And what's more, I don't give a damn about speaking ill of the dead!'

'Hush now.' Blodwen Meredith stroked the copper-coloured hair gently. 'Like I said, I should have told you more direct, like, and not pussyfooted around it like I'm doing now. Because you're wrong. It wasn't Fan who got herself into trouble. It was me! You're mine, Lyndis, not Fan's . . .'

'*What?* You mean that *you* are my mother? *You*, Auntie Blod? Then why was I never told? And I think I have the right, don't you, to ask why you gave me to *her* to bring up! Why didn't you keep me?' All at once, Lyn's heart began a furious thudding.

'Because I didn't have the money and besides, your father had a right to you, too. Yes, Jack is your father, your *real* father. He was engaged to our Myfanwy and in love with me. I didn't know you were on the way until it was too late and they were married and them all taken up with the good job he'd got in Kenya.

'And then Fan found out about him and me and she said she'd take you with her when she followed him to Kenya – when he'd got himself settled into his job and found somewhere for them to live. You were eight weeks old when she took you from me.'

For a little while there was an aching silence all around the room, then Lyn whispered, 'I'll bet my father was surprised when she got off the boat with me in her arms!'

'No. She'd told him in a letter there was a baby on the way – his and mine. He'd had time to get used to it, and ask her understanding for what the two of us did. I never saw him nor her from that day to this, and when they

584

wrote to say you were coming to school in England and would I keep an eye on you and have you for school holidays if they sent me money for your keep, I said I would.

'I hadn't much money – just what I earned going out cleaning and doing washing – but money for the food you ate when you were with me didn't come into it. I was getting you back for a little while and that was all I cared about it.

'Don't be upset, lovely girl, because you *aren't* illegitimate. Never let me hear you use that word again. You're a love-child and that's why you are so beautiful. Love-children are always especially beautiful. Stands to sense, now doesn't it?'

'So that's why they didn't send my fare back to Kenya when I was sixteen? They'd decided, by then, to let me take pot luck with you?'

'I don't know why it was. Maybe they felt that I could give you love, and that was better than money. And anyway, I'd grown so fond of you that if they hadn't decided to leave you with me, if they'd wanted you back when your schooling was over, I'd made up my mind to tell you who you really belonged to, and let you make your own mind up.'

'But the choice was made for us, Auntie Blod. The war came. All this explains why, though, my father was nicer to me than *she* was, I suppose. And if you think about it, it was best I was sent back to England to school. Every time she looked at me it must have reminded her of you; reminded my father, too.'

'So you aren't ashamed of what I did? You still love your Aunt Blodwen Meredith?'

'I still love you, but it's going to take a bit of getting used to – calling you Mother, I mean.' She reached for Blodwen Meredith's hand and laid it to her cheek.

'Then call me Auntie Blod, like always?'

'No. I want something special. How about *cariad*? It's

almost as nice as Mother, isn't it, and it means darling, or dearest, or whichever love word you want it to mean. Will *cariad* do?'

'It'll do very nicely, girl. And thank you for being so nice about it. Don't suppose I'd ever have told you if Fan hadn't died.'

'Then thank you for being my mother and for loving me when no one else did. But what do I tell my father, when I write back?'

'I think you should tell him that you know, Lyndis. It'll be up to him then. Maybe when this old war is over, he'll come and see you and maybe me, too, for old times' sake.'

'Would you like that? Do you still love him, in spite of what happened?'

'Yes, I still care for him. Real love isn't something you can turn off. It stays there in a little secret corner inside you for the rest of your life.'

'Like I love Drew Sutton, you mean?'

'Daisy's brother? The one you've got it bad for?'

'Yes, and I think he likes me quite a bit. Not as much as I like – *love* – him, but I can wait. I'll always love him, so I've got all the time in the world to wait – just as you have done, *cariad*.'

'And shall you tell your Drew about me?'

'Of course I will. He'll understand. Oh, dear.' She got to her feet, all at once smiling and happy because now she really did belong; belonged to Auntie Blod who was lovely and cuddly and who knew what it was really like to love. 'But I don't know what you saw in my father. He wasn't bad-looking, I'll grant you that, but in other ways he's quite well – *ordinary*.'

'Ah, yes, but then you aren't me, are you?'

'No, I suppose not. But tell me just one more thing, will you? Who chose my name?'

'I did. Why?'

'Because Drew thinks it's a beautiful name, that's why . . .'

Later that night, when she lay snuggled in the nest of feathers she had wriggled for herself in the fat, floppy mattress, Lyn wondered if anyone had the right to be this happy.

She should, she supposed, feel shame because her mother and father had not married; hedge children, by-blows – call them what you wanted – were required by polite society to share the shame of the man and woman who had got them in sin, because love between two people was wrong unless sanctioned and blessed by the rites of the Church. Given the public avowal of everlasting love and fidelity and the blessing of a priest, love between two people all at once became very right and correct – was expected of them, even, because of the offspring they were supposed to procreate.

Yet she, whose real birth certificate, had she ever seen it, would have stated that her name was Lyndis, daughter of Blodwen Meredith and an unknown father, realized with a small smile that she should be Lyndis Meredith or even Lyndis Unknown. She decided, though, that since she had obviously acquired a more respectable birth certificate showing her to be the daughter of John and Myfanwy Carmichael – Jack and Margot no less – she should stick with Carmichael, since if her desperate wish was granted she would one day end up Lyndis Sutton. And what was in a name wasn't of much importance – until you got the name you really wanted, of course!

Dear, lovely Auntie Blod. *Cariad*, her new mother. Life, if she counted Drew as another of her blessings, was all at once very good. It would be good to tell Daisy at great length about the amazing turn her life had taken in the space of forty-eight hours. And how good, too, it would be to see Drew whose little *Maggie* was due to dock any time now to take on fuel and fresh water.

She wondered what Drew was doing. There was no wind tonight, so it shouldn't be too rough out there. Maybe he was keeping listening-watch, maybe sleeping away his four hours off duty. But whatever he was doing, and where, she sent her love to him in great, warm, loving gusts. Drew would understand when she told him about Auntie Blod because Drew loved her – did he but know it.

The death of Margot Carmichael *was* sad news, Lyn acknowledged. It was sad when anyone died, especially before their expected time, and for the first time she felt sorrow at the passing of the woman she had thought to be her mother; sorrow, even though that woman had not truly loved her. But then how could she have loved the living, breathing evidence of her husband's infidelity?

She closed her eyes tightly and sent a small prayer winging, just in case there really was a heaven; sent it by way of an apology to God for having misjudged the woman who brought her up. Her father, Jack Carmichael, she dismissed completely from her thoughts. She would write him a letter tomorrow – or the next day – and tell him that Auntie Blod had taken the news of her twin's death sadly but bravely. It would be up to Auntie Blod to tell him the rest, as she surely would.

Instead, Lyn spared a thought for Keth, wondering at which part of Somewhere in England he was stationed and how soon he would get long leave so that he and Daisy could marry.

Not quite yet, she hoped, remembering the ball gown being altered to look like a bridesmaid's dress and which she would wear with her hair hanging loose from a coronet of flowers, and Drew thinking how very beautiful she looked.

A June wedding Lyn hoped it would be, with Rowangarth's lawns summer-green and the air warm and sweet-scented. Just to think of it made her feel so at peace with her world, her *belonging* world, that it didn't matter one iota if sometimes Drew took Gracie dancing. Lyndis Carmichael's life had taken such a wonderful turn for the better that nothing could spoil the absolute contentment she felt this night.

Her head was filled with the triumphant booming of the Wedding March and she saw herself, as chief bridesmaid, walking up the aisle with Drew, behind Daisy and Keth. Keth tall, very dark, very handsome; Daisy exquisite in white silk.

Her eyes closed sleepily, dreamily . . .

Keth dropped the unsealed envelope he had just addressed to Daisy into the censor's basket. His head ached. It often did now, because of the noise of the *bombes* and the constant, often frustrating concentration.

Today had been especially frustrating although some days went well, he supposed. That was how it was in code-breaking and at least he wasn't at sea this bitter February night, nor flying in one of the bombers he had heard passing high overhead two hours ago, taking the war to Berlin, or Essen maybe. Indeed, it was reasonable to hope he might survive this war, allowing he didn't die of boredom because that, sometimes, was what a lot of his job entailed. He turned his thoughts to Daisy.

It was easy to think of darling, adorable Daisy. He lay back on his bed to savour the warmth of her, remember in his mind her small, round breasts and the hollow that was her stomach. There were times he thought himself a fool for not insisting they be married at once, even if it took place on one of her weekends and supposing, of course, he too could manage a similar couple of days. But they were not generous, here, when it came to giving out leave. He pulled himself back from the borders of sleep as a knock sounded on the door.

'The major's compliments, sir, and will you see him at once – in the Mess?' asked a batman.

So what did his major want at this time of night? Keth fretted, as he attached his collar to his shirt, knotted the khaki tie and buttoned his jacket at record speed. Nothing formal, or the interview would have taken place in the major's office and he would have been asked to take his cap with him.

Something informal, he hoped; something to do with his progress here to date – which was next to nothing, in his own opinion – or maybe the condescending chat that officers of higher rank gave occasionally to those of lower rank. He would soon know.

The major always sat at a small table in a window alcove at the far end of the large room. He considered it his own particular place and no one challenged his right to it. He always placed his chair so his back faced the room. It was, Keth supposed, so no one could see the expression on his face nor, from a distance, make out any of the words he spoke. One or two men here, he had been warned, were adept at lip-reading, but they were the bods from Army Intelligence and not to be fraternized with unless you wanted the bother of having to watch every word you said.

Keth made his way to the window alcove, stood a little to the major's right hand, then coughed discreetly.

'Ah, Purvis, isn't it? Sit down, man.' He lifted a finger to summon the mess steward. 'What are you drinking?'

'Soda water, please,' then at a raising of eyebrows, hastened to explain that he had just taken tablets for a headache and that soda water might be best on this particular occasion.

'You'll be wondering why I sent for you,' the major said when the drink had been set on the table. 'Well, in a nutshell, it's to tell you to pack your full kit – *now*. You're moving on. Take-off at 04.00 hours from Hendon. Transport will be here in three hours.'

'*Take off,*' Keth gasped. 'But where to?'

'You'll know when you're airborne. The pilot will carry sealed orders. You'll have been told by the time you touch down where and to whom you are to report – at the other end, that is.'

'So I'm going overseas – just like that? With respect, sir, might I know why the urgency?'

'Nothing urgent exactly, Purvis. It's just that Transport Command has room on an aircraft so you might as well fill it, now as next week. Not airsick, are you?'

'No, sir.' Where was he going? Abroad, almost certainly, so what the hell went on? 'I don't suppose I could make a phone call?' In his bewilderment he still knew that almost any time now, Daisy would be finishing her watch.

'Just try it, Purvis, and I'll have your guts for garters and that'll only be for starters! You can write a letter, though. The censor will release it when he thinks fit, so be careful what you say in it. And make it brief. You haven't got much time.'

'I suppose it isn't any use asking why?' Keth took a gulp of the liquid in his glass and wished he had asked for whisky.

'No use at all. Just get your kit together and be ready to leave as soon as possible – is that understood?'

'Yes, sir!' The interview was over. Keth pushed back his chair, though he hadn't understood a word of what had been said, save that he was flying somewhere and that he couldn't tell Daisy or, more to the point, he couldn't be trusted to make a phone call because he might let slip something he shouldn't!

He returned to his room, heels banging angrily on the linoleum-covered floor, disgusted with himself for even daring to think of weddings.

He slammed the door behind him, then reached for pen and pad. At least the shock of his departure had not robbed him of the ability to get his priorities right. First things first. He unscrewed the top of his pen, though what he was going to say to Daisy that the censor would allow in his letter, he was damned if he knew! Hell, but he wanted her, needed her in his arms, in his bed, *now*!

'My darling love,' he began . . .

39

Keth sat at the tail end of a Dakota aircraft, thinking about Daisy, wanting Daisy, needing to touch her, take her. No, dammit! This miserable moment he would settle for just one 'I love you, Keth,' whispered over the phone; that, and to know where he was being sent and for how long.

He wondered when the censor would release the tongue-in-cheek letter he had left behind and how Daisy would feel when she got it. He had wanted to tell her he was being drafted at a few hours' notice and couldn't tell her where he was going because *They* had thought fit not to tell him; wanted to write how desperately he loved her and how he wished, now, they had been married, however hurriedly. Instead, he had written,

> My darling love,
> If you don't get a letter for a couple of weeks, don't worry because I shall be on yet another of those stupid courses I can't tell you about.
> Keep the letters coming. Keep telling me you love me. I'll get a letter to you as soon as I possibly can. Take care of yourself and don't [he had underlined the word don't three times] worry.
> I love you, my darling. Never forget for a minute you belong to me.
> Always,
> Keth.

Lies, of course. So trite a letter that even the slant-eyed censor would find no fault in what he had written.

He stretched a cramped leg, thinking that tomorrow Daisy would be starting a week of night watches and that on the Friday following she would be at Keeper's on one of her weekends.

The engines made an irritating, throbbing noise that vibrated in his head and he closed his eyes, willing sleep to come. But sleep, when you were cold and cramped and sitting between cargo and the rear gunner's turret, did not come to order. He shifted his buttocks and straightened his back and thought instead about the war he had become a part of.

How much longer would it last? His father's war had gone on for four years; this time around it would be longer – even a fool knew it. First Germany, then Japan to be reckoned with and the war stretching over almost all the world. Japanese armies moved on without hindrance, threatening even Australia; a bomb-weary Malta was still almost cut off, their food supplies so low that soon they would be at starvation point, like the people of Leningrad.

On the plus side, he considered, pulling off his gloves and blowing on the ends of his numbed fingers, Hitler's drive on Moscow had been halted. The once-arrogant Wehrmacht had frostbitten fingers and feet, and empty bellies because no one, least of all Hitler, had bargained for the bitterness of a Russian winter.

An airman walked, back bent, along the fuselage and Keth watched his slow progress with interest if only because it was preferable to thinking about how Daisy would feel when finally she realized he had left England without a goodbye.

The airman was dressed against the cold in flying boots and a fur-lined leather jacket, and he carried a large vacuum flask and two white-enamelled mugs, handing them to Keth, asking him to hold them steady while he poured.

'Any idea where we are going?' Keth asked casually.

594

'Dunno. Your guess is as good as mine.' The airman, who was a sergeant, paid little respect to Keth's rank. Why should he, he silently grumbled, when the lucky so-and-so was getting the hell out of England?

Carefully he replaced the top of the flask, turning it clumsily because his hands were cold. 'Want a relief, mate?' he asked the gunner.

'Not half! Been bursting for one for the last half-hour.' He stepped down and went in search of the Elsan toilet. He was quickly back, taking his mug, lifting it in silent toast to Keth.

The coffee was hot and sweet and laced with rum and Keth smiled a reply as the liquid touched his mouth and throat and ended in a brief, warm glow just below his ribcage.

The airman grumbled his way to the front, again, the gunner took up his position, traced an arc of the sky then grinned again because here all was quiet and if his estimation of the situation was correct, they were in little danger from Luftwaffe fighters.

'You wanted to know where we were going,' he offered. 'Reckon we took on enough fuel for a long crossing.'

'America?' Something behind Keth's nose tingled.

'That's where I think we're heading. Bit of a rush trip, this one, though it counts as an op. There's a VIP up front – a civilian – and his sort usually end up in Washington.'

'Well, what d'you know?' Keth drained his mug then wrapped his fingers round it to feel its last vestiges of warmth. 'I only left there nine months ago!'

'Then it looks as if you're going back again, you lucky sod.' The gunner manipulated another sweep of the star-bright sky.

'My girl won't think so when she finds out. We were going to be married as soon as I could get long leave. I'd rather have stayed in England.'

'Ah, well – it takes all sorts . . .' Given the choice, a

posting to Washington for the duration would suit the air gunner nicely. In Washington there was food, beer and street lights, still, and no blackout curtains at windows. He knew all about it. This – if Washington it was to be – was his second flight there and the pongo needed his head examined if he wasn't pleased about it, wedding or not!

The aircraft hit an air pocket and at once he focused his attention on his gun, reminding himself that this milk run was one more operation towards his tour of thirty, after which he would be given time off flying for a few months.

'My thirteenth op. this one,' he confided, feeling the benefit already of the coffee and what it contained.

'Did you have to tell me that?' Keth grinned.

'Not really.' Usually, aircrews did not talk too much about their thirteenth operational flight until it was behind them. 'I feel lucky tonight, though. I felt lucky when I flew my first one. They say that when you've got the first and the thirteenth out of the way, you've a good chance of making it to the end of a tour.' A few more milk runs like this one and life would be one lovely piece of cake. 'Does your girl know about this?'

'She does not! They let me leave a letter behind, but there's no knowing when the censor will release it. She'll be worrying before very much longer – not hearing from me, I mean.'

'What's her name?'

'Daisy. She's a Wren.'

The engines took on a different sound and Keth held his breath, listening. The rear-gunner leaned towards the dim blue light, pulling back the sleeve of his jacket, squinting at his watch.

'We're losing height. Reckon I was right. It's somewhere in America. Usually we know where we're heading, but we've got this civvy bod on board, so only the pilot and navigator were briefed.'

'What makes you so certain?'

'Oh, flying time, plus speed and the position of the stars – when I could see them. Simple, really. Looks as if you've landed yourself a cushy number, mate.'

'Depends on the way you look at it,' Keth shrugged as the aircraft shuddered and bucked. 'What the hell was that?'

'Crosswind. No problem. Look – lights! Over to the right.'

Keth rose stiffly to his feet, inching towards the gun turret, peering with inexperienced eyes through the mist on the Perspex as the window ice began to melt. He could see only the faintest glow and intermittently, too, as they slipped into and out of cloud.

'I'll take your word for it.' He inched back to his small, cramped space, wishing he were important enough to have merited a seat.

The air gunner relaxed. Already he felt warmer. They would make a good touchdown. It had been a lucky thirteenth op.

'Daisy, you said? What's she like? A cute blonde popsy?'

'As a matter of fact she is.' Keth closed his eyes, holding tightly to a metal rib at his side as crosswinds hit them again. He heard the *clunk* of the undercarriage dropping in readiness for landing. The mixture as before, he thought. Washington, here I come! Again!

And for how long, this time?

Alice climbed the stairs to find Daisy in the spare bedroom, gazing unblinking at the wedding dress, the sheet that had covered it on the floor at her feet.

'It's a pity, Mam,' she whispered, making no effort to disguise the unhappiness that dulled her eyes, 'that you worked so hard to finish it.'

'Worked so hard? To my way of thinking some things are a joy to do, young lady. But hadn't you better tell me what's bothering you? You've hardly said a word since you got home. Has something happened at Epsom House?'

'No. Nothing changes there, except the Plot – and the watches. Nothing would *dare* happen.' Tears filled her eyes and she brushed them away impatiently. 'Sorry, Mam, it's just that we had a pig of a watch last night.' And made worse that they seemed to have been up and down all night to street level for air, because the air-conditioning had broken down completely. 'I'll go to bed early tonight. I'll be fine after a decent night's sleep. You never sleep properly in the daytime, you know.'

'I do know,' Alice said obliquely. 'And is it because of Keth that you're sighing over that dress?'

'Why? How did –' Daisy spun round. 'I mean, what makes you think there's something the matter between Keth and me?'

'Don't evade the issue.' Begging questions was not allowed. 'And before you turn your back on me so you needn't look me in the face, let me tell you that Polly is worried, too.'

'She is?'

'Polly was saying only this morning that there hasn't been a letter nor a phone call from Keth for well over a week and that's never happened before – not since he came back to England. And you haven't heard, either, have you?'

'I have now. There was a letter from him yesterday, but it was only a short note. I suppose you'd call it a be-careful-what-you-write letter, telling me I wasn't going to hear from him for a couple of weeks because he was off on another of his courses. But it wasn't like his usual letters. He wanted me to read between the lines, I know it.'

'So did you?'

'Yes, and I think I'm not going to see him for a long time. That's why I came to look at my dress, I suppose.'

'And weep?'

'All right – and have a little grizzle.'

598

'So how long is this dress going to hang here, then?' Alice picked up the sheet, draping it carefully over the wedding dress. 'How long will Keth be away?'

'I don't know. I haven't even got an address to write to yet. Maybe when I do there'll be a way of getting past the censor – a word here, a hint there . . .'

'And what do you really think?'

'I don't know, Mam. A week's leave last June on my birthday and then none since, unless you count those two days. All I'm sure about is that I'm never going to know the half of what Keth is up to.'

'You can't mean he's spying!' Alice's eyes flew wide with concern.

'No. I'm as sure as I can be that he isn't in Intelligence. But we were tempting fate, getting the dress finished. It was asking for bad luck.'

'Well, there you are wrong, miss, because it *isn't* finished,' Alice announced triumphantly. 'Do you really think I would be so stupid?' She fumbled for a sleeve, holding it up. 'Look! A button not sewn on yet, and the same on the other sleeve. And those two buttons won't be sewn on till your wedding morning! Now that's taken care of the bad luck, so what have you to say about that?'

'I'd say,' Daisy's smile transformed her face, 'that I've got the best mother in the world who always makes it come right. And I'm going to give her a hug and a kiss, then go and tell Polly about the letter I got yesterday. And I won't let her think I'm worried because I *will* hear again soon. You never know, he might really be on a course.'

'And after the bothy?' Meaningfully, Alice quirked an eyebrow.

'After that, Mam, I'll talk a walk as far as the elms, and tell it to the rooks . . .'

When Daisy returned to Hellas House she checked the letterboard, something she did automatically, then let go a gasp of relief at the sight of the envelope with the red stamp of the censor on it.

'Keth!'

He was back at his code-breaking place! Sheer happiness pumped through her. How silly of her to have worried! A smile lifted the corners of her mouth. Spying, indeed!

She wondered if Lyn was back yet from Llangollen and decided to read her letter in a quiet corner of the common room. And when she had read it, then disbelievingly read it again, she closed her eyes tightly and breathed in and out slowly and deeply, to steady the despairing thudding of her heart.

Snatching up her greatcoat and respirator she ran up the stairs. She needed to weep, to slam doors or maybe, if Lyn was there, to share her anguish. Perhaps telling would be better than weeping because Keth *was* safe. Miles and miles away from her, but safe. And she had known, hadn't she, when an inexplicable need made her want to look at her wedding dress, that all was not well? She and Keth were too close for her not to know, not to reach out with her heart and gather in his unhappiness.

Lyn was sitting cross-legged on the top bunk. She looked very happy and smiled and said, 'You're back, then?'

'Of course I'm back! Who do you think this is – Marley's ghost?'

'Okay. Keep your hair on. I refuse to let you get me rattled because I had an absolutely wonderful forty-eight, and not even your sour face is going to spoil it. By the way, there's a letter from Keth. That should cheer you up!'

'Yes. I got it, thanks.'

'And?'

'And still no news.' There was, but she couldn't tell Lyn; not just yet when tears still threatened. And Lyn looked so happy that there must be good news for the telling and good news was so rare, these days, that no one had the right to spoil it. 'So tell me – why the dreamy expression?'

She lifted her chin and forced a smile. 'Have you heard a buzz? Is the *Maggie* due in?'

'The *Maggie* has been in, over the weekend. They'll be back at sea, by now.'

'So that's why you said you might give Llangollen a miss? You guessed?'

'Sort of.' Lyn had not guessed. She had known and said nothing. The despatch rider from Cabin 2 told her.

'Took signals to HMS *Penrose* this afternoon – she's just berthed in Salthouse Dock, Lyn. Thought you and Daisy would want to know.'

Only she hadn't told Daisy, which wasn't sneaky, exactly, all being fair in love and war. Besides, she had wanted Drew to herself. She had something to tell him, *must* tell him; something she hadn't told Daisy yet. But you couldn't sweep the fact of being illegitimate under the rug; not in a family like the Suttons of Rowangarth. Best Drew should know, she had decided; give him the chance to back away from someone whose pedigree might disqualify her from being an acceptable Sutton wife. She belonged to Auntie Blod – really belonged, now – but if having a skeleton in the family cupboard wasn't on, then best she should know it whilst it was still just possible for her to cope with the despair of losing Drew.

'Sort of,' she said again. 'Lucky, wasn't I? Drew and I hitched a lift to Auntie Blod's; only for the day, but she was tickled pink to meet him. And I wanted them to meet because – well, there's something you should know, you see. I should have told you before but –'

'But you didn't, so you're going to tell me now,' Daisy whispered, all at once apprehensive, because *that* couldn't have happened between Lyn and Drew; it just couldn't!

'I found out when I got the forty-eight hours' compassionate and I decided I wanted to tell Drew first. I thought it was important that I should. I saw the setup at Rowangarth when I stayed at your place, Daisy. It almost threw me – that old house and Drew being Sir Andrew, really, and not just the Drew I knew.'

'So? What was it that Drew must know?' Daisy ran her tongue round her lips. 'You and he – you didn't – well, did something happen, I mean, and you never told me?'

'Happen? Oh, *that*!' She laughed as if she thought it funny. 'You mean *did* we – *have* we? Oh, Daisy! You think I wanted to tell Drew I might be pregnant? Now what chance has there been of that ever happening?'

'None, come to think of it. Anyway, Drew wouldn't be so stupid.'

'No.' Lyn's laughter ended abruptly. 'I reckon you're right. Your brother would marry a girl before he bedded her. It's the way he is and I admire him for it. But then I wondered, once he knew, if it would have to be all over between us.'

'Knew *what*, for heaven's sake?' Daisy flung, because whatever it was had been said over the weekend at Auntie Blod's. 'And what do you mean about it being all over between you?'

'Not being socially acceptable – that's what I mean.'

'But why shouldn't you be? They've never been snobbish – well, not the Rowangarth Suttons. You should know that, Lyn. And why should you be socially unacceptable? *Tell me!*'

'Okay. Do you want it straight between the eyes, or will you have it gently in words of one syllable?'

'*Whichever!*'

'Right, then!' Lyn straightened her long legs, then slipped elegantly from the top bunk to face her cabin-mate. 'I'm illegitimate.'

'I see. So what?' Daisy felt mildly cheated. 'Someone had you and you were adopted. Sad, I suppose, but hardly your fault, Carmichael.'

All at once she realized that Lyn's news was nowhere

near so traumatic as she had feared. Drew and Lyn hadn't been lovers. The affair that was mostly one-sided had not developed into a mutual blazing passion.

'So you don't want to know, then? Can I have your attention for just long enough to explain that –'

'Sorry, Lyn. And I really do want to know – why you think being illegitimate matters so much, I mean.'

'Think? I *know* it matters. Having a child out of wedlock just isn't on and you know it! And being illegitimate isn't on, either. And I suppose that if I'd been *ordinary* illegitimate and shoved into an orphanage for adoption it might not have mattered quite so much, but I'm Auntie Blod's, you see.'

'*Auntie Blod had you?* But I don't understand!'

'I'm really Lyndis Meredith, father unknown – or that's how it was, it seems, in the home for unmarried mothers where I was born. But I got adopted, didn't I?'

'By your mother's – your natural mother's sister. You thought all along she and her husband were your real mother and father and not your aunt and uncle? Perfectly understandable I'd say.'

'Except that my father really was – *is* – my father, you see. Rather messy, don't you think? That's why I had to tell Drew.'

'But your father and Auntie Blod! It must have been awful for her, giving you up. But she's got you back now, hasn't she?'

'She has. And I'm very happy about it. But do you want to know about – *all* about it?'

'Of course I do.' Her unhappiness pushed to the back of her mind, Daisy lay back on her bunk, hands behind her head. 'But before you go any further, you're still socially acceptable to me – you and Auntie Blod both.'

'Bless you, lovely girl!' Lyn looked at her watch. 'But it's time for standeasy. What say we eat it downstairs – it'll be warmer in the common room.'

'Anywhere you say,' Daisy murmured. 'And after that, I've got news for you, Lyn – about Keth.'

'Who else?' Lyn grinned, suddenly happy. 'Let's get a move on, though, before the gannets scoff the lot!'

'So tell me,' Daisy demanded when they were settled in the quietest corner of the room, 'how did Drew take it?'

'He was just fine. And he likes Auntie Blod, by the way. When we were alone – we got shooed off to wait for the travelling fish-and-chip van, would you believe – Drew told me something similar had happened before to you and him.'

'It did. I can still remember it. Aunt Julia and Drew were staying at Windrush with us – in Hampshire, that was. Looking back, it was obvious that Mam and Aunt Julia had arranged it between them to tell us that Drew wasn't really Aunt Julia's. He'd started asking questions, you see. Drew took it quite well that Mam was his real mother, but I couldn't bear to think there had been anyone else in Mam's life, you see. She and Dada were so in love I simply couldn't understand why she had been married before.

'So I slammed out and found Dada and he sat me on his knee and explained everything – how he had been reported killed in action and oh, it must have been awful, Lyn, him getting home eventually when the war was over and finding her a widow. It was Drew, really, who made me accept it and made me glad I had a brother. He's an absolute love – so gentle. Like his father, Mam always says. Sir Giles was a good man – even Dada isn't jealous that he and Mam were once married.' She licked her finger, sticky from jam, then said, very softly, 'So do you want my news, now?'

'About Keth's letter, you mean?'

'Keth's letter from America!'

'America!' Lyn gasped, then lowering her voice she said,

'But how do you know? Did he tell you so? If he wrote that the censor would've cut it out. I thought he was going on another course.'

'Well, he wasn't. They sent for him at eleven o'clock at night and told him to get his kit packed; said he could write a letter and that it would be released later.'

'When they would know he'd have arrived?'

'Yes. The one I got last Thursday.' She dipped in her pocket for the letter. 'Listen to this bit, then tell me where you think he is.

'". . . I rang Mrs Amelia. I'd forgotten how easy it is to get through on the phone there. We had a long chat and she said I was to go and see them; that my bed was still ready and waiting . . ." He lived with them when he wasn't in college, you see. I suppose he'll spend some of his leaves in Kentucky, now.'

She stopped, screwing up her eyes against the tears, because the pain was back; the pain of losing him again and not knowing when she would see him and hold him and close her eyes when he whispered that he loved her.

'It mightn't be for long, old love.' Lyn reached for her hand, wishing she hadn't been so smug, so happy about Drew not caring that she was illegitimate. 'And can you be sure he's in America?'

'I'm sure.' Daisy sniffed inelegantly then turned over a page of Keth's letter. 'He says that Bas is still doing his training. He'd volunteered for the Army Air Corps – I think that's the same as being aircrew, over here – and Bas's hands failed him, it seems. Mrs Amelia was very glad about it, Keth said, though she couldn't understand why his hands had got him through veterinary school – using instruments, I suppose she meant – yet weren't fit for flying.'

'You're talking about the fire at Pendenys Place when his grandmother died?'

'That's it. Seems everything happens for a purpose. Anyway, Bas is fit enough to drive, Keth said, so he's going into Transport – something like our Royal Army Service Corps. And Keth said Mrs Amelia told him that Bas had volunteered for service overseas and that Kitty said if he was going to get in on the war, then so was she!'

'She's volunteered for the Wrens!'

'No. That would be too tame for our Kitty – and I believe they call them Waves over there. She's volunteered to entertain American servicemen overseas. I suppose it's like our ENSA.'

'So both Bas and his sister could end up over here?'

'They could. On the other hand, they could end up on the other side of the world or serve out the war in America. It might be nice, though, if the Clan could get together just once, though it can't if Keth is on the other side of the Atlantic. What *is* he doing in America, Lyn, because even though he didn't actually say so in his letter it's obvious that he's back there.'

'Reckon he is, and you'll just have to tell yourself that at least he's out of harm's way. I know the place he was stationed down south was very hush-hush, but the Krauts might have got wind of it and that would have been that! They'd have wiped it out – just like Coventry! And I'm sorry for being so happy about the weekend. I wouldn't have been so cockahoop if I'd known, truly I wouldn't.'

'That's okay, Lyn. I must just tell myself that he might have been in Singapore, or Hong Kong, or even be fighting in North Africa, or the Burma jungle. Only I hope that Mam will have taken my wedding dress to Rowangarth and hung it in the sewing room, or somewhere. If she doesn't, it's going to be murder going home and seeing it there. I'm going to be old and past it before we can get married. I wish we'd taken the plunge and had a quiet wedding.'

'Well, you know what they say about wishes being horses and beggars riding, don't you? But cheer up. He went suddenly and he can come back every bit as quickly. It's the way They work. It's a funny old war.'

'It's a bloody awful war and I'm sick of it!'

Daisy jumped to her feet, took the stairs two at a time and flung into Cabin 4A, throwing herself on the bottom bunk with such anger that the flimsy structure rattled and shook.

Then she buried her face in her pillow and wept.

40

In a mellow mood, Tom made for the fallen tree. Daisy was coming home on long leave next week and Alice already fussing and airing her bed with hot-water bottles, and bricks heated in the fire oven.

It would be good to have the lass back for a little while and now she seemed to have accepted Keth's being sent abroad, though none of them was supposed to know he'd landed on his feet, safe in America again.

Tom unscrewed the vacuum flask Alice had put in his game bag. Alice was like that. If the breakfast teapot had not been emptied, then he got it in a flask with orders for it to be drunk, every drop, since young men were being torpedoed every day and night to bring it to us!

He liked to sit on the fallen tree. Just to sit. Not even thinking, though it was hard not to think, these days. The war got into your head and it was the very devil pushing it out so he could concentrate on the ploughman and his team of shire horses, plodding, heads nodding, up and down the far field.

He blew on the steaming, sugarless liquid, realizing that even though they were into the first week of March, things were very backward. Not a daffodil out yet, though he had seen celandines and snowdrops and pussy willow catkins and, beside the stile that divided Brattocks Wood from Rowangarth's wild garden, a clump of coltsfoot, glowing brightly like little yellow stars.

He shook open the morning paper Alice had obligingly put in his game bag with the flask. A five-minute read, then he would finish walking the rounds, making a note of any new nests and if the pheasants were sitting tightly and undisturbed. The weather was still cold and vixens suckling young cubs; a hen pheasant, sitting wild and reluctant to leave her nest, was fair taking for a marauding fox with young to feed.

The first thing to note in the morning paper, of course, was the time of the blackout. Tonight, it began at eight o'clock, which was a heartening sign when in November it had started a little after five. And then he saw the headline and gave a howl of rage.

So Alice had been right all along! It was why, like as not, she had slipped the paper in with his flask. Knowing him as she did, she was giving him time to read and digest it and be over the worst of his anger before he got back to Keeper's for his dinner.

'CONSCRIPTION FOR WOMEN' said the headline. 'All women between the ages of twenty and thirty are to be asked' – 'Asked!' Tom snorted – 'to register at their local Labour Exchange for direction into war work.'

It went on to report that it was widely accepted in Whitehall that a great proportion of those registering would be directed into the armed forces.

Directed, indeed! His mellow mood was gone. How about young lasses brought up sheltered as his own daughter had been, all at once pitchforked into uniform and mixing with men – aye, and some of them wed and missing their wives! – and without the eyes of caring parents on them?

But your own daughter, you great daft-head, has been in the armed forces for more than a year, whispered a voice that sounded uncommonly like that of his wife, *and no harm has come to her.*

No *moral* harm, Tom conceded, folding the paper. He did not want to read any more, and right as Alice was and had been, he still didn't hold with young lasses having to wear uniforms and march and salute and be able to stay out late without first asking permission of their parents!

And that was only the tip of the iceberg. When he got home Alice would say to him, 'But *I* went to war, Tom. I was on active service. And you've got to remember that this is 1942, and young ladies aren't chaperoned any longer!'

He rose to his feet, clicked his tongue for his dogs to follow him, then set off towards the pastures. Women went to war. Women got killed, sometimes, or maybe landed in trouble by men with no thought for tomorrow. It had been like that in his war and now, happen, it could well be the same again. Nothing changed. The seasons came and went; hen pheasants still nested and hungry vixens still hunted to feed their young. And wars happened. It was the way of the world.

'I see,' said Olga Petrovska, 'that we are to have our clothing coupons cut by six at the next issue. How are we supposed to clothe ourselves decently, will you tell me? I buy a coat and I have a miserable four coupons left to last for six months! What can I buy with four coupons?'

'You could,' Anna Sutton considered, 'buy four ounces of knitting wool or two pairs of stockings. Or you could buy more clothes if you were to do without a winter coat. Do you really need one? You have your furs.'

'I brought my furs with me from Petersburg a quarter of a century ago!'

'Furs last, Mama. The sable still looks good. Some women I know would sell their souls for it. You don't need a winter coat!'

'Are you lecturing your mother?'

'Do you know,' Anna smiled, 'I rather think I am. You should think of Tatiana and that London is being bombed again. I very much doubt the Londoners will worry too much about six clothing coupons.'

'Your daughter, Anna Petrovska, left home of her own accord and against the advice of her elders! It is her own fault, but she is stubborn and will never admit how wrong she was.'

'It would make no difference now if she went down on her knees and begged to be allowed to come home. She is doing work of national importance and if she were to leave it she would have to register at the Labour Exchange and could well end up in London again, helping manhandle a barrage balloon! Soon, Mama, women of thirty to forty will have to register for war work. The newspapers say so. Even I might find myself being directed into a factory!'

The Countess threw her newspaper to the floor, because there was no answer to foolish remarks such as that!

'In Russia, in my day, a newspaper editor dared not have printed such dreadful news. The Czar would have –'

But the Czar-God-rest-him was dead and now her beloved St Petersburg was dying just as surely. Stubborn to the end, her beautiful city still held out against the Nazis. She wondered if her house on the riverbank near the Admiralty was still there or if it had been blasted into rubble. Once, just to think of her house, and of Peterhof, and that Igor and Anna or Tatiana, maybe, might one day return to claim them had sustained her in her darkest, most homesick hours. Now, perhaps, what remained of their homes might not be worth the paper the title deeds were written on. It was a very sad world; especially so when she had never once thought that the world she took for granted could ever come to an end. Resolutely she closed her eyes.

'I think I will sleep a little,' she whispered.

'Well, what do you know, Reverend!' Julia smiled as she laid down the morning paper. 'I've just been counting. It's the third time I've done it and there is no doubt at all about it!'

'Tell me.' Nathan folded his napkin then pushed back his chair.

'That Mother Nature is up to her tricks again. In our war, it was a known fact that more boy babies than girls were born – as if she knew, sort of –'

'That there is a balance to be righted, you mean?'

'I mean that today,' Julia pointed to the births announcements in the paper, 'of seventeen babies born, ten were boys. And yesterday it was nine boys and six girls and the day before – it must have been a busy night for the midwives – of twenty-one announcements, twelve were boys and –'

'Nine were girls,' Nathan interrupted, 'which will be absolutely lovely for those girl babies a few years from now, because there'll be a ratio of four men to three of them. But more important right now is where is the key to the church safe? I'm always losing the damn thing!'

Since the plane crash when the church might have ended up a smoking ruin with the parish hall, the silver and valuables from All Souls' had been brought to Rowangarth and kept deep in the meat cellar because, as Julia reasoned, there was little use for meat cellars when a week's ration could be eaten at one meal.

'The key is kept with all the house keys – you know it is.' She had tied a label to it with 'Stableyard lavatory' written on it, just to confound anyone with designs on silver too precious and beautiful ever to be stolen and melted down.

'Ah, yes. I remember.' The smile he was unable to suppress lighted his face and all at once he was young again, Julia thought, and he and Giles telling her that Denniston House was haunted because she was intruding on the closeness that was theirs. 'I'll skip Communion this morning,' she said. 'Think I'll bike into Creesby instead, and have a word with the butcher.'

'What about?' he called absently, already halfway through the door, in search of the church silver.

'The rabbits we let him have. He just might find his

supply drying up if Rowangarth doesn't get a few more sausages in future!' she called after him.

He hadn't heard her, of course, which was maybe as well since he'd best not know his less-than-saintly wife was about to indulge in a spot of double-dealing. After all, the wife of a vicar should never stoop to blackmail; not even for a pound of off-the-ration sausages! Or should she?

'Want to see the paper?' Lyndis asked.

'No thanks.' Lyndis was an avid reader of newspapers; Daisy was not. 'You tell me . . .'

'Well, just listen to this!' Lyn smiled wickedly. 'A bloke has been sentenced to five years' hard labour for getting sugar on the black market. And serve him right!'

Selling – or buying, come to that – on the black market was simply not done, despite the shortages. Auntie Blod said she wouldn't touch so much as a grain of sugar or anything else that had to be brought in by sea. It was like helping the Germans to sink our merchant ships, she said.

Yet many with a lesser conscience bought sugar with little thought for merchant seamen, Lyn brooded, and margarine and butter and cheese and anything they could get their grubby little hands on. And she agreed with the judge who declared that when the new Act, allowing a maximum sentence of fourteen years' hard labour for black-market dealings, became law, anyone found guilty of such crimes in *his* courtroom could expect that maximum sentence!

'Mm. Couldn't agree more.'

'And it says here,' Lyn continued, 'that more United States troops have arrived in Britain. I suppose they'll be part of a build-up for when we go back.'

'Go back to Europe? Invade?' Daisy squeaked. 'When we still might be invaded ourselves?'

'We won't, you know; not now Hitler's got himself in a mess in Russia.'

'So one day you think we'll invade France, or Holland?'

'We'll have to or the war is never going to end, though how we'll manage it,' Lyn frowned, 'I'll be blowed if I know. And it says that six troopships full of GIs have landed in Melbourne to help defend Australia against the Japs. Damn' stupid when Australia sent their troops here to help fight Hitler. What a crazy way to fight a war!'

'Then I think they should send the Australian soldiers and airmen back home,' Daisy considered. 'I mean – would you want to come halfway across the world to fight for a country you'd never seen; a country that probably sent your great-great-grandfather there in chains in the first place!'

'Mm. But be fair. Nobody thought for a minute the Japs would come into the war, now did they?'

'Nobody thinks about anything. Nobody thought Hitler would march into Poland. Mr Chamberlain said he wouldn't, but he did!' Daisy folded her sheets and pillow cases and towels neatly. Thursday was clean sheets and towels day. 'And hurry up with your bunk, then I'll take your stuff down with mine, and collect the clean ones.

'By the way, how are you fixed for cash? *Gone with the Wind* is coming to the Forum, soon, and they are taking advance bookings. What say we work our watches out and book for when we are on mornings? They say it's going to be in Liverpool for at least two months. Minnie from Cabin 4 told me she saw it twice in London when she was on leave and she's going to see it again here.'

'She would.' They were all slightly loopy in Cabin 4. 'I mean, who would want to see a flick *three* times?'

'Well – it *is* in colour, Lyn, and it lasts for three hours, so they have an interval for you to stretch your legs and have a wee if you want to, I believe.'

'If it lasts for three hours we're going to need a late pass, had you thought? What say we book an extra seat, then if the *Maggie* is alongside, Drew can come too.' To think of three hours holding hands with Telegraphist Sutton in the intimate darkness of the Forum picture house was little short of bliss.

'And what if he isn't in dock? We've got a ticket on our hands then, and they don't come cheap.'

'Oh, live dangerously!' Lyn scolded, bundling up her sheets and towels. 'We'd soon get rid of the ticket. You take these downstairs and I'll turn the mattresses.'

'Had you thought,' Daisy said from the doorway, 'that Bas might be amongst the American soldiers who have landed here?'

'I hadn't, but he well might. On the other hand, of course, he might just now be eyeing up the talent in Melbourne.' Sebastian Sutton was of no interest to Lyndis Carmichael. No man was, but Drew.

Drew sat in the kitchen rocker and let the feeling of home-coming wash over him.

'This was always Mrs Shaw's chair,' he said softly.

'Aye, and she'd have baked cherry scones, today, you being home on leave,' replied Tilda. 'You can have scones, but my stock of cherries was used up long ago. There hasn't been a sign of a glacé cherry since Lord knows when. Not even on the black market.'

'It doesn't matter, Tilda. I'm home for ten days. You've no idea how good it is.'

'I can imagine. You'll have heard, though,' she confided, 'that Keth has been sent overseas, and just when we were all looking forward to a wedding?'

'Daisy wrote to me. There was a letter waiting when we docked. She didn't tell me much, except that Keth had gone without so much as a forty-eight-hour embarkation leave. But I'll call in at the bothy. Maybe Polly will have more to tell me.'

'It's a nasty old war,' sniffed Tilda, who was chopping two of her precious hoard of prunes into tiny pieces resembling currants for the scones. 'But never mind. You're home on leave, so we'll not mention it again. And the hens have come out of the moult and are laying nicely again, so you'll be able to have a fresh egg for your breakfast, thanks to Gracie.'

'I'll look in on the garden when I've seen Polly.' Drew smiled, just to think of Gracie, who seemed always to be available to partner him at dances.

Gracie was fun – but then, so was Lyn. No! Lyn was more than fun. Sometimes, when they kissed it was – well, it wasn't like kissing your sister! Gracie was good to be with and a great dancer, but Lyn was altogether different. For one thing, she was head-turning attractive and the more so in civilian clothes, with her hair tumbling over her shoulders and not rolled into a tight pleat as regulations demanded, when in uniform.

That was how he had last seen her at her aunt's house, the day they hitched a lift to Llangollen. That was when she told him about not being who she thought she was and how she had felt to learn, after so long, who she really belonged to. She had been frank and honest about it and he understood because he, too, had two mothers . . .

'Er – sorry, Mary. What was that? Afraid I was miles away.'

'I said I'd give you a penny for your thoughts, but from the expression on your face, young sir, you were thinking about girls!'

'I was, actually.' He felt his cheeks flush red. 'Sorry.'

Tilda grinned. 'The time to be sorry is when a red-blooded, good-looking young lad like yourself *doesn't* think about girls. And talking about Daisy's wedding, I think it's about time we were talking about *yours*! And don't tell me you don't have a girl in every port,' she teased with the familiarity of one who had known him from the moment he was born.

'Every port! The only port I sail into and out of is Liverpool – but I do date a couple of Wrens, there. One called Daisy and the other one –'

'Yes?' Mary prompted.

'Well, the other one is very nice and very attractive and,' he laughed, rising to his feet, 'when I propose to her, *if* I propose to her, I promise you'll both be amongst the first to know.'

'And what is she called? Is she the girl Daisy brought home?' Tilda wanted to know, but Drew was already running, smiling, up the wooden stairs that led to the small, concealed door in the great hall. *When* he proposed to Lyn? Did he really find her so attractive?

He recalled her smile and her hair, swinging free; remembered wondering what it would be like in bed with her. Then he realized he knew nothing about making love and had been relieved to recall that Lyn once said that neither did she.

It must, he considered as he walked down the long, narrow path that led to the bothy, be a pretty traumatic thing for a girl – the first time, that was. But neither was it going to be all that easy for someone like himself, especially if he made a mess of it.

But what the heck! He was home for ten days and Gracie was fun to be with so it were best, he decided, to postpone the matter of losing his virginity until such time as it could be postponed no longer.

A land girl smiled her thanks and winked as he held the gate for her. And smiling, he winked back.

'Now tell me,' Daisy said when they were seated in the British Restaurant, 'what happened on your leave, Drew? And was Aunt Julia upset you came back a day early?'

'We-e-ll, Rowangarth doesn't change, of course.' He said it with a lightness he far from felt because unchanging Rowangarth meant more to him than ever he would have believed. Each time he went on leave the sense of home-coming was almost suffocating; each time he left it, the ache of parting became worse. 'And Mother understood – about us all coming here tonight, I mean. She said she can't wait to see the film. It's coming to York very soon. And she sent you both her love, as did Polly and Lady and Tilda and Mary. And by the way, Daiz, your wedding dress is hanging up in the sewing room at Rowangarth now, and I didn't see it,' he hastened. 'It was covered over with a sheet.'

'Then I'm glad.' Daisy let go a shuddering sigh. 'It's so beautiful that I want to wear it, you see. For Keth. It's like being very thirsty and all you are allowed is to look at a glass of water. This shepherd's pie isn't half bad, you know.' She swallowed hard on the surge of tears that seemed always there when she spoke about Keth. 'Soup, shepherd's pie and jelly for afters. And for only one-and-sixpence. Better than we get at Hellas House.'

'It's okay, Daiz. You don't have to do the stiff-upper-lip act with me.' Drew reached out for her hand. 'And I know this might sound a bit stupid, but had you thought of volunteering for overseas service? You might just end up at Washington because I'm sure that's where Keth is.'

'And do you think I haven't thought about it? There's a teleprinter at Epsom House. It's a direct line to Washington and I'm allowed to operate it now. Wouldn't it be wonderful,' she sighed, 'if I could type out a message to him on it and he was there, at the other end, and could send one back?'

'And you'd get your head in your hands if you were caught talking on teleprinter lines, especially to Washington! Even I know that,' Lyn protested. 'You'd be at defaulter's before you could say Careless Talk Costs Lives!'

'I know, but wouldn't it be great. And I wouldn't ask for an overseas draft because you never get the place you want to go to. They do it on purpose.'

'Is Keth still code-breaking?' Drew asked because Daisy's

voice had gone trembly and there were two bright red spots high on her cheeks.

'I can't be sure, though he did say in a letter that he was doing exactly the same job as before, and the censor didn't cut it out of his letter. I suppose that now America is in the war, they are at it, too – poaching enemy signals and trying to break their code.'

'But can you tell me *how*?' Lyn demanded, a frown creasing her forehead. 'What I'm trying to say is that the Japs are first and foremost America's enemy, so it's likely they will be monitoring *their* signals. But the Japs write in funny little squiggles – so is their morse code the same as ours or do they transmit in squiggly morse, so to speak?'

'That is something I can't tell you, but it'll be worth finding out when I get back on board. And talk about being lucky. I reported back to Flag Officer, the *Maggie* being at sea, or so I thought, and they told me she had just come in again. So I dumped my kit on board and found she won't be sailing again till tomorrow, on the evening tide.'

'But what do they do when you are on leave, Drew? I know you work watch about, you and your oppo., but he can't be expected to stay awake twenty-four hours a day, now can he? Or you, for that matter, when Knocker's on leave.'

'Agreed. But even the Admiralty get it right, sometimes. There's a pool of spare crew at Flag Officer's. They sent a relief for me.' Drew reached for his dish of utility jelly. 'So you don't think you'll be applying for foreign, Daisy?'

'No. I shall just sit tight and hope he gets back, somehow.'

'Then cheer up, and eat up, and we'll see if we can find a pub with beer to sell. What time do we have to be there?'

'It starts at half-past six, so we'd better be in our seats pretty soon if we are to catch the organ and the cartoon. And there might be a Newsreel.' Never having seen a three-hour-long film in glorious technicolor, Lyn could not be sure. 'But do let's hurry. They say *Gone with the Wind* cost the earth to make; millions and millions, I believe. And the dresses are out of this world! I did hear that Scarlett O'Hara is more in love with an old house than any of the men in her life. Can you believe that, now?'

And Drew, when they were settled in the cosy half-dark in the Forum picture house and he had entwined Lyn's fingers in his own and kissed their tips, secretly, so that Daisy should not see, thought about what she had said. And yes, he *could* believe that someone could be in love with an old house. His grandmother had loved Rowangarth and his mother loved it deeply for a while because there had been nothing else to give her love to, except himself. And Kitty was once supposed to have said – though not in his hearing – 'I just love that old Rowangarth. Guess I love it so much I'd even marry Drew to get it!' Dear Kitty. Such a show-off she had been.

The soul-tearing sound of *Gone with the Wind*'s theme music rose and swelled to fill the auditorium and Lyn sang softly to it, loving Drew, loving the whole world. Then she turned to smile at him, leaning closer.

And it made him wonder whether, when he asked her to marry him, as one day he might, she would come to love Rowangarth too. As he and Kitty loved it.

41

Julia unfastened her headscarf and flopped down in the sagging leather chair in the corner of the library. She liked this room. Sometimes she would sit here, unspeaking, whilst Nathan wrote sermons or letters or frowned over the parish accounts with too little to show on the credit side.

She liked the library because in it she could be near to Giles, her brother. Here, before the war – the Great War – turned their lives upside down, was where Giles had liked to be. He liked the smell of it, he always said; of musty books, mostly in need of repair, and applewood fires and beeswax polish. Yet mostly, Julia yearned, he had liked the quiet of it and being shut away from an estate he didn't really want to run and which, he had thought then, would never be his.

Yet now Rowangarth belonged to Drew, the rape child Giles had taken for his son; Drew, who had grown up Sutton fair and bore no resemblance to the man who fathered him.

'Faces?' Nathan said softly, laying down his pen. 'What is so awful to make you frown so? Your face will stay like it, you know,' he teased. 'Want to tell me?'

'I was thinking about Giles and how he loved this room and how he was so very much against war, and killing.'

'Yet he went to war, Julia.'

Nathan did not like her to dwell on her own war and the awfulness of it. Usually, it meant she was worrying about Drew.

'Yes.' She shut down her thoughts. 'I'm going to the

village to collect the new ration books for one or two who can't queue for them. I do try to be a good vicar's wife – well, sometimes.'

'Then don't try too hard. I might stop wanting you if you got too holy. Now be off, woman, and let me finish this sermon. And don't forget to post Drew's letter. Charity begins at home, remember. By the way, Mrs Sutton – I love you!'

He smiled. She had not heard him, but he would tell her tonight – or tomorrow, or tomorrow night. When you were getting older, it seemed there was all the time in the world. Not like the young. For them, there was no tomorrow. All at once, he was glad he was fifty-five.

The phone began to ring and through the open door he heard Julia answering it.

'Hullo! Rowangarth. Yes, Winnie, I'll hold on.'

He laid down his pen again. Drew, perhaps? He pushed back his chair and walked into the hall.

'Long-distance, from Liverpool – will we accept the charge? It'll be Drew – out of money,' Julia whispered, hand over the receiver. 'Who is that? *Who* . . . ?'

'Darling!' She turned excitedly. 'It's Bas! He's in England! Sorry, Bas. Just telling Uncle Nathan. Now for goodness' sake, how did you land up in Liverpool, of all places? You did? *No* . . . !'

Nathan, smiling broadly, sat down on the bottom stair, watching his wife's joy with pleasure.

'Bas! Of course you can!' Julia smiled. 'Rowangarth is your home whilst you are over here, don't forget. And Bas! Try to remember this number? Lark Lane, 1322. It's Daisy's phone number. She'll be at home at Keeper's this weekend, but if you get to Liverpool again, try to phone her? Oh Bas, I just can't believe it . . .'

She wiped away a tear, replacing the phone as the pips sounded and the line went dead.

'I take it,' Nathan smiled, 'that we are about to be

occupied by the United States Army. Was that really Bas? In England?'

'It was. He arrived two days ago with the US 8th Air Force, not the Army. He didn't say where he's stationed, but he'll be writing. Anyway, he said he'd driven his colonel to Liverpool and was stooging around waiting for him when he saw the phone box. He reversed the charges because he hasn't got any English money yet. And Nathan, he said could he come and see us when he gets leave and I said I'd be very annoyed if he didn't! Don't you see – I've been hoping and wishing and praying for my Clan to be together again, and there's Bas planning to visit us!'

'But one of your Clan, darling, is on the wrong side of the Atlantic, still. Two, if you count Kitty.'

'Kitty will get over here! She'll find a way!'

'So how about Keth, then?' Nathan cupped her face in his hands, whispering a kiss on the tip of her nose. 'It won't be a proper Clan without Keth, now will it?'

'Then I'll have to hope and wish and pray him back home again, won't I? And there's one good thing about it all – from Bas's point of view, that is. He won't have to stay at Pendenys, this time around!'

She was through the door and away, doubtless to tell Alice, Nathan smiled. And who was to know that before so very much longer, the entire village, starting with the ration-book queue in Winnie Hallam's front room, would know that Sebastian Sutton was in England and planning to visit Rowangarth.

He turned, shaking his head, making for the library again and a sermon that was going to take a lot of writing today, because another of the Sutton Clan was back and Bas would be the topic of conversation for a long time to come.

There was a tap on the study door, which opened to admit Mary, carrying a tea tray. Yet again he laid down his pen.

'Your elevenses, Mr Nathan. Shall I pour for you?'

'Please, Mary. And hold the pot very carefully because you'll never believe this.'

'So tell me,' Mary smiled. 'That phone call . . . ?'

'Was from Bas. He's in England!'

'Young Sebastian? From Kentucky?' She put down the teapot with a clatter. 'You wouldn't mind pouring for yourself, Reverend? Just this once? I've got to tell Tilda!' With a whisk of blue cotton skirts, she was gone.

Nathan picked up the teapot. 'Women! What were you thinking about, God,' he whispered, 'when you started messing around with that rib?'

But he was smiling, when he said it.

The bow of HMS *Penrose* came down with a slap and the little ship shuddered, then sailed on towards the port of Liverpool. It was always choppy, Drew reasoned, where the River Mersey met the sea, and especially when the tide was on the turn.

He swung the dial of his set to port-wave frequency then turned as the door of the confined space that was the wireless office opened.

'Hi.' Drew greeted his opposite number. 'Can't sleep or something?'

'No point. We'll be alongside in a couple of hours, provided we get a berth sharpish.' Like Drew, he wore old, comfortable clothes. Bell-bottom trousers and a navy polo-neck sweater. Best uniforms were only worn on official occasions and for going ashore in. It was one of the things Drew liked about being on a small ship – and they didn't come much smaller than the *Maggie*. Little ships were friendly, though with a small crew you had to get on with everyone or it was a bad job all round. On a boat as small as the *Maggie*, there was nowhere to hide.

'Going ashore, Knocker?' Eric White, the *Maggie*'s other telegraphist, had not heard his baptismal name since first entering Plymouth Barracks as a raw recruit.

'You bet. There's this lovely little Waaf got a passion for me.'

'Nice, is she?'

'She'll do, until something better comes along.'

'Is that what you do, then – play the field?' Drew fidgeted with the carbon paper in the signal pad beside him.

'Of course. Just like you. 'Strewth, Andy, isn't one at a time enough for you – though I wouldn't mind a run ashore with either of your bits of stuff. The redhead is a stunner, but really I fancy your little blonde piece.'

'The little blonde piece,' Drew grinned, 'happens to be my sister and –'

'Your *sister*? Then how about an intro? What's her name?'

'Daisy. And no introductions. She's very much engaged to a pongo. Sorry, chum.'

'Ah, well. Worth a try, I suppose.' The telegraphist shrugged. 'I suppose the redhead is your steady?'

'Well, that's just it.' Drew felt his cheeks flush. 'I'm not sure, you see. When I'm with her, it's great. It's only times like now that I wonder.'

'Wonder what?' Knocker's eyes were bright with interest.

'You know – wonder if I want to – well . . .'

'Spend a dirty weekend with her?'

'I wouldn't put it quite like that but yes, something on those lines.' Drew shifted uncomfortably.

'Well, there's only one way to find out, isn't there?'

'It isn't as easy as that. For one thing, I don't know if she would and for another – well, I don't know if *I* would – or could.'

'Flamin' Norah! You mean you've never – you're a –' He found it hard to say the word.

'I haven't even tried. Haven't wanted to till now.' Drew looked fixedly at the dial in front of him, wishing all at once he had not started the conversation.

'But you *are* interested, Andy? You're not – well, not *pansy*, I mean?' Now Knocker's cheeks were bright red.

'Of course I'm not. It's just that the right girl hasn't come along before. At least I think Lyn's the right one. We went, once, to see her aunt. On our own. Usually, my sister comes along, so being alone with Lyn was pretty good.'

'She's taken you to meet her auntie?' Knocker shook his head dolefully. 'Well, that's it, old chum! If you aren't dead serious about a girl, you cut and run when they start taking you to meet the family. Mind, I reckon you ought to fill your boots, first. You might find you like it!'

'And I might make a mess of it. Did you make a mess of it, Knocker – the first time, I mean?'

'Can't rightly remember, Andy. I was very drunk and she was very ugly. That night was best forgotten. But you'll know, when you meet the right one. There'll be just the two of you and you'll know it's on. Best not leave it till your wedding night, if you want my opinion. It's too late then if she turns out to be frigid.'

'Lyn isn't frigid – neither am I, but as for knowing . . .' He shrugged, leaving the statement hanging in the air . . .

'Well, the way I see it, Andy, you'll know whether or not she's the right one when you realize you'll go stark, raving mad if you have to sleep another night without her.'

'I see. Thanks for the advice. Can't say I've ever got to that point, though things might sort themselves out if I spent a night *with* her.'

'Put like that, I reckon you're halfway there already, especially as you've met her auntie. Why don't you try telling your sister to stop playing gooseberry, then take it from there?'

'Because tonight, when we get ashore, my sister will be on a forty-eight-hour stand down and Lyn will have already gone to North Wales, so I'll find a room ashore, have a decent bath, then get my head down.'

'In that case, you'd better have a run ashore with me,

Andy. My Waaf could bring a friend along – make up a foursome.'

'No, thanks. Think for once I'd prefer an early night and a proper bed – *alone*! Now push off, will you! If the signal log isn't up to date when we come alongside, the old man will blow his top.'

'If that's what you really want, mate. But you don't know what you're missing. You really don't,' Knocker grinned. 'And if that redhead of yours ever gets tired of waiting – well, just point her in my direction, uh?'

'I will,' Drew laughed. 'If she ever does. Now clear off and give me a shout when you see the Liver birds.'

When, through the land haze a ship's lookout could see the birds perched atop the massive Liver Building at the Pierhead, he knew that before very much longer his ship would be safely tied up in a Liverpool dock. And those funny, fat birds made more sense, Drew frowned, than the soul-searching conversation he'd just had with Knocker, because he wasn't at all sure that filling his boots was what he wanted to do until he was sure that Lyn was the one he wanted to spend the rest of his life with.

Sleeping with a girl just for the heck of it, to carve another notch on the bedpost, so to speak, just wasn't on. On the other hand, he was becoming increasingly curious to know what life was all about; just once, maybe, before he got blown out of the water – as well he might.

There was one thing, though, that now he was very sure about. It would seem that Telegraphist Sutton was the only virgin in the ship's company – he'd bet a week's pay on it – and before so very much longer, the entire ship's company would know it!

He adjusted his head set, wiped all thoughts of Lyndis Carmichael from his mind and thought, instead, of a hot bath ashore. Or maybe a cold one would be more beneficial!

*　　*　　*

Daisy sat alone in what must once have been a very beautiful summerhouse but which now had begun to rot and break up under the untamed vigour of a creeper. Here and there were signs that the garden behind Hellas House had been beautiful, too. Grecian statues, slimed green, still showed through overgrown shrubs and bushes, and sometimes in winter it was possible to see where paths had led to stone seats and what must once have been an ornamental pond.

It was sad; just as the park opposite Hellas House was sad. Acres of it ploughed up for crops; allotments biting out areas of grass; the huge ornate Palm House in which exotic plants were slowly dying because almost all the panes of glass had been shattered by air raids.

Today, the sky was very blue, but then it was June now: 20 June, her birthday and Mam's birthday, too. It was why she was here; in case a phone call came from Mam or the call she had booked to Keeper's early this morning came through.

There had been birthday cards, of course, from Mam and Dada and Aunt Julia. And Tatty had remembered, and Drew. Yet there was nothing from Keth.

When last he was in America, when he was done with college and trying all ways he knew to get back home, he had always posted a card extra early with 'Open on 20 June' written across the back of the envelope. But no such card had arrived and she could only think that the ship carrying it had been torpedoed and sunk, which was far, far worse when you thought about it, than Keth forgetting her birthday.

'We always thought you would grow up never to know war,' Dada said the day they listened to Mr Chamberlain telling them it was to be conflict with Germany again. 'That war of ours was so terrible, people called it the war to end all wars.'

Sometimes Daisy resented her own war. It had parted

her from her parents, though she had volunteered to go, just as Mam and Dada did. And now it was parting her from Keth and parting husbands from wives and fathers from their children. And in a little place called Lidice in Czechoslovakia, the entire village had been wiped out and every man in it killed because someone had assassinated a Nazi called Reinhard Heydrich. In Poland, too, as a warning to partisans who fought a secret war against their occupiers, eighteen men were hanged and the population forced to watch it. The bodies hung there in the summer heat until they stank, said the article in the newspaper.

She closed her eyes and began to cry softly because Mam and Dada would be thinking about her just as she was thinking about them and about Brattocks Wood and the peace of it with the sun slanting long shadows through the trees; wept because of Lidice and the poor, hanging bodies in Poland and because she wanted Keth until it was like a pain inside her.

'Dwerryhouse!' called the duty Wren through an open window of the common room. 'Phone call for you. Chop chop! It's long-distance!'

'Mam!' She dashed away her tears because suddenly it was all right: whatever happened, Keeper's Cottage would always be there, and Rowangarth, no matter how long it took to beat the Germans and the nasty little Japs.

And one day, Keth *would* come back to her. Of course he would.

Today Gracie was in absolute control of Rowangarth kitchen garden. It was left in her keeping because Rowangarth's gardener and his wife had gone to Whitby to the wedding of a favourite nephew on leave from the Army. After much thought, Jack Catchpole had decided that the lass was entitled to a bit of responsibility, now and then, her being an apt pupil – and pleasant, with it.

So Gracie had fed the hens at Keeper's Cottage, unlocked

the high iron gate in the red-brick garden wall, and unlocked the potting sheds and opened the ventilation windows in the glass houses long before eight that morning.

Today, the swallows flew high in a summer-blue sky, which promised a good day to come. The higher they flew, the better the weather. Gracie was learning to read the weather as if she had been born to the country life.

By midday she had done all Mr Catchpole had asked of her; had hoed and weeded the gravelled path that ran the length of the garden, cut the dead heads from the rose that climbed over the gate-arch and barrowed the load of manure Home Farm had dumped beside the gate to a more discreet situation at the back of the potting sheds. Then she washed her hands in the rainwater butt, slipped off her heavy shoes and made herself comfortable to eat her sandwiches.

Gracie looked around the garden, her garden and Mr Catchpole's, and wondered how any one person could be so contented with her life; contented when there was a war on, which was even worse, though if it wasn't for the bombers flying low overhead and the dreary winter black-out, she could easily dismiss the war from her life and pretend that this was where she had been born and would continue to live and work for all time.

This garden, which was really her war work, she looked upon as a place of sheer enchantment, hidden away from the outside world by a nine-foot-high wall, where vegetables grew in their season and orchids still flowered.

True, it was very unpatriotic of Mr Catchpole to grow orchids because the orchid house could have produced even more tomatoes and cucumbers for the war effort. Yet the Ministry of Food could issue directives till they were blue in the face, he'd said; that orchid house stayed, no matter what, and they could send him to prison before he would uproot even one of them!

'Them orchids,' Mr Catchpole said – and especially the

creamy white ones – 'are her ladyship's memorial,' and as far as he was concerned, there the matter ended.

Gracie was considering how she should fill the afternoon when she heard footsteps on the gravel.

She was, she was to recall later, not only extremely untidy, her dungarees being in need of scrubbing and her pale blue shirt not as clean as it might have been, but she was barefoot, too, and smelled, still, of the manure she had just shifted. To put it plainly, she was in no condition to meet the young man who walked smiling towards her – had she been interested, of course, in meeting him.

The smartly-dressed American soldier took in every detail of the girl who rose to her feet at his approach and felt as if someone had delivered a blow to his insides.

Her fair hair clung in damp curls to her face, her skin was the colour of an apricot and her eyes the bluest he had ever seen. And someone should tell her that it wasn't playing fair to leave her shirt unbuttoned at the neck because above it her throat rose to an exquisite jawline and below it he dared not trust himself to look.

He knew already that this was Gracie and that she was the provider of the breakfast egg he had eaten this morning; that Aunt Julia liked her a lot because she not only worked long and willingly, but because she got on very well with Catchpole, which was a miracle in itself.

But no one had thought to tell him how absolutely beautiful she was nor how perfect the smile that tilted her lips when she rose to greet him.

'I'm sorry, but Mr Catchpole is away for the day.' He would remember her first words, huskily spoken, for all time. 'He left me in charge, though, so if there's anything I can do to help . . . ? Are you lost?' she prompted, when he did not speak. 'Were you looking for someone?'

'No, not really . . .' *I wasn't* said a voice inside him, *but I think I've just found her.* 'I'm staying at Rowangarth till Tuesday. Bas Sutton.'

'Not Bas from Kentucky?' *Any minute now he will smell the manure!*

'That's me. Not long been over here. I'm stationed at Burtonwood – advance party, sort of. It'll be an airfield, one day.' *Why did no one tell me she is such a doll?*

'Is it far from here?' *Stop blushing, you idiot!*

'Only a spit. Between Liverpool and a place called Warrington.' *Near enough to visit often!* 'Mind if I stay a while, and talk?'

'N-no. Not at all. Would you like to see the garden?' *Pull yourself together, girl! It's only Drew's cousin, not Clark Gable!*

'Seen it, actually, though not since the summer of 'thirty-seven. It won't have changed a lot, though, if I know Catchpole.' *And I don't want to talk about gardens. I want to talk about you!*

'I'll get you something to sit on. And since Mr Catchpole isn't here, I suppose it'll be all right for you to stay a while.' *Calm down! You've seen a Yank before, haven't you? And no, you mustn't call him a Yank – not when he's from the deep south!*

She returned with the green wooden chair, unfolding it, placing it at a distance because of the smell.

'This was Lady Helen's special chair. She had been sitting on it in the orchid house the day she died – but I suppose you'll know that?' *Surely Mr Catchpole won't mind him sitting on her ladyship's chair?*

'No. I didn't know. We knew she had died suddenly – were all upset, back home, to hear about it. She was a very lovely lady.' *Fair, just like you. Only Aunt Helen looked at a person, always, when she spoke to them but you won't look at me, Gracie. Why won't you look at me?*

'Yes, she was. We used to talk. She missed Sir John so much. She had one of his white orchids in her hand when she died. I thought it was so beautiful. Your Aunt Julia was very glad about it, too. She said it meant they were together again. It comforted her. I was the last one to talk to her, you know. Doctor Pryce said her ladyship wouldn't have known a thing about it.' *I wonder if I ever fall in love it will be like she did. I hope so. For ever. Will you fall in love for ever, Bas Sutton, or do you play the field?*

'The thing I remember most about Aunt Helen was her smile. She had a beautiful smile.' *Like yours, Gracie.*

'Mm. I used to like talking to her. She often came to the orchid house; said it was nice and warm there on cold days.'

She glanced at her feet. Goodness! Her shoes! Hastily she pushed her feet into them, taking a long time to tie the laces because she was unable to look at him. *These shoes stink!*

'Gracie.' *We've had enough of this messing about. I've only got a seventy-two-hour furlough!* 'Aunt Julia says you like dancing and there's always a dance in Creesby, Saturday nights. Will you come with me? Please? I could call for you at the bothy. Aunt Julia said if we are going to be late back, it's best we take the bikes.'

'But you've come to see her and the Reverend. Won't they mind you going out?'

'No. It was she suggested it.' *And I want to dance with you, hold you.*

'The last bus leaves Creesby at half-past nine. They've had to cut down – the petrol, you see.' *Why am I making such a fool of myself? Why don't I just say no, I'm meeting someone else or washing my hair?*

'Then I guess it'll have to be the bikes. You won't mind getting your hair blown about?' *Most girls do.*

'Not a bit. Everyone cycles everywhere these days. Besides, my hair is naturally curly, so it doesn't matter.'

'I'll call at six-thirty, then?'

'No! Could you make it seven?' *I must wash my hair and scrub the muck from my fingernails and, above all else, get rid of the smell of manure!*

She rose to her feet, all at once in a turmoil because she

knew she was in danger of doing something she had said time and time again she would never do. Never would she fall in love; *never*, until the war was over! Yet now she was acting like a girl on her first date and leaving herself wide open to Bas Sutton's very obvious charms.

'How long did you say you were staying?' she whispered.

'Until Tuesday, early, so we've got plenty of time to see each other.'

'But I don't think Mr Catchpole will let me have time off,' she protested weakly.

'Want to bet?' he grinned. 'I've got a tin of pipe tobacco with me that says he will!'

'You can get tobacco? *A whole tin of it?*'

'Sure. I've brought some for Uncle Nathan and cigarettes for Aunt Julia. We can get most things in the PX canteen. I'd like it if you'd show me York, Gracie.'

'But you must have been to York oodles of times.'

'Not with you, I haven't.'

'I'd have to ask Mr Catchpole and the forewoman at the bothy.'

Here was trouble in the shape of a GI who could charm the birds from the trees, given the chance. She could resist that charm; she would make herself resist it, but how would Mr Catchpole resist a whole tin of tobacco?

'And I'm sorry about the manure – the smell, I mean.'

'Think nothing of it. I'm a vet. We breed horses back home. Guess I've shovelled more manure than you have! But is it a date for tonight and Monday then?'

She fidgeted with her work-roughened hands. And whilst she should have said no it wasn't, thanks all the same, she heard herself whisper, 'Okay. It's a date.'

'You're early,' Polly laughed when Bas, who had crept up behind her, put his hands over her eyes and asked her to guess who. 'Gracie said you wouldn't be here till seven.' She turned to gather him to her, hugging him tightly, her cheek on his. 'My, but you've grown, and you an officer, an' all!'

'I meant to surprise you and sorry, I'm just a private. This uniform is general issue. But it's lovely to see you, Polly, after so long. I called in on Daisy's Mom and took her some candies and these are for you. And I have news for you – strictly between you and me, of course.' The careless-talk thing pertained in America, too, since Pearl Harbor. 'Keth phoned Mom. He's just fine.'

'So he *is* in America?'

'Yup. In Washington, and doing exactly the same, he told Mom, as he was doing here, in England – whatever that was. Mom didn't find out.'

'No. She wouldn't. Very airy-fairy Keth was when I tried to get it out of him. Said he dusted the colonel's desk, would you believe!'

'I guess it's more important than that, but Mom said I was to try and see you, let you know that things are just as before. Keth is welcome at our place as often as he can get time off to go there. She specially wanted you to know that.'

'Then tell her, when you write, that I'm grateful. I'm only sorry I can't ask you here, Bas, but you know the way it is. Men strictly not allowed. Keth had to sleep at Keeper's when he was home.

'But sometimes, when I hear those bombers taking off, I'm glad Keth has been sent back to America. It's selfish of me I know, and you over here, fighting for our country and your mother missing you. Good job she's got Kitty!'

'But that's just it. She hasn't; Kitty only went and volunteered to entertain US troops overseas, would you believe? Said she was going to try to team up with ENSA. Pa hit the roof, but it was too late, of course!'

'What's ENSA?' Polly placed the chocolates on the kitchen table, staring almost mesmerized at so enormous a box.

'It means Entertainments National Service Association, I think. They put on shows for the troops – give their services free, though it counts as war work. And they must be prepared to go anywhere.'

'Like Vera Lynn, you mean, singing to our lads in North Africa?'

'Like that, only Kitty isn't much of a singer – more a dancer, though she'll try her hand at anything if it'll get her noticed. My terrible little sister hasn't changed much!'

'And where are you stationed, Bas, or can't you tell me?'

'It's no secret. I'm here with the advance party at a place called Burtonwood. It's quite near to Liverpool.'

'So you'll be able to see Drew, when he's in port?'

'I sure will. We'll have five years' catching up to do. Guess he'll have grown some, too.' He glanced at his watch, eager to see Gracie, and when she walked into the room he said, '*Wow!*'

'They told me Polly was entertaining in the kitchen,' she smiled.

'There now,' said Polly, 'don't you look just lovely? It's a crying shame that bonny young girls should have to wear trousers and jumpers and go round looking like farm men. Doesn't she look lovely, Bas?'

'Lovely,' was all he could say because he was taking in the blue of the dress that matched her eyes exactly, unstockinged legs, browned by the sun, and newly washed hair he was sure would smell of scented soap. And since he must report back to Burtonwood by noon on Tuesday, suddenly it seemed important not to waste a minute of the time they had together.

'I've brought us a couple of bikes from Rowangarth,' he smiled. 'Tyres checked. See you, Polly.'

'Have a good time. And thanks for the sweeties, Bas.'

Gracie tied a scarf over her hair, put her dancing shoes and handbag in the bicycle basket then looked sharply up, cheeks blazing as a long-drawn wolf-whistle came from an open bedroom window.

'Ooh! Aren't they awful?' she choked, but Bas grinned and whistled back because he felt a million dollars. Was only to be expected, he supposed, when before so very much longer you would be holding a girl like Gracie in your arms – maybe even dancing cheek to cheek.

Being in uniform hadn't figured in his plans when he graduated, but if a guy had to go to war, then there were worse places to be than England, especially when a land girl called Grace was a part of the deal.

Strange, he frowned, how the sight of her had awakened something tender and yearny inside him; made him want to touch her and kiss her – boy, how he wanted to kiss her!

And then, just as they reached the crossroads a thought so awful hit him that he called ahead to her, 'Hey, Gracie! Stop! There's something I forgot to ask you!'

'Yes?' She raised an eyebrow.

'Are you engaged, or going steady? Is there a special guy in your life?'

For a moment she did not speak, then she said, very quietly, 'No! To all three! And there won't be any special guy in my life till the war is over. Remember what happened to Tatty? Well, it isn't going to happen to me, Bas!'

'Tatty? What *did* happen? Nobody told me anything.'

'Tatty fell for an airman called Tim. She met him at a dance at the aerodrome at Holdenby Moor and it was what I call a hook, line and sinker job. They were mad about each other right from the start. Daisy and I used to alibi her, so they could meet without Mrs Anna knowing.'

'And he ditched her, poor kid?'

'No. He was killed. Shot down by a hit-and-run fighter as they were taking off. Tatty's folks didn't know anything about it until afterwards. They had three months together, that's all. She'll be a long time getting over him.'

'Gee – poor little Tatty. I still think of her as a kid, y'see. No one told me, though, about her boyfriend. That's tough.'

'Like I said, she kept it quiet. And she's no longer a child, Bas. She'll be twenty-one, soon, and she's working in London, getting blitzed, most nights. But that's why there's no man in my life – not until I know he won't get killed. I'm what you might call a sensible Lancashire lass.'

'But if you *did* meet someone . . . ?'

'Then I'd do my very best,' she whispered, looking him straight in the eyes for the very first time, 'to stop myself getting too fond of him – okay?'

Then she pressed hard on the pedals and rode off, head high, heart thumping wildly because why she had made so completely foolish a statement she had no idea.

'Now is that so, Gracie Fielding?' Bas whispered tight-lipped to her straight, indignant back. 'Then it's going to be real interesting between you and me, because I shall do *my* very best to make sure you do get fond of me – real fond!'

And in that moment, he knew that if he couldn't have her, then no other would do. He was, he supposed, another hook, line and sinker job and there could be no changing it.

42

They sat on the grass at the top of Holdenby Pike. The evening was warm and it was still light because double summertime gave an extra hour of daylight and saved electricity for the war effort, the Government said.

The day spent in York had been pleasant. They had wandered up and down streets so narrow it was said that people leaning from the overhanging upstairs windows could shake hands, were they of a mind to do so; streets built, Bas marvelled, long before the *Mayflower* set sail for America. They visited the ages-old Minster that had stood witness to the start of more wars than people could begin to imagine and walked the entire city walls and found, too, the house in which Guy Fawkes was born.

'Yorkshire people don't hold him a criminal; rather more the most sensible man who ever had designs on Parliament,' Gracie had giggled on one of the rare occasions she let down her guard.

Because guarded she knew she must be. Bas Sutton had been nice, this far, to be with and being so close when they danced would have been nicer than nice had she allowed herself to enjoy it. Bas was everything a girl could want, in fact, and it was a pity about her solemn, oft-renewed vow never to fall in love for the duration.

'Let's go back to Holdenby,' Bas said all at once as they walked under Micklegate Bar, trying not to look at the bomb-damaged convent. 'I want to see Pendenys Place. We'll catch the next train, if we run.'

So here they sat, he relaxed and she with arms round

knees bent to her chin because that way she felt she was shutting out his nearness.

'You won't be able to see Pendenys,' she had said as the train neared Holdenby. 'You can only climb the pike and look down on it.'

'That's as near as I want to be,' he grinned. Looking down was all he wanted. 'Those army bods who commandeered it are welcome to it as far as I'm concerned.' And now, as he looked down, he was glad he would not – for a long time, at least – have to walk its echoing passages nor climb the winding tower steps to Grandmother Clementina's room.

'There was once a tower, y'know. Grandfather had most of it pulled down, after the fire. He only left two floors – level with the rest of the house. Pendenys furniture is stored there, now, and the tower door padlocked. I hated that tower door.'

'Why, Bas?'

'Because it meant that through it I was summoned to the presence, sort of. Grandmother Sutton spent a lot of her time in the tower, after Uncle Elliot was killed. The servants used to call it Madam's sulking room. She took to drink, in the end.' He held out his hands. 'Keth got me out of that tower, when she set it alight. He saved my life. It's why my hands are like this.'

'Yes. I'd heard, sort of, only I didn't like to ask.' Gently she took his hands in hers.

'Then why didn't you ask me? The scars don't bother me, you know. They remind me I'm alive when I could have died along with Grandma. And they didn't stop me getting to be a vet – only being a pilot.'

'Then be glad about that. Aircrews have a terrible time of it, you know.'

'So you wouldn't want me to be killed, Gracie?'

'I wouldn't want anyone to be killed!' She let go his hands suddenly. 'I've often wondered what goes on, at

Pendenys,' she hastened, eager to talk of other things. 'Daisy's dada said two guards he met one night told him that the Fannies stationed there threw hand grenades.'

'They *what*?'

'Fannies. They are army drivers – or supposed to be. First Aid Nursing Yeomanry. F-A-N-Y.' She spelled it out patiently. 'Daisy's mother said the Fannies drove ambulances in *her* war. Anyway, you can't get near Pendenys for love nor money.'

'Seems Daisy's pa did.'

'That was because he knows Rowangarth and Pendenys land. Daisy said that when he went back, afterwards, the way he'd got in by had been blocked up. The guards must have reported it. But it's a peculiar place.'

'Don't I just know it. I hated it as a kid. Kitty loved it, though. I'll give it to her, if she wants it. It'll be mine one day – did you know that?'

'*Yours?* That great place?' Gracie was shocked.

'Sure. By rights, Tatty's pa should've had it and Tatty would have had to live there. She was afraid of Grandmother Clementina, too. Kitty was the only one who wasn't.'

'All you Suttons are rich, aren't you?'

'No. I guess the Kentucky Suttons were comfortable, kind of, till Uncle Elliot died. Then Grandmother Clementina made another Will – while she still had her wits about her – and left Pendenys to Grandfather for his lifetime and then to Uncle Nathan. And her money was shared between Uncle Nathan and my pa, and provision made for Tatiana, so I guess that makes us better than comfortable, now, since Mom has a fair few dollars of her own. Does having money upset you, Gracie?'

'How would I know? I've never had any. I suppose *money* doesn't upset me, really. It's just usually that rich people think they are Almighty God. Now that *does* make me mad!'

'But Uncle Nathan is very rich. Now Grandfather is dead, Pendenys is his. And Aunt Julia isn't what you'd call hard up – yet they are two of the nicest people I've ever met,' Bas defended.

'So they are an exception! But before you say any more, I want you to know that my folks aren't rich. They aren't even comfortable. Mum worked in the cotton mills – she still does, as war work. But she left me with Gran when I was little and worked for years to pay for me to go to grammar school so I could end up a clerk – have a ladylike job.

'And do you know what became of me, Bas? I ended up a clerk, all right – in the wages department of the mill my mother works in, would you believe! Now *that's* what I am and you should know it!'

'So you're ashamed of your grass roots? Why, Gracie? In America it isn't who you are born to, or where, but where you end up that matters! Just because Mom owns one of the biggest studs in Kentucky didn't stop me having to start at the bottom, even though I'd been through college and got a degree. I had to sweep stables and barrow manure, so don't get all sassy about your mother working in a mill!'

'I'm not getting sassy and I'm not ashamed of my folks – far from it! It's just that you should know, that's all.'

She had jumped to her feet and was walking away from him but he caught her arm and roughly pulled her to face him.

'Okay – so I know! Do you think it makes one blind bit of difference to me? I only know I want to marry you! And I must be the only guy in this man's army who's proposed to a girl before he's even got to kiss her! I need my head looking at!'

'Marry you? *Marry you*, did you say?' Her voice sounded strange, and high above her head.

'You got it in one!'

'But you don't know me and I don't know you! A day in York and Saturday night at the dance – that's all! And I told you, didn't I, that I don't think it's very clever to fall in love when there's a war on. I couldn't risk getting hurt. I *won't*!'

'Tatty did.'

'Yes, and she'll never get over it. And there's no such thing as love at first sight! Physical attraction – that's all it is!' She was shaking in every limb. She wanted him to let go of her arm. 'And you're hurting me. Let me go, please.'

'Not on your life, Gracie! Not till you give me a reason – a *good* reason – for turning me down!' His face was white, his mouth traplike. 'Is it my hands? Are they so repulsive?'

'No,' she said softly, shaking her head. She wouldn't want him to think his hands made any difference, because they didn't. 'They aren't repulsive at all; only scarred a little.' With her free hand she took his and laid it to her cheek. 'And you aren't repulsive, either, Bas Sutton. When I first saw you in the kitchen garden, my stomach went *boing*, sort of, and I felt really awful – because of the manure. I suppose, really, I didn't want it to put you off me . . .'

'And it damn well didn't put me off you! It couldn't have. Nothing about you could! People *do* fall in love in wartime. Tatty did, and Keth and Daisy are making the best of things. What's so different about you and me that we can't make a go of it?'

'Tatty got hurt – how many more times do I have to tell you? And do you think Keth and Daisy are laughing their heads off right now?'

'No, I don't. But Tatty has something to remember – at least I hope she has. Were they lovers, Gracie?'

Mutely, she nodded her head.

'Then I'm glad about that, at least. And Daisy and Keth

643

have something to hold on to. Tell me – what is so wrong being in love? I love you, Gracie, and you love me, I know it. Say, "I love you, Bas." At least say that?'

'No, Bas. No, no, *no*! Thanks for asking me to marry you,' she added almost as an afterthought. 'But it's getting late. I'll have to go.'

'It's only a little after ten, but if that's what you want, then okay.' He tucked the arm he held in his, then twined her fingers in his as if he were afraid that if he let her go she would run from him and he would lose her completely. 'But think about what I've said, won't you, when you've had a little more time to get used to it? It's easier for me, you see. I've had almost three days to get used to loving you. Think about it, then if you change your mind – when the shock has worn off, I mean – then let me know, uh?'

'But I don't know your address!'

'I mean let me know in the morning – before I leave Holdenby.'

'But how?' He mustn't do this to her!

'That's up to you, Gracie. You'll find a way somehow, if you really want to.'

They walked in silence to the bothy gates. More than once, Gracie admitted as they stood there in the half-dark, she had wanted to tell him how she felt; that her stomach really had done a somersault when he walked into the kitchen garden. And was it only two days ago? Could people fall in love in two days? In two minutes, truth known.

'So this is it, Gracie? You won't say you'll marry me – you won't even say you love me, so how about goodbye and a goodbye kiss, maybe?'

'All right.' She owed him that, at least; owed it to herself, really. 'And I have enjoyed being with you, Bas. I really have.' She reached for his hand – the left one, more scarred than the right – and laid her lips to it. Then she reached on tiptoe and kissed his cheek. 'If there hadn't been a war on . . .'

'If there hadn't been a war on you and me wouldn't have met. And I meant a real kiss!'

He reached for her, pulling her close, kissing her mouth, and she made her lips into a little round so neither of them would enjoy it, and held herself rigid in his arms because if she let her guard down, just once . . .

'Sweetheart.' His voice was husky with need and she took a deep breath as his lips found hers again, and because his nearness was so disturbing she relaxed her body against his and parted her lips because she, too, like Daisy and Keth, wanted something to hold on to. When Bas was gone, the memory of just one kiss would be better than nothing.

'I love you, Gracie. I love you so much,' he whispered, then claimed her mouth again, silencing any protests she might have made. And her head swam and strange, disturbing pulses began to beat inside her and if she did not leave him now, then all the good Lancashire common sense that had filled her head since the day she could ever spell the words, would fly high and away and she would be lost.

'Good night, Bas. Take care of yourself,' she gasped, then ran up the path and round the corner of the house to the back door, shutting it with a slam behind her.

She was in bed, the blankets pulled up to her chin and feigning sleep, when the land girl who shared her room opened the door quietly at eleven o'clock. She heard midnight chime on the clock in the hall downstairs, and one o'clock, and two. And oh, what a God-forsaken hour was two in the morning when you had just made a mess of your life and sent the most marvellous man out of it. And all because she said she would never fall in love in wartime!

Yet she *had* fallen in love, or fallen victim to instant attraction, call it what you liked. All she really knew was that it had been a hook, line and sinker job the minute

Bas Sutton's feet crunched the gravel of the kitchen-garden path. And Gracie Fielding, who was so very sure of herself and where she was going and when she would fall in love, even, had made a mess of it, and all because of her stupid stubbornness.

You'll find a way somehow. . . But how was she to do it? Bas was getting the 6.30 train out of Holdenby; he would probably be walking to the station because Mrs Sutton would have no petrol left to drive him there until she got her July coupons. So if he walked, what time would he leave Rowangarth? Wouldn't it be better if she were to get up early, take the short cut through Brattocks Wood and across Home Farm pastures to the track that led to the station?

She could even walk up it as far as the platform. Trespassing on railway property it would be if she were caught, but that would be the least of her worries.

It must have been then, about three o'clock, that she fell asleep, because she was awakened by the banging of the bedroom door and sat bolt-upright, staring at the alarm clock she had forgotten to set. The hands pointed to six o'clock. *Six* dammit! How was she to dress and get to Holdenby in time to tell him?

She wasn't! She would never make it! She wasn't intended to. She had been right all along about not falling in love. Fate had settled it for her.

She closed her eyes and remembered their kiss; the lovely, suffocating closeness of him, the way he held her when they danced and the happy smile that could charm the birds out of the trees; remembered all that, then threw back her bedclothes, pulled on her shirt, dungarees and canvas pumps, and ran up Bothy Lane as if her life depended on it.

Bas checked the station clock with his watch. It was two minutes slow which gave him, he supposed, two more minutes to spend with Gracie. If she came.

The platform was deserted but for himself and an airman, going on leave he shouldn't wonder, and the porter, of course, manhandling a trolley with six milk churns on it and a mailbag.

Aunt Julia had wanted to drive him to the station, but he refused because it wasn't right when petrol was rationed and so precious. He would walk, he told her. He had little to carry and it wasn't all that far. He knew the short cut across the fields, now didn't he?

Yet he had walked on the road, instead, because if Gracie was coming she would surely use one of the bothy cycles. He had left Rowangarth early so as to arrive at the station early, because if Gracie were already there . . .

But she had not been there when he arrived and now the porter was closing the crossing gates. The train was coming, and on time, too. He could hear it clearly on the fresh morning air way down the track and in just half a minute he would see it rounding the bend. In less than three minutes it would have taken on passengers, churns and mailbag and started back to York, and by seven o'clock he would be sitting on the Liverpool-bound train and this weekend would mean nothing, because Gracie wasn't coming. She had meant what she said, even though she clung to him when he kissed her and had kissed him back, too.

Silly, stupid girl with a head full of Lancashire common sense. But which sensible man or woman fell in love in wartime and which sensible man or woman did *not* fall in love in wartime?

The signal fell noisily and he glared at it. The train would arrive on time and leave on time and he had just four minutes left; *they* had just four minutes left, yet Gracie was throwing them all away.

Well, he didn't want a woman with a head full of common sense. He wanted the woman who had kissed him goodbye last night, and he wanted her here, right now, on the platform beside him, telling him she loved him.

What was so wrong, he demanded of the minute hand of the station clock that was jerking forward with awesome speed, in saying, 'I love you'? She had refused to say it, even though her body had said it, silently, and the mouth that clung to his. But the most important words she had steadfastly refused to say.

'Stand back, if you *please*,' called the porter.

The airman picked up his kitbag and heaved it on to his shoulder. Bas picked up his grip and looked towards the ticket barrier. She wasn't coming.

Reluctantly, he stepped on board, leaving the door open, because there might just be time to get off again, kiss her, and hear her say, 'I love you.'

He placed his grip on the seat and stepped down on the platform once more, eyes sweeping its length.

'All aboard, sir, *if you please*,' insisted the porter, who had loaded the milk churns and the mailbag with super-human speed and was now walking the length of the train, banging compartment doors with officious zeal.

The train let out a hoot, the porter, deputizing for the stationmaster at so early an hour, blew a whistle and waved his green flag importantly.

The wheels began to turn slowly. The train juddered and strained. Bas threw a last despairing glance at the ticket barrier as slowly they slid past it. She had not come.

Had Keth felt like this, the day they all left for Kentucky in the late summer of 'thirty-seven? Keth had looked sad, kind of, until they had asked him which side of the compartment the little clearing in Brattocks Wood would be on because he and Kitty had known, hadn't they, that Daisy would be standing there for one last glimpse, a final wave as the train passed it.

Brattocks! He jumped to his feet and grasping the leather strap, let down the window with a bang. Leaning out as far as he dare, he looked down the track to the clearing in

648

the trees and saw a distant flash of pale blue. She was there, at the waving place.

'Gracie!' he yelled. 'I love you!'

She was standing on the bottom rung of the fence, the better for him to see her, wearing the same overalls and pale blue shirt as on the morning they met and though he knew she could not hear his words over the clatter of the train, he had to say them again, for all that. 'Gracie, I love you!'

She held up her hand and her smile told him she had read the words on his lips.

She had come, he exulted, as he asked her to! It took just five seconds for the train to slip by, but *she had come*!

'She loves me!' he yelled to the empty compartment, his fist punching the air. And tonight he would ring her, tell her again that he loved her and would ask her to say she loved him too.

He was a fool. They were both fools to fall in love in wartime. They knew so little about each other, yet in wartime having someone to love was all that mattered.

He leaned back and closed his eyes and thought about a land girl he had met just three days ago.

Gracie of the lovely smile, with manure on her boots and a pale blue shirt, open at the neck. How easy she was to love.

Tonight, HMS *Penrose* would be late docking. It was the fault of the massive aircraft carrier which had come to Liverpool on a courtesy visit and was proving hard to manoeuvre from the dockside. Tugs fussed and pushed and heaved. A ship so swift and formidable when at sea was clumsy and helpless in dock. And what was really annoying, Drew thought as he leaned on the *Maggie*'s rail to await the passing of the carrier, was that being stuck in mid-river awaiting a berth was boring and time-wasting.

Below deck, Knocker had tuned in to port-wave

frequency. Soon, when the carrier that was causing all the bother got speed up and sailed past them, they would get the signal to proceed.

Tired of gazing, he opened the wireless-cabin door where his opposite number listened with half an ear for the *Maggie*'s call sign.

'We're going to be too late to go ashore – you realize that Andy, don't you? Flaming carrier! Never mind showing the flag in port; it should be out there clobbering U-boats!'

'Won't be long, now,' Drew shrugged. 'I'll make up the signal log for you, if you want.'

'It's done. Everything's close-up.' Knocker had even managed to change into his number-one uniform in readiness for a skylark ashore. 'It'll be eight, near enough, before we tie up alongside and God knows when we'll get into Liverpool. What use is that!'

No use at all to sailors who had to catch up with their wenching and drinking. By the time they were through the dock gates, Knocker reasoned, there'd be no wenches for the taking and no ale for the drinking!

'We could go to the ENSA show,' Drew offered, knowing it was useless to ring Daisy. Both she and Lyn, according to the marks in his diary, were on duty tonight – and for the remainder of the week – until midnight. Lates, from six o'clock until midnight, was the most disliked watch of all and by far the busiest. Or so Daisy said. 'I'm dateless tonight. Think I'll look in on the show, then grab a bed ashore for the night and get my head down.'

'In that case, I'll come with you – to the show, at least.' Pay parade was not until Thursday and Knocker's Waaf girlfriend liked to drink gin and lime, which made a nasty hole in a sailor's pocket! And the ENSA shows cost nothing, he reasoned, so nothing would be lost if it wasn't up to much because a hastily erected stage in a damp and gloomy warehouse didn't exactly measure up to the

Windmill Theatre! 'You'll not be meeting your Jennies, then?'

'They're on watch.'

'Very inconsiderate of them – but that's women for you. So are you going to shove off, and get yourself changed?'

If they were going to the dockside show, Knocker reasoned, they must get there early enough to get a front seat. A front seat was essential in order to get a good view of things; things pertaining to chorus girls, that was, and especially the high-kickers in scanty knickers! Because life in wartime was a gamble, he always said, and you had to store up memories and anything else that was sugar and spice, because you were a long time dead, especially if you copped it up on the next sweep!

'Okay,' Drew grinned, glad to be going ashore. They wouldn't put to sea again until late tomorrow. He could meet Lyn and Daisy in the afternoon, buy them a meal – or maybe even take in the tea dance – and still have them at Epsom House for six o'clock duty.

He winked at the sepia photograph of Margaret Penrose outside the wardroom door, and thanked her silently for another sweep safely over.

He hoped, as he shaved, that the ENSA show wouldn't be a load of old gash. Impromptu concerts in dockside warehouses could sometimes be a pain in the neck. But they cost nothing, so what the heck . . . ?

When they arrived at the warehouse, the front row of seats, to Knocker's disgust, bore a notice 'Reserved. Officers only', a fact made worse because they were decent chairs and not the rickety, uncomfortable benches provided for the lower decks. But when the lighting dimmed and the chairs were still unoccupied, they were immediately filled by enterprising sailors, two of whom were Drew and Knocker.

They sat, arms folded, to let off steam with a sing-song

of saucy sea shanties, conducted by a pianist who was resigned to the legitimate words being substituted for the Navy's own version, then settled down to the innuendoes of an equally saucy comic until, starved of that for which they had come, the entire audience began a slow and persistent handclapping. 'We want the dancing girls!'

'Gentlemen! Gentle-*men*!' The compere, whose career in entertainment had consisted of pier-end shows in the summer season and pantomime from Christmas to February, held up his hands in mock distress. He was heavily made up and wore the striped pants and colourful jacket left over from his summer-season days. 'Now let's have order. Girls you want, then a girl – a young lady – you will get! She has travelled thousands of miles to be with you tonight, and are you lucky?'

'Let's be having her, then!' came the raucous demand. 'Gerroff, Phyllis, and let's see somethin' worth lookin' at!' Ear-shattering whistles followed their demands. Smiling, the man bowed himself to the edge of the stage, then flung wide his arms in a dramatic gesture.

'Gentlemen, please give a warm welcome to a beautiful little lady from America – Kate from Kentucky!'

The curtains parted a few inches, the clapping stopped. A foot appeared in a bright red, high-heeled shoe. A leg followed it; a long, slim, beautiful leg wearing a black fishnet stocking.

'Come on out then, darling. Let's see yer face!'

The leg disappeared, the curtains opened wider and a bottom, scantily covered in a leotard of red lace, pushed through the opening and wiggled provocatively. There was a tumultuous roar. Knocker placed two fingers in his mouth and let go a frenzied whistle.

Then holding wide the curtains, standing posing, smiling, simpering in a costume that showed more than was ladylike of two exquisitely rounded breasts, she flung wide her arms and cried, 'Well, hi, guys! Ah'm Kate. How've ya been?'

She said it in an exaggerated southern drawl. She sounded like Scarlett O'Hara and looked every bit as provocative, except that Scarlett would have been whipped out of town had she appeared so scantily dressed.

The audience showed its approval with a stamping of feet. Here was something worth seeing! And see it they near as dammit could!

'Well, how about that for a lovely bit of crackling?' Knocker, red-faced with delight, dug his elbow into Drew's ribs. 'Cor, look at them legs, Andy! And that lovely little bottom! How about a basinful of that, then?'

'Shut your mouth!' Drew's face was white, his mouth set traplike. 'And keep your dirty little remarks to yourself! She doesn't give it away in basinfuls!'

'Bet you anything you like she does! I've ten bob that says she'd go to bed with anybody!'

'Well, she won't! I guarantee it!' Drew lapsed into simmering silence, defeated by the noise and still trying to accept the near-riot Kate from Kentucky had caused. He sucked in a deep breath, took in the violet eyes, the black hair, cut short now in feathery curls that clung to her head, and knew she was once more in her element, centre stage.

'I still say –'

'And I said shut your mouth! That's my cousin up there, so watch what you say!'

'She's *what*, Andy . . . ?'

Kate from Kentucky held up her hands and there was instant silence.

'Wa-a-a-ll, thanks, guys, for that welcome. It was worth crossing the Atlantic for. 'S a matter of fact, I only just got here yest'day, but I sure would've come sooner if I'd known you were such a genteel crowd!' She winked saucily. 'Now, I'm going to sing you a song, but I'm gonna need one of you lovely sailors to help me – so who's goin' to volunteer, uh?'

'Here y'are!' Knocker was on his feet, determined to call

Drew's bluff. 'This bloke here says he'll come up! Says he knows you!'

She shaded her eyes against the glare of the makeshift footlights, bending over, which was a mistake, though appreciated by her audience who cheered and whistled at a still more revealing glimpse of her breasts.

'Why, gentlemen – *please*!' Modestly she covered her cleavage with fingers spread. 'And since one volunteer is worth two pressmen, then I'd be obliged, sir, if you'd come on to the stage and bring your chair with you.'

'All right, Andy – now's your chance.' Knocker pushed Drew on to the stage; another sailor passed up his chair. Drew stood unmoving, unwilling to join her.

'Aw, c'mon, sailor. Don't tell me you're shy of little Kate!'

She swayed towards him, holding out her arms, the audience urging her on. Momentarily she hesitated, pulled in a sharp breath, then held out her arms again, clasping them around his neck, hissing, 'Drew! I didn't know it was you! The footlights. Couldn't see . . .'

'Come on, then! Give the lady a kiss!' The Navy demanded action.

'Why, guys!' There was another immediate, expectant silence. 'Don't embarrass the nice sailor!'

The cheering began again. Knocker stood on his chair, turning to demand the attention of the back rows.

'That one on the stage, that fancy sparker, says he knows the lady!'

'And so he does, sailor!' Kate called, then turning back to Drew, lifted her mouth to his. 'He's ma cousin. He's ma kissin' cousin!'

She whispered her lips across his cheek, saying softly, 'Bear with me, Drew? It's only a bit of fun.'

'Fun!' he hissed, so she kissed him again before his protests could be allowed to spoil her act.

He jerked away, shaking with anger. The audience

interpreted it as embarrassment and urged him on.

'Now, tell all those nice sailors your name, uh?'

'Be damned if I will!' He made to leave the stage and she caught his arm, begging him with her eyes to stay, but he shook her hand away. 'Sorry, Kitty. Make a fool of yourself if you want.' He said it so quietly that only she heard. 'But don't expect me to watch you!'

To a barrage of derision he jumped from the stage and made for the way out. Hand on the door he turned to see another sailor already seated there, Kitty on his knee. He stood as she began to sing teasingly to him, his face cupped in her hands, and he saw with complete revulsion that the sailor's hands were already on her bottom.

With a strength aided by rage he pulled back the heavy sliding door and flung out, and along the dockside. He had left his cap behind, but what the hell?

The shaking inside him continued, part rage, part confusion. How could she? How could she dress like a tart – yes, like a bloody tart! – and wiggle her bottom and wear a top that showed her breasts. And her breasts were small and rounded and he felt dismayed that the first time he had ever seen them, *really* seen them, they should be displayed so provocatively.

And what was she doing here, anyway? How had she managed to make the crossing and hadn't she the sense, if she wanted to do war work, to do it at home? But that was Kitty all over. Always the actress; always needing an audience. He recalled their youth and the performances she gave to the Clan; remembered the sheer naughtiness of her, hiding in cupboards and behind sofas, listening to grown-ups talking, passing on her highly embroidered version of what had been said. Lovely, funny Kitty.

But that did not justify behaving as she had done tonight; didn't give that leering, three-badge stoker the right to hold her on his knee, maybe even kiss her!

Kiss her! He stopped in his tracks. Kitty had kissed him,

hadn't she; called him her kissing cousin whilst whispering to him to go along with her act. Because that was all it had been, really. An act. Kitty Sutton up to her old tricks again and she hadn't meant that kiss, had she?

But what a kiss! He had never before thought of her as his kissing cousin. Was it that in five years she had grown into a beauty or had he never before bothered to notice that her legs, especially in black fishnet stockings held up by red satin suspenders, were just about the longest, most elegant, most sexy he had ever seen!

All at once, he wondered what it would be like to kiss her properly; properly as in Rowangarth garden, perhaps, on a flower-scented evening and the blackbird singing 'Sunset'.

Or would he settle for that kiss here, on a bleak, litter-strewn, bomb-damaged dockside? He would! Oh, too right he would!

He turned to walk back to the warehouse. He was still angry with her, but he had to retrieve his cap – and that was as good an excuse as any!

Her act was over and a noisy interval in progress when he returned.

'I've come for my cap,' he said by way of explanation. 'See you, Knocker.'

'Andy – sorry, mate. I shouldn't have said what I did but you can't blame me. She did put it all on show, y'know.'

'Leave it, Knocker! I'm going backstage. I want words with Kitty Sutton. See you in the morning.'

He jumped lightly on to the stage and pushed aside the flimsy backcloth. Behind a curtained-off corner he guessed at once was the female dressing room.

'Hey! You!' the compere called after him. 'You aren't allowed here!'

'I want to see Kitty Sutton.'

'Who?'

'Kate from Kentucky. Tell her it's Drew.'

'Tell her yourself!' He nodded indignantly in the direction of the curtained corner. 'And no messing about!'

Drew glared. He didn't like the little man. Pansy, he'd take bets on it. He was looking for a way in when the curtain parted and Kitty stepped out. She wore trousers and a black sweater. Brightly painted toenails peeped out of her sandals. Over her arm she carried a duffel coat.

'Drew,' she whispered.

'That's me! Is the – er – *show* over?'

'I'm sorry.' She grasped his meaning at once. 'It wasn't my costume, you see. I borrowed it until my own gear arrives. It was a little on the small side.'

'I'll say. You oozed out of it all over!'

'I said I was sorry.' Her face was pale and scrubbed clean of stage make-up, her eyes looked larger than ever. 'I suppose you couldn't walk me back to my digs? I haven't got my bearings here, yet. Or do you have to go back to your ship?'

'No, I don't and yes, I'll see you back. Seems to me you need looking after!'

'Well, you know me, Drew. Still the same old Kitty! And I must say I like your uniform.'

'Flattery will get you nowhere,' he snapped.

'Look – I've said I'm sorry! What more do you want – sackcloth and ashes?'

They were walking towards the dockyard gates. Drew reached for her arm, warning her to be careful of the railway lines.

'I'm staying at Ma MacTaggart's in Roscoe Lane – theatrical digs.'

'Where's that?'

'Turn right at the top of Renshaw Street, then right again, that's all I know. Ma told me to be careful in the blackout.'

'It won't be dark until eleven tonight.'

'Okay – so don't walk me back! I'll find my own way!'

'I'll take you, I said. Besides, I want to talk to you. I shouldn't have walked off the stage like I did. I'm sorry.'

'I asked for it, I guess. Like I said – still the show-off. The guys enjoyed it, though.'

'They did! Only just don't show so much, next time!'

'I won't.' She slipped an arm through his. 'Can we start again?'

'I suppose so . . .' He wanted to, dammit.

'Right, then. Well hi, Drew! Fancy running into you after all this time! Five years, isn't it?'

'Five years. We've grown up, you and me. And I like your hair cut short, Kitty.'

'So don't I get a kiss? After five years, don't I?'

'You had your kiss, on the stage.' His mouth had gone very dry and he stared ahead, knowing that if he looked into those amazing eyes, anything might happen. 'In public, you had it!'

'Then could we do it again in private? Properly, I mean.' She glanced up and down the street. 'There's no one around.' She reached up, pulling his head down and he gathered her close, slipping his hands under her loose sweater. She wore nothing beneath it and he wanted to reach for her small, round breasts.

Her mouth was soft and warm when they kissed, and in that instant he wanted her and he didn't care about being a virgin because he knew it would be all right with Kitty.

'I usually get a room at the Adelphi when I'm ashore,' he said huskily, his cheek resting on her hair.

'No. Not there. Come back to my place, Drew. Ma's all right. She'll let you stay. And Drew, I *am* sorry about tonight.'

'Ssssh,' he whispered, and kissed her again.

'Hey!' Startled by the intensity of their embrace, she drew back from him, picked up her coat from where it had fallen then said, unsteadily, 'What's news then, Drew? We've got five years to catch up on.'

News, when their kiss, their private kiss, had set him rocking on his heels? 'I suppose you'll know Bas is over here. There was mail waiting when we docked. He was spending last weekend at Rowangarth, Mother said.'

'The so-and-so. He beat me to it!'

'How did you get over, Kitty?'

'Sailed. On a trooper, mostly with GIs and medical staff. It was a bit frightening. But where is Bas stationed?'

'At a place called Burtonwood – not far from here, it seems. I've got his address on board – I'll give it to you tomorrow. You'll be here tomorrow?' he asked, all at once anxious.

'For about a month. I think it'll be fine, joining up with ENSA. They're desperate for artistes.'

'They'd have to be to take you,' he smiled.

They began to walk slowly towards Roscoe Street, though the turmoil still raged inside him, and the strangeness of wanting her so desperately.

'No ifs. It's settled. I'll get some sort of a uniform, eventually. And when my gear arrives, I promise you my act won't be so revealing. Do you suppose, if I can get time off, I could stay with Aunt Julia, too?'

'She'll hit the roof, if you don't. Me, too. We could try and arrange to be there together. And I hope you'll be based permanently around here – did you know Daisy is stationed here, too? I see her often.' See *them* often. Daisy and Lyn. Oh, God – Lyn! He pushed her from his thoughts. 'Are you sure it'll be all right for me to stay at your digs, Kitty?'

'Sure. Ma's got a couple of empty rooms tonight. Theatricals come and go. You could take one of them – you don't have to sleep in it.'

'You mean you want to, as well?' All at once, he wasn't sure he could cope.

'If you mean do I want to sleep with you – yes, I do.'

Her directness unnerved him and even though he wanted

her so desperately he said, 'I haven't – well, it'll be the first time for me. Have you – ever . . . ?'

'Course I have!'

'*Kitty!*' That another man had touched her shocked and angered him. 'When, for God's sake?' She *couldn't* have!

'Oh, yonks ago, in college. Everybody was trying it, so I did.'

'But –'

'But *nothing*, Drew Sutton! You asked me and I told you! It was a giggle, that's all. It meant nothing.'

'And you haven't since?'

'No. I wished I hadn't, afterwards, truth known. D'you know, I can't remember his name, but I think it might have been Oscar.'

'Oscar? Oh my Lord – *Oscar!*'

They began to laugh because all at once a dim and distantly remembered Oscar didn't really matter.

'And you, Drew? No one?'

'Like I said – no one. There's a girl called Lyn – she and Daisy share a cabin. I thought she might've been the first, but something held me back. I'm glad, now. I think I was waiting for you.'

'And what's she like, this Lyn?'

'Very attractive and quiet, sort of, to be with. Good fun, though. My opposite number fancies her. Red hair and green eyes.' He felt uneasy, talking about Lyn.

'And I've got black hair and blue eyes. And I'm a show-off and you were mad at me tonight. I'm truly sorry, Drew.'

'Don't keep saying sorry! Anyway, you've got Mary Anne Pendennis hair and your mother's eyes and I was only mad at you because they were all ogling you and leering, and I wanted to kill them! And as for that three-badge stoker who got up on the stage with you . . .'

'He was fun, Drew – a good sport. He said afterwards that he'd enjoyed it – had played to the gallery, just as I was doing. Said his wife would've murdered him if she'd seen us, so I understand how you must have felt, loving me.'

'Who said I love you?' They stopped walking again to stand close and he tweaked her nose and this time, when they kissed, they did not bother to look up and down the street. 'I do, of course. I think I always did. I suppose this is what Gracie would call a hook, line and sinker job. It feels good.'

'And who is Gracie?' she demanded indignantly. 'My, Drew Sutton, you sure do get around!'

'Gracie is Rowangarth's land girl. She helps Jack Catchpole in the kitchen garden, digging for victory. I usually go dancing with her when I'm on leave, but she isn't going to fall for anyone, she told me, till the war is over. It suited me fine. No complications.'

'Okay,' she said, mollified, kissing him again. 'And I'm sure I can get some time off before so very much longer. When d'you think you'll be getting leave?'

'Not for about six weeks. Seven days, it'll be. Shall we keep it our secret, till then – well, only tell Daisy, perhaps.'

'Mm. It's hard luck about Keth – them sending him back to America, I mean. I didn't get to see him, but Mom told me he'd said on the phone that he intends trying to get back to England.'

'It's a funny old war, isn't it?'

'Sure is. But wonderful, you and me meeting like this. Are you sure you want to marry me, Drew?'

'Take it easy, Kitty! You'll be telling me you're pregnant, next! But I do love you! Don't ever change?'

She kissed him and snuggled close again, and all at once the dingy street with its bomb-damaged buildings that stood bleak and ugly against a sinking sun became a magic place he would remember when he and Kitty were old and the war was over and nothing more than memories.

'Is this the place?' he asked softly when they stopped outside a small terraced house.

'This is it, darling.'

At ten o'clock exactly, just as Drew and Kitty pushed open the door of the small, shabby bedroom; just as Grace Fielding was going to bed, the phone at the foot of the bothy staircase rang.

'For you, Gracie,' called the land girl who answered it.

'For *me*? Now who can it be?' But the speed at which she ran down the stairs, the sudden flushing of her cheeks, told anyone who was there it was the call she had been waiting all evening for.

'Hullo? Bas?'

'Hi, Gracie. Thanks for being there this morning!'

'I nearly didn't make it,' she laughed shakily. 'I couldn't get to sleep, then I must've overslept. I just made the waving place in Brattocks in time.'

'So what would you have said to me if you'd made it to the station?'

'What do you mean?' Her voice sounded breathless and didn't deceive anyone, he thought fondly.

'I mean would you have said it – said you love me?'

'I don't know. I might've.'

'Then say it now, sweetheart?'

'No. Not over the phone. But some day, I might.'

'What the heck d'you mean – some day? It doesn't take a lot of doing, Gracie. First you inhale, then you move your tongue about a bit and open your mouth and it comes out, real easy.'

'I'm sure it does.' There was laughter in her voice now. 'But remember I told you about Lancashire common sense? Well, there's something else you should know about Lancashire women, Bas Sutton. They like to be courted! Oh, I know it's an old-fashioned word and when there's a war on, courting can be a bit complicated. But that's what I want!'

'You want to be courted,' he said flatly. 'Okay – so it's a deal. So how long will it be before you finally get around to saying it, then?'

'Your guess, Bas, is as good as mine,' she said primly, 'but you might find you get quite to like it – courting, I mean.'

Bas opened his mouth to tell her he was sure he would; ask her if she knew there was a war on, though, and courting over the phone and by letter wasn't half as good as the real eyeball to eyeball, hands on, thing. But the operator interrupted to say, 'Your time is up, caller. Do you wish to pay for an extra three minutes?'

'Hell!' Bas wailed, 'haven't any more money – only a dollar bill.'

'Then ring me tomorrow? Good night, darling,' Gracie had time to whisper before the pips sounded and the line went dead.

Drew held the phone in his hand, staring at it mesmerized. Darling, she had called him. *Darling!* And she had said it all gentle, sort of, as if she meant it!

Darling. It was almost as good as 'I love you!'

43

So it was done now. Think about it, he had been told. What is so wrong being here in Washington, he had been asked.

Nothing at all, Keth was bound to admit. There were no shortages, no blackout, no bombing. Shops had goods for sale, not hidden under the counter; food was virtually unrationed, and clothing, too. Any sane young man of twenty-five would have been grateful for such a posting, he admitted it without reservation.

But sanity didn't enter into it when he was in America and Daisy was in England; not only too far away from him but putting up with shortages, bombing and the discipline of life in the armed forces. Besides which, he needed her. If things had gone to plan, they would have had their first wedding anniversary by now, maybe even their first child. And they would live in some nice house – not too far away from Holdenby, of course – and have a phone and almost certainly a car. But plans count for nothing in wartime, because the war had trampled all over their hopes and dreams.

Keth recalled the talk he had had with his immediate superior; once an Oxford don, recruited now into the secret life of Enigma.

'I thought you were settled here, Purvis.'

'I am, I suppose. But I'm doing almost exactly the same job as I did at Bletchley and it makes me wonder why I was sent here.'

'But you know why. We are part of the liaison staff now that America is at war. America gave us a lot when we were up against it; the least we can do in return is share what we know with them.'

'Share Enigma.'

'Amongst other things – yes. And you are here to help pass on that knowledge. It's a posting a lot of young men in North Africa would give a great deal for.'

'I'll grant you that, Professor, but why me? There were others who knew far more than I did.'

'Maybe so, but you were the one who was sent here. It isn't for us to question what Whitehall thinks to do. So tell me – why is it so important to get back to England when you've hardly had time to settle in?'

'I want to get married, sir.'

'Married?' The shaggy eyebrows shot up. 'You'd leave a first-class position like yours, and all it might lead to, to get *married*?'

Keth looked at him pityingly. Too old, the professor; his head too full of figures and codes and ciphers to remember the tearing need to love.

'Yes, I would. You know I went to university here and I got a job at the British Embassy because I couldn't get a passage home. Then I was offered a job in England and I couldn't get back there quickly enough. I'd never have thought I'd be sent back to Washington.'

'It isn't always what we want in wartime. At least you're alive.'

'Yes, sir. I did think my fiancée might apply for a posting over here, but there isn't a chance, she said. I believe they are notorious for being awkward about overseas drafts. If she asked for Washington she would almost certainly end up in Ceylon.'

'What does she do, Purvis?'

'She's a teleprinter-operator.'

'Hmm.' The professor drummed with his fingers on the desktop. He always drummed when he was thinking.

'She's a Wren, sir.'

'Ah, then I can't help.' The drumming stopped. 'This is an army setup. We wouldn't have any pull with the Navy.'

'So you don't hold much hope – for either of us?'

''Fraid not. You are making yourself useful, here. There's no valid reason for you to return to Bletchley. Sorry, but that's the way I see it.'

He had expected it, Keth frowned. Although the uniform he wore was merely a cover for what he did, he was getting used to the way the Army thought and acted.

'Then I would like your permission to put in an official request,' Keth said quietly. 'Not going over your head, of course, but . . .'

'Entirely up to you! And thanks for confiding in me. But if you want my advice you'll drop it – forget it.'

'Yes, sir,' Keth had said from the doorway. 'Thanks for your time.'

He had closed the door quietly behind him then immediately written his request to see the commanding officer. And no matter what any of them said, no matter how many times they turned him down, he would go on trying.

He blotted the sheet of paper, folded it and put it in an envelope. He wondered what Daisy was doing now. Time in England was ahead of here. Soon it would be tomorrow in Liverpool. He wondered if she had been able to get home for her birthday or if it had been just the same as any other day.

And why he was wasting time with requests for a posting to England, he didn't know. They would never let him go back, he knew it. He would sit out the war here and by the time it was over he would be too old to care. Just like his professor.

He reached for his pen and began to write, urgently, desperately.

My darling, I miss you so, need you so much. I want us to be together. I want to hold you and kiss you and hear you saying you love me.

'Oh, what the hell!' He tore the page from the pad, ripped it angrily into tiny pieces and threw it in the waste-paper basket. Then he looked at his request in the brown manila envelope and wondered if it wouldn't be better to tear that up, too.

Best sleep on it, because he knew that tomorrow he would place it on the commanding officer's desk. And tonight, just for the hell of it, he would get drunk. He would go to his room and get very drunk because he wanted Daisy so much it hurt.

He wished he had never heard the name Enigma.

Drew opened his eyes and lay still, taking in the outline of a cheap, ornate wardrobe, a dressing table with an old-fashioned mirror hanging above it, and dimly, on the pillow next to his own, Kitty's head.

So it was true? Last night had happened. She was real. They had been lovers and he hadn't made a mess of it. With Kitty it had been easy and wonderful and better than he had ever thought it could be. He reached to pull back the blackout curtain and she stirred, yawned, then opened her eyes.

'Good morning, darling,' she said huskily.

'Hullo.' He leaned over her, touching her lips with his own.

'Ouch! You need a shave!'

'Sorry, sweetheart.' He looked at her shoulders and the shape of her round, hard breasts beneath the thin sheet. She had never looked so beautiful as she did now, and she was his. 'I love you,' he whispered, reaching for her and she wriggled herself comfortable in his arms then kissed the hollow at his throat. 'Do you realize that this time yesterday, I had just handed over the watch to Knocker and you were my Kentucky cousin and for all I knew that was where you still were? My life was reasonably uncomplicated. I had a fair chance of surviving the war, I thought, and Rowangarth was always there, and Mother and Nathan and Lady. And Daisy, of course. I dated girls. I even wondered what it would be like to make love to them – one of them, especially.'

'Lyn, uh?'

'Lyn. And then you came back into my life, you in your outrageous costume, and I knew it was you I'd been waiting for; realized you were my past, my present and, if I make it through the war, I want you to be my future. So will you marry me?'

'That was a real pretty speech, Drew. The answer is yes. When?'

'As soon as we can make it.'

'I suppose you could call us married, now . . .'

'I suppose so. But I'd like it to be official and legal. And I'd like it a whole lot better if you had a wedding ring on your finger when you're doing your Kate from Kentucky act. And what your pa would say if he'd seen you last night, I just daren't imagine.'

'Well, the way I look at it is this. I'm over twenty-one so what Pa don't see he don't need to bother over, and if my fiancé doesn't mind my act, then what the heck!'

'But I *do* mind, Kitty! They were leering at you last night and I saw red. I don't suppose you could show a bit less?'

'I could wear a knitted muffler,' she giggled.

'Better than that, how about marrying me and giving up your ENSA lark?'

'No chance. Not till I'm pregnant, anyway.'

'Then I'll have to do my best to get you – hell!' He sat bolt-upright. 'Kitty! Last night – I didn't – I mean, well, you *could* be –'

'Pregnant already? Suppose I could. We were a bit

careless. Guess you'd better do something about it before another time. I'd kind of like not to be pregnant when I walk down the aisle. And I hear clothes are rationed, here, and wedding dresses hard to come by. What say I write Mom and get her to send one over. I'd like to be married in white, war or no war.'

'I thought we weren't going to say anything about us – not yet, that was.'

'That was last night. This morning I want everyone to know. What time do you have to be back on board?'

'Noon. We go out again, tonight. And if it isn't going to be a secret, then I'd like to tell Daisy this morning. She'll probably know we're in dock. She'll be expecting me to ring her.'

'Okay. Then before you do –' she reached up, pulling him closer – 'love me again?' Her lips were softly parted, her eyes dreamy.

'I need a shave,' he said huskily, kissing her softly. 'And do you think we should? We agreed that next time –'

'I think we should. You know you want to. If I get pregnant, we can always have a shotgun wedding.'

Her warm, soft body was touching his. Somehow, nothing mattered but having her.

'Shall I close the curtain?'

'No. I want to look at you.' She leaned over him, kissing his nose, the tip of his chin, his eyelids.

'I love you,' he said as he took her and in that moment of coupling, he wondered how he had lived so long without her or what life would be like if suddenly he was to awaken and find all this was nothing more than a dream.

'Hi, Drew!' Daisy smiled into the phone. 'What's news?'

'News is we got in late last night. I didn't ring, of course.'

'No. Well you wouldn't, us being on lates. So where shall we meet?'

'Well – that's just it,' he hesitated. 'Exactly what are you doing, right now?'

'This very minute, you mean? I'm standing in the hall with a mop and dusters and a tin of floor polish in my hand. We're going to clean the cabin. Why do you ask?'

'Are you near a chair? Can you sit down because I think you'd better.'

'Drew! You're leaving the *Maggie*!'

'No, I –'

'You've got your hook up? You're a leading-telegraphist!'

'No, Daisy. *No!* Just *listen*. We can't meet. I've got a date, this afternoon – with Kitty.'

'Not *our* Kitty – Kitty Sutton?' She gave a laugh of delight.

'Kitty's over here – based in Liverpool for a few weeks at least. She's joining up with ENSA, you see, and I –'

'But Drew – why can't we make it a foursome? I'm longing to see her. It's years and years since we met. How is she?'

'She's fine.' More than fine. She was his, and she loved him.

'We aren't on duty till six. Couldn't we meet up somewhere? Just imagine – Kitty *here*, in Liverpool! And Bas is near, too! Mam told me last night. He's been staying with Aunt Julia. Isn't it wonderful! We only need Keth, now, and –' She stopped, suddenly aware of what she had said. 'Oh, dear. Wouldn't it have been just perfect if Keth could be here, too?'

'Daisy. Please listen. I know you aren't going to believe this – I can hardly believe it myself – but I've asked Kitty to marry me, and she said yes!'

'You – have – what? *Marry you?* When did all this happen, then?' Her jaw sagged.

'I met her last night on the dockside and I asked her to marry me, this morning – in bed.'

'You mean you've – you and her? *Already?* Well, I must say you're a quick worker, Drew Sutton! I mean – well, I don't know what to say!'

'How about "Congratulations", Daiz, and "I hope you'll both be very happy"?'

'Drew – what about Lyn? How is she going to take this?' She stared at the tin of floor polish in her hand, and the duster; at ordinary things because they made more sense, really, than what she had just heard. 'You know she's mad about you?'

'I knew she liked me – yes. And I like her a lot. But Kitty is the one, Daiz. Be glad for me?'

'Ssssh! Got to go! Lyn's coming downstairs!'

'Then let me speak to her?'

'No! I'll tell her! 'Bye, Drew! Take care!' She slammed down the phone, then turned to face Lyn.

'That was Drew.'

'Good. I was coming to see what had kept you.' She picked up the mop and Daisy followed her up the stairs. 'Where are we meeting him?'

'We aren't. Lyn – there's something you must know.' She took her arm and pulled her inside the cabin, closing the door, leaning on it as if she were afraid that once she knew, Lyn would run away and do something awful. 'Drew can't meet us, this afternoon.'

'Why not? Is he in the rattle, or something?'

'No. He's meeting Kitty. Kitty Sutton.'

'The one from America, you mean? She's over here?'

'Yes. And I'm sorry, Lyn, but there's no other way to say this. Drew says they're engaged. He asked her to marry him, and she said yes.'

'B-but I don't understand.' White-faced, she sat with a bump on Daisy's bunk. 'You're having me on? It *was* Drew on the phone? You're sure?'

'It was Drew. I told him you were coming downstairs and he asked to speak to you, but I hung up on him.'

'Why? What gives you the right to do that? I'd have liked to speak to him, tell him – tell him I'm glad and that I hope – hope . . . Oh God, Daisy!'

She closed her eyes tightly, biting on her lip to stop the sobs that had risen in her throat and were hurting like hell.

'Sssssh. It's all right, Lyn. It's all right.' She sat down beside her, gathering her close, hugging her. 'I'm sorry.'

'But when did it happen? Has he been seeing her and not saying anything?'

'No. They met last night. She's just come over. On the dockside, it was. And they spent the night together.'

There, she had said it. Lyn knew everything now. Best she should, though if Drew were here right now, she would gladly wring his neck. Not for falling in love with Kitty – you couldn't blame any man for falling in love with Kitty – but for doing it so suddenly and thoroughly!

The door opened. The duty-Wren poked her head round the door.

'Call for you, Dwerryhouse! A man.'

'Drew!' Daisy hissed. Drew ringing back because she had hung up on him! 'Look – be a love and tell whoever it is that you can't find me?'

'No! I'll take it.' Lyn rose to her feet. 'I want to talk to him, if that's okay with you, Daisy?'

'Don't, Lyn! Don't be a fool!'

But Lyn was out of the room and running downstairs.

'Well! What was all that about?' asked the duty-Wren.

'Don't ask, because I don't know! I honestly don't know, but it's my guess my brother is in for an ear-bashing!'

They walked across the landing and leaned over the banister rail, looking down at Lyn who was smiling into the phone.

'Drew! It's Lyn.' Her voice came up to them clearly. 'Daisy has just told me that congratulations are in order. They are? Then I hope you'll be – I hope you'll *both* be very happy!'

She hesitated, still smiling, and Daisy closed her eyes and waited, breath indrawn.

'For goodness' sake, Drew – what do you mean you hope I understand? Of course I understand. Why shouldn't I? You and I had fun, but that's all it was. Just fun, Drew.'

Another pause.

'That's just fine, then. And I mean it – every happiness. Now do you want to speak to Daisy? Okay, you don't. Well, careful how you go, sailor! See you around, sometime!'

She replaced the phone then walked slowly across the hall to sit on the bottom stair. Then she covered her face with her hands and sobbed; sobbed as if her heart would never be whole again.

'Drew! I'll murder him!' In a flash, Daisy was at Lyn's side, holding her, hushing her. 'Lyn, don't cry? Please don't cry?'

But the sobs went on, and on . . .

High summer was Alice's time for bedding washing. She had used all her precious soap flakes, but now the blankets hung on the line, carefully pegged to keep their shape. Tonight, she would take them down and bury her face in their fluffiness, sniffing their new-washed cleanness, and when they had hung another day in tomorrow's sun to air, she would fold them into her blanket chest, lavender bags between them, to await winter.

There was something satisfying about heaping blankets on the beds against the cold of winter, to remember the sunny summer day on which she washed them; remember squinting up into a sun-filled sky when she hung them to dry, and the air filled with the scent of elderflower blossom.

'Alice! Thank heaven you're in!' Julia, red-faced from running, arrived to interrupt her daydreaming.

'In? And why *thank heaven*? Shall I put the kettle on?' The expression on Julia's face seemed to warrant it.

'I should have phoned, but I wanted to come. And no thanks, don't bother. It would only be a waste of a spoonful of tea! But I've just got to tell you. It's Drew!'

'Y-yes?' Alice pushed the prop under the clothes line then picked up the clothes basket and the peg basket very carefully. In times of stress, doing ordinary things seemed somehow to make it not quite so bad. And what Julia was about to say, she knew, was of importance. 'Drew?'

'Yes! And don't look so anxious! But I can't make head nor tail of it. We didn't have long on the phone – well, you know how it is with long-distance. But in the space of three minutes he's only got himself engaged!'

'Engaged?' Alice stood stock-still but Julia took her arm, guiding her towards the kitchen door.

'Yes. And I think I'd better have that cup of tea. They've decided they want everybody to know. Daisy knows already, he told me.'

'But – *who*? Lyndis, is it? And why so sudden?'

'It's Kitty. Kitty Sutton, that's who! Oh, Daisy, he sounded so happy, so excited. Just like I feel, now. He'll be ringing you, I shouldn't wonder . . .'

'So Kitty's got herself over here, too? Well, Bas said she would. But when did she arrive?'

'Two days ago, it seems. Drew met her last night on the dockside. She was with a concert party. And that was it, he said. He asked her to marry him and she said yes and he says can they have one of Grandmother Whitecliffe's rings as there aren't any decent ones in the shops now. He'll be bringing her with him on his next leave, I suppose. He just knew she was the right one, he said. But is he *sure*, Alice? I mean, how can he be?'

'Oh, Julia Sutton! How can you!' Alice began to laugh. Whether it was reaction to the shock of Julia's news or whether she thought it really funny, she didn't know. But she laughed, then said, 'Oh, how *can* you? How dare old kettles call young pots black? What do you mean – is he sure? How sure were you that morning when you went, black eye and all, looking for a young doctor whose wife might well have opened the door to you? But you went and you wouldn't let me go with you, even though I was supposed to be maiding you! Love at first sight you said it was, so what's so strange about it happening again?'

'You're right, Alice. You always are,' Julia sighed. 'We Suttons are good at it, it would seem. Now Drew has done it. And d'you know what? I can't wait for them to get married, wartime wedding or not!'

'You'll wait until they tell you they're good and ready,' Alice said as severely as she was able. 'And I'm pleased for him. I always liked Kitty, tomboy though she was. She'll be good for him. Drew was always inclined to seriousness as a little boy.'

'Oh! I'm forgetting! Kitty will be your daughter-in-law, too, won't she, Alice? Well, I suppose she'll have to find out that when you marry a sailor with two mothers, you get two mothers-in-law. You're sure you're happy about it, Alice? Even if it is so sudden – are you?'

'I'm very happy. Another cousins' wedding in the family, had you thought? And since we are talking weddings – what about young Bas?'

'What about him?' Julia pulled out a chair then sat, chin on hands, still smiling.

'Well, I don't want you to think that Polly is a gossip because you know she isn't – but the land girls have gone out to work long before the mail van comes, so the letters are stuck there all day on the board for everyone to see. And there have been two letters for Gracie since you know who had a weekend at Rowangarth. And phone calls, too. I think Bas is smitten, an' all. But not one word about what I've told you, mind!'

'I won't. Promise. But, Alice, how is Daisy going to take all this, poor love? Drew getting engaged, I mean, and Bas halfway there, it would seem. How is she going to feel when Keth is so far away? And him going without warning, either. It's a good thing her wedding dress is at Rowangarth. Out of sight, out of mind . . .'

'Well, that's the way it is when there's a war on. And who's to say Keth might not get back home again just as suddenly as he went?'

'Do you think there's a chance he might, then? I'd so love my Clan together again, just once.'

'No, I don't. And I suppose it's wrong of me, but I hope he stays in America for the duration, though it'll be sad for Daisy, seeing all the Clan so happy.'

'And sadder still, for poor little Tatty. She'll be twenty-one, in March. I wonder if she'll come home for her birthday or if she'll let it pass? She seems happier with Sparrow than ever she was at home. And she'll come into her inheritance then. She'll be rich, just like Daisy. Does Daisy ever talk about her money, Alice?'

'No. Hardly at all, though she did say last time she was home that she's had a cheque book for a year and never written a cheque yet. Nothing to spend it on, she says. And girls in the Forces don't get clothing coupons. But let's have that cup of tea? I think we need it and we've got to drink to Drew and Kitty, now haven't we?'

But drink a toast to her son's future happiness in tea? Oh, my word, no! All at once happy, she opened the cupboard door and took out a brown bottle. Still three inches of medicinal brandy in it, she was pleased to discover.

'I think we should have a drop of this in our tea, Julia. A snifter, as Aunt Sutton used to say.'

Carefully Alice poured a capful into each cup, then eyes brimming with happy tears she whispered, 'To Drew and Kitty, and to all those we love.'

'And to all those we have loved.' Julia's smile was serene.

To her mother who was with Pa, now; to Andrew, her first love; to Aunt Sutton and Giles and Robert – and to Uncle Edward.

'And those we have loved,' Alice echoed. To Reuben and and Mrs Shaw and Jin Dobb, and to Dickon. And especially to dear, gentle Giles who would be happy, were he alive, for the son he called his own. 'You and I are very lucky, Julia. Even with another dratted war to contend with, we're lucky.'

And that summer evening, when she had told Tom about it and taken her blankets from the line and folded them carefully, she knew that in winter, when she took them out all lavender-scented and put them on the beds, she would not only remember the sunny day on which she washed them, but that it was the day, too, on which Drew and Kitty became engaged.

'It's going to be a stinker down there, tonight,' Daisy mourned. Another week of night watches had come round and afterwards, their forty-eight-hour rest period.

'They owe us our crafty weekends, after night watches. You'll be going to Yorkshire, I suppose?'

'What do you think?'

'Hm. I'll be away to Auntie Blod's.' Lyn's new-found mother was still Auntie Blod. 'Look, Daisy, I've got to tell you this; been meaning to for a while now. I've seen my divvy; asked for a draft.'

'Lyn! *No!* I thought –' She stopped. Lyn was getting over Drew and Kitty, she had thought. The weeping had stopped and Lyn's eyelids were no longer swollen. Only her sad eyes and the way she steered away from any conversation that might, eventually, have mention of Drew in it, told Daisy who knew her so well that she was still hurting inside.

'Daisy! *Yes!* Look – I can't go on living each day trying not to think of Drew and wondering if the *Maggie* is in, or if he'll phone you. And I can't take being dropped – avoided. Because we each have to avoid the other, now. Imagine how it would be if I were to come across them in

Liverpool? How would I smile and act like nothing had happened when all the time I would want to pull my fingernails down her face? Oh, it was all one-sided. Looking back, I know I thought more about Drew than he did about me. But I've had it, Daisy. I saw Ma'am and told her all about it – asked for a draft to anywhere she wanted to send me. I even thought about volunteering for overseas, but then I remembered Auntie Blod and realized I didn't want to leave her. She's all I have left now.'

'But had you thought – if you leave here you might be miles and miles away from Llangollen? No more crafty weekends every four weeks.'

'I realize that. I've thought about it a lot. Anyway, Ma'am said it wasn't on; that I couldn't have a draft from here for no reason at all because it seems that having your heart broken isn't a reason. But I think she understood, for all that, because she asked me how long I'd been in the Wrens and I told her two and a half years. "Time to put in for your hook, then," she said. And she said she'd have a look at my record sheet and probably recommend me for it.'

'I see. Your divisional officer recommends you for promotion so you automatically get a draft chit?' It was the way the Navy always did it.

'Yes. Leading-Wren Carmichael – what about that? No more duty-stooging in the Wrennery, and extra late passes.'

'And seven bob a week more and your hook up.' A hook; a killick anchor sewn on her left arm to show she would have had two stripes, if she had been in khaki, in the ATS.

'Wonder where they'll send me – if it happens, that is.'

'Don't even talk about it! Do you think I want someone else in your bunk?'

'Maybe not – but had you thought? You could grab the top one before my relief came.'

'I don't want the top bunk! Oh, Lyn, you were so good to me when I first came here, running a temperature –

remember? And there has just been the two of us, sharing this little cabin.'

'And sharing Drew, when the *Maggie* came in.'

'I hate this blasted war!' Keth thousands of miles away, Drew all at once taken up with Kitty and now Lyn might be going, too. And to cap it all, a week of sweltering, airless night watches. 'How long do you think we can stand it?'

'Longer than the Jews, that's for sure.'

'I know. And at least Keth is safe.' Daisy was all at once contrite, though her world seemed to be crumbling into little useless pieces and suddenly she wanted Keeper's Cottage and Brattocks Wood, and Dada taking her on his knee and telling her it would all come right. Only she was too big, now, and too grown up to sit on Dada's knee and not even Dada could bring Keth back home or make things come right for Lyn.

'I think,' she said very earnestly, 'that when next we are on early watches, we should do a pub crawl in Liverpool and get as drunk as skunks.'

'On weak beer? Grow up, Dwerryhouse!'

44

'At ease, Purvis.' The commanding officer looked up from his desk. 'Take off your cap. This isn't official yet.'

Keth sat down, noisily clearing his throat. 'Thank you, sir,' he said because some response, he supposed, was expected of him.

He hoped it was not his request for a draft back to England they were about to discuss because it was barely two weeks since he had made it and Authority never moved *that* fast. So soon after, it could only be an uncompromising refusal. A yes would have taken much, much longer to ponder upon.

A pity, really, the refusal could not have happened yesterday, or tomorrow. Pity to spoil his birthday, which this far had been good; had started with a letter that arrived three days ago marked 'Open on the 12th' written on the back.

This morning, he had read Daisy's letter; a loving, wanting, yearning letter that made him close his eyes and hold his indrawn breath so he could hear her voice, remember the sweet, soft scent of her.

A drawer closed with a bang, invading Keth's thoughts. He straightened his shoulders as a folder was opened and read through very slowly. Then the senior officer closed the file and laid it to his left, as if he were discarding it.

Keth felt a surge of disappointment, even though he hadn't expected a resounding yes; not the first time of asking. But he would ask again! Formally and officially he would request to be sent back to England and would keep on asking. Water dripping on a stone. They would get so sick of him that –

'You'll know what this is about, Purvis?'

'Well yes, sir.' He had thought of little else lately. 'It's about my request to be sent back to England.'

'Hm. So do you want the good news first, or the bad?'

'Whichever, sir.' They really *had* turned him down!

'The bad news is that your request has been approved, but with conditions attached.'

'*Approved!*' Conditions? Some remote Scottish island, signal-gathering from Scandinavia perhaps? Another Enigma, more *bombes*, but in some isolated place? So did it matter? 'Thank you, sir. Am I to know the details?'

'That's just it. The bad news. I don't know what they are. The move back to Blighty comes with conditions attached, that's all it says. Looks to me like a take-it-or-leave-it deal. Don't ask me to explain the way the Army thinks. I'm only a boffin in khaki!'

'Sir, I'll take it! And thank you,' he added hastily because which conditions could be so awful that they weren't worth getting back to Daisy again?

'You're sure about it?'

'I'm sure, sir. I'll take a chance on it.' Bet your life he would!

'Then the good news is that when, *if*, you go back, you'll be promoted to captain. Congratulations, Purvis.'

'Captain?' He felt his face flush. A more responsible job, that was what it amounted to. So wasn't his back broad and didn't he know what he was doing – as well as the next man, that was? 'I suppose it's too much to ask when?'

'When you'll be going back? That I don't know. Might be weeks, might be months. There'll be your relief to organize and get over here and you'll have to hand things over to him – put him in the picture, I would think. But there must be no mention of this in letters home. No hints between the lines and all that sort of thing. When I hear things are on the move you'll know at once, and you'll be in the queue for a seat on a plane over. Or you might have to sail – okay?'

It had been wonderfully, unbelievably okay! He hadn't been able to stop himself grinning every time he thought about it. He had even allowed himself to wonder if being a captain would earn him a seat on the plane or if he would have to wedge himself in again, between cargo and the tail-end gunner.

But did it matter? He found himself thinking about a Christmas wedding. Vague conditions? So what? He was going home with another pip on his shoulder! Now, for the first time in months, he could think about Daisy and wonder what she was doing without feeling resentment.

All at once, life was good, again!

Daisy was rinsing underwear in the wash house when Lyn came in, her cheeks bright red, a frown on her forehead.

'There you are!'

'Of course I'm here! You always say that!' Daisy said crossly. 'And why weren't you on the transport?'

'Because I had to see Ma'am after watch was over and I couldn't get to let you know!'

'You've seen your divvy? What did she say?' All at once, Daisy was sorry she had snapped because she knew exactly what Lyn would tell her. 'Your draft – it's approved?' She carried her washing across to the mangle. 'That's what it was about?'

'Yes. Sort of. My promotion to Leading-Wren is official. Ma'am gave me a chit to draw hooks from stores. I'm to sew them up as from the beginning of August.'

'So you'll be leaving, then? I wish you weren't, Lyn. I'm glad about your hook, but things won't be the same, will they? We've had some good times together.'

'Yup! Only don't get designs on my bunk, Dwerryhouse, because I shall still want it, would you believe?'

'But They always draft you, when you get promotion.' Of course They did!

'Yes, and They have. Technically, that is. It's all come about very suddenly.'

'You can say that again!'

'It's all come about very suddenly,' Lyn smiled. 'I'm drafted to Flag Officer, you see, which takes care of the move – technically, as I said . . .'

'So all it entails is shifting from Commander-in-Chief's to Flag Officer's setup?'

'Mm. To the Liver Building. Sixth floor. To Flag Officer in Chief, Port of Liverpool. I'm leaving Epsom House and going down the road, that's all. And it could only happen to me! I'd hoped to put this place behind me, but it seems it's not to be. I'm not even leaving Hellas House. It won't be necessary, Ma'am said. I'm not even changing watches, so it's going to be almost the same as before.'

'Then don't expect me to be sorry because I really hated it, thinking you were going. Only don't pull rank on me, will you?'

'I won't. Promise. And all this has come about because there's an urgent need of a leading-telephonist. The one I'm replacing is going overseas so they want her relief as soon as possible.'

'It was meant to be, Lyn. You weren't meant to go.'

'The only thing is that the Liver Building is right on the Pierhead, so there'll be a risk of bumping into Drew.'

'Then when – *if* – you do, you'll have to grin and bear it, just like you did when you stood there and wished them both every happiness, that morning on the phone. And don't say you didn't, because I was there listening.'

'I won't ever stop loving him.' Lyn's eyes were all at once sad.

'I know that.'

'I won't ever get over him, either,' she warned, 'even though Auntie Blod says the pain does get bearable in time.

She was very much in love with my father, you know.'

'Then what say I hang this stuff to dry and we go for a walk in the park? It's a lovely afternoon; a shame to be in. And it's Keth's birthday today, so I'd be glad of your company, Leading-Wren, to stop me having a whinge. I've been feeling a bit sorry for myself today. Or we could skip supper and go to town. We might even do a pub crawl; get as drunk as a pair of skunks.'

'On weak beer? Grow up, Dwerryhouse!'

And they began to giggle, because there was nothing else to do, really, but giggle. And it was a whole lot better than being miserable.

'You are looking very pleased with yourself, Mrs Sutton.' Nathan kissed his wife's cheek. 'What have you been up to?'

'I've been counting my blessings as befits a parson's missus. I've been thinking all day that something wonderful is going to happen.'

'Like what?'

'We-e-ll, you know I've always wished and wanted and prayed for my young ones to be together – just once, even, so I can take a snap of them, just as I did that Christmas before the war – have something to keep for ever and ever?'

'What do you mean – keep for ever?' he frowned. 'That sounds a bit fatalistic.'

'No, it's just something I want to happen – have all my Clan together whilst they are still mine, sort of. Before Daisy marries Keth, and Drew marries Kitty, and –'

'And before Bas marries Gracie, because that young man is never away these days. Three times he's been here and you can't tell me it's out of concern for his aged aunt and uncle!'

'Agreed. But isn't it lovely to think that however awful war is, it can't stop people falling in love? I think Drew and Kitty might be home very soon. Drew is due his long leave any time now, so surely Kitty will be able to get time off, too? And Bas can get colour films in their canteen, remember.'

'But you can't take a picture of your precious Clan, my darling, because Keth isn't here. It wouldn't be right to take one without him, now would it?'

'No. But he might come home. I know he would want to, if ever he got the chance.'

'And if he's got the sense, he'll stay where he's safe. Goodness, you'd think the world was going to end, all the young ones getting married. Because they *are* young, Julia, and so impatient! Look how old you and I were when we got hitched, for goodness' sake!'

'No comment,' she said drily. 'And have you forgotten what it's like to be in love in wartime – oh, sorry, Nathan!' When would she ever learn to watch her tongue? 'That wasn't very kind of me, was it?'

'No, it wasn't, because I was in love with a married woman, remember?'

'I remember. Thank you for waiting all those years for me. But I'm so happy, today. Something good is going to happen, just see if it doesn't! I *will* get my snaps of the Clan, I know it! I felt a sort of Jinny Dobb inside me. It was at Keeper's, actually. Alice was saying that she wondered if Keth had got her card in time for his birthday and suddenly I got this warm, happy feeling about him.'

'Julia, be careful. Don't raise Daisy's hopes, will you, because miracles don't happen often – not even little ones. And the Clan being all here together – now that would be a miracle, wouldn't it?' He gathered her into his arms, loving her as he had always loved her for the best part of his life and in all her moods; in every high and every awful low. 'Don't hope for too much, Julia?' he smiled, kissing her gently.

'Oh ye of little faith,' she teased. 'But I suppose it isn't any use expecting a man to understand. And you won't stop me wishing and hoping and praying Keth home, so don't dare try!'

Daisy replaced the phone, frowning. Drew, it had been, telling her he was going on leave – that he and Kitty were going on leave – and were there any messages?

'Nothing in particular. Just tell them I'm fine. And by the way, I'll be home myself on Friday, Drew – just the usual quick weekend,' she said, lowering her voice.

'Then you'll meet Kitty at last, Daiz! That's great!'

Great – even though she was between two stools; happy for Drew, sad for Lyn. Happy for Kitty, too, because Kitty was special and fun to be with and was a part of their enchanted youth when there was never going to be another war. How wonderful that life once was; how innocently uncomplicated. How unbelievable they had made plans without ever having to look over their shoulders or cross their fingers as they did now.

Reluctantly Daisy opened the door of Cabin 4A.

'I – er . . .'

'That was Drew on the phone,' Lyn said matter-of-factly.

'Well – yes.'

'And he's going on leave? I suppose he's taking – Kitty.' She hesitated only slightly before saying the name.

'Look, Lyn, it's very –'

'Awkward for you? I understand, Daisy. Well, it's okay. Things will be different when I'm not at Epsom House any more.'

'Things *won't* be different, Lyn, and you know it! We're both still on D-watch. All that will change is that you'll get off the transport before me and pick it up again from the Pierhead.'

'There's my hook, remember.'

'Okay – so you'll be a Leading-Wren.' Lyn had already sewn the blue anchors on her left sleeves. 'It won't make any difference to you and me, will it?'

'Of course it won't. But Drew *is* taking her home to meet his folks?' Lyn pressed.

'She's met them, dozens of times. They are cousins, don't forget – but yes, it seems he is . . .'

'Making it official. Making plans,' Lyn said lightly. Too lightly. 'Choosing a ring from the Sutton hoard?'

'Don't – *please*. Don't make things worse for yourself.'

'But I've got to, don't you see? I can't go on pretending it didn't happen between Drew and me – that I really fell for him and I thought he'd feel the same for me, given time. But instead he met Kitty Sutton, and wham!'

'No, Lyn. Kitty came back into his life, and he knew. They grew up together, remember.'

'I suppose so. She had a head start on me and I'll say she's a fast worker. He stayed at her digs that same night, didn't he? That's what makes me really mad – me, I mean, practically offering it on a plate . . .'

'Lyn – stop it! You can't turn the clock back!'

'No. But if I could, I would! And if I had any say in the matter I'd be pregnant now, and he'd *have* to marry me.'

'But it didn't happen between you, did it? It wasn't meant to.'

'No! But if it had I wouldn't have been like Auntie Blod. She kept her mouth shut till it was too late. And look what happened to her. She lost both him and me!'

'Yes. She really had something to moan about!' Daisy walked over to the window, shutting it with a bang. 'And it's starting to rain.'

'Hell! That's all I need! That, and a week of nights!'

'So let's wash our hair?' There was usually hot water, afternoons. 'We can have it pinned up and dry before we go on watch.'

'I haven't got any shampoo.'

'Well I have, so you can share mine. Come on, Carmichael. Snap out of it!'

'Okay. I'm sorry. I must be an awful drip these days.'

'Yes, you are. But I understand, truly I do.' She gave Lyn a brief, comforting hug.

But she didn't understand, not really, because to truly understand she would have to lose Keth to another woman and that would never happen.

But it *could* happen. Keth might be away for years and years because everybody accepted, now, that the war would go on for far longer than the last one; more than four years!

So there were more years to be endured; more years of young men getting killed and husbands parted from their wives and children and having no say at all in the matter; rationing going on and on and merchant seamen getting killed bringing those rations to us. *And* the blackout!

But Keth wouldn't get tired of waiting any more than she would. And at least he had a better chance of making it home alive than most men could ever hope for.

'Penny for them,' Lyn offered. 'If they're worth a penny, that is. You were miles away and looking miserable.'

'I *was* miles away. And I was counting my blessings.'

'Is that a dig at me, then?'

'No. But I was thinking about Keth and realizing he's pretty safe in America. Tim Thomson would've given his eye teeth for a draft like that – and Tatty would, too.'

'So let's wash our hair, Dwerryhouse, before we're weeping on each other's shoulders.'

It was good, sound advice, Daisy was bound to admit. And what else was there to do on a wet afternoon in Liverpool!

'Here! Catch!' Smiling, Kitty Sutton passed her case to Drew, then stepped down from the train. 'Oh, almost there. Does the Holdenby train still leave from –' She stopped, all at once shocked. 'Hey! What happened?' She gazed at the smoke-blackened station roof, open to the sky, the platforms where repair gangs worked. 'Was there a fire? What gives?'

'I thought you knew. I know Mother wrote to tell you.'

'We sometimes got letters with bits sliced out . . .'

'Then the censor must have cut it out. York was bombed in April – quite badly. They hit the station here – the London-to-Edinburgh train had just pulled in; a bomb got the platform and there were terrible casualties.'

'Just the station, Drew?'

'No. A lot more besides. But they didn't get the Minster, though goodness knows how they missed it. It was bright moonlight.'

'But that's terrible!' Kitty's homecoming was all at once saddened.

'It happens, darling. You've seen Liverpool; wait till you see London. And Plymouth and Coventry and –'

'But what did York do to deserve this?' Lovely, ages-old, precious York, the part of her that was English protested.

'Why should Norwich and Exeter be bombed either? Or Coventry? Because they were old, I suppose, and had cathedrals or minsters. Because of what our bombers did to Cologne, Hitler said. But they didn't bomb the Holdenby Flyer,' he comforted, pointing in the direction of the little local train, hissing steam, ready to leave from its same side platform. 'Come on! Holdenby next stop!'

'Mm.' She turned to smile up at him. 'Seeing Rowangarth after all this time away. How long, Drew?'

'Almost exactly five years. 'It was 'thirty-seven when you were last here.'

'Too long! And say, did I ever tell you I love you – on York station, I mean?'

'Idiot! And hurry!' He took her case. 'It's leaving.'

Doors were banging. The guard was looking at his watch. The little Holdenby train always left on time!

*   *   *

They called, 'Thanks, chum,' to the driver of an army truck who dropped them at Rowangarth gates, then they left their cases and respirators at the gate lodge to be collected later because nothing, Drew insisted, must be allowed to spoil the absolute joy of walking the tree-lined drive, of rounding the bend and seeing Rowangarth all at once, unchanged and welcoming as if they had never been away. For a little while, a sheltering, loving haven from the world at war outside.

And so Kitty Sutton, her hand in Drew's, saw the old house again that late-summer afternoon, warm and lazy in the sun, and tears filled her eyes and she whispered, 'Oh, darling, I do so love it!'

'And I should hope so, too. It's a part of the deal – love me, love Rowangarth,' he said sternly, mopping her tears. 'Blow your nose,' he ordered, 'and stop grizzling.'

'I'm *not* grizzling. Just unbearably happy. And I always did – love Rowangarth, I mean.'

'And me?'

'Reckon I must've always loved you too, Drew. Think I only realized it, though, the night of the concert when I kissed you. You were so mad at me! Something just hit me and I thought, *Gee whiz!* Guess it was your sailor suit. But do hurry.'

She held out her hand and they began to run, just as Julia opened the door and waved to them because she had been waiting impatiently all afternoon, looking for them from upstairs windows. Now she stood at the top of the steps, smiling a welcome, hearing their distant laughter and was all at once so happy that it hurt. Drew was home, and Kitty.

He's home, Mother, with Kitty, she whispered with her heart, *and they are so in love*.

She sent her thoughts high and wide because a joy such as she felt at that moment had to be shared. Then, arms wide, she ran the last few yards to meet them, her dearly loved son and the girl he was to marry.

In that moment, she knew complete happines.

'Oh, come in, do, and let me have a look at you!' Alice hugged Kitty to her, then gazed at her, long and frankly. The young girl with a mop of black curls tied up in ribbons was gone. Here was a beautiful, violet-eyed woman. Small wonder Drew had fallen head over heels in love. 'You've grown up real pretty, Kitty Sutton.'

'You reckon?' Kitty's cheeks pinked. 'Well, thanks. Oh, and Drew said I was to remember specially to tell you that we called last night, and no one was in. Nor at the bothy.'

'No. Me and Polly both were out. Mothers' Union meeting at the vicarage, and Tom away Home Guarding. Sorry about that, love. So where is Drew this morning?'

'Gone to Creesby with Aunt Julia. Estate business at the bank – and Drew wants me to have a ring.'

'Ah, yes. Julia keeps the stuff at the bank. So you're to have one of your great-grandmother Whitecliffe's rings? Pity there aren't any decent diamond rings in the shops now.'

'But I'd rather have an old ring, Mrs Dwerryhouse. Kind of traditional, isn't it? And I can't go on calling you Mrs Dwerryhouse, now that I'm almost a Rowangarth Sutton. Drew calls you Lady – can I call you Lady, too?'

'Of course you can! And poor old you, getting two mothers-in-law.' Alice laughed.

'Yes, but they're both lovely! And what do I call Aunt Julia, now? Not that she's really my aunt.'

'No. She's your father's cousin – but I'd go on with the Aunt Julia bit until you and Drew are married, then see what pops out. When I was married to Giles I felt real peculiar, trying not to call his mother milady. So I called her mother-in-law – with great difficulty, I might add, me once being a servant there.'

'So what popped out in the end?'

'We-e-ll, Giles often called Lady Helen "Dearest", so that's what I called her. And she was still my dearest mother-in-law right until she died, even though I was married to Tom.'

'Mm. She was a love. I half expected to see her there – especially when we had afternoon tea in the conservatory. I go into rooms and deep down I'm really wanting her to be there. It seems wrong somehow.'

'No, not really. She's never far away. Julia refuses to mourn her. Says she and Sir John are together again . . . But I believe you're based in Liverpool. You and Daisy will have met?'

'Only once, I'm afraid. It was kind of awkward, you see. Drew used to date her friend, Lyndis and – well . . .'

'Yes, I know about that. But Daisy almost always went along, too, on those dates.'

'Tell me about it, Lady? Did he love her a lot?' Kitty pulled up a chair to the table then sat, chin on hands, gazing at Alice with questioning eyes.

'Not *love* exactly. Well, that's what Daisy had me to believe. Lyn has been here to stay, and I liked her. She's tall and slim and her hair is so beautiful – chestnut, I suppose you'd call it. Drew liked dancing with her and taking her out, but which sailor doesn't like having a bonny lass on his arm? *Two*, it usually was!'

'But was he gone on her?'

'Not as much as she was on him – well, according to what Daisy said. I think Lyn was in love with him, but it wasn't like that for Drew. Oh, he liked her very much, but not enough to – well, he must have known, mustn't he, that you were just around the corner?'

'Thank goodness for that, anyway!' Kitty smiled her relief. 'Because I'll be leaving Liverpool soon, maybe – being based in the south. London, perhaps.'

'Well, you'll not need to worry about Drew.'

'Even though it was so sudden between him and me?'

'Even though,' Alice said comfortably. 'The Rowangarth Suttons have a history for falling in love at first sight – and falling hard, too.'

'So what's this I hear about my brother? He mentioned a girl called Grace in his last letter to me, and Uncle Nathan says his visits here are very frequent! Tell me about Grace: is she pretty?'

'Well, now – see for yourself!' Alice pulled aside the kitchen curtain. 'That's her, at the hen run.'

'Wow! She's good-looking all right!'

'She's a nice girl, Kitty, though how serious she is about Bas I can't say. But go down and introduce yourself whilst I put the kettle on. Tell her there'll be a cup for her, if she wants it. Only mind how you go! Don't ask her if you can be bridesmaid. If there's anything between her and Bas, she's saying nothing. Don't go frightening her off.'

'Now would I do a thing like that!'

'Yes you would, Kitty Sutton, unless you've changed a lot,' Alice laughed, 'so be careful what you say!'

Later, when she called to them that the tea was ready, Alice felt pleasure to see them talking so eagerly together. Kitty was such a beautiful young woman and right in every way for Drew, but as for Bas and Gracie – well, that was anybody's guess. Mind, Nathan was right: Bas was smitten, nothing was more certain, yet Gracie, it seemed, was more on the cautious side and that was a pity, Alice's romantic soul yearned.

'Tea up, you two,' she called from the kitchen doorway, all at once feeling near-contentment, for wouldn't Daisy be home, too, on Friday and likely Bas, an' all? The lad, she smiled, seemed to be able to manage even more crafty weekends than Daisy!

It would be lovely, seeing them together again. Almost like old times, if only Keth were here, and Tatty.

*   *   *

Julia took a large brown envelope from her shopping bag and tipped the contents on the study desk with a casualness that belied the pleasure it gave her.

'There you are! I picked out the four best. There are a few dress rings, but they aren't so valuable.'

'But I don't want a valuable ring, Aunt Julia – just something that's special between Drew and me. It's kind of you to offer one, though,' she hastened, gazing at the old-fashioned ring boxes.

'Well, it's second-hand or nothing these days. The war, I'm afraid . . .'

'Sorry, darling,' Drew smiled when Julia had left them. 'I know it must be marvellous to go to a jeweller's and look at trays of rings and –'

'Drew Sutton, I really want a Whitecliffe ring! Your great-grandmother was my great-grandmother, too, don't forget! And I hope one of them fits. Victorian ladies had small, dainty hands, didn't they?' She looked at her own hands, strong and capable, that had held reins and carried feed buckets and brushed out stables. 'Mine are working hands.'

'Do you miss home, Kitty – and the horses?'

'Of course I do, especially the morning rides, but I always felt I had two homes and the English half of me is happy here. Now do let me see them. Can I really have any one I like?'

'Have the four, if you want them! Mother says they'll all be yours anyway one day. And I'm afraid they aren't modern . . .' He flicked open the boxes, standing them side by side. 'You choose, but I like this one – it matches your eyes.'

The sapphire ring was beautiful; a perfect stone set round with diamonds. Kitty put it on her finger and it stuck at the knuckle.

'It's too small, Drew.'

'Push it then.'

'No, I don't want it.' She discarded the ruby and the emerald rings, too. 'This is the one and I know it will fit. Put it on for me, please?'

'This one?' Drew frowned. 'But it's quite – *ordinary*.'

'It isn't, because it's the one I want.' She held out her left hand and the ring slid on easily.

'You're sure?' Drew kissed her gently.

'Very sure, darling.' She held her hand to the light and three opals shone creamily. 'And the tiny pearls between are so right. Thank you, Drew. I won't ever take it off – well, not till our wedding day. And how soon can we be married?'

'Hey! That's something I should ask *you*,' Drew laughed. 'But soon, I hope.'

'Yes, *please*. In All Souls' and Uncle Nathan to marry us. Oh, Drew, I'm so happy I could weep in case I lose you!'

'You won't lose me, I promise.'

'Had you thought, darling, I won't be changing my name. I'll still be Kitty Sutton. But it'll be nice, for all that, being a Mrs.'

'Sorry, but you'll have to be Lady Sutton. Lady Kathryn. I like it. Shall you mind? I know titles don't go down very well in America.'

'The English half of me will like it, so don't worry none. Now please, *please* kiss me and tell me you'll always love me – then we'll go and tell Aunt Julia it's official!'

'It's a crying shame,' Tilda sniffed, her romantic soul still a little on the weepy side because people getting engaged was lovely and brave an' all, when there was a war on. 'A shame, that's what! There should have been a dinner-dance to celebrate.'

She dabbed at her eyes and envisaged a world at peace and splendid gowns, a glittering dining table and dancing in the conservatory. And lanterns and champagne, bottles of it, and corks popping all over the place.

'Still, it was nice and traditional, Kitty having a White-cliffe ring,' she sighed, even if tonight the celebration would consist of pigeon-breast pie with a suet crust and the last of the strawberries for dessert with not even sugar and cream to put on them!

'That ring,' Mary sniffed, 'wouldn't have done for me!'

'You'd have chosen different? Well, I liked it. Unusual, that's what, and it looked real pretty on her hand.'

'So it might have.' Mary picked up her carrier bag and reached for her coat. 'But I'd certainly have chosen different – *luckier.*'

'What do you mean – luckier? Old Lady Whitecliffe as once wore it never had any bad luck. Those Whitecliffes were well-heeled and all of them lived into ripe old age! Don't spoil it, Mary. Be glad for them.'

'Spoil it? Me – not be glad for them? *Me,* that has watched them both grow up! I wish them all the happiness in the world!'

And with that she whisked out and up the stairs in search of Will who had given her three diamonds, which was sensible and a good investment should times of need arise.

But weren't opals said to be unlucky, she brooded as she crossed the stableyard. And didn't pearls stand for tears?

Ah, well; it had been Miss Kitty's choice and there was no accounting for taste and she did wish them well; with all her heart and soul she wished them happiness and bairns and a long life together.

Come to think of it, Kitty Sutton would make a lovely mistress of Rowangarth. Lady Helen would have approved. Oh my word, yes!

'Hullo, you two – had a good walk?' Julia glanced up from her book as Drew and Kitty came hand in hand into the conservatory. 'You're just in time for tea.'

'We climbed the pike. It's years and years since I was up there.'

'She said she wanted to show her ring to Pendenys,' Drew teased.

'And so I should! Pendenys was a part of being young and I wanted to see the old place, anyway – even from a distance.'

'Young? And you're an old, old lady now,' Nathan teased, laying aside his newspaper, because he defied anyone to concentrate upon serious matters when Kitty's personality filled any room she entered.

'Not old, exactly, but more sensible, I guess; and serious about getting married, Uncle Nathan, and having children and all that sort of thing. But today Pendenys looked strange, kind of. Just the same as always, yet different, like it was waiting for something to happen. Maybe it wants Grandmother Clementina back. Y'know, just for a minute I understood why Bas never liked it.'

'He's going to have to like it some day. All things being equal,' Nathan said comfortably, 'it will come to him.'

'So I guess he'll sell it – or give it away. You know my brother . . .'

'Afraid he can't do that. It's entailed for two more generations after me.'

'Gee. Tough. Does Bas know?'

'Sebastian never speaks about it,' Julia supplied, 'and talking about your brother, Kitty, he was on the phone and I had to tell him you were both out. I told him about you and Drew and the ring and that Daisy would be here, too, on Friday and he said so would he!'

'Bas coming? Great! It's ages since I've seen him.'

'Bas gets more leave than any young man I know,' Nathan observed to no one in particular. 'Just how does he manage it?'

'Guess it's 'cos he's got a crush on your garden girl.'

'Land girl,' Drew corrected, 'and he won't be able to get

away so often when Burtonwood gets finished and properly operational – he told me so. But won't it be amazing, all four of us here together after so long? Can you cope, Mother?'

'Of course she can. She'll love every minute of it, won't you, darling?' Nathan smiled at Julia and it made Kitty think it was just beautiful the way he loved her and wondered if Drew would smile at her that way when he was as old as Uncle Nathan.

'No trouble at all, and Tilda and Mary will manage very well if you all make your own beds and help clear away after meals. But I'll be booking a call to Montpelier. I'm going to ask Tatty to try to get home, too. Anna was saying it was about time she paid another visit. They don't see as much of her as they would like at Denniston.'

'Do you blame her, Mother?' Drew defended. 'The Petrovska can be a bit overpowering.'

'I'll say! "Your reenk! It ees very charmink, I suppose, but the Petrovskys always have diamonds, very *beeg* ones," Kitty mimicked. 'And when I told her that I chose this one because I liked it she said that a young lady should insist upon the biggest and best ring or it would look poverty-stricken!' Kitty laughed, not in the least put out.

'Well, I shall ask Tatty when I phone for all that. It would be really something, having all the Clan together again – well, almost all.'

'Then I suggest you don't ask outright,' Nathan said softly. 'Just mention it in passing and let her make up her own mind. Don't make an issue of it.'

'I won't. And it won't seem obvious because I always ring every week to make sure Sparrow is all right. Tatty might want to come, you know.'

'And she might not. Seeing Drew and Kitty so happy and by all accounts Bas and Gracie, too, might just rub on a raw nerve.'

'When I first met Gracie,' Kitty said brightly, 'I could

understand Bas falling for her. She wouldn't talk about him, though. When I asked her if it was serious between them she just smiled and said they seriously like going dancing and being together when he comes over. And what a smile! I sure hope she's not messing about with my brother's feelings, that's all!'

'Gracie is a sensible girl, Kitty, and we all like her a lot. She even gets on well with Jack Catchpole and you know how crusty he can be. But Polly says there are letters and phone calls all the time so I don't think that Gracie is leading Bas up the garden path. Maybe she just wants to be sure.'

'I get it! She's giving him a run for his money before she lets him catch her,' Kitty smiled sunnily.

'N-no. I think she realizes that people can fall in love too easily in wartime, though it's natural to want someone to love when you've got to live your life from one day to the next,' Julia said softly. 'But like you say, I think he'll catch her, one day. And here comes tea!'

'Mm. Afternoon tea at Rowangarth,' Kitty sighed blissfully. 'One of the things I remembered all those years we couldn't get over. Cherry scones and –'

'No cherry scones now,' Julia smiled.

'How come?'

'No cherries. And no sugar.'

'Gee! I'm sorry. Guess I haven't really taken in the food shortage yet. Tell you what, though. I'll write Mom to send cherries over in her next food parcel. And would you like me to pour, Aunt Julia?'

'Please. But don't ask your mother for things. Amelia is the most thoughtful person I know and the food she sends is really appreciated. But we mustn't ask for things in letters. The censor would cut it out anyway. It's called soliciting and we aren't allowed to do it.'

'Now is that so?' Kitty was genuinely surprised; the more so because the British who had once, her mother said, occupied the best part of the world, including North America, should accept the privations of war without question. Why, they even stood in orderly queues for hours on end without grumbling! 'Well, I'll just have to find a way round it – hint, sort of.'

'You could try,' Nathan chuckled. Kitty Sutton was the one person he knew in all the world who could outwit the censor's office if she put her mind to it. 'Now, are we to get our cup of tea, young lady, before it goes cold?'

'I think,' said Julia to Alice, 'that it's just lovely to have almost all my Clan together. I felt quite full up, seeing them in the wild garden on the way here. Just like they used to do when they were little. They'd lie there, laughing and chattering under the rowan trees. It was their favourite meeting place. Only Keth was missing and I'm really willing him home, you know. I do so want to see Daisy married.'

'Even though the war isn't over?'

'Even though. But do you know, even yet Tatty seems the odd one out, just as she used to be when they were all growing up.'

'That's because she was mollycoddled when she was a bairn. She's got a bit of backbone, now. It must have taken a lot of doing, coming here this weekend, knowing she was going to have to see Drew and Kitty all happy.'

'Yes, and Daisy already engaged and Bas and Gracie heading for it, if I'm any judge. So she's still the odd one out.'

'You think so, Julia – about Bas and Gracie, I mean?'

'I'd take bets on it. And another thing I'd take bets on is that Keth will be home sooner than we think. I feel it inside me.'

'You're sure you're not just *wanting* it to happen?'

'Oh, I want it to happen. I want nothing more than to see Daisy in her beautiful dress – well, perhaps to see Drew married takes priority. But Keth getting home is something

I feel, though I wouldn't say a word about it to Daisy.'

'No. Best not raise her hopes. She's coming to accept that they might have to wait till the end of the war. But are you going to take a snap of the five of them whilst they are together?'

'No! It's all of them, or nothing! I've got the film that Bas gave me in my camera and I won't use even one up because goodness only knows when I'll get another – and in colour, too. I shall use my precious snaps for Drew's wedding and Daisy's wedding – that's when I'll take the six of them together again. I shall take it in the conservatory like I did all those years ago.'

'When we thought none of them would have to go to war, you mean?'

'Yes, but even then, something inside me told me to get a picture of them all, because they were mine, I always pretended, and so very precious. And that feeling inside is there about Keth getting home – well, before the end of the war, that is.'

'Then it's fingers crossed your hunch is right,' Alice frowned, taking more time than she should arranging cups and saucers on the tea tray. 'But isn't there something more important we are both forgetting? Something you and me hoped and prayed would never happen?' She stood with her back to Julia, stirring the liquid in the pot as if reluctant to say what was in her mind. 'I'm talking about Drew and Tatty. There was always the chance they would fall in love. Cousins can marry – you and Nathan did, and Drew and Kitty will.'

'Drew and Kitty are second cousins.'

'So are Drew and Tatiana – or so they've always thought. But they aren't. They're half-brother and -sister, did they but know it. Them wanting to marry would have blown things sky-high, wouldn't it? Thank God it won't happen now. I used to wonder whether her father's wickedness would come out in Tatty but it hasn't. There's a great deal of her Grandfather Sutton in her, thank God.'

'Mm. Dear Uncle Edward. Tatty *is* like him. I think that's why he saw to it that she got Denniston and enough money to make her independent. It was brave of her coming home for the weekend, and her being so sad, still, about her young man. I'll make a point of being especially nice to her whilst she's here, though she gets a lot of loving from Sparrow, you know.'

'There's a quietness about her, now, and she's learned how to stand on her own two feet. It must have taken a bit of doing, breaking away from home, but like you say, we'll be especially nice to her. We both know what it's like to lose the man we loved – our first loves.'

'Yes.' For the fleeting of a second, Julia was a nurse again and young and headstrong, tilting at life defiantly. 'But things work out, don't they, though it makes me angry with the war when I see the young ones trying to make the best of it – falling in love even though, like Tatty, they could be torn apart. Why did we let this war happen, Alice, and how much longer is it going to go on?'

'That's what we said last time and it lasted for four years. This one is going to take longer, Tom says. And we've got to invade somewhere in Europe – go back.'

'That's what I mean! My Clan. The war is taking their green years. It's stealing their right to be young.'

'Aye. They've had to grow up a lot faster – those who are lucky, that is.'

'You're right. You usually are.' Julia glanced up at the dear, familiar mantelpiece with the clock in the centre, the tea caddy to the left and photographs either side of Daisy and Drew in uniform. 'But this far, we've been lucky, Alice.'

'Yes. This time Rowangarth is in credit, you might say. The Garth Suttons paid dearly, last time; both sons and Andrew. But Drew saved the line. He was meant to be and the fates will look kindly on him, I know it.

'It's a long tunnel we're going down, Julia, and as yet we can't see even a glimmer of light at the end of it – but we will!'

'You think so?'

'I *know* so.' Alice smiled lovingly up at her son and daughter. 'Those two will come safely home. And soon there'll be that light at the end of the tunnel and we'll know we are going to win.'

All at once Alice felt very sure, though she couldn't for the life of her explain why. She just knew inside her that Drew would come home to plant more rowan trees and that Daisy would walk down the aisle at All Souls' on Tom's arm, her silk wedding dress swishing deliciously.

'A light? Soon?' Julia whispered. 'Are you sure?'

'As sure as I know that night follows day and that after winter spring comes. We'll muddle through, you and me.'

'Yes, we *will*! Just as we've always done. Oh, how would I have managed all these years without you, Alice Hawthorn? Thank you for being there, for being my sister. Like you say, it's been a funny old quarter of a century and I don't think I could have endured it without you. Don't ever leave me? Always be there – please?'

'It works both ways, Julia Sutton. There have been times when I couldn't have coped without you. And don't be bothering yourself,' she said matter-of-factly. 'Rowangarth is where I belong. I'm not going anywhere.'

Not when there was a wedding dress hanging in the sewing-room and a daughter to see down the aisle – aye, and grandchildren to look forward to. Home was where the heart was and Alice Dwerryhouse was staying put. Oh my word, yes!

What would happen in the years before peace came she couldn't even begin to guess, but Daisy and Drew would come back safely to Rowangarth; in her heart she was sure of it.

'Drink your tea,' she said. 'It's going cold . . .'